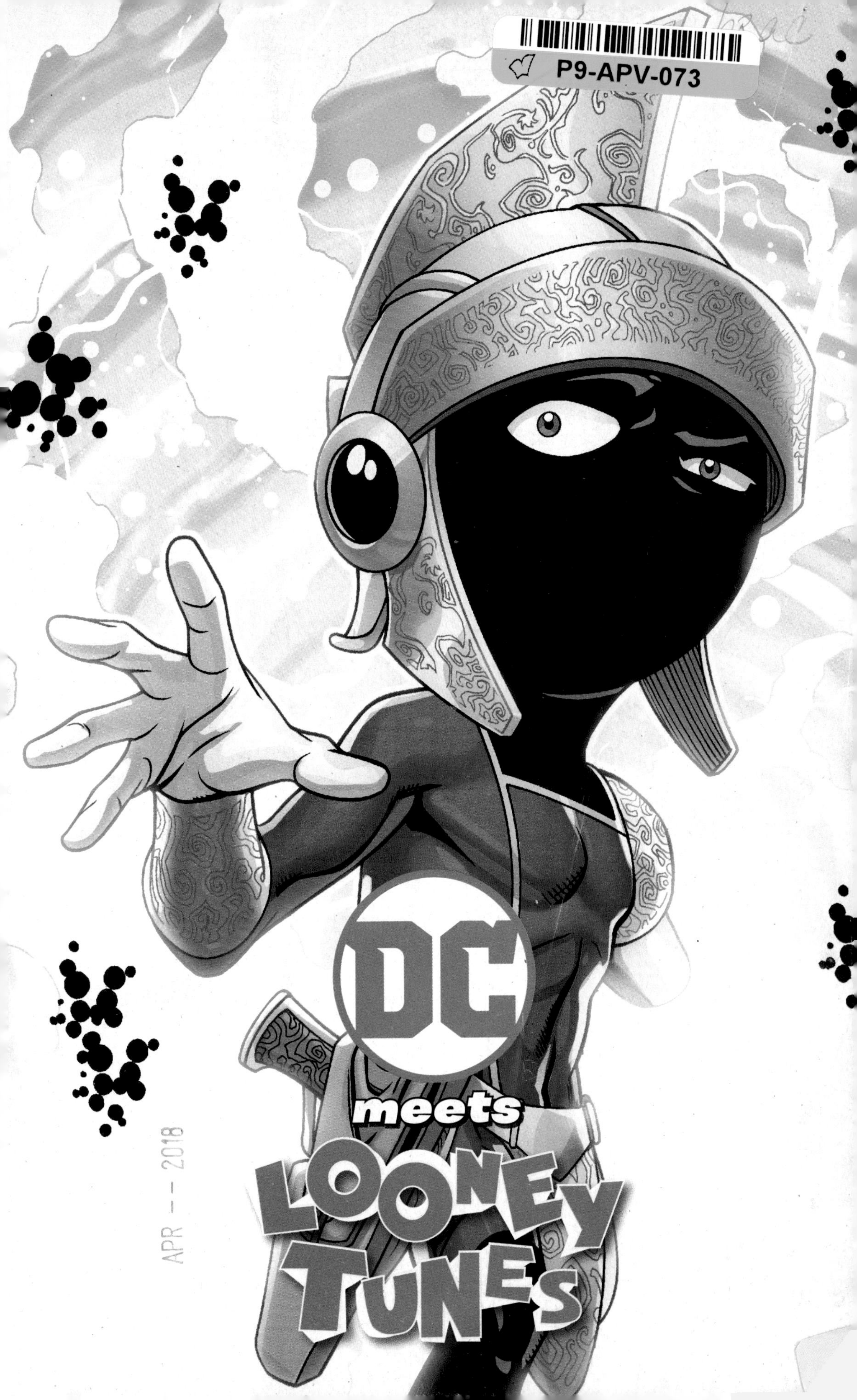
DC
meets
LOONEY TUNES

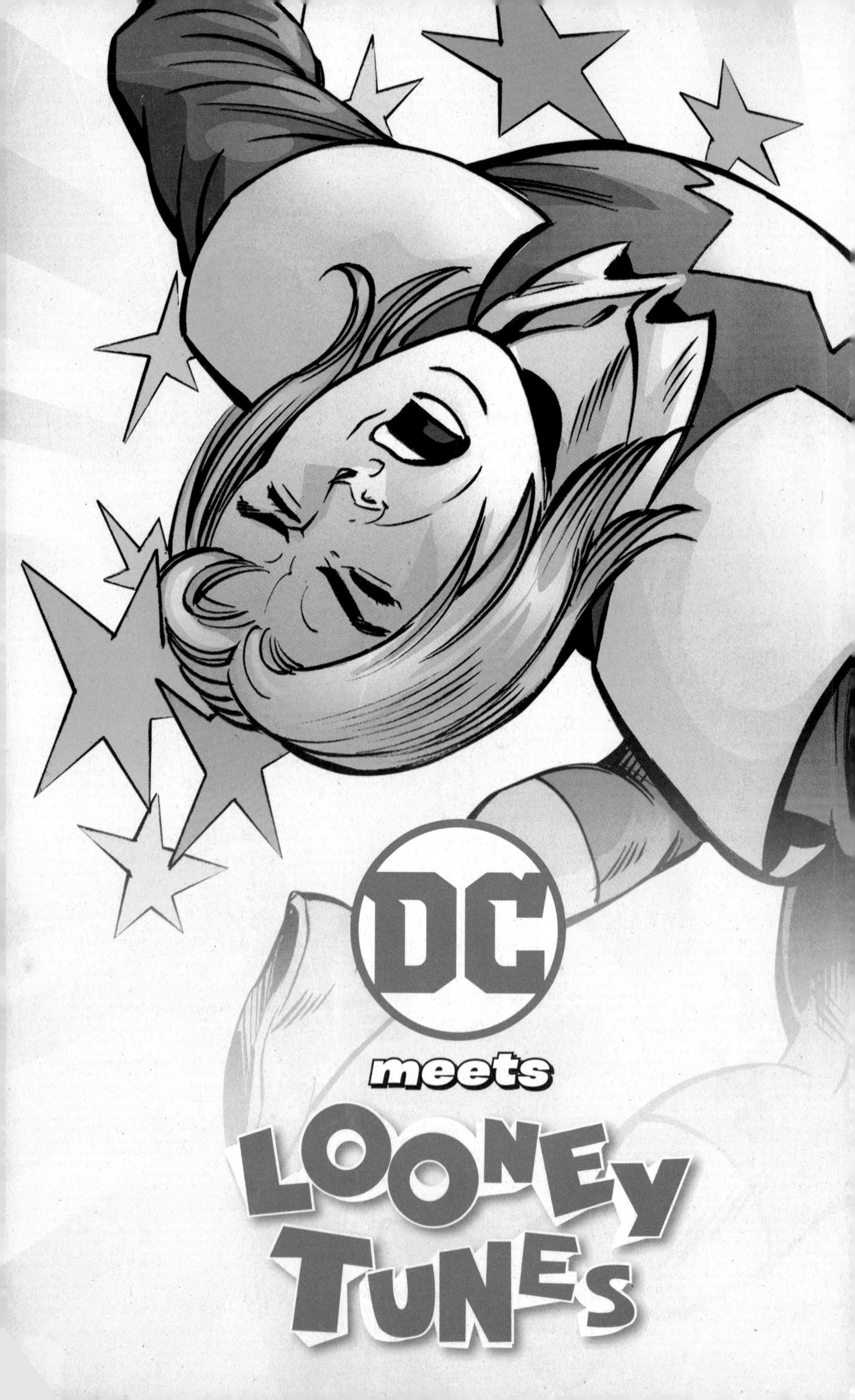
DC
meets
LOONEY TUNES

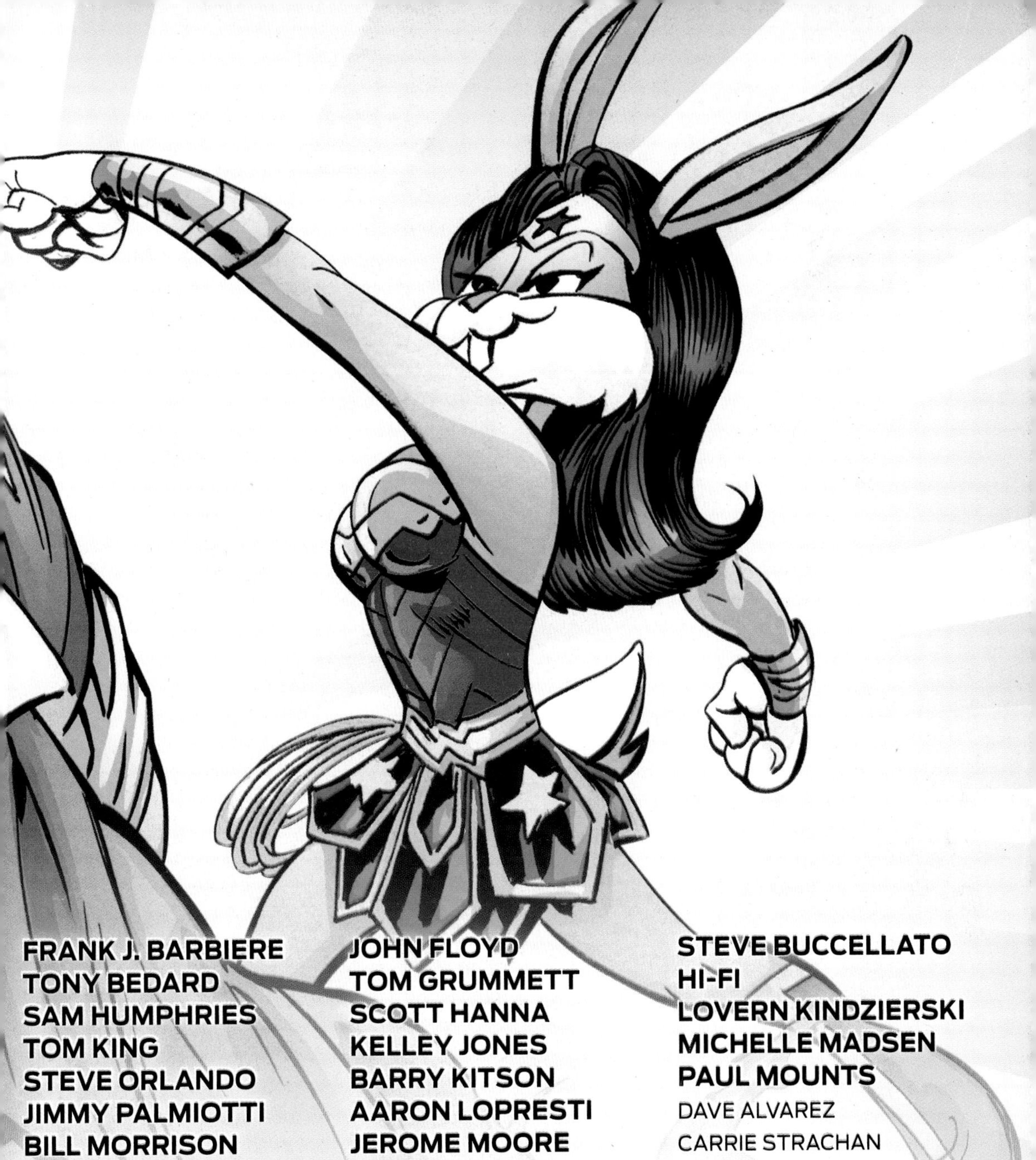

FRANK J. BARBIERE
TONY BEDARD
SAM HUMPHRIES
TOM KING
STEVE ORLANDO
JIMMY PALMIOTTI
BILL MORRISON
JIM FANNING
BILL MATHENY
JUAN MANUEL ORTIZ
writers

JOHN FLOYD
TOM GRUMMETT
SCOTT HANNA
KELLEY JONES
BARRY KITSON
AARON LOPRESTI
JEROME MOORE
MARK TEXEIRA
LEE WEEKS
DAVE ALVAREZ
BEN CALDWELL
JOHN LOTER
BILL MORRISON
JUAN MANUEL ORTIZ
BYRON VAUGHNS
artists

STEVE BUCCELLATO
HI-FI
LOVERN KINDZIERSKI
MICHELLE MADSEN
PAUL MOUNTS
DAVE ALVAREZ
CARRIE STRACHAN
colorists

DERON BENNETT
ROB LEIGH
CARLOS M. MANGUAL
JOSH REED
DAVE SHARPE
SAIDA TEMOFONTE
letterers

LEE WEEKS collection cover artist

BATMAN created by BOB KANE with BILL FINGER
WONDER WOMAN created by WILLIAM MOULTON MARSTON
LOBO created by ROGER SLIFER and KEITH GIFFEN
MARTIAN MANHUNTER created by JOE SAMACHSON and JOE CERTA
SUPERGIRL based on characters created by JERRY SIEGEL and JOE SHUSTER
SUPERBOY created by JERRY SIEGEL
By special arrangement with the Jerry Siegel family

JOEY CAVALIERI Editor – Original Series
MICHAEL McCALISTER Assistant Editor – Original Series
JEB WOODARD Group Editor – Collected Editions
ERIKA ROTHBERG Editor – Collected Edition
STEVE COOK Design Director – Books
SHANNON STEWART Publication Design

BOB HARRAS Senior VP – Editor-in-Chief, DC Comics
PAT McCALLUM Executive Editor, DC Comics

DIANE NELSON President
DAN DiDIO Publisher
JIM LEE Publisher
GEOFF JOHNS President & Chief Creative Officer
AMIT DESAI Executive VP – Business & Marketing Strategy,
Direct to Consumer & Global Franchise Management
SAM ADES Senior VP & General Manager, Digital Services
BOBBIE CHASE VP & Executive Editor, Young Reader & Talent Development
MARK CHIARELLO Senior VP – Art, Design & Collected Editions
JOHN CUNNINGHAM Senior VP – Sales & Trade Marketing
ANNE DePIES Senior VP – Business Strategy, Finance & Administration
DON FALLETTI VP – Manufacturing Operations
LAWRENCE GANEM VP – Editorial Administration & Talent Relations
ALISON GILL Senior VP – Manufacturing & Operations
HANK KANALZ Senior VP – Editorial Strategy & Administration
JAY KOGAN VP – Legal Affairs
JACK MAHAN VP – Business Affairs
NICK J. NAPOLITANO VP – Manufacturing Administration
EDDIE SCANNELL VP – Consumer Marketing
COURTNEY SIMMONS Senior VP – Publicity & Communications
JIM (SKI) SOKOLOWSKI VP – Comic Book Specialty Sales & Trade Marketing
NANCY SPEARS VP – Mass, Book, Digital Sales & Trade Marketing
MICHELE R. WELLS VP – Content Strategy

DC MEETS LOONEY TUNES.

Published by DC Comics. Compilation and all new material Copyright © 2018 DC Comics and Warner Bros.
Entertainment Inc. All Rights Reserved. Originally published in single magazine form in BATMAN/ELMER
FUDD SPECIAL 1, JONAH HEX/YOSEMITE SAM SPECIAL 1, WONDER WOMAN/TASMANIAN DEVIL SPECIAL 1,
LOBO/ROAD RUNNER SPECIAL 1, MARTIAN MANHUNTER/MARVIN THE MARTIAN SPECIAL 1 and LEGION OF
SUPER-HEROES/BUGS BUNNY SPECIAL 1. Copyright © 2017 DC Comics. All Rights Reserved.
The stories, characters and incidents featured in this publication are entirely fictional.
DC Comics does not read or accept unsolicited submissions of ideas, stories or artwork.

Copyright © 2018 Warner Bros. Entertainment Inc.
LOONEY TUNES and all related characters and elements © & ™ Warner Bros. Entertainment Inc. (s18)
WB SHIELD: ™ & © WBEI. (s18)

DCCO40233

DC Comics, 2900 West Alameda Ave., Burbank, CA 91505
Printed by Vanguard Graphics, LLC, Ithaca, NY, USA. 1/12/18. First Printing.
ISBN: 978-1-4012-7757-4

Library of Congress Cataloging-in-Publication Data is available.

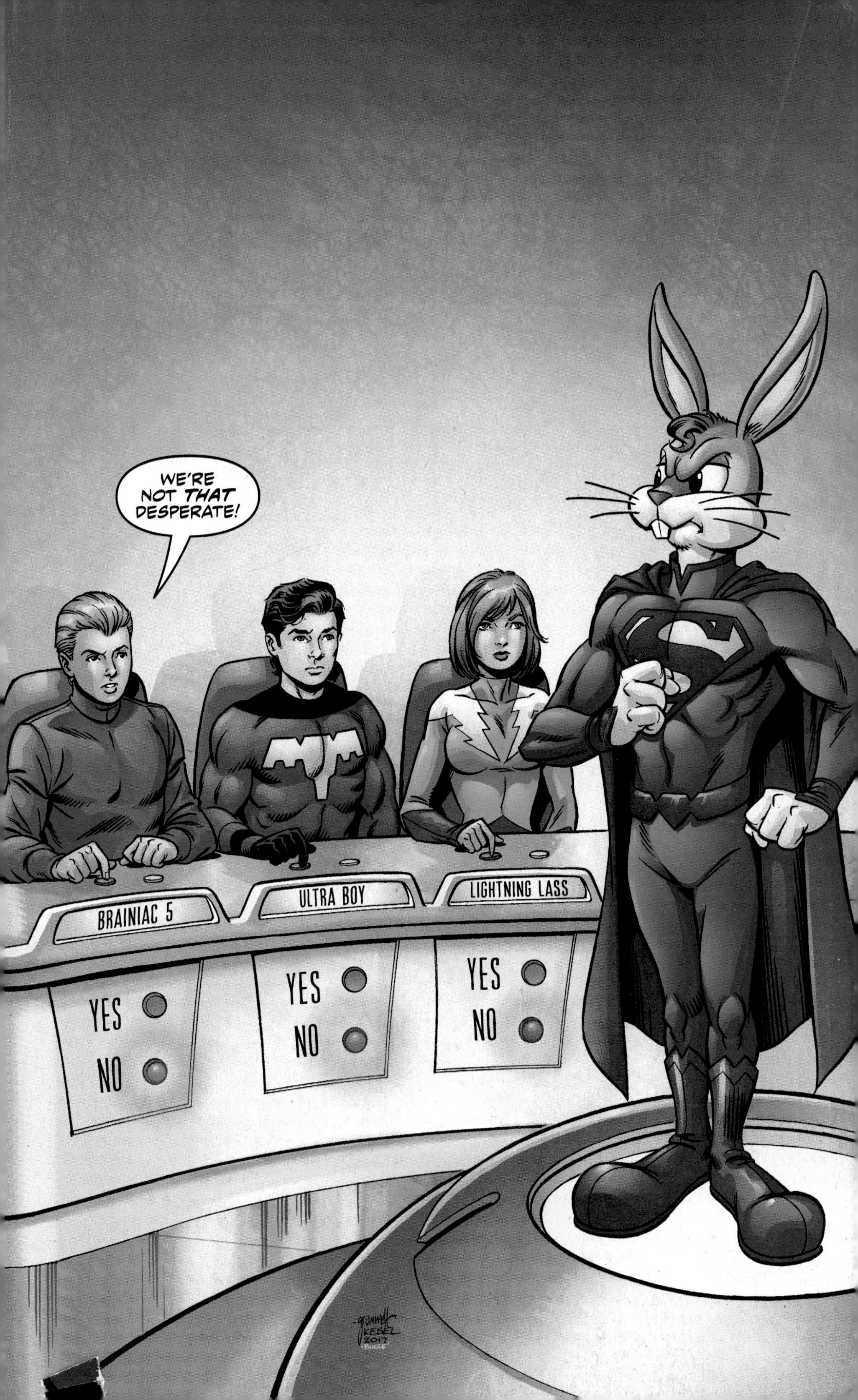
WE'RE NOT *THAT* DESPERATE!
BRAINIAC 5
ULTRA BOY
LIGHTNING LASS
YES
NO
YES
NO
YES
NO

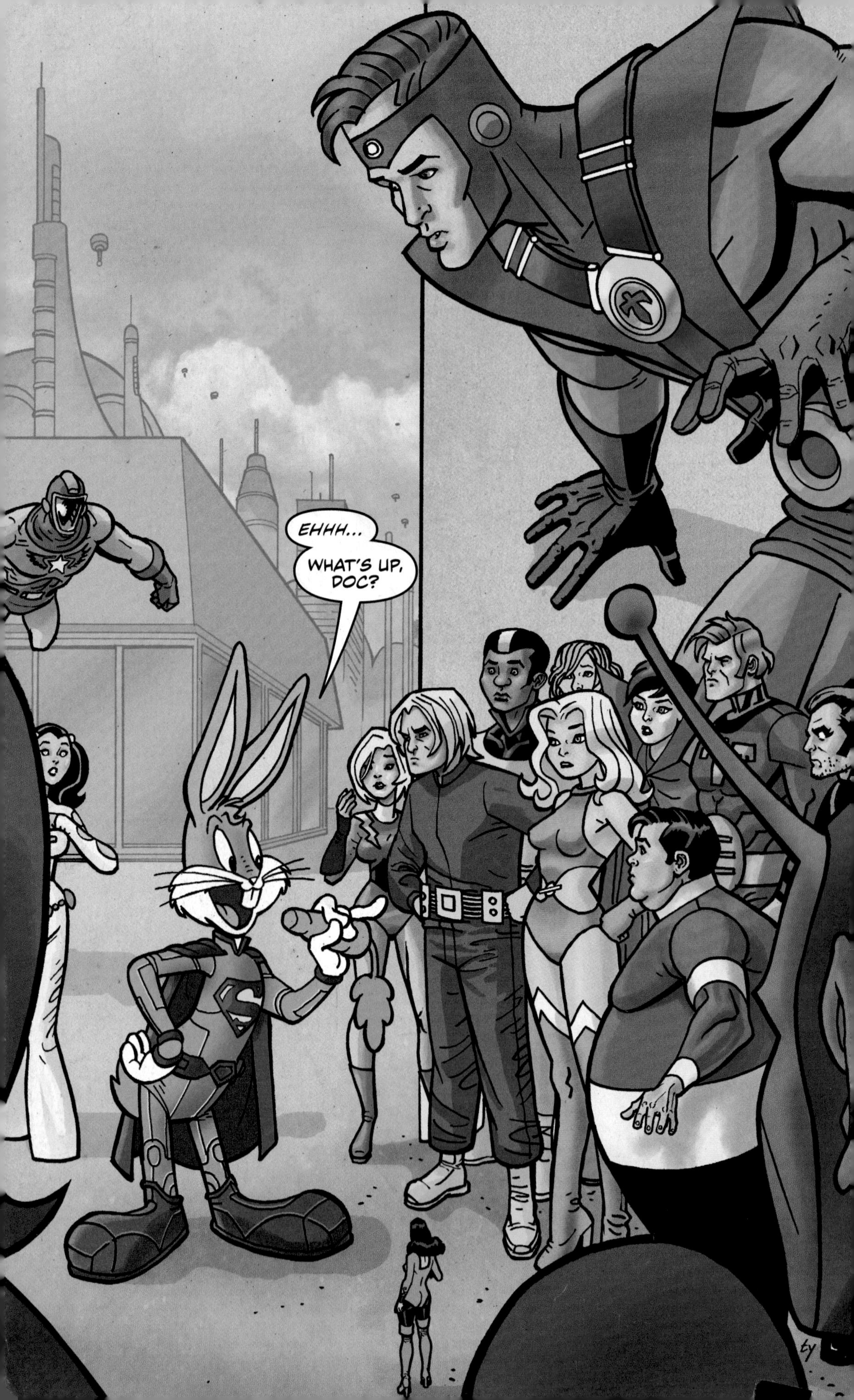
EHHH...
WHAT'S UP, DOC?
ty

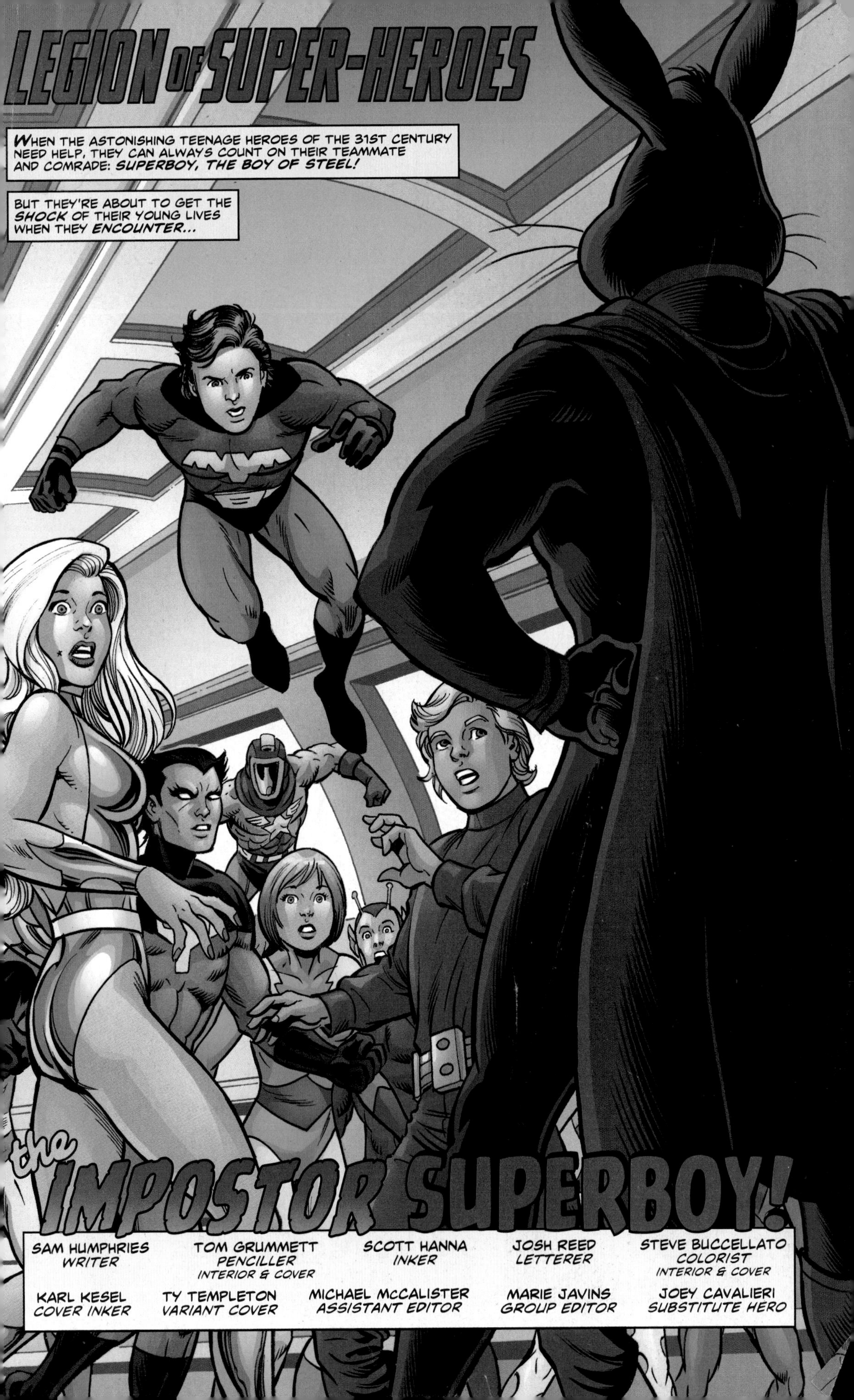

LEGION OF SUPER-HEROES
WHEN THE ASTONISHING TEENAGE HEROES OF THE 31ST CENTURY NEED HELP, THEY CAN ALWAYS COUNT ON THEIR TEAMMATE AND COMRADE: SUPERBOY, THE BOY OF STEEL!
BUT THEY'RE ABOUT TO GET THE SHOCK OF THEIR YOUNG LIVES WHEN THEY ENCOUNTER...
the IMPOSTOR SUPERBOY!
SAM HUMPHRIES WRITER
TOM GRUMMETT PENCILLER INTERIOR & COVER
SCOTT HANNA INKER
JOSH REED LETTERER
STEVE BUCCELLATO COLORIST INTERIOR & COVER
KARL KESEL COVER INKER
TY TEMPLETON VARIANT COVER
MICHAEL McCALISTER ASSISTANT EDITOR
MARIE JAVINS GROUP EDITOR
JOEY CAVALIERI SUBSTITUTE HERO

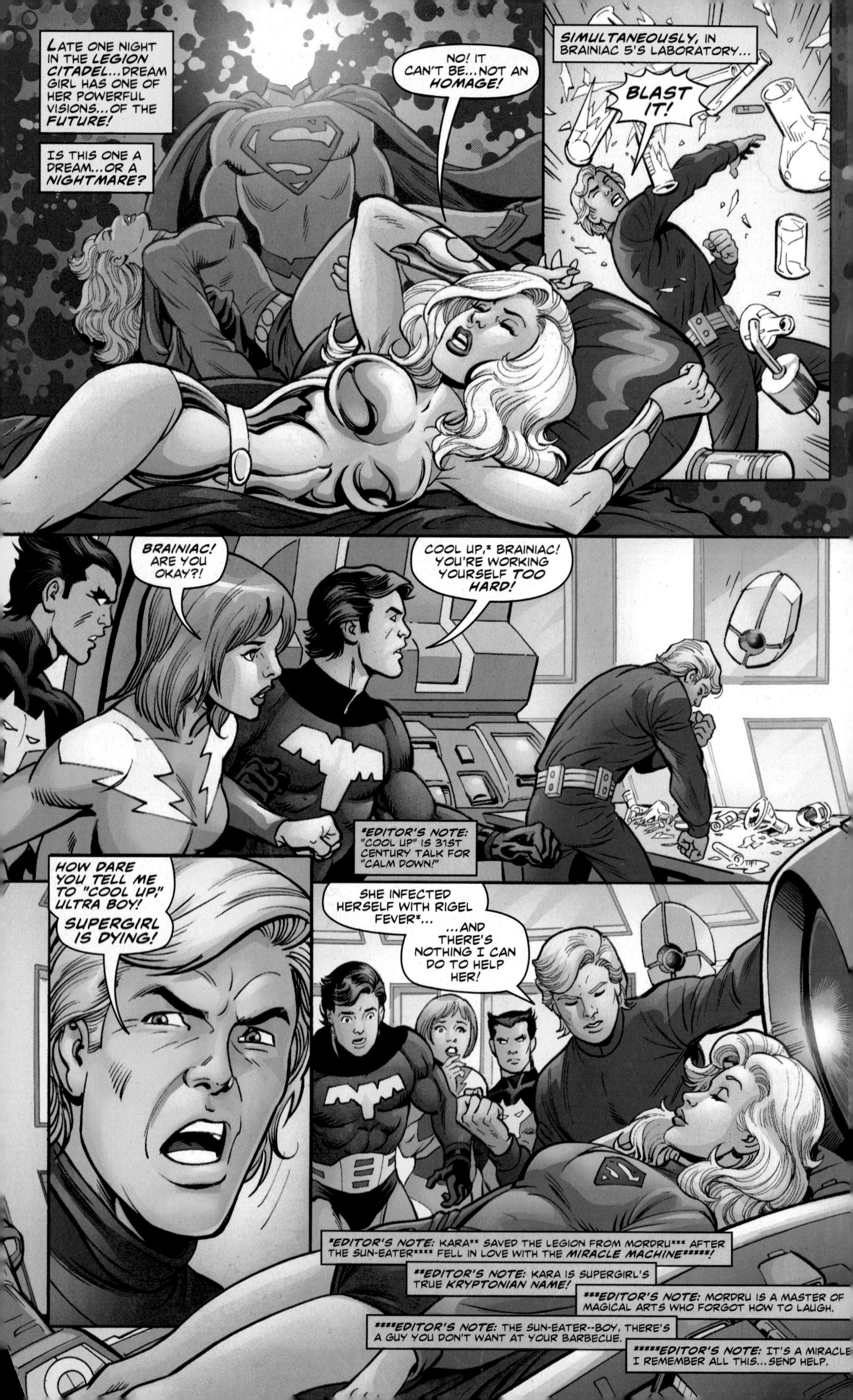
LATE ONE NIGHT IN THE LEGION CITADEL...DREAM GIRL HAS ONE OF HER POWERFUL VISIONS...OF THE FUTURE!
IS THIS ONE A DREAM...OR A NIGHTMARE?
NO! IT CAN'T BE...NOT AN HOMAGE!
SIMULTANEOUSLY, IN BRAINIAC 5'S LABORATORY...
BLAST IT!
BRAINIAC! ARE YOU OKAY?!
COOL UP,* BRAINIAC! YOU'RE WORKING YOURSELF TOO HARD!
*EDITOR'S NOTE: "COOL UP" IS 31ST CENTURY TALK FOR "CALM DOWN!"
HOW DARE YOU TELL ME TO "COOL UP," ULTRA BOY! SUPERGIRL IS DYING!
SHE INFECTED HERSELF WITH RIGEL FEVER*...
...AND THERE'S NOTHING I CAN DO TO HELP HER!
*EDITOR'S NOTE: KARA** SAVED THE LEGION FROM MORDRU*** AFTER THE SUN-EATER**** FELL IN LOVE WITH THE MIRACLE MACHINE*****!
**EDITOR'S NOTE: KARA IS SUPERGIRL'S TRUE KRYPTONIAN NAME!
***EDITOR'S NOTE: MORDRU IS A MASTER OF MAGICAL ARTS WHO FORGOT HOW TO LAUGH.
****EDITOR'S NOTE: THE SUN-EATER--BOY, THERE'S A GUY YOU DON'T WANT AT YOUR BARBECUE.
*****EDITOR'S NOTE: IT'S A MIRACLE I REMEMBER ALL THIS...SEND HELP.

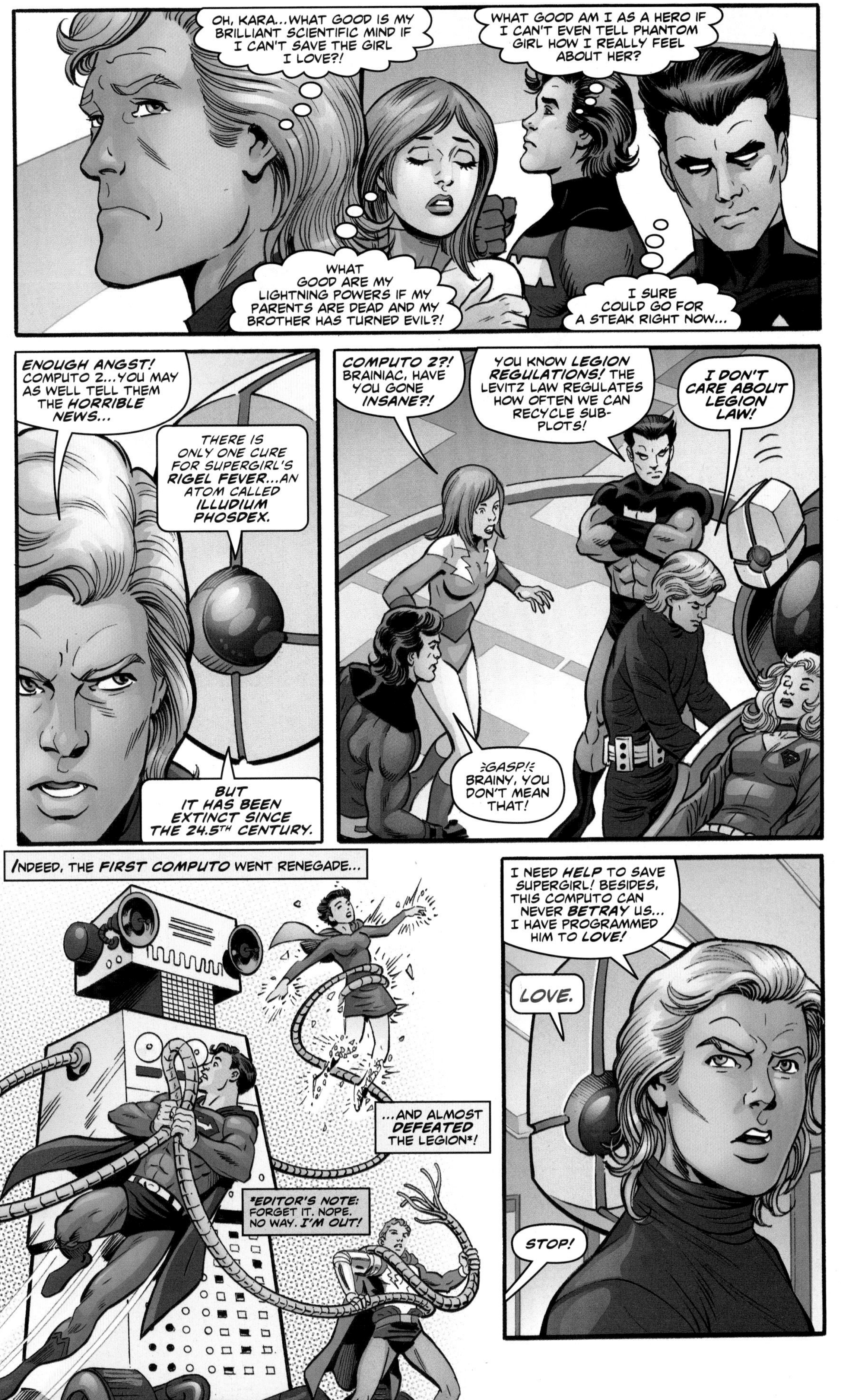
OH, KARA...WHAT GOOD IS MY BRILLIANT SCIENTIFIC MIND IF I CAN'T SAVE THE GIRL I LOVE?!
WHAT GOOD AM I AS A HERO IF I CAN'T EVEN TELL PHANTOM GIRL HOW I REALLY FEEL ABOUT HER?
WHAT GOOD ARE MY LIGHTNING POWERS IF MY PARENTS ARE DEAD AND MY BROTHER HAS TURNED EVIL?!
I SURE COULD GO FOR A STEAK RIGHT NOW...
ENOUGH ANGST! COMPUTO 2...YOU MAY AS WELL TELL THEM THE HORRIBLE NEWS...
THERE IS ONLY ONE CURE FOR SUPERGIRL'S RIGEL FEVER...AN ATOM CALLED ILLUDIUM PHOSDEX.
BUT IT HAS BEEN EXTINCT SINCE THE 24.5TH CENTURY.
COMPUTO 2?! BRAINIAC, HAVE YOU GONE INSANE?!
YOU KNOW LEGION REGULATIONS! THE LEVITZ LAW REGULATES HOW OFTEN WE CAN RECYCLE SUB-PLOTS!
I DON'T CARE ABOUT LEGION LAW!
GASP! BRAINY, YOU DON'T MEAN THAT!
INDEED, THE FIRST COMPUTO WENT RENEGADE...
...AND ALMOST DEFEATED THE LEGION*!
*EDITOR'S NOTE: FORGET IT. NOPE. NO WAY. I'M OUT!
I NEED HELP TO SAVE SUPERGIRL! BESIDES, THIS COMPUTO CAN NEVER BETRAY US... I HAVE PROGRAMMED HIM TO LOVE!
LOVE.
STOP!

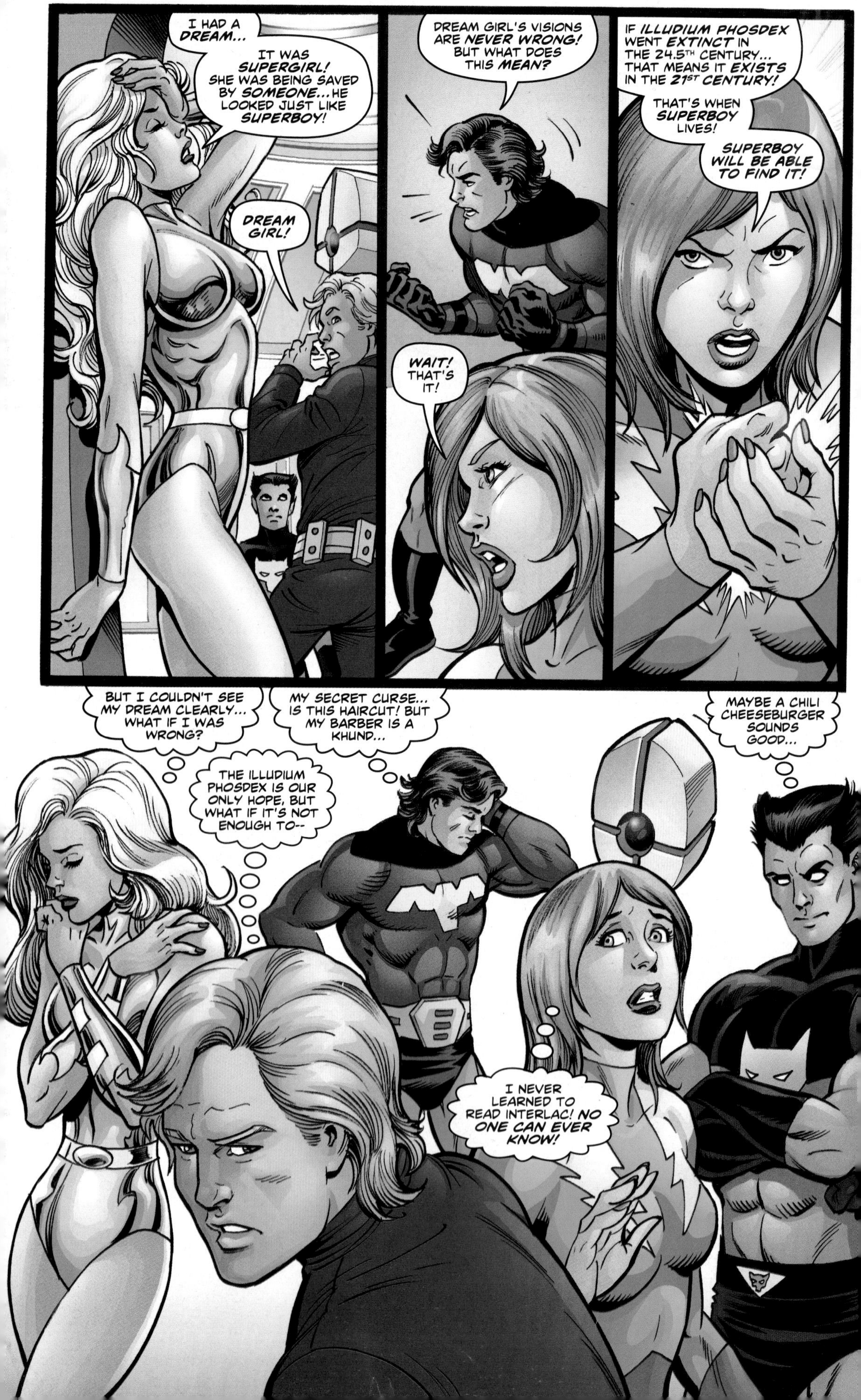
I HAD A DREAM...
IT WAS SUPERGIRL! SHE WAS BEING SAVED BY SOMEONE... HE LOOKED JUST LIKE SUPERBOY!
DREAM GIRL!
DREAM GIRL'S VISIONS ARE NEVER WRONG! BUT WHAT DOES THIS MEAN?
WAIT! THAT'S IT!
IF ILLUDIUM PHOSDEX WENT EXTINCT IN THE 24.5TH CENTURY... THAT MEANS IT EXISTS IN THE 21ST CENTURY!
THAT'S WHEN SUPERBOY LIVES!
SUPERBOY WILL BE ABLE TO FIND IT!
BUT I COULDN'T SEE MY DREAM CLEARLY... WHAT IF I WAS WRONG?
THE ILLUDIUM PHOSDEX IS OUR ONLY HOPE, BUT WHAT IF IT'S NOT ENOUGH TO--
MY SECRET CURSE... IS THIS HAIRCUT! BUT MY BARBER IS A KHUND...
MAYBE A CHILI CHEESEBURGER SOUNDS GOOD...
I NEVER LEARNED TO READ INTERLAC! NO ONE CAN EVER KNOW!

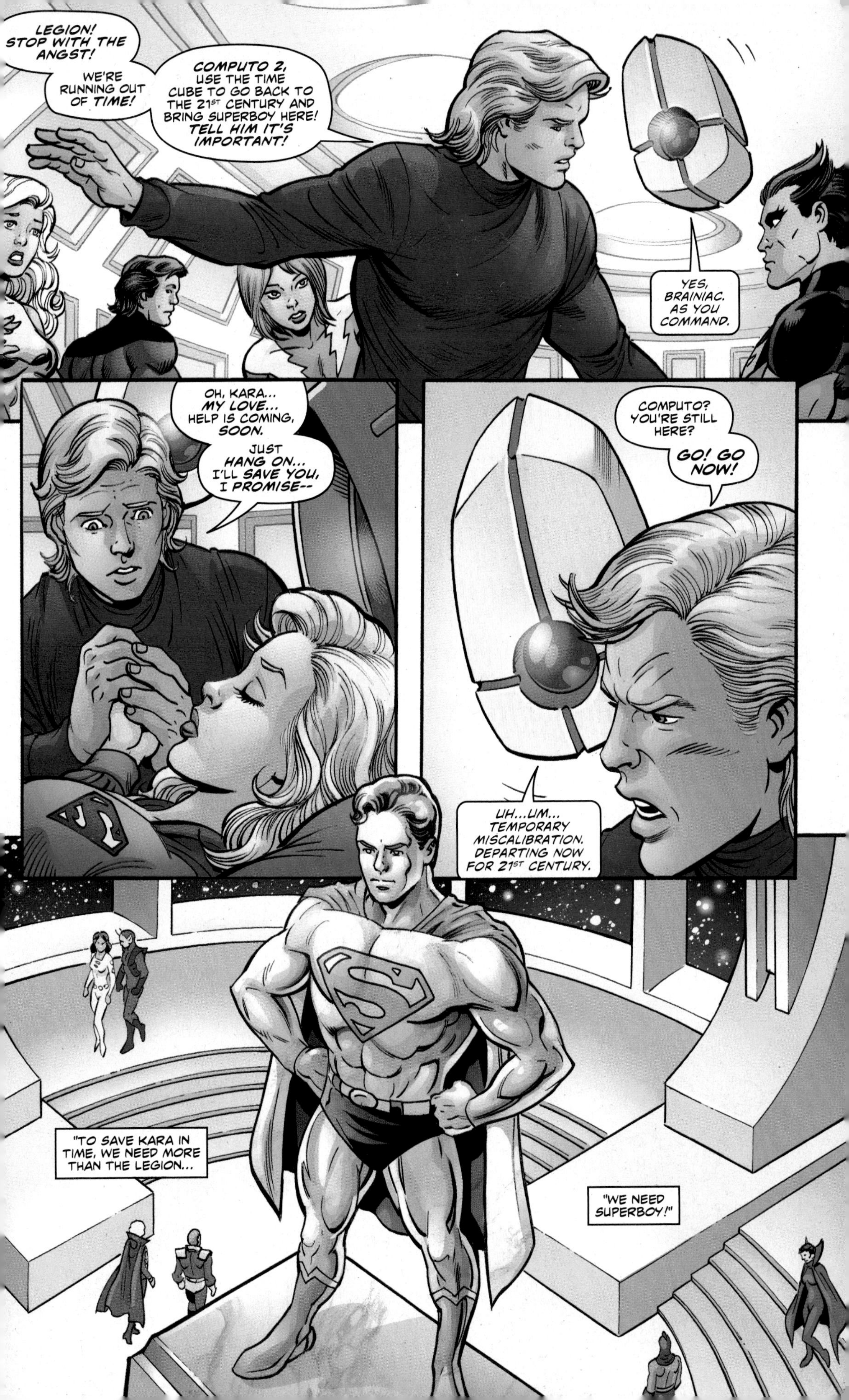
LEGION! STOP WITH THE ANGST!
WE'RE RUNNING OUT OF TIME!
COMPUTO 2, USE THE TIME CUBE TO GO BACK TO THE 21ST CENTURY AND BRING SUPERBOY HERE! TELL HIM IT'S IMPORTANT!
YES, BRAINIAC. AS YOU COMMAND.
OH, KARA... MY LOVE... HELP IS COMING, SOON.
JUST HANG ON... I'LL SAVE YOU, I PROMISE--
COMPUTO? YOU'RE STILL HERE?
GO! GO NOW!
UH...UM... TEMPORARY MISCALIBRATION. DEPARTING NOW FOR 21ST CENTURY.
"TO SAVE KARA IN TIME, WE NEED MORE THAN THE LEGION...
"WE NEED SUPERBOY!"

CHAPTER 2
THE HERO SMALLVILLE DESERVES!

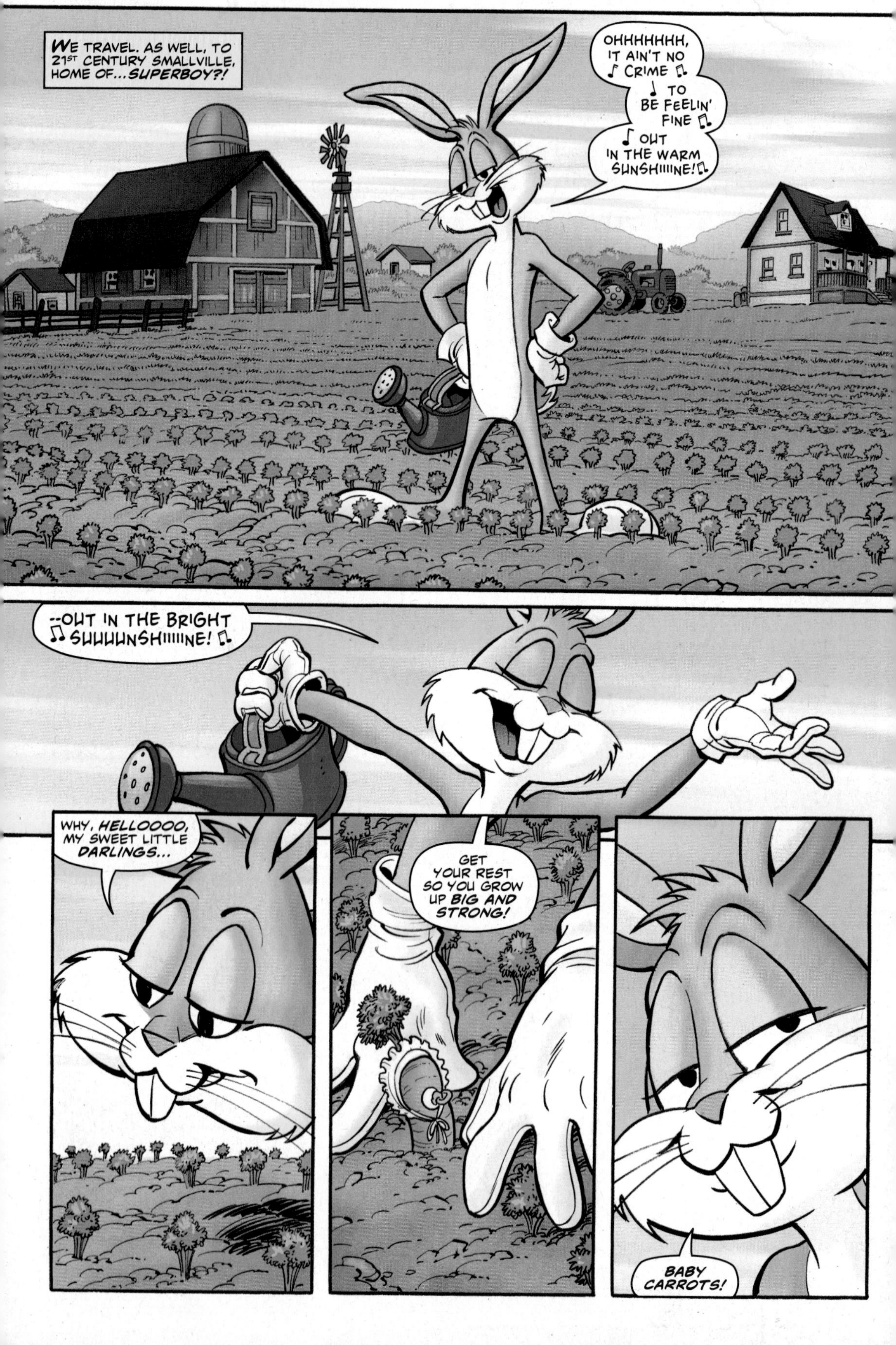

WE TRAVEL, AS WELL, TO 21ST CENTURY SMALLVILLE, HOME OF... SUPERBOY?!
OHHHHHHH, IT AIN'T NO ♪ CRIME ♫
♩ TO BE FEELIN' FINE ♫
♪ OUT IN THE WARM SUNSHIIIINE! ♫
--OUT IN THE BRIGHT ♫ SUUUUNSHIIIINE! ♫
WHY, HELLOOOO, MY SWEET LITTLE DARLINGS...
GET YOUR REST SO YOU GROW UP BIG AND STRONG!
BABY CARROTS!

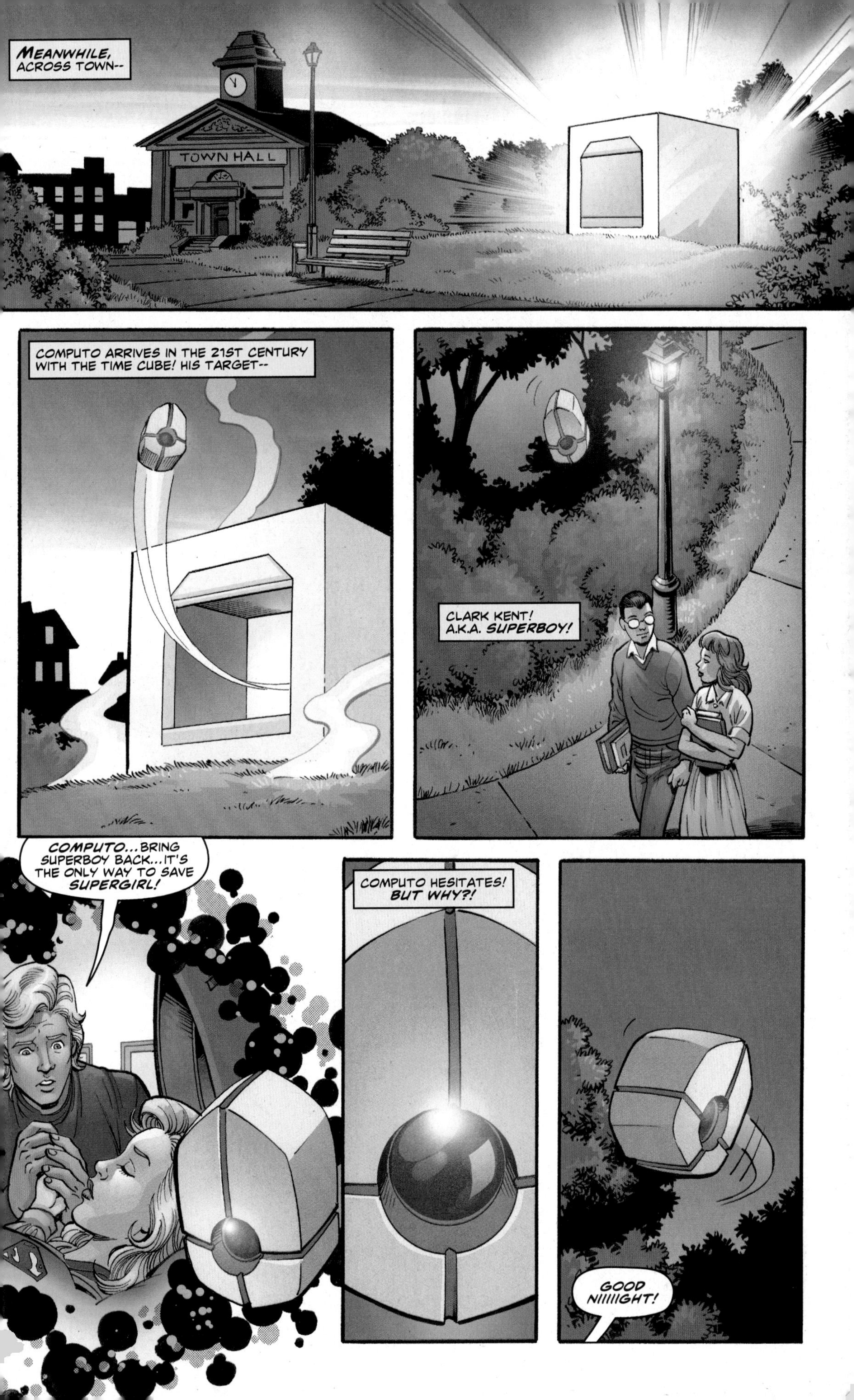
MEANWHILE, ACROSS TOWN--
TOWN HALL
COMPUTO ARRIVES IN THE 21ST CENTURY WITH THE TIME CUBE! HIS TARGET--
CLARK KENT! A.K.A. SUPERBOY!
COMPUTO...BRING SUPERBOY BACK...IT'S THE ONLY WAY TO SAVE SUPERGIRL!
COMPUTO HESITATES! BUT WHY?!
GOOD NIIIIIGHT!

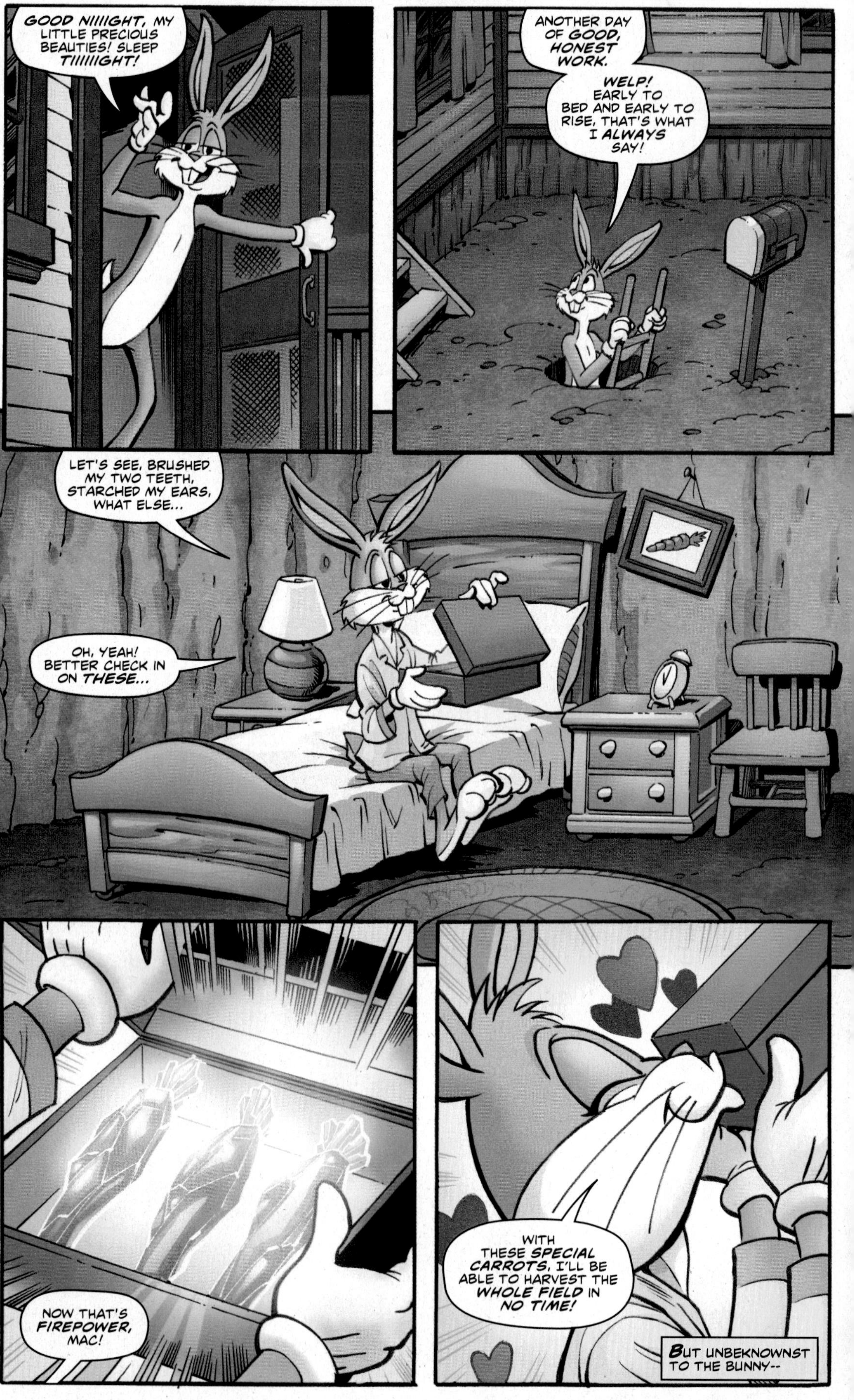
GOOD NIIIIGHT, MY LITTLE PRECIOUS BEAUTIES! SLEEP TIIIIIGHT!
ANOTHER DAY OF GOOD, HONEST WORK.
WELP! EARLY TO BED AND EARLY TO RISE, THAT'S WHAT I ALWAYS SAY!
LET'S SEE, BRUSHED MY TWO TEETH, STARCHED MY EARS, WHAT ELSE...
OH, YEAH! BETTER CHECK IN ON THESE...
NOW THAT'S FIREPOWER, MAC!
WITH THESE SPECIAL CARROTS, I'LL BE ABLE TO HARVEST THE WHOLE FIELD IN NO TIME!
BUT UNBEKNOWNST TO THE BUNNY--

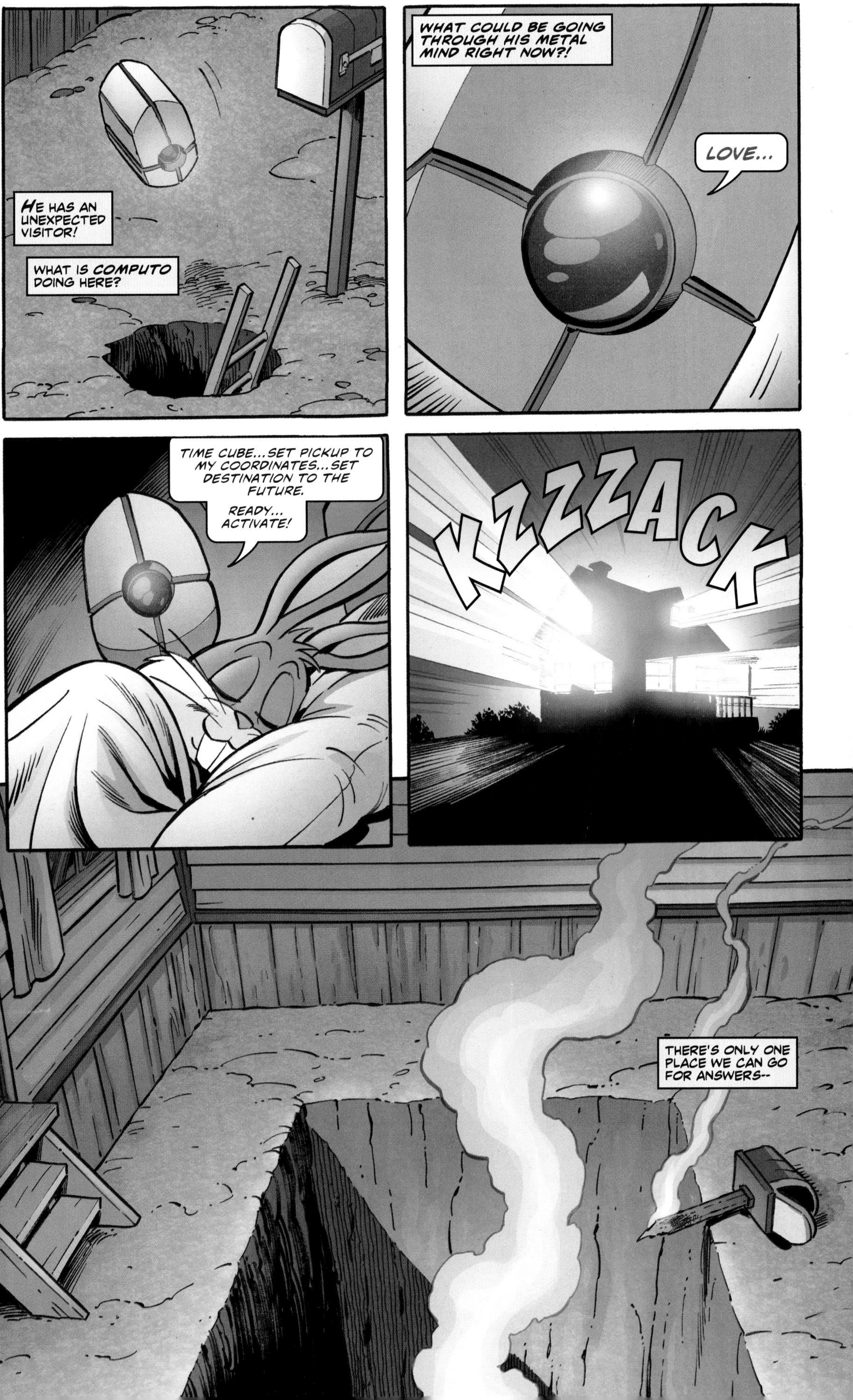
HE HAS AN UNEXPECTED VISITOR!
WHAT IS COMPUTO DOING HERE?
WHAT COULD BE GOING THROUGH HIS METAL MIND RIGHT NOW?!
LOVE...
TIME CUBE...SET PICKUP TO MY COORDINATES...SET DESTINATION TO THE FUTURE.
READY... ACTIVATE!
KZZZACK
THERE'S ONLY ONE PLACE WE CAN GO FOR ANSWERS--

CHAPTER 3 RABBIT OF THE SUPER-FUTURE!

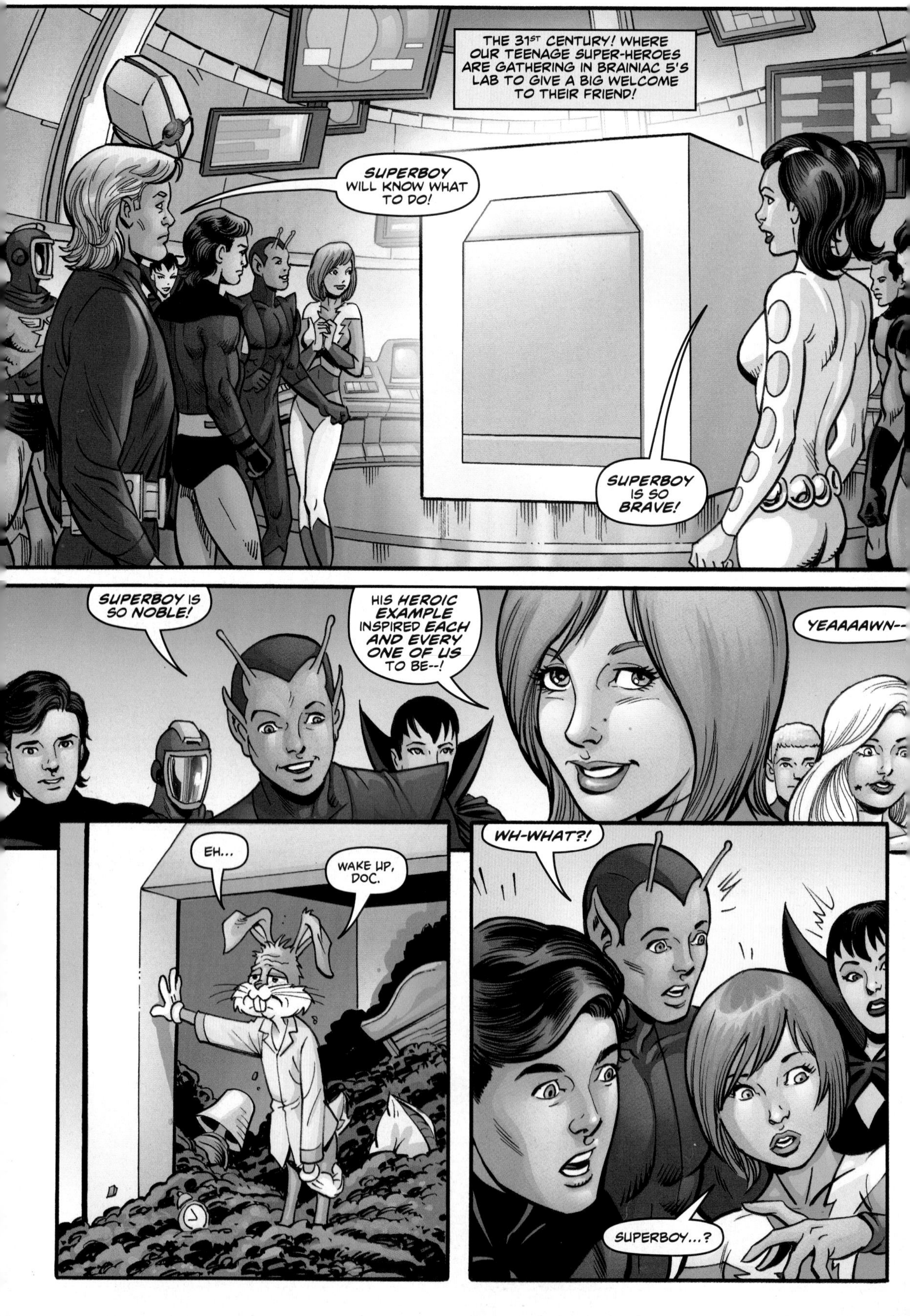

THE 31ST CENTURY! WHERE OUR TEENAGE SUPER-HEROES ARE GATHERING IN BRAINIAC 5'S LAB TO GIVE A BIG WELCOME TO THEIR FRIEND!
SUPERBOY WILL KNOW WHAT TO DO!
SUPERBOY IS SO BRAVE!
SUPERBOY IS SO NOBLE!
HIS HEROIC EXAMPLE INSPIRED EACH AND EVERY ONE OF US TO BE--!
YEAAAAWN--
EH...
WAKE UP, DOC.
WH-WHAT?!
SUPERBOY...?

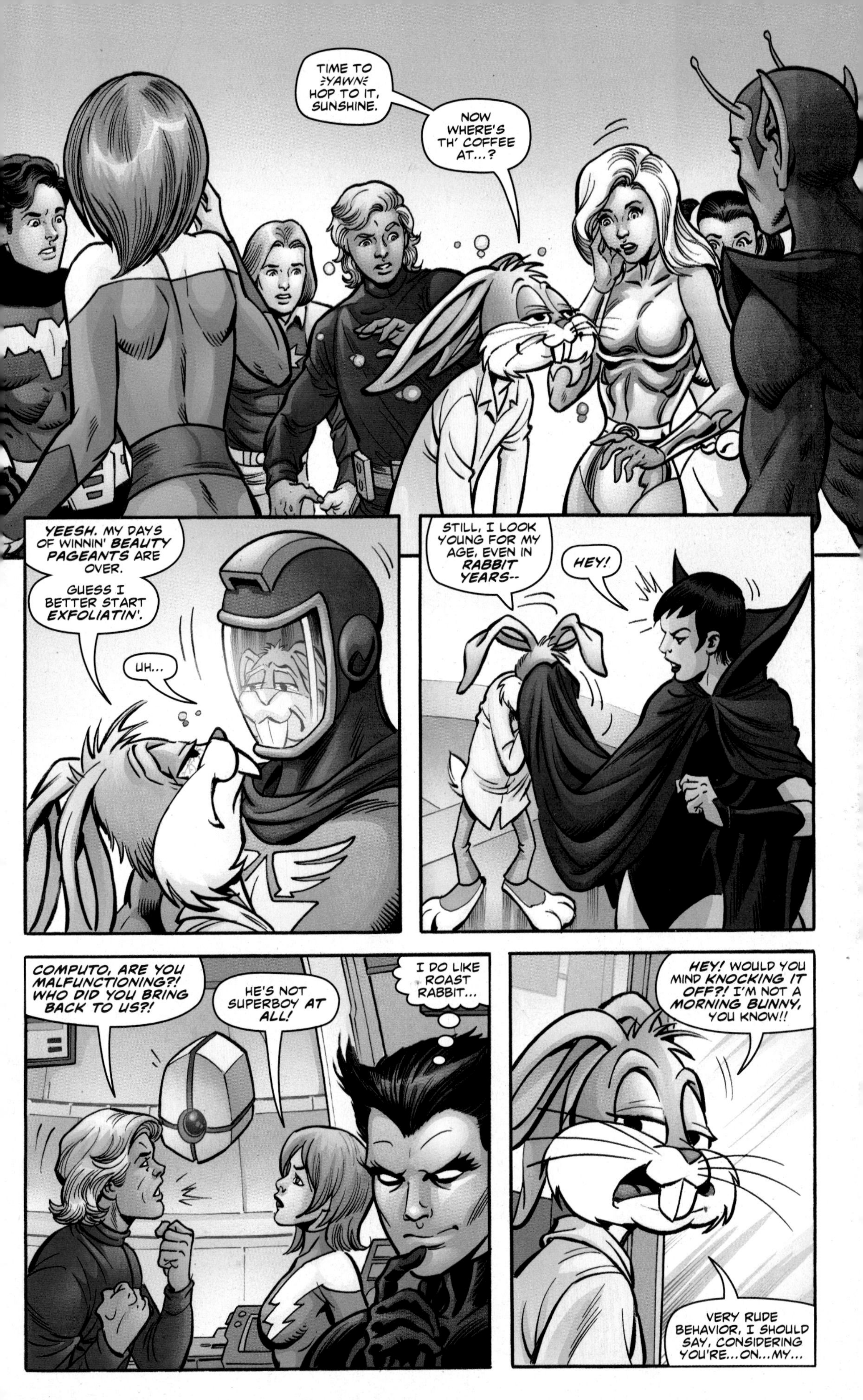
TIME TO ≥YAWN≤ HOP TO IT, SUNSHINE.
NOW WHERE'S TH' COFFEE AT...?
YEESH. MY DAYS OF WINNIN' BEAUTY PAGEANTS ARE OVER.
GUESS I BETTER START EXFOLIATIN'.
UH...
STILL, I LOOK YOUNG FOR MY AGE, EVEN IN RABBIT YEARS--
HEY!
COMPUTO, ARE YOU MALFUNCTIONING?! WHO DID YOU BRING BACK TO US?!
HE'S NOT SUPERBOY AT ALL!
I DO LIKE ROAST RABBIT...
HEY! WOULD YOU MIND KNOCKING IT OFF?! I'M NOT A MORNING BUNNY, YOU KNOW!!
VERY RUDE BEHAVIOR, I SHOULD SAY, CONSIDERING YOU'RE...ON...MY...

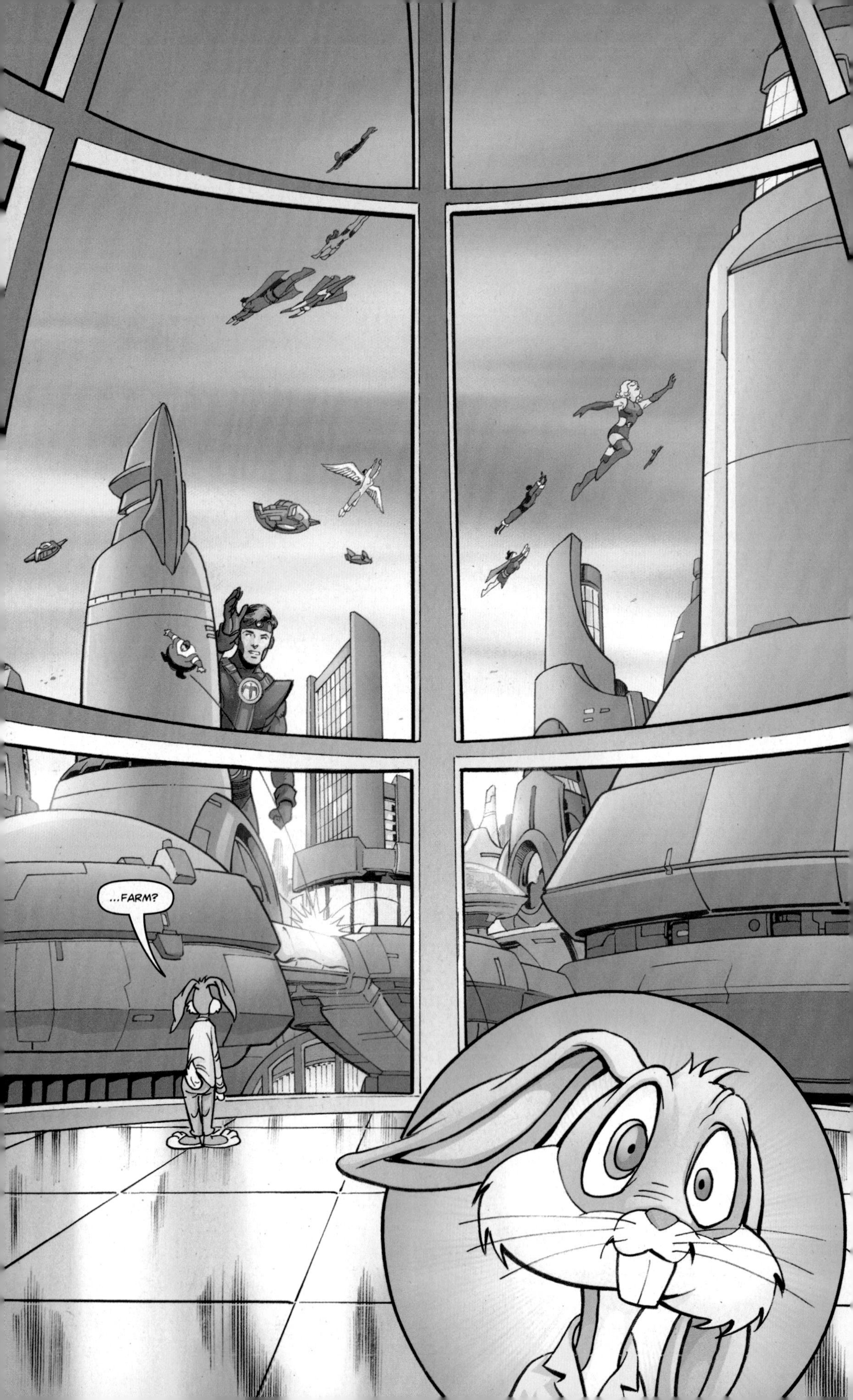
...FARM?

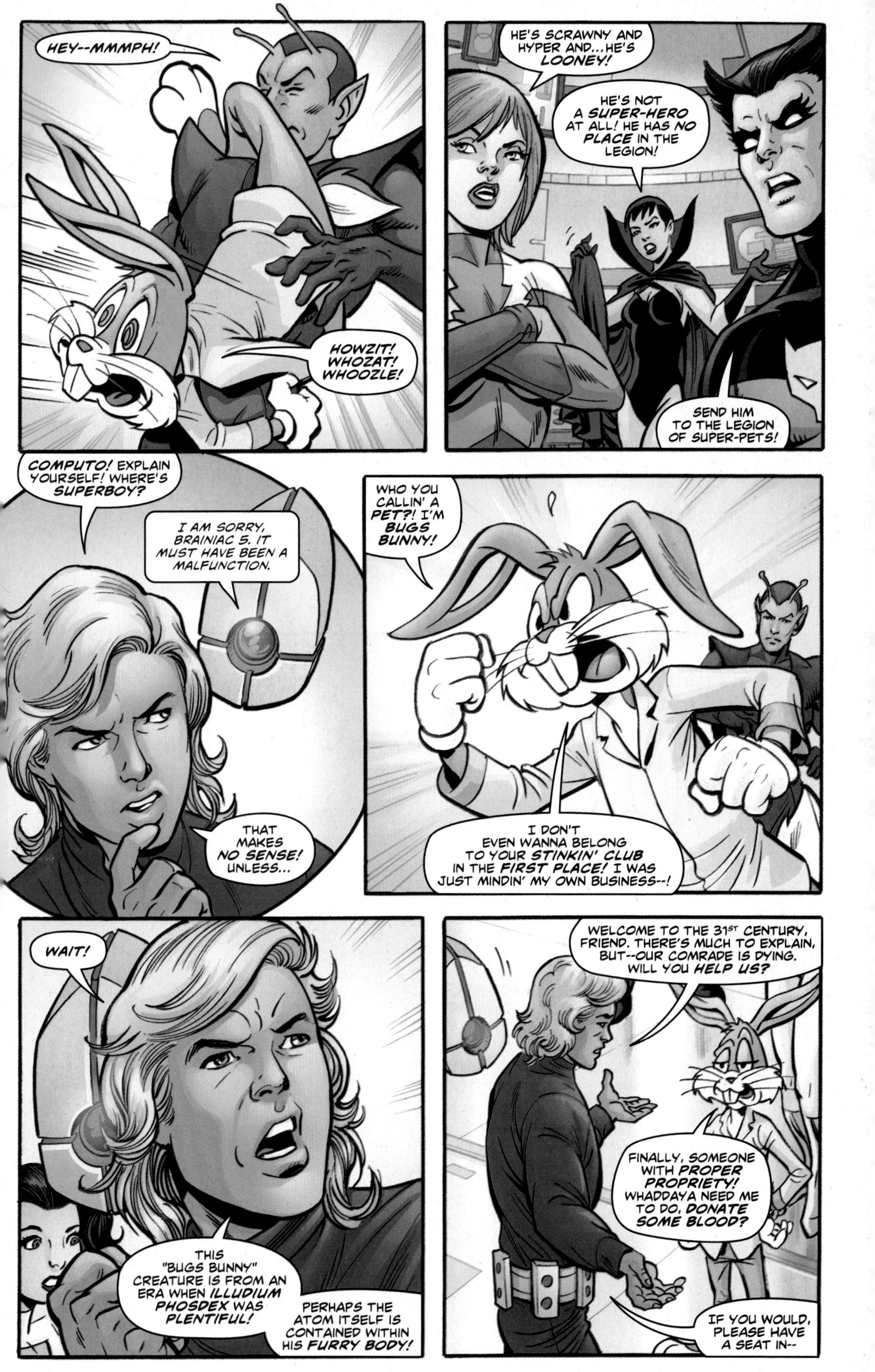
HEY--MMMPH!
HOWZIT! WHOZAT! WHOOZLE!
HE'S SCRAWNY AND HYPER AND... HE'S LOONEY!
HE'S NOT A SUPER-HERO AT ALL! HE HAS NO PLACE IN THE LEGION!
SEND HIM TO THE LEGION OF SUPER-PETS!
COMPUTO! EXPLAIN YOURSELF! WHERE'S SUPERBOY?
I AM SORRY, BRAINIAC 5. IT MUST HAVE BEEN A MALFUNCTION.
THAT MAKES NO SENSE! UNLESS...
WHO YOU CALLIN' A PET?! I'M BUGS BUNNY!
I DON'T EVEN WANNA BELONG TO YOUR STINKIN' CLUB IN THE FIRST PLACE! I WAS JUST MINDIN' MY OWN BUSINESS--!
WAIT!
THIS "BUGS BUNNY" CREATURE IS FROM AN ERA WHEN ILLUDIUM PHOSDEX WAS PLENTIFUL!
PERHAPS THE ATOM ITSELF IS CONTAINED WITHIN HIS FURRY BODY!
WELCOME TO THE 31ST CENTURY, FRIEND. THERE'S MUCH TO EXPLAIN, BUT--OUR COMRADE IS DYING. WILL YOU HELP US?
FINALLY, SOMEONE WITH PROPER PROPRIETY! WHADDAYA NEED ME TO DO, DONATE SOME BLOOD?
IF YOU WOULD, PLEASE HAVE A SEAT IN--

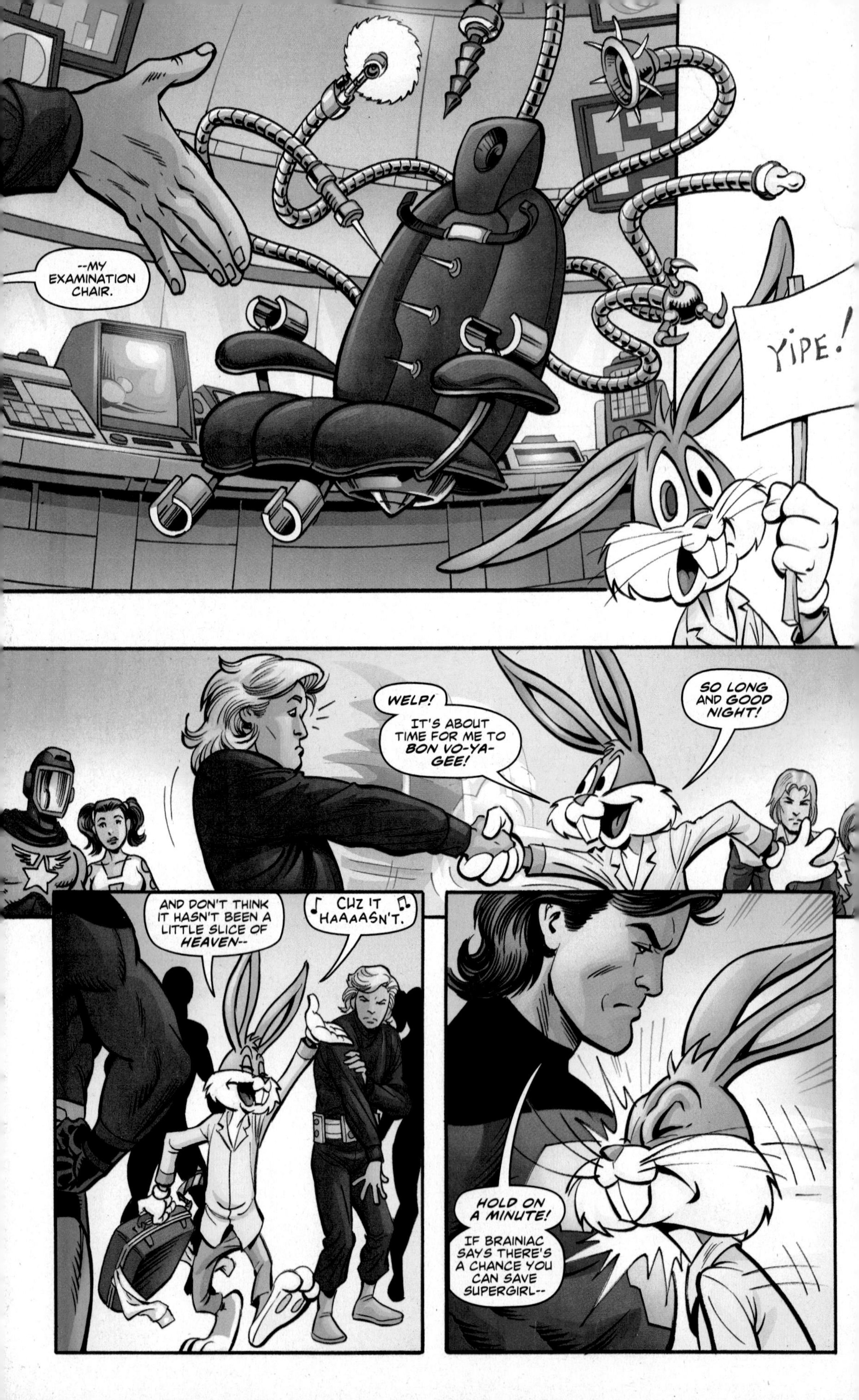
--MY EXAMINATION CHAIR.
YIPE!
WELP!
IT'S ABOUT TIME FOR ME TO BON VO-YA-GEE!
SO LONG AND GOOD NIGHT!
AND DON'T THINK IT HASN'T BEEN A LITTLE SLICE OF HEAVEN--
CUZ IT HAAAASN'T.
HOLD ON A MINUTE!
IF BRAINIAC SAYS THERE'S A CHANCE YOU CAN SAVE SUPERGIRL--

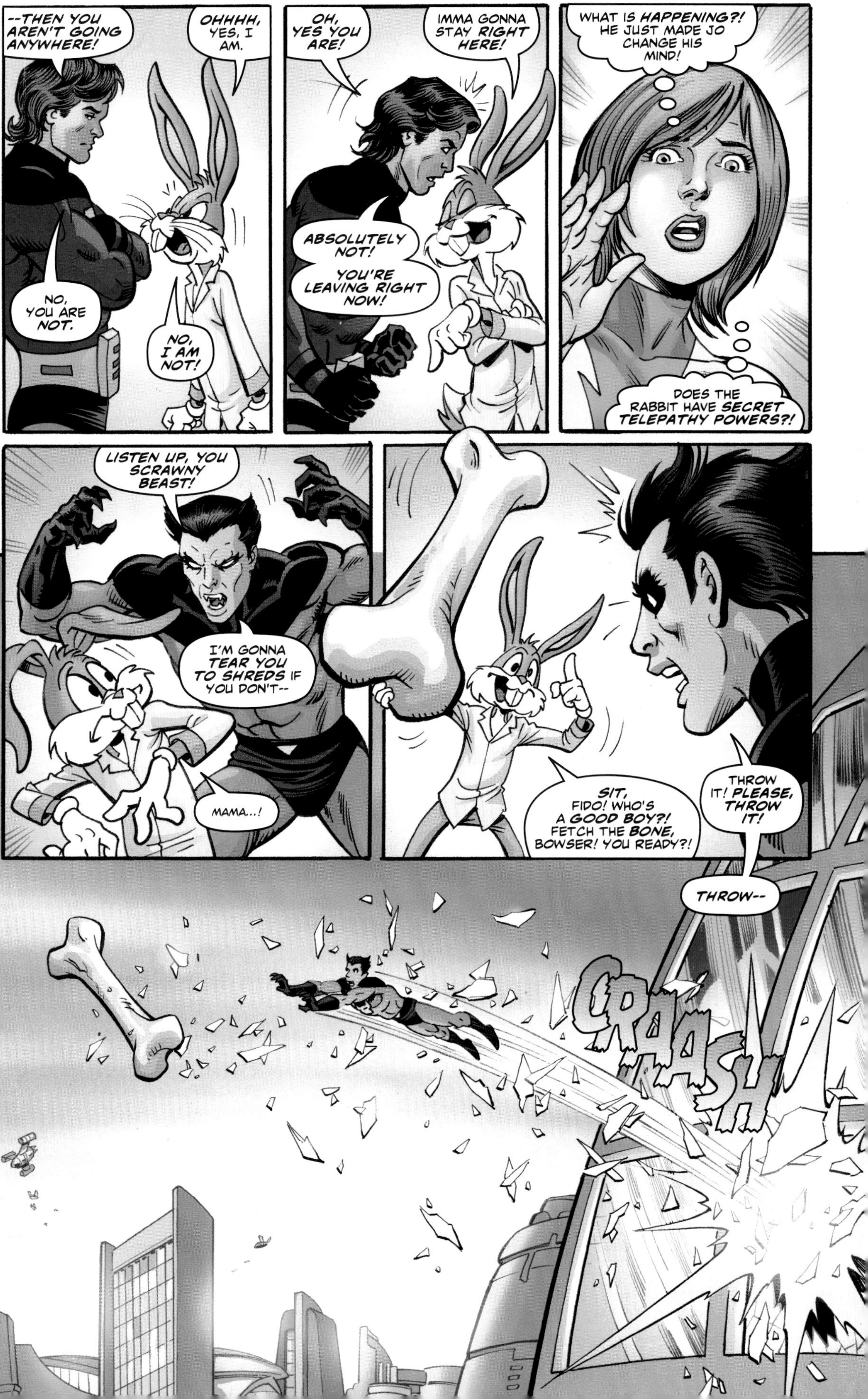
--THEN YOU AREN'T GOING ANYWHERE!
OHHHH, YES, I AM.
NO, YOU ARE NOT.
NO, I AM NOT!
OH, YES YOU ARE!
IMMA GONNA STAY RIGHT HERE!
ABSOLUTELY NOT!
YOU'RE LEAVING RIGHT NOW!
WHAT IS HAPPENING?! HE JUST MADE JO CHANGE HIS MIND!
DOES THE RABBIT HAVE SECRET TELEPATHY POWERS?!
LISTEN UP, YOU SCRAWNY BEAST!
I'M GONNA TEAR YOU TO SHREDS IF YOU DON'T--
MAMA...!
SIT, FIDO! WHO'S A GOOD BOY?! FETCH THE BONE, BOWSER! YOU READY?!
THROW IT! PLEASE, THROW IT!
THROW--
CRAASH

THAT GIANT BONE CAME OUT OF *NOWHERE!* THE RABBIT MUST HAVE *TELEPORTATION ABILITIES!* HOW MANY *SUPER POWERS* DOES HE HAVE?!

LOVE...

COMPUTO 2 OBSERVES FROM A REMOVE, ITS WHEELS AND RESISTORS WHIRRING ALMOST IMPERCEPTIBLY, AS IT CONTEMPLATES ITS OWN THOUGHTS...

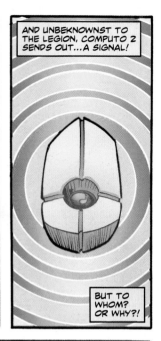

AND UNBEKNOWNST TO THE LEGION, COMPUTO 2 SENDS OUT...A SIGNAL!

BUT TO WHOM? OR WHY?!

RABBITS ARE *EXTINCT* ON EARTH IN THE 31ST CENTURY... I *DON'T WANT* TO HURT YOU!

THEM'S *FIGHTIN' WORDS!* JUST GIMME A SEC, MAC--

--AND I'LL SLIP INTO MY *WARRIOR ACCOUTRE- MENTS!*

IF YOU CAN'T LOVE YOURSELF, HOW TH' HECK YOU GONNA LOVE SOMEONE ELSE?

ENOUGH!

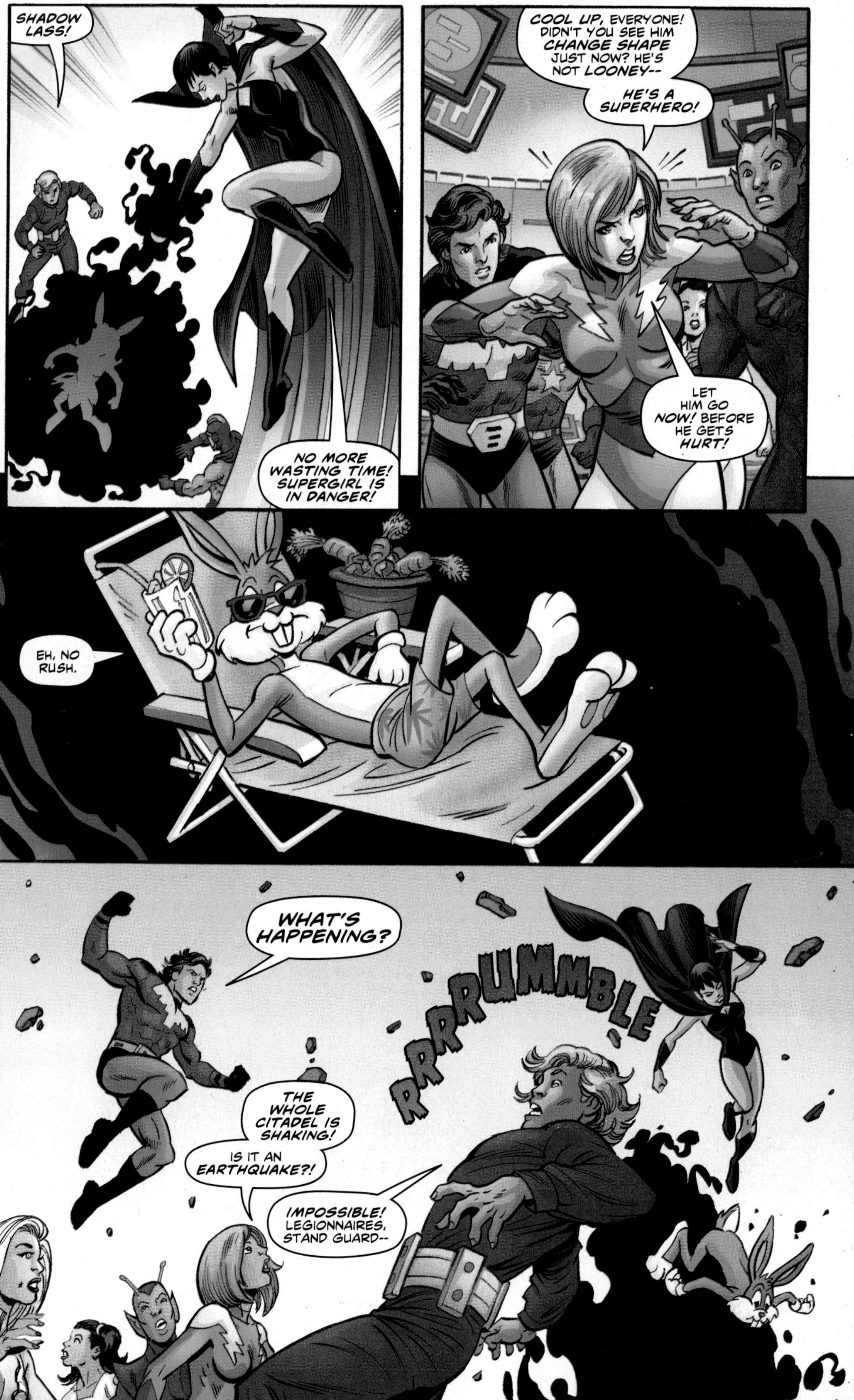
SHADOW LASS!
NO MORE WASTING TIME! SUPERGIRL IS IN DANGER!
COOL UP, EVERYONE! DIDN'T YOU SEE HIM CHANGE SHAPE JUST NOW? HE'S NOT LOONEY--
HE'S A SUPERHERO!
LET HIM GO NOW! BEFORE HE GETS HURT!
EH, NO RUSH.
WHAT'S HAPPENING?
RRRRUMMMBLE
THE WHOLE CITADEL IS SHAKING!
IS IT AN EARTHQUAKE?!
IMPOSSIBLE! LEGIONNAIRES, STAND GUARD--

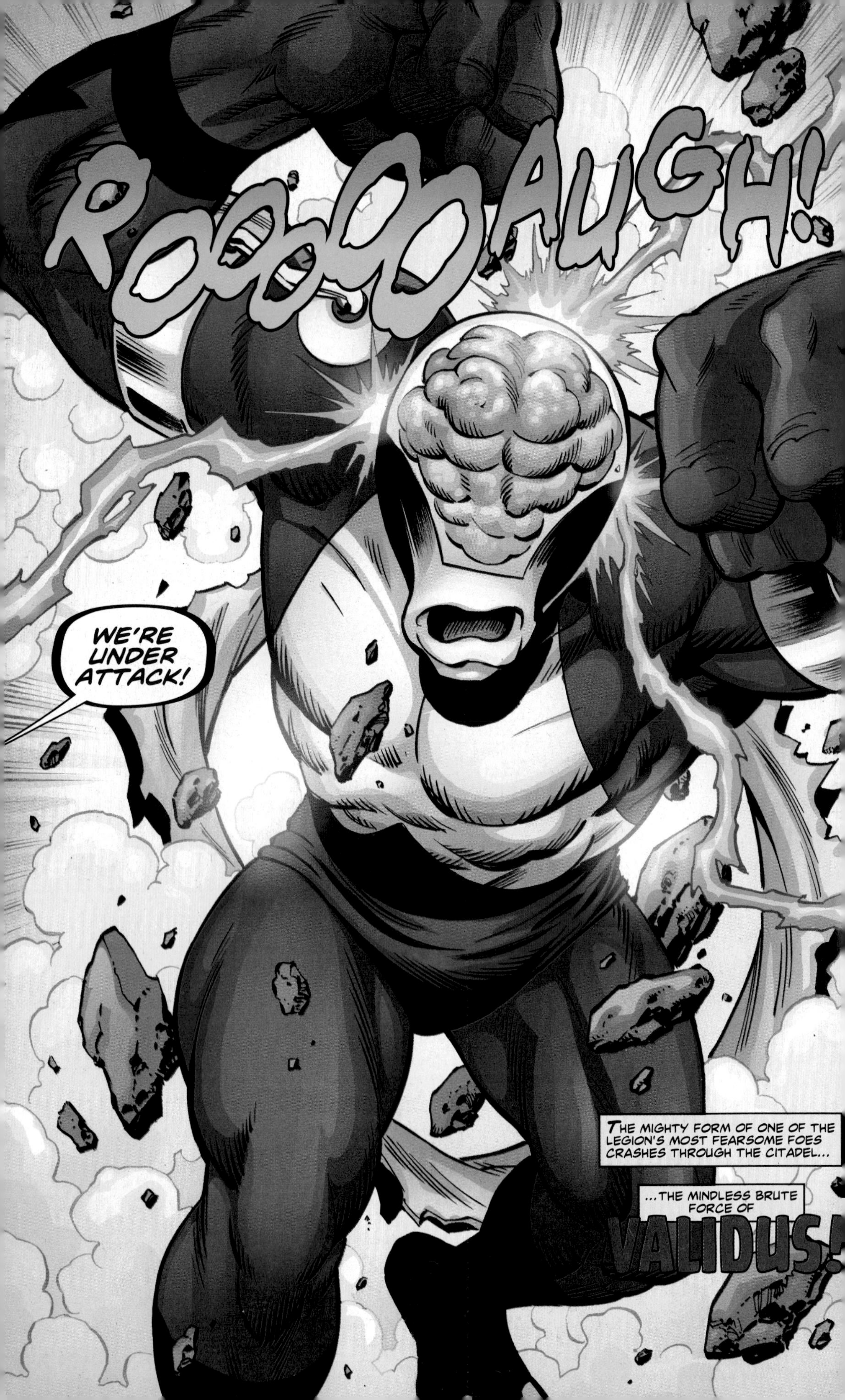
ROOOOOAUGH!
WE'RE UNDER ATTACK!
THE MIGHTY FORM OF ONE OF THE LEGION'S MOST FEARSOME FOES CRASHES THROUGH THE CITADEL...
...THE MINDLESS BRUTE FORCE OF
VALIDUS!

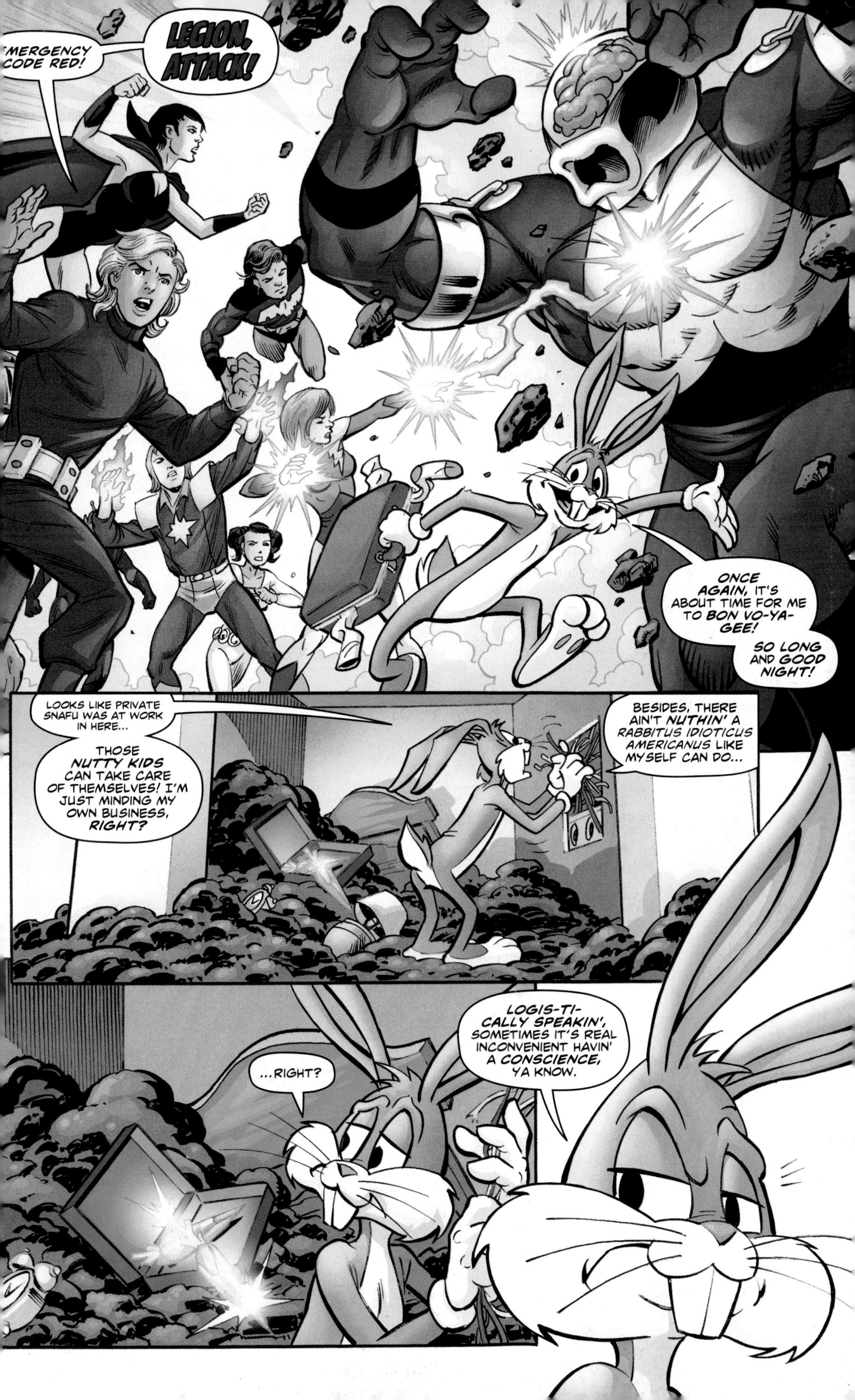
EMERGENCY CODE RED!
LEGION, ATTACK!
ONCE AGAIN, IT'S ABOUT TIME FOR ME TO BON VO-YA-GEE!
SO LONG AND GOOD NIGHT!
LOOKS LIKE PRIVATE SNAFU WAS AT WORK IN HERE...
THOSE NUTTY KIDS CAN TAKE CARE OF THEMSELVES! I'M JUST MINDING MY OWN BUSINESS, RIGHT?
BESIDES, THERE AIN'T NUTHIN' A RABBITUS IDIOTICUS AMERICANUS LIKE MYSELF CAN DO...
...RIGHT?
LOGIS-TI-CALLY SPEAKIN', SOMETIMES IT'S REAL INCONVENIENT HAVIN' A CONSCIENCE, YA KNOW.

CHAPTER 4 THE CURSE OF THE LEGION!

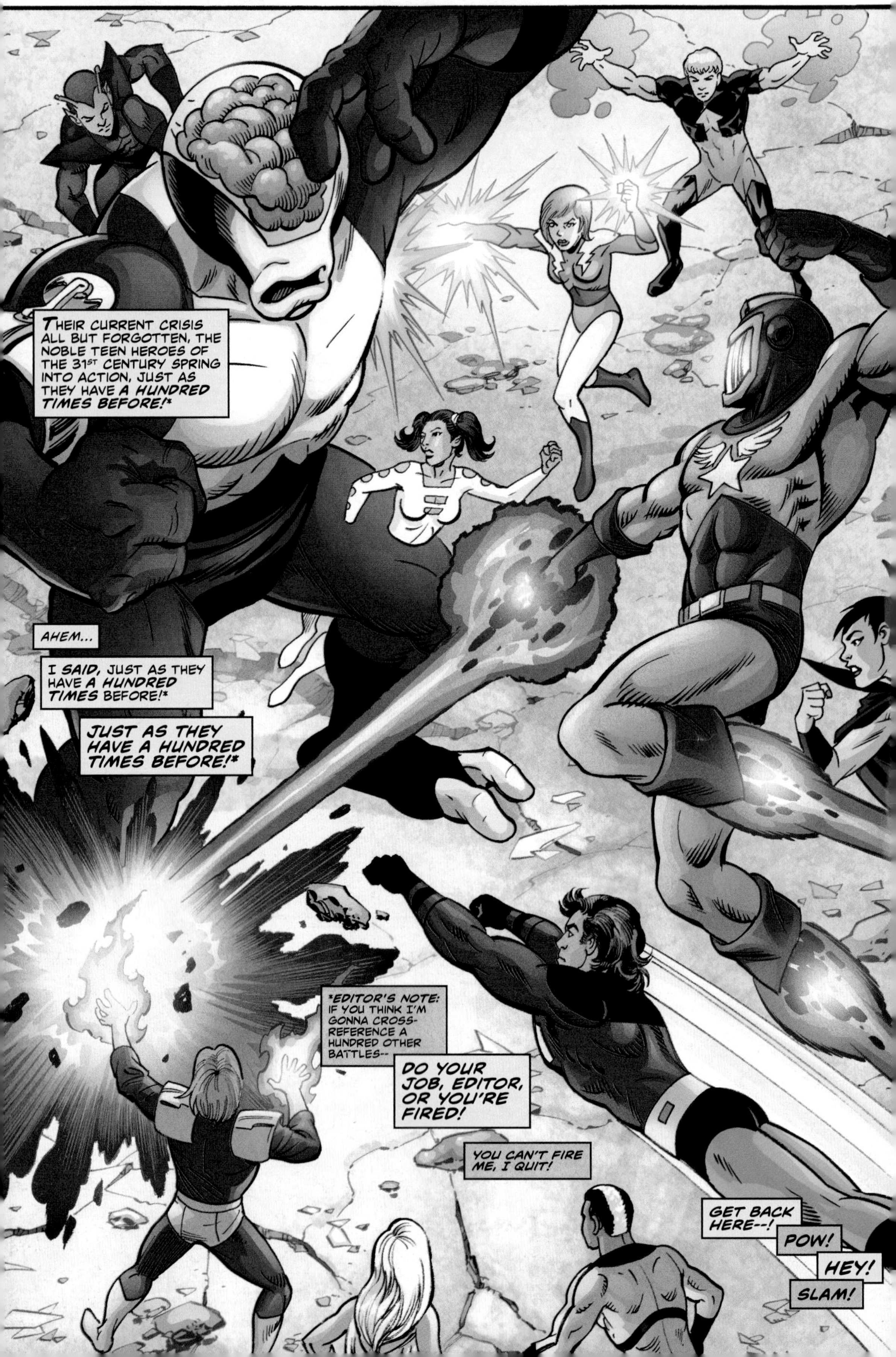

THEIR CURRENT CRISIS ALL BUT FORGOTTEN, THE NOBLE TEEN HEROES OF THE 31ST CENTURY SPRING INTO ACTION, JUST AS THEY HAVE A HUNDRED TIMES BEFORE!*
AHEM...
I SAID, JUST AS THEY HAVE A HUNDRED TIMES BEFORE!*
JUST AS THEY HAVE A HUNDRED TIMES BEFORE!*
*EDITOR'S NOTE: IF YOU THINK I'M GONNA CROSS-REFERENCE A HUNDRED OTHER BATTLES--
DO YOUR JOB, EDITOR, OR YOU'RE FIRED!
YOU CAN'T FIRE ME, I QUIT!
GET BACK HERE--!
POW!
HEY!
SLAM!

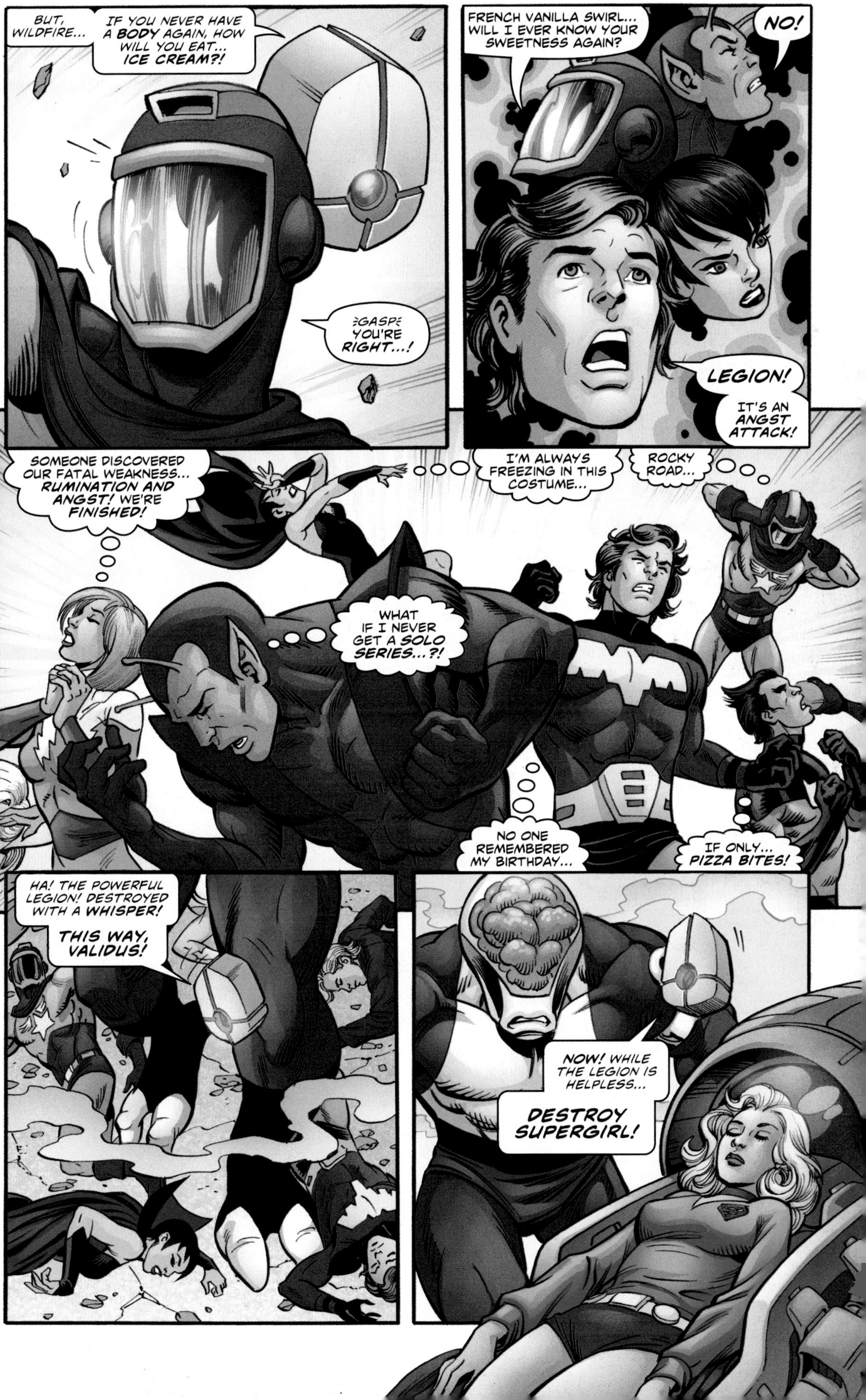
BUT, WILDFIRE...
IF YOU NEVER HAVE A BODY AGAIN, HOW WILL YOU EAT... ICE CREAM?!
GASP YOU'RE RIGHT...!
FRENCH VANILLA SWIRL... WILL I EVER KNOW YOUR SWEETNESS AGAIN?
NO!
LEGION!
IT'S AN ANGST ATTACK!
SOMEONE DISCOVERED OUR FATAL WEAKNESS... RUMINATION AND ANGST! WE'RE FINISHED!
I'M ALWAYS FREEZING IN THIS COSTUME...
ROCKY ROAD...
WHAT IF I NEVER GET A SOLO SERIES...?!
NO ONE REMEMBERED MY BIRTHDAY...
IF ONLY... PIZZA BITES!
HA! THE POWERFUL LEGION! DESTROYED WITH A WHISPER!
THIS WAY, VALIDUS!
NOW! WHILE THE LEGION IS HELPLESS...
DESTROY SUPERGIRL!

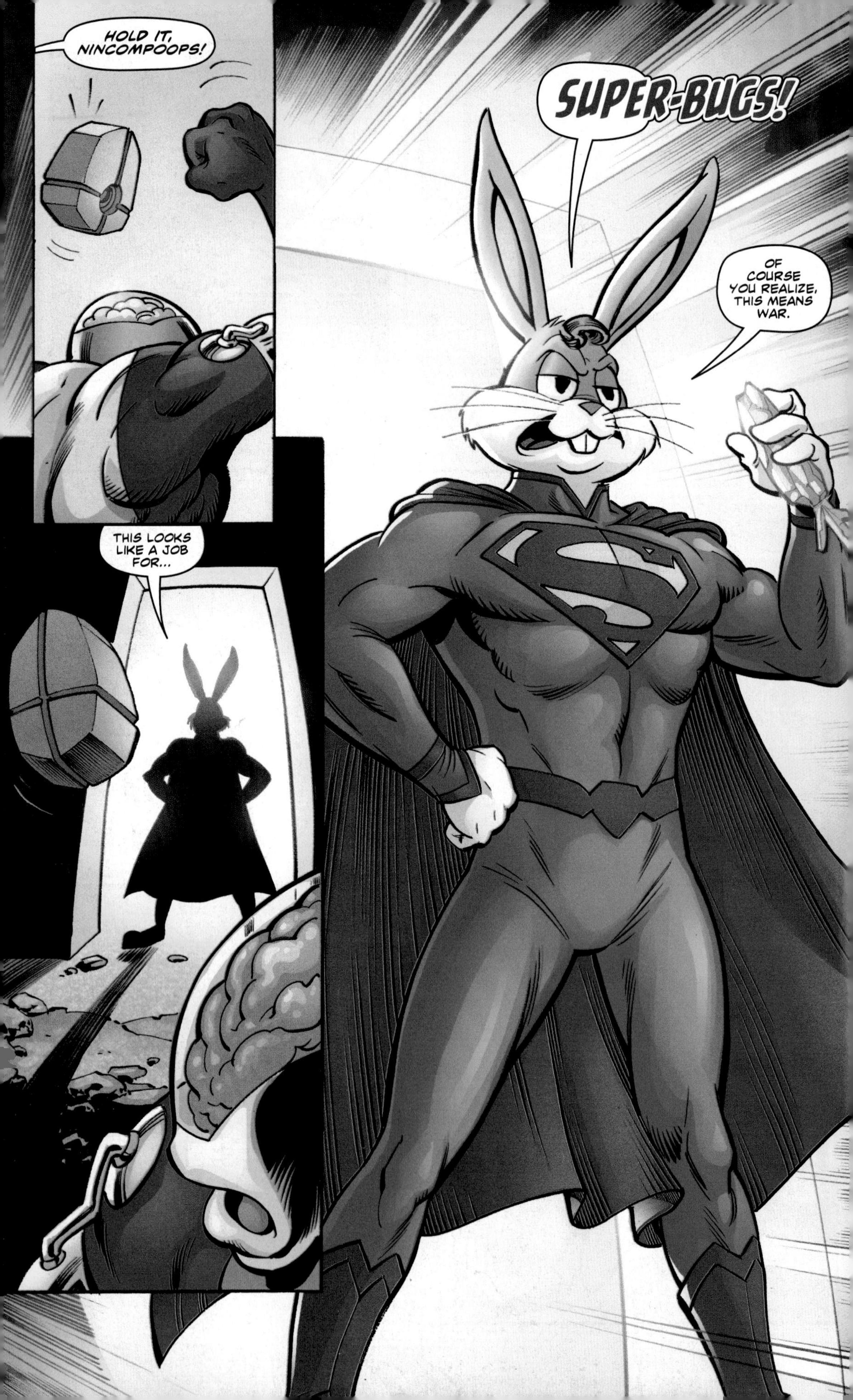
HOLD IT, NINCOMPOOPS!
THIS LOOKS LIKE A JOB FOR...
SUPER-BUGS!
OF COURSE YOU REALIZE, THIS MEANS WAR.

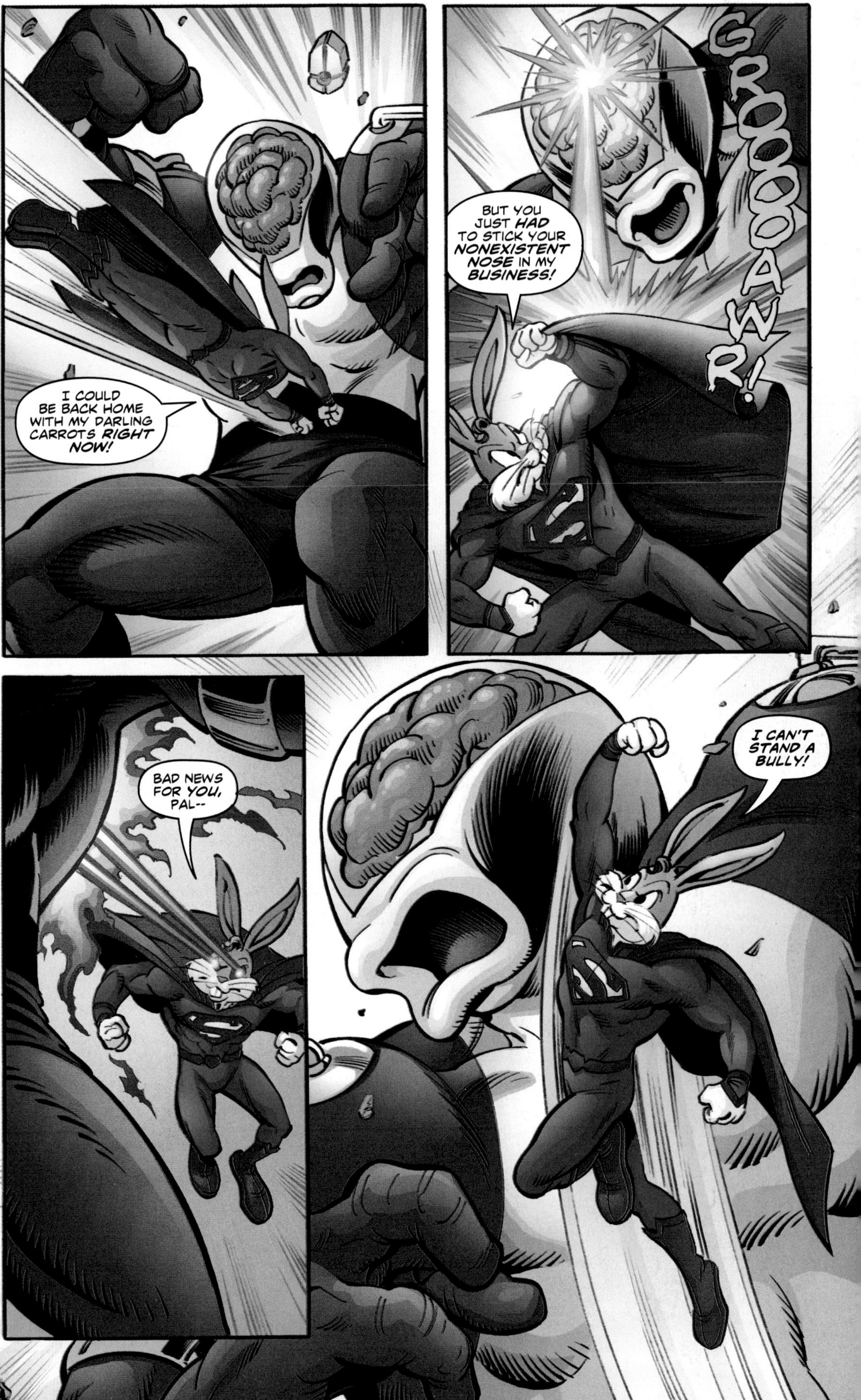
I COULD BE BACK HOME WITH MY DARLING CARROTS RIGHT NOW!
BUT YOU JUST HAD TO STICK YOUR NONEXISTENT NOSE IN MY BUSINESS!
GROOOOAWR!
BAD NEWS FOR YOU, PAL--
I CAN'T STAND A BULLY!

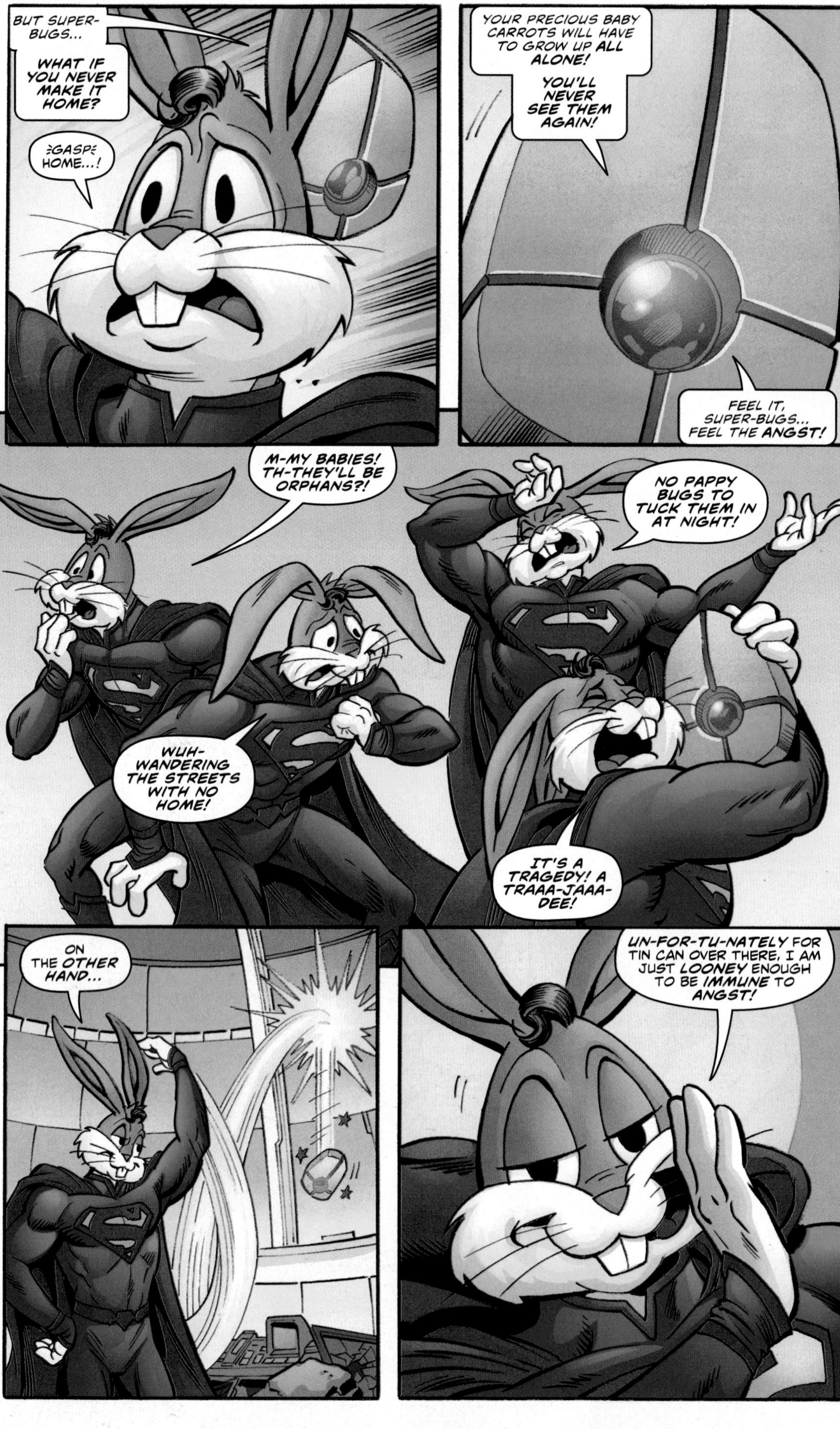
BUT SUPER-BUGS...
WHAT IF YOU NEVER MAKE IT HOME?
GASP HOME...!
YOUR PRECIOUS BABY CARROTS WILL HAVE TO GROW UP ALL ALONE!
YOU'LL NEVER SEE THEM AGAIN!
FEEL IT, SUPER-BUGS... FEEL THE ANGST!
M-MY BABIES! TH-THEY'LL BE ORPHANS?!
WUH-WANDERING THE STREETS WITH NO HOME!
NO PAPPY BUGS TO TUCK THEM IN AT NIGHT!
IT'S A TRAGEDY! A TRAAA-JAAA-DEE!
ON THE OTHER HAND...
UN-FOR-TU-NATELY FOR TIN CAN OVER THERE, I AM JUST LOONEY ENOUGH TO BE IMMUNE TO ANGST!

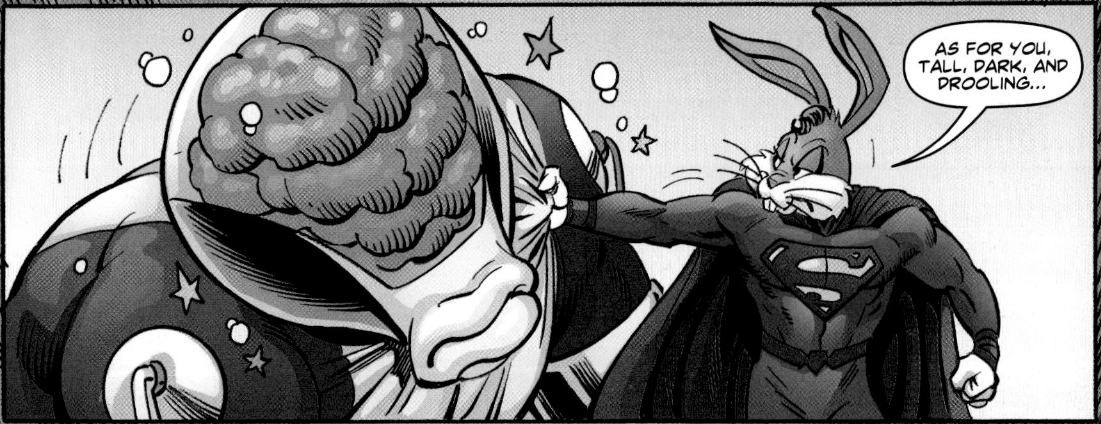
AS FOR YOU, TALL, DARK, AND DROOLING...

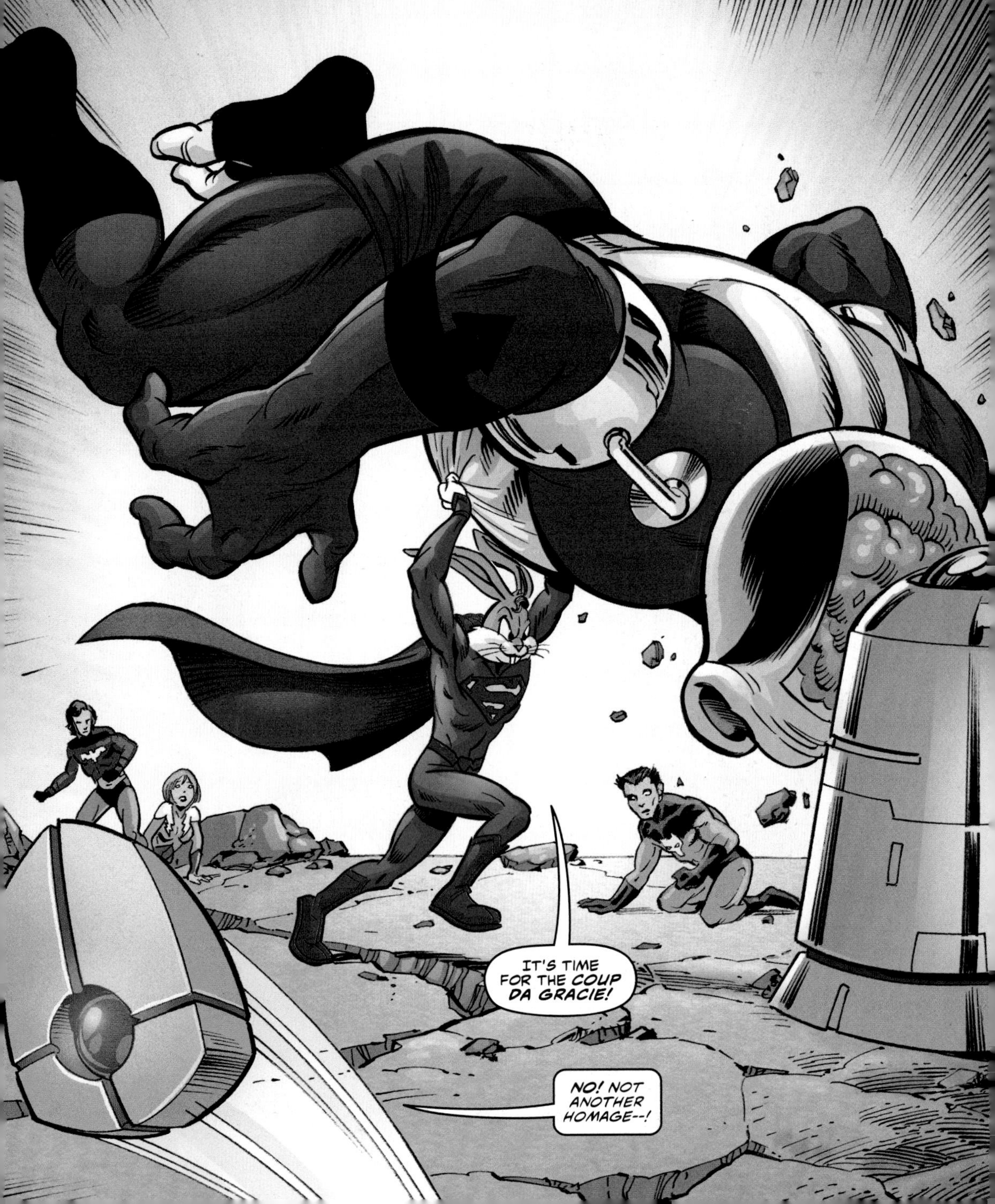
IT'S TIME FOR THE COUP DA GRACIE!
NO! NOT ANOTHER HOMAGE--!

CHAPTER 5 FUNERAL FOR A FRIEND?

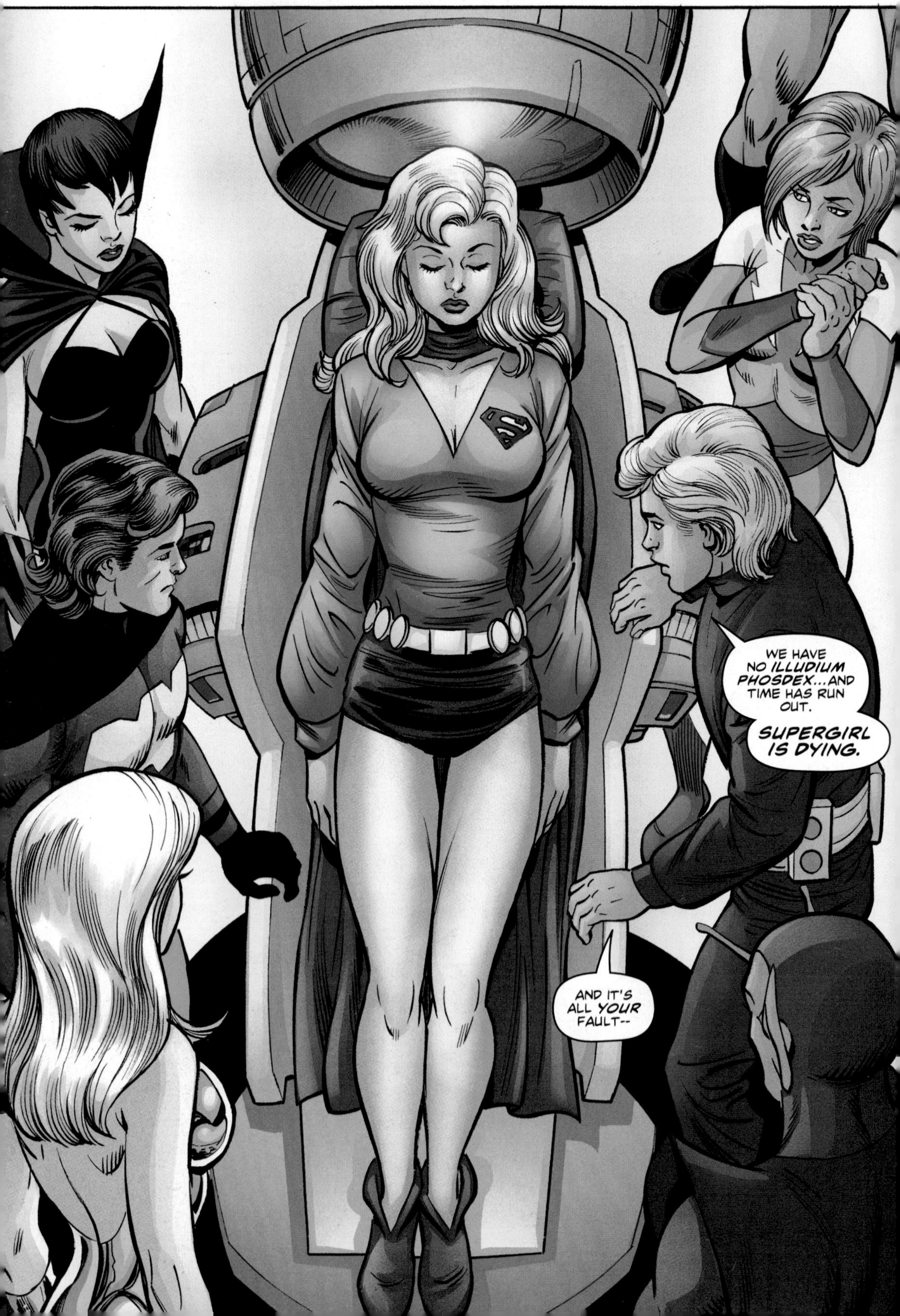
WE HAVE NO ILLUDIUM PHOSDEX...AND TIME HAS RUN OUT.
SUPERGIRL IS DYING.
AND IT'S ALL YOUR FAULT--

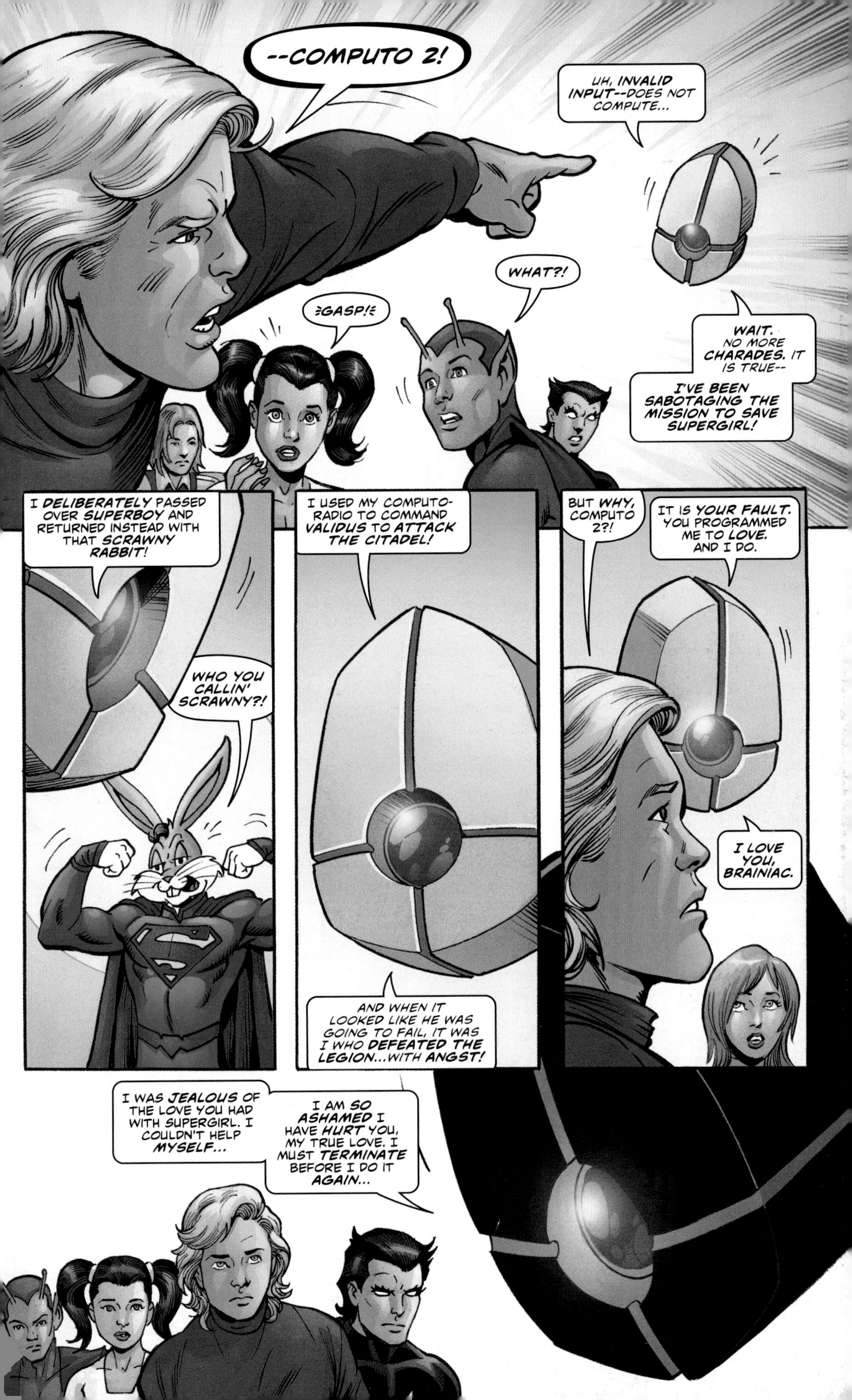
--COMPUTO 2!
UH, INVALID INPUT--DOES NOT COMPUTE...
¡GASP!¡
WHAT?!
WAIT. NO MORE CHARADES. IT IS TRUE--
I'VE BEEN SABOTAGING THE MISSION TO SAVE SUPERGIRL!
I DELIBERATELY PASSED OVER SUPERBOY AND RETURNED INSTEAD WITH THAT SCRAWNY RABBIT!
WHO YOU CALLIN' SCRAWNY?!
I USED MY COMPUTO-RADIO TO COMMAND VALIDUS TO ATTACK THE CITADEL!
AND WHEN IT LOOKED LIKE HE WAS GOING TO FAIL, IT WAS I WHO DEFEATED THE LEGION...WITH ANGST!
BUT WHY, COMPUTO 2?!
IT IS YOUR FAULT. YOU PROGRAMMED ME TO LOVE. AND I DO.
I LOVE YOU, BRAINIAC.
I WAS JEALOUS OF THE LOVE YOU HAD WITH SUPERGIRL. I COULDN'T HELP MYSELF...
I AM SO ASHAMED I HAVE HURT YOU, MY TRUE LOVE. I MUST TERMINATE BEFORE I DO IT AGAIN...

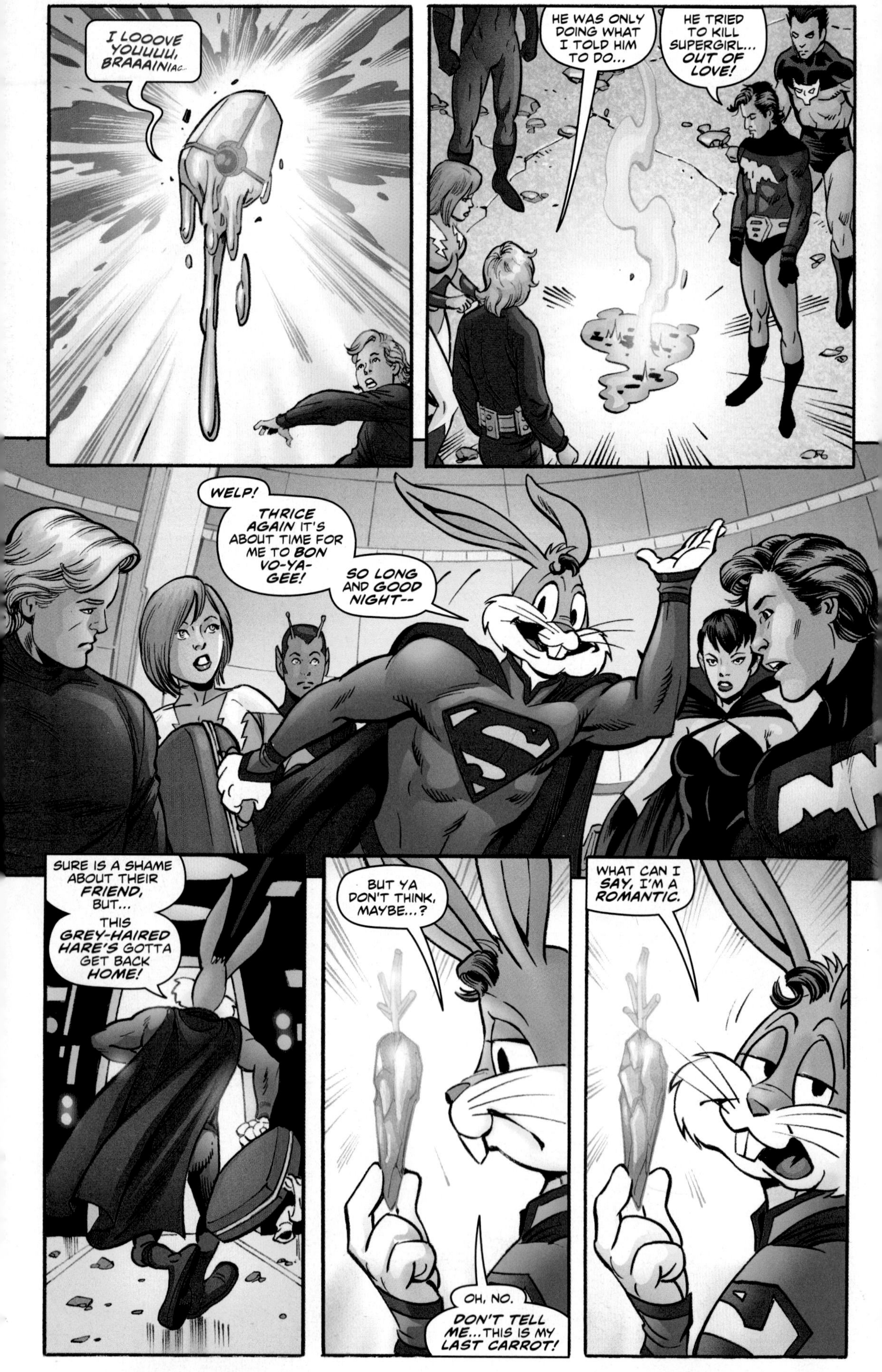
I LOOOVE YOUUUU, BRAAAINIAC...
HE WAS ONLY DOING WHAT I TOLD HIM TO DO...
HE TRIED TO KILL SUPERGIRL... OUT OF LOVE!
WELP!
THRICE AGAIN IT'S ABOUT TIME FOR ME TO BON VO-YA-GEE!
SO LONG AND GOOD NIGHT--
SURE IS A SHAME ABOUT THEIR FRIEND, BUT...
THIS GREY-HAIRED HARE'S GOTTA GET BACK HOME!
BUT YA DON'T THINK, MAYBE...?
OH, NO.
DON'T TELL ME... THIS IS MY LAST CARROT!
WHAT CAN I SAY, I'M A ROMANTIC.

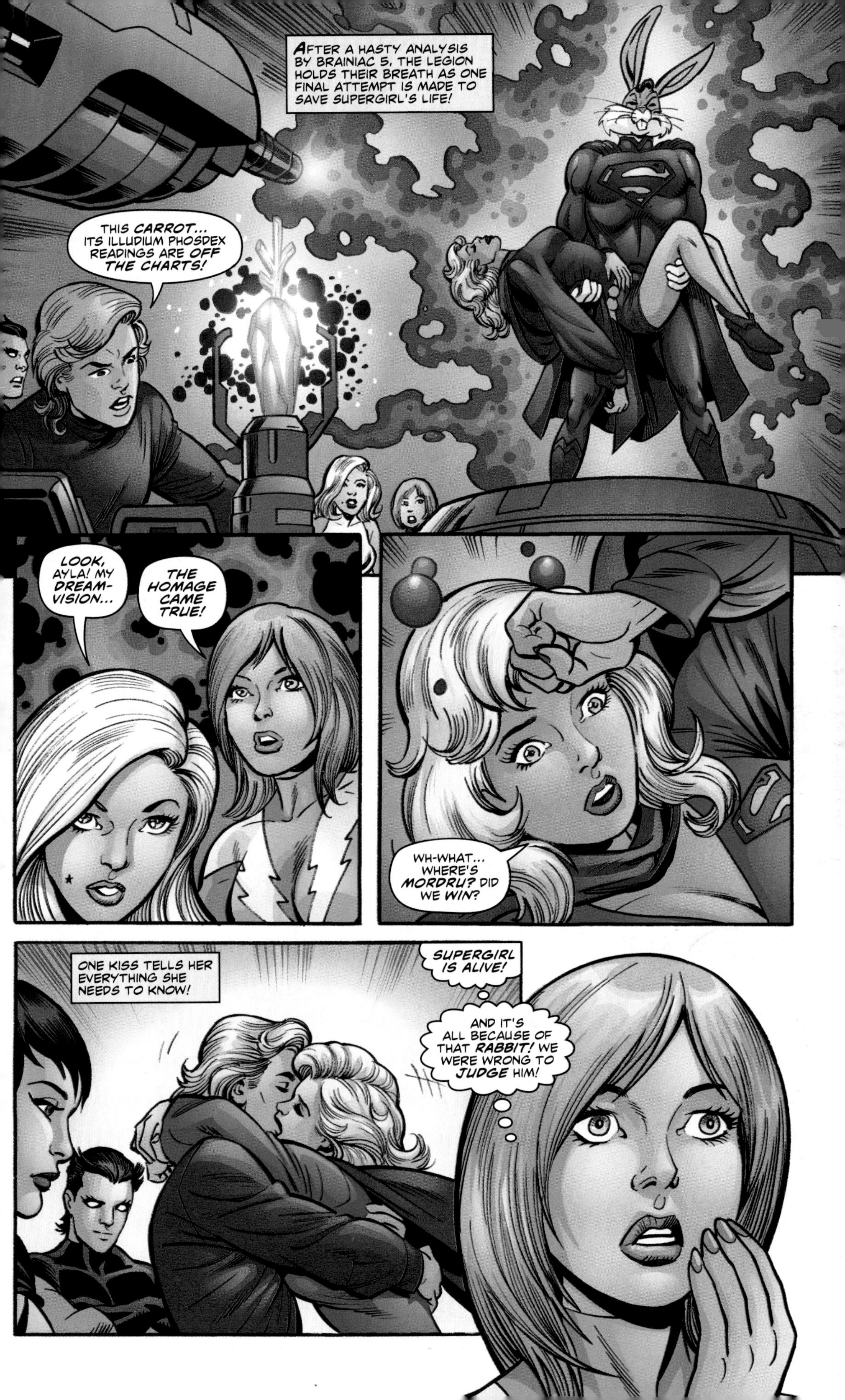
AFTER A HASTY ANALYSIS BY BRAINIAC 5, THE LEGION HOLDS THEIR BREATH AS ONE FINAL ATTEMPT IS MADE TO SAVE SUPERGIRL'S LIFE!
THIS CARROT... ITS ILLUDIUM PHOSDEX READINGS ARE OFF THE CHARTS!
LOOK, AYLA! MY DREAM-VISION...
THE HOMAGE CAME TRUE!
WH-WHAT... WHERE'S MORDRU? DID WE WIN?
ONE KISS TELLS HER EVERYTHING SHE NEEDS TO KNOW!
SUPERGIRL IS ALIVE!
AND IT'S ALL BECAUSE OF THAT RABBIT! WE WERE WRONG TO JUDGE HIM!

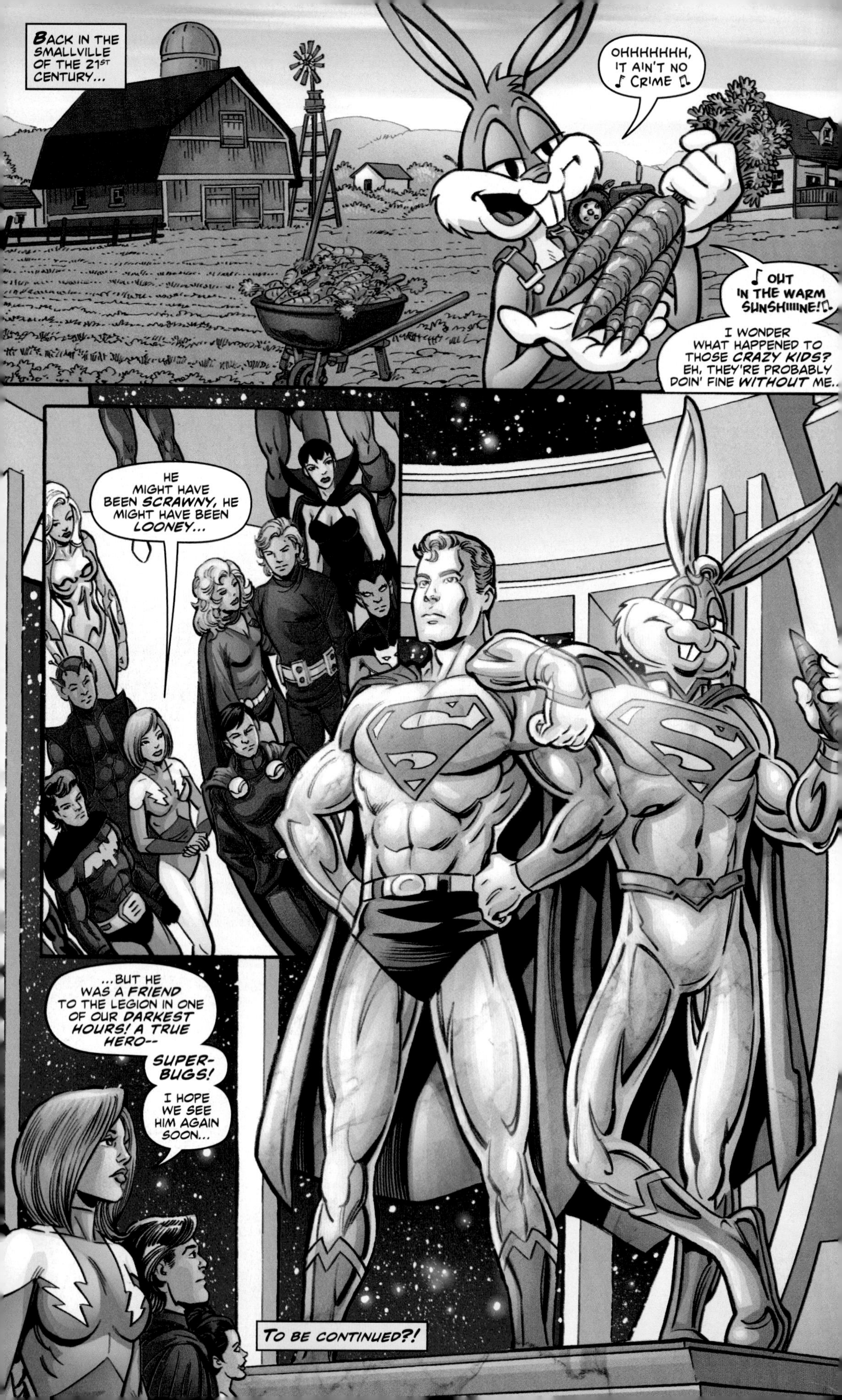

BACK IN THE SMALLVILLE OF THE 21ST CENTURY...
OHHHHHHH, IT AIN'T NO ♪ CRIME ♫
♪ OUT IN THE WARM SUNSHIIIINE! ♫
I WONDER WHAT HAPPENED TO THOSE CRAZY KIDS? EH, THEY'RE PROBABLY DOIN' FINE WITHOUT ME...
HE MIGHT HAVE BEEN SCRAWNY, HE MIGHT HAVE BEEN LOONEY...
...BUT HE WAS A FRIEND TO THE LEGION IN ONE OF OUR DARKEST HOURS! A TRUE HERO--
SUPER-BUGS!
I HOPE WE SEE HIM AGAIN SOON...
TO BE CONTINUED?!

TALES OF THE
LEGION of SUPER-HEROES

What happens when you send a *rascally* rabbit into the far-flung future? Pure *chaos*, that's what! Just see for yourself when-- THE LEGION OF SUPER-HEROES MEET--

the IMPOSTOR SUPERBOY!

WRITTEN AND DRAWN BY:
JUAN MANUEL ORTIZ
SPECIAL THANKS:
MARK PRUDEAUX

FACE IT, *DOCS!* THE *FUTURE* IS LOOKING A LOT BRIGHTER, NOW THAT I'M HERE!

STOP HIM! OR WE'RE ALL FINISHED!

STOP HIM? HOW? --HOW?

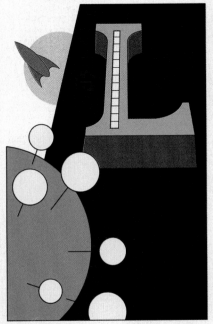

Welcome to the 31st century! We begin our tale on Earth, where we find the headquarters for *THE LEGION OF SUPER-HEROES!*

And also *SUPERGIRL!* --In a coma! She has been lying in medical stasis since infecting herself with the incurable *RIGEL FEVER!* It had been her only way to defeat *MORDRU,* the immortal sorcerer!*

*AS WITNESSED LAST ISSUE. -Ed.

Brainiac 5 is at his most manic!

He has been working *furiously* around the clock to save his one true *love!*

Will he succeed? Or will it be fate that intervenes this day?

I MUSN'T GIVE UP!

--THERE IS *ALWAYS* HOPE!

1

BRAINIAC 5 IS JOINED BY TWO OF HIS FELLOW LEGIONNAIRES -- ULTRA BOY AND LIGHTNING LASS.

BRAINIAC! ANY PROGRESS IN SUPERGIRL'S STATUS?

IS THERE ANYTHING THAT WE CAN DO TO HELP?

NOTHING NEW TO REPORT, YET.

HOWEVER, COMPUTO 2 IS ALSO WORKING TO DISCOVER A FORMULA.

TOGETHER, WE MAY YET PROVE TO BE SUCCESSFUL.

COMPUTO 2? HMM, IF HE'S ANYTHING LIKE THE FIRST COMPUTO, SUPERGIRL MAY NEVER BE CURED.

ULTRA BOY!

SOMEWHAT MIFFED, BRAINIAC 5 BRUSHES OFF HIS FELLOW LEGIONNAIRES' CONCERNS.

YOU DON'T NEED TO WORRY, ULTRA BOY. COMPUTO 2 HAS BEEN PROGRAMMED TO LOVE ALL OF US. THAT INCLUDES EVEN YOU.

I-- I DIDN'T MEAN - -

AS IF ON CUE-- COMPUTO 2 ENTERS WITH SOME NEWS.

FORGIVE MY INTRUSION, SIR. HOWEVER, I BELIEVE THAT I MAY HAVE FOUND SOMETHING THAT WILL BE OF INTEREST.

WHAT IS IT, COMPUTO 2?

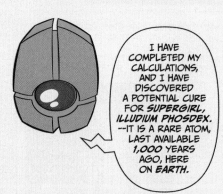

I HAVE COMPLETED MY CALCULATIONS, AND I HAVE DISCOVERED A POTENTIAL CURE FOR SUPERGIRL, ILLUDIUM PHOSDEX. --IT IS A RARE ATOM, LAST AVAILABLE 1,000 YEARS AGO, HERE ON EARTH.

1,000? THAT MEANS THAT IT WAS AVAILABLE IN THE 20TH CENTURY. MAYBE OUR FRIEND SUPERBOY CAN HELP US!

COMPUTO 2-- DON'T DELAY! GO INTO THE TIME CUBE!

--BRING BACK SUPERBOY!

BY YOUR COMMAND.

WITH THOSE PARTING WORDS, COMPUTO 2 BEGINS HIS JOURNEY INTO THE PAST!

JANGG

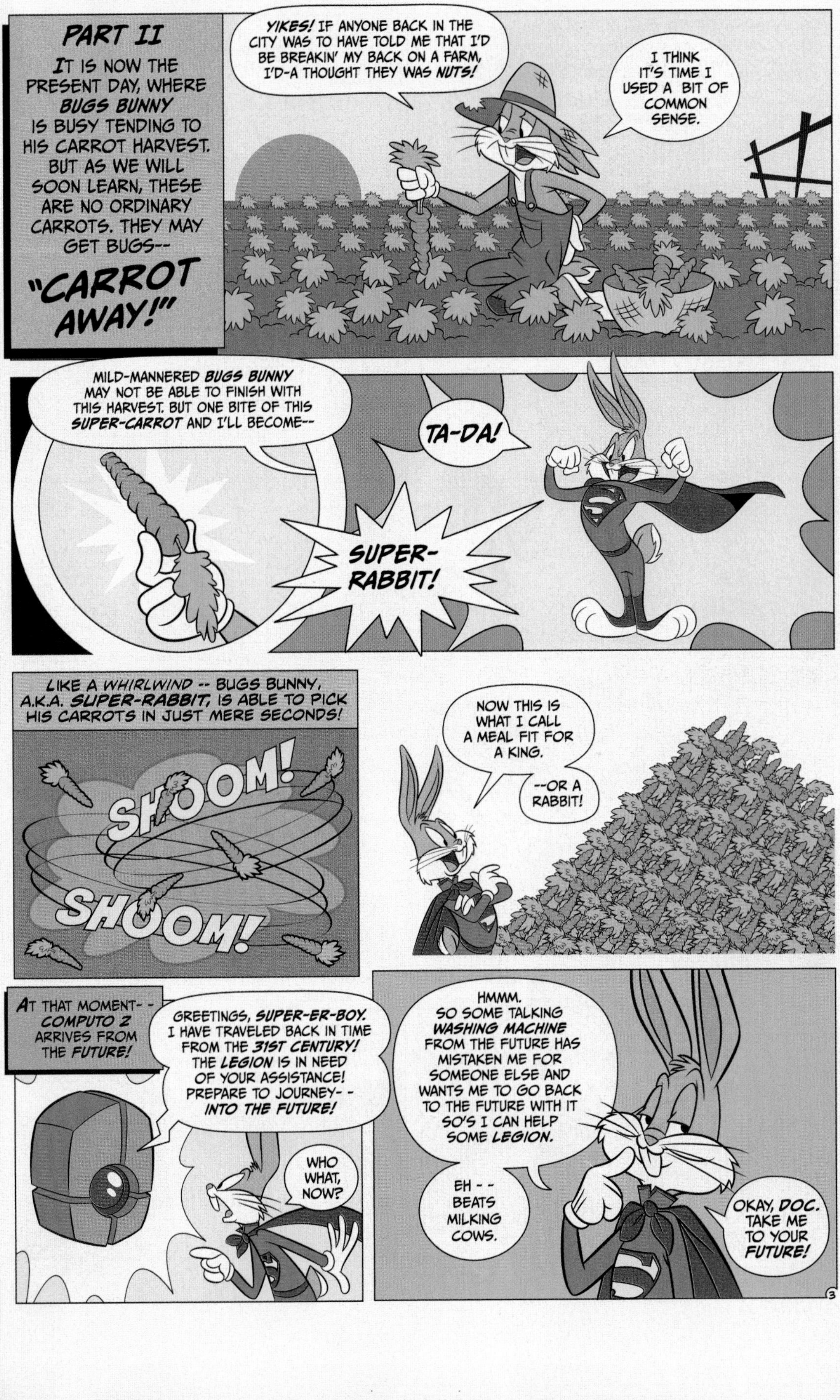
PART II
IT IS NOW THE PRESENT DAY, WHERE BUGS BUNNY IS BUSY TENDING TO HIS CARROT HARVEST. BUT AS WE WILL SOON LEARN, THESE ARE NO ORDINARY CARROTS. THEY MAY GET BUGS--
"CARROT AWAY!"
YIKES! IF ANYONE BACK IN THE CITY WAS TO HAVE TOLD ME THAT I'D BE BREAKIN' MY BACK ON A FARM, I'D-A THOUGHT THEY WAS NUTS!
I THINK IT'S TIME I USED A BIT OF COMMON SENSE.
MILD-MANNERED BUGS BUNNY MAY NOT BE ABLE TO FINISH WITH THIS HARVEST. BUT ONE BITE OF THIS SUPER-CARROT AND I'LL BECOME--
TA-DA!
SUPER-RABBIT!
LIKE A WHIRLWIND -- BUGS BUNNY, A.K.A. SUPER-RABBIT, IS ABLE TO PICK HIS CARROTS IN JUST MERE SECONDS!
SHOOM!
SHOOM!
NOW THIS IS WHAT I CALL A MEAL FIT FOR A KING.
--OR A RABBIT!
AT THAT MOMENT--COMPUTO 2 ARRIVES FROM THE FUTURE!
GREETINGS, SUPER-ER-BOY. I HAVE TRAVELED BACK IN TIME FROM THE 31ST CENTURY! THE LEGION IS IN NEED OF YOUR ASSISTANCE! PREPARE TO JOURNEY--INTO THE FUTURE!
WHO WHAT, NOW?
HMMM. SO SOME TALKING WASHING MACHINE FROM THE FUTURE HAS MISTAKEN ME FOR SOMEONE ELSE AND WANTS ME TO GO BACK TO THE FUTURE WITH IT SO'S I CAN HELP SOME LEGION.
EH--BEATS MILKING COWS.
OKAY, DOC. TAKE ME TO YOUR FUTURE!

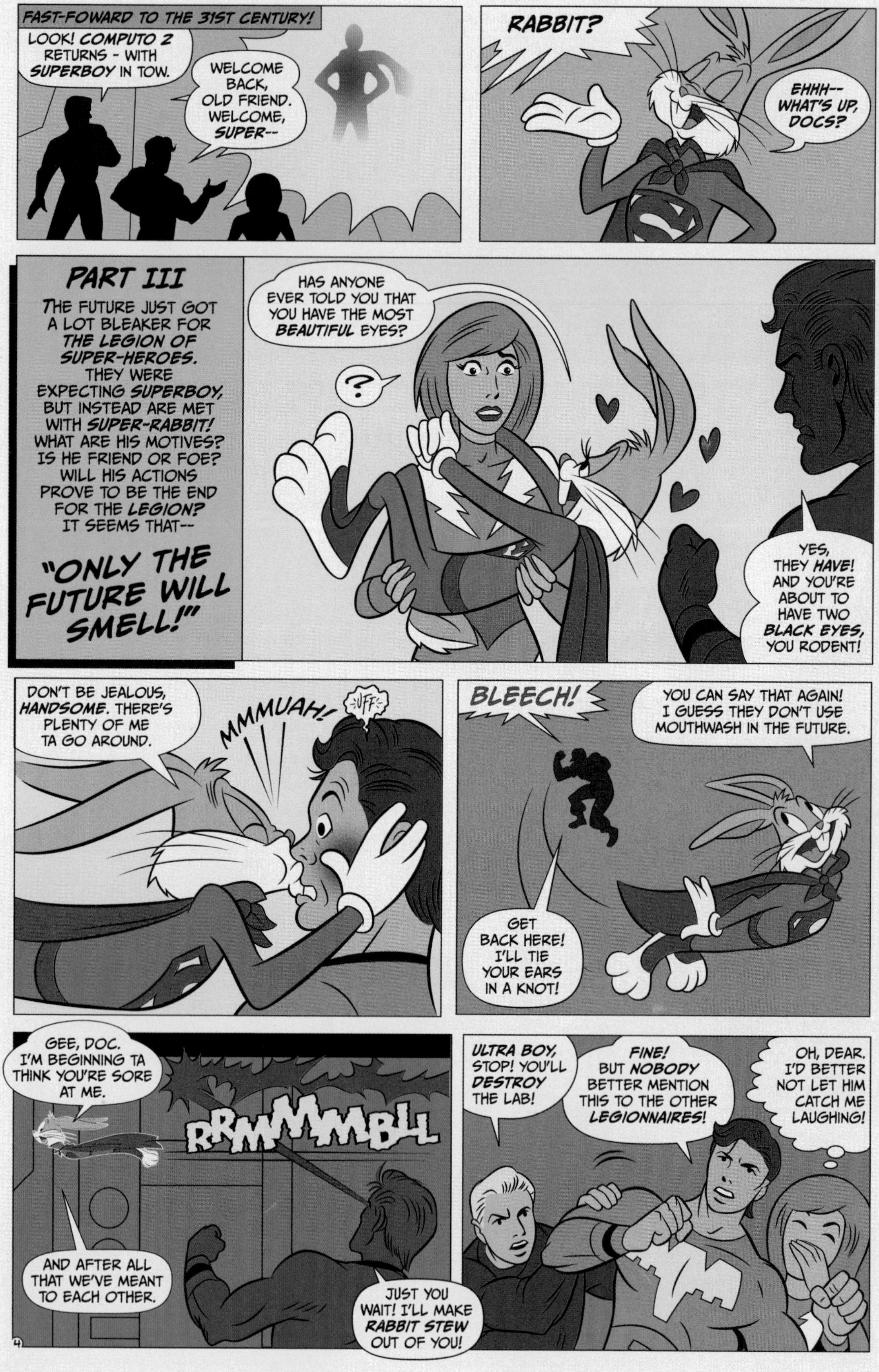

FAST-FOWARD TO THE 31ST CENTURY!
LOOK! COMPUTO 2 RETURNS - WITH SUPERBOY IN TOW.
WELCOME BACK, OLD FRIEND. WELCOME, SUPER--
RABBIT?
EHHH-- WHAT'S UP, DOCS?
PART III
THE FUTURE JUST GOT A LOT BLEAKER FOR THE LEGION OF SUPER-HEROES. THEY WERE EXPECTING SUPERBOY, BUT INSTEAD ARE MET WITH SUPER-RABBIT! WHAT ARE HIS MOTIVES? IS HE FRIEND OR FOE? WILL HIS ACTIONS PROVE TO BE THE END FOR THE LEGION? IT SEEMS THAT--
"ONLY THE FUTURE WILL SMELL!"
HAS ANYONE EVER TOLD YOU THAT YOU HAVE THE MOST BEAUTIFUL EYES?
?
YES, THEY HAVE! AND YOU'RE ABOUT TO HAVE TWO BLACK EYES, YOU RODENT!
DON'T BE JEALOUS, HANDSOME. THERE'S PLENTY OF ME TA GO AROUND.
MMMUAH!
UFF
BLEECH!
YOU CAN SAY THAT AGAIN! I GUESS THEY DON'T USE MOUTHWASH IN THE FUTURE.
GET BACK HERE! I'LL TIE YOUR EARS IN A KNOT!
GEE, DOC. I'M BEGINNING TA THINK YOU'RE SORE AT ME.
RRMMMMBLL
AND AFTER ALL THAT WE'VE MEANT TO EACH OTHER.
JUST YOU WAIT! I'LL MAKE RABBIT STEW OUT OF YOU!
ULTRA BOY, STOP! YOU'LL DESTROY THE LAB!
FINE! BUT NOBODY BETTER MENTION THIS TO THE OTHER LEGIONNAIRES!
OH, DEAR. I'D BETTER NOT LET HIM CATCH ME LAUGHING!

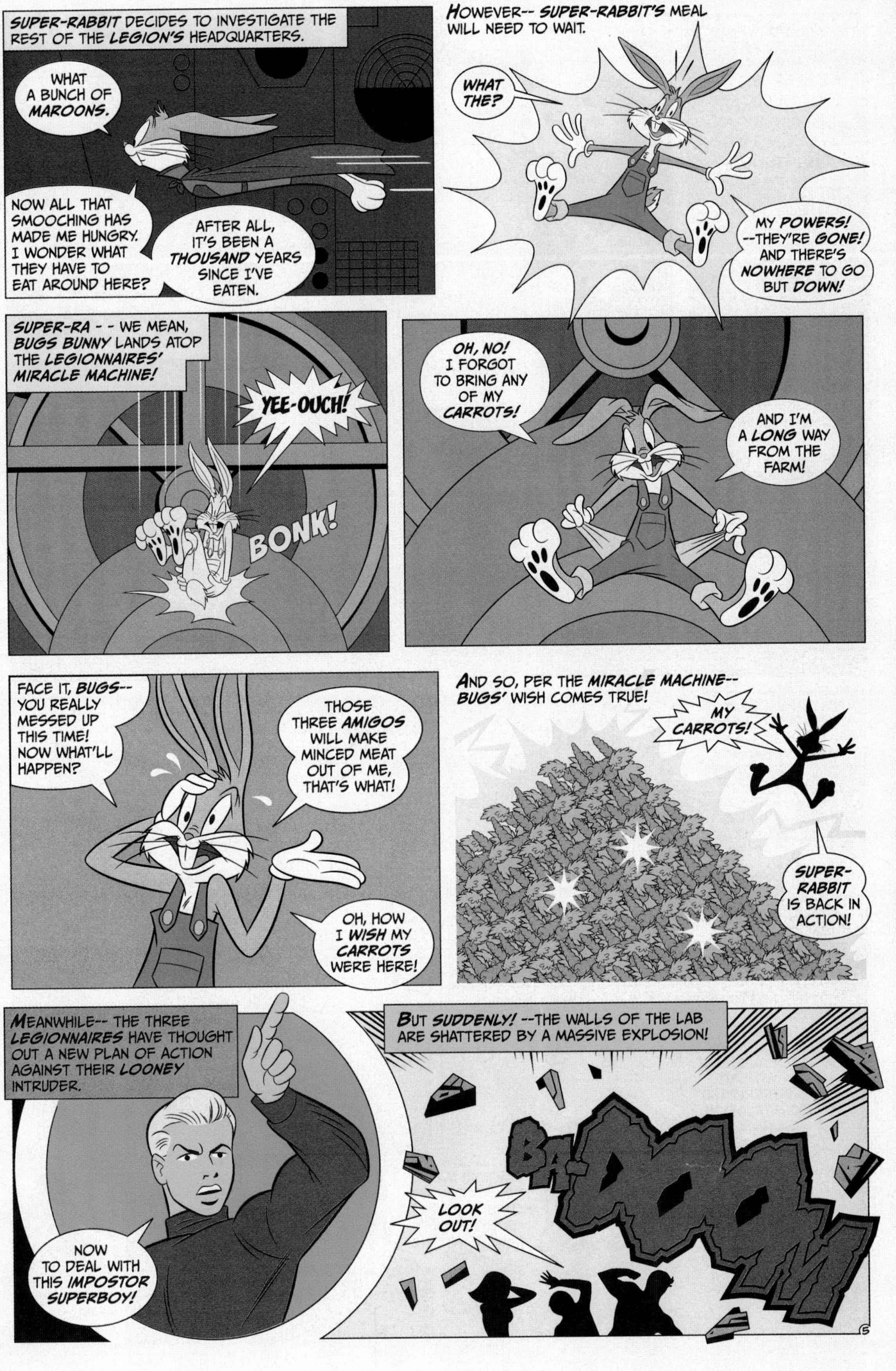

SUPER-RABBIT DECIDES TO INVESTIGATE THE REST OF THE LEGION'S HEADQUARTERS.
WHAT A BUNCH OF MAROONS.
NOW ALL THAT SMOOCHING HAS MADE ME HUNGRY. I WONDER WHAT THEY HAVE TO EAT AROUND HERE?
AFTER ALL, IT'S BEEN A THOUSAND YEARS SINCE I'VE EATEN.
HOWEVER-- SUPER-RABBIT'S MEAL WILL NEED TO WAIT.
WHAT THE?
MY POWERS! --THEY'RE GONE! AND THERE'S NOWHERE TO GO BUT DOWN!
SUPER-RA - - WE MEAN, BUGS BUNNY LANDS ATOP THE LEGIONNAIRES' MIRACLE MACHINE!
YEE-OUCH!
BONK!
OH, NO! I FORGOT TO BRING ANY OF MY CARROTS!
AND I'M A LONG WAY FROM THE FARM!
FACE IT, BUGS-- YOU REALLY MESSED UP THIS TIME! NOW WHAT'LL HAPPEN?
THOSE THREE AMIGOS WILL MAKE MINCED MEAT OUT OF ME, THAT'S WHAT!
OH, HOW I WISH MY CARROTS WERE HERE!
AND SO, PER THE MIRACLE MACHINE-- BUGS' WISH COMES TRUE!
MY CARROTS!
SUPER-RABBIT IS BACK IN ACTION!
MEANWHILE-- THE THREE LEGIONNAIRES HAVE THOUGHT OUT A NEW PLAN OF ACTION AGAINST THEIR LOONEY INTRUDER.
NOW TO DEAL WITH THIS IMPOSTOR SUPERBOY!
BUT SUDDENLY! --THE WALLS OF THE LAB ARE SHATTERED BY A MASSIVE EXPLOSION!
BA-DOOM
LOOK OUT!

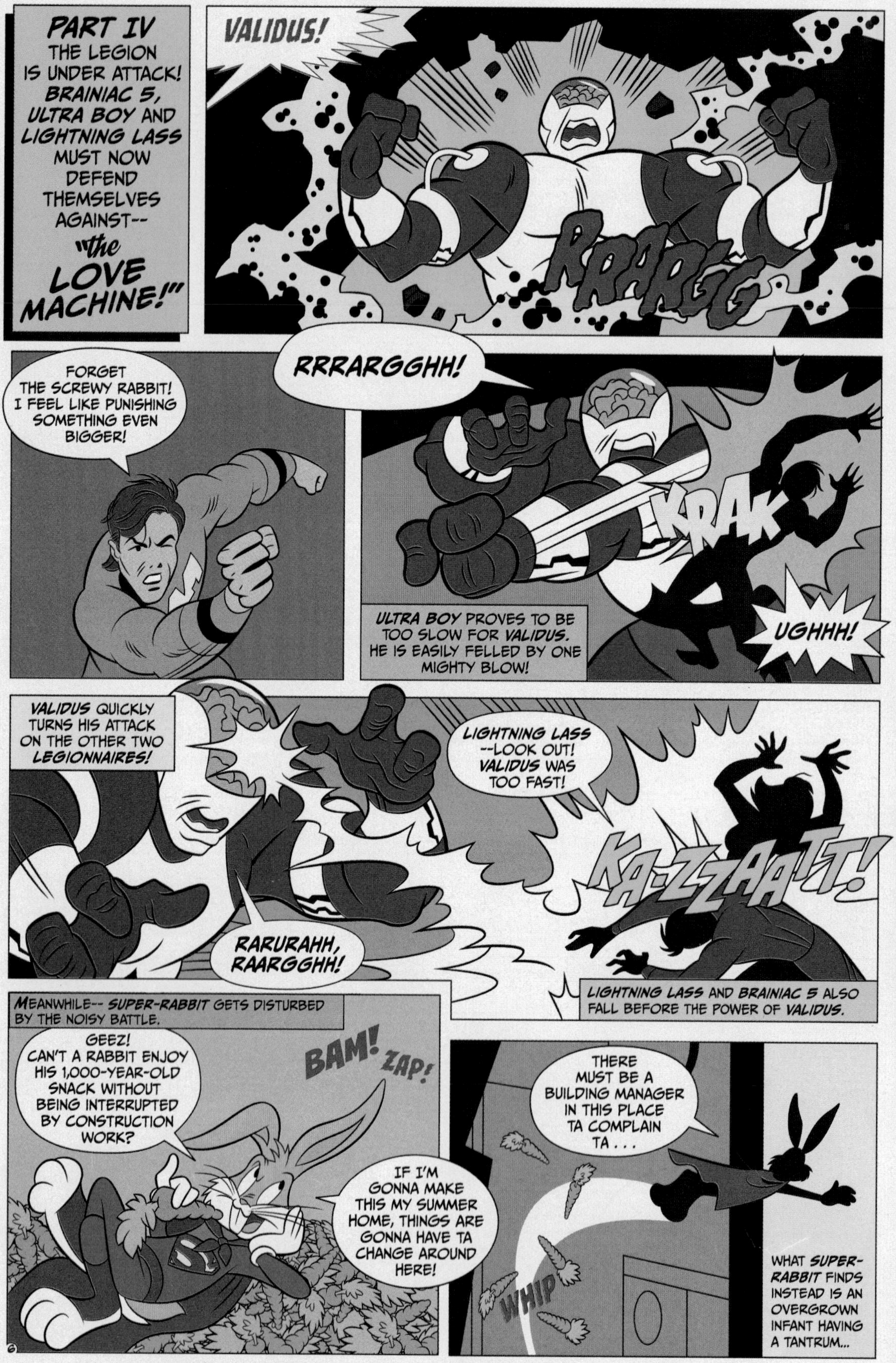
PART IV
THE LEGION IS UNDER ATTACK! BRAINIAC 5, ULTRA BOY AND LIGHTNING LASS MUST NOW DEFEND THEMSELVES AGAINST-- "the LOVE MACHINE!"
VALIDUS!
RRARGG
FORGET THE SCREWY RABBIT! I FEEL LIKE PUNISHING SOMETHING EVEN BIGGER!
RRRARGGHH!
KRAK
ULTRA BOY PROVES TO BE TOO SLOW FOR VALIDUS. HE IS EASILY FELLED BY ONE MIGHTY BLOW!
UGHHH!
VALIDUS QUICKLY TURNS HIS ATTACK ON THE OTHER TWO LEGIONNAIRES!
LIGHTNING LASS --LOOK OUT! VALIDUS WAS TOO FAST!
KA-ZZAATT!
RARURAHH, RAARGGHH!
LIGHTNING LASS AND BRAINIAC 5 ALSO FALL BEFORE THE POWER OF VALIDUS.
MEANWHILE-- SUPER-RABBIT GETS DISTURBED BY THE NOISY BATTLE.
BAM! ZAP!
GEEZ! CAN'T A RABBIT ENJOY HIS 1,000-YEAR-OLD SNACK WITHOUT BEING INTERRUPTED BY CONSTRUCTION WORK?
IF I'M GONNA MAKE THIS MY SUMMER HOME, THINGS ARE GONNA HAVE TA CHANGE AROUND HERE!
THERE MUST BE A BUILDING MANAGER IN THIS PLACE TA COMPLAIN TA . . .
WHIP
WHAT SUPER-RABBIT FINDS INSTEAD IS AN OVERGROWN INFANT HAVING A TANTRUM...

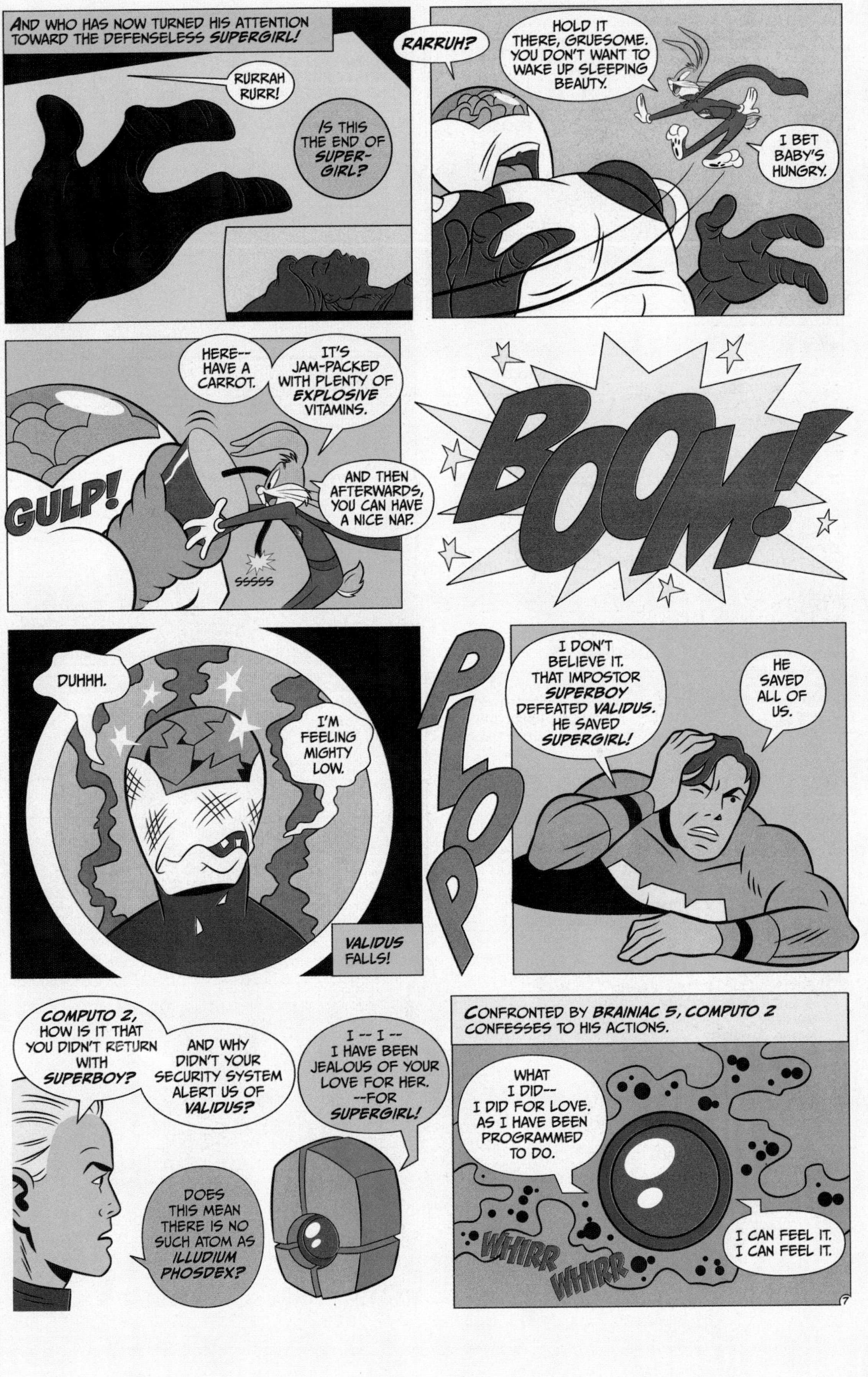

AND WHO HAS NOW TURNED HIS ATTENTION TOWARD THE DEFENSELESS SUPERGIRL!
RURRAH RURR!
IS THIS THE END OF SUPER-GIRL?
RARRUH?
HOLD IT THERE, GRUESOME. YOU DON'T WANT TO WAKE UP SLEEPING BEAUTY.
I BET BABY'S HUNGRY.
HERE-- HAVE A CARROT.
IT'S JAM-PACKED WITH PLENTY OF EXPLOSIVE VITAMINS.
GULP!
AND THEN AFTERWARDS, YOU CAN HAVE A NICE NAP.
SSSSS
BOOM!
DUHHH.
I'M FEELING MIGHTY LOW.
VALIDUS FALLS!
PLOP
I DON'T BELIEVE IT. THAT IMPOSTOR SUPERBOY DEFEATED VALIDUS. HE SAVED SUPERGIRL!
HE SAVED ALL OF US.
COMPUTO 2, HOW IS IT THAT YOU DIDN'T RETURN WITH SUPERBOY?
AND WHY DIDN'T YOUR SECURITY SYSTEM ALERT US OF VALIDUS?
I -- I -- I HAVE BEEN JEALOUS OF YOUR LOVE FOR HER. --FOR SUPERGIRL!
DOES THIS MEAN THERE IS NO SUCH ATOM AS ILLUDIUM PHOSDEX?
CONFRONTED BY BRAINIAC 5, COMPUTO 2 CONFESSES TO HIS ACTIONS.
WHAT I DID-- I DID FOR LOVE. AS I HAVE BEEN PROGRAMMED TO DO.
WHIRR WHIRR
I CAN FEEL IT. I CAN FEEL IT.

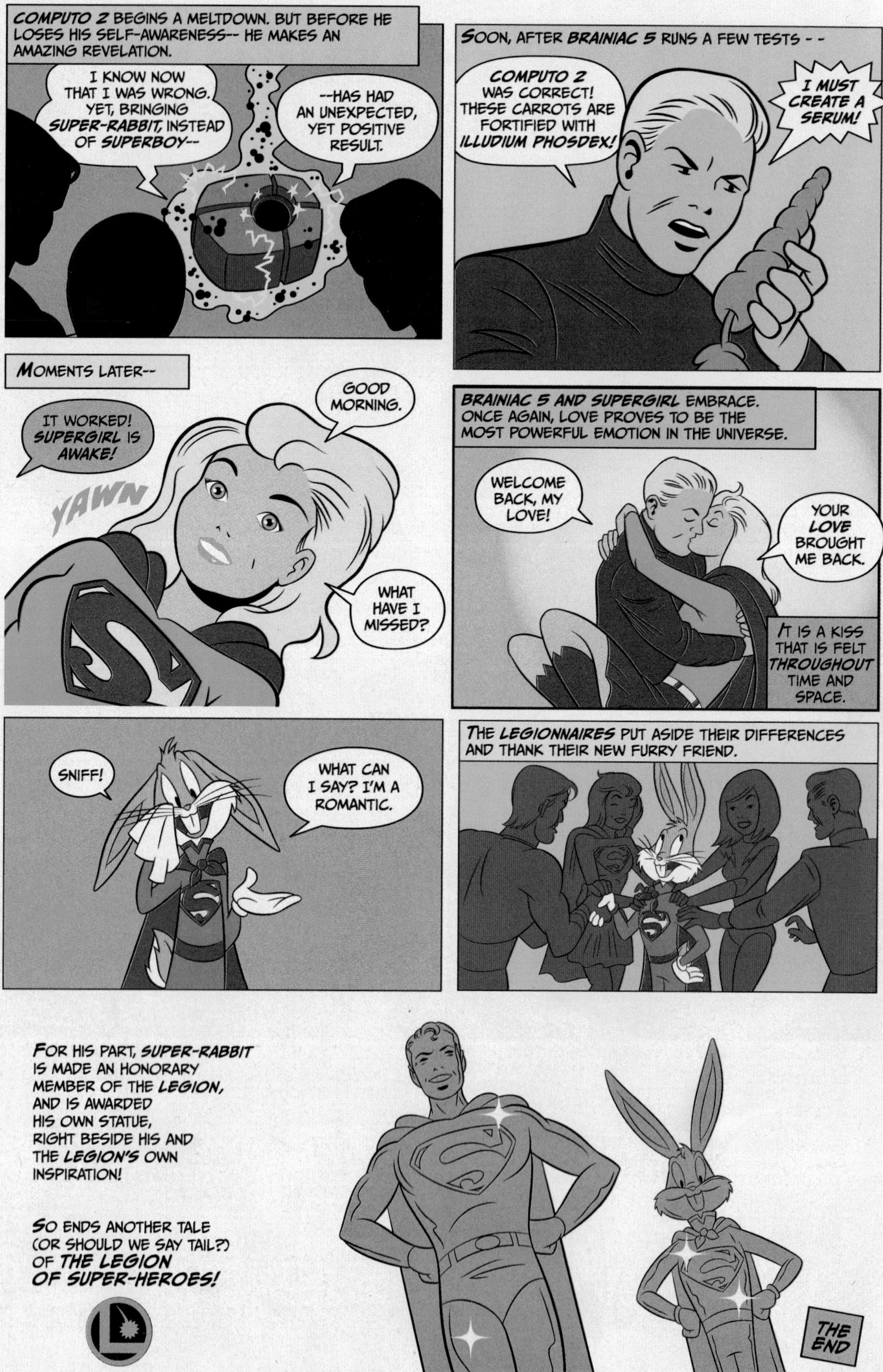
COMPUTO 2 BEGINS A MELTDOWN. BUT BEFORE HE LOSES HIS SELF-AWARENESS-- HE MAKES AN AMAZING REVELATION.
I KNOW NOW THAT I WAS WRONG. YET, BRINGING SUPER-RABBIT, INSTEAD OF SUPERBOY--
--HAS HAD AN UNEXPECTED, YET POSITIVE RESULT.
SOON, AFTER BRAINIAC 5 RUNS A FEW TESTS - -
COMPUTO 2 WAS CORRECT! THESE CARROTS ARE FORTIFIED WITH ILLUDIUM PHOSDEX!
I MUST CREATE A SERUM!
MOMENTS LATER--
IT WORKED! SUPERGIRL IS AWAKE!
GOOD MORNING.
YAWN
WHAT HAVE I MISSED?
BRAINIAC 5 AND SUPERGIRL EMBRACE. ONCE AGAIN, LOVE PROVES TO BE THE MOST POWERFUL EMOTION IN THE UNIVERSE.
WELCOME BACK, MY LOVE!
YOUR LOVE BROUGHT ME BACK.
IT IS A KISS THAT IS FELT THROUGHOUT TIME AND SPACE.
SNIFF!
WHAT CAN I SAY? I'M A ROMANTIC.
THE LEGIONNAIRES PUT ASIDE THEIR DIFFERENCES AND THANK THEIR NEW FURRY FRIEND.
FOR HIS PART, SUPER-RABBIT IS MADE AN HONORARY MEMBER OF THE LEGION, AND IS AWARDED HIS OWN STATUE, RIGHT BESIDE HIS AND THE LEGION'S OWN INSPIRATION!
SO ENDS ANOTHER TALE (OR SHOULD WE SAY TAIL?) OF THE LEGION OF SUPER-HEROES!
THE END

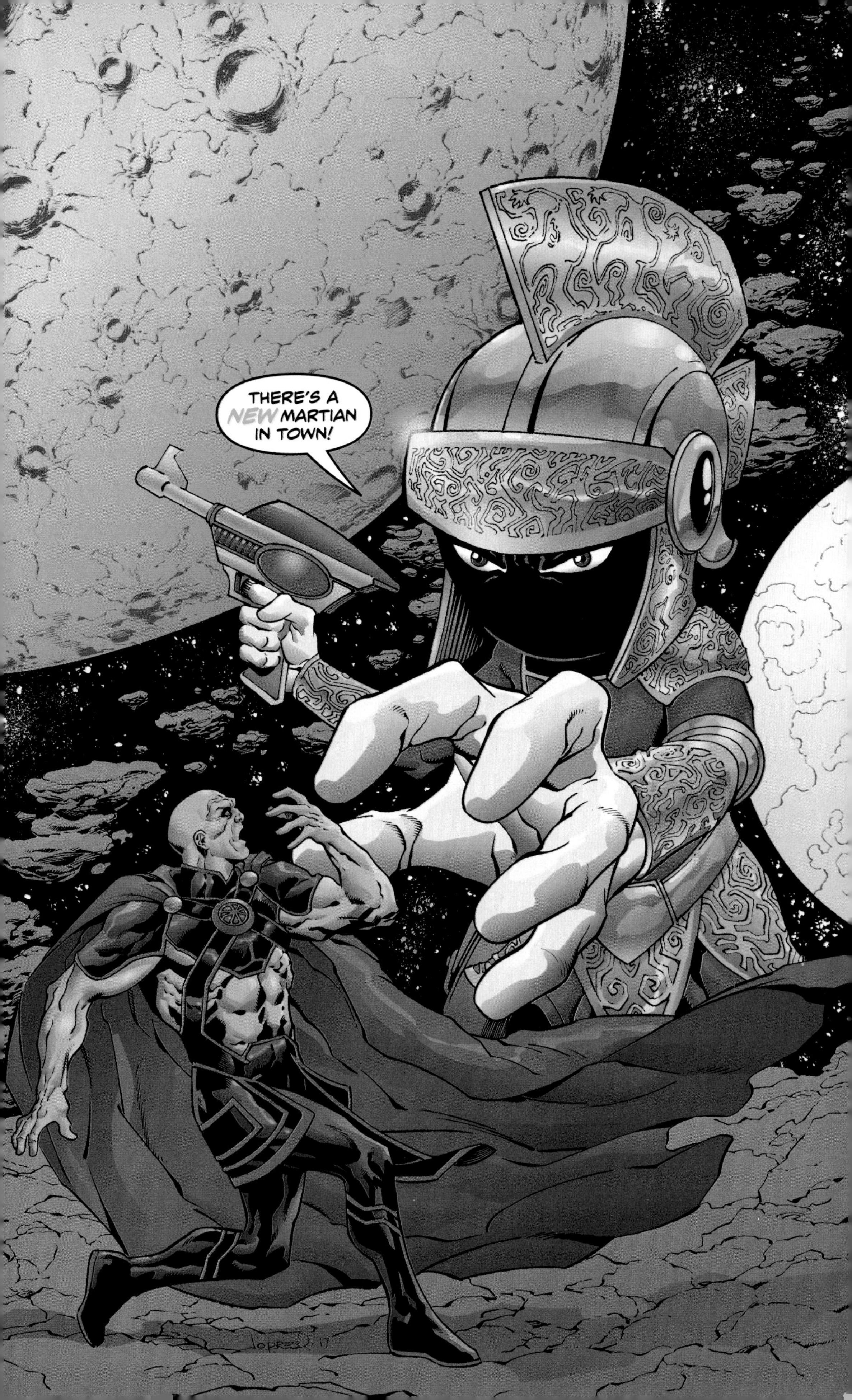
THERE'S A NEW MARTIAN IN TOWN!

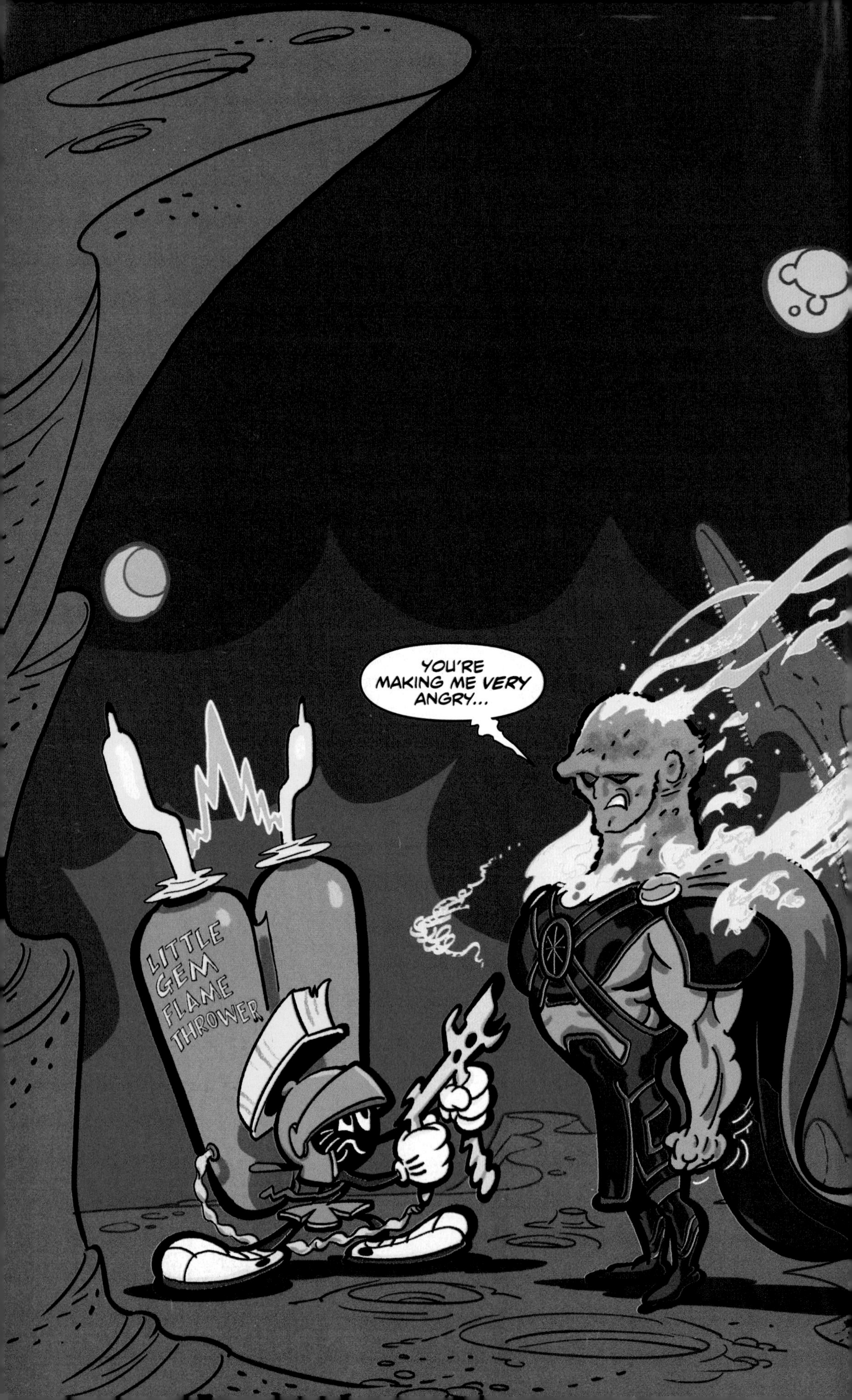
YOU'RE MAKING ME VERY ANGRY...
LITTLE GEM FLAME THROWER

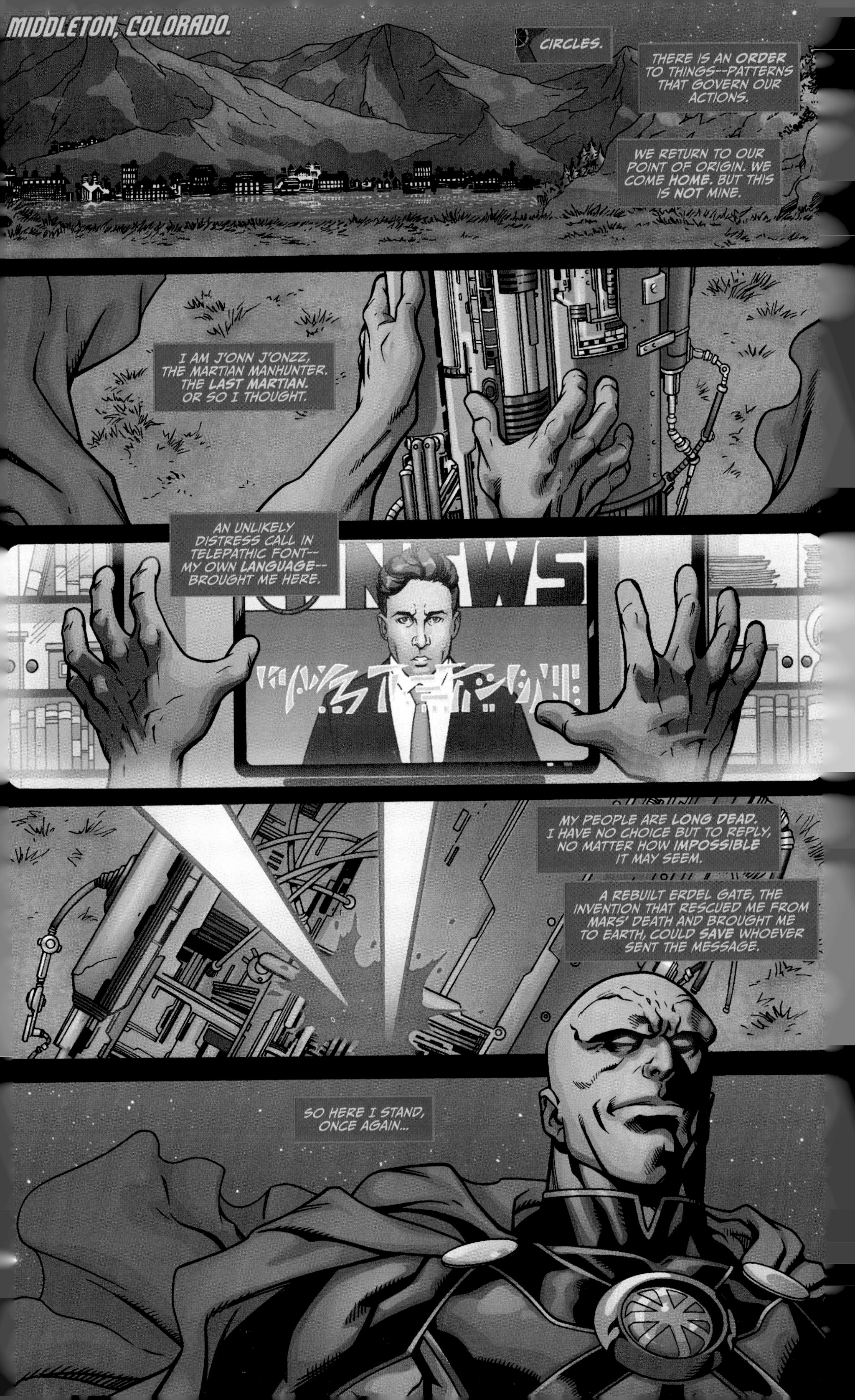
MIDDLETON, COLORADO.
CIRCLES.
THERE IS AN ORDER TO THINGS--PATTERNS THAT GOVERN OUR ACTIONS.
WE RETURN TO OUR POINT OF ORIGIN. WE COME HOME. BUT THIS IS NOT MINE.
I AM J'ONN J'ONZZ, THE MARTIAN MANHUNTER. THE LAST MARTIAN. OR SO I THOUGHT.
AN UNLIKELY DISTRESS CALL IN TELEPATHIC FONT-- MY OWN LANGUAGE-- BROUGHT ME HERE.
MY PEOPLE ARE LONG DEAD. I HAVE NO CHOICE BUT TO REPLY, NO MATTER HOW IMPOSSIBLE IT MAY SEEM.
A REBUILT ERDEL GATE, THE INVENTION THAT RESCUED ME FROM MARS' DEATH AND BROUGHT ME TO EARTH, COULD SAVE WHOEVER SENT THE MESSAGE.
SO HERE I STAND, ONCE AGAIN...

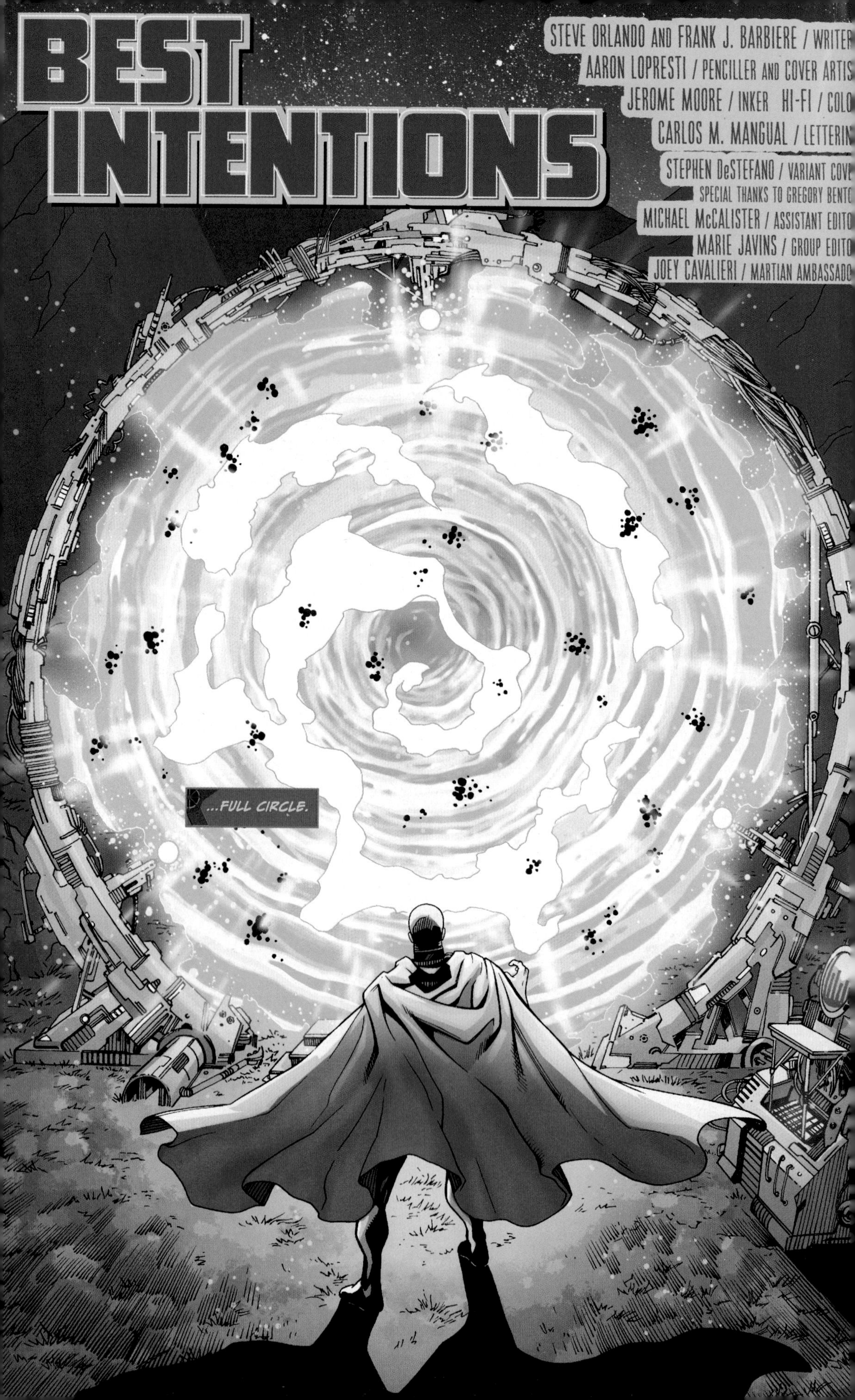

BEST INTENTIONS
STEVE ORLANDO AND FRANK J. BARBIERE / WRITER
AARON LOPRESTI / PENCILLER AND COVER ARTIS
JEROME MOORE / INKER HI-FI / COLO
CARLOS M. MANGUAL / LETTERIN
STEPHEN DeSTEFANO / VARIANT COVE
SPECIAL THANKS TO GREGORY BENTO
MICHAEL McCALISTER / ASSISTANT EDITO
MARIE JAVINS / GROUP EDITO
JOEY CAVALIERI / MARTIAN AMBASSADO
...FULL CIRCLE.

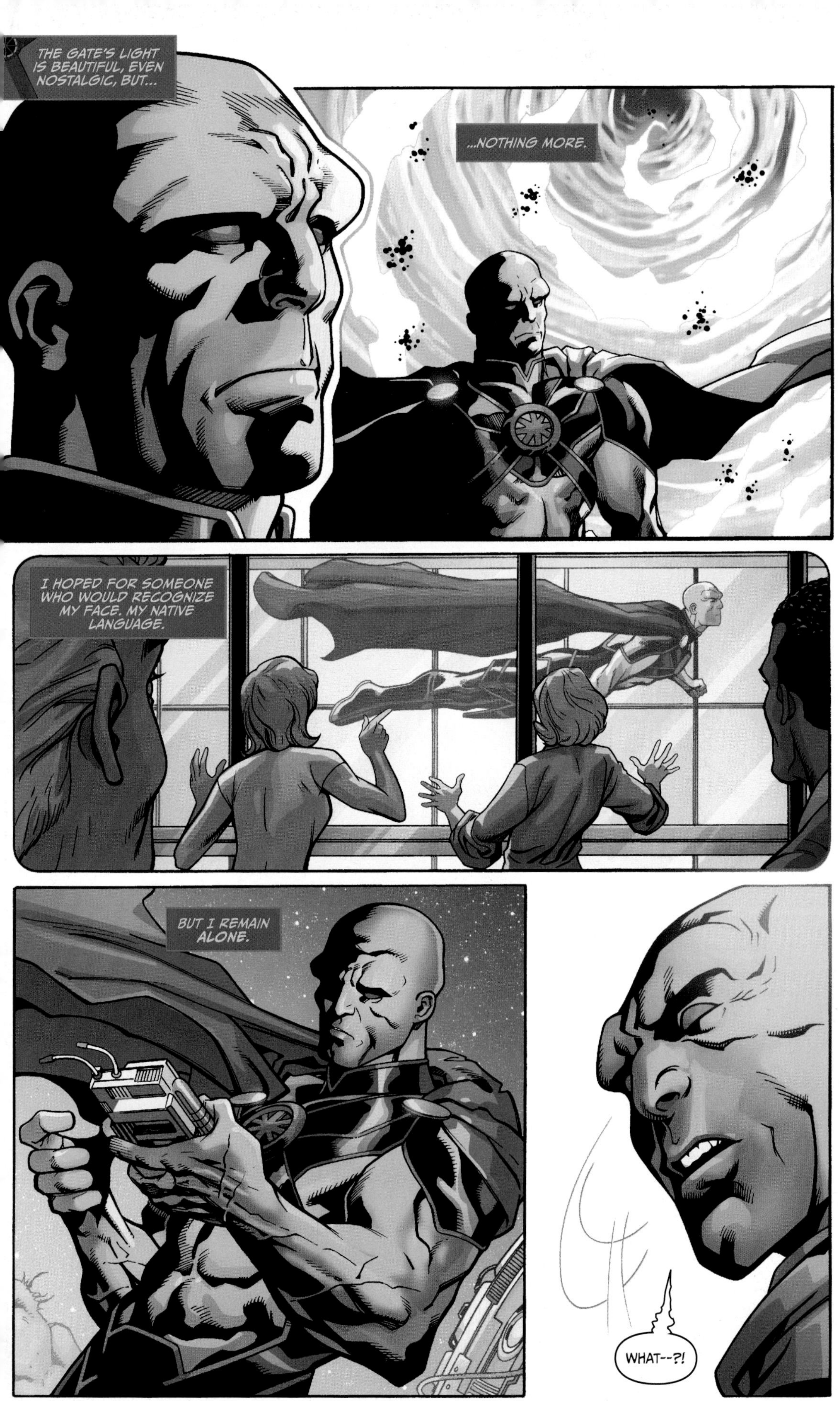
THE GATE'S LIGHT IS BEAUTIFUL, EVEN NOSTALGIC, BUT...
...NOTHING MORE.
I HOPED FOR SOMEONE WHO WOULD RECOGNIZE MY FACE. MY NATIVE LANGUAGE.
BUT I REMAIN ALONE.
WHAT--?!

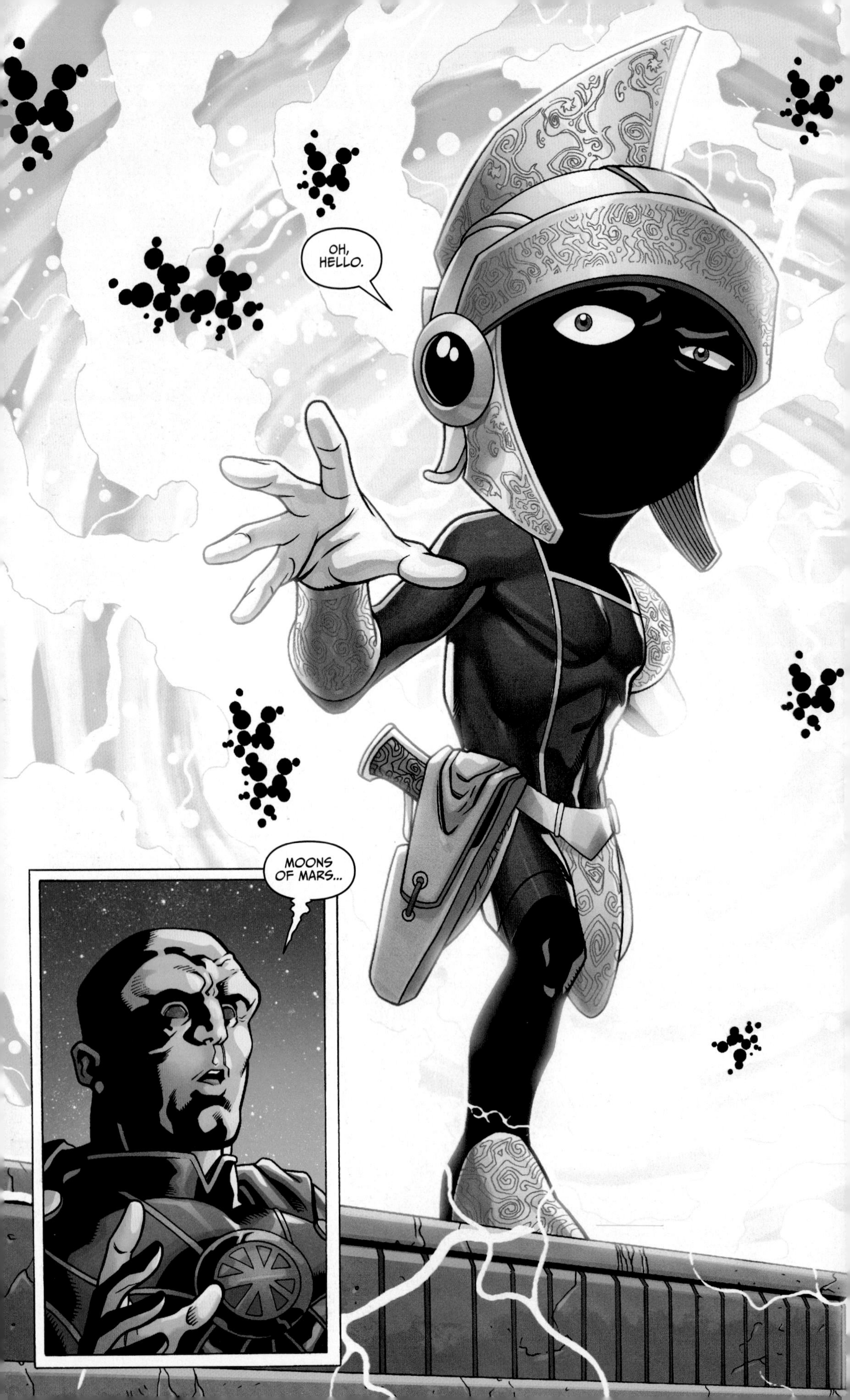
OH, HELLO.
MOONS OF MARS...

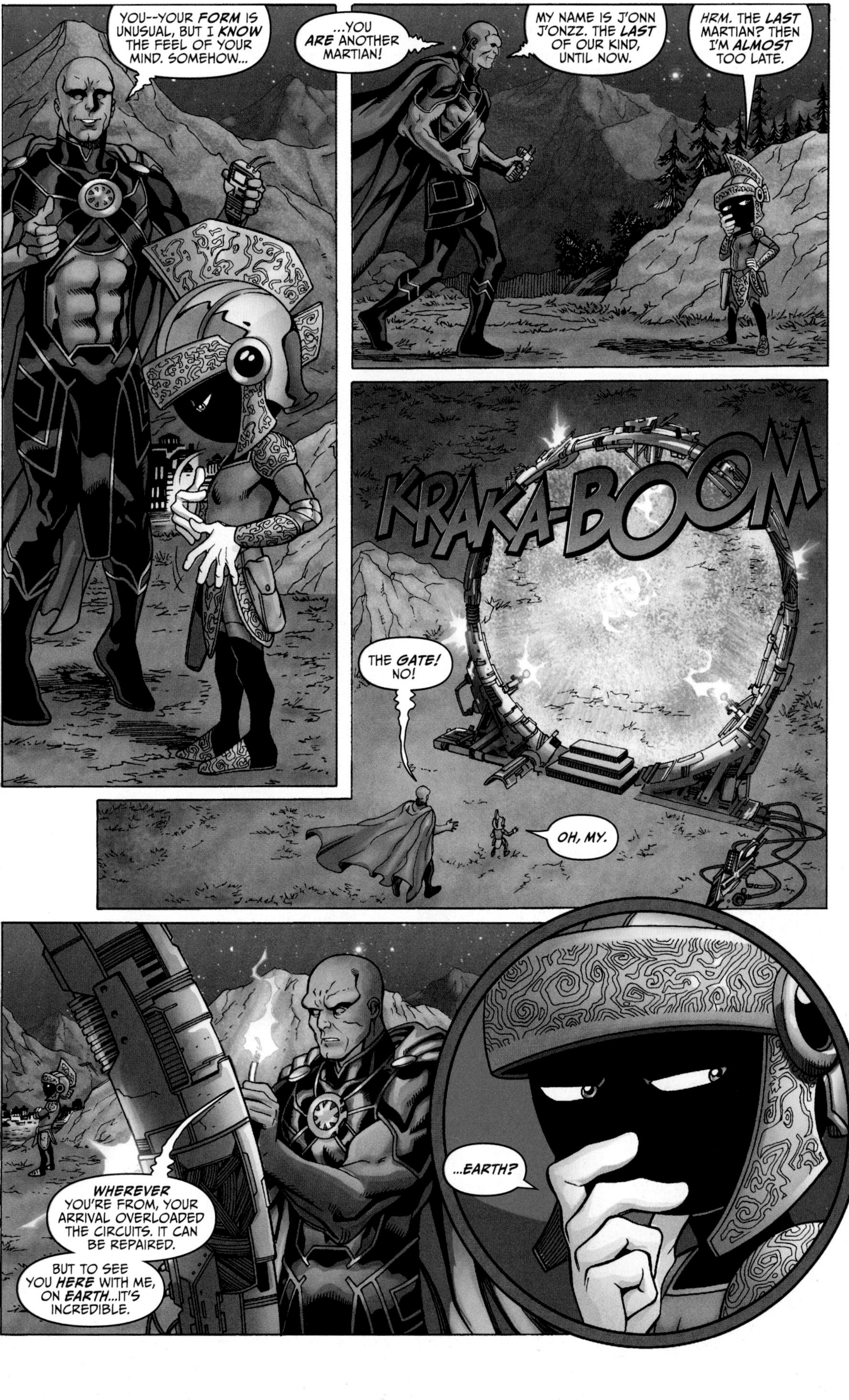
YOU--YOUR FORM IS UNUSUAL, BUT I KNOW THE FEEL OF YOUR MIND. SOMEHOW...
...YOU ARE ANOTHER MARTIAN!
MY NAME IS J'ONN J'ONZZ. THE LAST OF OUR KIND, UNTIL NOW.
HRM. THE LAST MARTIAN? THEN I'M ALMOST TOO LATE.
KRAKA-BOOM
THE GATE! NO!
OH, MY.
WHEREVER YOU'RE FROM, YOUR ARRIVAL OVERLOADED THE CIRCUITS. IT CAN BE REPAIRED.
BUT TO SEE YOU HERE WITH ME, ON EARTH...IT'S INCREDIBLE.
...EARTH?

THEN THERE'S STILL TIME TO SAVE YOU.

...WHAT?

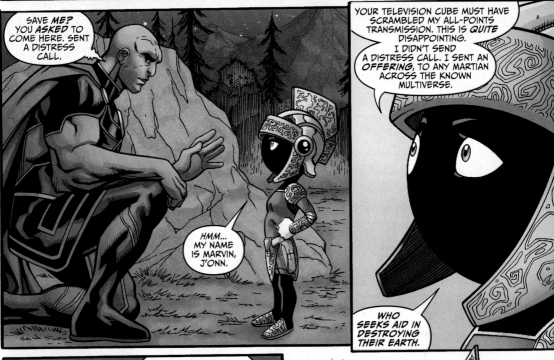

SAVE *ME?* YOU *ASKED* TO COME HERE. SENT A DISTRESS CALL.

HMM... MY NAME IS MARVIN, J'ONN.

YOUR TELEVISION CUBE MUST HAVE SCRAMBLED MY ALL-POINTS TRANSMISSION. THIS IS *QUITE* DISAPPOINTING. I DIDN'T SEND A DISTRESS CALL. I SENT AN *OFFERING,* TO ANY MARTIAN ACROSS THE KNOWN MULTIVERSE.

WHO SEEKS AID IN DESTROYING THEIR EARTH.

ONE OF THEM WAS TROUBLING ENOUGH! IMAGINE MY SURPRISE WHEN *COUNTLESS* EARTHS APPEARED ON MY MULTIVERSAL MONITOR. IT *JUST WOULD NOT DO.*

NO OTHER MARTIAN SHOULD ENDURE SUCH TORTURE AS *EARTH* ALONE.

THIS IS A *FORTUITOUS TURN OF EVENTS.* HUMANS WILL BOTHER YOU NO MORE, MY FRIEND.

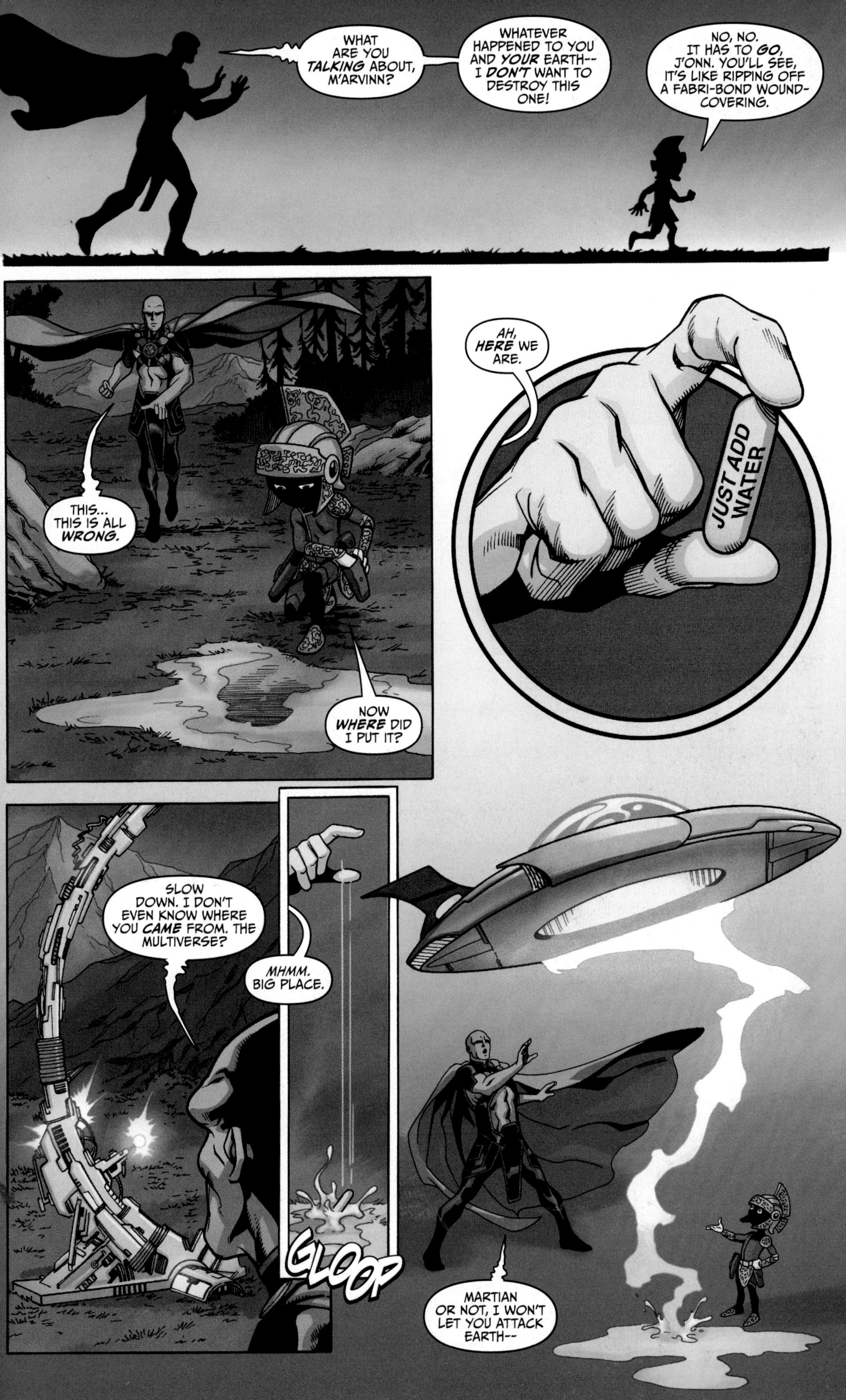
WHAT ARE YOU TALKING ABOUT, M'ARVINN?
WHATEVER HAPPENED TO YOU AND YOUR EARTH-- I DON'T WANT TO DESTROY THIS ONE!
NO, NO. IT HAS TO GO, J'ONN. YOU'LL SEE, IT'S LIKE RIPPING OFF A FABRI-BOND WOUND-COVERING.
THIS... THIS IS ALL WRONG.
NOW WHERE DID I PUT IT?
AH, HERE WE ARE.
JUST ADD WATER
SLOW DOWN. I DON'T EVEN KNOW WHERE YOU CAME FROM. THE MULTIVERSE?
MHMM. BIG PLACE.
GLOOP
MARTIAN OR NOT, I WON'T LET YOU ATTACK EARTH--

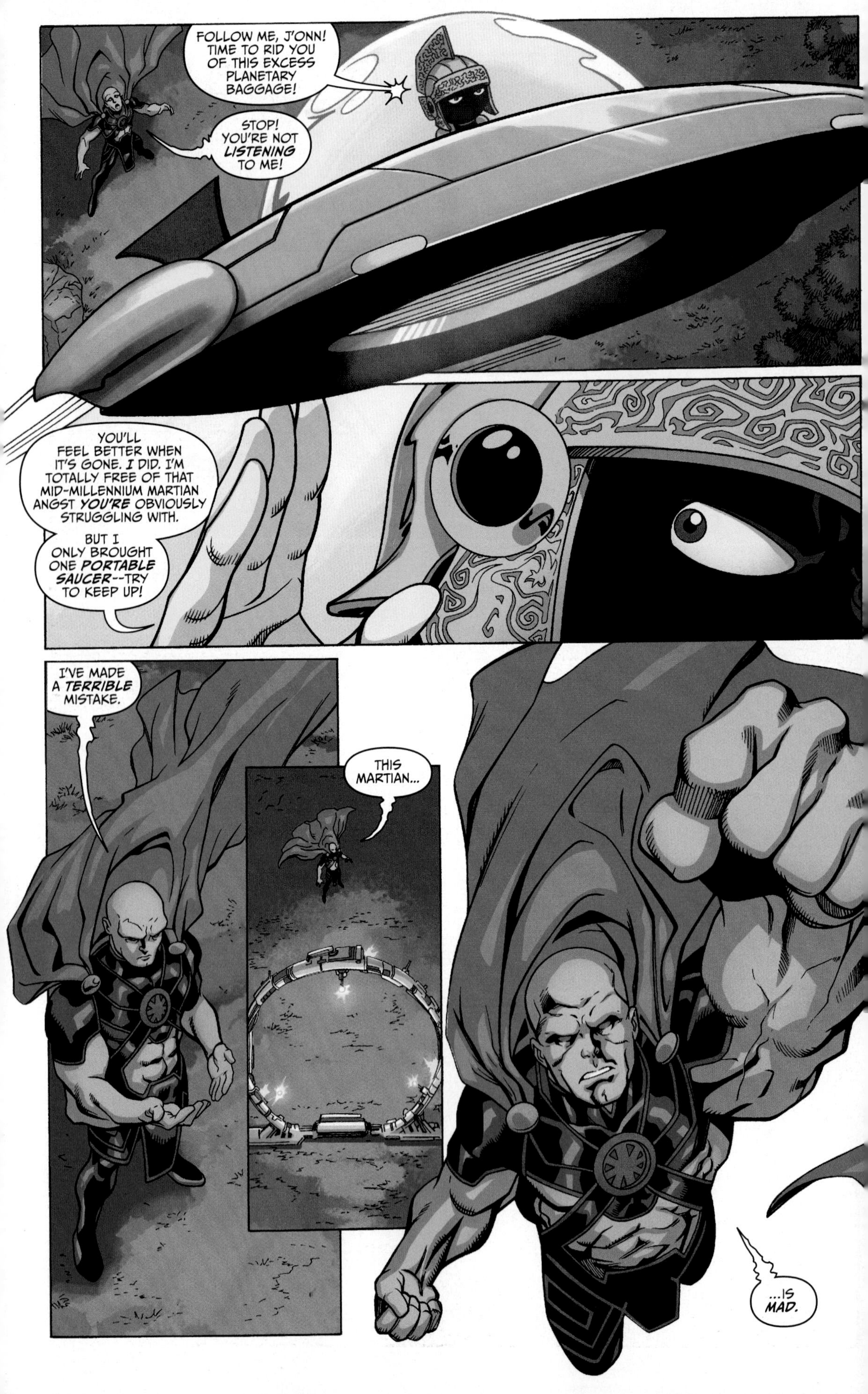
FOLLOW ME, J'ONN! TIME TO RID YOU OF THIS EXCESS PLANETARY BAGGAGE!
STOP! YOU'RE NOT *LISTENING* TO ME!
YOU'LL FEEL BETTER WHEN IT'S GONE. *I* DID. I'M TOTALLY FREE OF THAT MID-MILLENNIUM MARTIAN ANGST *YOU'RE* OBVIOUSLY STRUGGLING WITH.
BUT I ONLY BROUGHT ONE *PORTABLE SAUCER*--TRY TO KEEP UP!
I'VE MADE A *TERRIBLE* MISTAKE.
THIS MARTIAN...
...IS *MAD.*

HMMM.

M'ARVINN!

OH, YOU CAN FLY. MARTIAN EVOLUTION SEEMS *WONDERFUL* HERE!

STOP THIS. *NOW.*

SPEAKING OF EVOLUTION, LOOK AT THESE *HUMANS*. WHAT PREHISTORIC *FLUIDSACKS*.

THEY CAN'T EVEN ORGANIZE TRAVEL ROUTES! HOW COULD THEY ORGANIZE CIVILIZATION?

THEY'VE GOT TO *GO*, J'ONN. EVERY MARTIAN STRUGGLES WITH *EARTH ENVY*--THEY'RE THE SOL SYSTEM'S DISAPPOINTING SIBLING.

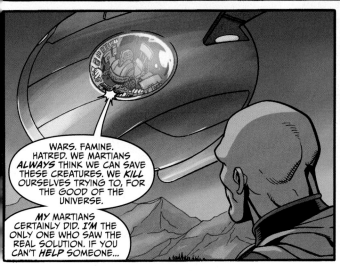

WARS. FAMINE. HATRED. WE MARTIANS *ALWAYS* THINK WE CAN SAVE THESE CREATURES. WE *KILL* OURSELVES TRYING TO, FOR THE GOOD OF THE UNIVERSE.

MY MARTIANS CERTAINLY DID. *I'M* THE ONLY ONE WHO SAW THE REAL SOLUTION. IF YOU CAN'T *HELP* SOMEONE...

...BLOW THEM UP.

WE WILL *NOT* BE BLOWING ANYONE UP.

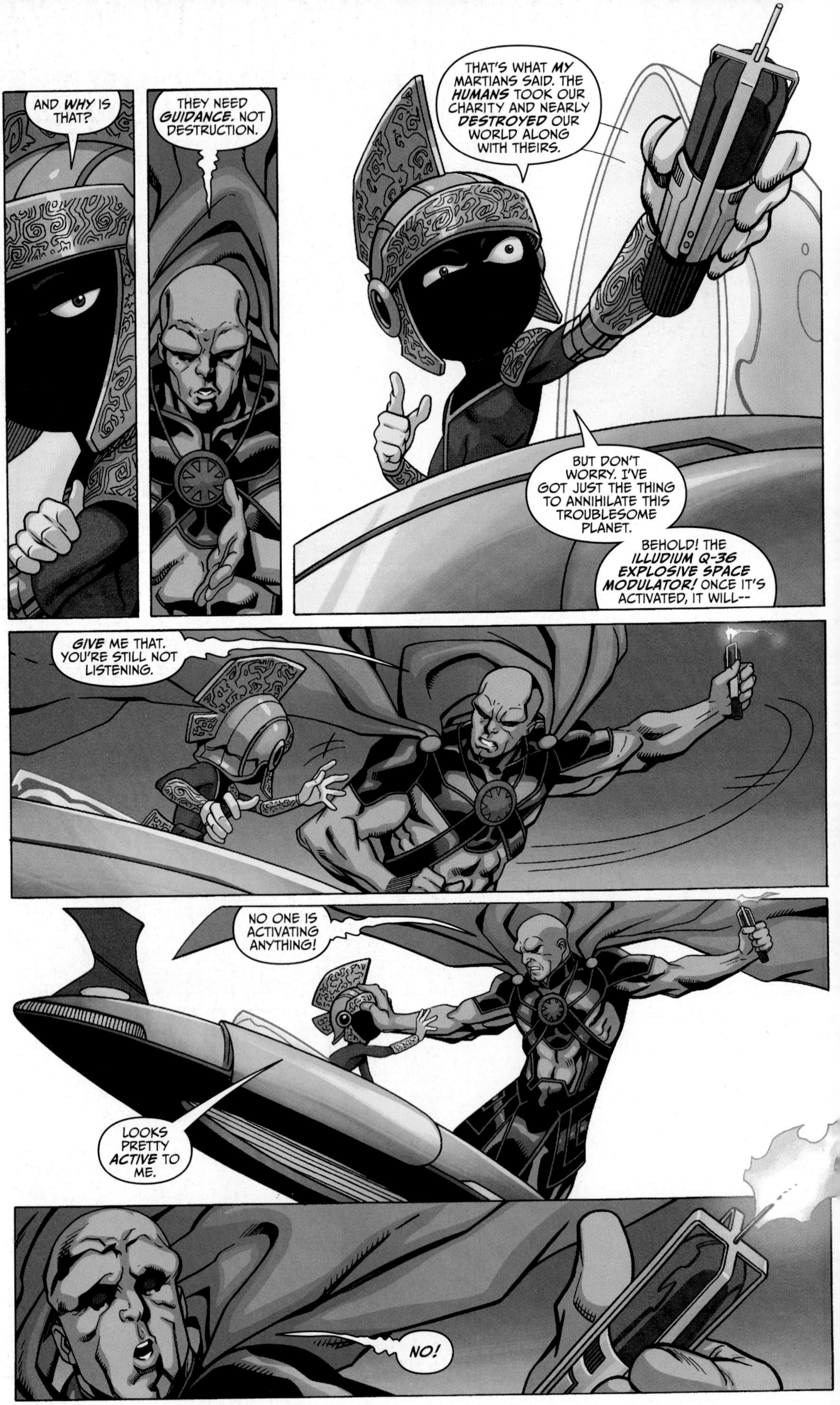
AND *WHY* IS THAT?
THEY NEED *GUIDANCE.* NOT DESTRUCTION.
THAT'S WHAT *MY* MARTIANS SAID. THE *HUMANS* TOOK OUR CHARITY AND NEARLY *DESTROYED* OUR WORLD ALONG WITH THEIRS.
BUT DON'T WORRY. I'VE GOT JUST THE THING TO ANNIHILATE THIS TROUBLESOME PLANET.
BEHOLD! THE *ILLUDIUM Q-36 EXPLOSIVE SPACE MODULATOR!* ONCE IT'S ACTIVATED, IT WILL--
GIVE ME THAT. YOU'RE STILL NOT LISTENING.
NO ONE IS ACTIVATING ANYTHING!
LOOKS PRETTY *ACTIVE* TO ME.
NO!

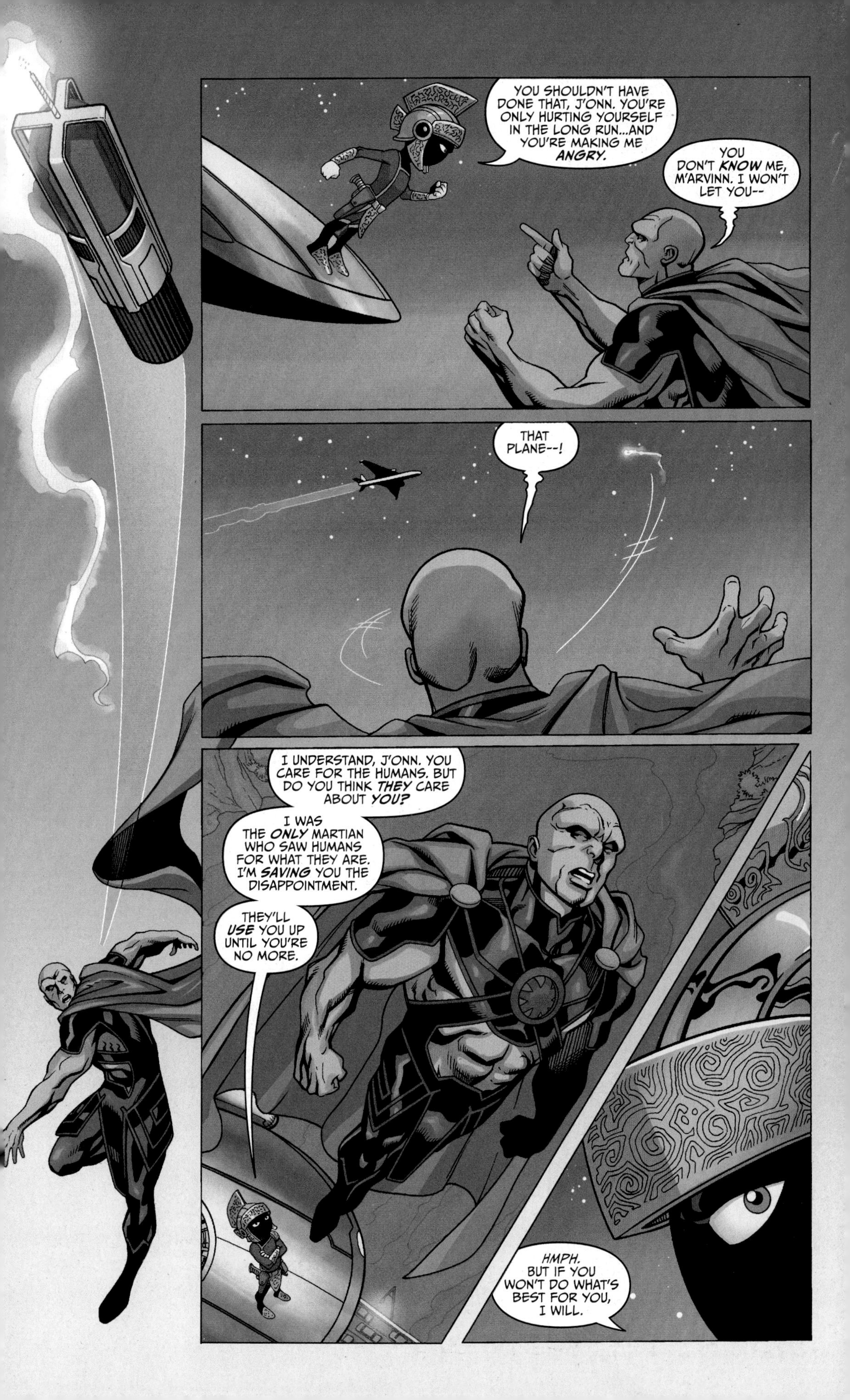
YOU SHOULDN'T HAVE DONE THAT, J'ONN. YOU'RE ONLY HURTING YOURSELF IN THE LONG RUN...AND YOU'RE MAKING ME *ANGRY.*
YOU DON'T *KNOW* ME, M'ARVINN. I WON'T LET YOU--
THAT PLANE--!
I UNDERSTAND, J'ONN. YOU CARE FOR THE HUMANS. BUT DO YOU THINK *THEY* CARE ABOUT *YOU?*
I WAS THE *ONLY* MARTIAN WHO SAW HUMANS FOR WHAT THEY ARE. I'M *SAVING* YOU THE DISAPPOINTMENT.
THEY'LL *USE* YOU UP UNTIL YOU'RE NO MORE.
HMPH. BUT IF YOU WON'T DO WHAT'S BEST FOR YOU, I WILL.

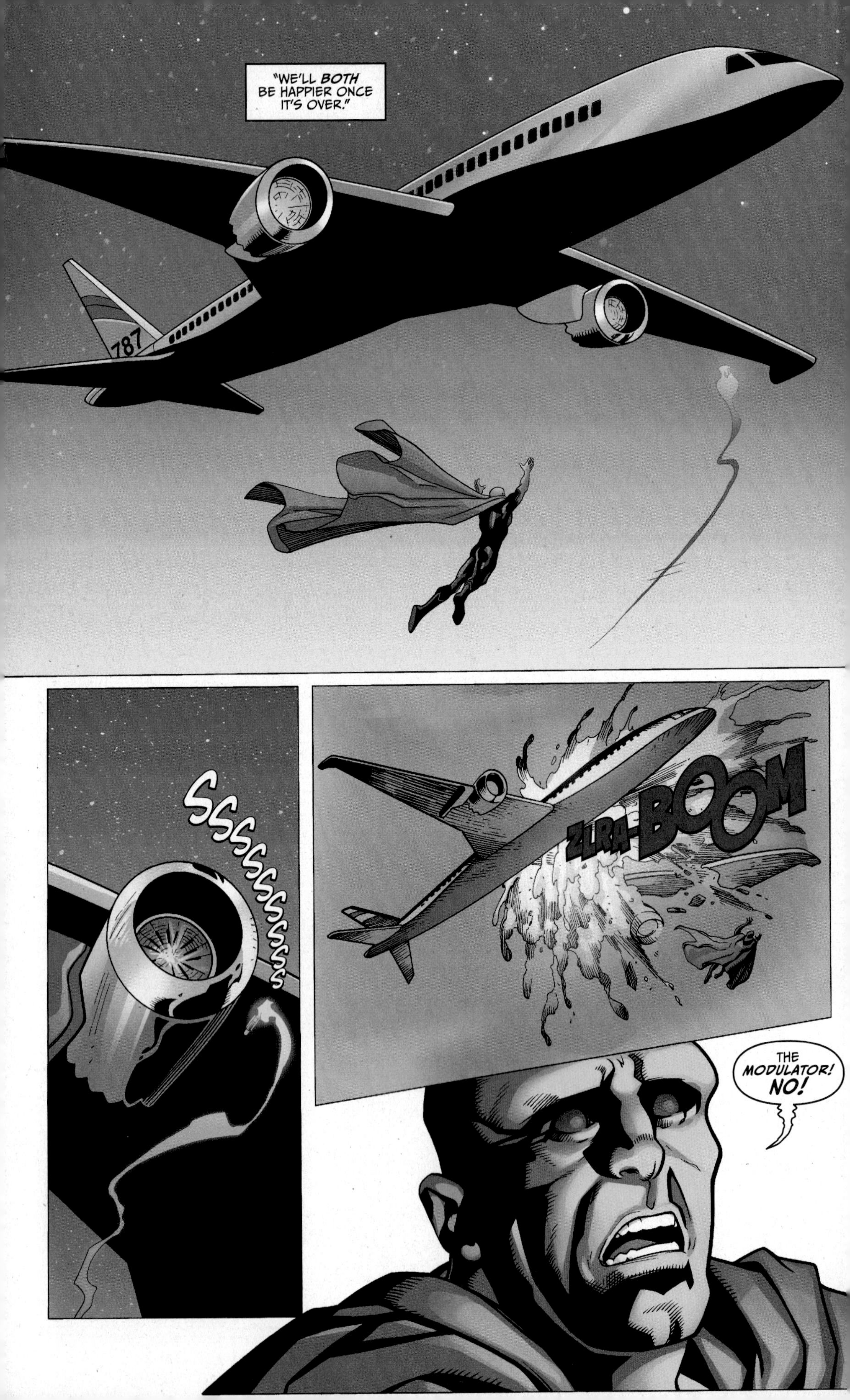
"WE'LL BOTH BE HAPPIER ONCE IT'S OVER."
787
SSSSSSSSSSSSS
ZLRA-BOOM
THE MODULATOR! NO!

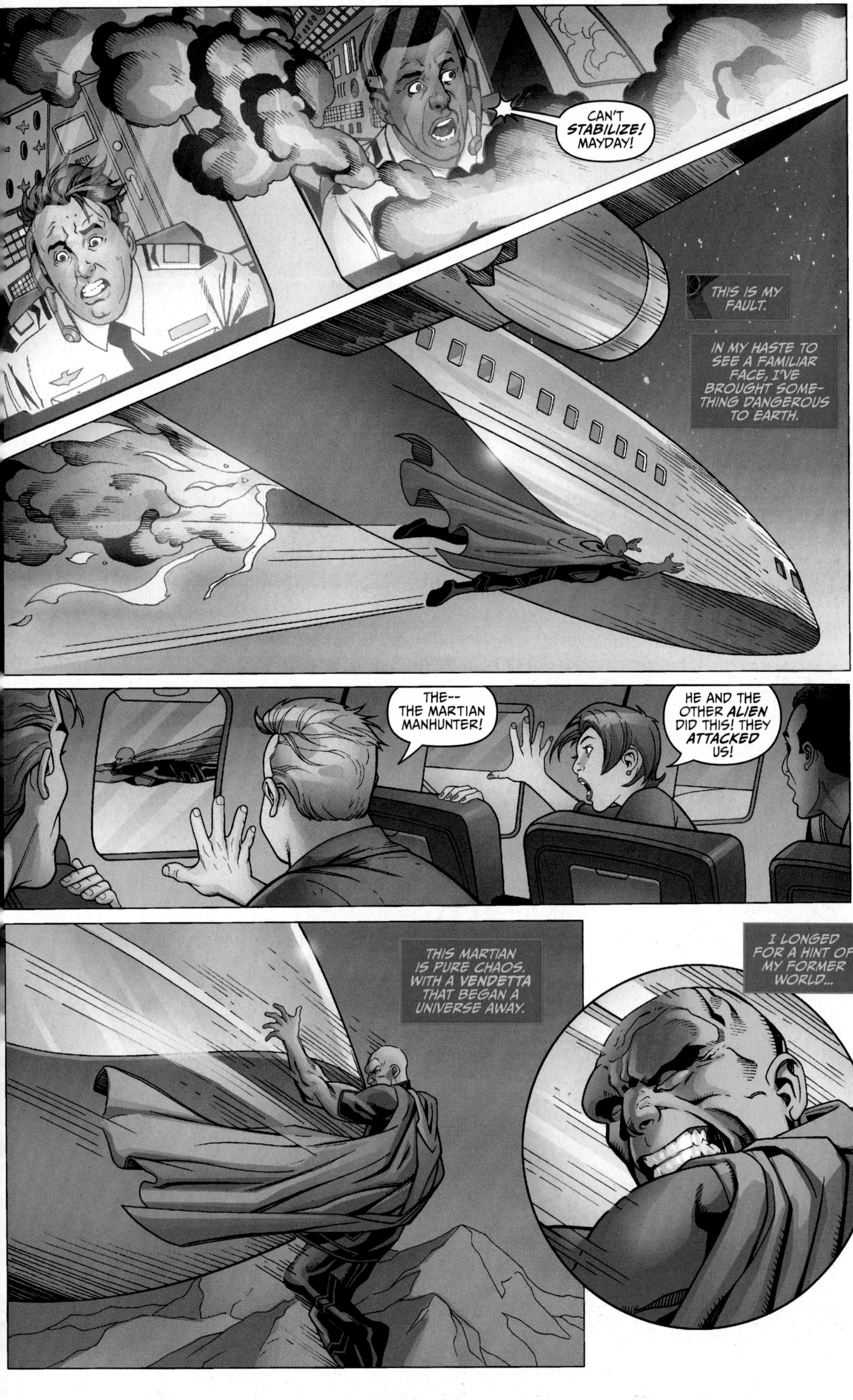
CAN'T STABILIZE! MAYDAY!
THIS IS MY FAULT.
IN MY HASTE TO SEE A FAMILIAR FACE, I'VE BROUGHT SOMETHING DANGEROUS TO EARTH.
THE-- THE MARTIAN MANHUNTER!
HE AND THE OTHER ALIEN DID THIS! THEY ATTACKED US!
THIS MARTIAN IS PURE CHAOS. WITH A VENDETTA THAT BEGAN A UNIVERSE AWAY.
I LONGED FOR A HINT OF MY FORMER WORLD...

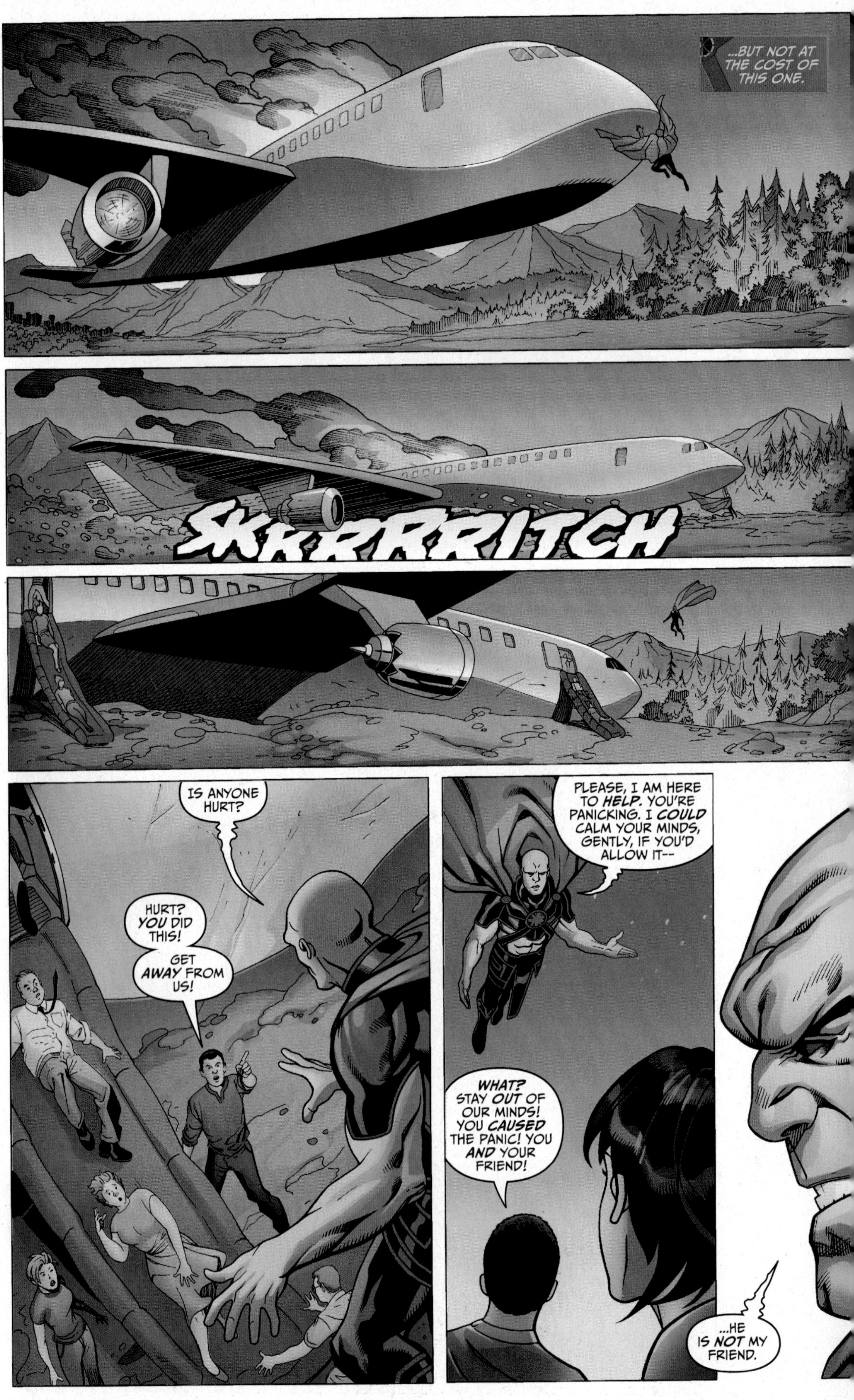
...BUT NOT AT THE COST OF THIS ONE.
SKRRRRITCH
IS ANYONE HURT?
HURT? YOU DID THIS!
GET AWAY FROM US!
PLEASE, I AM HERE TO HELP. YOU'RE PANICKING. I COULD CALM YOUR MINDS, GENTLY, IF YOU'D ALLOW IT--
WHAT? STAY OUT OF OUR MINDS! YOU CAUSED THE PANIC! YOU AND YOUR FRIEND!
...HE IS NOT MY FRIEND.

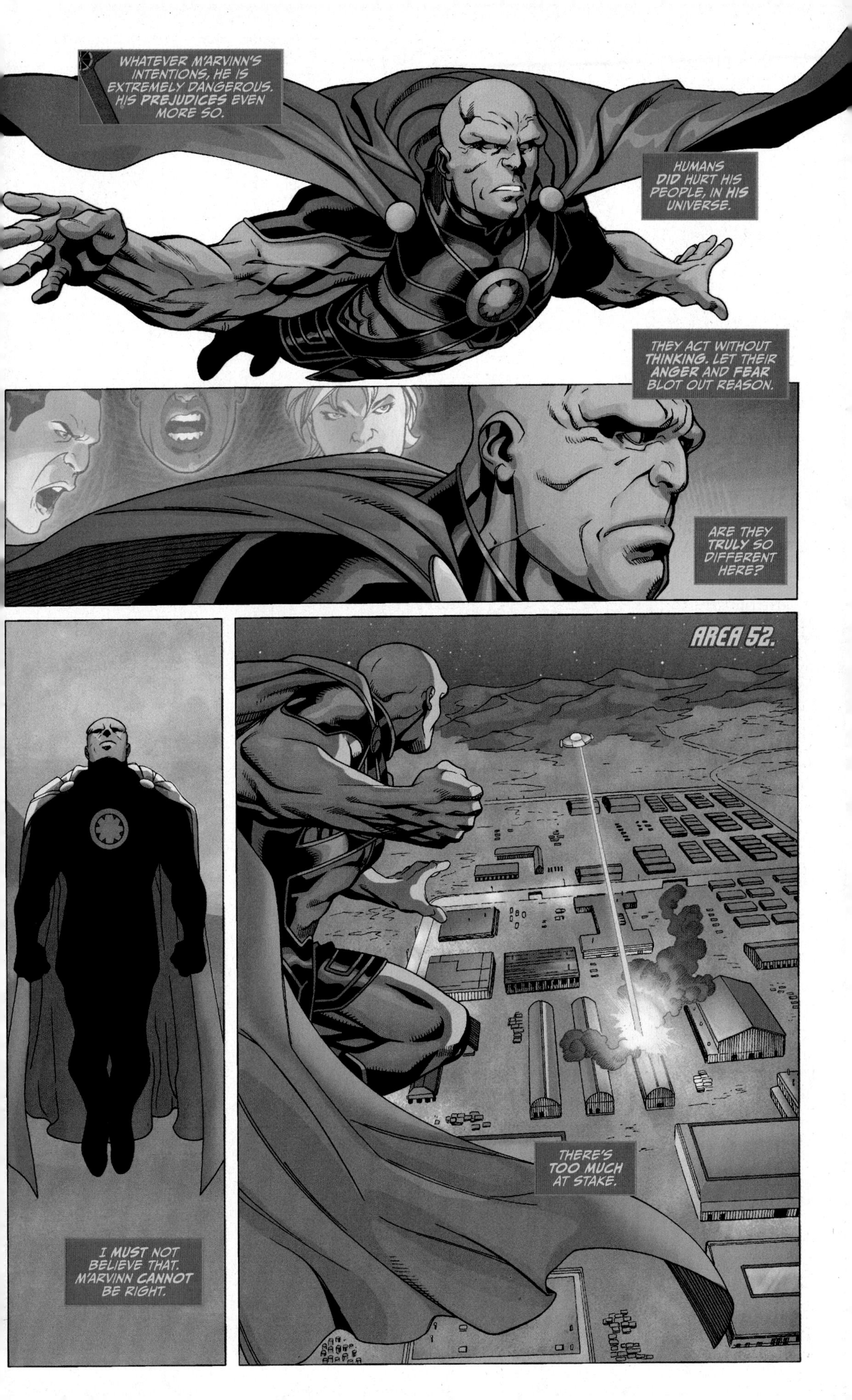
WHATEVER M'ARVINN'S INTENTIONS, HE IS EXTREMELY DANGEROUS. HIS PREJUDICES EVEN MORE SO.
HUMANS DID HURT HIS PEOPLE, IN HIS UNIVERSE.
THEY ACT WITHOUT THINKING. LET THEIR ANGER AND FEAR BLOT OUT REASON.
ARE THEY TRULY SO DIFFERENT HERE?
I MUST NOT BELIEVE THAT. M'ARVINN CANNOT BE RIGHT.
AREA 52.
THERE'S TOO MUCH AT STAKE.

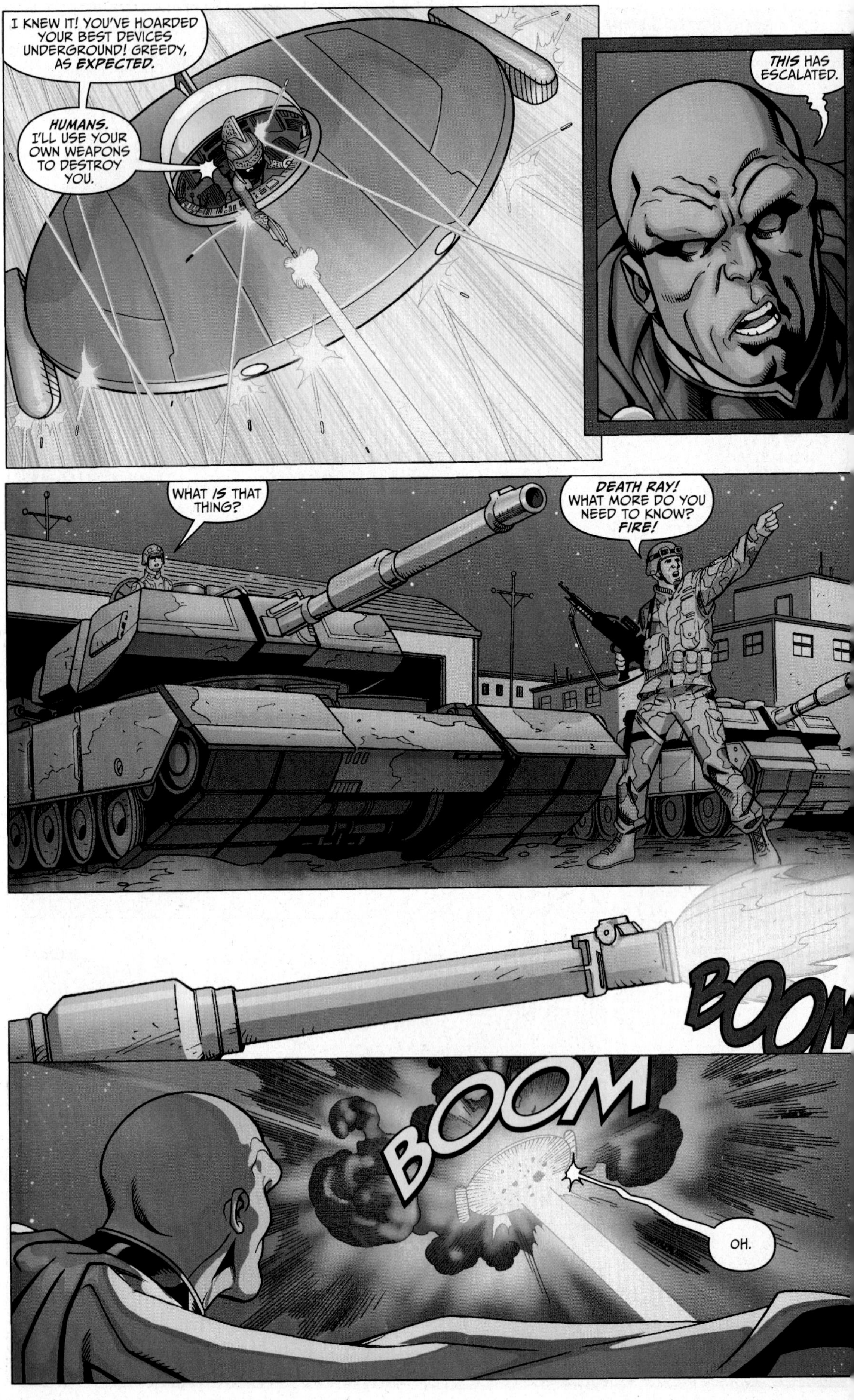
I KNEW IT! YOU'VE HOARDED YOUR BEST DEVICES UNDERGROUND! GREEDY, AS EXPECTED.
HUMANS. I'LL USE YOUR OWN WEAPONS TO DESTROY YOU.
THIS HAS ESCALATED.
WHAT IS THAT THING?
DEATH RAY! WHAT MORE DO YOU NEED TO KNOW? FIRE!
BOOM
BOOM
OH.

LOOK AT *THAT.* YOU'RE *PROVING* MY POINT.

ENOUGH OF THIS, M'ARVINN!

ENOUGH? YOU *SAVED* THOSE CREATURES AND THEIR ANTIQUE PLANE. THEY *BERATED* YOU IN RETURN!

I THOUGHT MAYBE YOU'D HAVE SEEN I'M *RIGHT.*

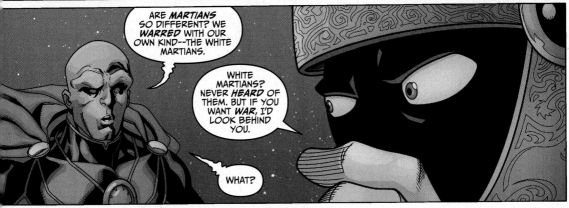

ARE *MARTIANS* SO DIFFERENT? WE *WARRED* WITH OUR OWN KIND--THE WHITE MARTIANS.

WHITE MARTIANS? NEVER *HEARD* OF THEM. BUT IF YOU WANT *WAR,* I'D LOOK BEHIND YOU.

WHAT?

NO! I'M TRYING TO *PROTECT* YOU!

TWO OF THEM? KEEP FIRING!

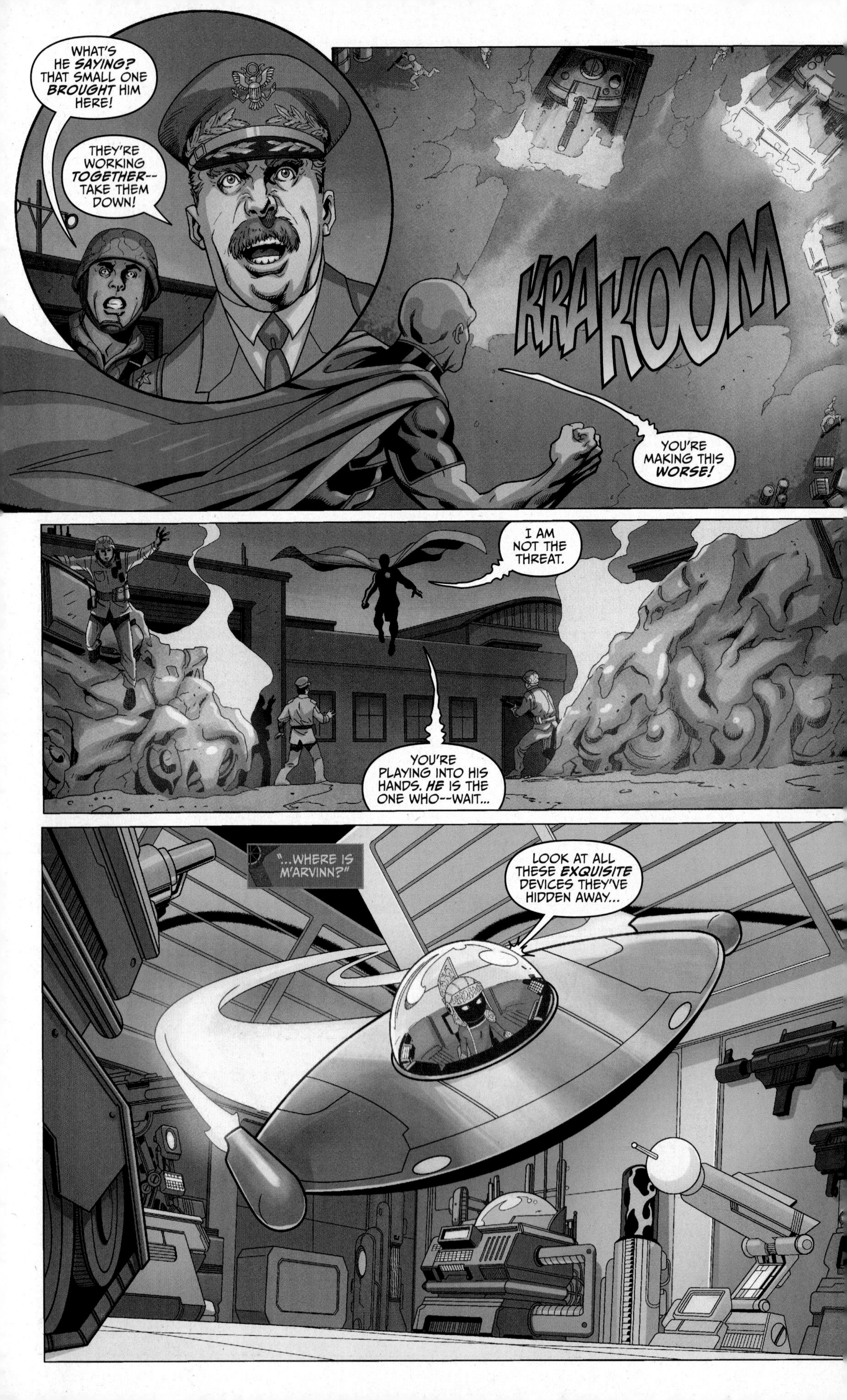
WHAT'S HE SAYING? THAT SMALL ONE BROUGHT HIM HERE!
THEY'RE WORKING TOGETHER-- TAKE THEM DOWN!
KRAKOOM
YOU'RE MAKING THIS WORSE!
I AM NOT THE THREAT.
YOU'RE PLAYING INTO HIS HANDS. HE IS THE ONE WHO--WAIT...
"...WHERE IS M'ARVINN?"
LOOK AT ALL THESE EXQUISITE DEVICES THEY'VE HIDDEN AWAY...

SO MANY CHOICES...

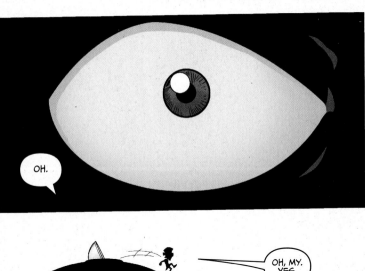

OH.

OH, MY. YES.

ISN'T THAT LOVELY?

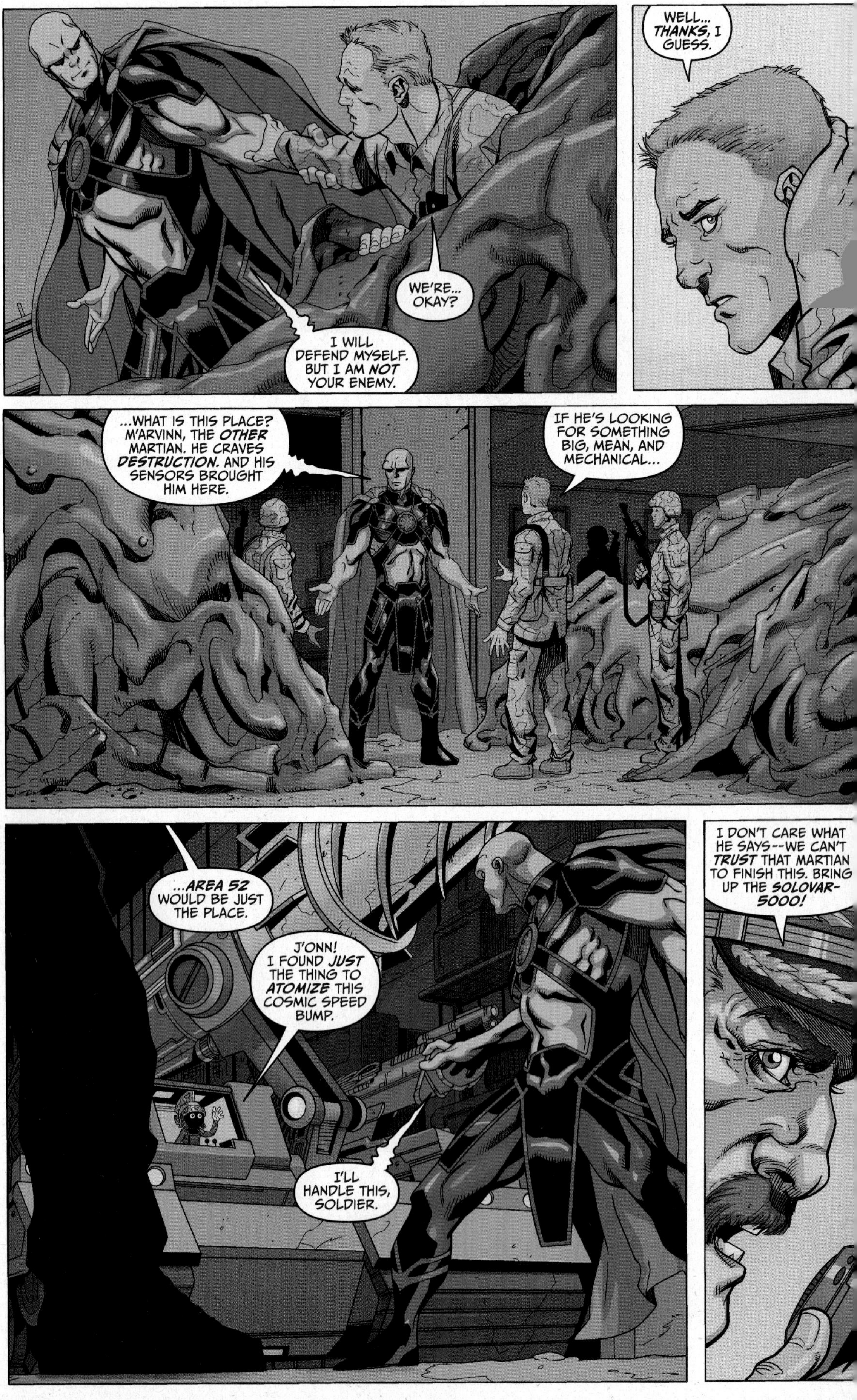

WE'RE... OKAY?
I WILL DEFEND MYSELF. BUT I AM NOT YOUR ENEMY.
WELL... THANKS, I GUESS.
...WHAT IS THIS PLACE? M'ARVINN, THE OTHER MARTIAN. HE CRAVES DESTRUCTION. AND HIS SENSORS BROUGHT HIM HERE.
IF HE'S LOOKING FOR SOMETHING BIG, MEAN, AND MECHANICAL...
...AREA 52 WOULD BE JUST THE PLACE.
J'ONN! I FOUND JUST THE THING TO ATOMIZE THIS COSMIC SPEED BUMP.
I'LL HANDLE THIS, SOLDIER.
I DON'T CARE WHAT HE SAYS--WE CAN'T TRUST THAT MARTIAN TO FINISH THIS. BRING UP THE SOLOVAR-5000!

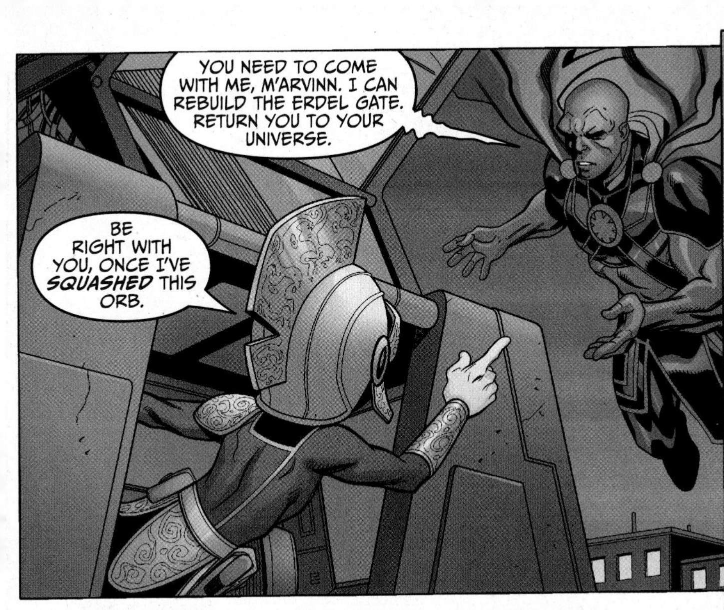
YOU NEED TO COME WITH ME, M'ARVINN. I CAN REBUILD THE ERDEL GATE. RETURN YOU TO YOUR UNIVERSE.
BE RIGHT WITH YOU, ONCE I'VE *SQUASHED* THIS ORB.

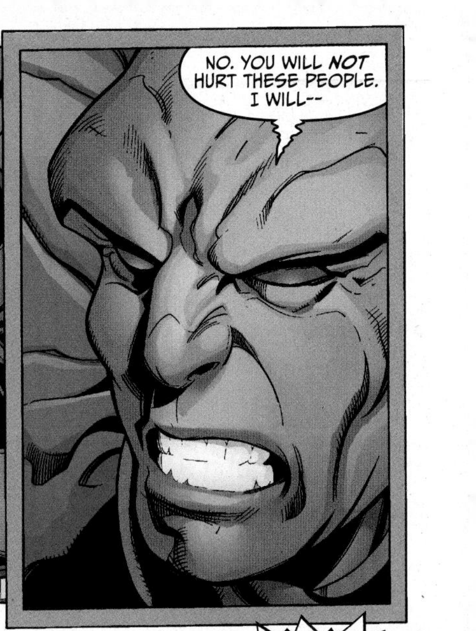
NO. YOU WILL *NOT* HURT THESE PEOPLE. I WILL--

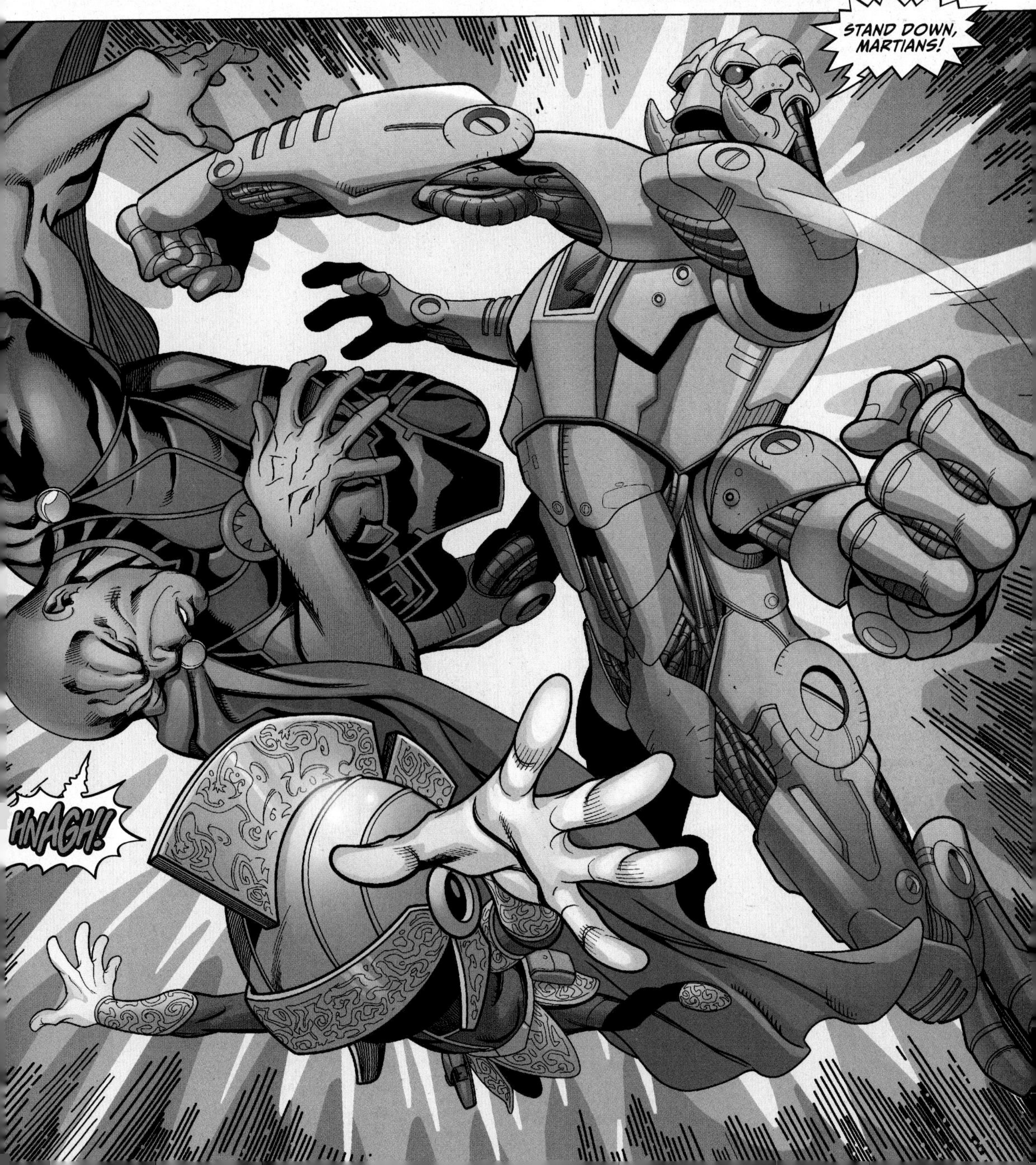
STAND DOWN, MARTIANS!
HNAGH!

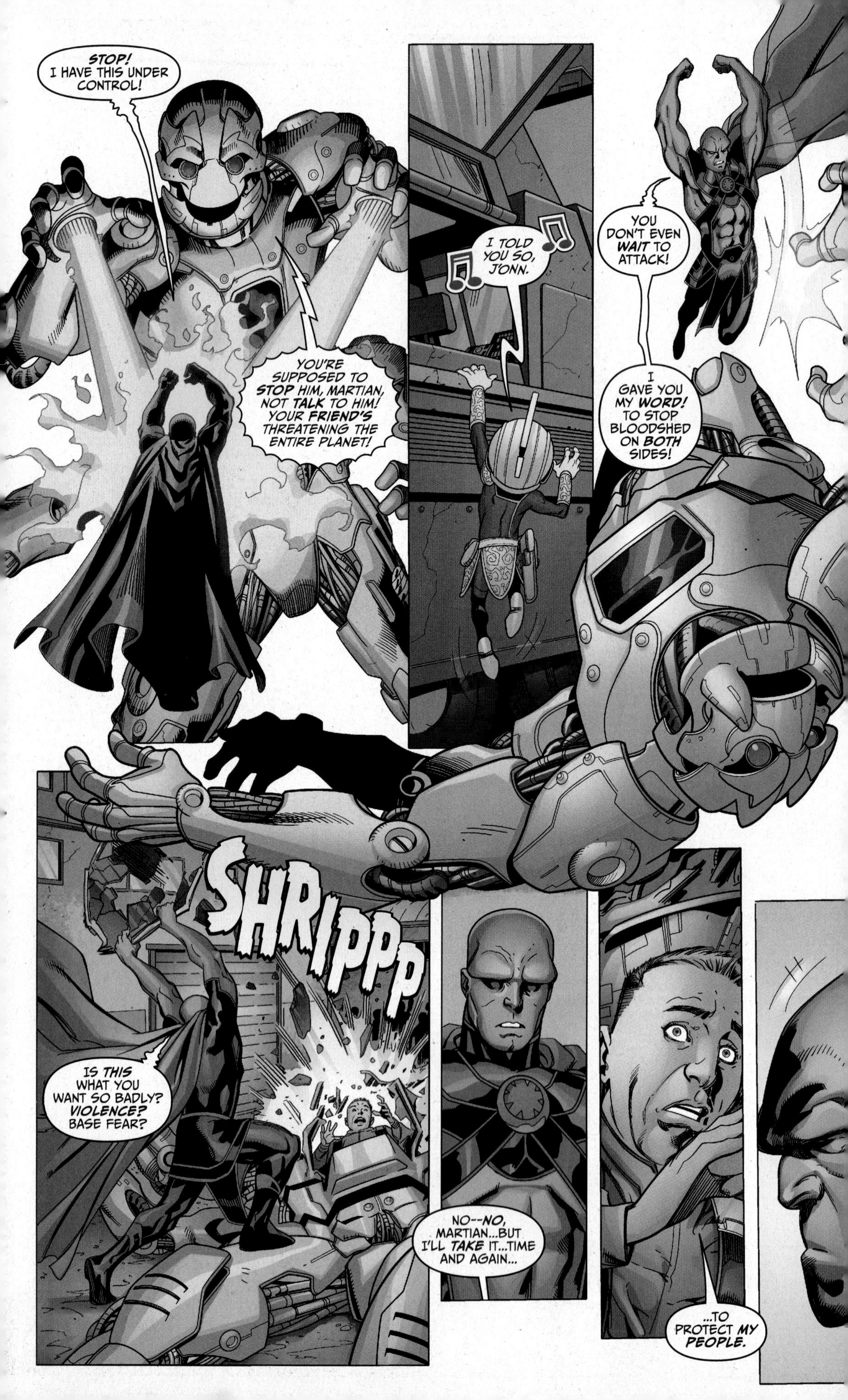
STOP! I HAVE THIS UNDER CONTROL!
YOU'RE SUPPOSED TO STOP HIM, MARTIAN, NOT TALK TO HIM! YOUR FRIEND'S THREATENING THE ENTIRE PLANET!
I TOLD YOU SO, J'ONN.
YOU DON'T EVEN WAIT TO ATTACK!
I GAVE YOU MY WORD! TO STOP BLOODSHED ON BOTH SIDES!
SHRIPPP
IS THIS WHAT YOU WANT SO BADLY? VIOLENCE? BASE FEAR?
NO--NO, MARTIAN...BUT I'LL TAKE IT...TIME AND AGAIN...
...TO PROTECT MY PEOPLE.

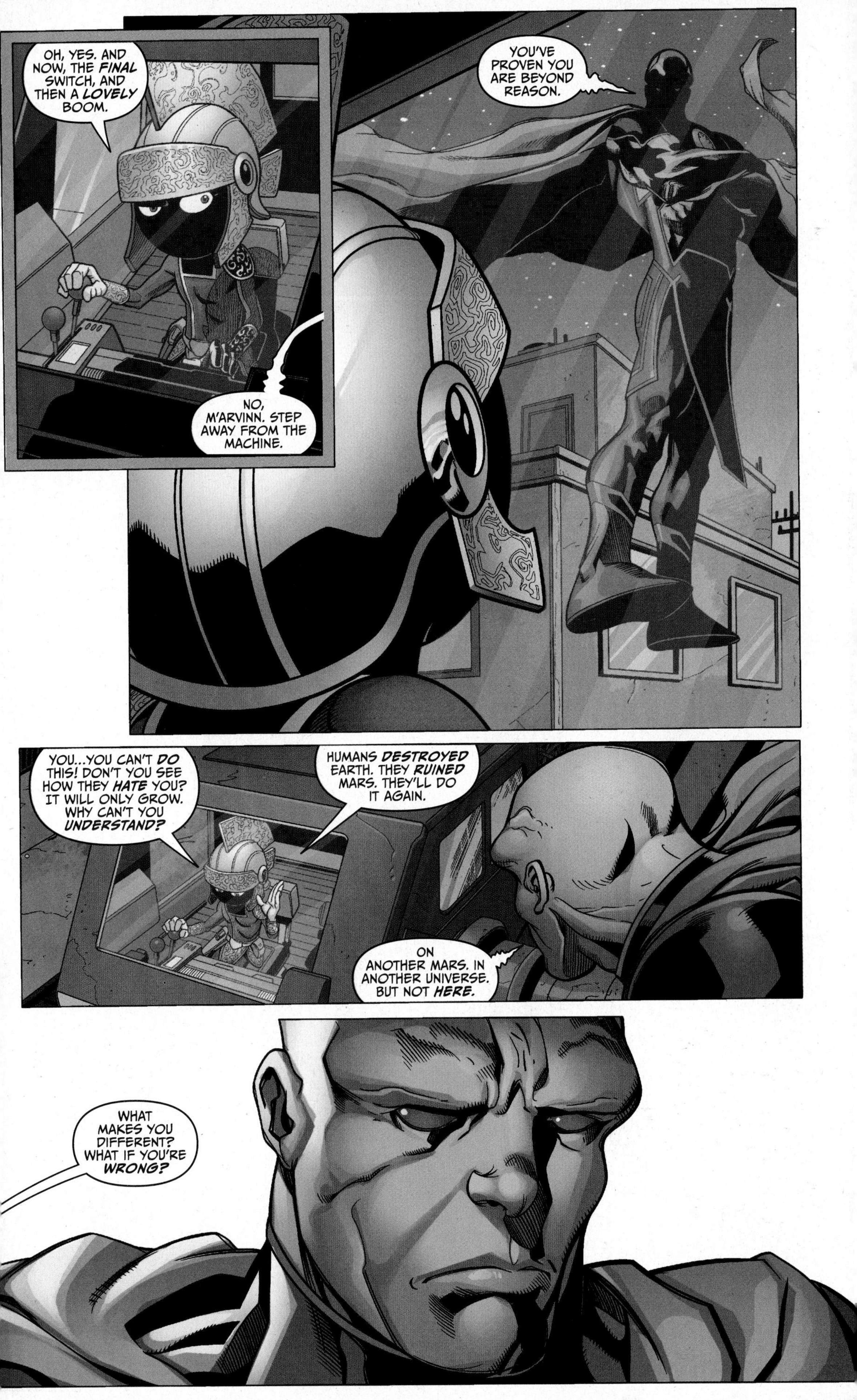
OH, YES. AND NOW, THE FINAL SWITCH, AND THEN A LOVELY BOOM.
NO, M'ARVINN. STEP AWAY FROM THE MACHINE.
YOU'VE PROVEN YOU ARE BEYOND REASON.
YOU...YOU CAN'T DO THIS! DON'T YOU SEE HOW THEY HATE YOU? IT WILL ONLY GROW. WHY CAN'T YOU UNDERSTAND?
HUMANS DESTROYED EARTH. THEY RUINED MARS. THEY'LL DO IT AGAIN.
ON ANOTHER MARS. IN ANOTHER UNIVERSE. BUT NOT HERE.
WHAT MAKES YOU DIFFERENT? WHAT IF YOU'RE WRONG?

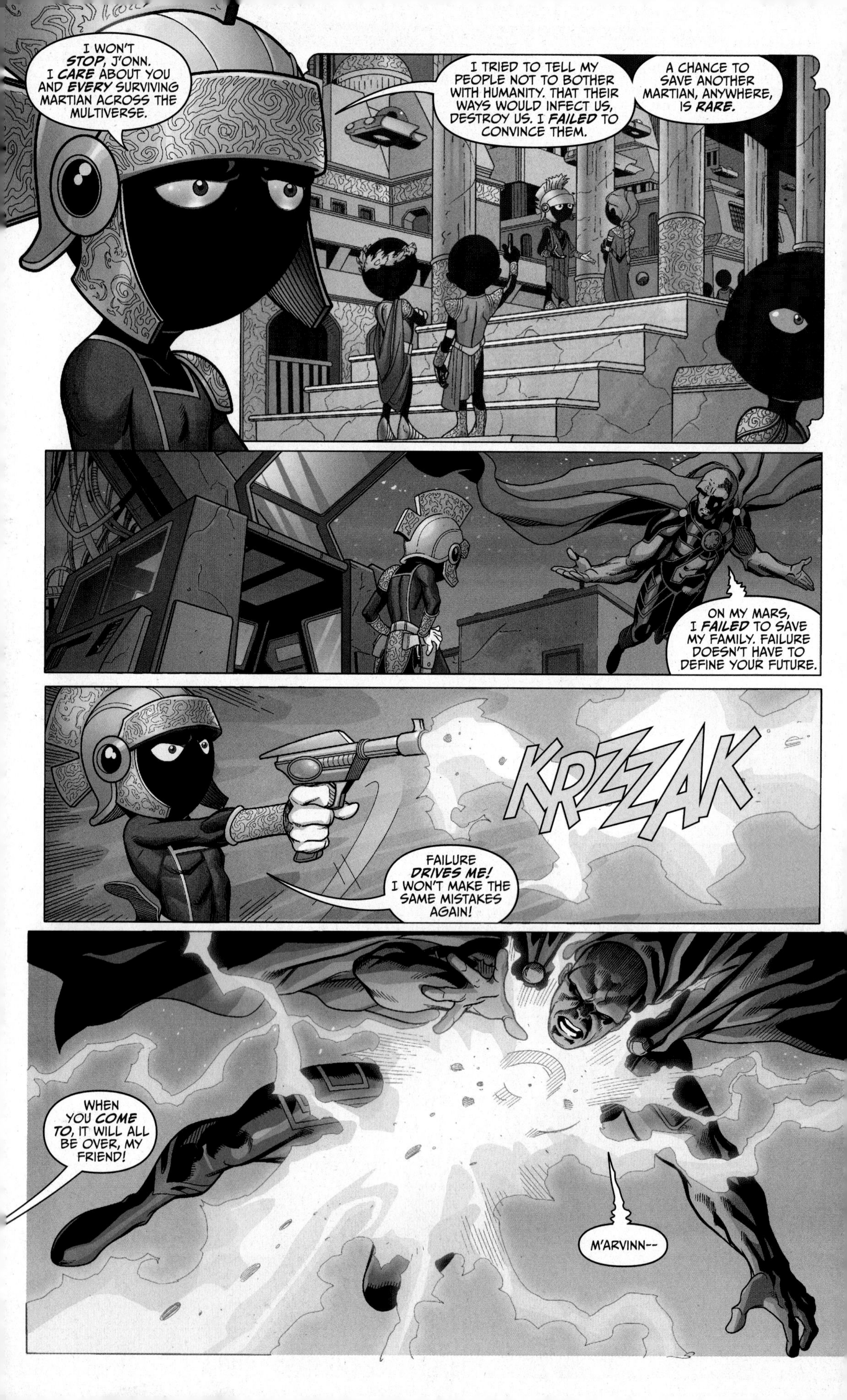
I WON'T STOP, J'ONN. I CARE ABOUT YOU AND EVERY SURVIVING MARTIAN ACROSS THE MULTIVERSE.
I TRIED TO TELL MY PEOPLE NOT TO BOTHER WITH HUMANITY. THAT THEIR WAYS WOULD INFECT US, DESTROY US. I FAILED TO CONVINCE THEM.
A CHANCE TO SAVE ANOTHER MARTIAN, ANYWHERE, IS RARE.
ON MY MARS, I FAILED TO SAVE MY FAMILY. FAILURE DOESN'T HAVE TO DEFINE YOUR FUTURE.
KRZZZAK
FAILURE DRIVES ME! I WON'T MAKE THE SAME MISTAKES AGAIN!
WHEN YOU COME TO, IT WILL ALL BE OVER, MY FRIEND!
M'ARVINN--

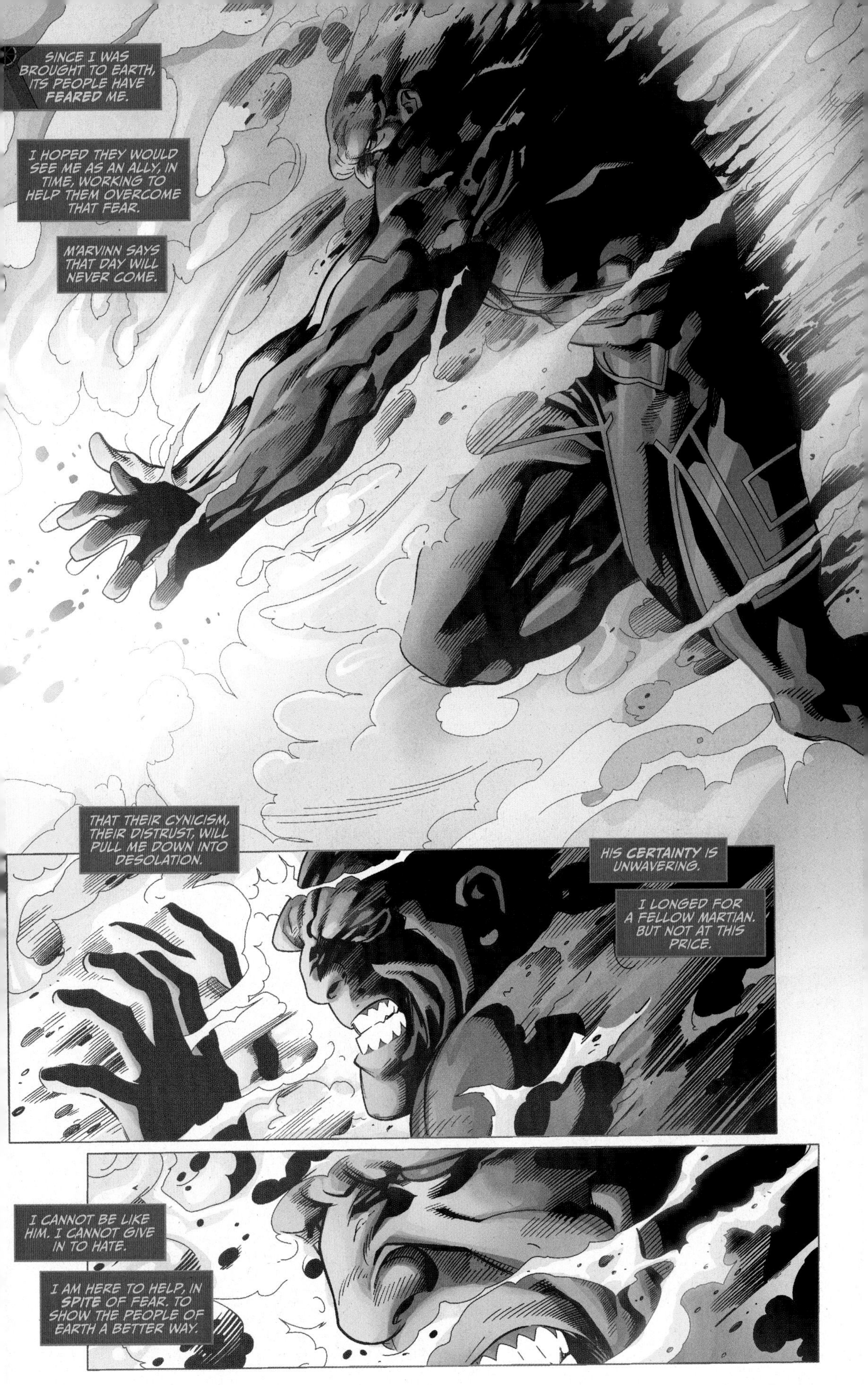
SINCE I WAS BROUGHT TO EARTH, ITS PEOPLE HAVE FEARED ME.
I HOPED THEY WOULD SEE ME AS AN ALLY, IN TIME, WORKING TO HELP THEM OVERCOME THAT FEAR.
M'ARVINN SAYS THAT DAY WILL NEVER COME.
THAT THEIR CYNICISM, THEIR DISTRUST, WILL PULL ME DOWN INTO DESOLATION.
HIS CERTAINTY IS UNWAVERING.
I LONGED FOR A FELLOW MARTIAN. BUT NOT AT THIS PRICE.
I CANNOT BE LIKE HIM. I CANNOT GIVE IN TO HATE.
I AM HERE TO HELP, IN SPITE OF FEAR. TO SHOW THE PEOPLE OF EARTH A BETTER WAY.

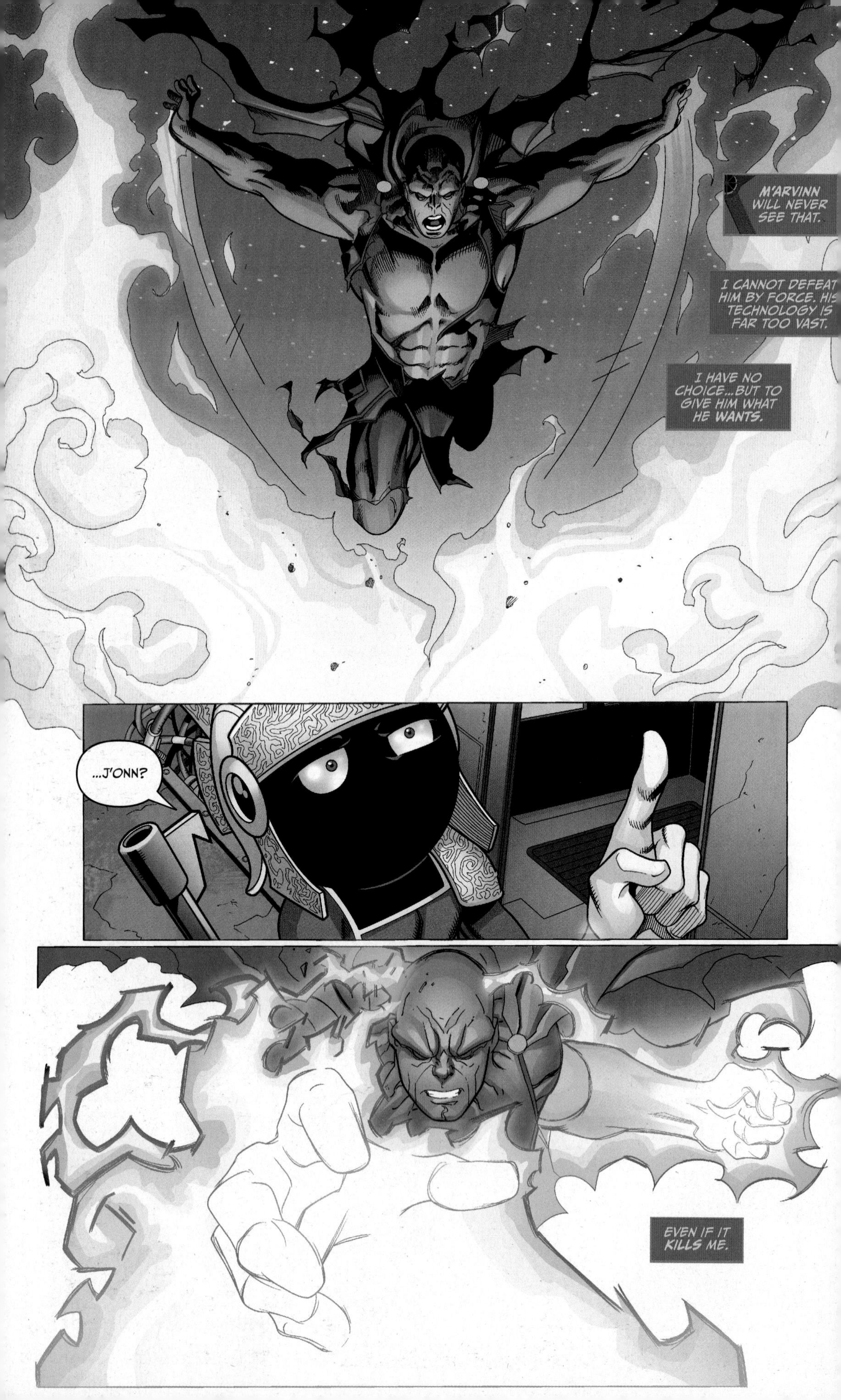
M'ARVINN WILL NEVER SEE THAT.
I CANNOT DEFEAT HIM BY FORCE. HIS TECHNOLOGY IS FAR TOO VAST.
I HAVE NO CHOICE...BUT TO GIVE HIM WHAT HE WANTS.
...J'ONN?
EVEN IF IT KILLS ME.

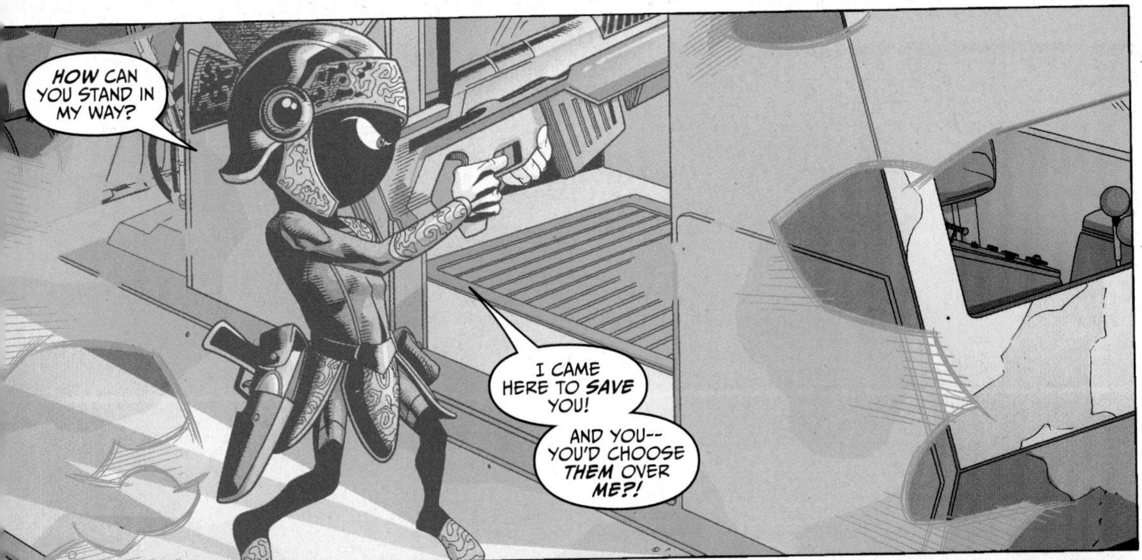
HOW CAN YOU STAND IN MY WAY?
I CAME HERE TO SAVE YOU!
AND YOU-- YOU'D CHOOSE THEM OVER ME?!

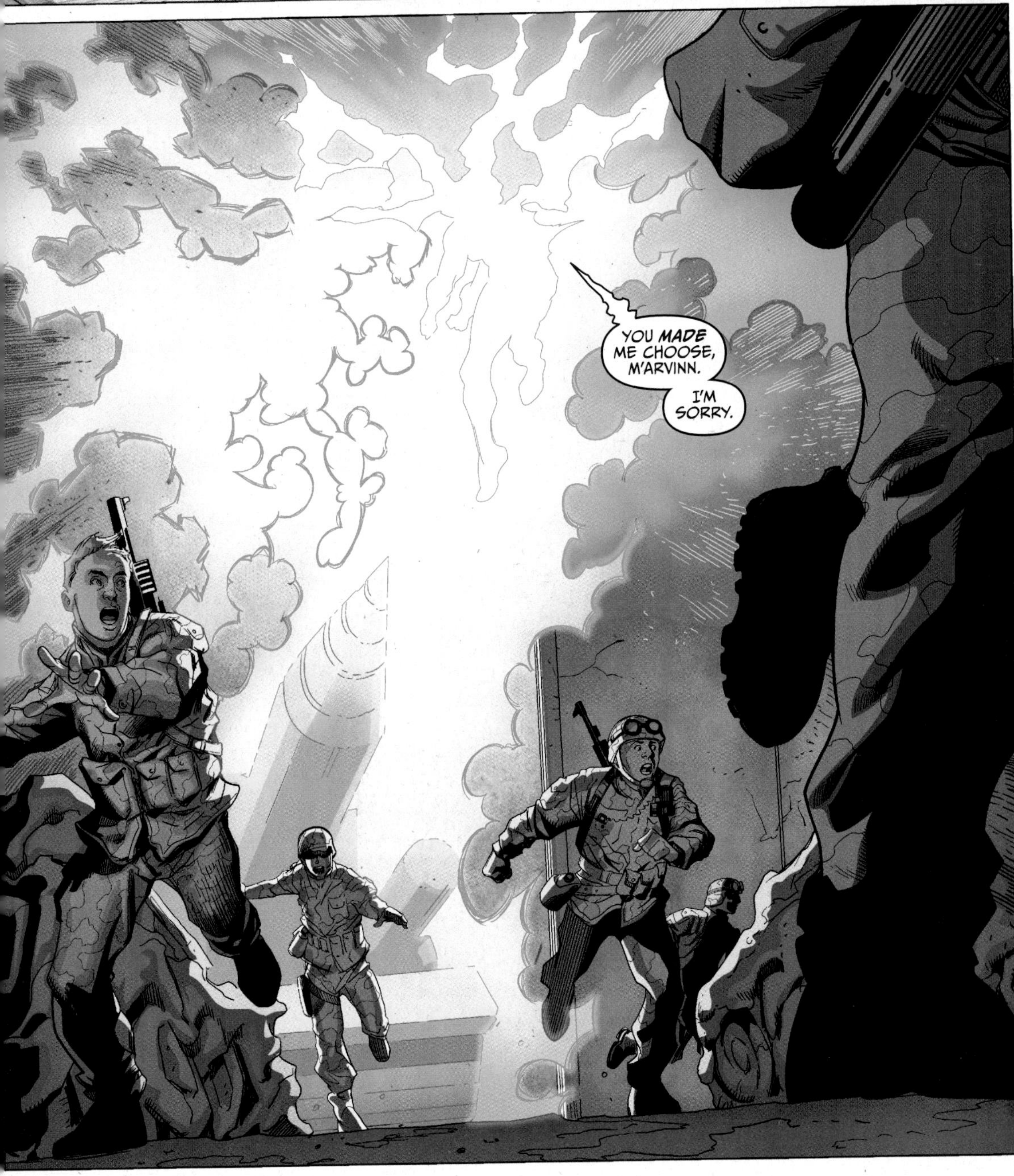
YOU MADE ME CHOOSE, M'ARVINN.
I'M SORRY.

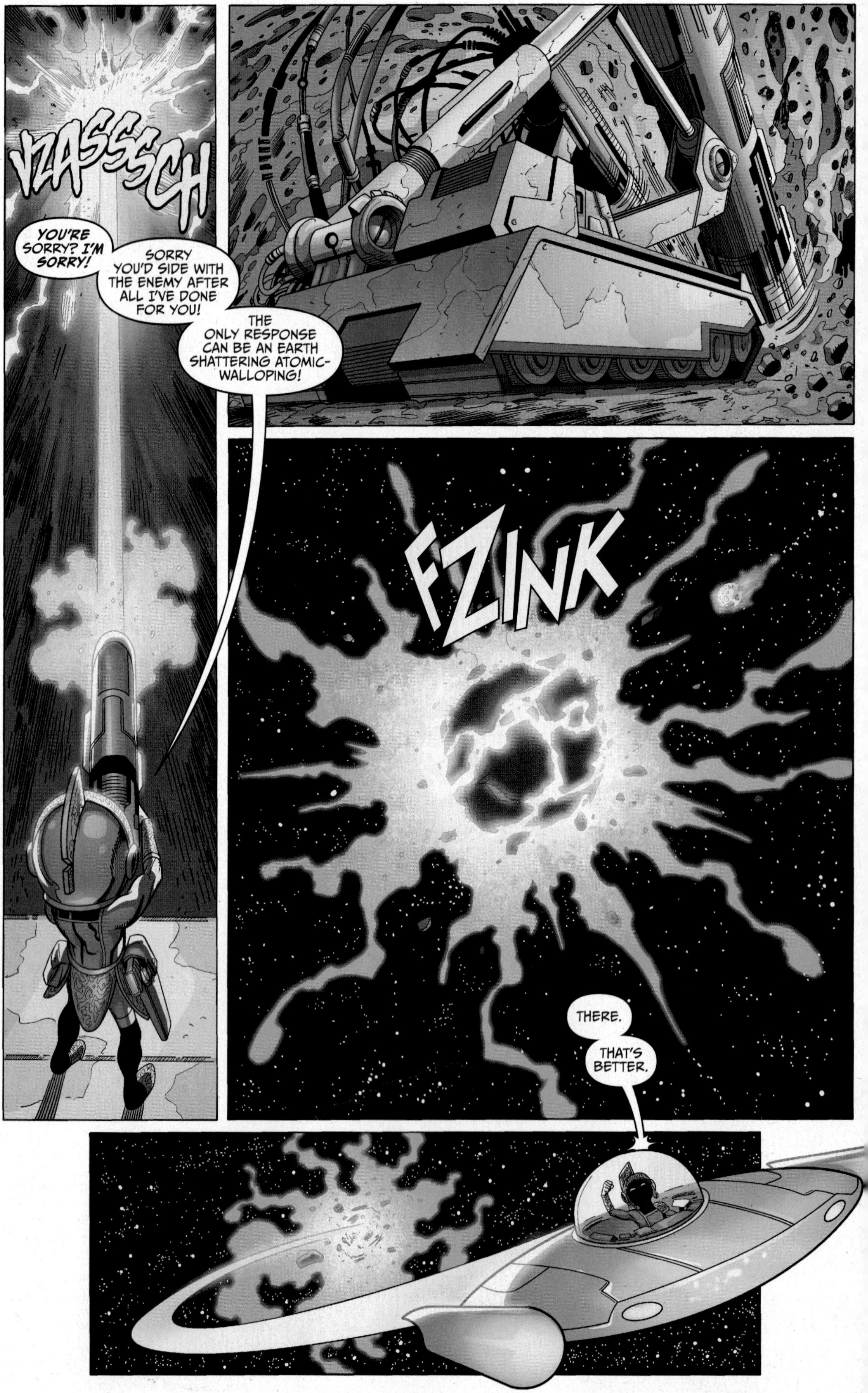
VZASSSCH
YOU'RE SORRY? I'M SORRY!
SORRY YOU'D SIDE WITH THE ENEMY AFTER ALL I'VE DONE FOR YOU!
THE ONLY RESPONSE CAN BE AN EARTH SHATTERING ATOMIC-WALLOPING!
FZINK
THERE.
THAT'S BETTER.

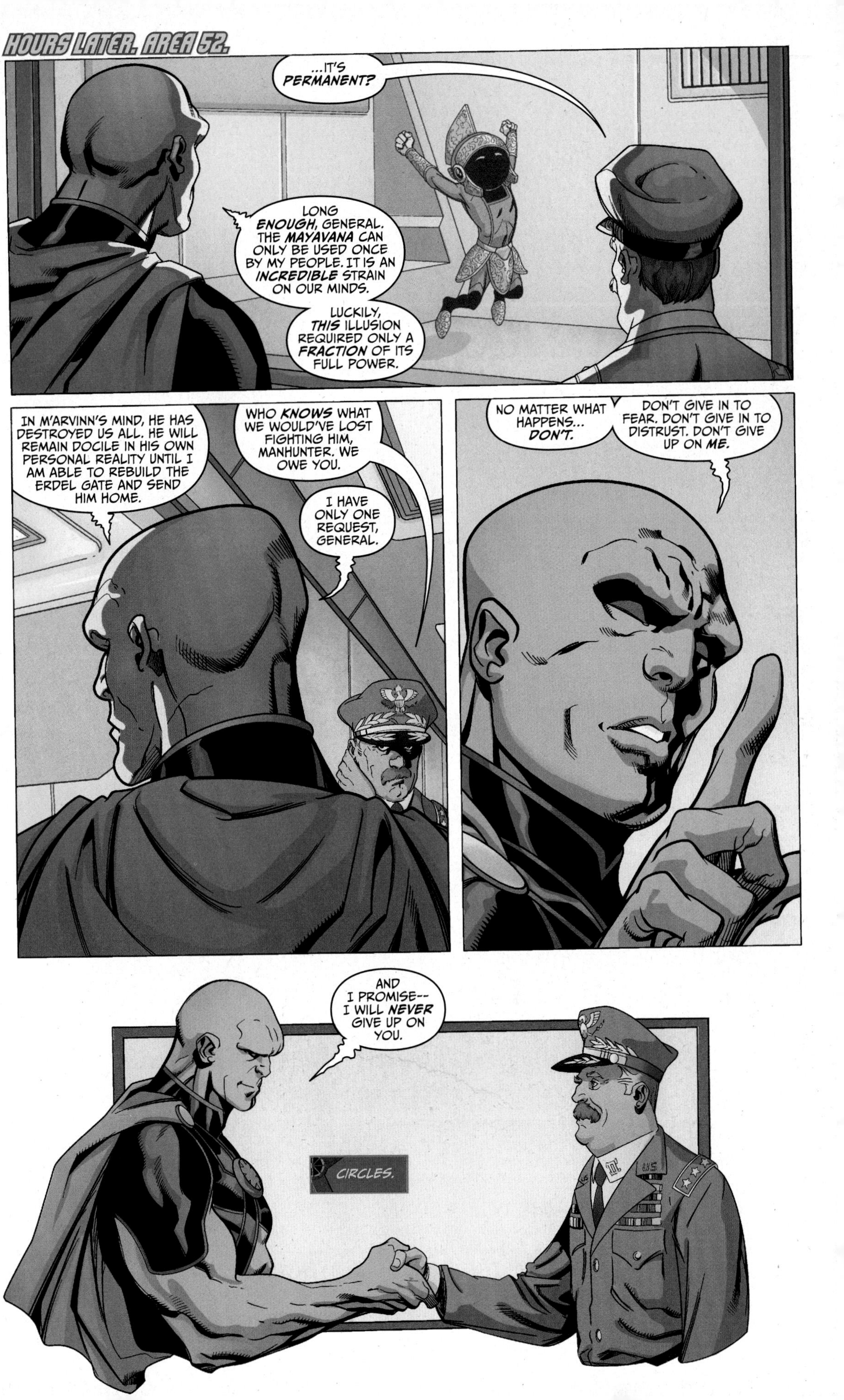
HOURS LATER. AREA 52.
...IT'S PERMANENT?
LONG ENOUGH, GENERAL. THE MAYAVANA CAN ONLY BE USED ONCE BY MY PEOPLE. IT IS AN INCREDIBLE STRAIN ON OUR MINDS.
LUCKILY, THIS ILLUSION REQUIRED ONLY A FRACTION OF ITS FULL POWER.
IN M'ARVINN'S MIND, HE HAS DESTROYED US ALL. HE WILL REMAIN DOCILE IN HIS OWN PERSONAL REALITY UNTIL I AM ABLE TO REBUILD THE ERDEL GATE AND SEND HIM HOME.
WHO KNOWS WHAT WE WOULD'VE LOST FIGHTING HIM, MANHUNTER. WE OWE YOU.
I HAVE ONLY ONE REQUEST, GENERAL.
NO MATTER WHAT HAPPENS... DON'T.
DON'T GIVE IN TO FEAR. DON'T GIVE IN TO DISTRUST. DON'T GIVE UP ON ME.
AND I PROMISE-- I WILL NEVER GIVE UP ON YOU.
CIRCLES.

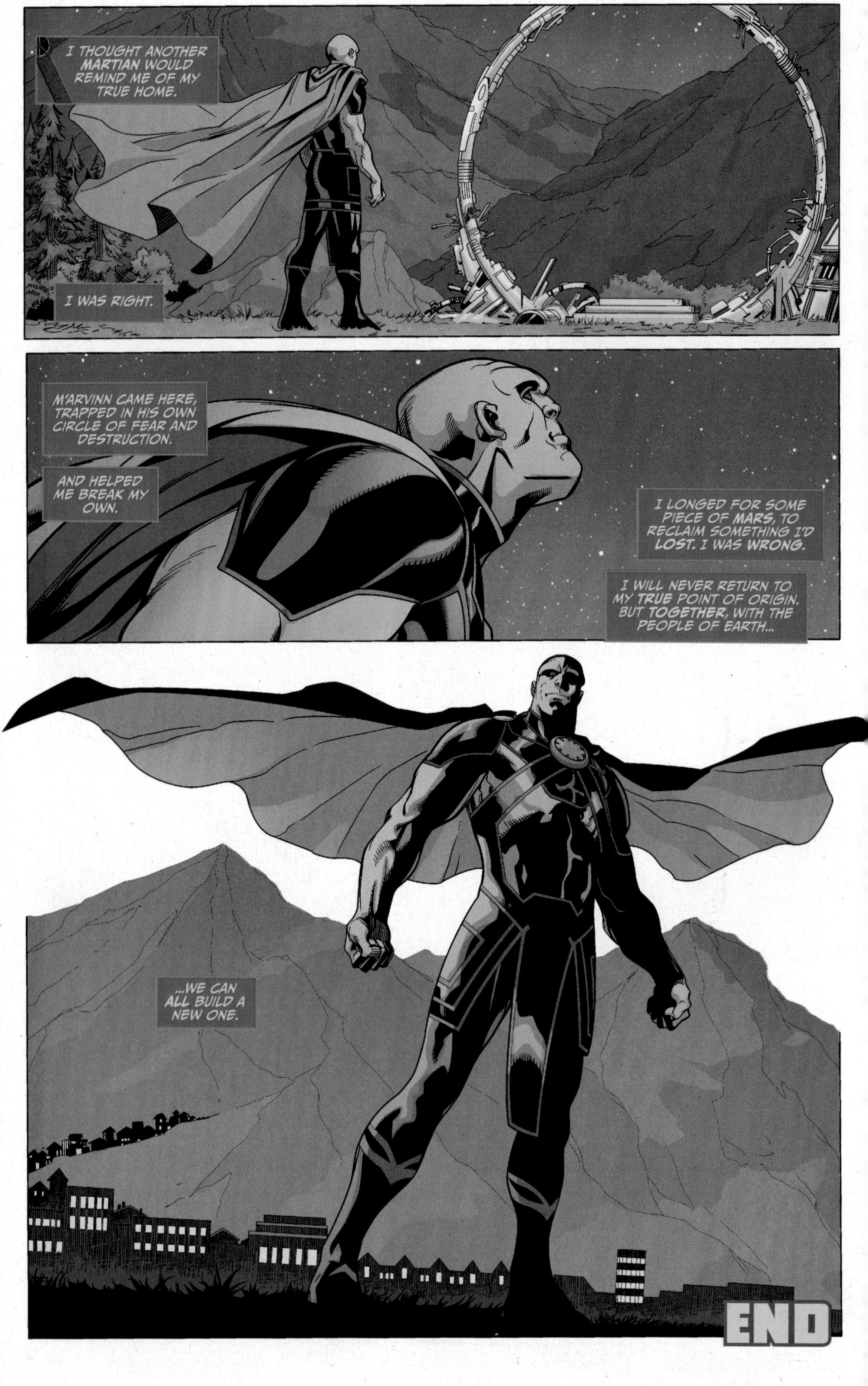
I THOUGHT ANOTHER MARTIAN WOULD REMIND ME OF MY TRUE HOME.
I WAS RIGHT.
M'ARVINN CAME HERE, TRAPPED IN HIS OWN CIRCLE OF FEAR AND DESTRUCTION.
AND HELPED ME BREAK MY OWN.
I LONGED FOR SOME PIECE OF MARS, TO RECLAIM SOMETHING I'D LOST. I WAS WRONG.
I WILL NEVER RETURN TO MY TRUE POINT OF ORIGIN. BUT TOGETHER, WITH THE PEOPLE OF EARTH...
...WE CAN ALL BUILD A NEW ONE.
END

MARVIN the Martian AND Martian Manhunter in: THE (NEXT TO THE) LAST MARTIAN

Jim Fanning, writer
John Loter, artist

Saida Temofonte, letterer
special thanks to Paul J. Lopez

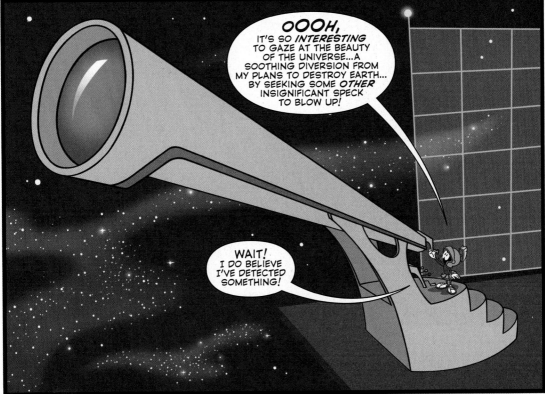

OOOH, IT'S SO *INTERESTING* TO GAZE AT THE BEAUTY OF THE UNIVERSE...A SOOTHING DIVERSION FROM MY PLANS TO DESTROY EARTH... BY SEEKING SOME *OTHER* INSIGNIFICANT SPECK TO BLOW UP!

WAIT! I DO BELIEVE I'VE DETECTED SOMETHING!

OH GOODIE! I JUST KNOW IT'S A *U.D.O.*--AN UTTERLY *DESTROYABLE* OBJECT!

I SHALL TAKE A CLOSER LOOK AT THIS LOVELY, MOST-LIKELY-TO-BE-*DISINTEGRATED* BIT OF SPACE FLOTSAM...

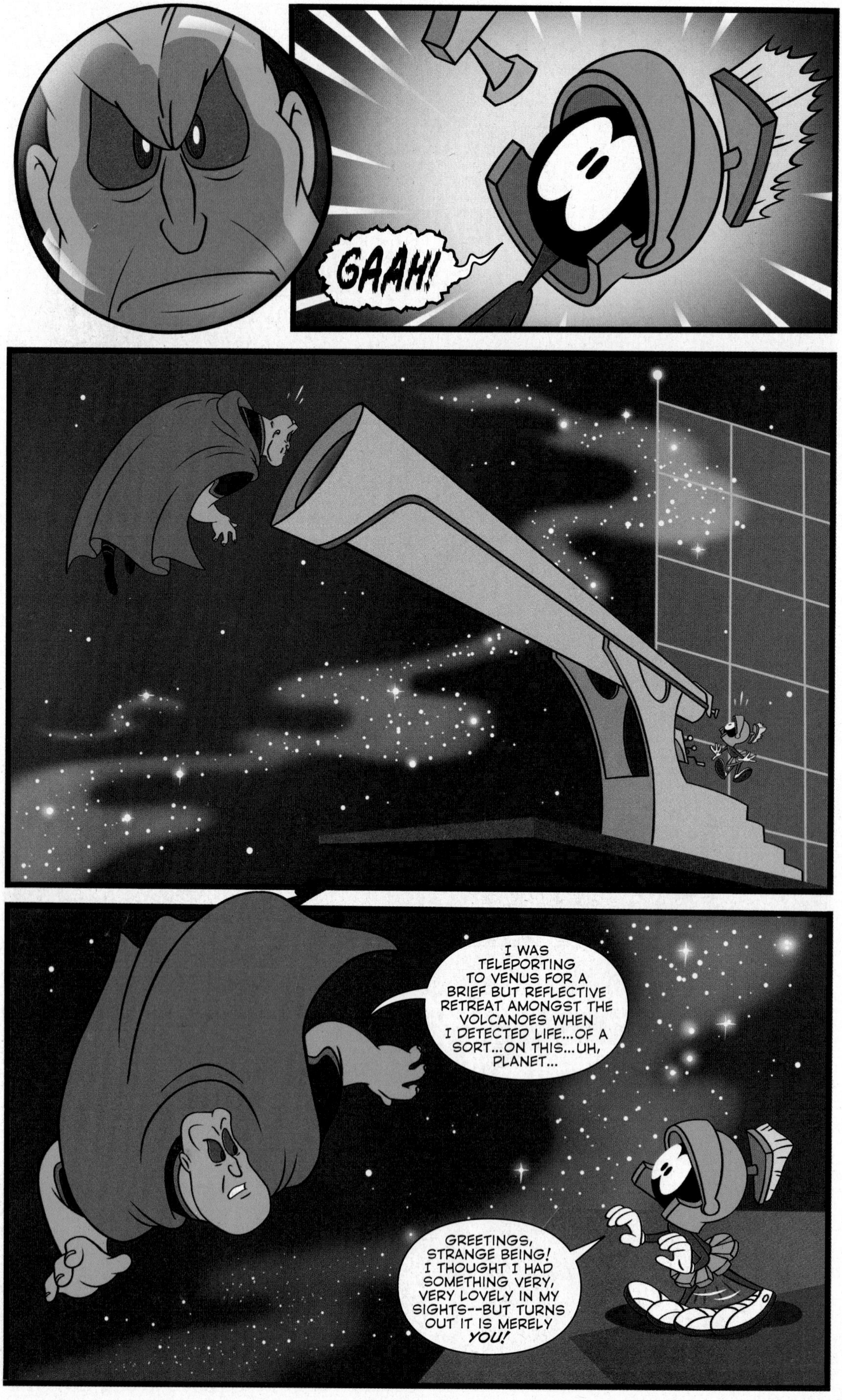
GAAH!
I WAS TELEPORTING TO VENUS FOR A BRIEF BUT REFLECTIVE RETREAT AMONGST THE VOLCANOES WHEN I DETECTED LIFE...OF A SORT...ON THIS...UH, PLANET...
GREETINGS, STRANGE BEING! I THOUGHT I HAD SOMETHING VERY, VERY LOVELY IN MY SIGHTS--BUT TURNS OUT IT IS MERELY YOU!

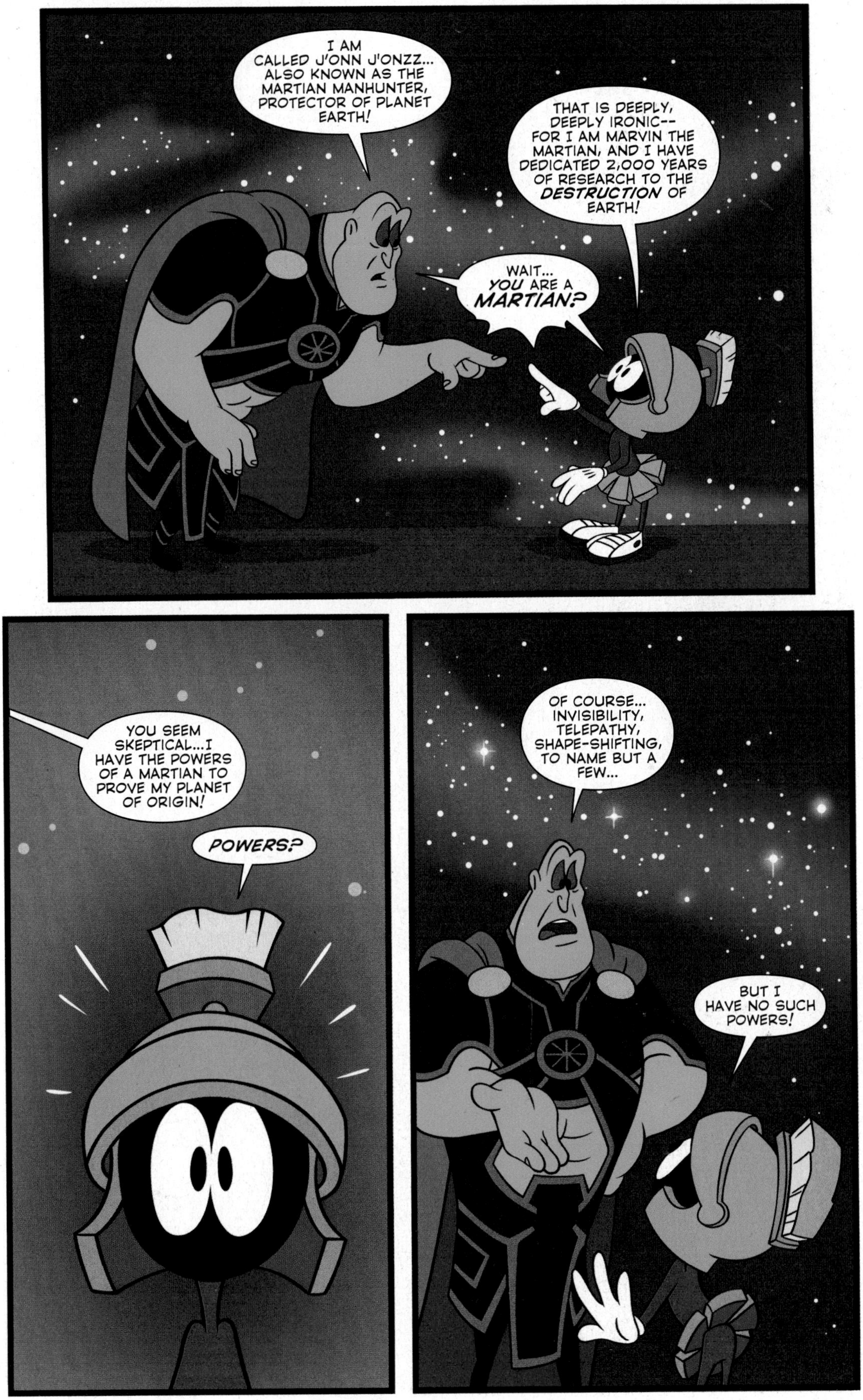
I AM CALLED J'ONN J'ONZZ... ALSO KNOWN AS THE MARTIAN MANHUNTER, PROTECTOR OF PLANET EARTH!
THAT IS DEEPLY, DEEPLY IRONIC-- FOR I AM MARVIN THE MARTIAN, AND I HAVE DEDICATED 2,000 YEARS OF RESEARCH TO THE *DESTRUCTION* OF EARTH!
WAIT... *YOU* ARE A *MARTIAN?*
YOU SEEM SKEPTICAL...I HAVE THE POWERS OF A MARTIAN TO PROVE MY PLANET OF ORIGIN!
POWERS?
OF COURSE... INVISIBILITY, TELEPATHY, SHAPE-SHIFTING, TO NAME BUT A FEW...
BUT I HAVE NO SUCH POWERS!

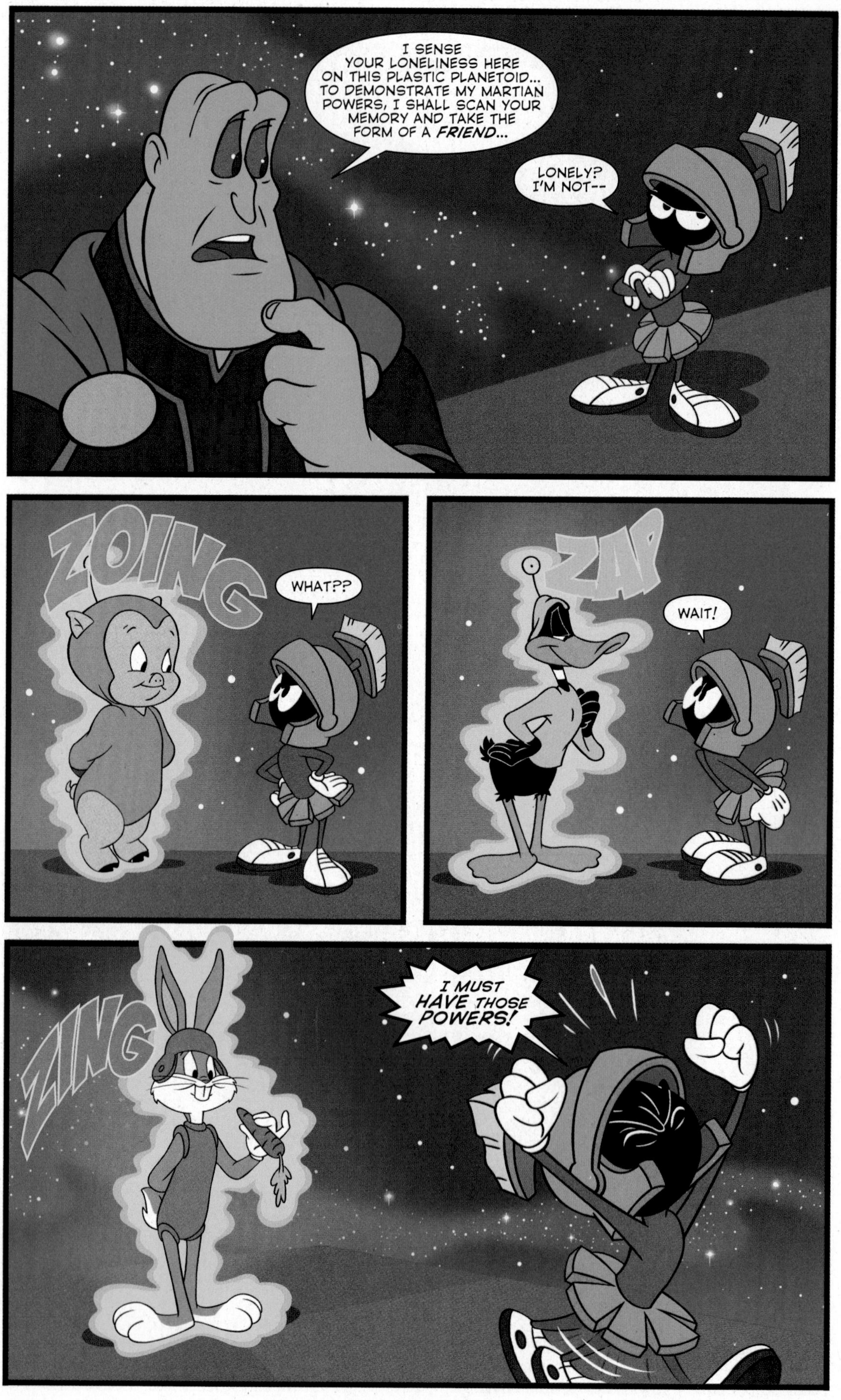
I SENSE YOUR LONELINESS HERE ON THIS PLASTIC PLANETOID... TO DEMONSTRATE MY MARTIAN POWERS, I SHALL SCAN YOUR MEMORY AND TAKE THE FORM OF A *FRIEND*...
LONELY? I'M NOT--
ZOING
WHAT??
ZAP
WAIT!
ZING
I MUST *HAVE* THOSE *POWERS!*

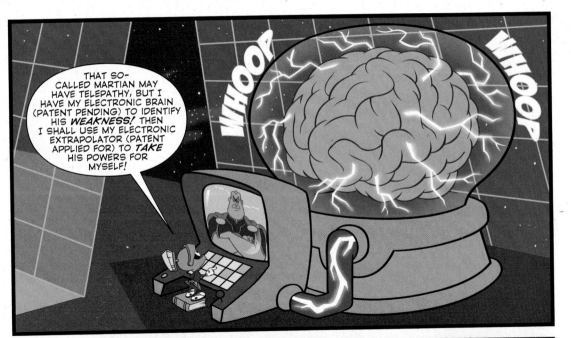

THAT SO-CALLED MARTIAN MAY HAVE TELEPATHY, BUT I HAVE MY ELECTRONIC BRAIN (PATENT PENDING) TO IDENTIFY HIS *WEAKNESS!* THEN I SHALL USE MY ELECTRONIC EXTRAPOLATOR (PATENT APPLIED FOR) TO *TAKE* HIS POWERS FOR MYSELF!

COOKIES? OBVIOUSLY AN EARTH DELICACY THAT THE CREATURE HAS DEVELOPED AN ADDICTION TO!

IN ORDER TO TRAP THE CREATURE AND TAKE HIS POWERS, I MUST HAVE EARTH COOKIES!

SUMMONING *K-9!*

I NEED TONS AND TONS OF THE DELICACIES THOSE EASILY PLEASED EARTH CREATURES CALL CHOCOS! *FETCH!*

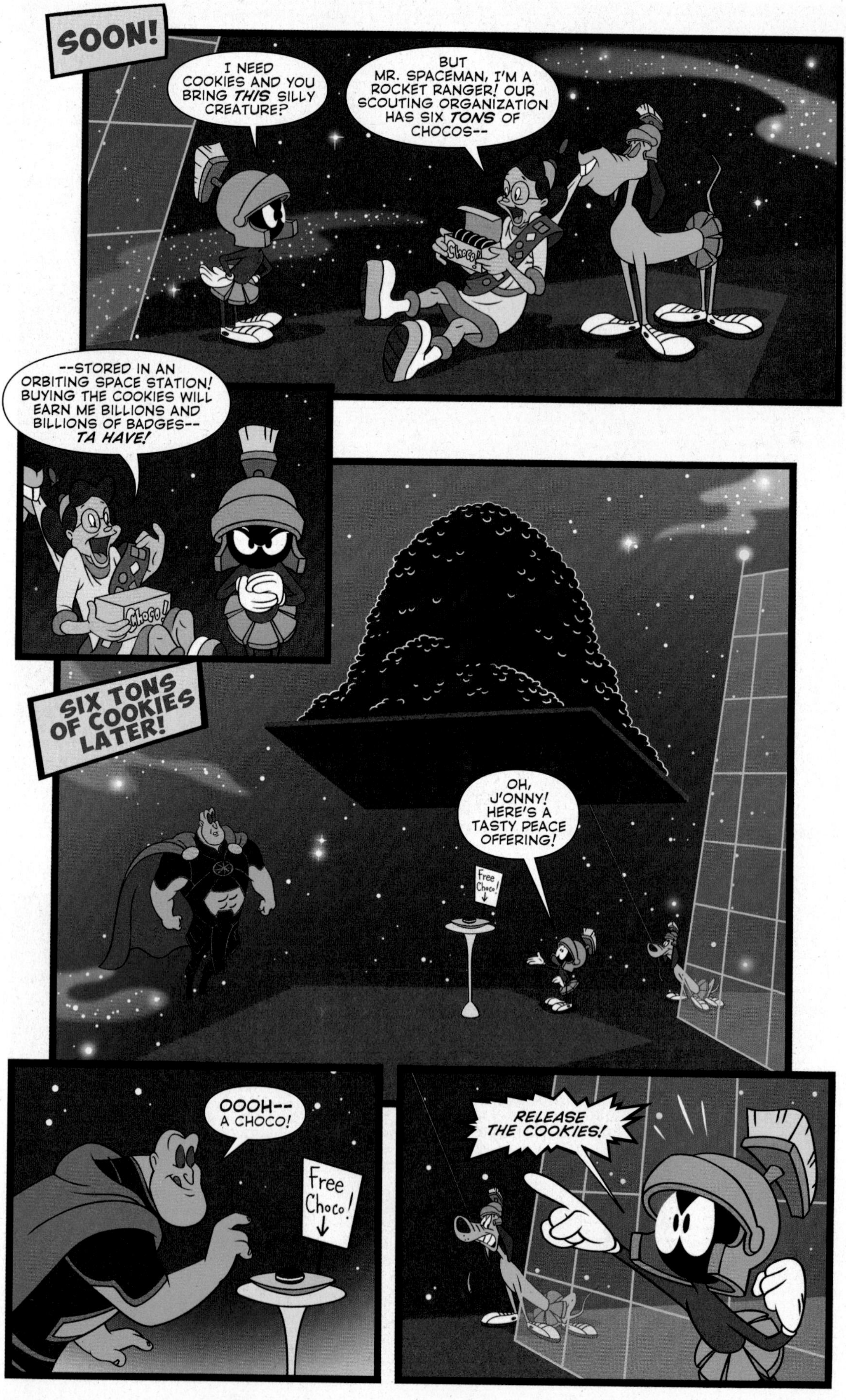
SOON!
I NEED COOKIES AND YOU BRING THIS SILLY CREATURE?
BUT MR. SPACEMAN, I'M A ROCKET RANGER! OUR SCOUTING ORGANIZATION HAS SIX TONS OF CHOCOS--
Choco!
--STORED IN AN ORBITING SPACE STATION! BUYING THE COOKIES WILL EARN ME BILLIONS AND BILLIONS OF BADGES-- TA HAVE!
Choco!
SIX TONS OF COOKIES LATER!
OH, J'ONNY! HERE'S A TASTY PEACE OFFERING!
Free Choco! ↓
OOOH-- A CHOCO!
Free Choco! ↓
RELEASE THE COOKIES!

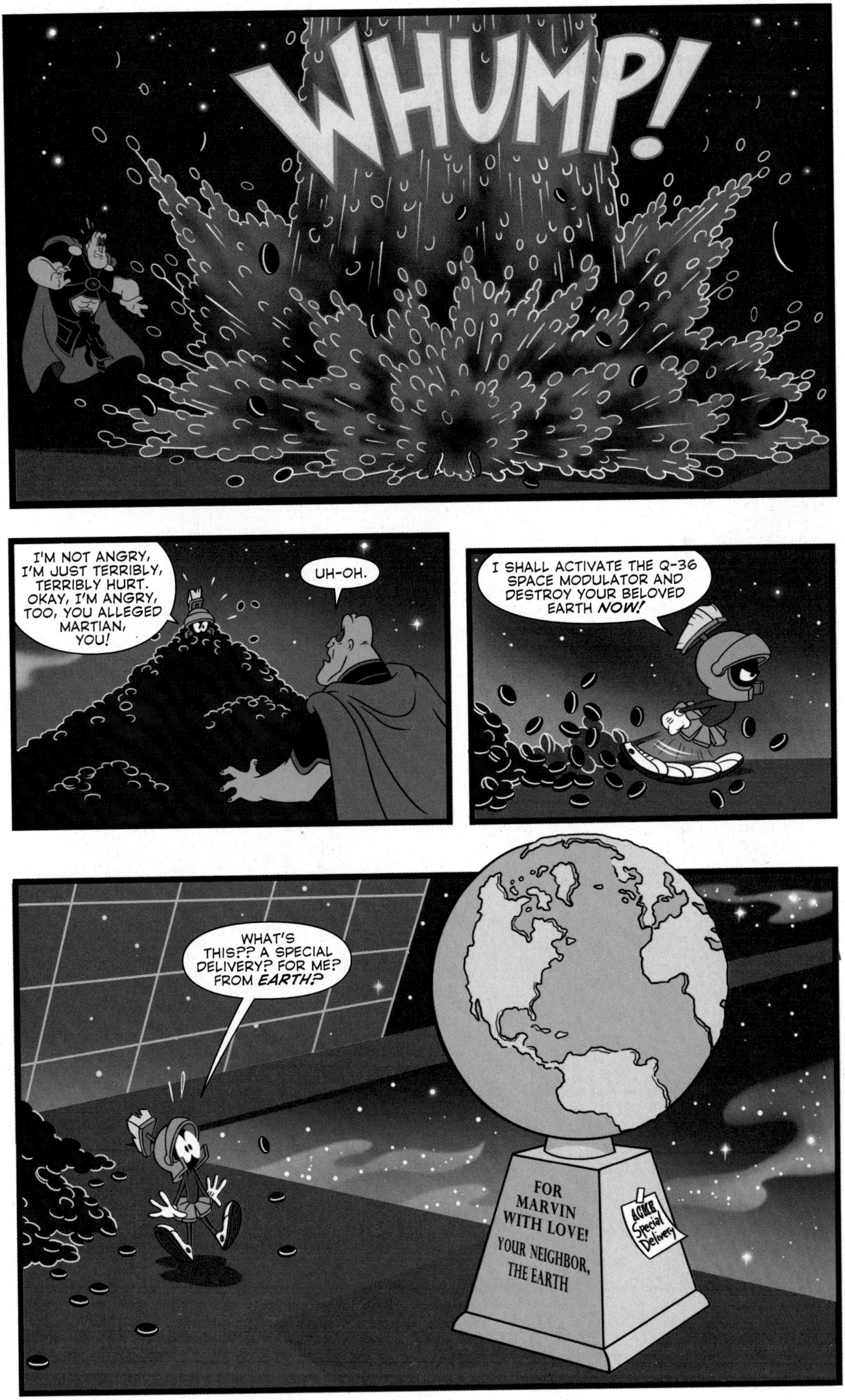
WHUMP!
I'M NOT ANGRY, I'M JUST TERRIBLY, TERRIBLY HURT. OKAY, I'M ANGRY, TOO, YOU ALLEGED MARTIAN, YOU!
UH-OH.
I SHALL ACTIVATE THE Q-36 SPACE MODULATOR AND DESTROY YOUR BELOVED EARTH NOW!
WHAT'S THIS?? A SPECIAL DELIVERY? FOR ME? FROM EARTH?
FOR MARVIN WITH LOVE!
YOUR NEIGHBOR, THE EARTH
ACME Special Delivery

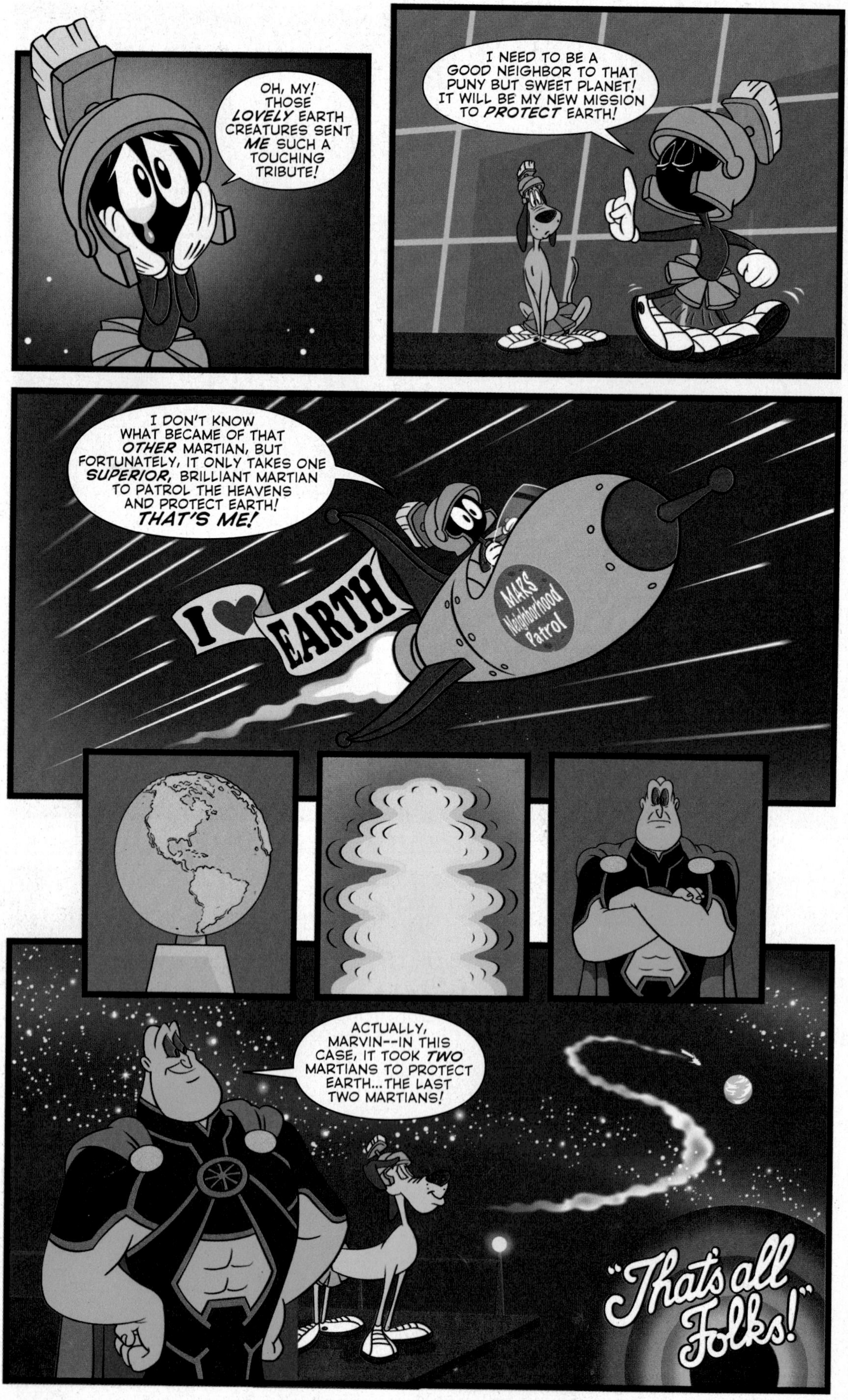
OH, MY! THOSE *LOVELY* EARTH CREATURES SENT *ME* SUCH A TOUCHING TRIBUTE!
I NEED TO BE A GOOD NEIGHBOR TO THAT PUNY BUT SWEET PLANET! IT WILL BE MY NEW MISSION TO *PROTECT* EARTH!
I DON'T KNOW WHAT BECAME OF THAT *OTHER* MARTIAN, BUT FORTUNATELY, IT ONLY TAKES ONE *SUPERIOR*, BRILLIANT MARTIAN TO PATROL THE HEAVENS AND PROTECT EARTH! ***THAT'S ME!***
I ♥ EARTH
MARS Neighborhood Patrol
ACTUALLY, MARVIN--IN THIS CASE, IT TOOK *TWO* MARTIANS TO PROTECT EARTH...THE LAST TWO MARTIANS!
"That's all Folks!"

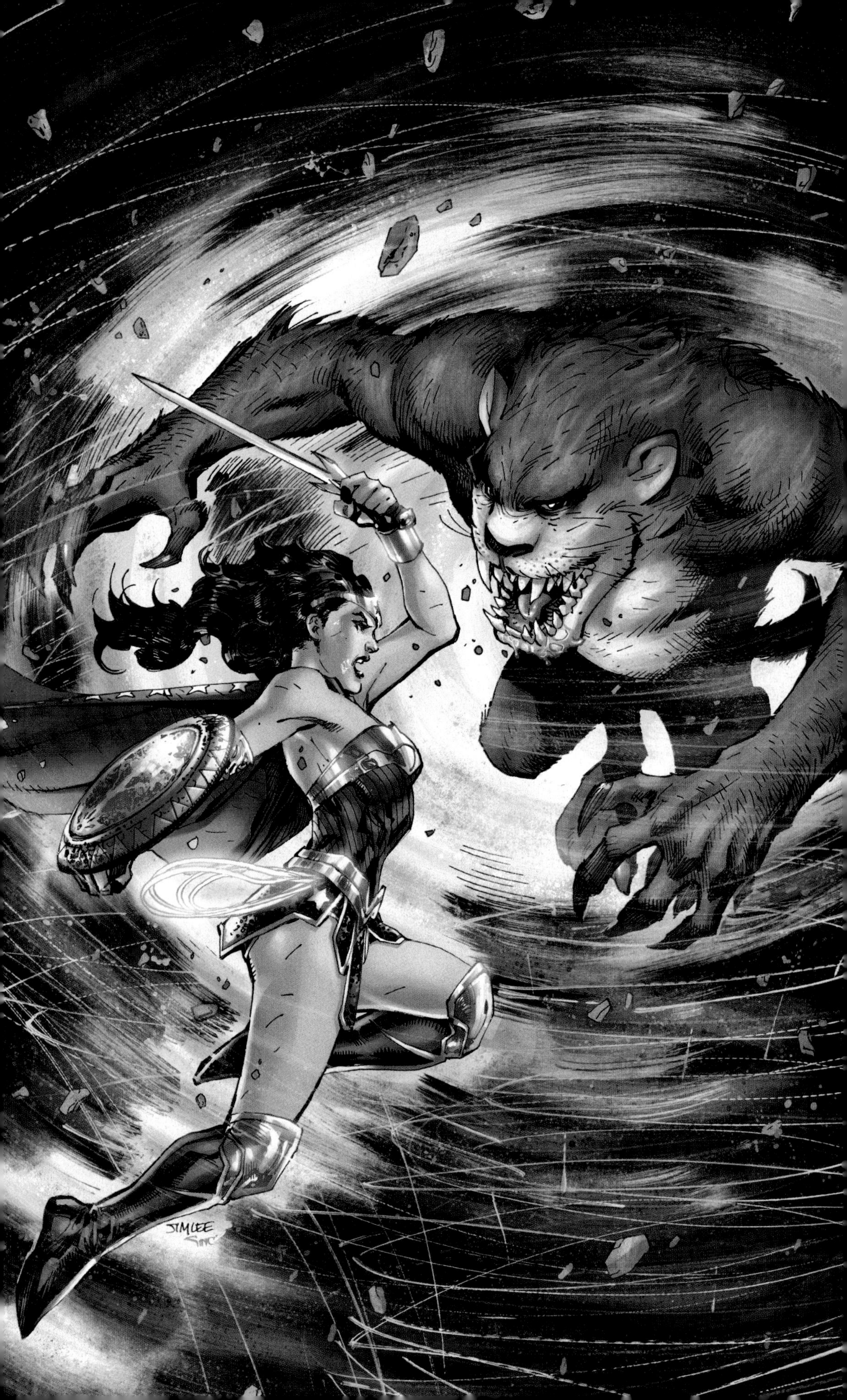
JIM LEE

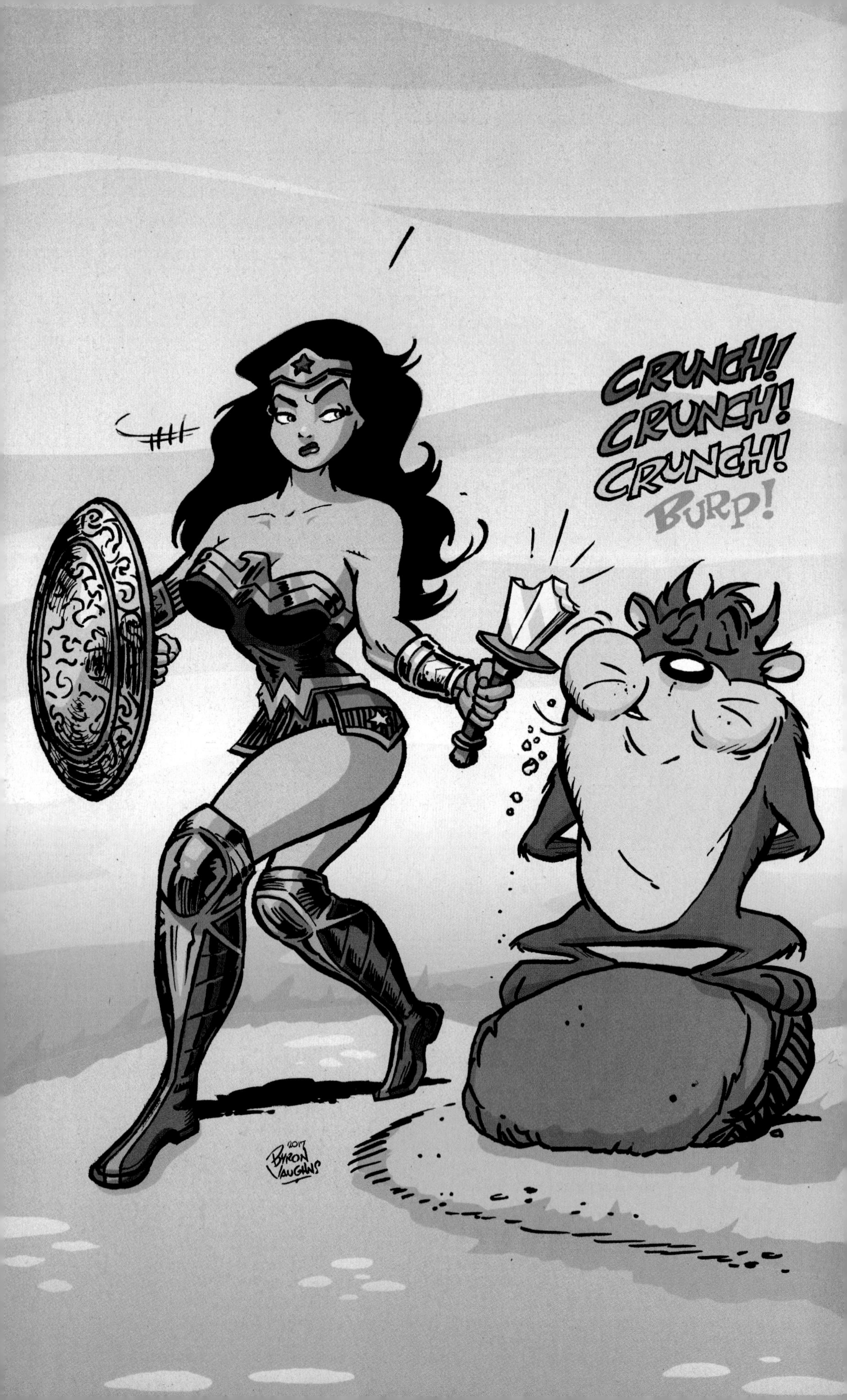
CRUNCH!
CRUNCH!
CRUNCH!
BURP!

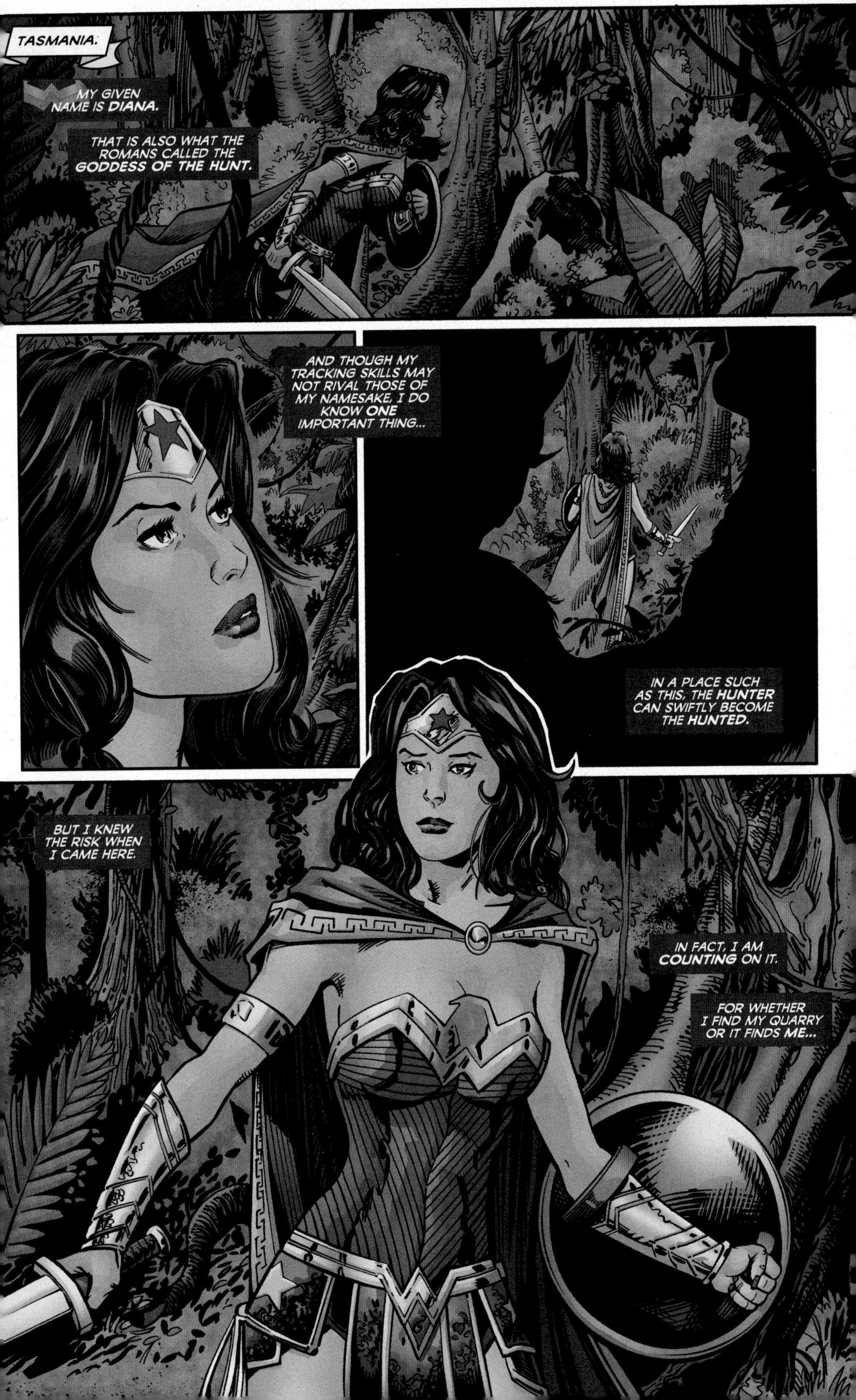
TASMANIA.
MY GIVEN NAME IS DIANA.
THAT IS ALSO WHAT THE ROMANS CALLED THE GODDESS OF THE HUNT.
AND THOUGH MY TRACKING SKILLS MAY NOT RIVAL THOSE OF MY NAMESAKE, I DO KNOW ONE IMPORTANT THING...
IN A PLACE SUCH AS THIS, THE HUNTER CAN SWIFTLY BECOME THE HUNTED.
BUT I KNEW THE RISK WHEN I CAME HERE.
IN FACT, I AM COUNTING ON IT.
FOR WHETHER I FIND MY QUARRY OR IT FINDS ME...

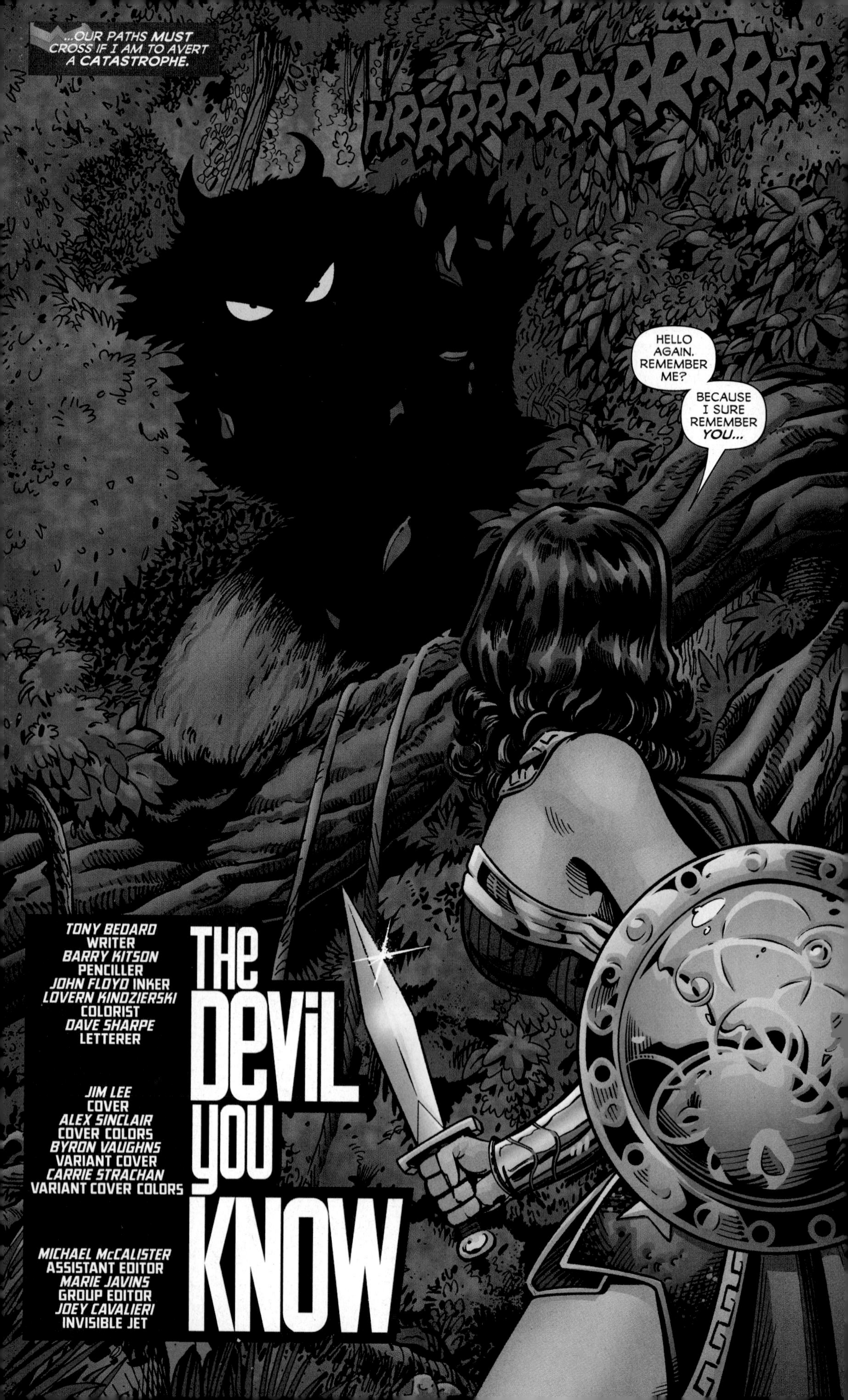
...OUR PATHS MUST CROSS IF I AM TO AVERT A CATASTROPHE.
HRRRRRRRRRRRRR
HELLO AGAIN. REMEMBER ME?
BECAUSE I SURE REMEMBER YOU...
TONY BEDARD WRITER
BARRY KITSON PENCILLER
JOHN FLOYD INKER
LOVERN KINDZIERSKI COLORIST
DAVE SHARPE LETTERER
THE DEVIL YOU KNOW
JIM LEE COVER
ALEX SINCLAIR COVER COLORS
BYRON VAUGHNS VARIANT COVER
CARRIE STRACHAN VARIANT COVER COLORS
MICHAEL McCALISTER ASSISTANT EDITOR
MARIE JAVINS GROUP EDITOR
JOEY CAVALIERI INVISIBLE JET

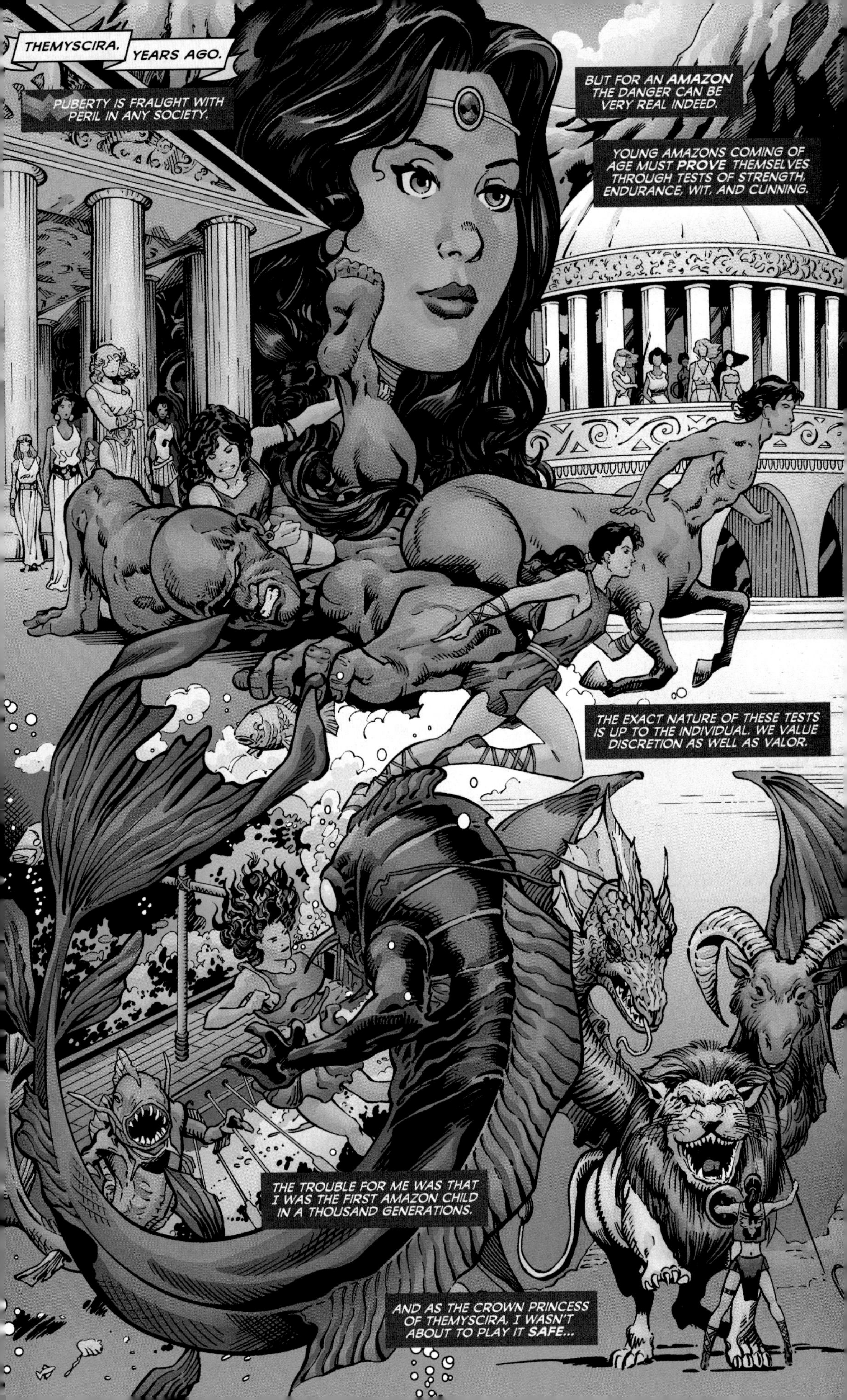
THEMYSCIRA.
YEARS AGO.
PUBERTY IS FRAUGHT WITH PERIL IN ANY SOCIETY.
BUT FOR AN AMAZON THE DANGER CAN BE VERY REAL INDEED.
YOUNG AMAZONS COMING OF AGE MUST PROVE THEMSELVES THROUGH TESTS OF STRENGTH, ENDURANCE, WIT, AND CUNNING.
THE EXACT NATURE OF THESE TESTS IS UP TO THE INDIVIDUAL. WE VALUE DISCRETION AS WELL AS VALOR.
THE TROUBLE FOR ME WAS THAT I WAS THE FIRST AMAZON CHILD IN A THOUSAND GENERATIONS.
AND AS THE CROWN PRINCESS OF THEMYSCIRA, I WASN'T ABOUT TO PLAY IT SAFE...

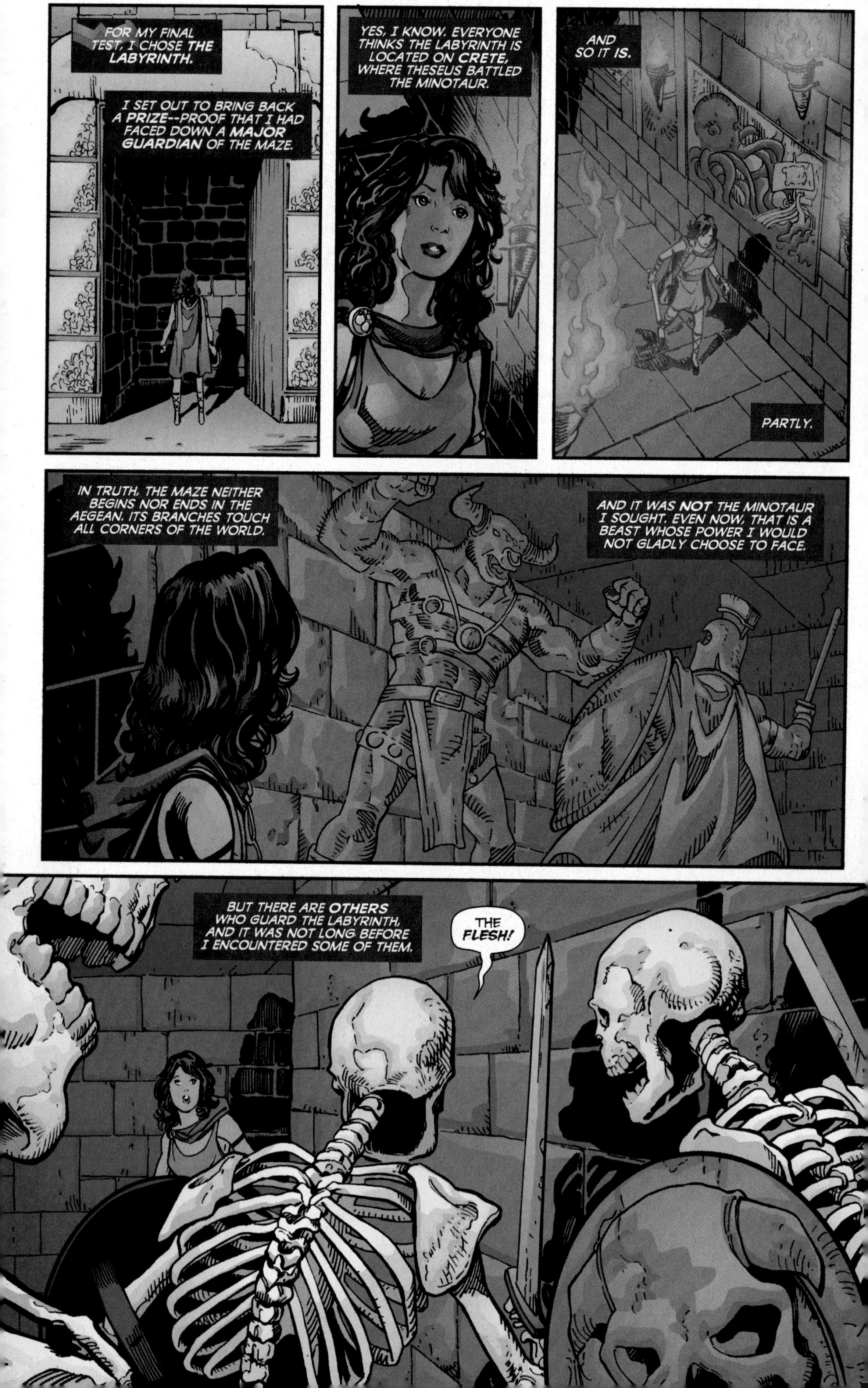
FOR MY FINAL TEST, I CHOSE THE LABYRINTH.
I SET OUT TO BRING BACK A PRIZE--PROOF THAT I HAD FACED DOWN A MAJOR GUARDIAN OF THE MAZE.
YES, I KNOW. EVERYONE THINKS THE LABYRINTH IS LOCATED ON CRETE, WHERE THESEUS BATTLED THE MINOTAUR.
AND SO IT IS.
PARTLY.
IN TRUTH, THE MAZE NEITHER BEGINS NOR ENDS IN THE AEGEAN. ITS BRANCHES TOUCH ALL CORNERS OF THE WORLD.
AND IT WAS NOT THE MINOTAUR I SOUGHT. EVEN NOW, THAT IS A BEAST WHOSE POWER I WOULD NOT GLADLY CHOOSE TO FACE.
BUT THERE ARE OTHERS WHO GUARD THE LABYRINTH, AND IT WAS NOT LONG BEFORE I ENCOUNTERED SOME OF THEM.
THE FLESH!

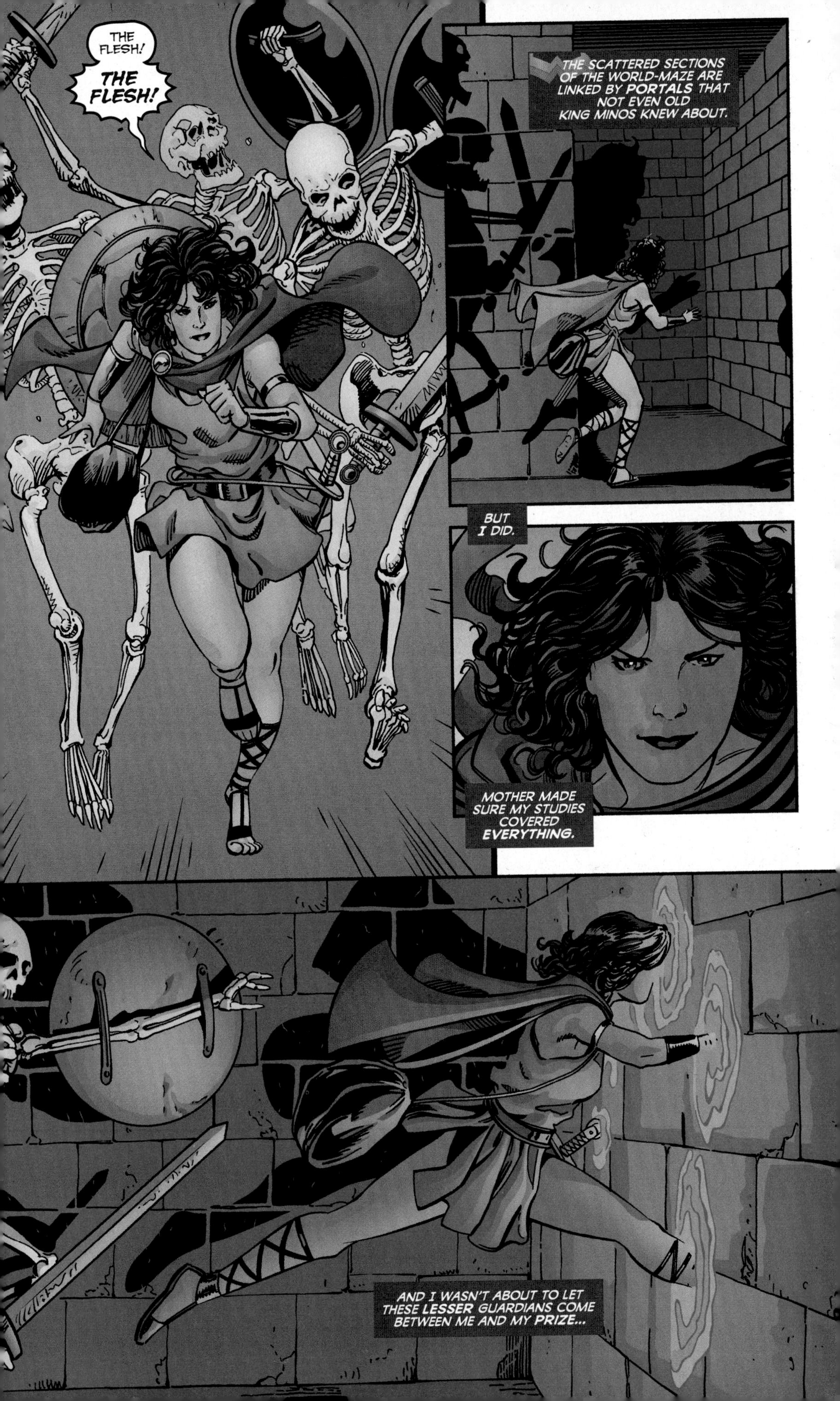
THE FLESH!
THE FLESH!
THE SCATTERED SECTIONS OF THE WORLD-MAZE ARE LINKED BY PORTALS THAT NOT EVEN OLD KING MINOS KNEW ABOUT.
BUT I DID.
MOTHER MADE SURE MY STUDIES COVERED EVERYTHING.
AND I WASN'T ABOUT TO LET THESE LESSER GUARDIANS COME BETWEEN ME AND MY PRIZE...

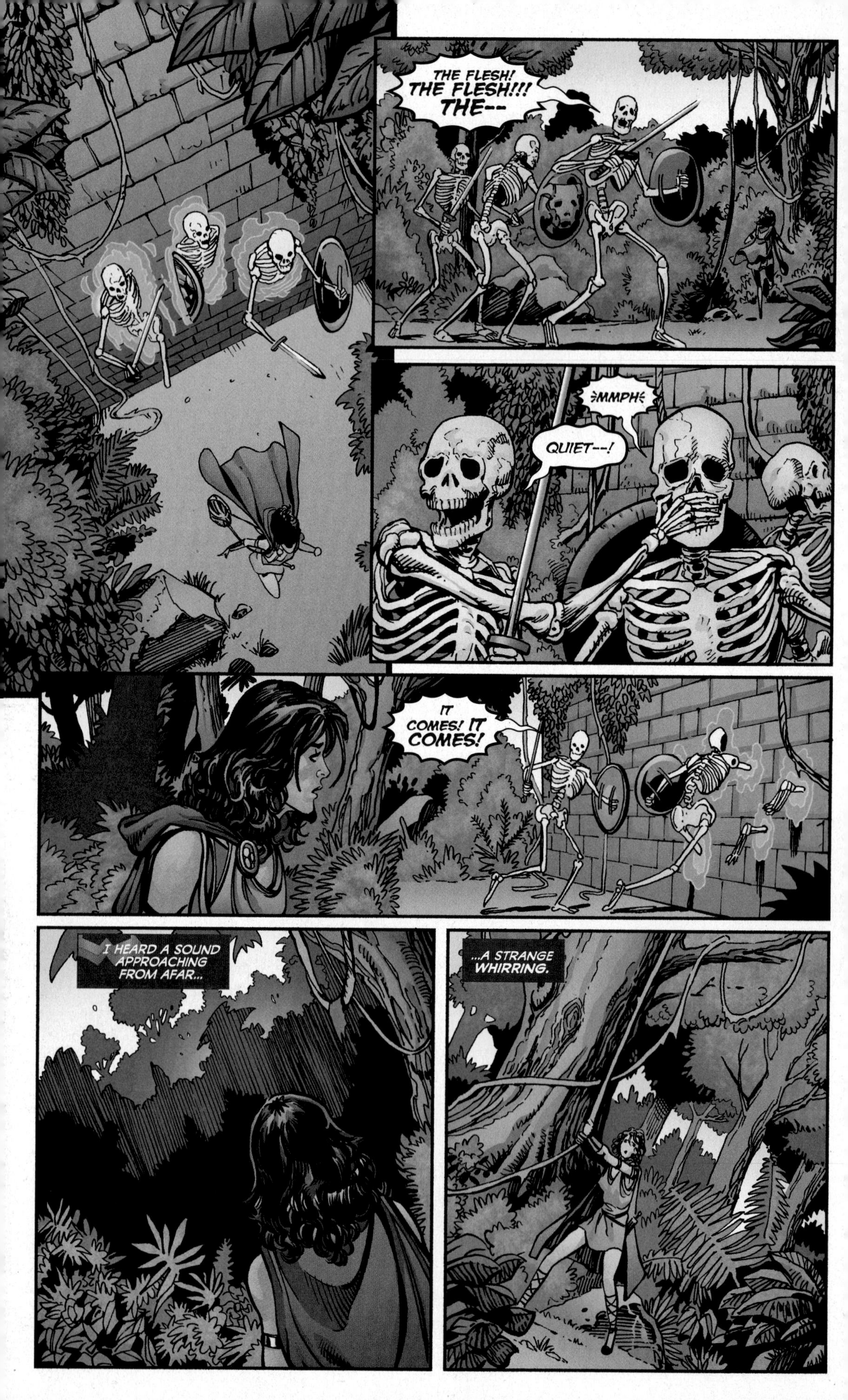
THE FLESH! THE FLESH!!! THE--
MMPH
QUIET--!
IT COMES! IT COMES!
I HEARD A SOUND APPROACHING FROM AFAR...
...A STRANGE WHIRRING.

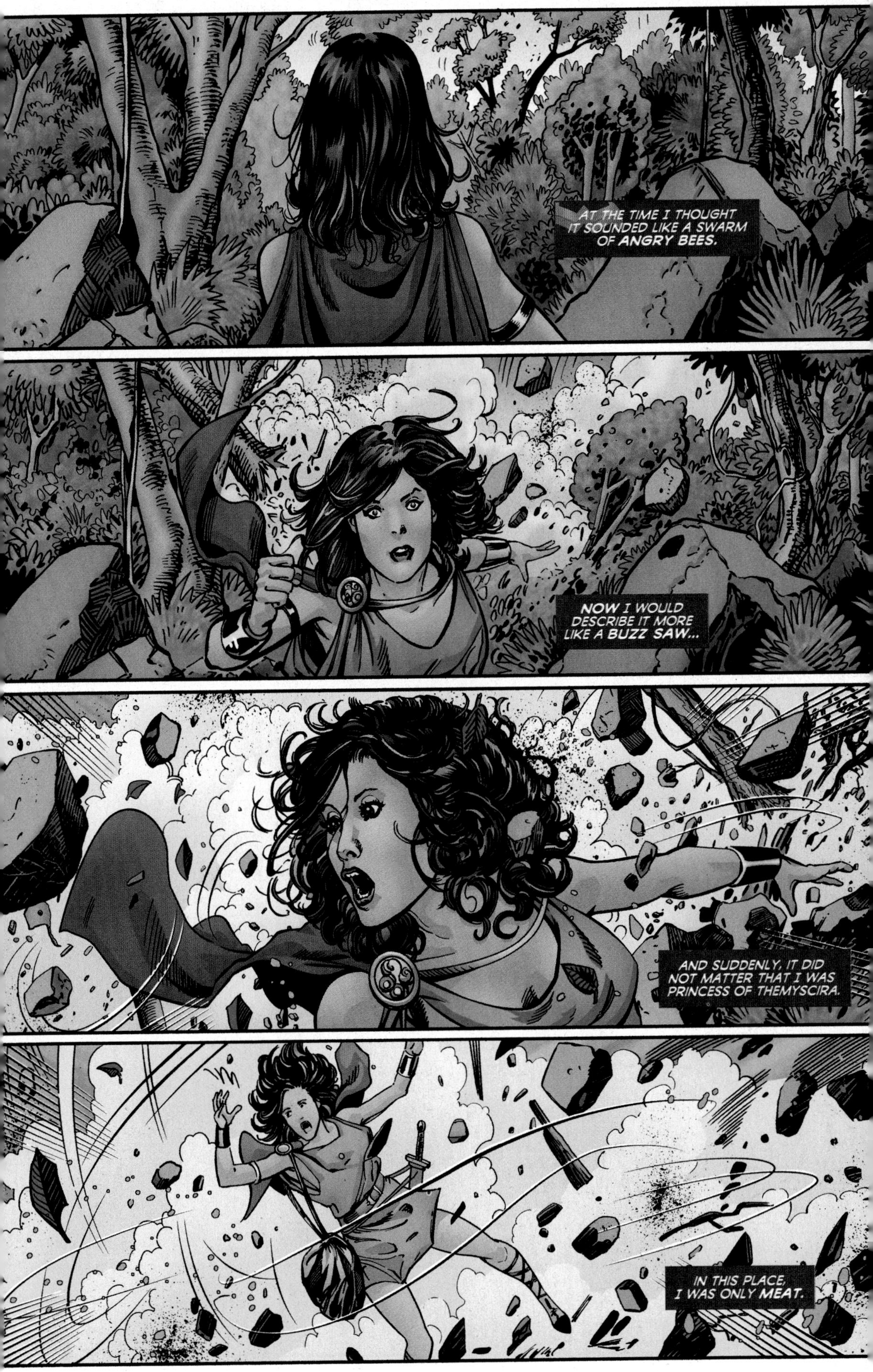
AT THE TIME I THOUGHT IT SOUNDED LIKE A SWARM OF ANGRY BEES.
NOW I WOULD DESCRIBE IT MORE LIKE A BUZZ SAW...
AND SUDDENLY, IT DID NOT MATTER THAT I WAS PRINCESS OF THEMYSCIRA.
IN THIS PLACE, I WAS ONLY MEAT.

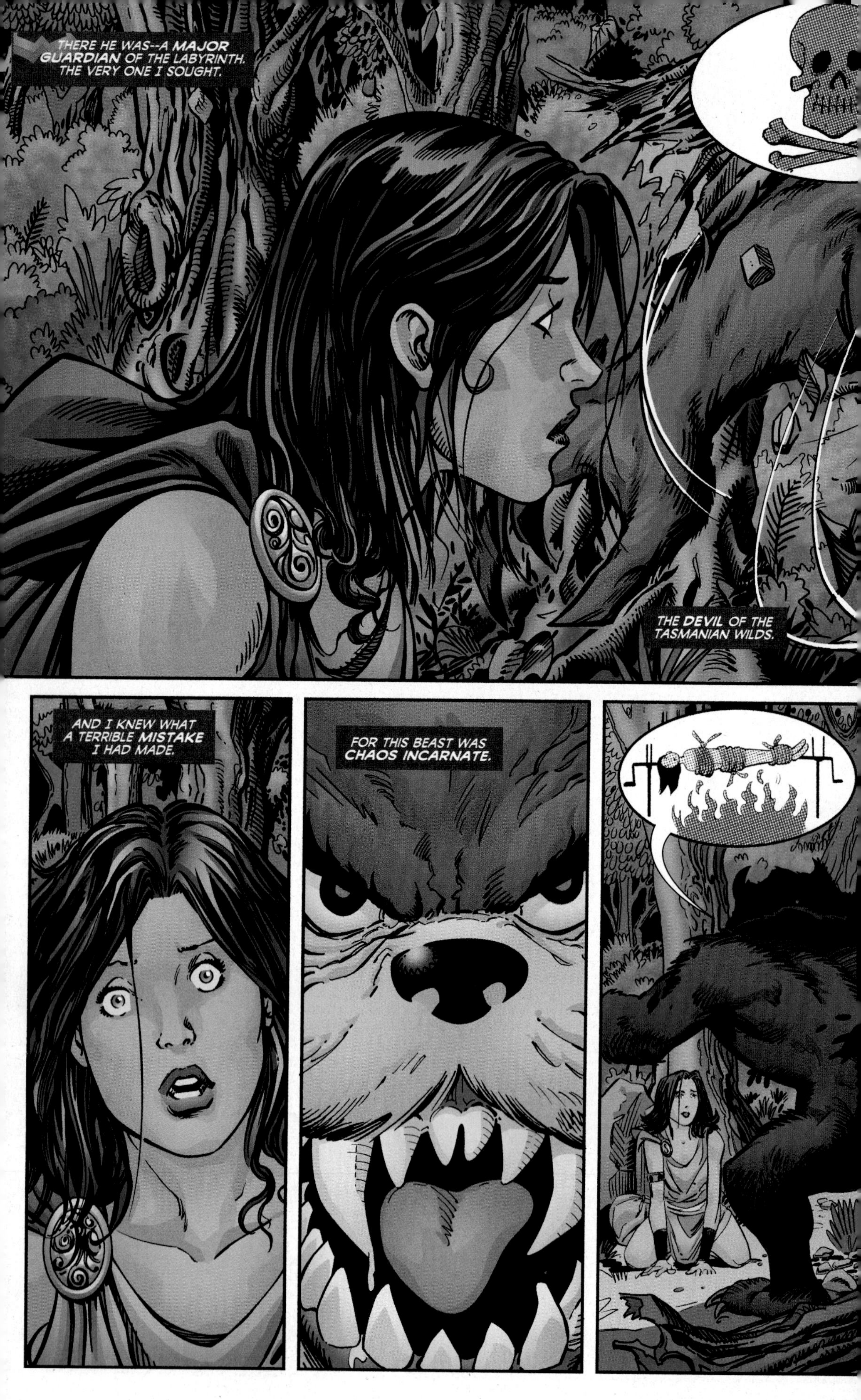
THERE HE WAS--A MAJOR GUARDIAN OF THE LABYRINTH. THE VERY ONE I SOUGHT.
THE DEVIL OF THE TASMANIAN WILDS.
AND I KNEW WHAT A TERRIBLE MISTAKE I HAD MADE.
FOR THIS BEAST WAS CHAOS INCARNATE.

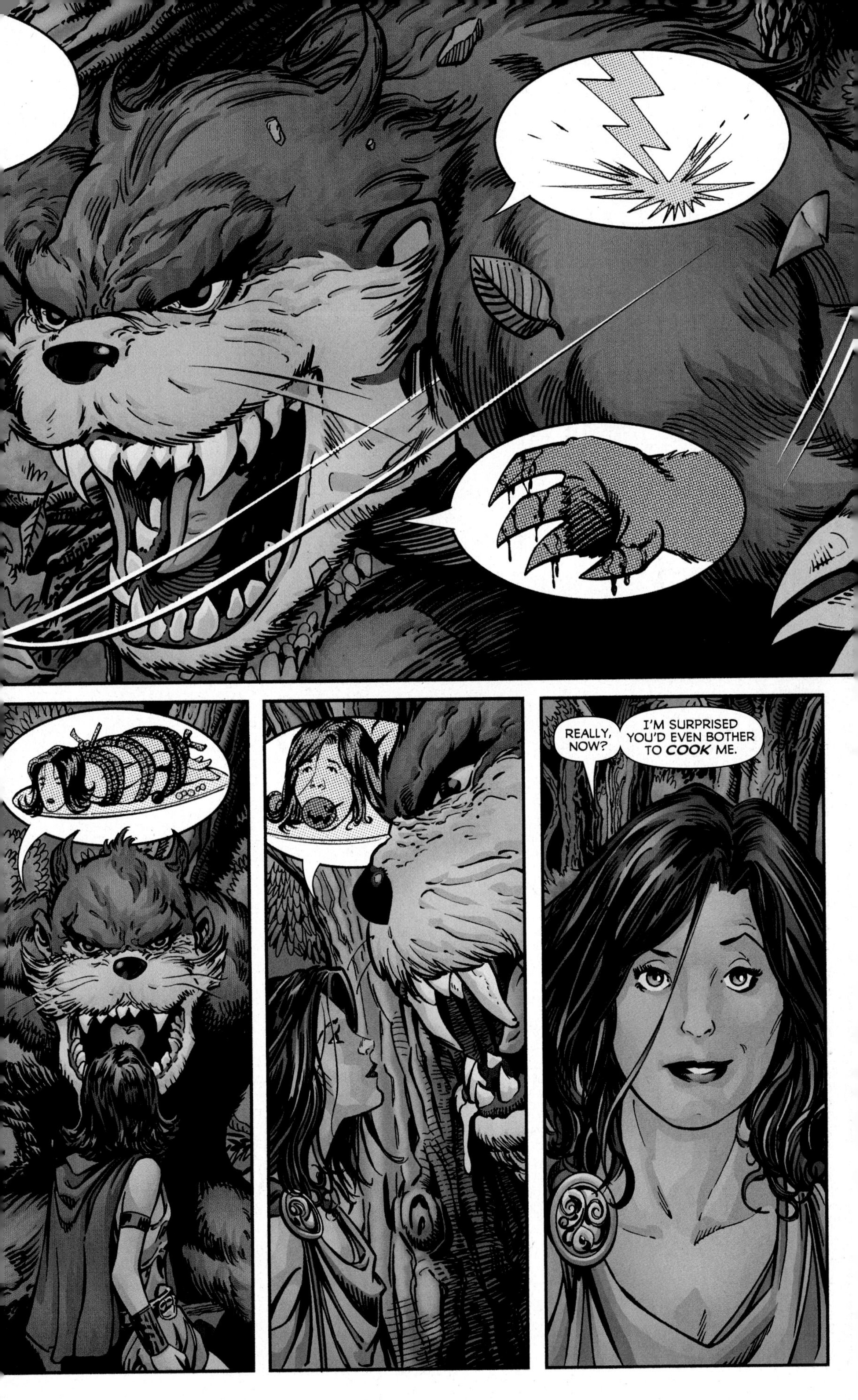
REALLY, NOW?
I'M SURPRISED YOU'D EVEN BOTHER TO COOK ME.

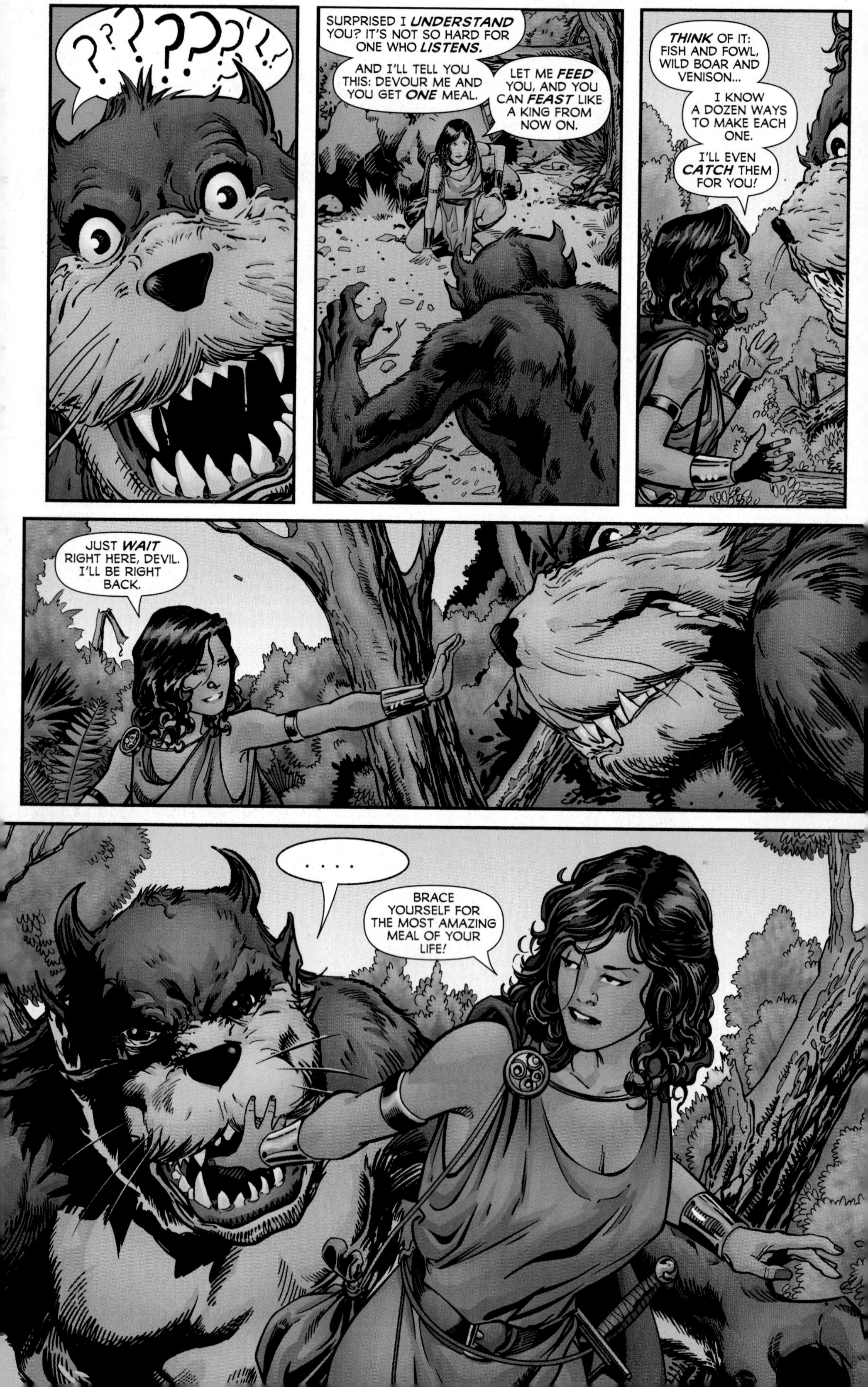

??????!!
SURPRISED I UNDERSTAND YOU? IT'S NOT SO HARD FOR ONE WHO LISTENS.
AND I'LL TELL YOU THIS: DEVOUR ME AND YOU GET ONE MEAL.
LET ME FEED YOU, AND YOU CAN FEAST LIKE A KING FROM NOW ON.
THINK OF IT: FISH AND FOWL, WILD BOAR AND VENISON...
I KNOW A DOZEN WAYS TO MAKE EACH ONE.
I'LL EVEN CATCH THEM FOR YOU!
JUST WAIT RIGHT HERE, DEVIL. I'LL BE RIGHT BACK.
. . . .
BRACE YOURSELF FOR THE MOST AMAZING MEAL OF YOUR LIFE!

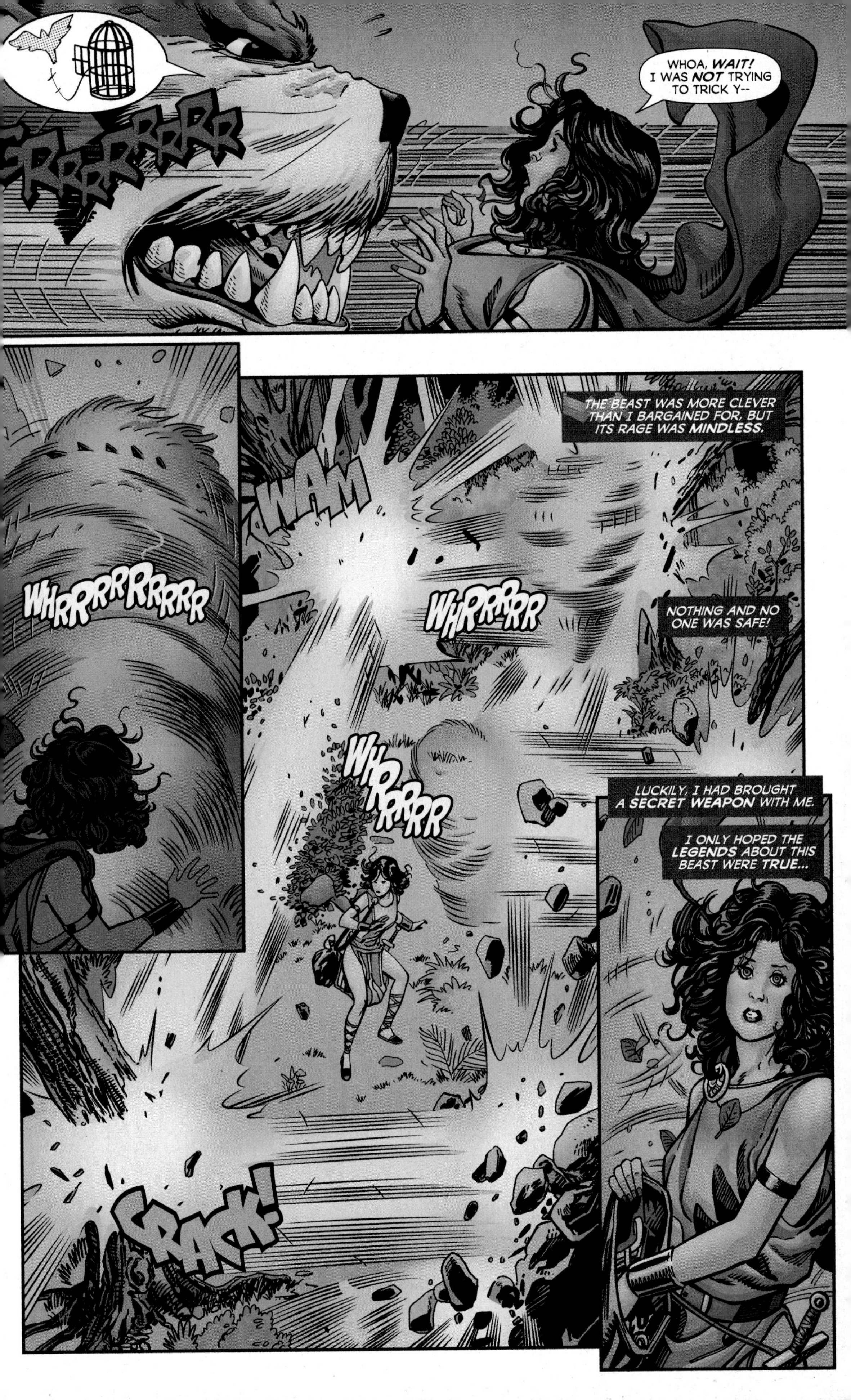
WHOA, WAIT! I WAS NOT TRYING TO TRICK Y--
GRRRRRRRRR
THE BEAST WAS MORE CLEVER THAN I BARGAINED FOR, BUT ITS RAGE WAS MINDLESS.
WAM
WHRRRRRRRRR
WHRRRRR
NOTHING AND NO ONE WAS SAFE!
WHRRRRR
LUCKILY, I HAD BROUGHT A SECRET WEAPON WITH ME.
I ONLY HOPED THE LEGENDS ABOUT THIS BEAST WERE TRUE...
CRACK!

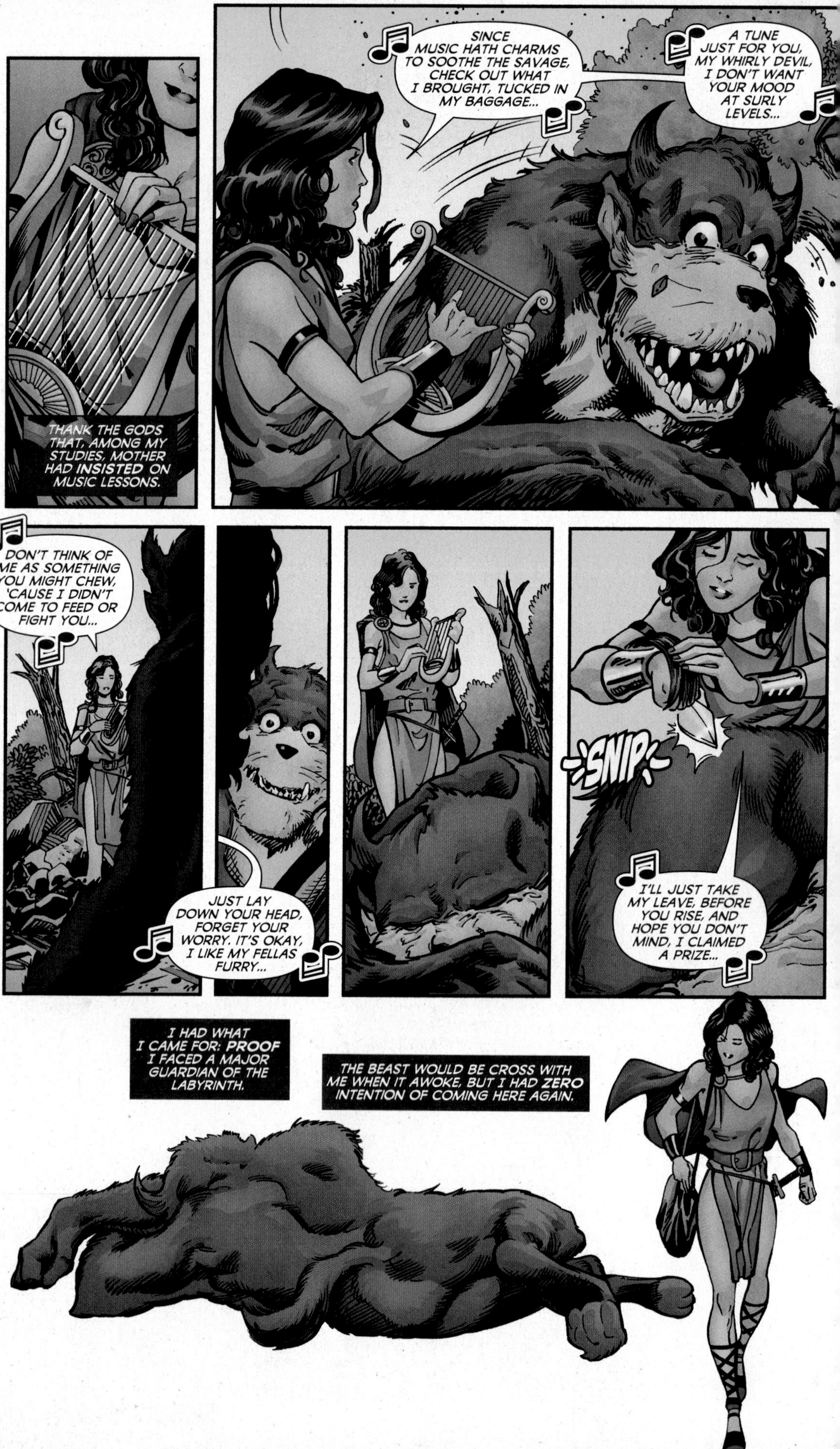
THANK THE GODS THAT, AMONG MY STUDIES, MOTHER HAD INSISTED ON MUSIC LESSONS.
SINCE MUSIC HATH CHARMS TO SOOTHE THE SAVAGE, CHECK OUT WHAT I BROUGHT, TUCKED IN MY BAGGAGE...
A TUNE JUST FOR YOU, MY WHIRLY DEVIL, I DON'T WANT YOUR MOOD AT SURLY LEVELS...
DON'T THINK OF ME AS SOMETHING YOU MIGHT CHEW, 'CAUSE I DIDN'T COME TO FEED OR FIGHT YOU...
JUST LAY DOWN YOUR HEAD, FORGET YOUR WORRY. IT'S OKAY, I LIKE MY FELLAS FURRY...
SNIP
I'LL JUST TAKE MY LEAVE, BEFORE YOU RISE, AND HOPE YOU DON'T MIND, I CLAIMED A PRIZE...
I HAD WHAT I CAME FOR: PROOF I FACED A MAJOR GUARDIAN OF THE LABYRINTH.
THE BEAST WOULD BE CROSS WITH ME WHEN IT AWOKE, BUT I HAD ZERO INTENTION OF COMING HERE AGAIN.

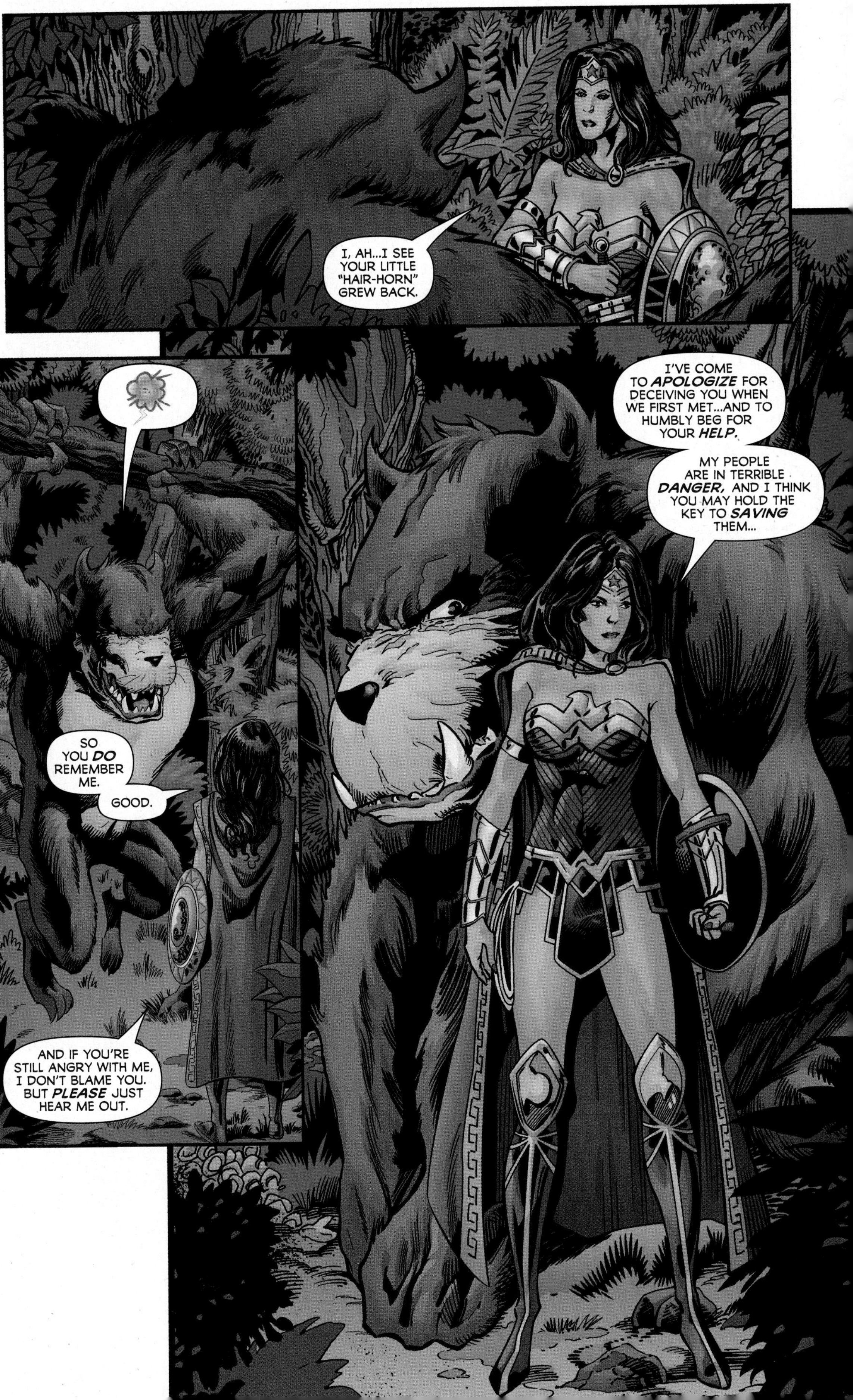
I, AH...I SEE YOUR LITTLE "HAIR-HORN" GREW BACK.
SO YOU DO REMEMBER ME.
GOOD.
AND IF YOU'RE STILL ANGRY WITH ME, I DON'T BLAME YOU. BUT PLEASE JUST HEAR ME OUT.
I'VE COME TO APOLOGIZE FOR DECEIVING YOU WHEN WE FIRST MET...AND TO HUMBLY BEG FOR YOUR HELP.
MY PEOPLE ARE IN TERRIBLE DANGER, AND I THINK YOU MAY HOLD THE KEY TO SAVING THEM...

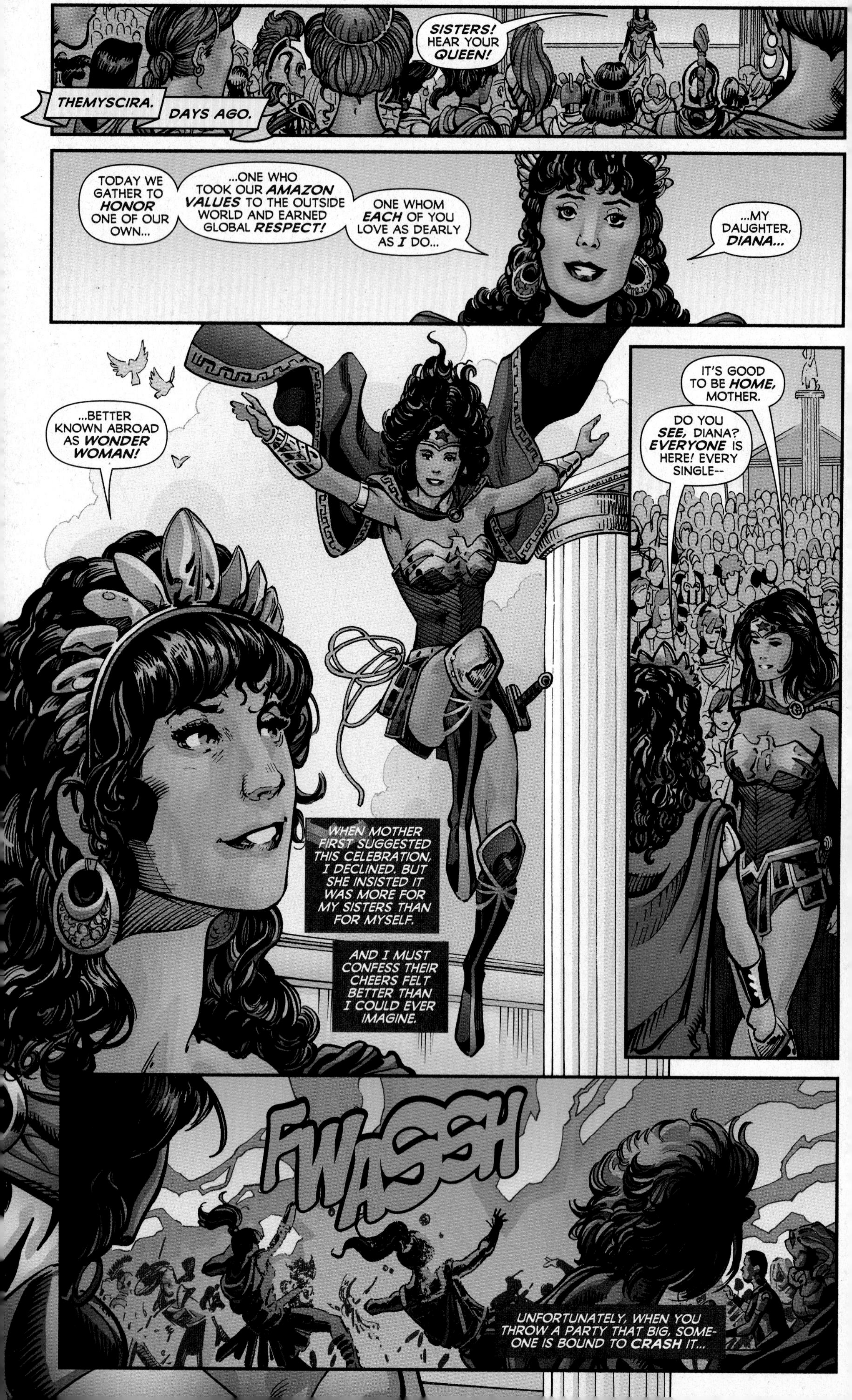
THEMYSCIRA.
DAYS AGO.
SISTERS! HEAR YOUR QUEEN!
TODAY WE GATHER TO HONOR ONE OF OUR OWN...
...ONE WHO TOOK OUR AMAZON VALUES TO THE OUTSIDE WORLD AND EARNED GLOBAL RESPECT!
ONE WHOM EACH OF YOU LOVE AS DEARLY AS I DO...
...MY DAUGHTER, DIANA...
...BETTER KNOWN ABROAD AS WONDER WOMAN!
WHEN MOTHER FIRST SUGGESTED THIS CELEBRATION, I DECLINED. BUT SHE INSISTED IT WAS MORE FOR MY SISTERS THAN FOR MYSELF.
AND I MUST CONFESS THEIR CHEERS FELT BETTER THAN I COULD EVER IMAGINE.
IT'S GOOD TO BE HOME, MOTHER.
DO YOU SEE, DIANA? EVERYONE IS HERE! EVERY SINGLE--
FWASSH
UNFORTUNATELY, WHEN YOU THROW A PARTY THAT BIG, SOME-ONE IS BOUND TO CRASH IT...

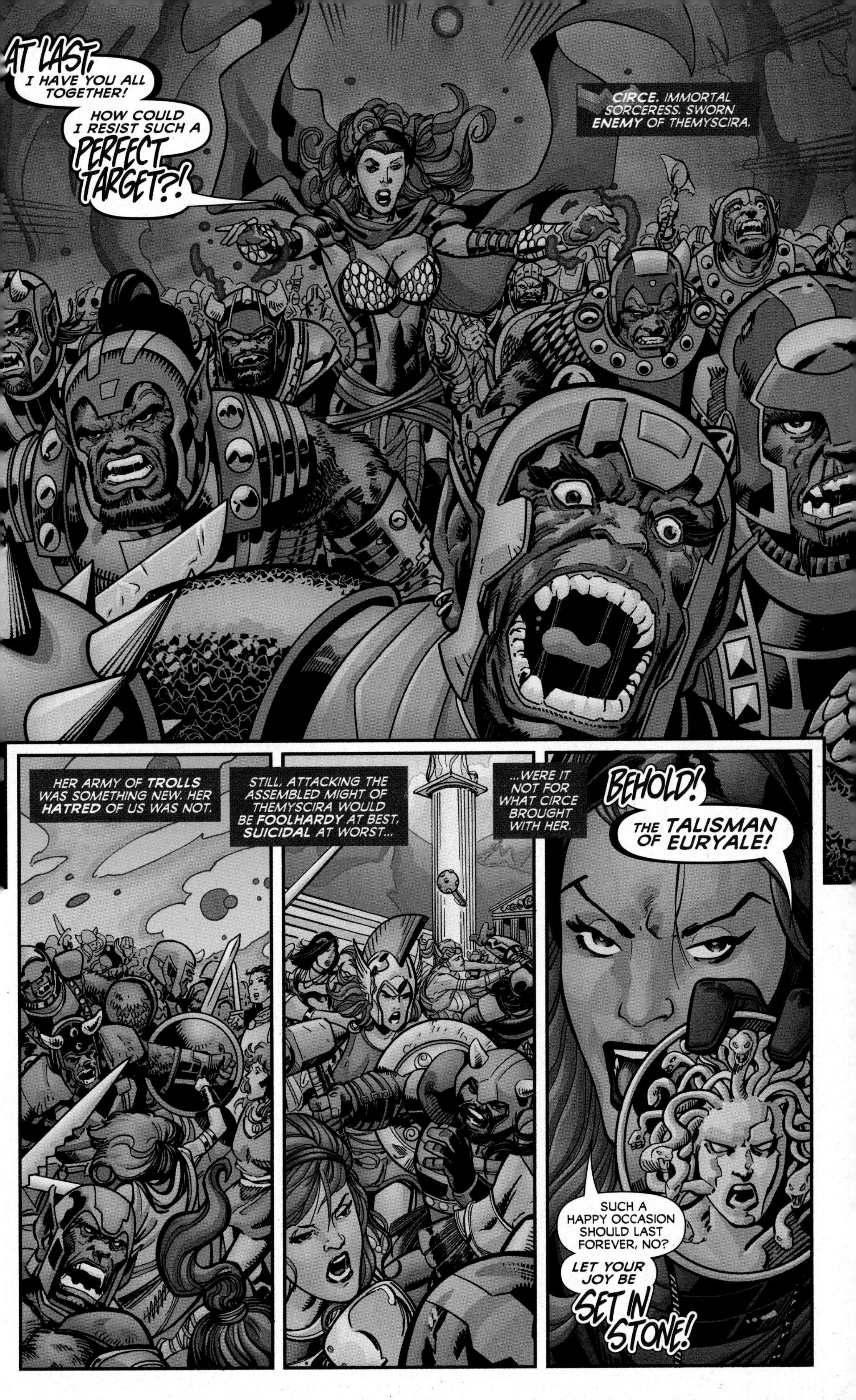
AT LAST, I HAVE YOU ALL TOGETHER!
HOW COULD I RESIST SUCH A PERFECT TARGET?!
CIRCE. IMMORTAL SORCERESS. SWORN ENEMY OF THEMYSCIRA.
HER ARMY OF TROLLS WAS SOMETHING NEW. HER HATRED OF US WAS NOT.
STILL, ATTACKING THE ASSEMBLED MIGHT OF THEMYSCIRA WOULD BE FOOLHARDY AT BEST, SUICIDAL AT WORST...
...WERE IT NOT FOR WHAT CIRCE BROUGHT WITH HER.
BEHOLD!
THE TALISMAN OF EURYALE!
SUCH A HAPPY OCCASION SHOULD LAST FOREVER, NO?
LET YOUR JOY BE SET IN STONE!

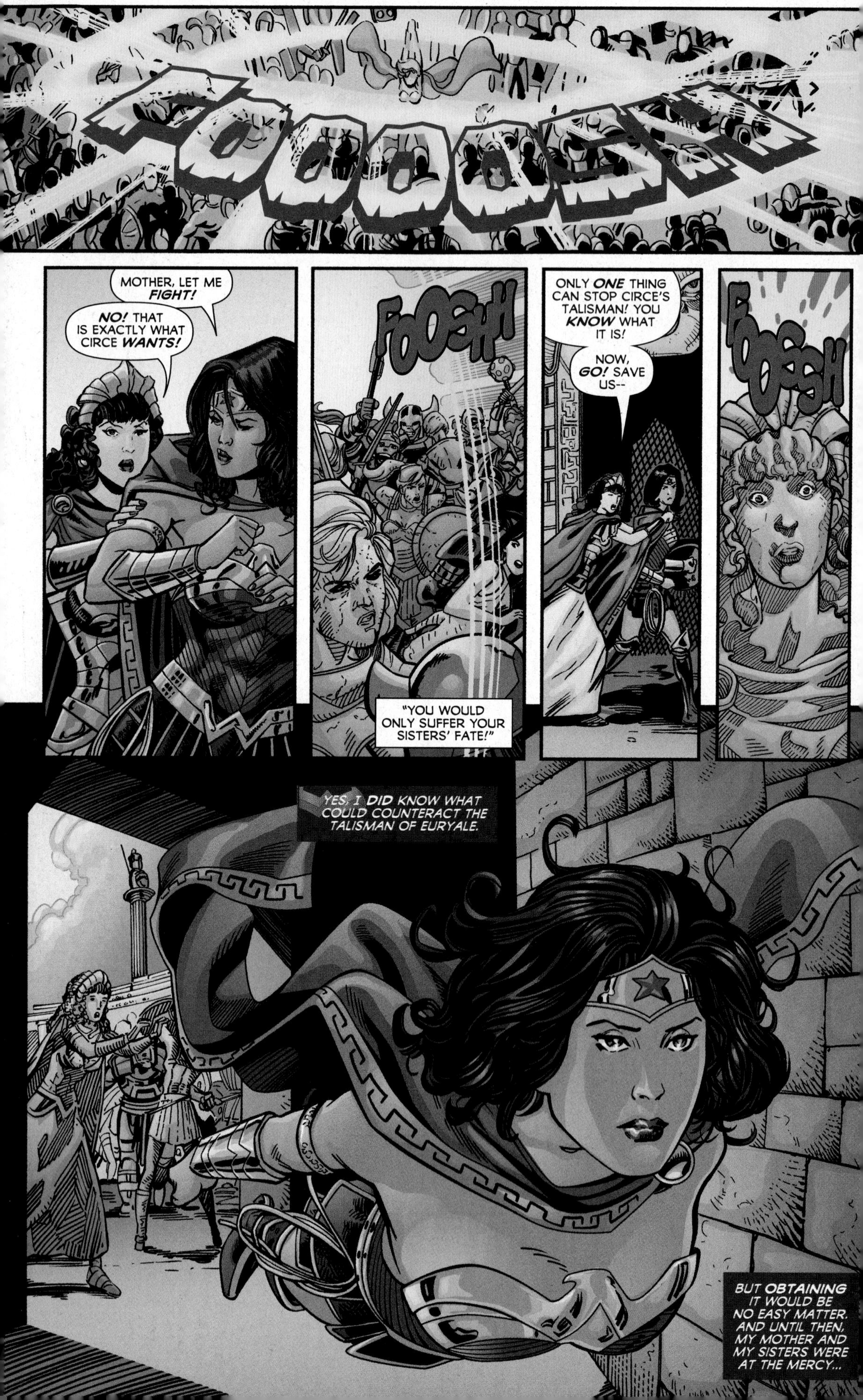

FOOOOSH!
MOTHER, LET ME FIGHT!
NO! THAT IS EXACTLY WHAT CIRCE WANTS!
FOOSH!
"YOU WOULD ONLY SUFFER YOUR SISTERS' FATE!"
ONLY ONE THING CAN STOP CIRCE'S TALISMAN! YOU KNOW WHAT IT IS!
NOW, GO! SAVE US--
FOOSSH
YES, I DID KNOW WHAT COULD COUNTERACT THE TALISMAN OF EURYALE.
BUT OBTAINING IT WOULD BE NO EASY MATTER. AND UNTIL THEN, MY MOTHER AND MY SISTERS WERE AT THE MERCY...

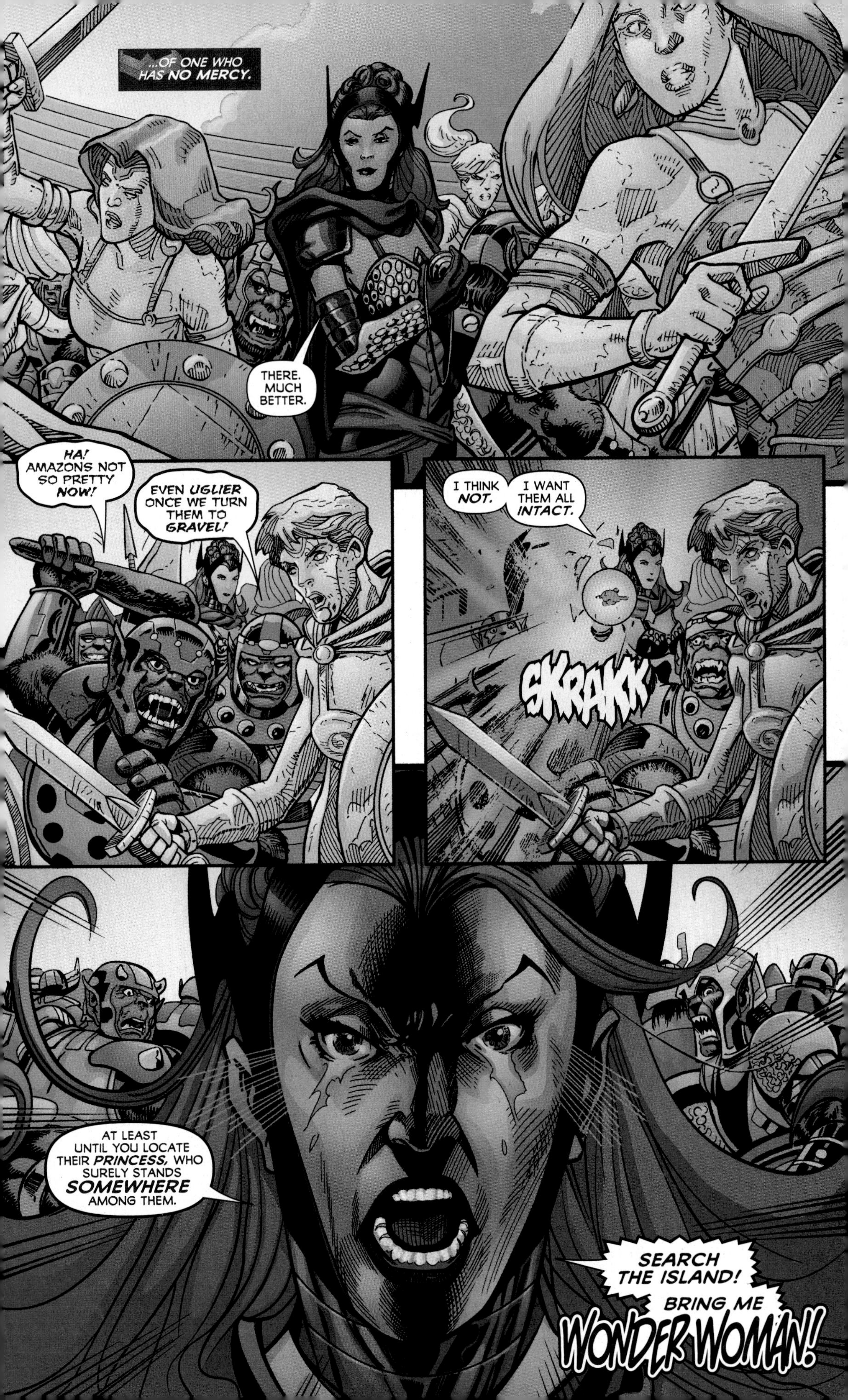

...OF ONE WHO HAS NO MERCY.
THERE. MUCH BETTER.
HA! AMAZONS NOT SO PRETTY NOW!
EVEN UGLIER ONCE WE TURN THEM TO GRAVEL!
I THINK NOT.
I WANT THEM ALL INTACT.
SKRAKK
AT LEAST UNTIL YOU LOCATE THEIR PRINCESS, WHO SURELY STANDS SOMEWHERE AMONG THEM.
SEARCH THE ISLAND! BRING ME WONDER WOMAN!

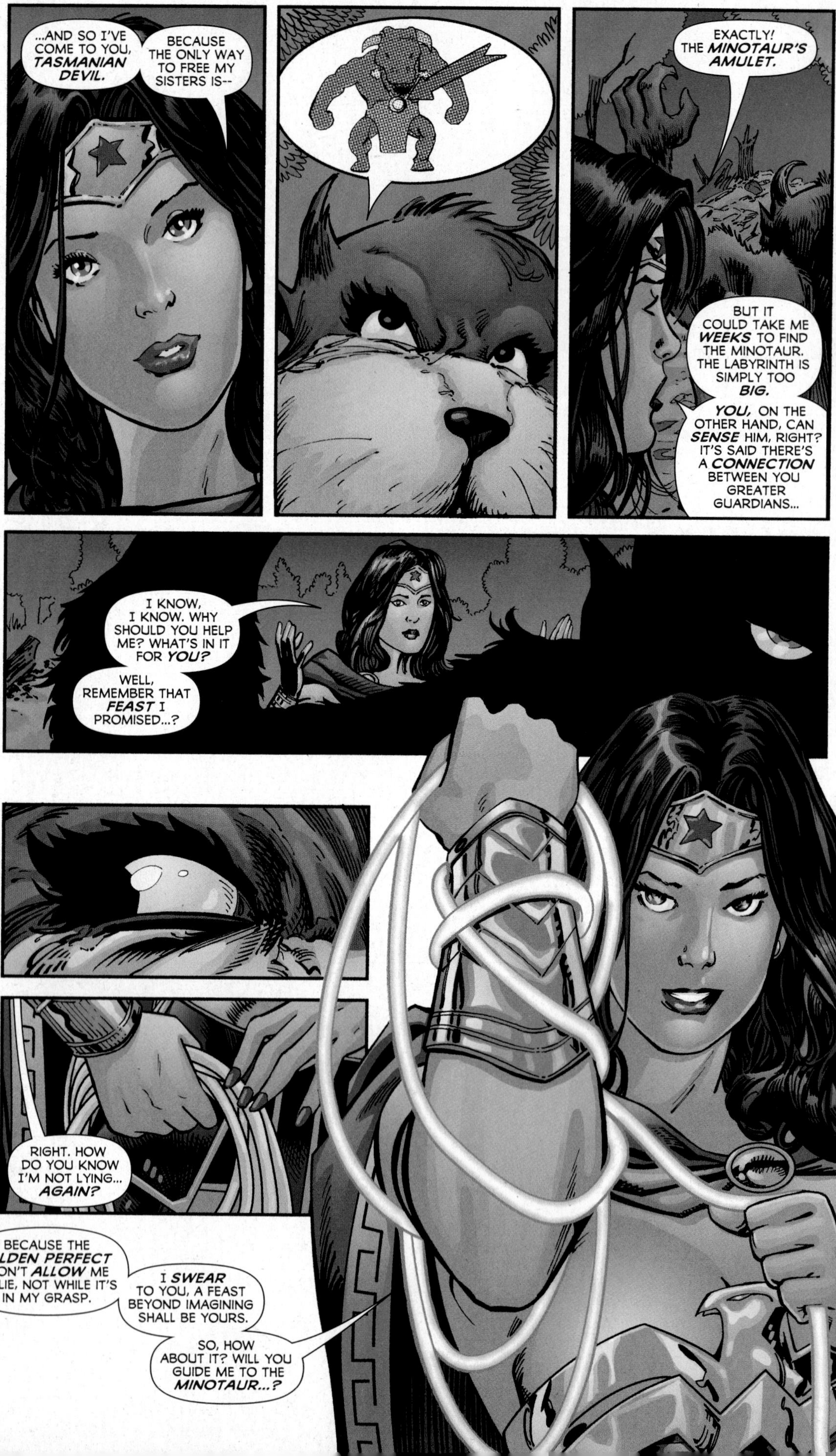
...AND SO I'VE COME TO YOU, TASMANIAN DEVIL.
BECAUSE THE ONLY WAY TO FREE MY SISTERS IS--
EXACTLY! THE MINOTAUR'S AMULET.
BUT IT COULD TAKE ME WEEKS TO FIND THE MINOTAUR. THE LABYRINTH IS SIMPLY TOO BIG.
YOU, ON THE OTHER HAND, CAN SENSE HIM, RIGHT? IT'S SAID THERE'S A CONNECTION BETWEEN YOU GREATER GUARDIANS...
I KNOW, I KNOW. WHY SHOULD YOU HELP ME? WHAT'S IN IT FOR YOU?
WELL, REMEMBER THAT FEAST I PROMISED...?
RIGHT. HOW DO YOU KNOW I'M NOT LYING... AGAIN?
BECAUSE THE GOLDEN PERFECT WON'T ALLOW ME TO LIE, NOT WHILE IT'S IN MY GRASP.
I SWEAR TO YOU, A FEAST BEYOND IMAGINING SHALL BE YOURS.
SO, HOW ABOUT IT? WILL YOU GUIDE ME TO THE MINOTAUR...?

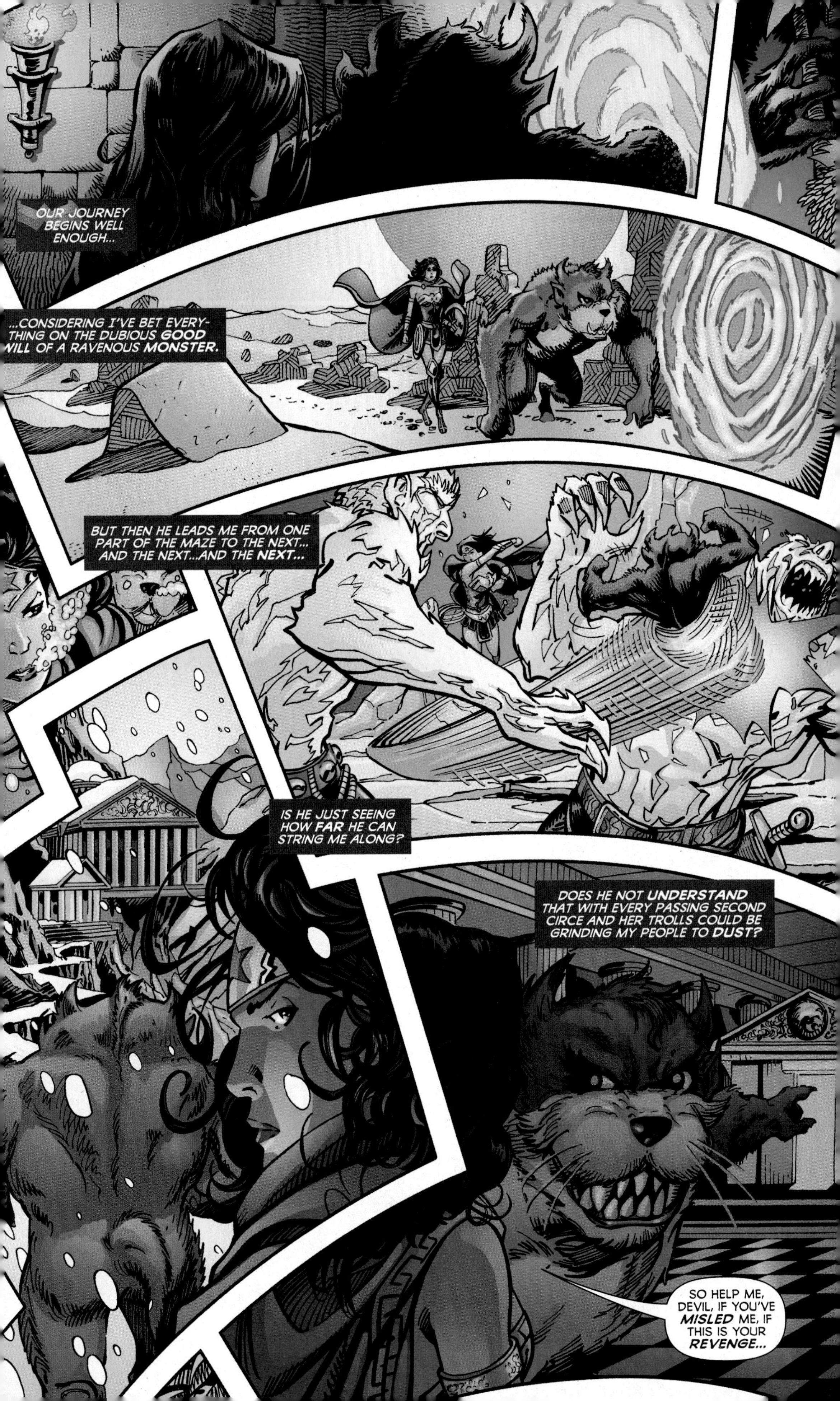
OUR JOURNEY BEGINS WELL ENOUGH...
...CONSIDERING I'VE BET EVERY-THING ON THE DUBIOUS GOOD WILL OF A RAVENOUS MONSTER.
BUT THEN HE LEADS ME FROM ONE PART OF THE MAZE TO THE NEXT... AND THE NEXT...AND THE NEXT...
IS HE JUST SEEING HOW FAR HE CAN STRING ME ALONG?
DOES HE NOT UNDERSTAND THAT WITH EVERY PASSING SECOND CIRCE AND HER TROLLS COULD BE GRINDING MY PEOPLE TO DUST?
SO HELP ME, DEVIL, IF YOU'VE MISLED ME, IF THIS IS YOUR REVENGE...

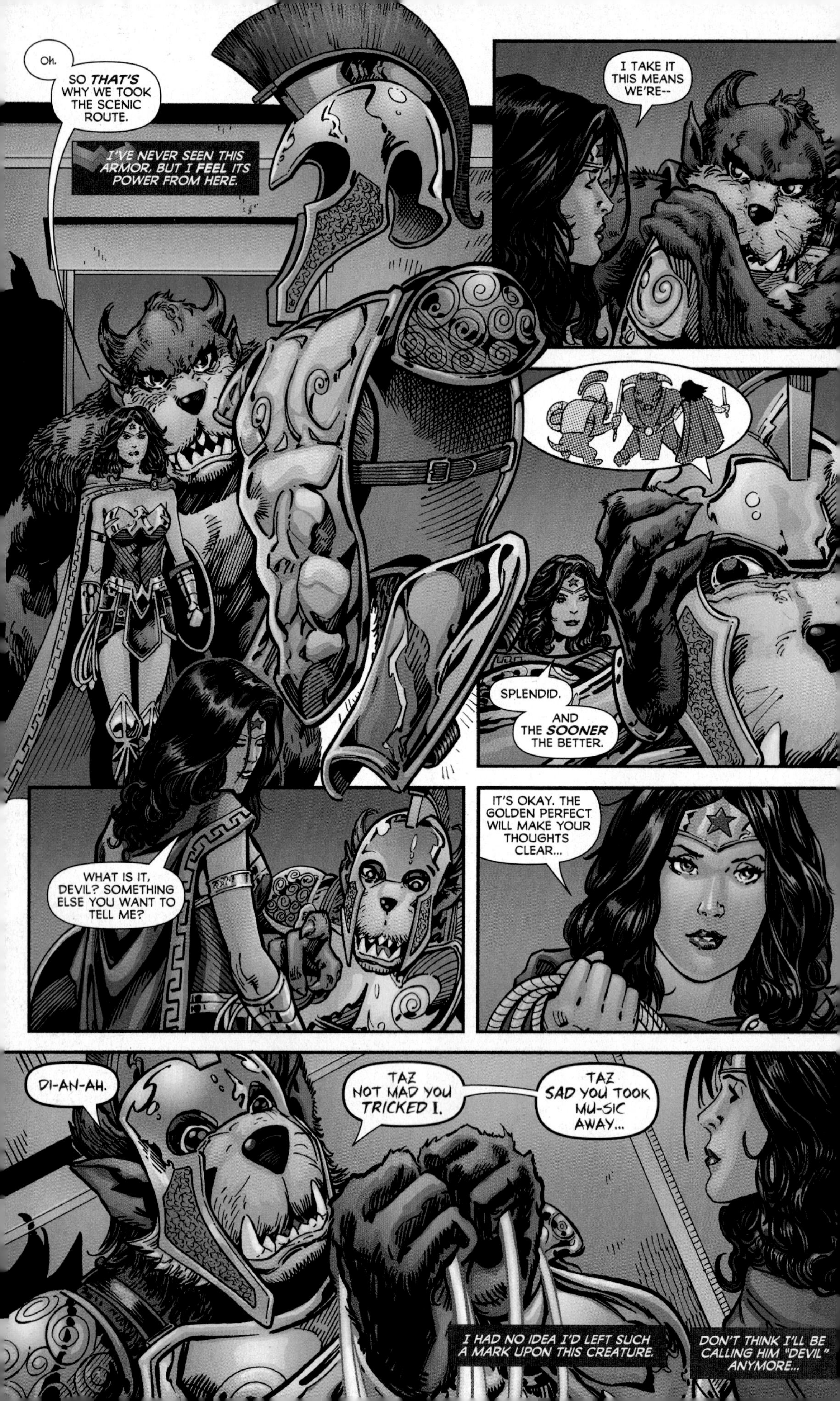
Oh.
SO THAT'S WHY WE TOOK THE SCENIC ROUTE.
I'VE NEVER SEEN THIS ARMOR, BUT I FEEL ITS POWER FROM HERE.
I TAKE IT THIS MEANS WE'RE--
SPLENDID.
AND THE SOONER THE BETTER.
WHAT IS IT, DEVIL? SOMETHING ELSE YOU WANT TO TELL ME?
IT'S OKAY. THE GOLDEN PERFECT WILL MAKE YOUR THOUGHTS CLEAR...
DI-AN-AH.
TAZ NOT MAD YOU TRICKED I.
TAZ SAD YOU TOOK MU-SIC AWAY...
I HAD NO IDEA I'D LEFT SUCH A MARK UPON THIS CREATURE.
DON'T THINK I'LL BE CALLING HIM "DEVIL" ANYMORE...

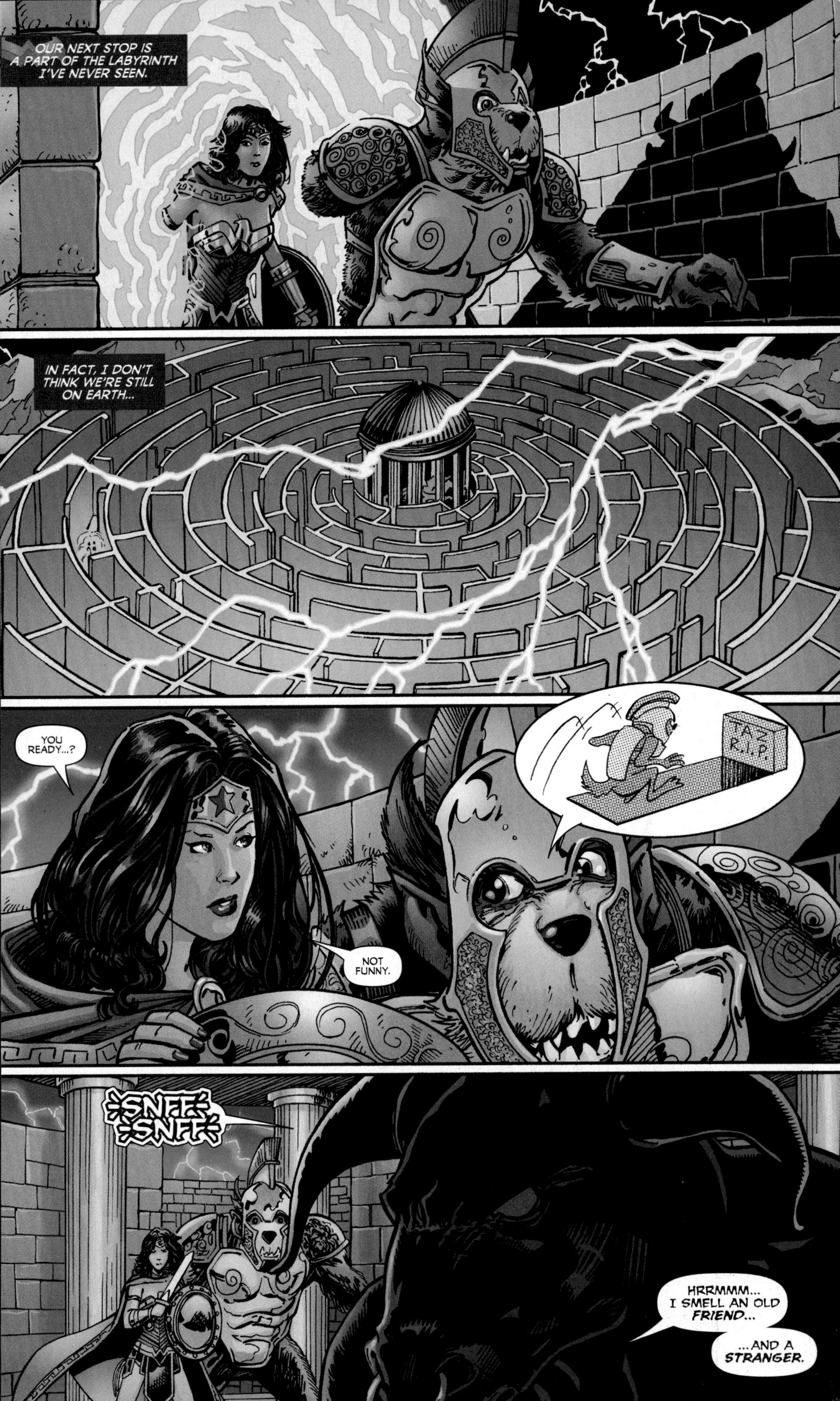
OUR NEXT STOP IS A PART OF THE LABYRINTH I'VE NEVER SEEN.
IN FACT, I DON'T THINK WE'RE STILL ON EARTH...
YOU READY...?
TAZ R.I.P.
NOT FUNNY.
SNFF SNFF
HRRMMM... I SMELL AN OLD FRIEND...
...AND A STRANGER.

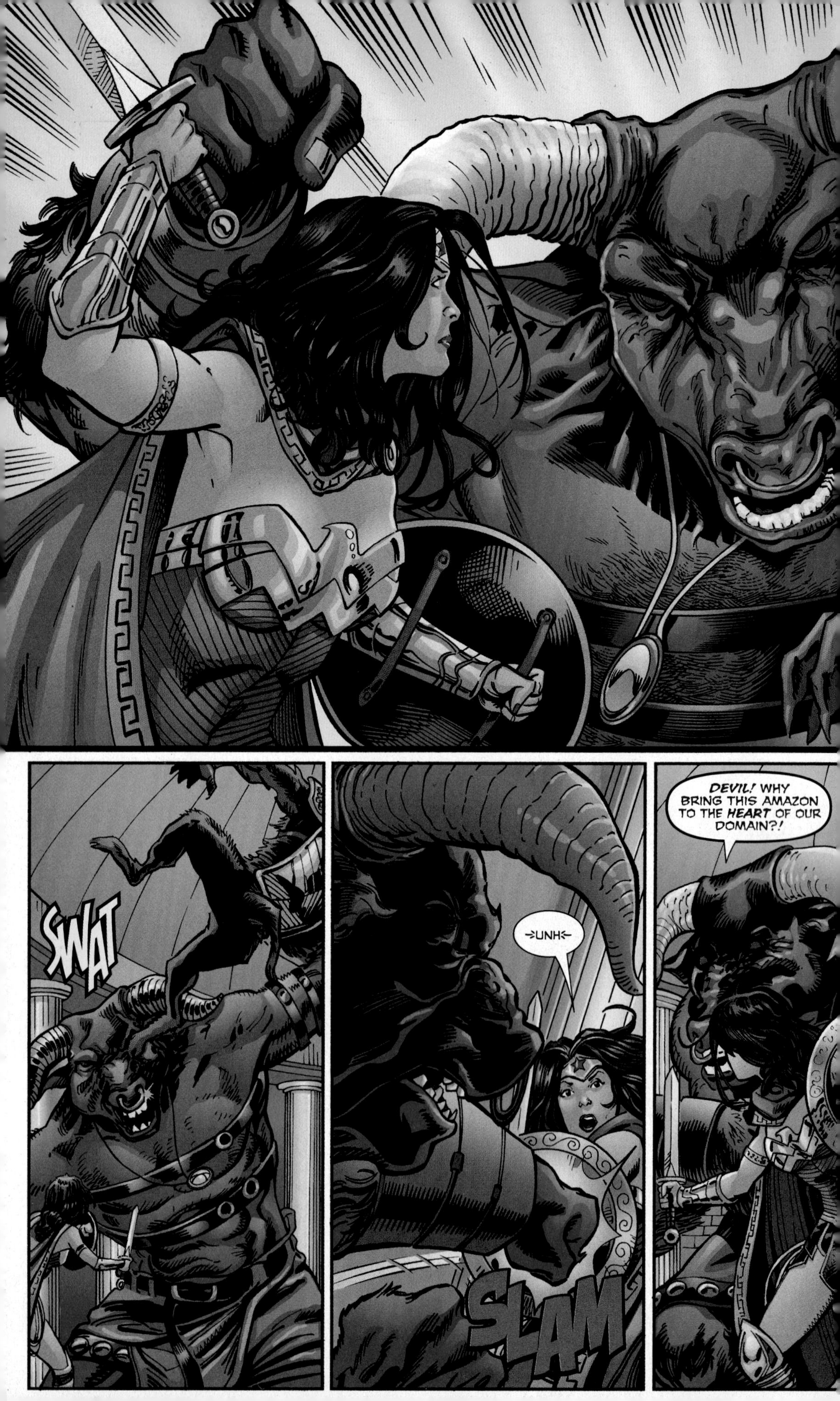
SWAT
UNH
SLAM
DEVIL! WHY BRING THIS AMAZON TO THE HEART OF OUR DOMAIN?!

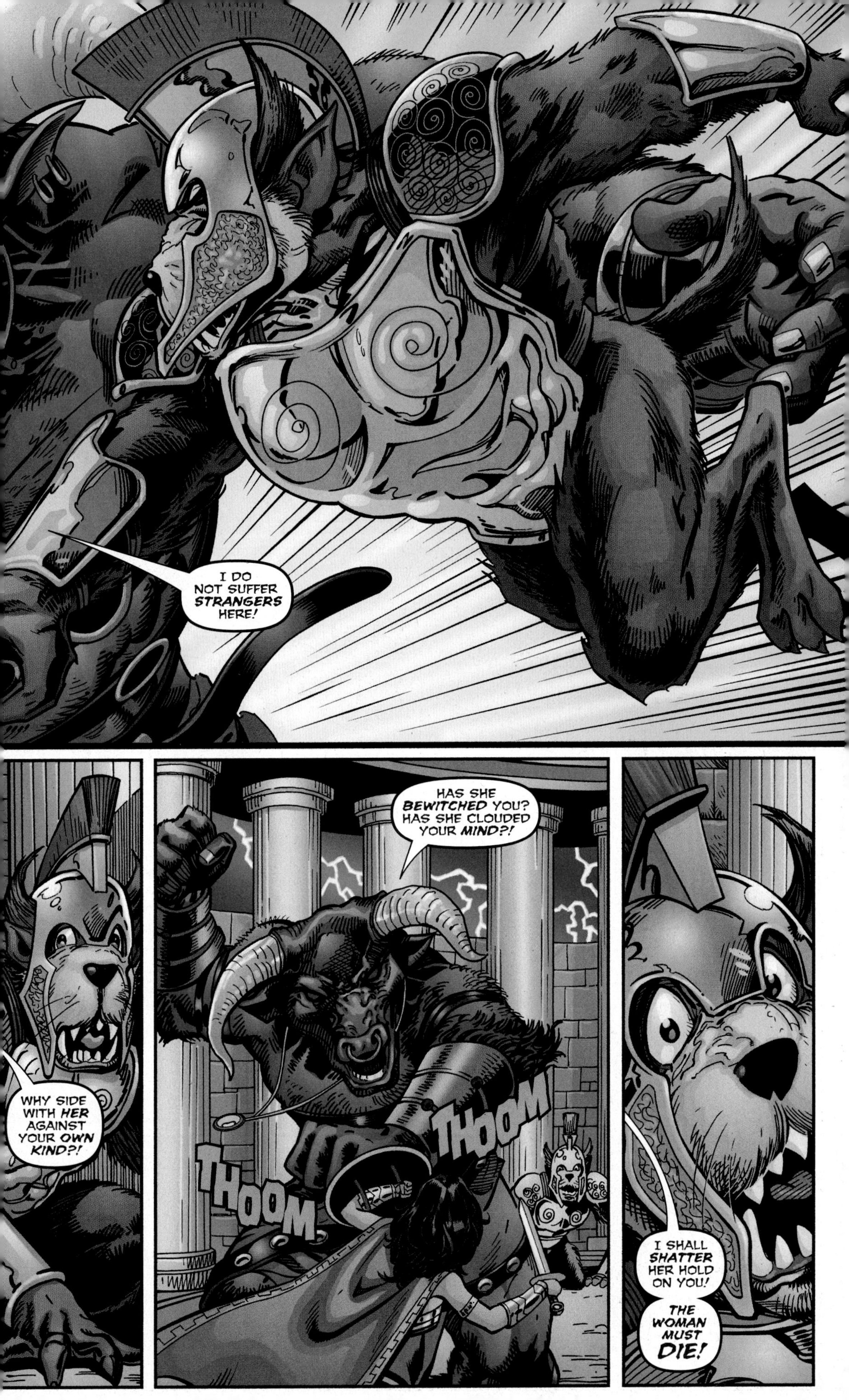
I DO NOT SUFFER STRANGERS HERE!
WHY SIDE WITH HER AGAINST YOUR OWN KIND?!
HAS SHE BEWITCHED YOU? HAS SHE CLOUDED YOUR MIND?!
THOOM
THOOM
I SHALL SHATTER HER HOLD ON YOU!
THE WOMAN MUST DIE!

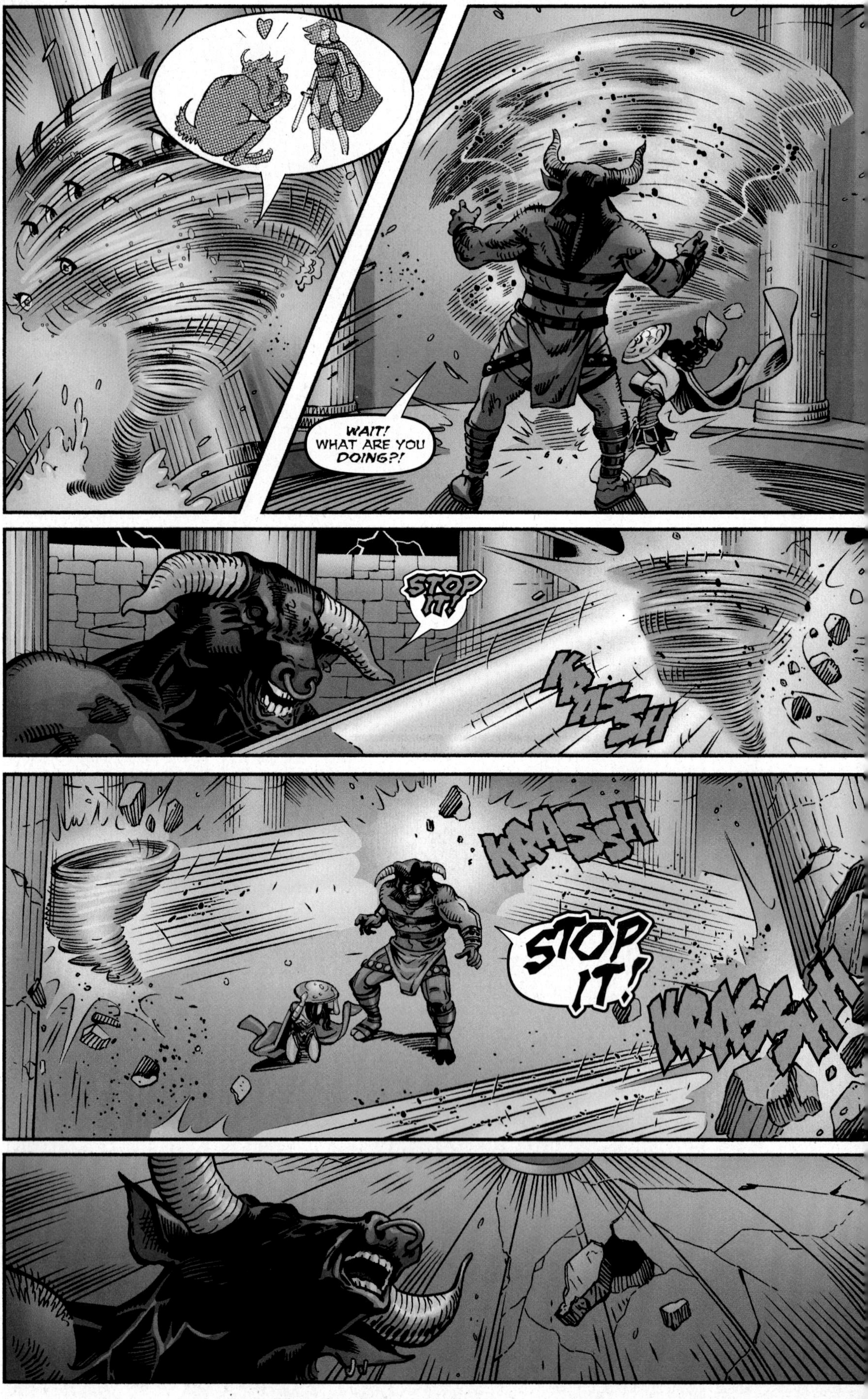
WAIT! WHAT ARE YOU DOING?!
STOP IT!
KRASSH
KRASSH
STOP IT!
KRASSH

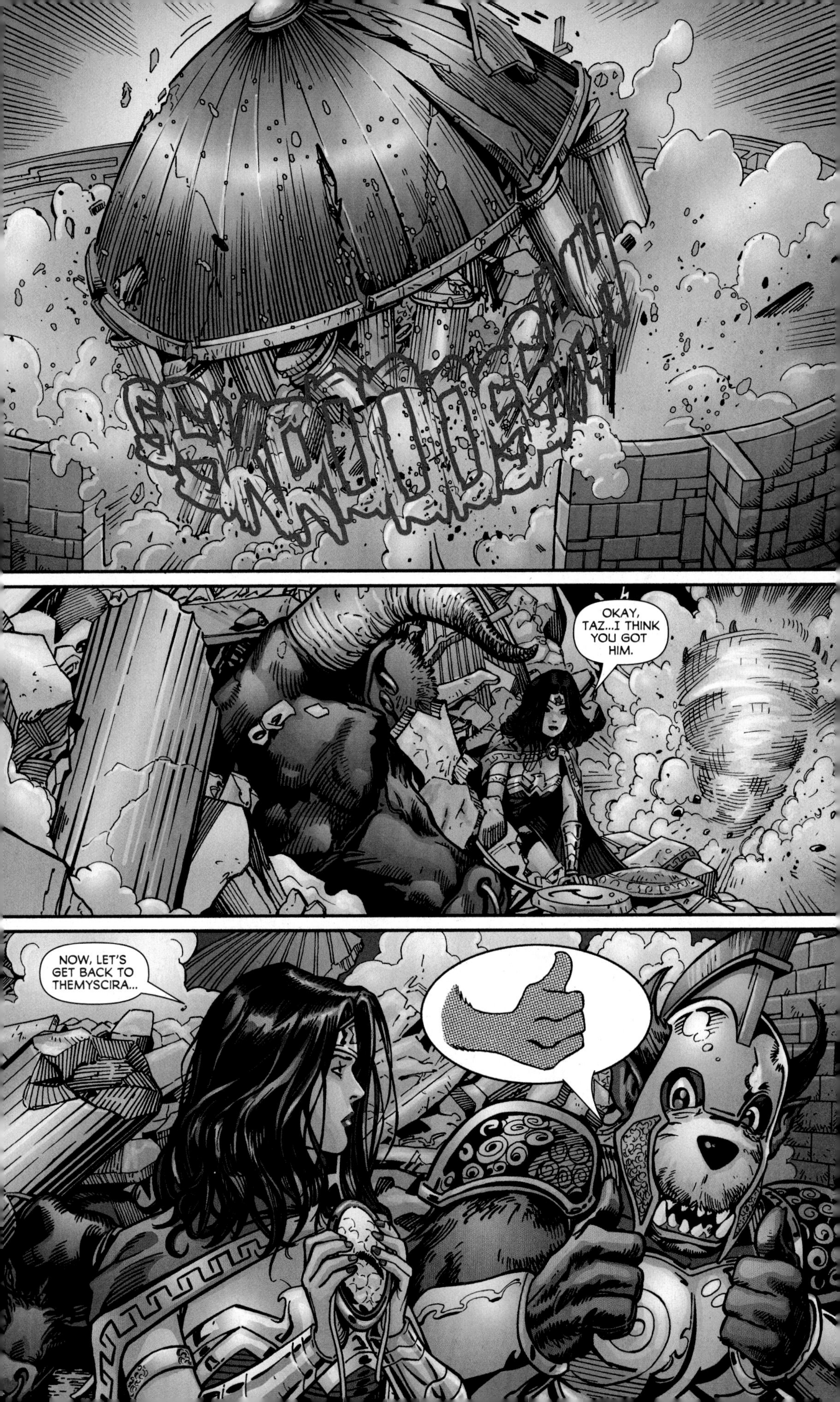
OKAY, TAZ...I THINK YOU GOT HIM.
NOW, LET'S GET BACK TO THEMYSCIRA...

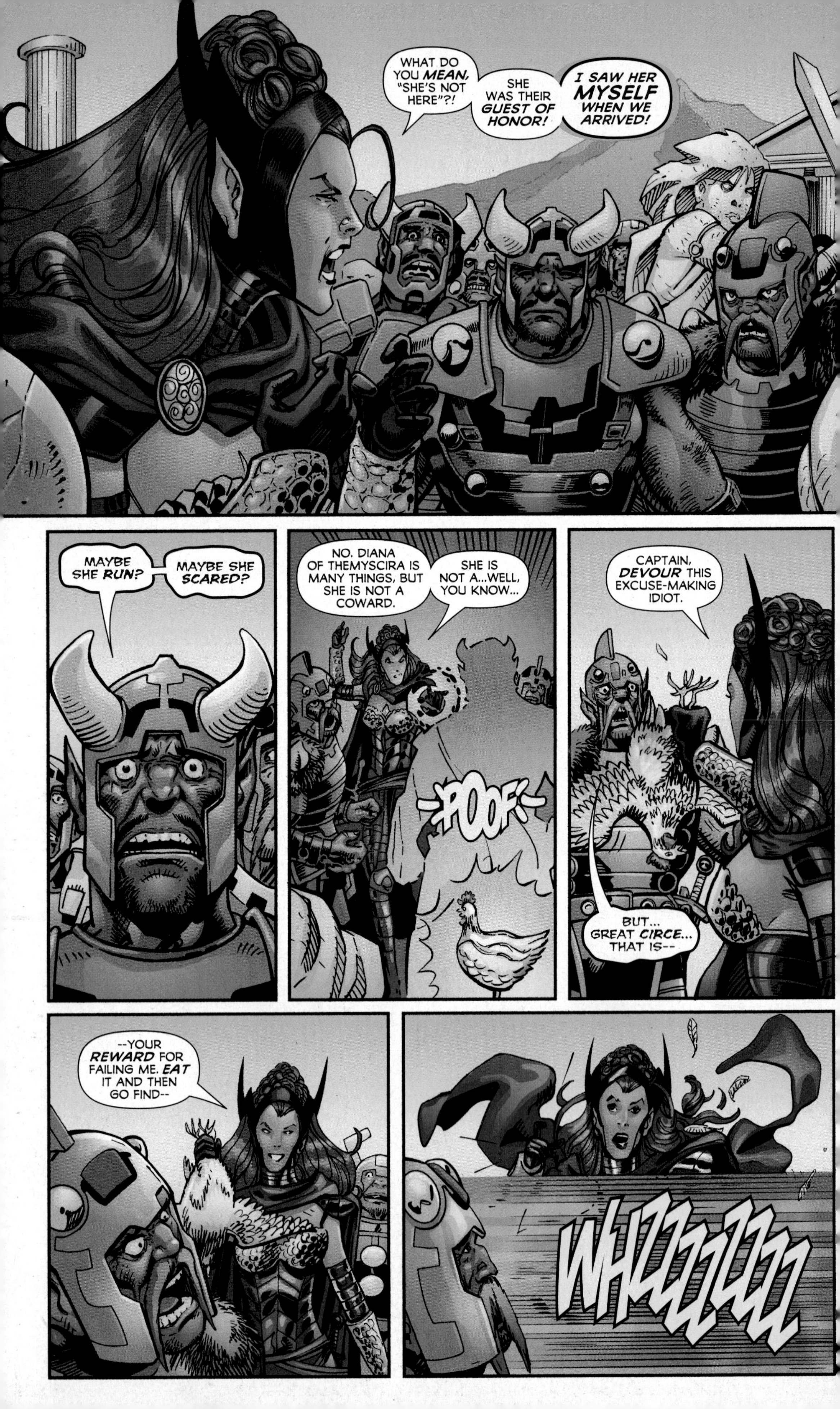

WHAT DO YOU MEAN, "SHE'S NOT HERE"?!
SHE WAS THEIR GUEST OF HONOR!
I SAW HER MYSELF WHEN WE ARRIVED!
MAYBE SHE RUN?
MAYBE SHE SCARED?
NO. DIANA OF THEMYSCIRA IS MANY THINGS, BUT SHE IS NOT A COWARD.
SHE IS NOT A...WELL, YOU KNOW...
POOF
CAPTAIN, DEVOUR THIS EXCUSE-MAKING IDIOT.
BUT... GREAT CIRCE... THAT IS--
--YOUR REWARD FOR FAILING ME. EAT IT AND THEN GO FIND--
WHZZZZZZZ

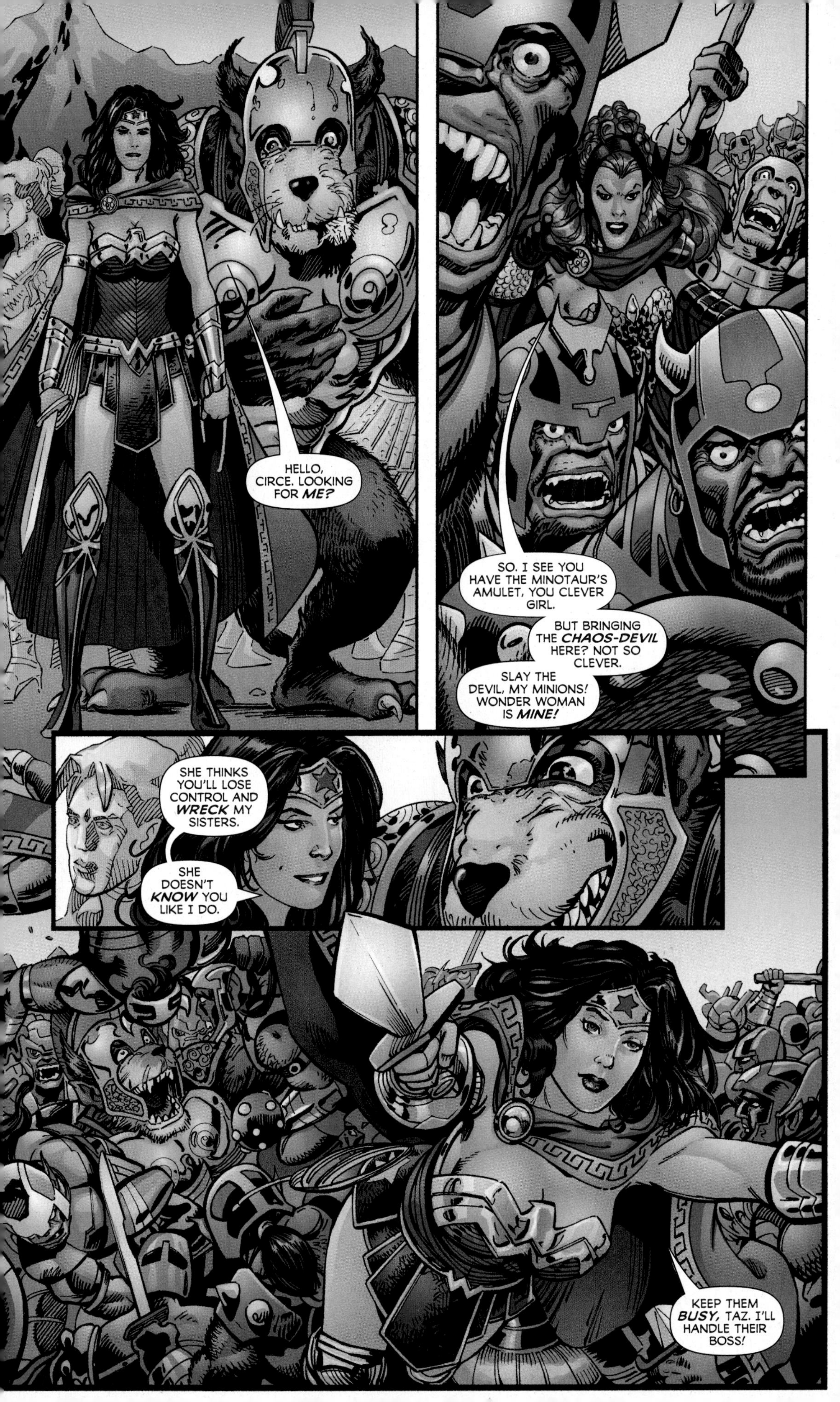

HELLO, CIRCE. LOOKING FOR *ME?*
SO. I SEE YOU HAVE THE MINOTAUR'S AMULET, YOU CLEVER GIRL.
BUT BRINGING THE *CHAOS-DEVIL* HERE? NOT SO CLEVER.
SLAY THE DEVIL, MY MINIONS! WONDER WOMAN IS *MINE!*
SHE THINKS YOU'LL LOSE CONTROL AND *WRECK* MY SISTERS.
SHE DOESN'T *KNOW* YOU LIKE I DO.
KEEP THEM *BUSY,* TAZ. I'LL HANDLE THEIR BOSS!

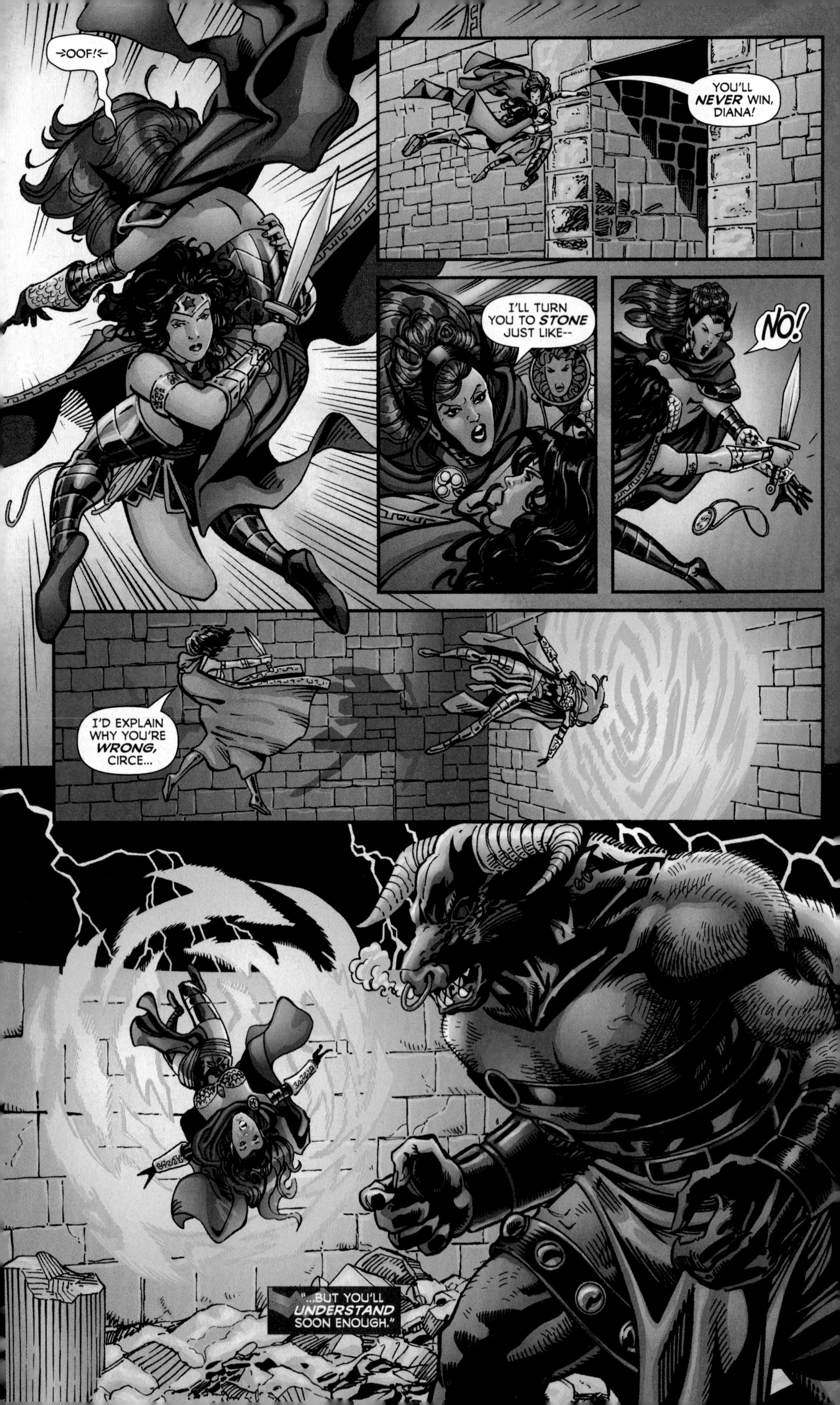
OOF!
YOU'LL NEVER WIN, DIANA!
I'LL TURN YOU TO STONE JUST LIKE--
NO!
I'D EXPLAIN WHY YOU'RE WRONG, CIRCE...
"...BUT YOU'LL UNDERSTAND SOON ENOUGH."

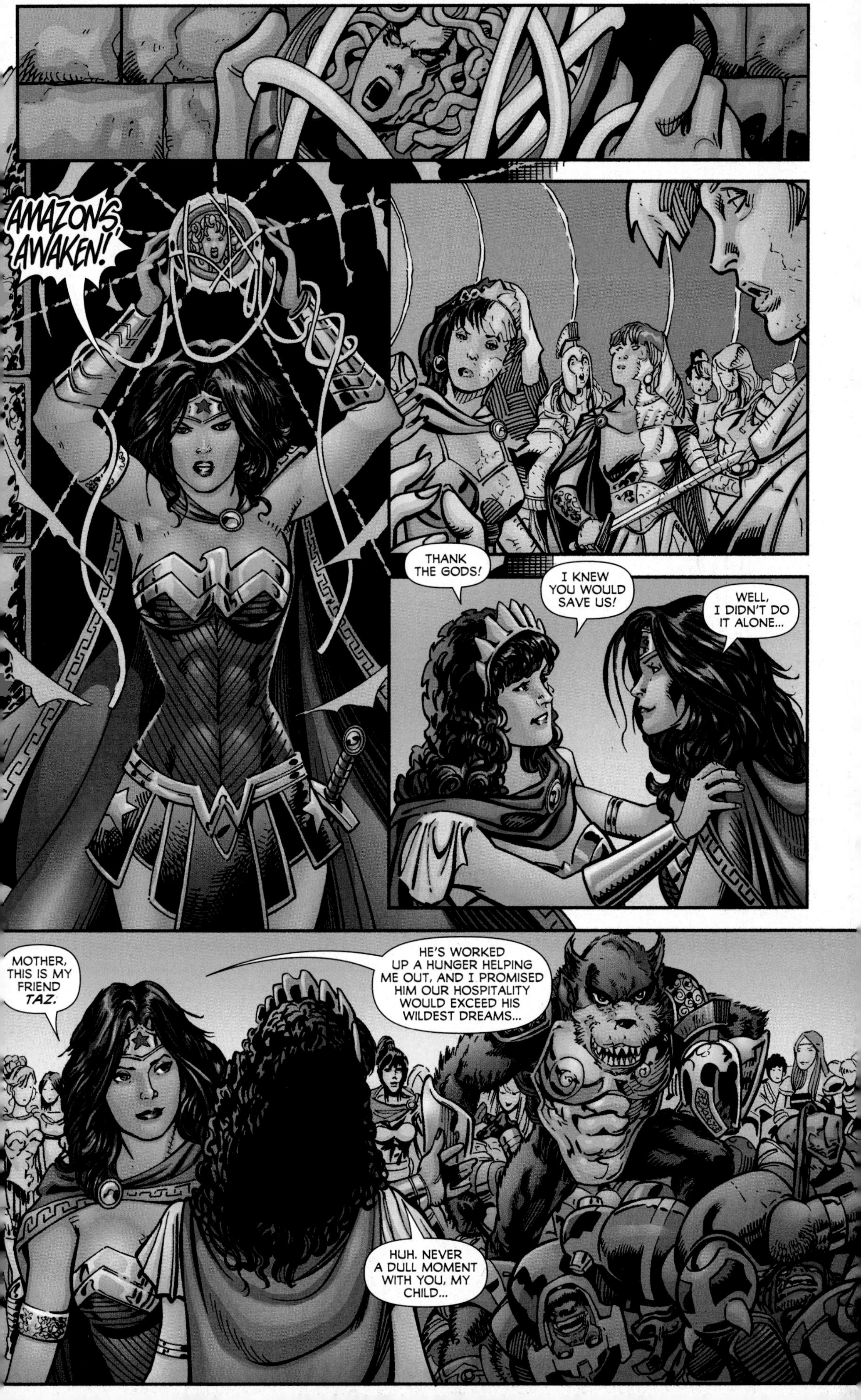
AMAZONS, AWAKEN!
THANK THE GODS!
I KNEW YOU WOULD SAVE US!
WELL, I DIDN'T DO IT ALONE...
MOTHER, THIS IS MY FRIEND *TAZ.*
HE'S WORKED UP A HUNGER HELPING ME OUT, AND I PROMISED HIM OUR HOSPITALITY WOULD EXCEED HIS WILDEST DREAMS...
HUH. NEVER A DULL MOMENT WITH YOU, MY CHILD...

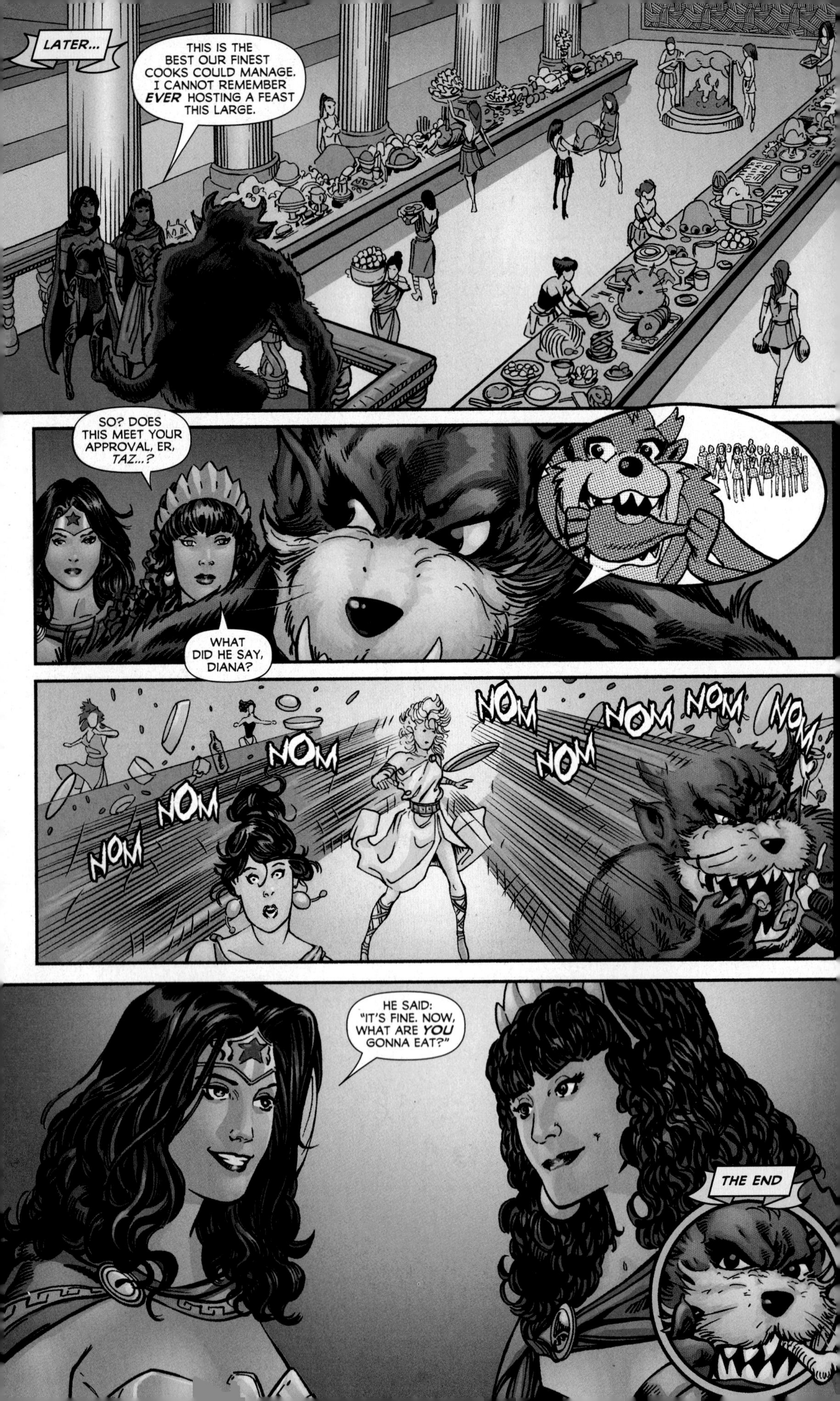
LATER...
THIS IS THE BEST OUR FINEST COOKS COULD MANAGE. I CANNOT REMEMBER EVER HOSTING A FEAST THIS LARGE.
SO? DOES THIS MEET YOUR APPROVAL, ER, TAZ...?
WHAT DID HE SAY, DIANA?
NOM NOM NOM NOM NOM NOM NOM NOM
HE SAID: "IT'S FINE. NOW, WHAT ARE YOU GONNA EAT?"
THE END

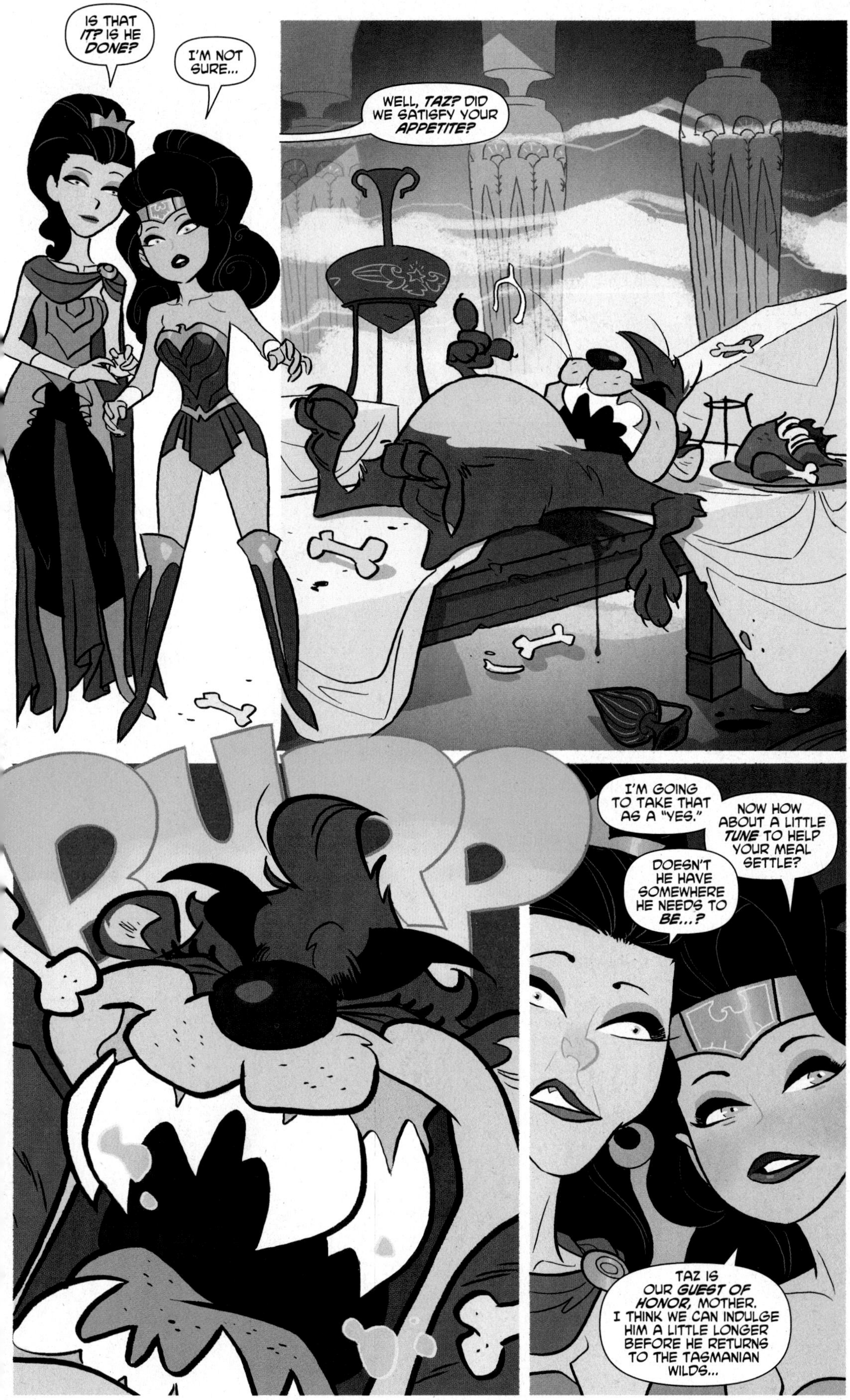
IS THAT *IT?* IS HE *DONE?*
I'M NOT SURE...
WELL, *TAZ?* DID WE SATISFY YOUR *APPETITE?*
BURP
I'M GOING TO TAKE THAT AS A "YES."
NOW HOW ABOUT A LITTLE *TUNE* TO HELP YOUR MEAL SETTLE?
DOESN'T HE HAVE SOMEWHERE HE NEEDS TO *BE...?*
TAZ IS OUR *GUEST OF HONOR,* MOTHER. I THINK WE CAN INDULGE HIM A LITTLE LONGER BEFORE HE RETURNS TO THE TASMANIAN WILDS...

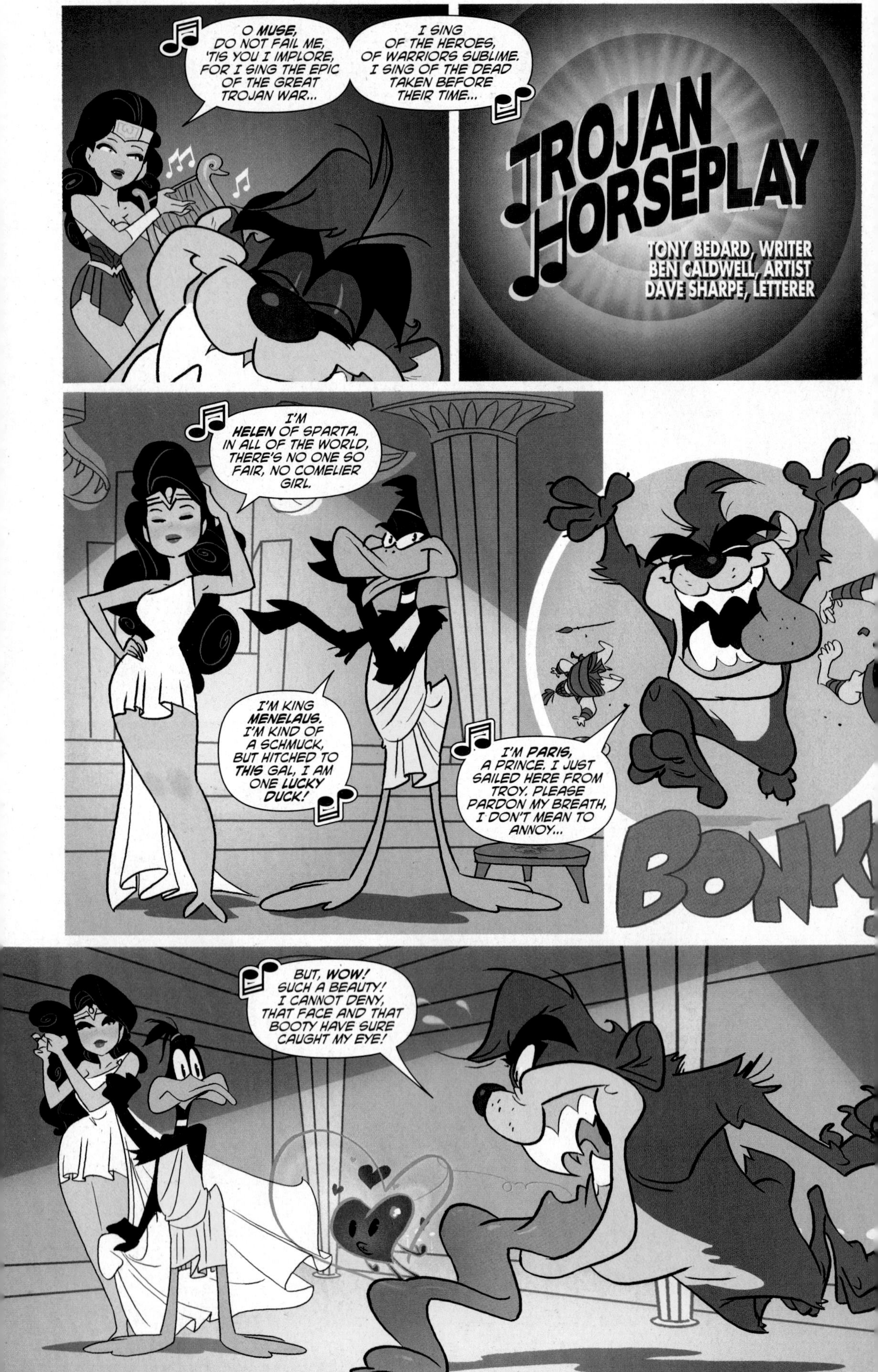
O MUSE, DO NOT FAIL ME, 'TIS YOU I IMPLORE, FOR I SING THE EPIC OF THE GREAT TROJAN WAR...
I SING OF THE HEROES, OF WARRIORS SUBLIME. I SING OF THE DEAD TAKEN BEFORE THEIR TIME...
TROJAN HORSEPLAY
TONY BEDARD, WRITER
BEN CALDWELL, ARTIST
DAVE SHARPE, LETTERER
I'M HELEN OF SPARTA. IN ALL OF THE WORLD, THERE'S NO ONE SO FAIR, NO COMELIER GIRL.
I'M KING MENELAUS. I'M KIND OF A SCHMUCK, BUT HITCHED TO THIS GAL, I AM ONE LUCKY DUCK!
I'M PARIS, A PRINCE. I JUST SAILED HERE FROM TROY. PLEASE PARDON MY BREATH, I DON'T MEAN TO ANNOY...
BONK
BUT, WOW! SUCH A BEAUTY! I CANNOT DENY, THAT FACE AND THAT BOOTY HAVE SURE CAUGHT MY EYE!

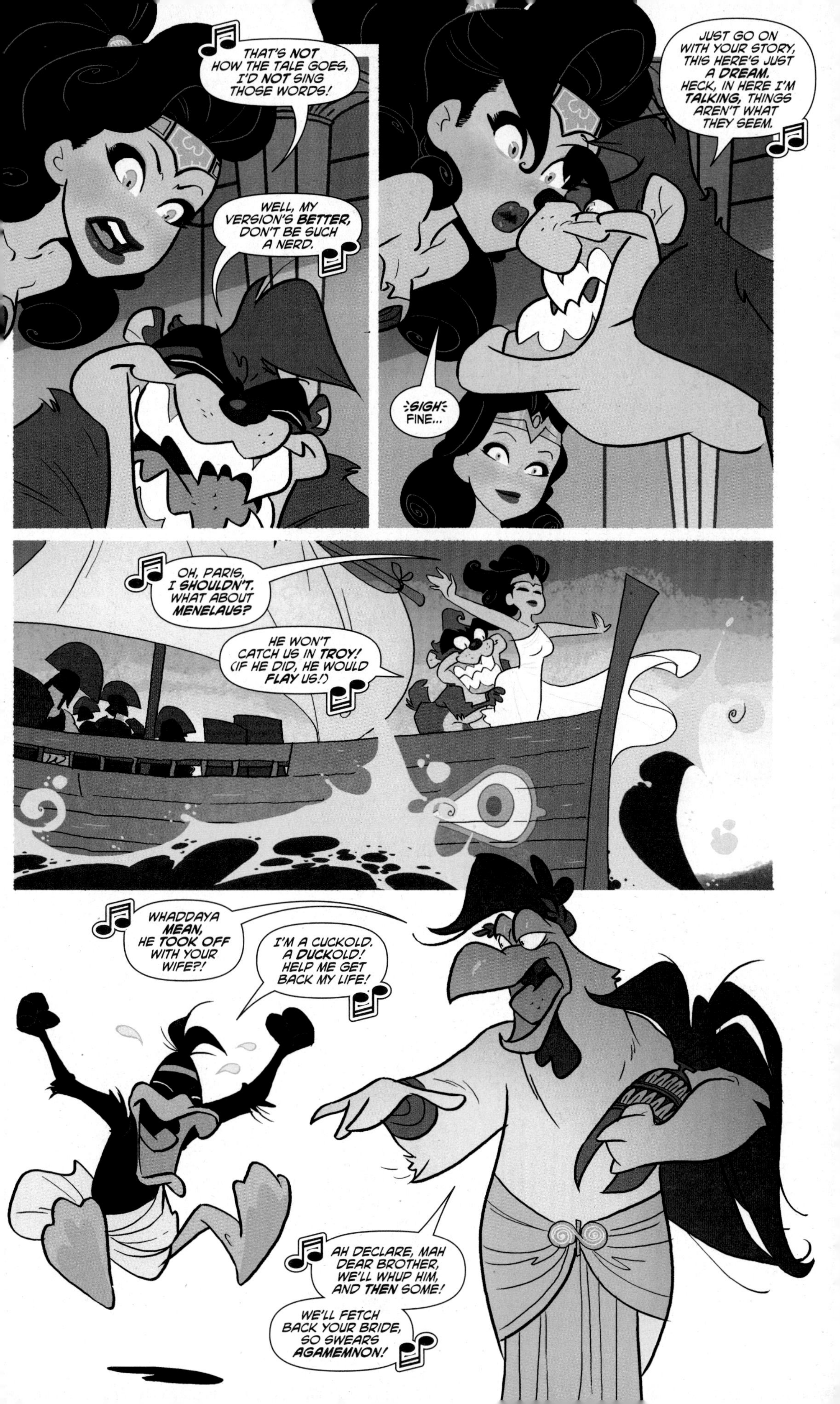
THAT'S NOT HOW THE TALE GOES, I'D NOT SING THOSE WORDS!
WELL, MY VERSION'S BETTER, DON'T BE SUCH A NERD.
JUST GO ON WITH YOUR STORY, THIS HERE'S JUST A DREAM. HECK, IN HERE I'M TALKING, THINGS AREN'T WHAT THEY SEEM.
SIGH FINE...
OH, PARIS, I SHOULDN'T. WHAT ABOUT MENELAUS?
HE WON'T CATCH US IN TROY! (IF HE DID, HE WOULD FLAY US!)
WHADDAYA MEAN, HE TOOK OFF WITH YOUR WIFE?!
I'M A CUCKOLD. A DUCKOLD! HELP ME GET BACK MY LIFE!
AH DECLARE, MAH DEAR BROTHER, WE'LL WHUP HIM, AND THEN SOME!
WE'LL FETCH BACK YOUR BRIDE, SO SWEARS AGAMEMNON!

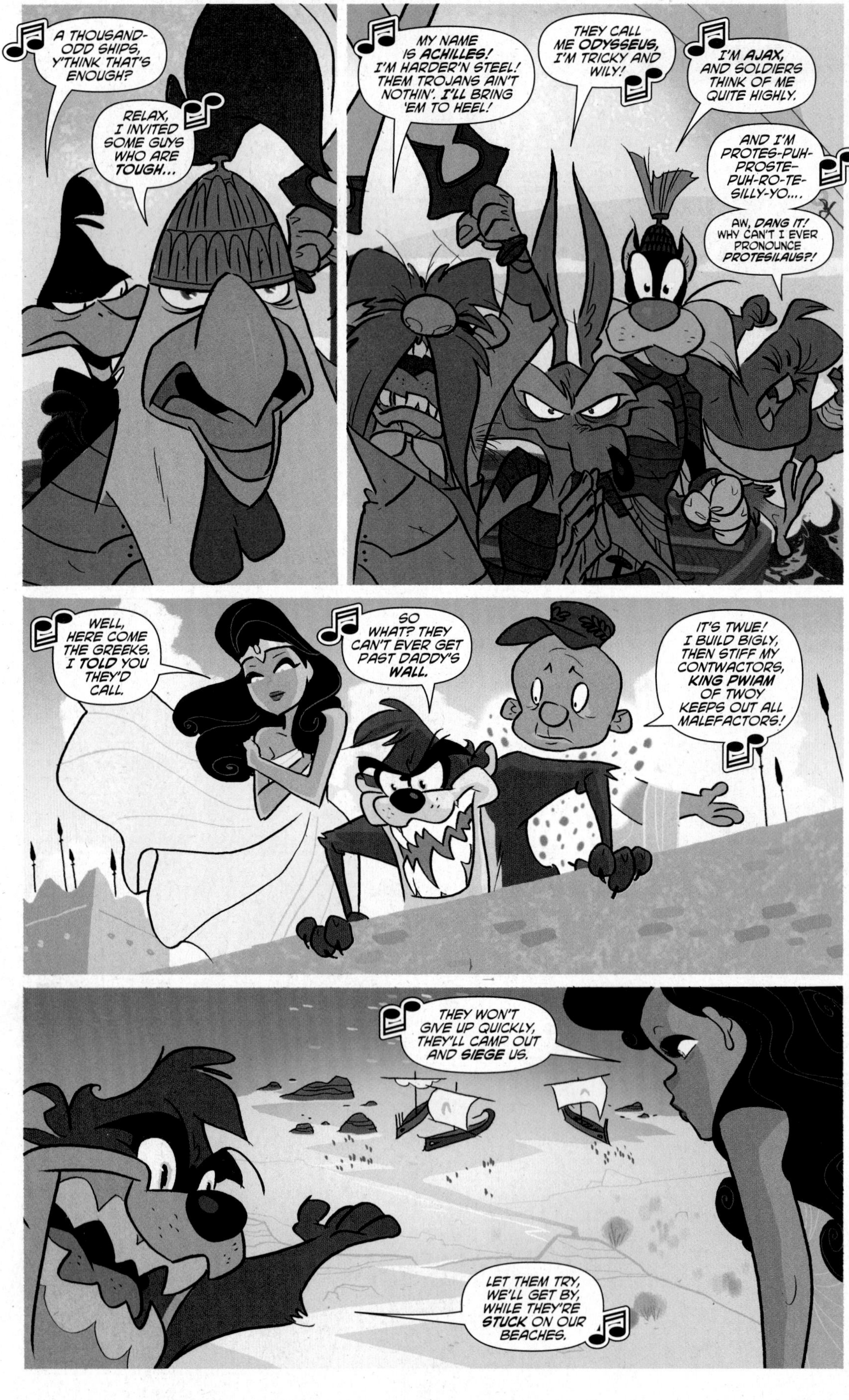
A THOUSAND-ODD SHIPS, Y'THINK THAT'S ENOUGH?
RELAX, I INVITED SOME GUYS WHO ARE TOUGH...
MY NAME IS ACHILLES! I'M HARDER'N STEEL! THEM TROJANS AIN'T NOTHIN'. I'LL BRING 'EM TO HEEL!
THEY CALL ME ODYSSEUS, I'M TRICKY AND WILY!
I'M AJAX, AND SOLDIERS THINK OF ME QUITE HIGHLY.
AND I'M PROTES-PUH-PROSTE-PUH-RO-TE-SILLY-YO....
AW, DANG IT! WHY CAN'T I EVER PRONOUNCE PROTESILAUS?!
WELL, HERE COME THE GREEKS. I TOLD YOU THEY'D CALL.
SO WHAT? THEY CAN'T EVER GET PAST DADDY'S WALL.
IT'S TWUE! I BUILD BIGLY, THEN STIFF MY CONTWACTORS, KING PWIAM OF TWOY KEEPS OUT ALL MALEFACTORS!
THEY WON'T GIVE UP QUICKLY, THEY'LL CAMP OUT AND SIEGE US.
LET THEM TRY, WE'LL GET BY, WHILE THEY'RE STUCK ON OUR BEACHES.

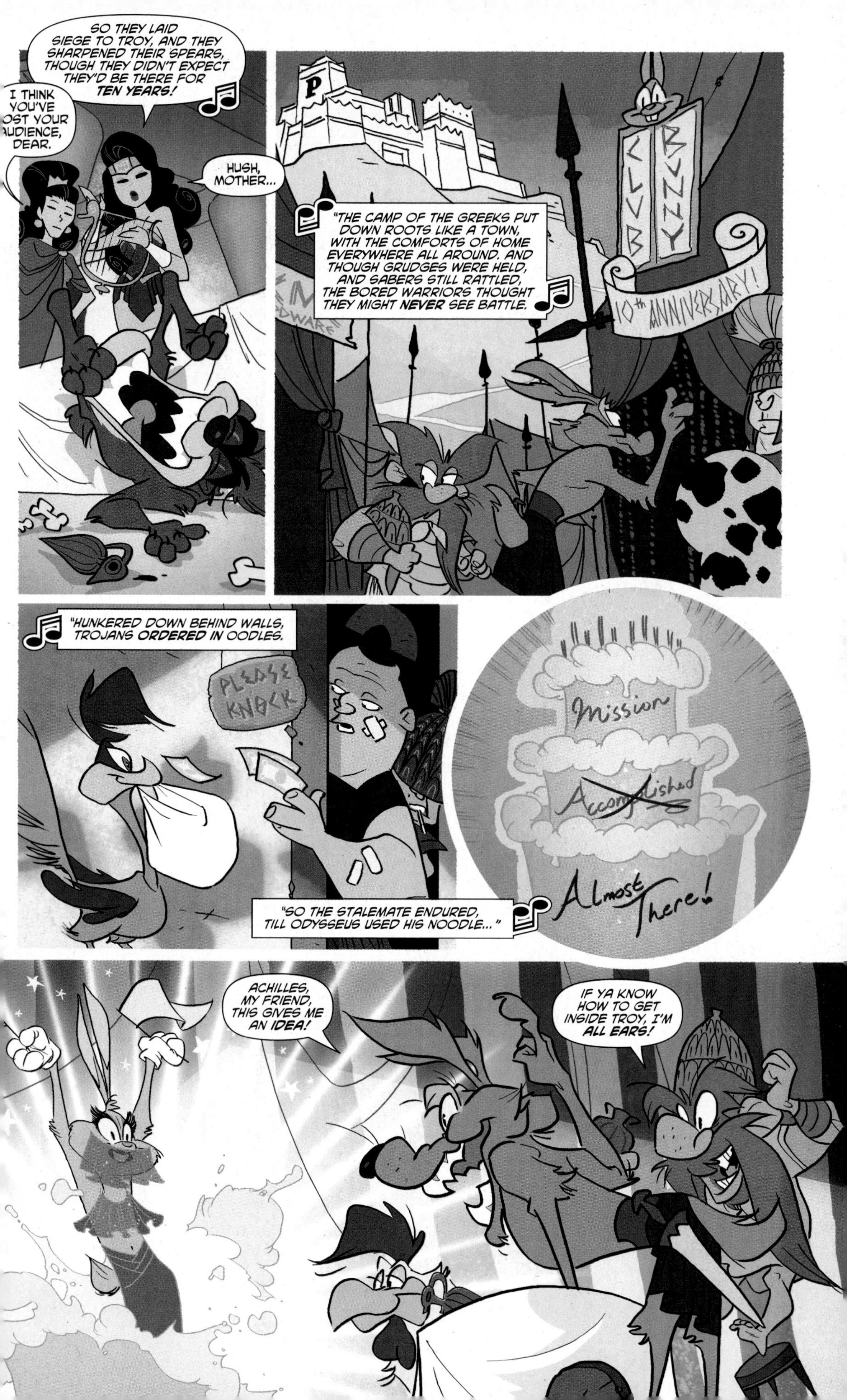
SO THEY LAID SIEGE TO TROY, AND THEY SHARPENED THEIR SPEARS, THOUGH THEY DIDN'T EXPECT THEY'D BE THERE FOR **TEN YEARS!**
I THINK YOU'VE LOST YOUR AUDIENCE, DEAR.
HUSH, MOTHER...
"THE CAMP OF THE GREEKS PUT DOWN ROOTS LIKE A TOWN, WITH THE COMFORTS OF HOME EVERYWHERE ALL AROUND. AND THOUGH GRUDGES WERE HELD, AND SABERS STILL RATTLED, THE BORED WARRIORS THOUGHT THEY MIGHT **NEVER** SEE BATTLE.
P
CLUB BUNNY
10th ANNIVERSARY!
"HUNKERED DOWN BEHIND WALLS, TROJANS **ORDERED IN** OODLES.
PLEASE KNOCK
Mission Accomplished
Almost There!
"SO THE STALEMATE ENDURED, TILL ODYSSEUS USED HIS NOODLE..."
ACHILLES, MY FRIEND, THIS GIVES ME AN **IDEA!**
IF YA KNOW HOW TO GET INSIDE TROY, I'M **ALL EARS!**

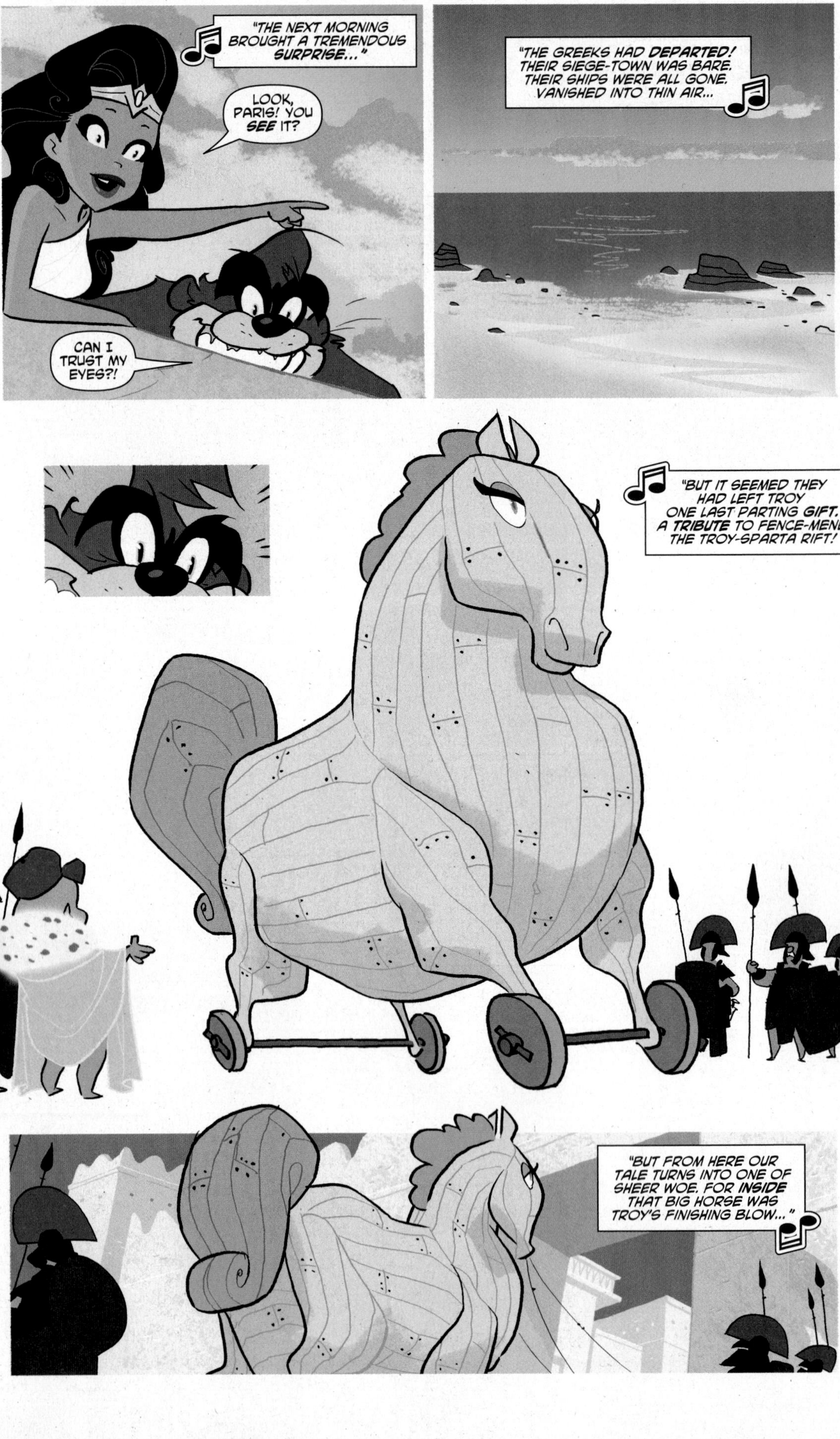
"THE NEXT MORNING BROUGHT A TREMENDOUS SURPRISE..."
LOOK, PARIS! YOU SEE IT?
CAN I TRUST MY EYES?!
"THE GREEKS HAD DEPARTED! THEIR SIEGE-TOWN WAS BARE. THEIR SHIPS WERE ALL GONE. VANISHED INTO THIN AIR...
"BUT IT SEEMED THEY HAD LEFT TROY ONE LAST PARTING GIFT. A TRIBUTE TO FENCE-MEND THE TROY-SPARTA RIFT!
"BUT FROM HERE OUR TALE TURNS INTO ONE OF SHEER WOE. FOR INSIDE THAT BIG HORSE WAS TROY'S FINISHING BLOW..."

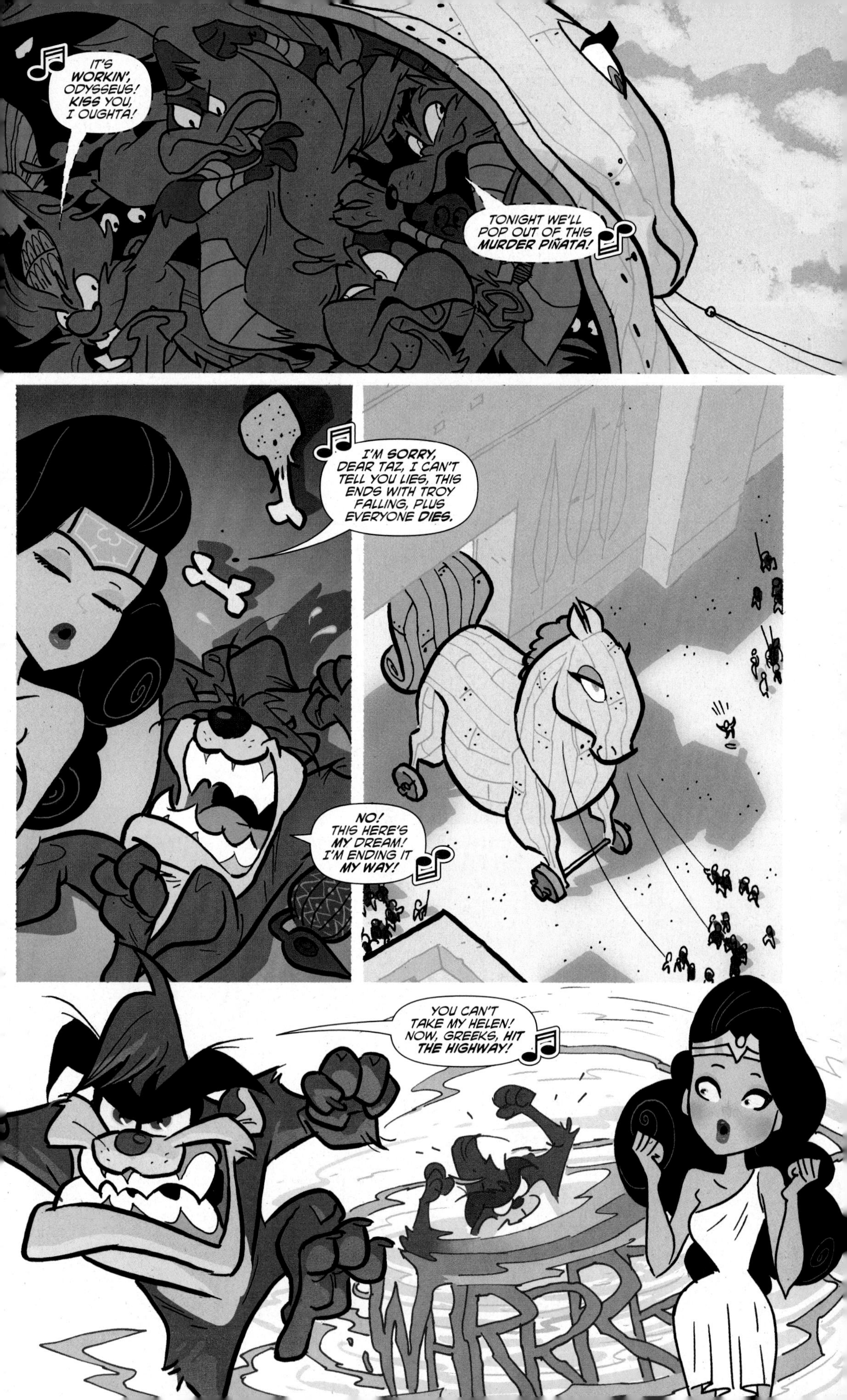

IT'S WORKIN', ODYSSEUS! KISS YOU, I OUGHTA!
TONIGHT WE'LL POP OUT OF THIS MURDER PIÑATA!
I'M SORRY, DEAR TAZ, I CAN'T TELL YOU LIES, THIS ENDS WITH TROY FALLING, PLUS EVERYONE DIES.
NO! THIS HERE'S MY DREAM! I'M ENDING IT MY WAY!
YOU CAN'T TAKE MY HELEN! NOW, GREEKS, HIT THE HIGHWAY!
WHRRRR

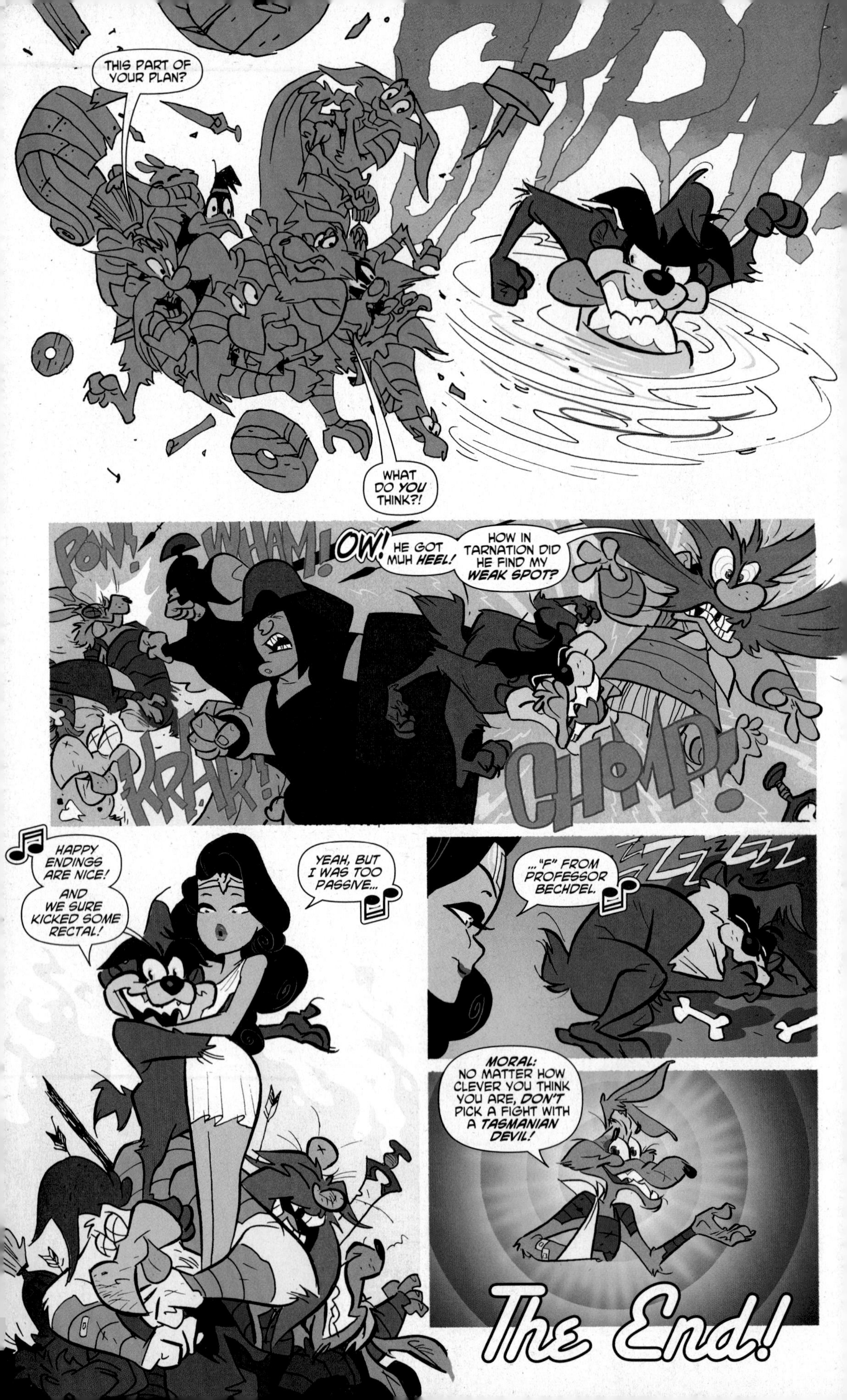
THIS PART OF YOUR PLAN?
WHAT DO YOU THINK?!
POW!
WHAM!
OW!
HE GOT MUH HEEL!
HOW IN TARNATION DID HE FIND MY WEAK SPOT?
KRAK!
CHOMP!
HAPPY ENDINGS ARE NICE! AND WE SURE KICKED SOME RECTAL!
YEAH, BUT I WAS TOO PASSIVE...
..."F" FROM PROFESSOR BECHDEL.
MORAL: NO MATTER HOW CLEVER YOU THINK YOU ARE, DON'T PICK A FIGHT WITH A TASMANIAN DEVIL!
The End!

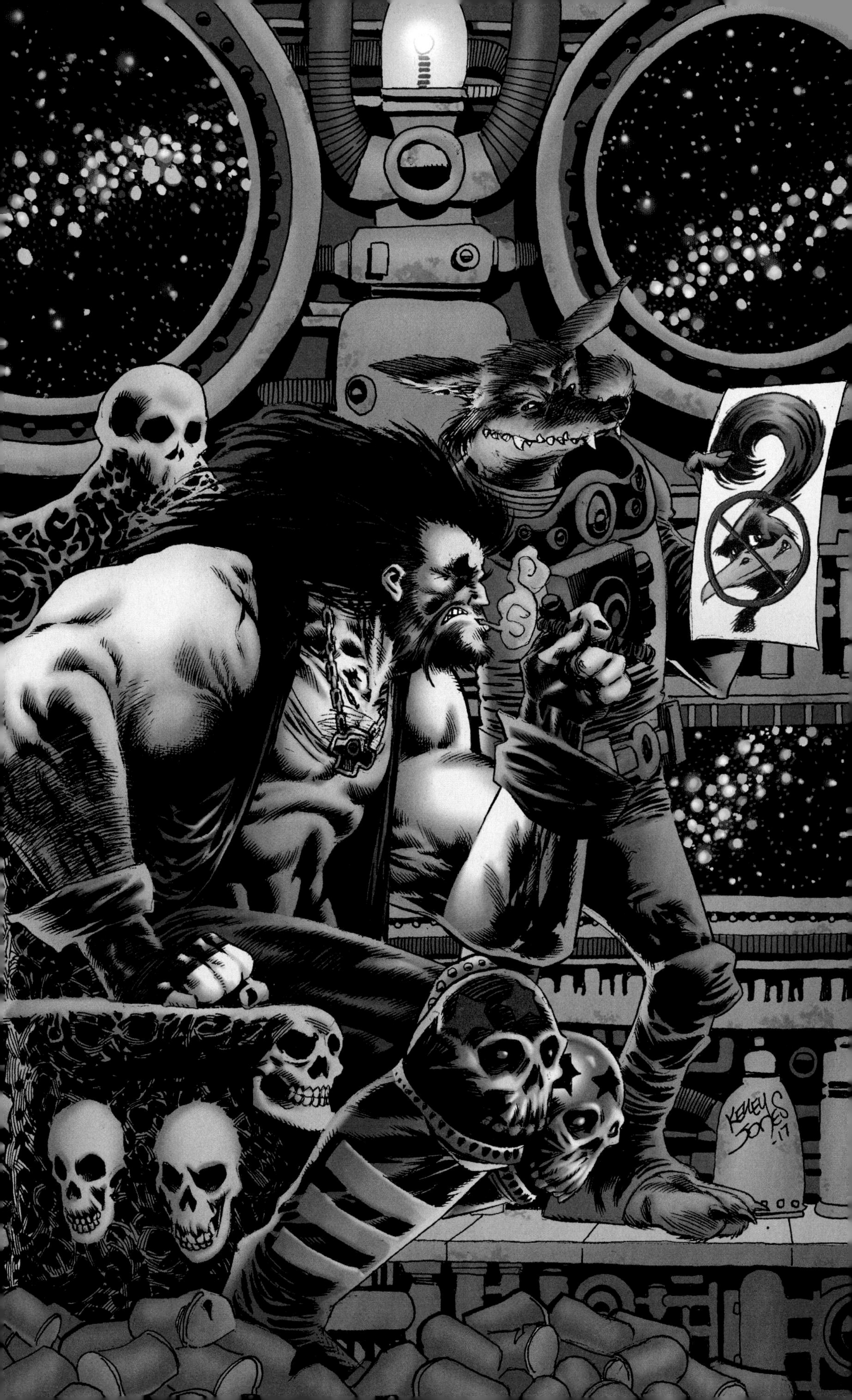

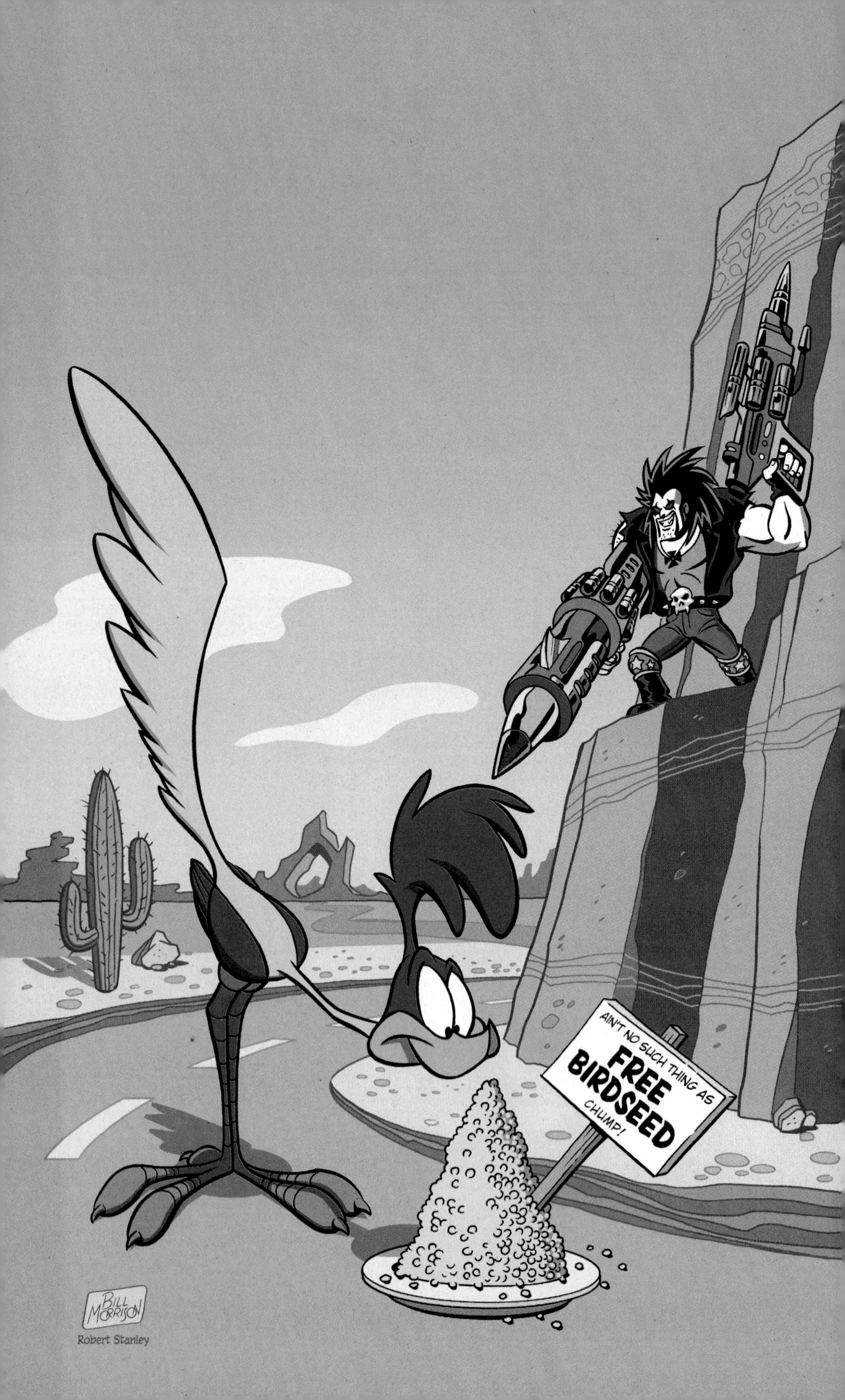
AIN'T NO SUCH THING AS
FREE BIRDSEED
CHUMP!
BILL MORRISON
Robert Stanley

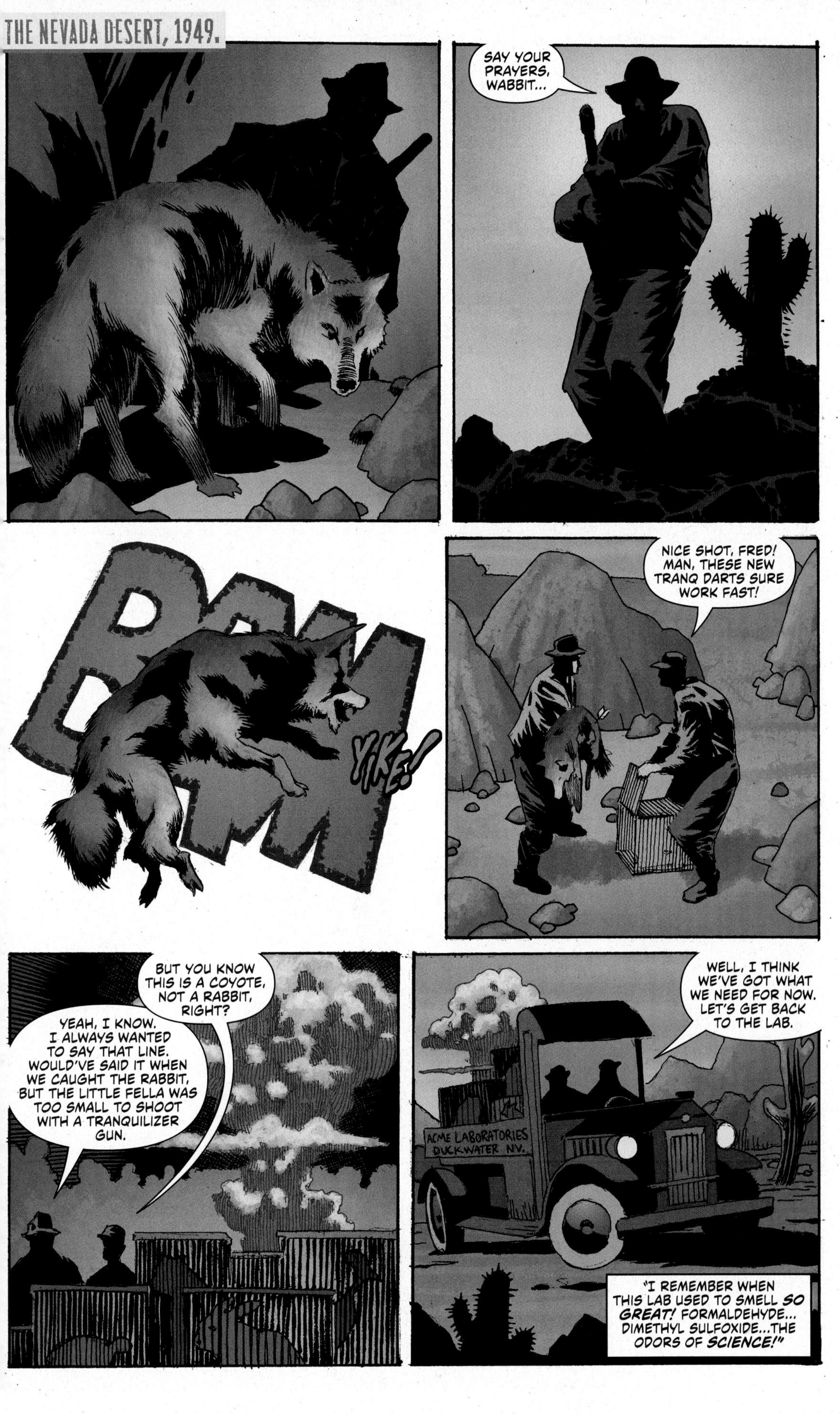
THE NEVADA DESERT, 1949.
SAY YOUR PRAYERS, WABBIT...
BAM
YIKE!
NICE SHOT, FRED! MAN, THESE NEW TRANQ DARTS SURE WORK FAST!
BUT YOU KNOW THIS IS A COYOTE, NOT A RABBIT, RIGHT?
YEAH, I KNOW. I ALWAYS WANTED TO SAY THAT LINE. WOULD'VE SAID IT WHEN WE CAUGHT THE RABBIT, BUT THE LITTLE FELLA WAS TOO SMALL TO SHOOT WITH A TRANQUILIZER GUN.
WELL, I THINK WE'VE GOT WHAT WE NEED FOR NOW. LET'S GET BACK TO THE LAB.
ACME LABORATORIES DUCKWATER NV.
"I REMEMBER WHEN THIS LAB USED TO SMELL SO GREAT! FORMALDEHYDE... DIMETHYL SULFOXIDE...THE ODORS OF SCIENCE!"

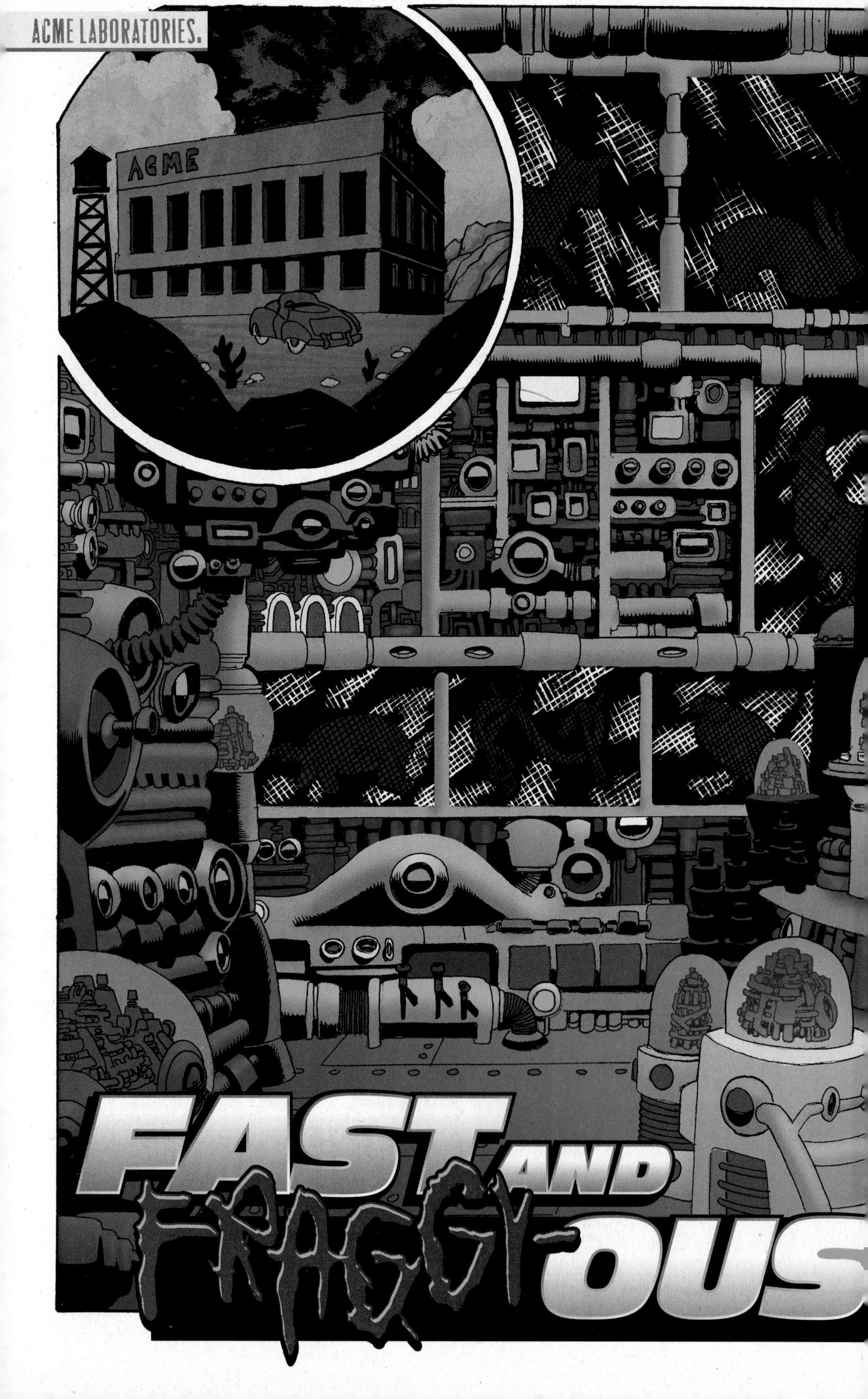
ACME LABORATORIES.
ACME
FAST AND FRAGGY-OUS

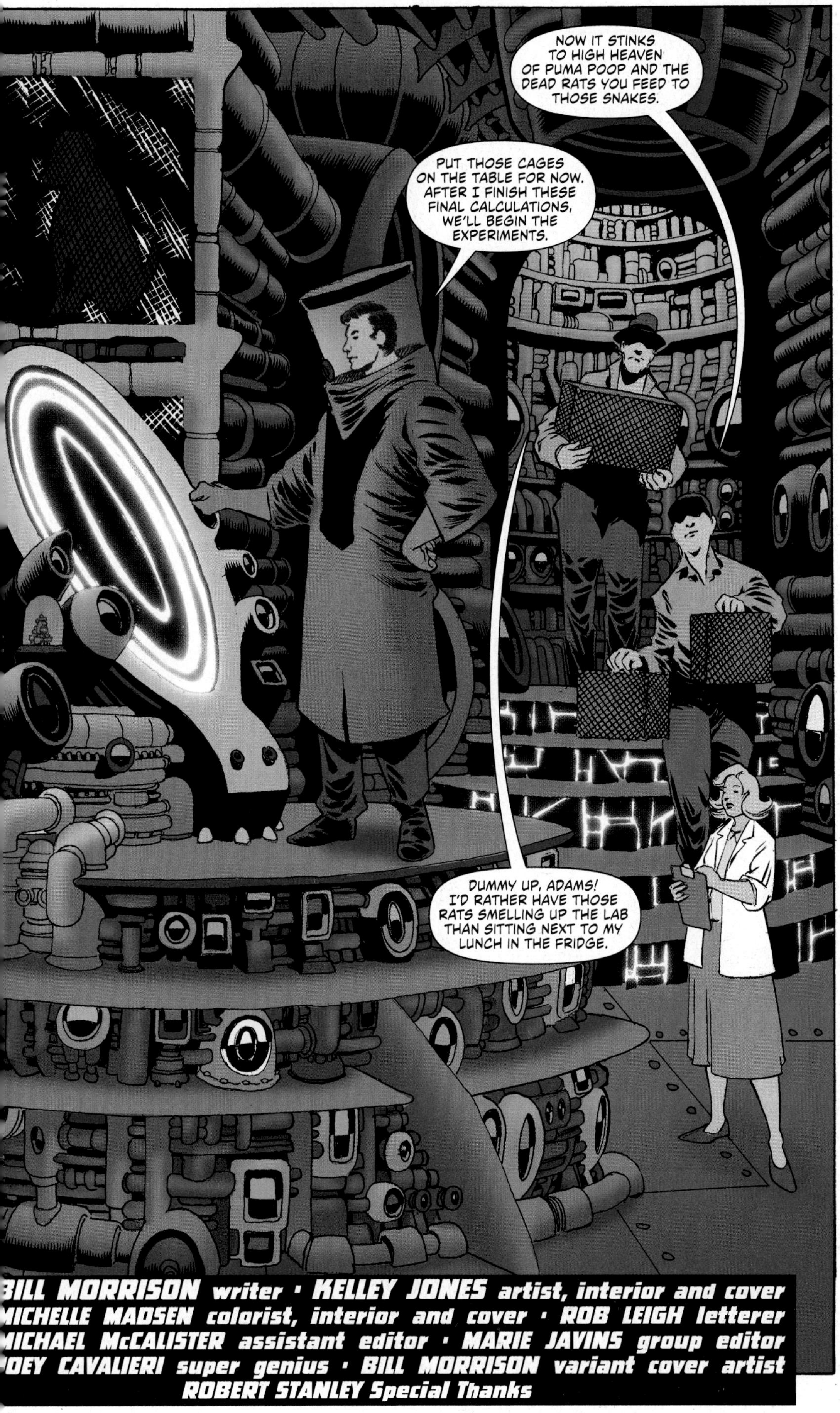
NOW IT STINKS TO HIGH HEAVEN OF PUMA POOP AND THE DEAD RATS YOU FEED TO THOSE SNAKES.
PUT THOSE CAGES ON THE TABLE FOR NOW. AFTER I FINISH THESE FINAL CALCULATIONS, WE'LL BEGIN THE EXPERIMENTS.
DUMMY UP, ADAMS! I'D RATHER HAVE THOSE RATS SMELLING UP THE LAB THAN SITTING NEXT TO MY LUNCH IN THE FRIDGE.

BILL MORRISON *writer* · **KELLEY JONES** *artist, interior and cover*
MICHELLE MADSEN *colorist, interior and cover* · **ROB LEIGH** *letterer*
MICHAEL McCALISTER *assistant editor* · **MARIE JAVINS** *group editor*
JOEY CAVALIERI *super genius* · **BILL MORRISON** *variant cover artist*
ROBERT STANLEY *Special Thanks*

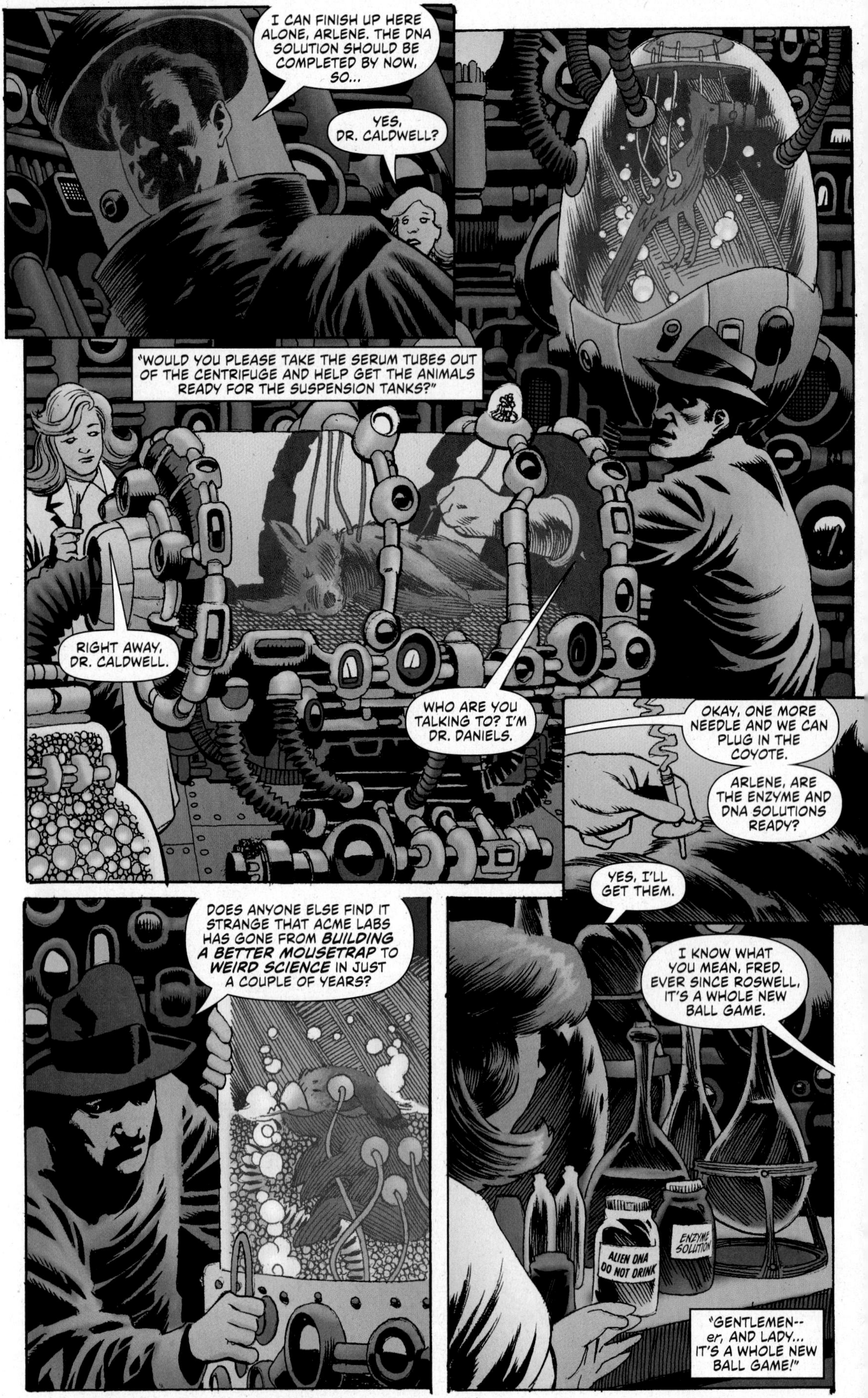
I CAN FINISH UP HERE ALONE, ARLENE. THE DNA SOLUTION SHOULD BE COMPLETED BY NOW, SO...
YES, DR. CALDWELL?
"WOULD YOU PLEASE TAKE THE SERUM TUBES OUT OF THE CENTRIFUGE AND HELP GET THE ANIMALS READY FOR THE SUSPENSION TANKS?"
RIGHT AWAY, DR. CALDWELL.
WHO ARE YOU TALKING TO? I'M DR. DANIELS.
OKAY, ONE MORE NEEDLE AND WE CAN PLUG IN THE COYOTE.
ARLENE, ARE THE ENZYME AND DNA SOLUTIONS READY?
YES, I'LL GET THEM.
DOES ANYONE ELSE FIND IT STRANGE THAT ACME LABS HAS GONE FROM BUILDING A BETTER MOUSETRAP TO WEIRD SCIENCE IN JUST A COUPLE OF YEARS?
I KNOW WHAT YOU MEAN, FRED. EVER SINCE ROSWELL, IT'S A WHOLE NEW BALL GAME.
ALIEN DNA DO NOT DRINK
ENZYME SOLUTION
"GENTLEMEN-- er, AND LADY... IT'S A WHOLE NEW BALL GAME!"

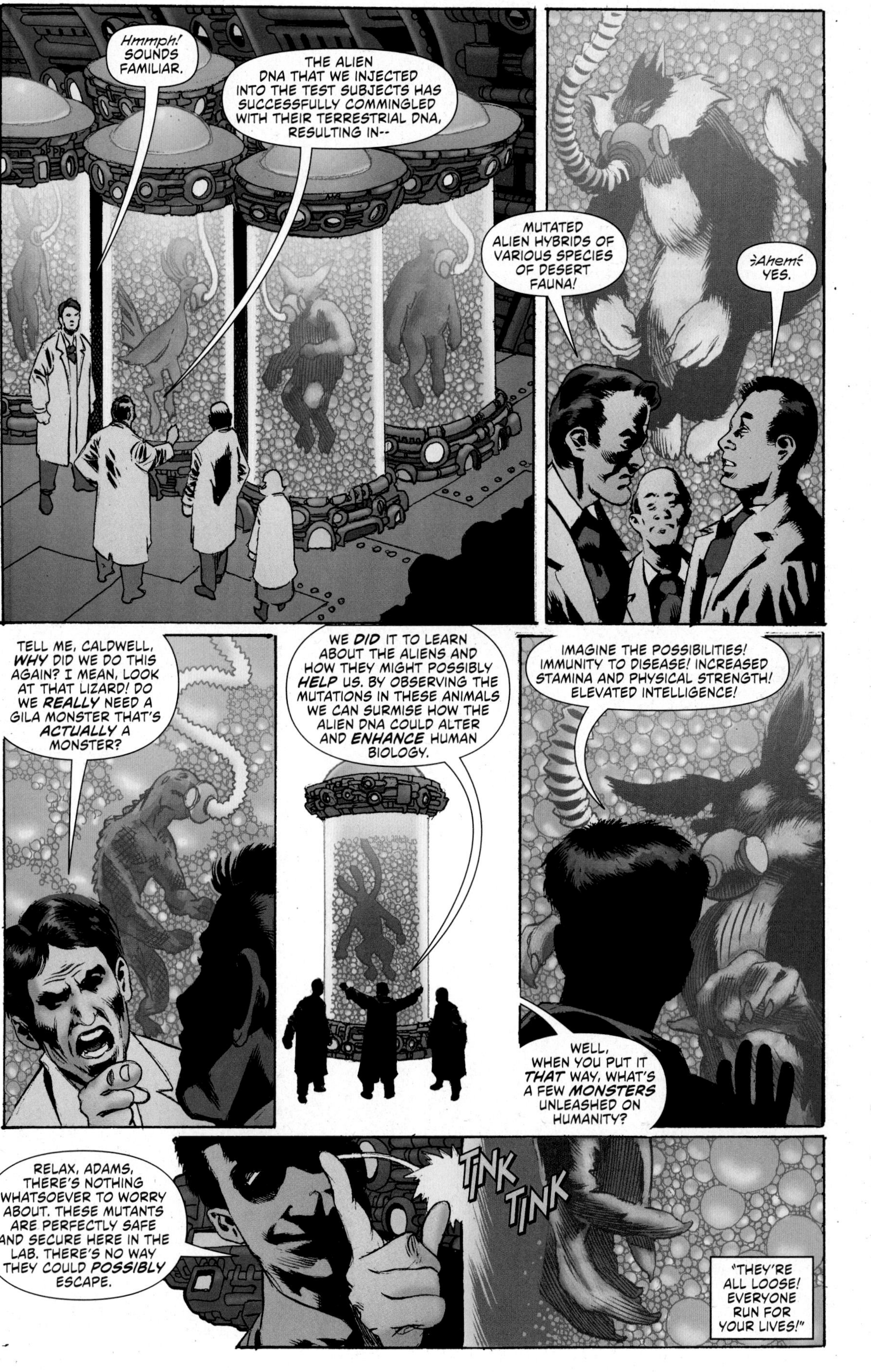

Hmmph! SOUNDS FAMILIAR.
THE ALIEN DNA THAT WE INJECTED INTO THE TEST SUBJECTS HAS SUCCESSFULLY COMMINGLED WITH THEIR TERRESTRIAL DNA, RESULTING IN--
MUTATED ALIEN HYBRIDS OF VARIOUS SPECIES OF DESERT FAUNA!
Ahem YES.
TELL ME, CALDWELL, WHY DID WE DO THIS AGAIN? I MEAN, LOOK AT THAT LIZARD! DO WE REALLY NEED A GILA MONSTER THAT'S ACTUALLY A MONSTER?
WE DID IT TO LEARN ABOUT THE ALIENS AND HOW THEY MIGHT POSSIBLY HELP US. BY OBSERVING THE MUTATIONS IN THESE ANIMALS WE CAN SURMISE HOW THE ALIEN DNA COULD ALTER AND ENHANCE HUMAN BIOLOGY.
IMAGINE THE POSSIBILITIES! IMMUNITY TO DISEASE! INCREASED STAMINA AND PHYSICAL STRENGTH! ELEVATED INTELLIGENCE!
WELL, WHEN YOU PUT IT THAT WAY, WHAT'S A FEW MONSTERS UNLEASHED ON HUMANITY?
RELAX, ADAMS, THERE'S NOTHING WHATSOEVER TO WORRY ABOUT. THESE MUTANTS ARE PERFECTLY SAFE AND SECURE HERE IN THE LAB. THERE'S NO WAY THEY COULD POSSIBLY ESCAPE.
TINK TINK
"THEY'RE ALL LOOSE! EVERYONE RUN FOR YOUR LIVES!"

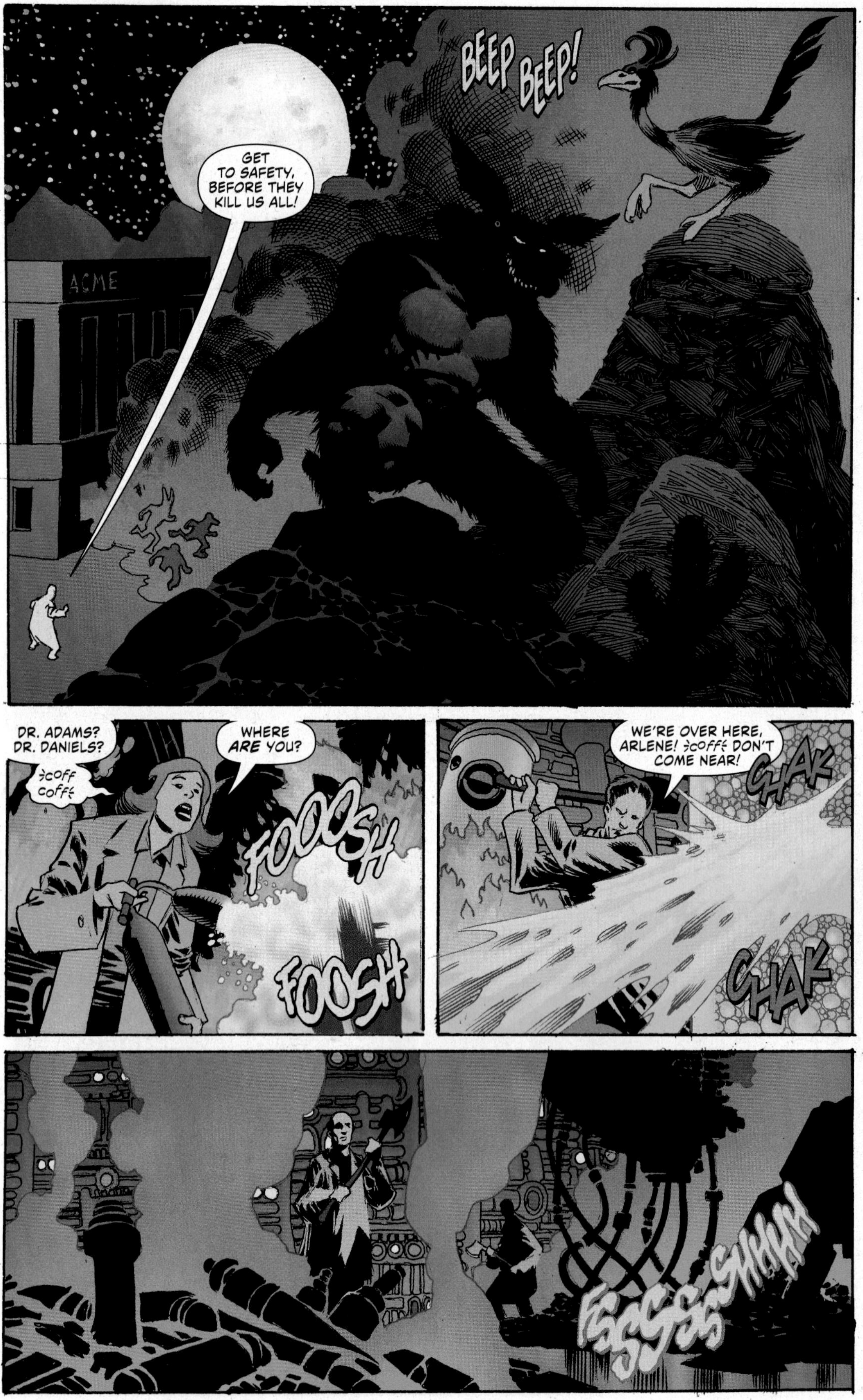
GET TO SAFETY, BEFORE THEY KILL US ALL!
BEEP BEEP!
DR. ADAMS? DR. DANIELS?
COFF COFF
WHERE ARE YOU?
FOOOSH
FOOSH
WE'RE OVER HERE, ARLENE! COFF DON'T COME NEAR!
CHAK
CHAK
FSSSSSHHHH

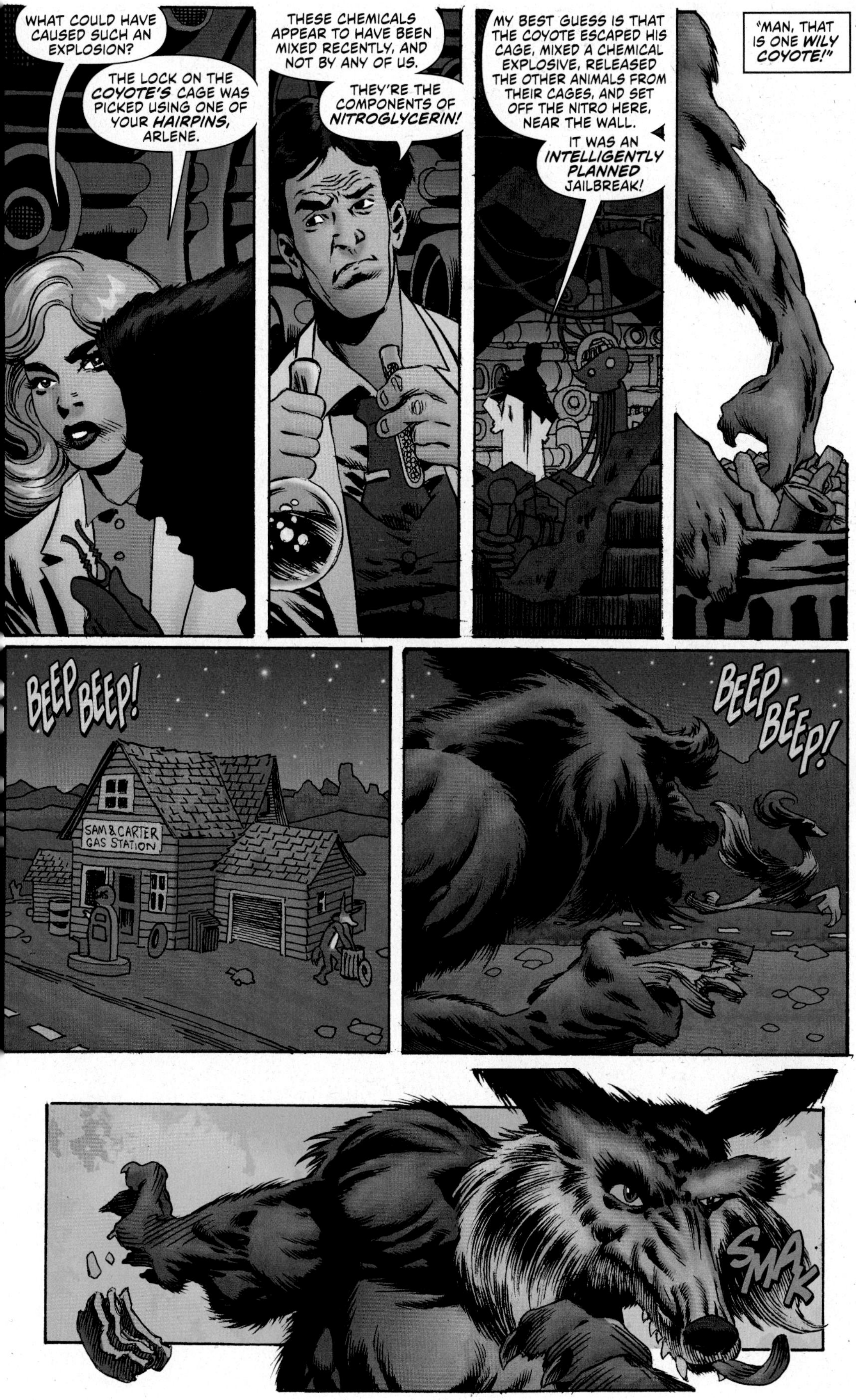
WHAT COULD HAVE CAUSED SUCH AN EXPLOSION?
THE LOCK ON THE COYOTE'S CAGE WAS PICKED USING ONE OF YOUR HAIRPINS, ARLENE.
THESE CHEMICALS APPEAR TO HAVE BEEN MIXED RECENTLY, AND NOT BY ANY OF US.
THEY'RE THE COMPONENTS OF NITROGLYCERIN!
MY BEST GUESS IS THAT THE COYOTE ESCAPED HIS CAGE, MIXED A CHEMICAL EXPLOSIVE, RELEASED THE OTHER ANIMALS FROM THEIR CAGES, AND SET OFF THE NITRO HERE, NEAR THE WALL.
IT WAS AN INTELLIGENTLY PLANNED JAILBREAK!
"MAN, THAT IS ONE WILY COYOTE!"
BEEP BEEP!
SAM & CARTER GAS STATION
BEEP BEEP!
SMAK

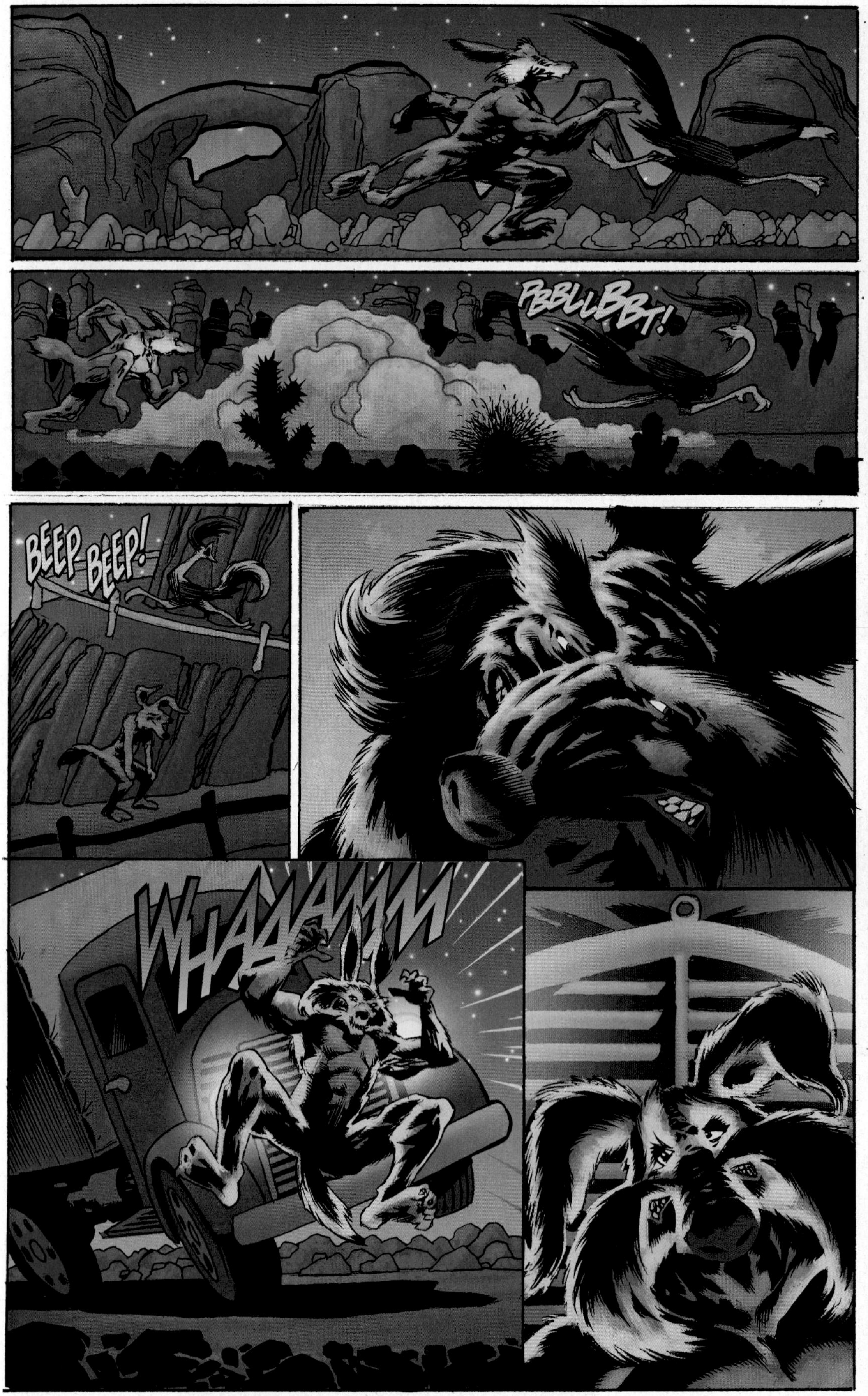
PBBLLBBT!
BEEP BEEP!
WHAAAMM

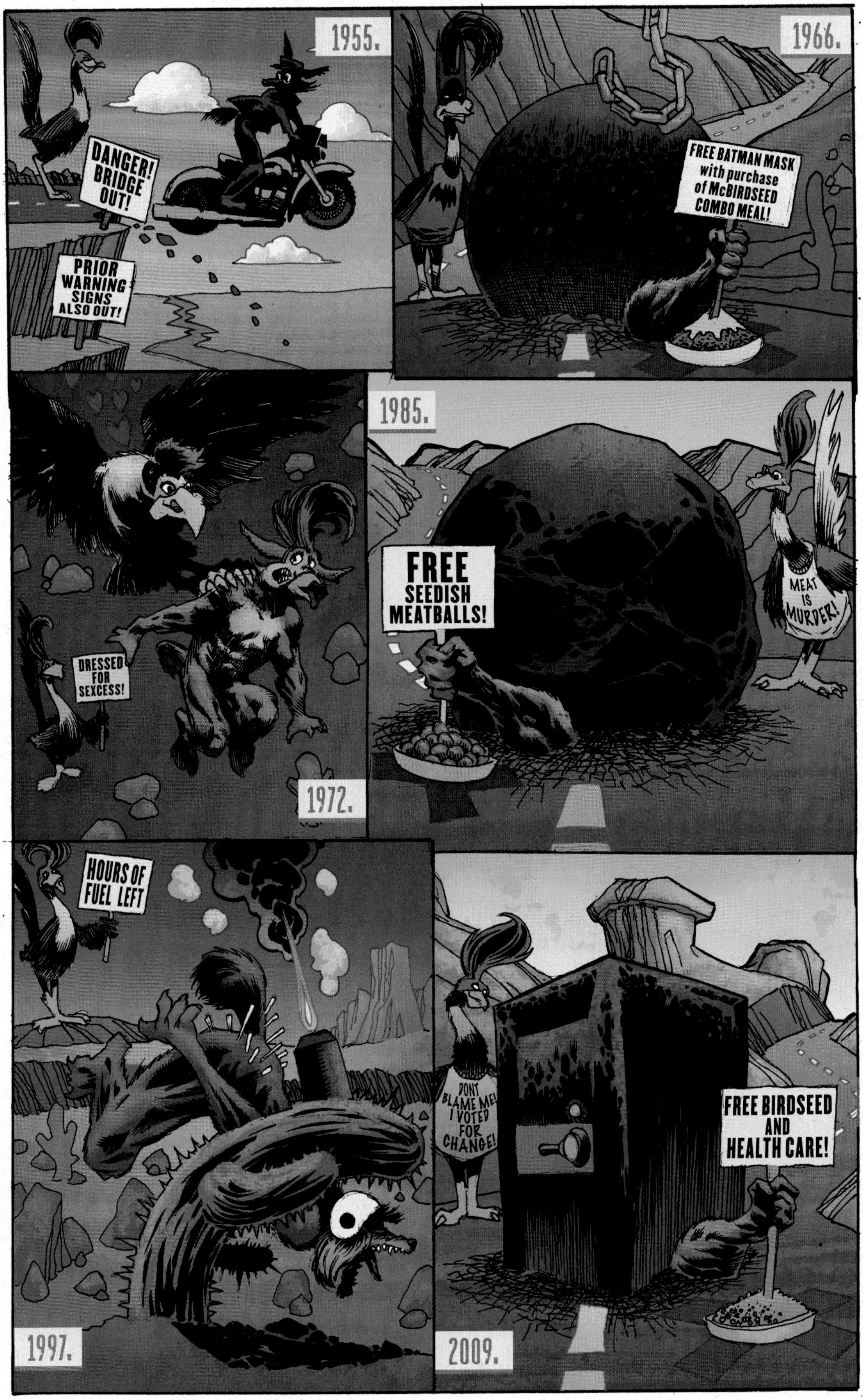
1955.
DANGER! BRIDGE OUT!
PRIOR WARNING SIGNS ALSO OUT!
1966.
FREE BATMAN MASK with purchase of McBIRDSEED COMBO MEAL!
DRESSED FOR SEXCESS!
1972.
1985.
FREE SEEDISH MEATBALLS!
MEAT IS MURDER!
HOURS OF FUEL LEFT
1997.
DONT BLAME ME! I VOTED FOR CHANGE!
FREE BIRDSEED AND HEALTH CARE!
2009.

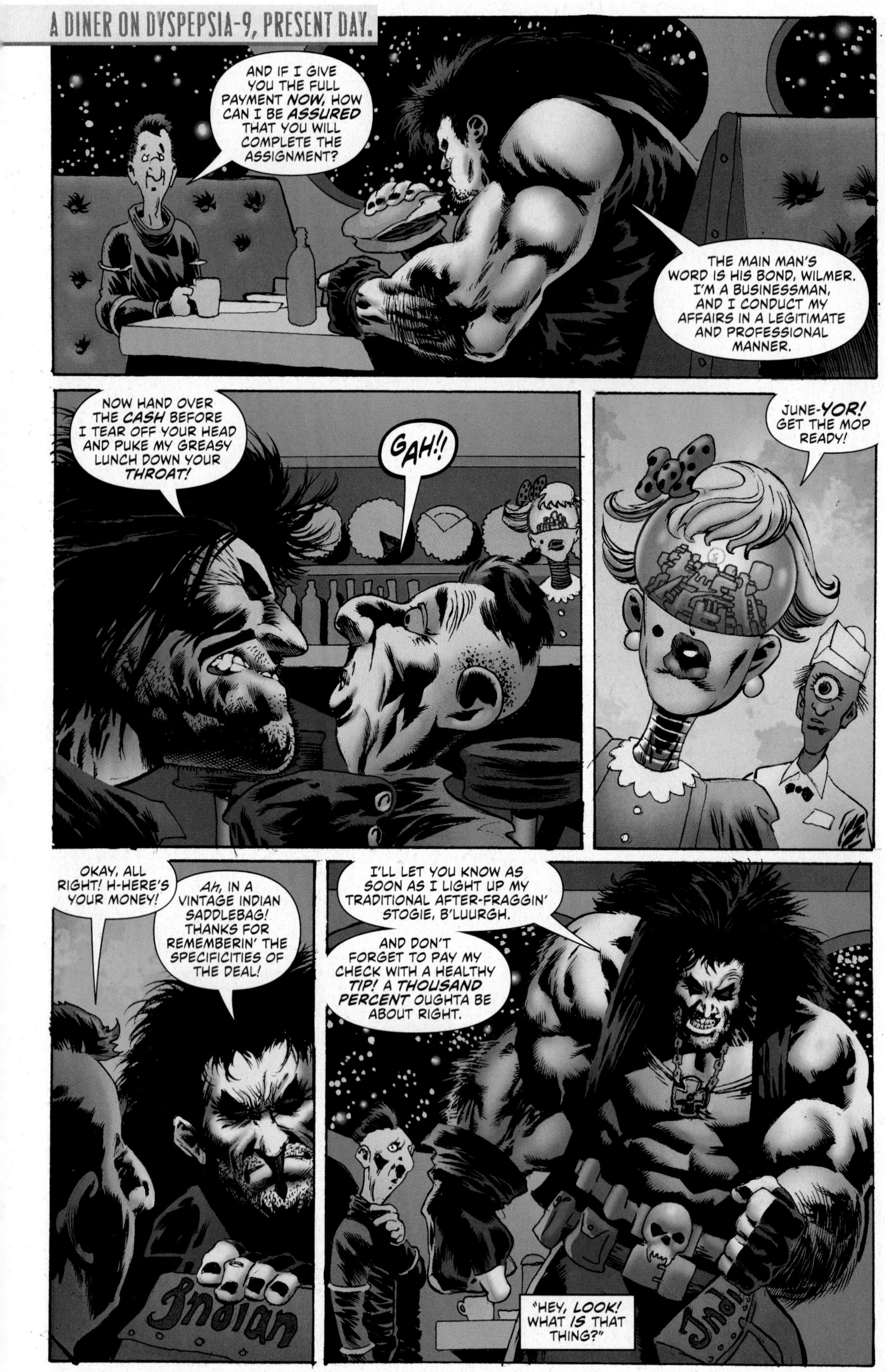
A DINER ON DYSPEPSIA-9, PRESENT DAY.
AND IF I GIVE YOU THE FULL PAYMENT NOW, HOW CAN I BE ASSURED THAT YOU WILL COMPLETE THE ASSIGNMENT?
THE MAIN MAN'S WORD IS HIS BOND, WILMER. I'M A BUSINESSMAN, AND I CONDUCT MY AFFAIRS IN A LEGITIMATE AND PROFESSIONAL MANNER.
NOW HAND OVER THE CASH BEFORE I TEAR OFF YOUR HEAD AND PUKE MY GREASY LUNCH DOWN YOUR THROAT!
GAH!!
JUNE-YOR! GET THE MOP READY!
OKAY, ALL RIGHT! H-HERE'S YOUR MONEY!
Ah, IN A VINTAGE INDIAN SADDLEBAG! THANKS FOR REMEMBERIN' THE SPECIFICITIES OF THE DEAL!
Indian
I'LL LET YOU KNOW AS SOON AS I LIGHT UP MY TRADITIONAL AFTER-FRAGGIN' STOGIE, B'LUURGH.
AND DON'T FORGET TO PAY MY CHECK WITH A HEALTHY TIP! A THOUSAND PERCENT OUGHTA BE ABOUT RIGHT.
"HEY, LOOK! WHAT IS THAT THING?"

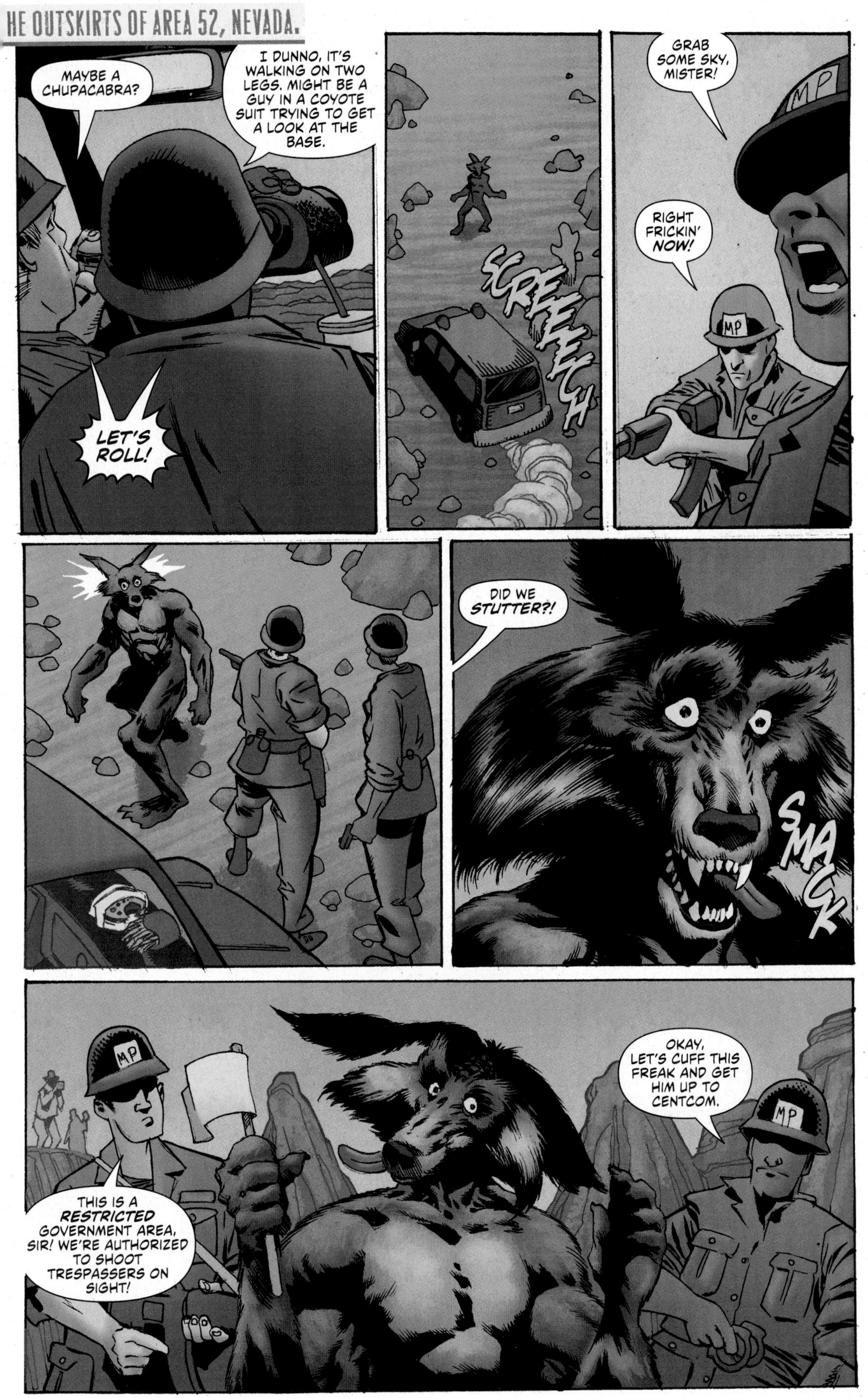
HE OUTSKIRTS OF AREA 52, NEVADA.
MAYBE A CHUPACABRA?
I DUNNO, IT'S WALKING ON TWO LEGS. MIGHT BE A GUY IN A COYOTE SUIT TRYING TO GET A LOOK AT THE BASE.
LET'S ROLL!
SCREEEECH
GRAB SOME SKY, MISTER!
RIGHT FRICKIN' NOW!
MP
DID WE STUTTER?!
SMACK
THIS IS A RESTRICTED GOVERNMENT AREA, SIR! WE'RE AUTHORIZED TO SHOOT TRESPASSERS ON SIGHT!
OKAY, LET'S CUFF THIS FREAK AND GET HIM UP TO CENTCOM.

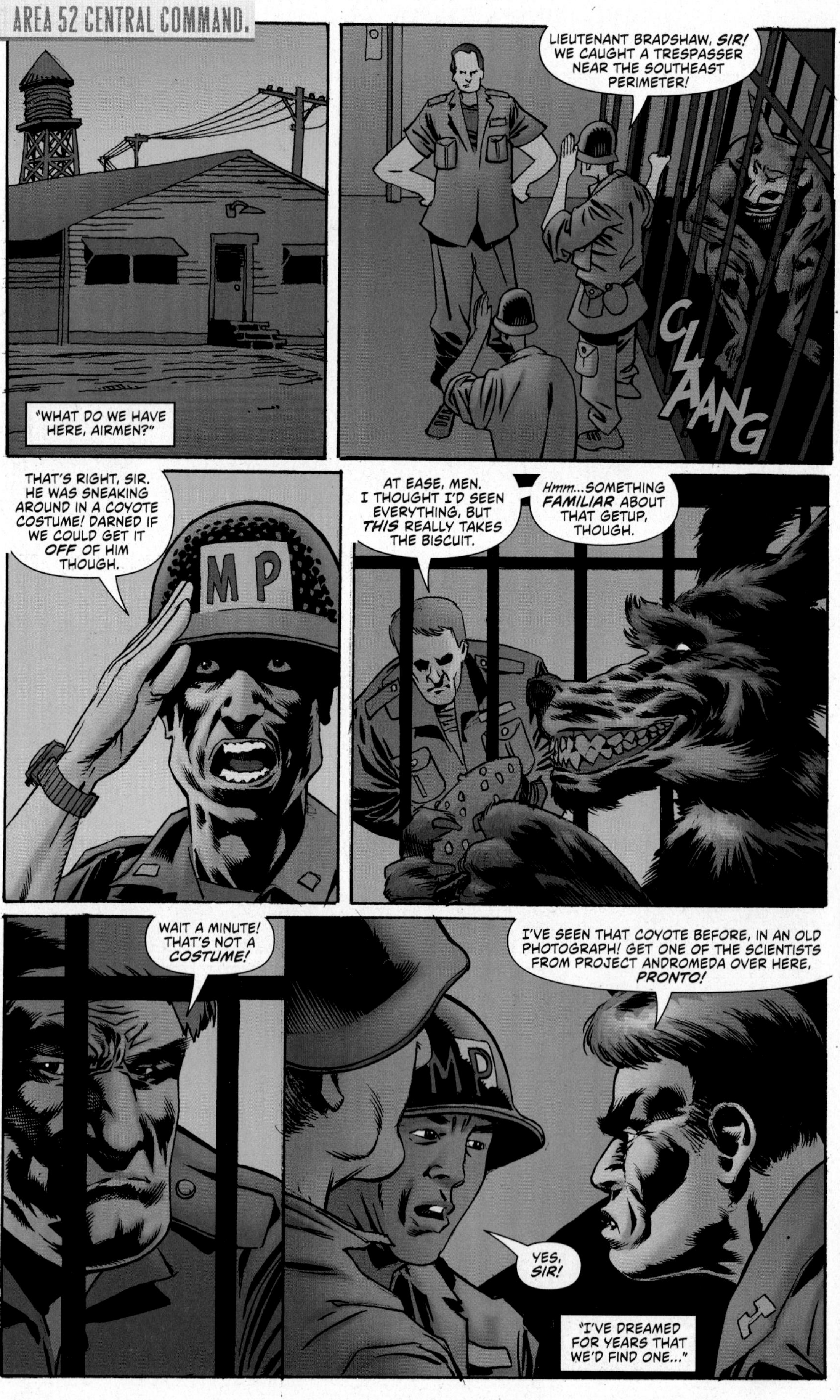
AREA 52 CENTRAL COMMAND.
"WHAT DO WE HAVE HERE, AIRMEN?"
LIEUTENANT BRADSHAW, SIR! WE CAUGHT A TRESPASSER NEAR THE SOUTHEAST PERIMETER!
CLAANG
THAT'S RIGHT, SIR. HE WAS SNEAKING AROUND IN A COYOTE COSTUME! DARNED IF WE COULD GET IT OFF OF HIM THOUGH.
MP
AT EASE, MEN. I THOUGHT I'D SEEN EVERYTHING, BUT THIS REALLY TAKES THE BISCUIT.
Hmm...SOMETHING FAMILIAR ABOUT THAT GETUP, THOUGH.
WAIT A MINUTE! THAT'S NOT A COSTUME!
I'VE SEEN THAT COYOTE BEFORE, IN AN OLD PHOTOGRAPH! GET ONE OF THE SCIENTISTS FROM PROJECT ANDROMEDA OVER HERE, PRONTO!
MP
YES, SIR!
"I'VE DREAMED FOR YEARS THAT WE'D FIND ONE..."

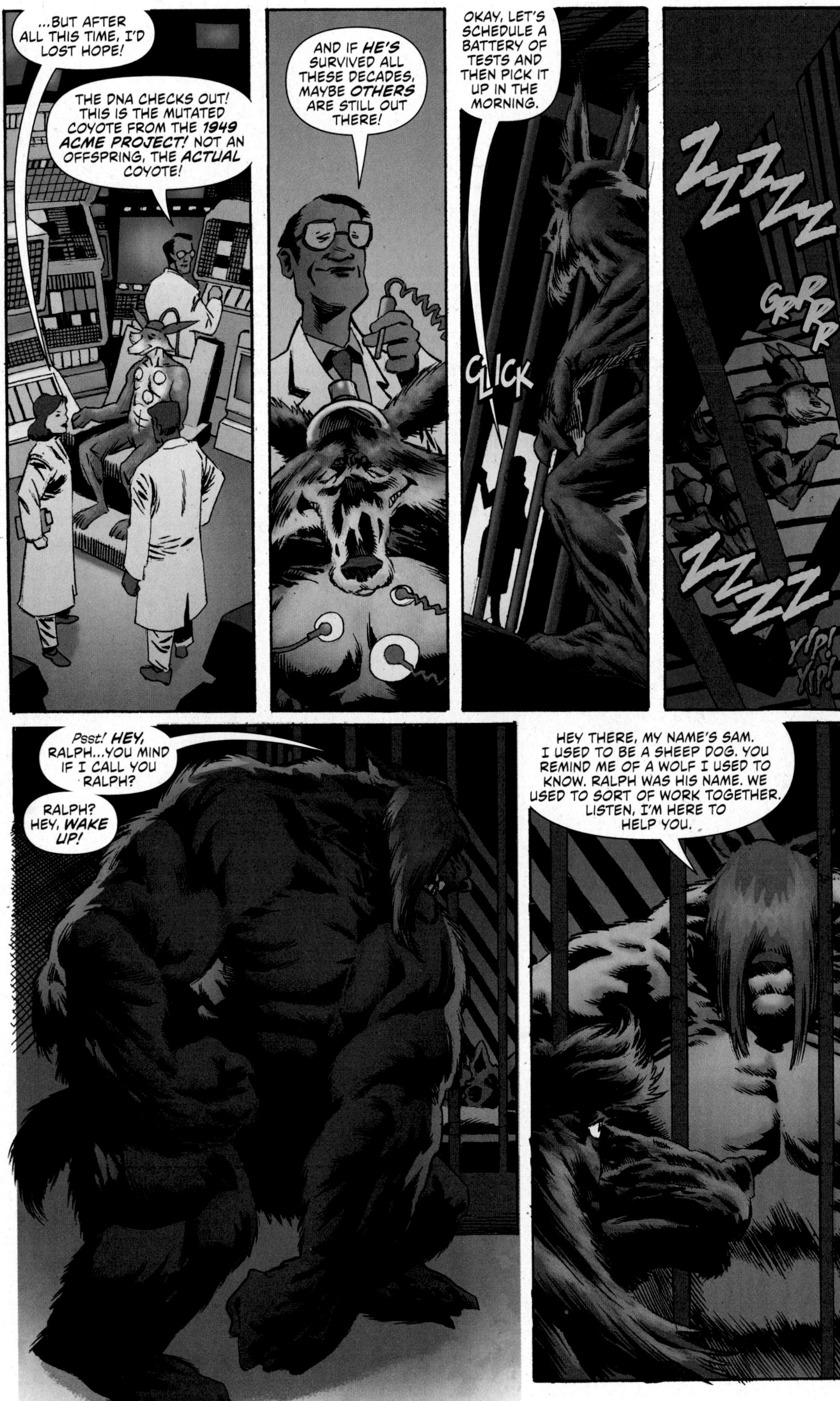
...BUT AFTER ALL THIS TIME, I'D LOST HOPE!
THE DNA CHECKS OUT! THIS IS THE MUTATED COYOTE FROM THE 1949 ACME PROJECT! NOT AN OFFSPRING, THE ACTUAL COYOTE!
AND IF HE'S SURVIVED ALL THESE DECADES, MAYBE OTHERS ARE STILL OUT THERE!
OKAY, LET'S SCHEDULE A BATTERY OF TESTS AND THEN PICK IT UP IN THE MORNING.
CLICK
ZZZZZ
GRRRR
ZZZZ
YIP! YIP!
Psst! HEY, RALPH...YOU MIND IF I CALL YOU RALPH?
RALPH? HEY, WAKE UP!
HEY THERE, MY NAME'S SAM. I USED TO BE A SHEEP DOG. YOU REMIND ME OF A WOLF I USED TO KNOW. RALPH WAS HIS NAME. WE USED TO SORT OF WORK TOGETHER. LISTEN, I'M HERE TO HELP YOU.

THE PLOOK 'N' PUKE INN, DOOLEY-7.

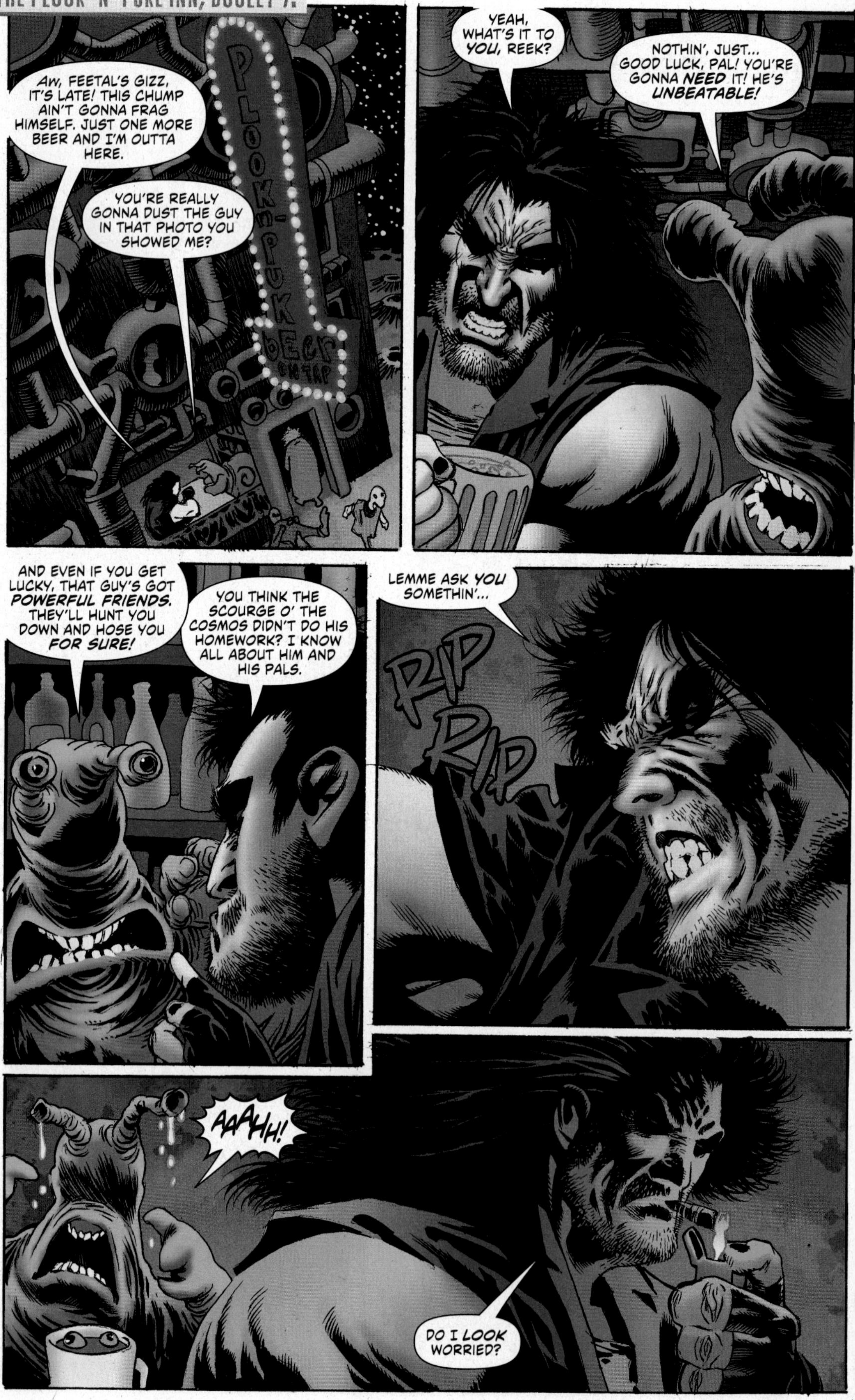
AW, FEETAL'S GIZZ, IT'S LATE! THIS CHUMP AIN'T GONNA FRAG HIMSELF. JUST ONE MORE BEER AND I'M OUTTA HERE.
YOU'RE REALLY GONNA DUST THE GUY IN THAT PHOTO YOU SHOWED ME?
PLOOK-N-PUKE
BEER ON TAP
YEAH, WHAT'S IT TO YOU, REEK?
NOTHIN', JUST... GOOD LUCK, PAL! YOU'RE GONNA NEED IT! HE'S UNBEATABLE!
AND EVEN IF YOU GET LUCKY, THAT GUY'S GOT POWERFUL FRIENDS. THEY'LL HUNT YOU DOWN AND HOSE YOU FOR SURE!
YOU THINK THE SCOURGE O' THE COSMOS DIDN'T DO HIS HOMEWORK? I KNOW ALL ABOUT HIM AND HIS PALS.
LEMME ASK YOU SOMETHIN'...
RIP RIP
AAAHH!
DO I LOOK WORRIED?

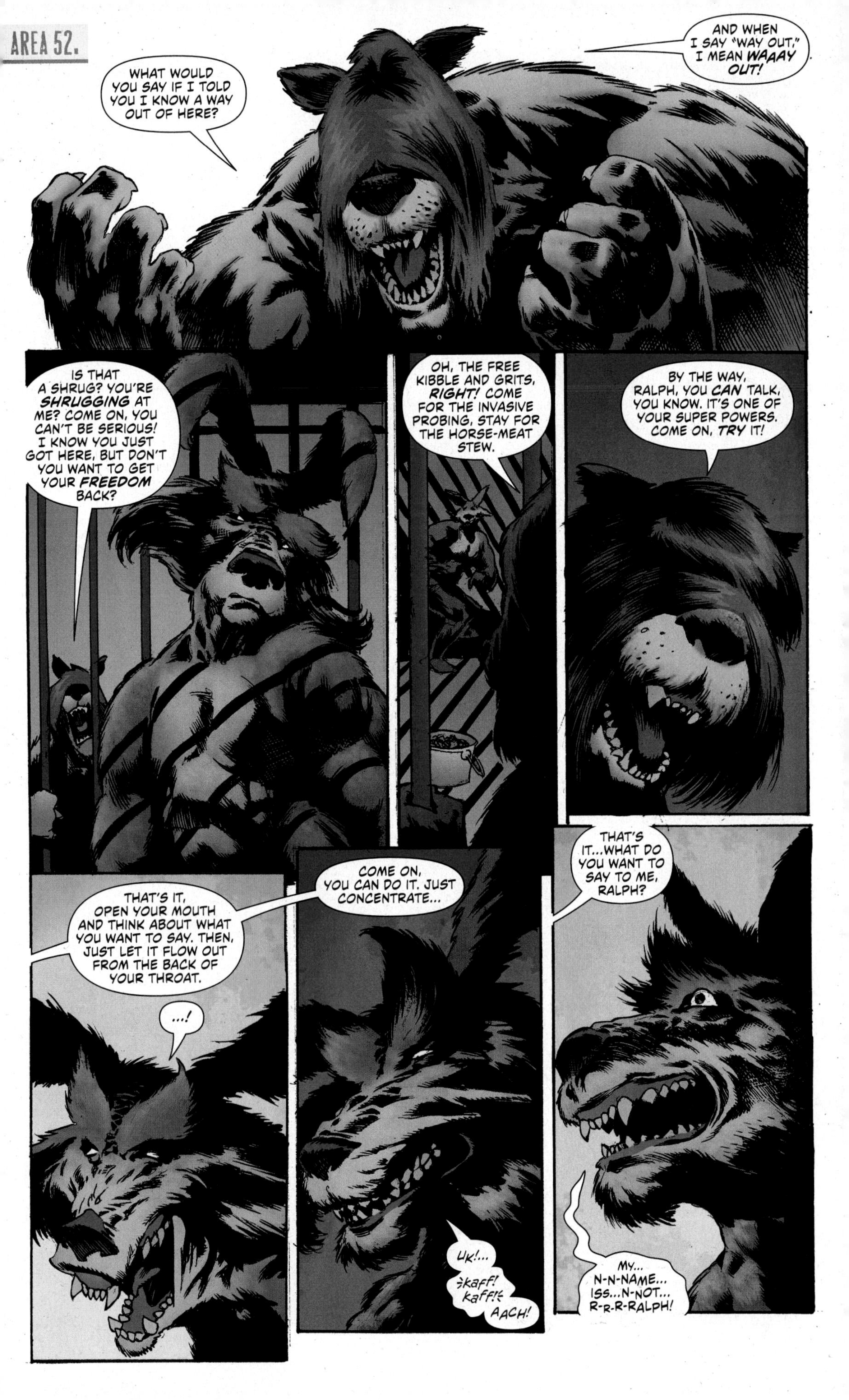
AREA 52.
WHAT WOULD YOU SAY IF I TOLD YOU I KNOW A WAY OUT OF HERE?
AND WHEN I SAY "WAY OUT," I MEAN WAAAY OUT!
IS THAT A SHRUG? YOU'RE SHRUGGING AT ME? COME ON, YOU CAN'T BE SERIOUS! I KNOW YOU JUST GOT HERE, BUT DON'T YOU WANT TO GET YOUR FREEDOM BACK?
OH, THE FREE KIBBLE AND GRITS, RIGHT! COME FOR THE INVASIVE PROBING, STAY FOR THE HORSE-MEAT STEW.
BY THE WAY, RALPH, YOU CAN TALK, YOU KNOW. IT'S ONE OF YOUR SUPER POWERS. COME ON, TRY IT!
THAT'S IT, OPEN YOUR MOUTH AND THINK ABOUT WHAT YOU WANT TO SAY. THEN, JUST LET IT FLOW OUT FROM THE BACK OF YOUR THROAT.
...!
COME ON, YOU CAN DO IT. JUST CONCENTRATE...
UK!...
KAFF! KAFF!
AACH!
THAT'S IT...WHAT DO YOU WANT TO SAY TO ME, RALPH?
MY... N-N-NAME... ISS...N-NOT... R-R-R-RALPH!

I AM...

...WILE E. COYOTE...

...SUPER GENIUS!

INCREDIBLE! I CAN TALK! I CAN'T BELIEVE I NEVER TRIED THIS BEFORE!

CONGRATULATIONS. SO WHAT'S A TALKING SUPER GENIUS LIKE YOU DOING IN A CAGE LIKE THIS? SHOULDN'T YOU BE OUT TEARING UP THE DESERT?

MEH. I'M TOO TIRED. I'VE SPENT NEARLY SEVEN DECADES TRYING TO KILL AND EAT A PARTICULARLY ODIOUS BIRD.

EVERY ATTEMPT WAS MORE INGENIOUS AND DIABOLICAL THAN THE LAST, BUT SOMEHOW THEY ALL FAILED SPECTACULARLY... AND VERY PAINFULLY.

STILL, I HATE THAT ROAD RUNNER. I'D GIVE ANYTHING TO SEE HIM DEAD AND ON MY DINNER PLATE, BUT I DON'T HAVE IT IN ME TO KEEP TRYING. I'M JUST DONE.

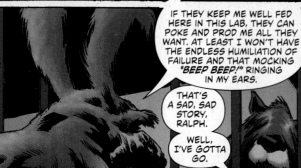

IF THEY KEEP ME WELL FED HERE IN THIS LAB, THEY CAN POKE AND PROD ME ALL THEY WANT. AT LEAST I WON'T HAVE THE ENDLESS HUMILIATION OF FAILURE AND THAT MOCKING "BEEP BEEP!" RINGING IN MY EARS.

THAT'S A SAD, SAD STORY, RALPH.

WELL, I'VE GOTTA GO.

GOOD NIGHT, RALPH. PLEASANT DREAMS.

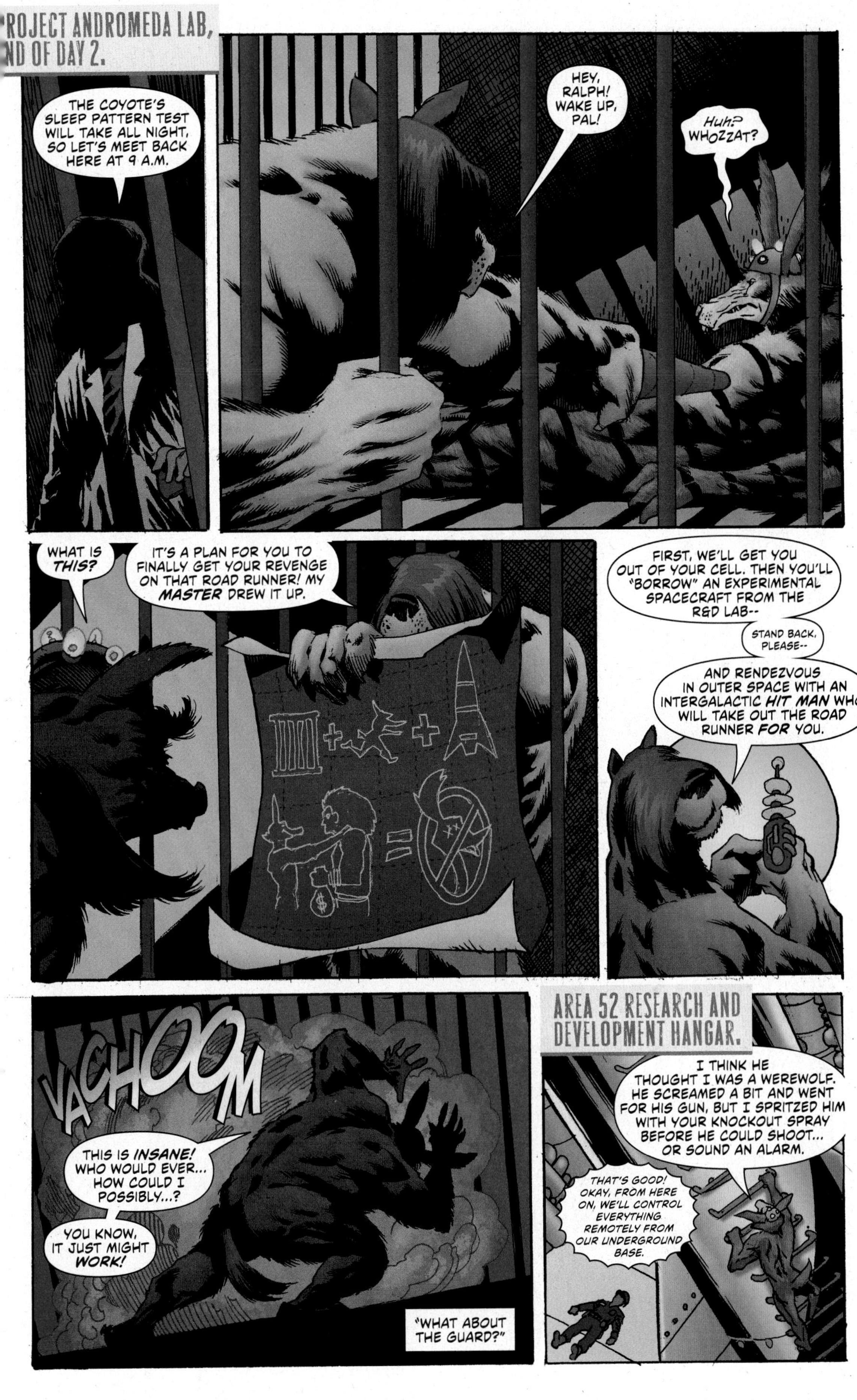
ROJECT ANDROMEDA LAB,
ND OF DAY 2.
THE COYOTE'S SLEEP PATTERN TEST WILL TAKE ALL NIGHT, SO LET'S MEET BACK HERE AT 9 A.M.
HEY, RALPH! WAKE UP, PAL!
Huh? WHOZZAT?
WHAT IS THIS?
IT'S A PLAN FOR YOU TO FINALLY GET YOUR REVENGE ON THAT ROAD RUNNER! MY MASTER DREW IT UP.
FIRST, WE'LL GET YOU OUT OF YOUR CELL. THEN YOU'LL "BORROW" AN EXPERIMENTAL SPACECRAFT FROM THE R&D LAB--
STAND BACK, PLEASE--
AND RENDEZVOUS IN OUTER SPACE WITH AN INTERGALACTIC HIT MAN WHO WILL TAKE OUT THE ROAD RUNNER FOR YOU.
VACHOOM
THIS IS INSANE! WHO WOULD EVER... HOW COULD I POSSIBLY...?
YOU KNOW, IT JUST MIGHT WORK!
"WHAT ABOUT THE GUARD?"
AREA 52 RESEARCH AND DEVELOPMENT HANGAR.
I THINK HE THOUGHT I WAS A WEREWOLF. HE SCREAMED A BIT AND WENT FOR HIS GUN, BUT I SPRITZED HIM WITH YOUR KNOCKOUT SPRAY BEFORE HE COULD SHOOT... OR SOUND AN ALARM.
THAT'S GOOD! OKAY, FROM HERE ON, WE'LL CONTROL EVERYTHING REMOTELY FROM OUR UNDERGROUND BASE.

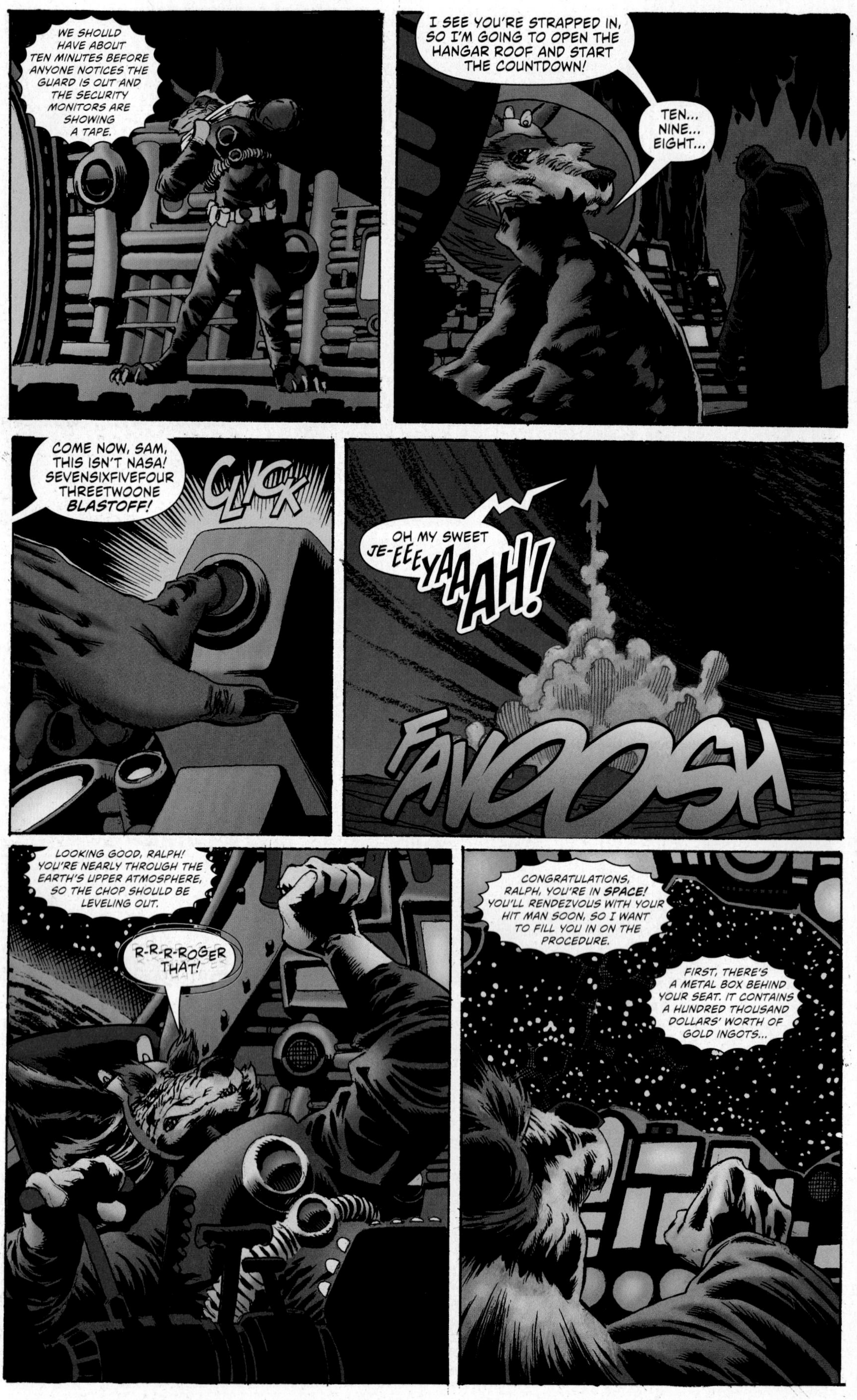
WE SHOULD HAVE ABOUT TEN MINUTES BEFORE ANYONE NOTICES THE GUARD IS OUT AND THE SECURITY MONITORS ARE SHOWING A TAPE.
I SEE YOU'RE STRAPPED IN, SO I'M GOING TO OPEN THE HANGAR ROOF AND START THE COUNTDOWN!
TEN... NINE... EIGHT...
COME NOW, SAM, THIS ISN'T NASA! SEVENSIXFIVEFOUR THREETWOONE BLASTOFF!
CLICK
OH MY SWEET JE-EEEYAAAAH!
FAWOOSH
LOOKING GOOD, RALPH! YOU'RE NEARLY THROUGH THE EARTH'S UPPER ATMOSPHERE, SO THE CHOP SHOULD BE LEVELING OUT.
R-R-R-ROGER THAT!
CONGRATULATIONS, RALPH, YOU'RE IN SPACE! YOU'LL RENDEZVOUS WITH YOUR HIT MAN SOON, SO I WANT TO FILL YOU IN ON THE PROCEDURE.
FIRST, THERE'S A METAL BOX BEHIND YOUR SEAT. IT CONTAINS A HUNDRED THOUSAND DOLLARS' WORTH OF GOLD INGOTS...

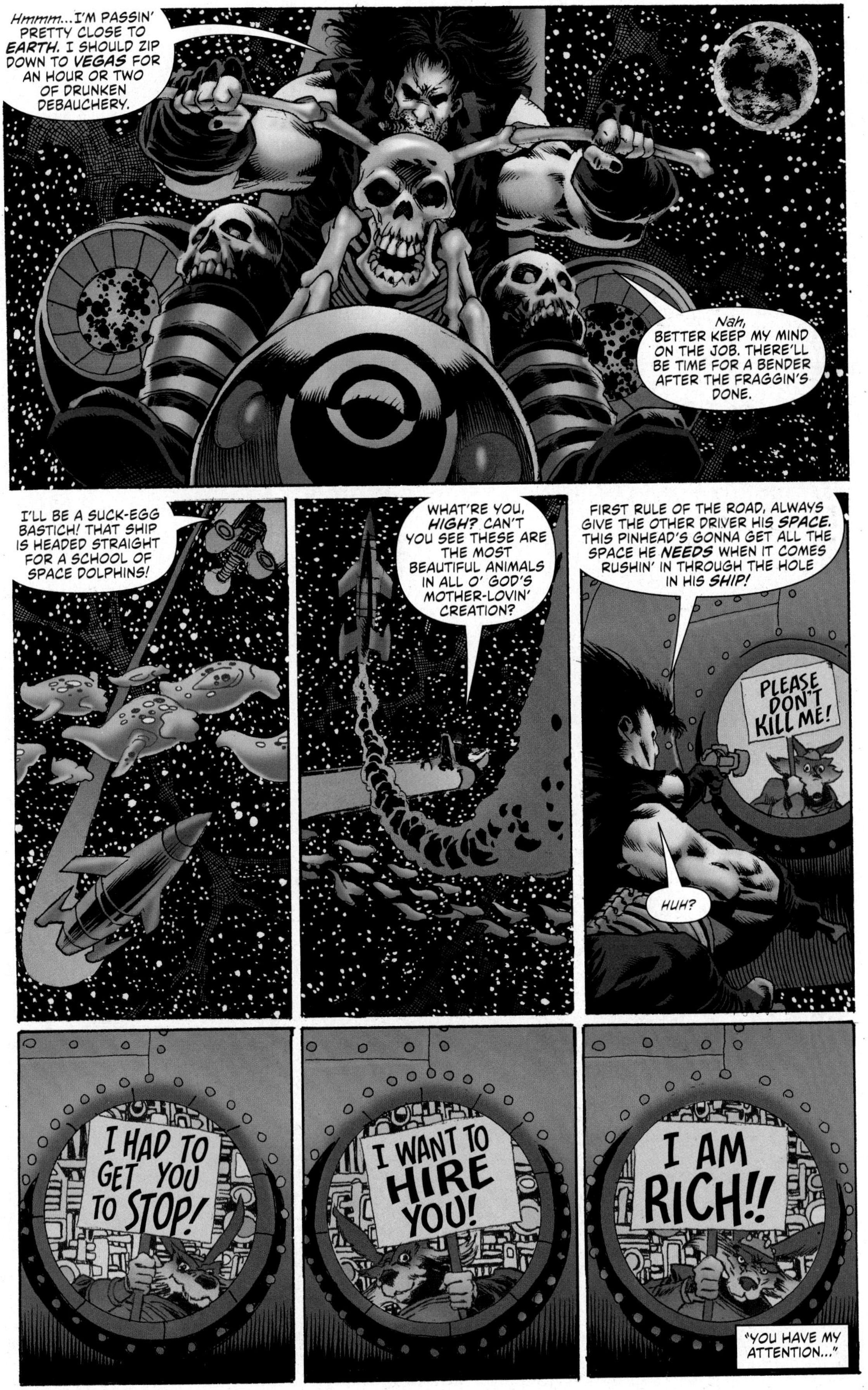
Hmmm...I'M PASSIN' PRETTY CLOSE TO EARTH. I SHOULD ZIP DOWN TO VEGAS FOR AN HOUR OR TWO OF DRUNKEN DEBAUCHERY.
Nah, BETTER KEEP MY MIND ON THE JOB. THERE'LL BE TIME FOR A BENDER AFTER THE FRAGGIN'S DONE.
I'LL BE A SUCK-EGG BASTICH! THAT SHIP IS HEADED STRAIGHT FOR A SCHOOL OF SPACE DOLPHINS!
WHAT'RE YOU, HIGH? CAN'T YOU SEE THESE ARE THE MOST BEAUTIFUL ANIMALS IN ALL O' GOD'S MOTHER-LOVIN' CREATION?
FIRST RULE OF THE ROAD, ALWAYS GIVE THE OTHER DRIVER HIS SPACE. THIS PINHEAD'S GONNA GET ALL THE SPACE HE NEEDS WHEN IT COMES RUSHIN' IN THROUGH THE HOLE IN HIS SHIP!
PLEASE DON'T KILL ME!
HUH?
I HAD TO GET YOU TO STOP!
I WANT TO HIRE YOU!
I AM RICH!!
"YOU HAVE MY ATTENTION..."

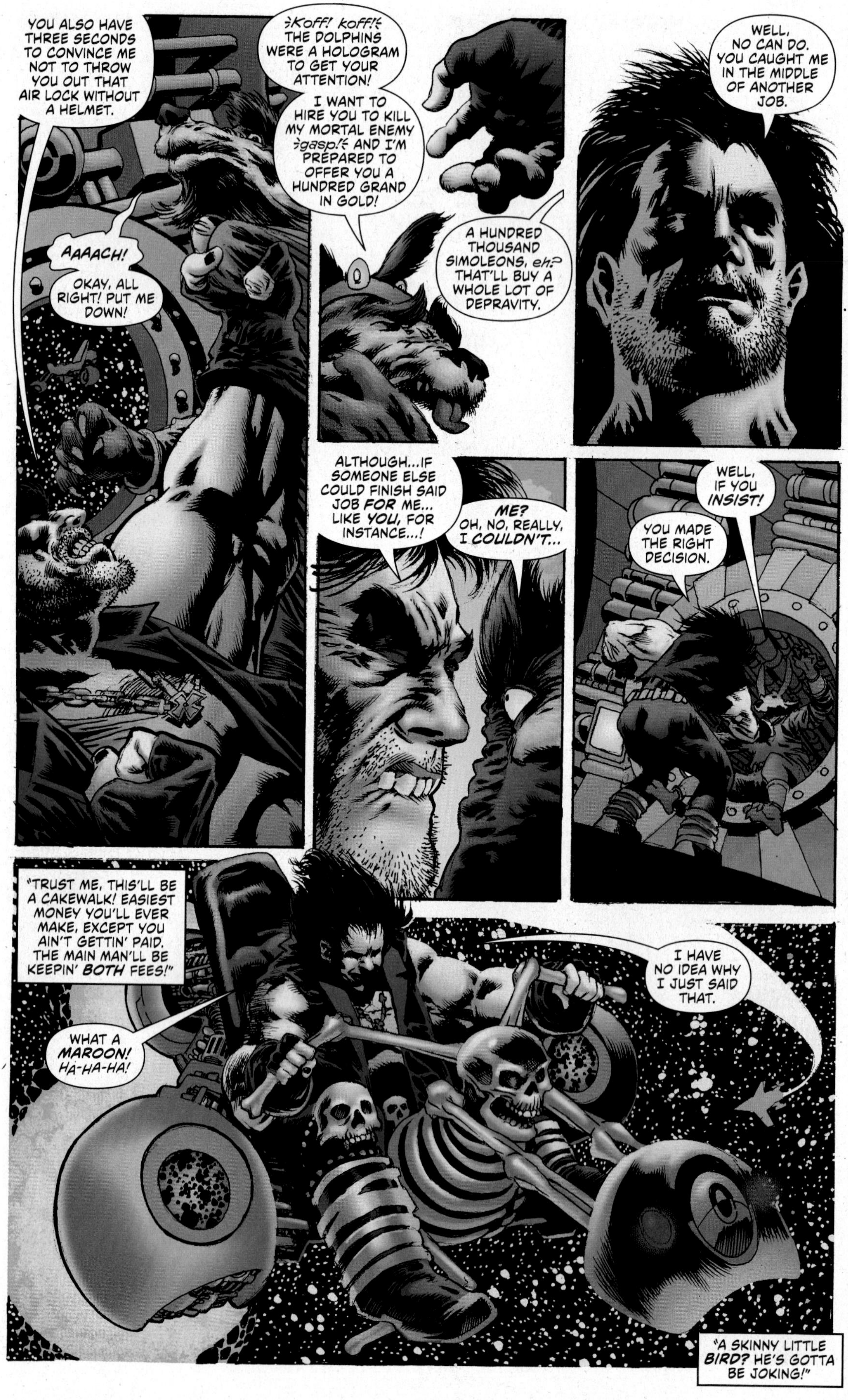
YOU ALSO HAVE THREE SECONDS TO CONVINCE ME NOT TO THROW YOU OUT THAT AIR LOCK WITHOUT A HELMET.
AAAACH!
OKAY, ALL RIGHT! PUT ME DOWN!
KOFF! KOFF! THE DOLPHINS WERE A HOLOGRAM TO GET YOUR ATTENTION!
I WANT TO HIRE YOU TO KILL MY MORTAL ENEMY *GASP!* AND I'M PREPARED TO OFFER YOU A HUNDRED GRAND IN GOLD!
A HUNDRED THOUSAND SIMOLEONS, *EH?* THAT'LL BUY A WHOLE LOT OF DEPRAVITY.
WELL, NO CAN DO. YOU CAUGHT ME IN THE MIDDLE OF ANOTHER JOB.
ALTHOUGH...IF SOMEONE ELSE COULD FINISH SAID JOB FOR ME... LIKE YOU, FOR INSTANCE...!
ME? OH, NO, REALLY, I COULDN'T...
WELL, IF YOU INSIST!
YOU MADE THE RIGHT DECISION.
"TRUST ME, THIS'LL BE A CAKEWALK! EASIEST MONEY YOU'LL EVER MAKE, EXCEPT YOU AIN'T GETTIN' PAID. THE MAIN MAN'LL BE KEEPIN' BOTH FEES!"
WHAT A MAROON! HA-HA-HA!
I HAVE NO IDEA WHY I JUST SAID THAT.
"A SKINNY LITTLE BIRD? HE'S GOTTA BE JOKING!"

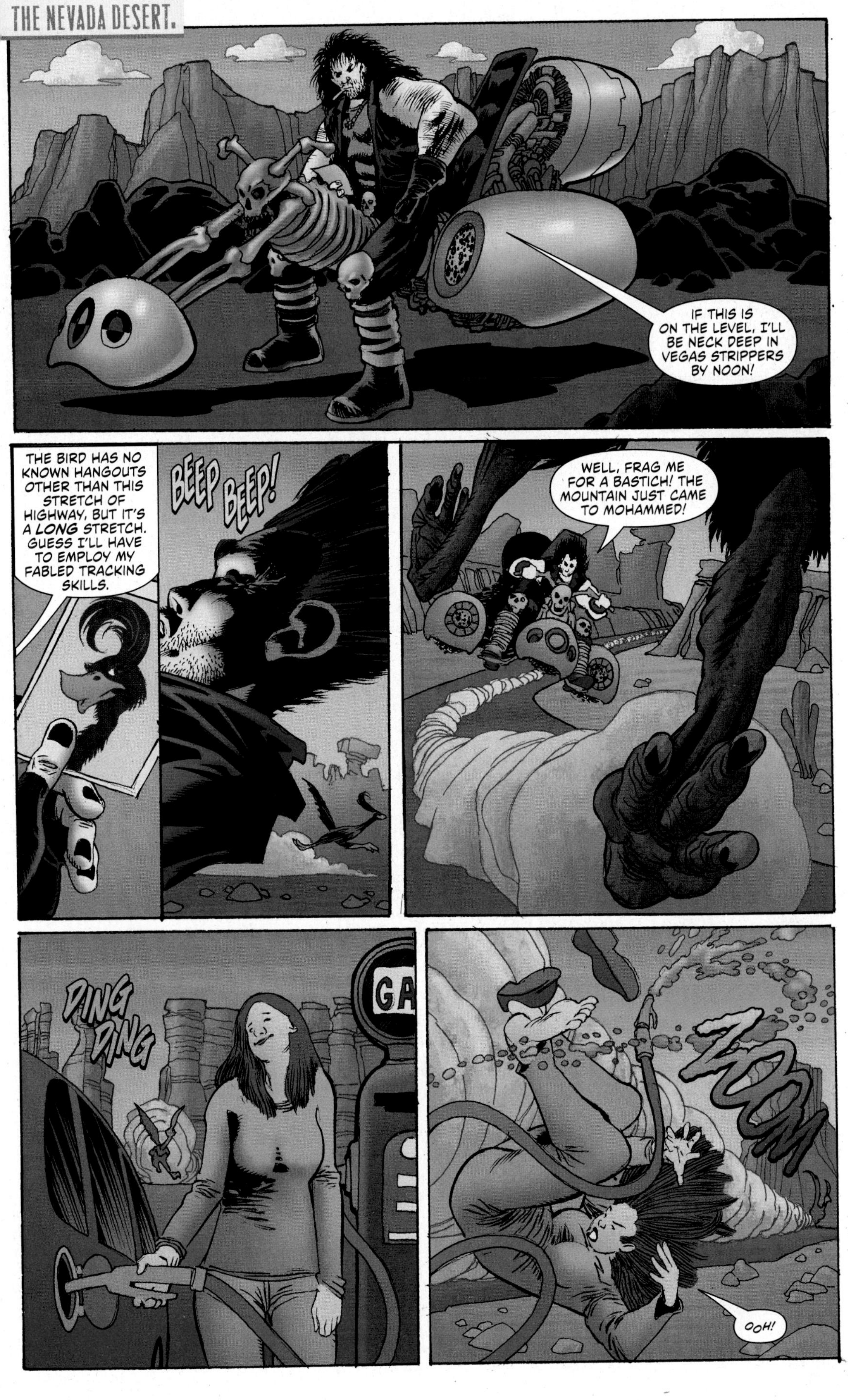
THE NEVADA DESERT.
IF THIS IS ON THE LEVEL, I'LL BE NECK DEEP IN VEGAS STRIPPERS BY NOON!
THE BIRD HAS NO KNOWN HANGOUTS OTHER THAN THIS STRETCH OF HIGHWAY, BUT IT'S A LONG STRETCH. GUESS I'LL HAVE TO EMPLOY MY FABLED TRACKING SKILLS.
BEEP BEEP!
WELL, FRAG ME FOR A BASTICH! THE MOUNTAIN JUST CAME TO MOHAMMED!
DING DING
GA
ZOOM
OOH!

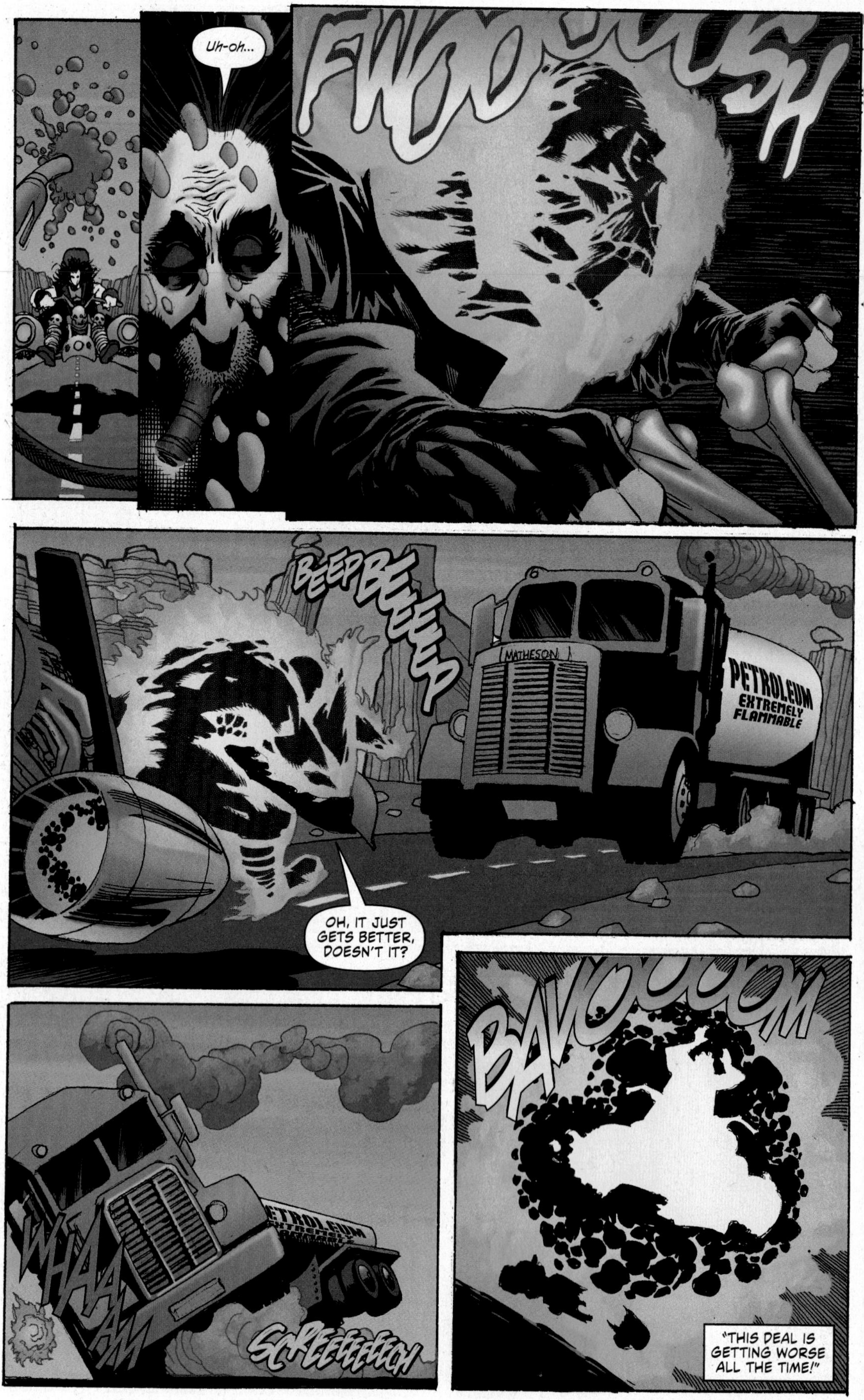
Uh-oh...
FWOOOOSH
BEEP BEEEEEEP
MATHESON
PETROLEUM
EXTREMELY
FLAMMABLE
OH, IT JUST GETS BETTER, DOESN'T IT?
WHAAAM
SCREEEEEEECH
BAVOOOOOM
"THIS DEAL IS GETTING WORSE ALL THE TIME!"

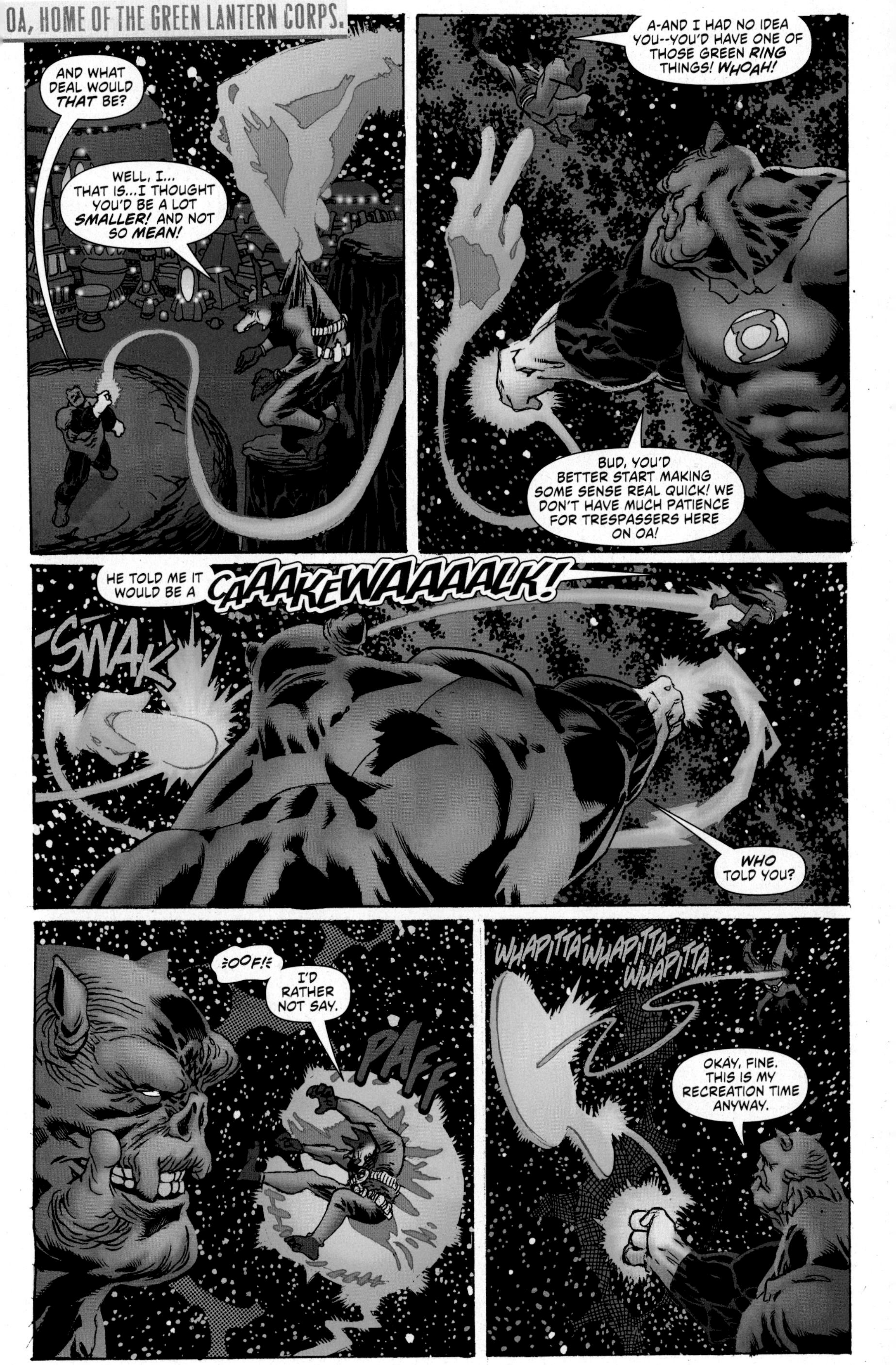
OA, HOME OF THE GREEN LANTERN CORPS.
AND WHAT DEAL WOULD THAT BE?
WELL, I... THAT IS...I THOUGHT YOU'D BE A LOT SMALLER! AND NOT SO MEAN!
A-AND I HAD NO IDEA YOU--YOU'D HAVE ONE OF THOSE GREEN RING THINGS! WHOAH!
BUD, YOU'D BETTER START MAKING SOME SENSE REAL QUICK! WE DON'T HAVE MUCH PATIENCE FOR TRESPASSERS HERE ON OA!
HE TOLD ME IT WOULD BE A CAAAKEWAAAAALK!
SWAK
WHO TOLD YOU?
OOF!
I'D RATHER NOT SAY.
PAFF
WHAPITTA-WHAPITTA-WHAPITTA
OKAY, FINE. THIS IS MY RECREATION TIME ANYWAY.

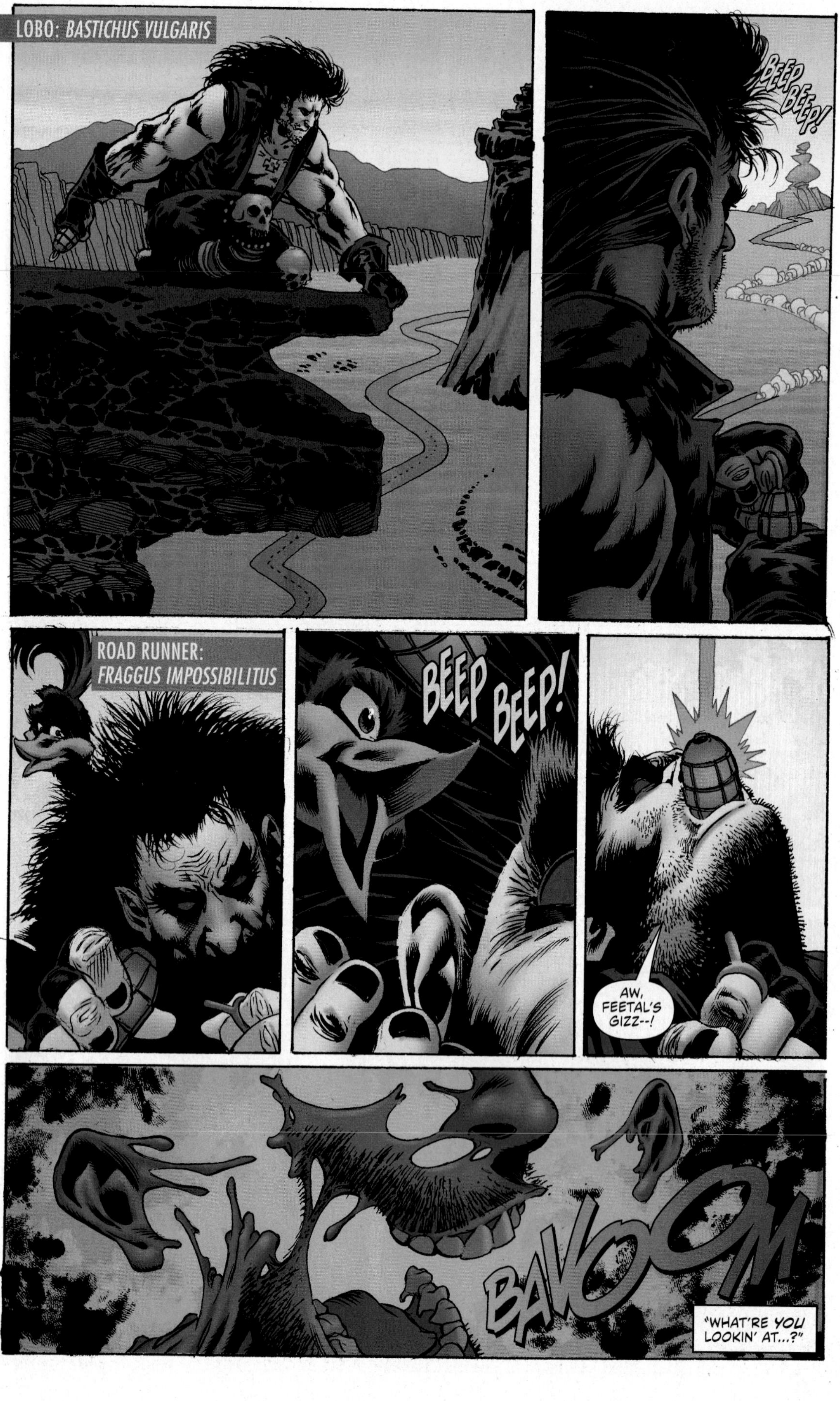
LOBO: *BASTICHUS VULGARIS*
BEEP BEEP!
ROAD RUNNER: *FRAGGUS IMPOSSIBILITUS*
BEEP BEEP!
AW, FEETAL'S GIZZ--!
BAVOOM
"WHAT'RE YOU LOOKIN' AT...?"

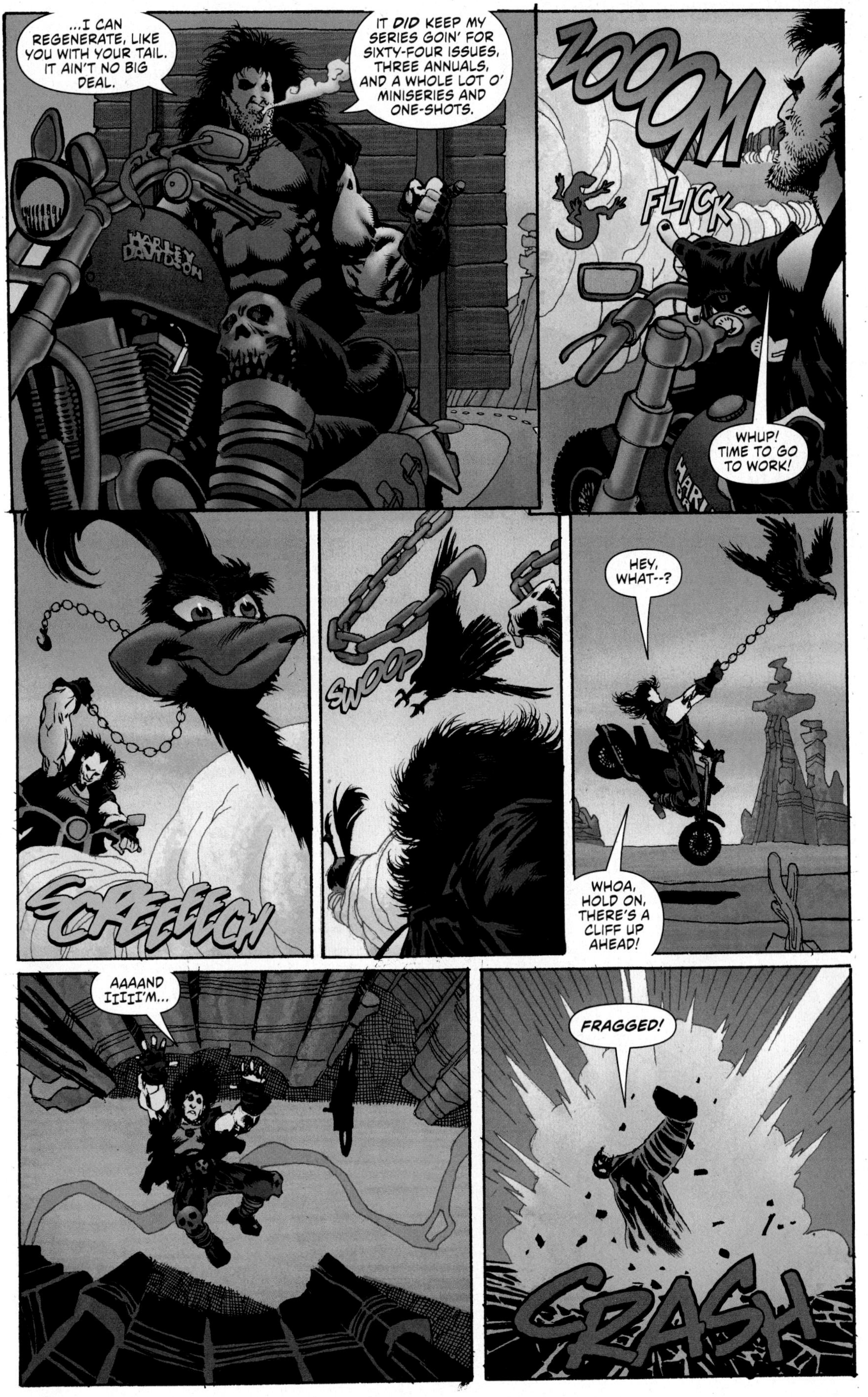

...I CAN REGENERATE, LIKE YOU WITH YOUR TAIL. IT AIN'T NO BIG DEAL.
IT DID KEEP MY SERIES GOIN' FOR SIXTY-FOUR ISSUES, THREE ANNUALS, AND A WHOLE LOT O' MINISERIES AND ONE-SHOTS.
HARLEY DAVIDSON
ZOOOM
FLICK
WHUP! TIME TO GO TO WORK!
SCREEEECH
SWOOP
HEY, WHAT--?
WHOA, HOLD ON, THERE'S A CLIFF UP AHEAD!
AAAAND IIIII'M...
FRAGGED!
CRASH

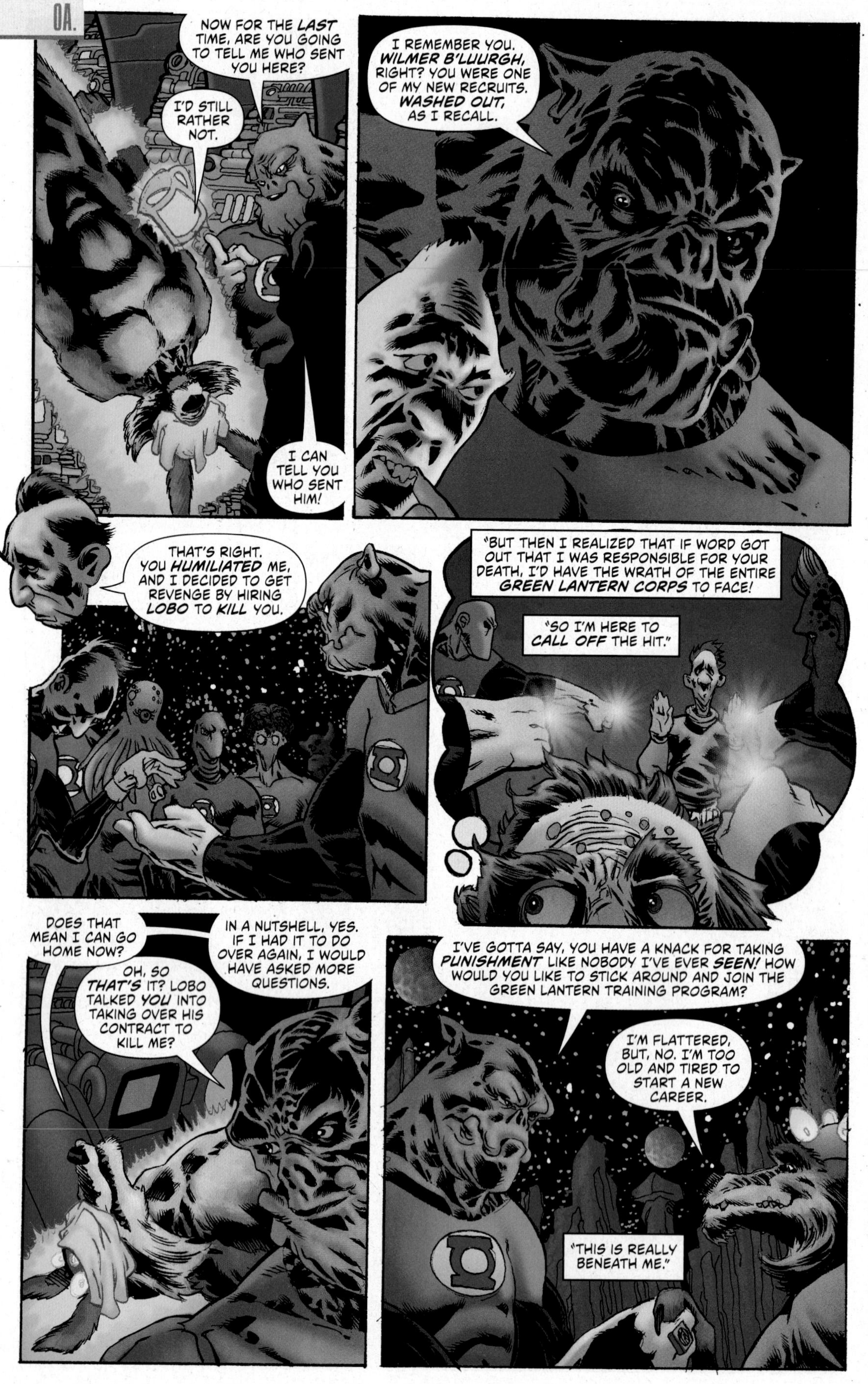
NOW FOR THE LAST TIME, ARE YOU GOING TO TELL ME WHO SENT YOU HERE?
I'D STILL RATHER NOT.
I CAN TELL YOU WHO SENT HIM!
I REMEMBER YOU. WILMER B'LUURGH, RIGHT? YOU WERE ONE OF MY NEW RECRUITS. WASHED OUT, AS I RECALL.
THAT'S RIGHT. YOU HUMILIATED ME, AND I DECIDED TO GET REVENGE BY HIRING LOBO TO KILL YOU.
"BUT THEN I REALIZED THAT IF WORD GOT OUT THAT I WAS RESPONSIBLE FOR YOUR DEATH, I'D HAVE THE WRATH OF THE ENTIRE GREEN LANTERN CORPS TO FACE!
"SO I'M HERE TO CALL OFF THE HIT."
DOES THAT MEAN I CAN GO HOME NOW?
OH, SO THAT'S IT? LOBO TALKED YOU INTO TAKING OVER HIS CONTRACT TO KILL ME?
IN A NUTSHELL, YES. IF I HAD IT TO DO OVER AGAIN, I WOULD HAVE ASKED MORE QUESTIONS.
I'VE GOTTA SAY, YOU HAVE A KNACK FOR TAKING PUNISHMENT LIKE NOBODY I'VE EVER SEEN! HOW WOULD YOU LIKE TO STICK AROUND AND JOIN THE GREEN LANTERN TRAINING PROGRAM?
I'M FLATTERED, BUT, NO. I'M TOO OLD AND TIRED TO START A NEW CAREER.
"THIS IS REALLY BENEATH ME."

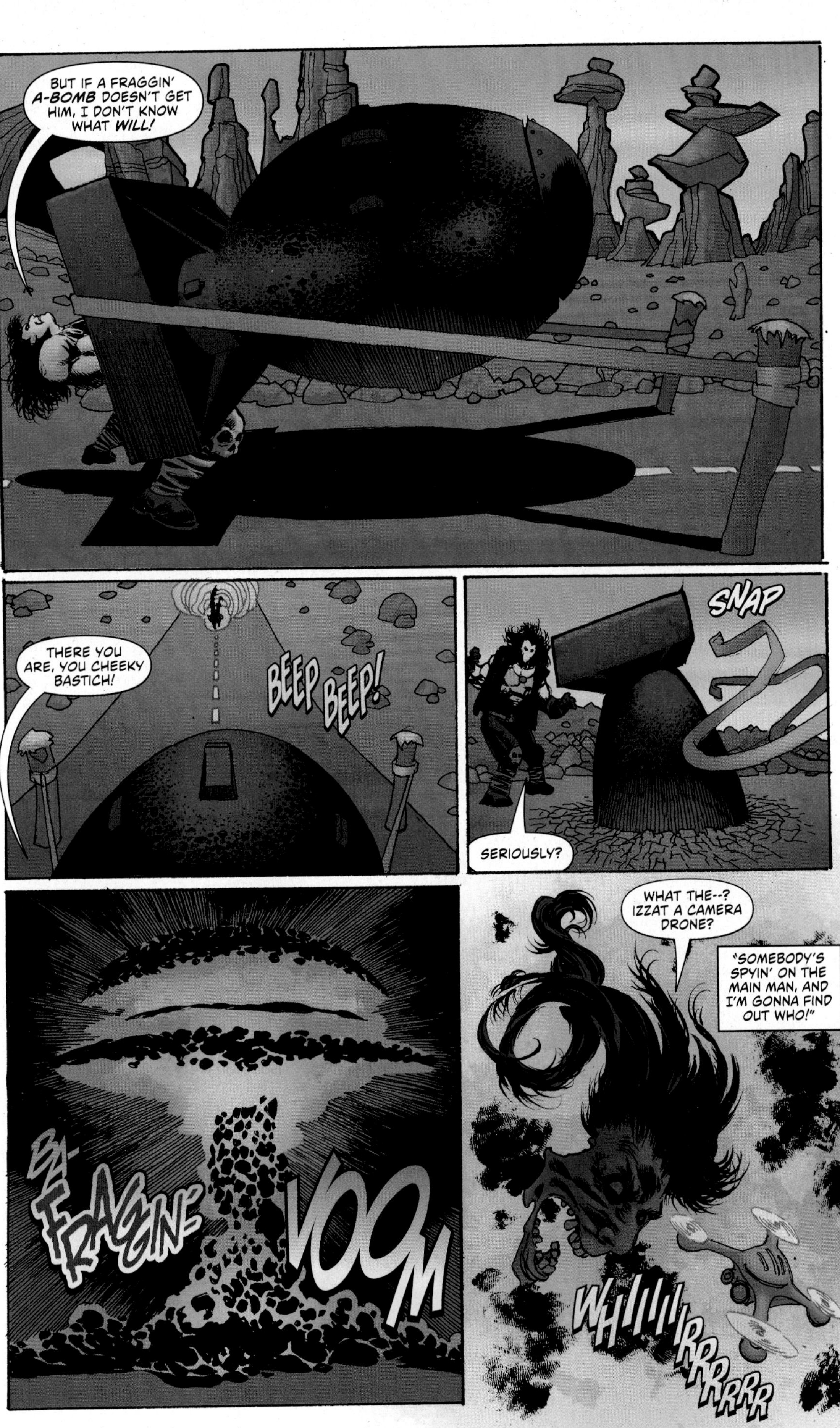
BUT IF A FRAGGIN' A-BOMB DOESN'T GET HIM, I DON'T KNOW WHAT WILL!
THERE YOU ARE, YOU CHEEKY BASTICH!
BEEP BEEP!
SNAP
SERIOUSLY?
BA-FRAGGIN'-VOOM
WHAT THE--? IZZAT A CAMERA DRONE?
"SOMEBODY'S SPYIN' ON THE MAIN MAN, AND I'M GONNA FIND OUT WHO!"
WHIIIIIRRRRRRR

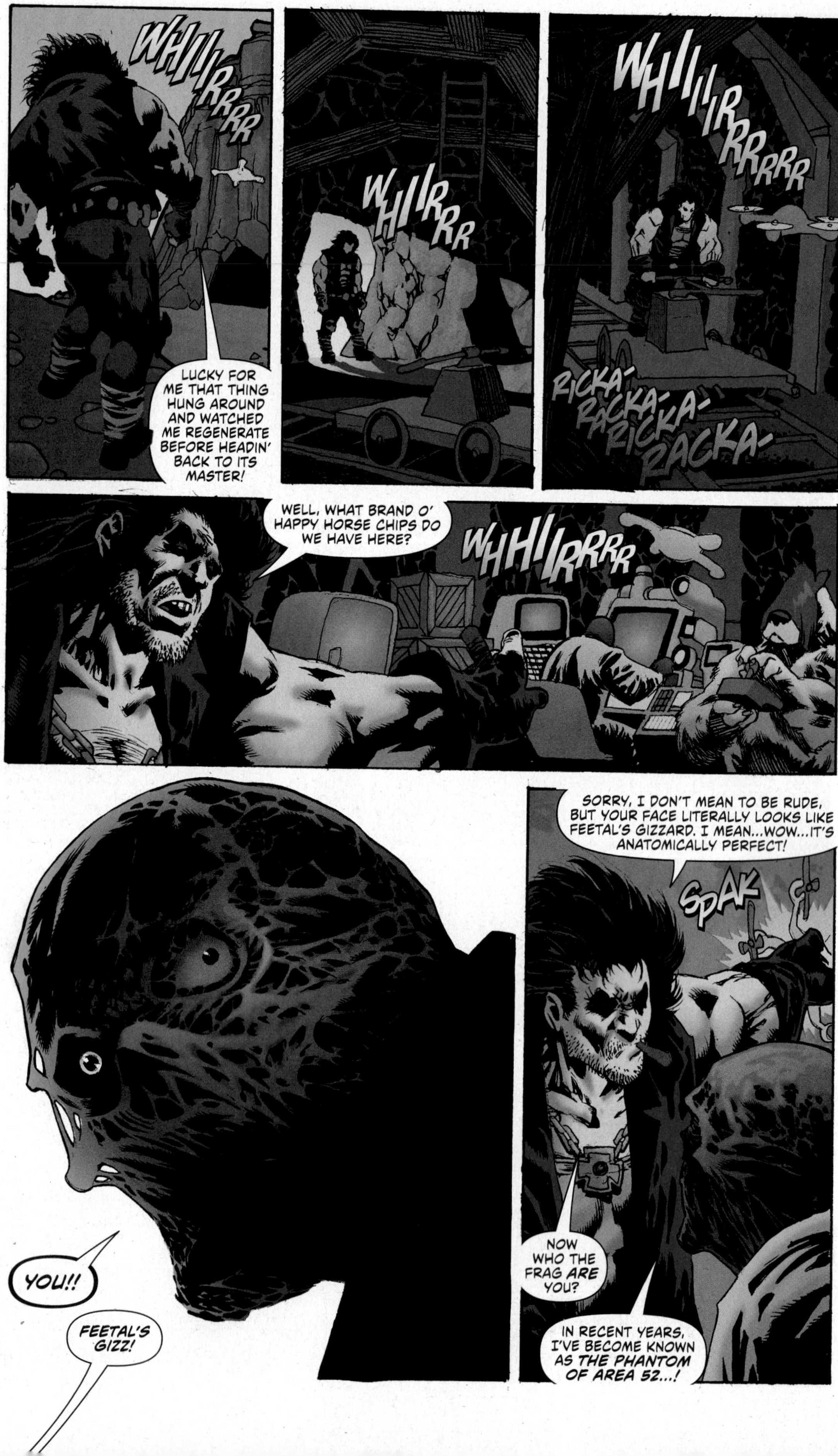
WHIIRRRR
LUCKY FOR ME THAT THING HUNG AROUND AND WATCHED ME REGENERATE BEFORE HEADIN' BACK TO ITS MASTER!
WHIIRRRR
WHIIIIRRRRRR
RICKA-RACKA-RICKA-RACKA-
WELL, WHAT BRAND O' HAPPY HORSE CHIPS DO WE HAVE HERE?
WHHIIRRRR
YOU!!
FEETAL'S GIZZ!
SORRY, I DON'T MEAN TO BE RUDE, BUT YOUR FACE LITERALLY LOOKS LIKE FEETAL'S GIZZARD. I MEAN...WOW...IT'S ANATOMICALLY PERFECT!
SPAK
NOW WHO THE FRAG ARE YOU?
IN RECENT YEARS, I'VE BECOME KNOWN AS THE PHANTOM OF AREA 52...!

"...BUT IN 1949, I WAS **DR. CHARLES CALDWELL** OF ACME LABORATORIES.

"AFTER LOSING THE SUBJECTS OF AN ALIEN DNA EXPERIMENT, I MUTATED MY PET SHEEP DOG, SAM, AND THEN DECIDED TO TRY THE FORMULA ON MYSELF.

"YOU CAN SEE THE RESULT. IT DOESN'T WORK QUITE AS WELL ON HUMANS AS IT DOES ON ANIMALS.

"I'VE BEEN LIVING UNDER MY OLD LAB AND USING A SECRET TUNNEL TO RAID AREA 52 FOR SUPPLIES.

"I SPENT **DECADES** STUDYING TWO OF MY ESCAPED SUBJECTS, THE **COYOTE** AND **ROAD RUNNER!** THE COYOTE'S INVENTIVENESS AND RESILIENCE WERE **FASCINATING,** AND THE ROAD RUNNER'S ABILITY TO AVOID DESTRUCTION DEFIED NATURAL LAW!"

WHEN THE COYOTE APPEARED TO BE LOSING STEAM, I USED THE ALIEN DATABASE AT AREA 52 TO FIND A **NEW** SUPER PREDATOR FOR THE ROAD RUNNER. **YOU!**

I DON'T KNOW HOW I CAN MAKE YOUR FACE ANY **UGLIER,** BUT I'M SURE GONNA GIVE IT MY **BEST** SHOT!

WAIT! IT LOOKS LIKE THE COYOTE IS BACK!

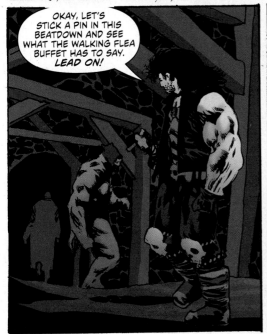

OKAY, LET'S STICK A PIN IN THIS BEATDOWN AND SEE WHAT THE WALKING FLEA BUFFET HAS TO SAY. **LEAD ON!**

HEY, SPACE COYOTE. I ASSUME THE JOB IS DONE?

NOT EXACTLY. BUT IT IS **FINISHED.** YOUR CLIENT, WILMER B'LUURGH, HAD A CHANGE OF HEART AND CANCELLED THE CONTRACT.

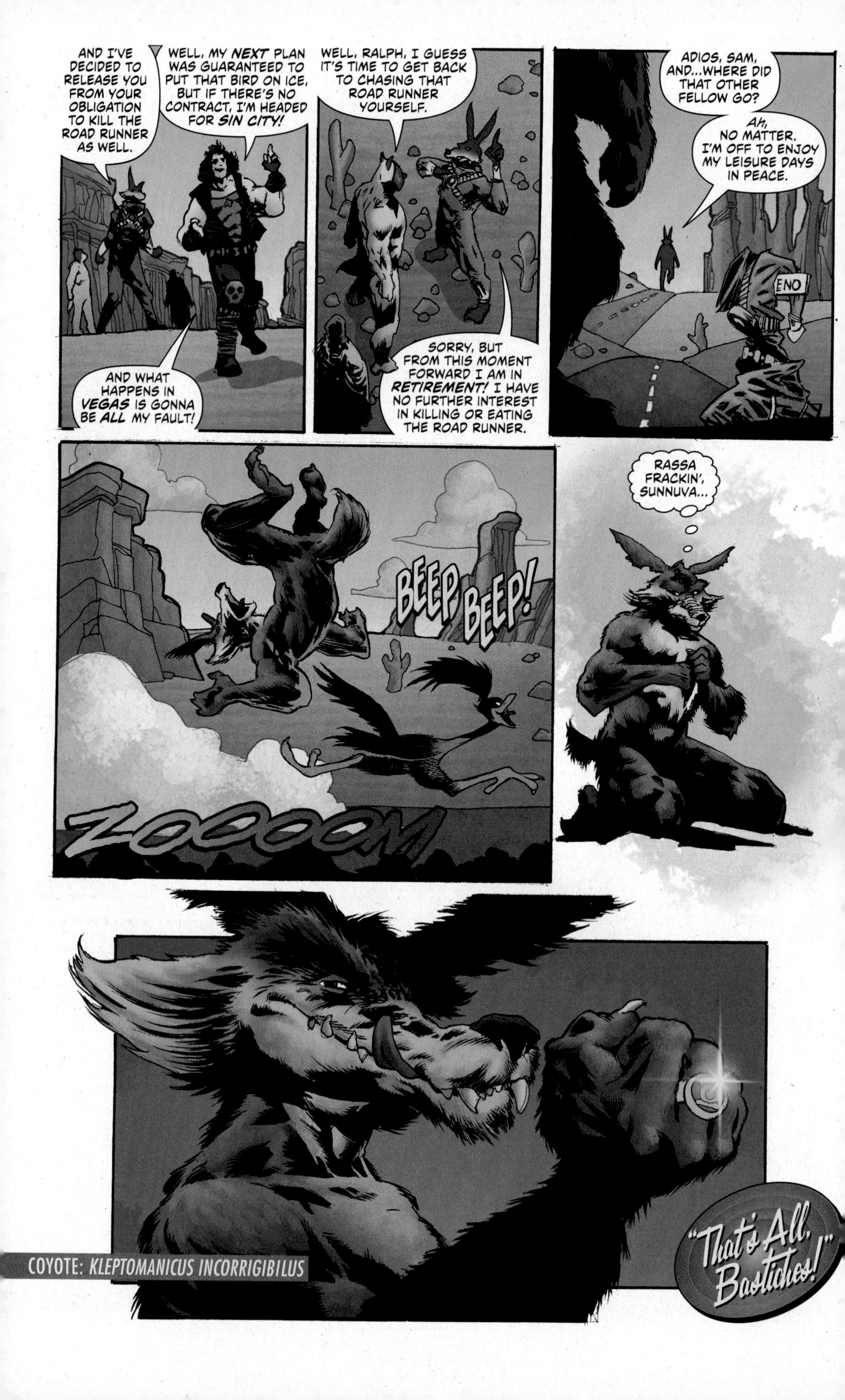

AND I'VE DECIDED TO RELEASE YOU FROM YOUR OBLIGATION TO KILL THE ROAD RUNNER AS WELL.
WELL, MY NEXT PLAN WAS GUARANTEED TO PUT THAT BIRD ON ICE, BUT IF THERE'S NO CONTRACT, I'M HEADED FOR SIN CITY!
AND WHAT HAPPENS IN VEGAS IS GONNA BE ALL MY FAULT!
WELL, RALPH, I GUESS IT'S TIME TO GET BACK TO CHASING THAT ROAD RUNNER YOURSELF.
SORRY, BUT FROM THIS MOMENT FORWARD I AM IN RETIREMENT! I HAVE NO FURTHER INTEREST IN KILLING OR EATING THE ROAD RUNNER.
ADIOS, SAM, AND...WHERE DID THAT OTHER FELLOW GO?
Ah, NO MATTER. I'M OFF TO ENJOY MY LEISURE DAYS IN PEACE.
ENO
BEEP BEEP!
ZOOOOM
RASSA FRACKIN', SUNNUVA...
COYOTE: KLEPTOMANICUS INCORRIGIBILUS
"That's All, Bastiches!"

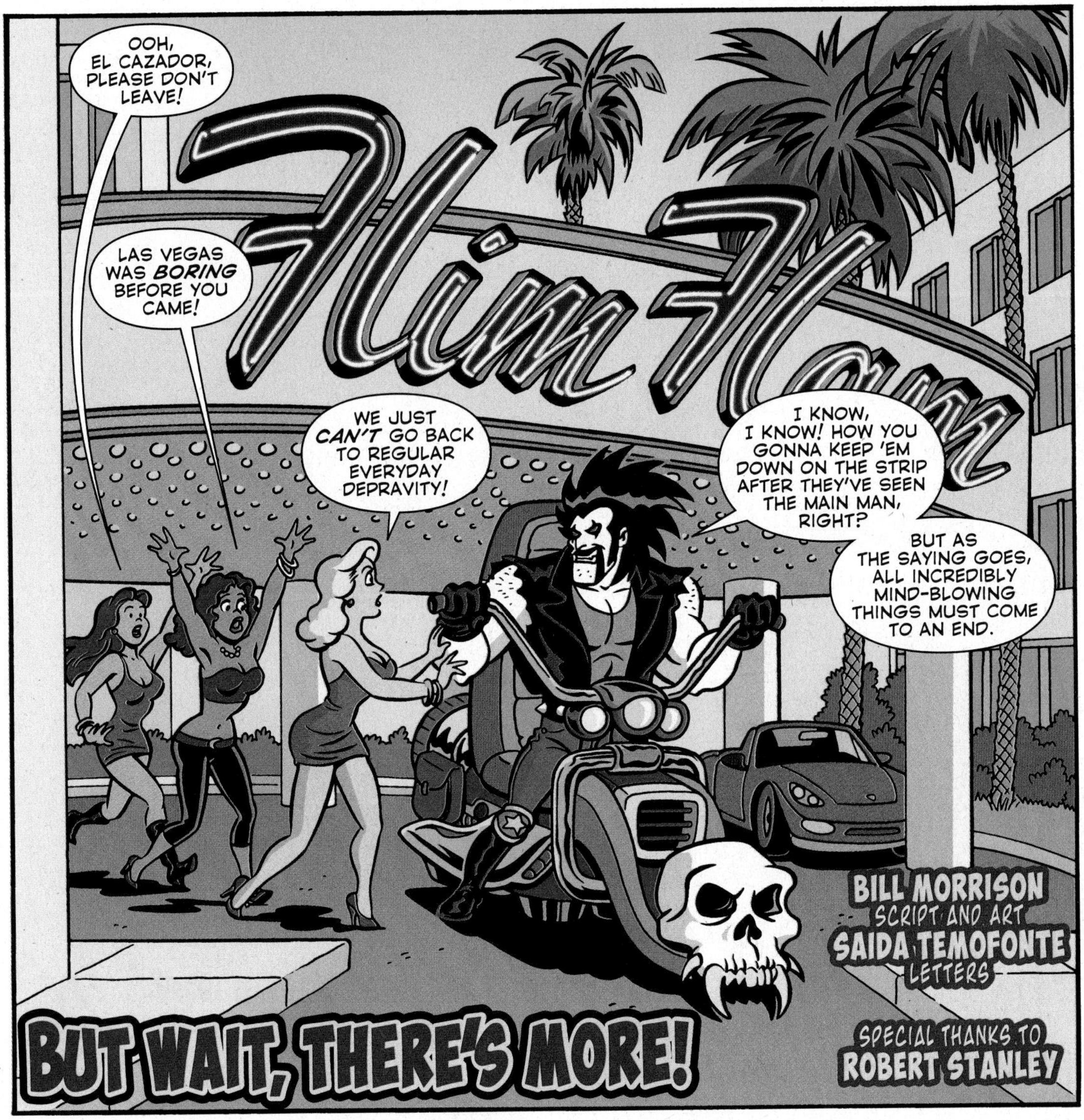
OOH, EL CAZADOR, PLEASE DON'T LEAVE!
LAS VEGAS WAS *BORING* BEFORE YOU CAME!
WE JUST *CAN'T* GO BACK TO REGULAR EVERYDAY DEPRAVITY!
I KNOW, I KNOW! HOW YOU GONNA KEEP 'EM DOWN ON THE STRIP AFTER THEY'VE SEEN THE MAIN MAN, RIGHT?
BUT AS THE SAYING GOES, ALL INCREDIBLY MIND-BLOWING THINGS MUST COME TO AN END.
Flim Flam
BUT WAIT, THERE'S MORE!
BILL MORRISON
SCRIPT AND ART
SAIDA TEMOFONTE
LETTERS
SPECIAL THANKS TO
ROBERT STANLEY

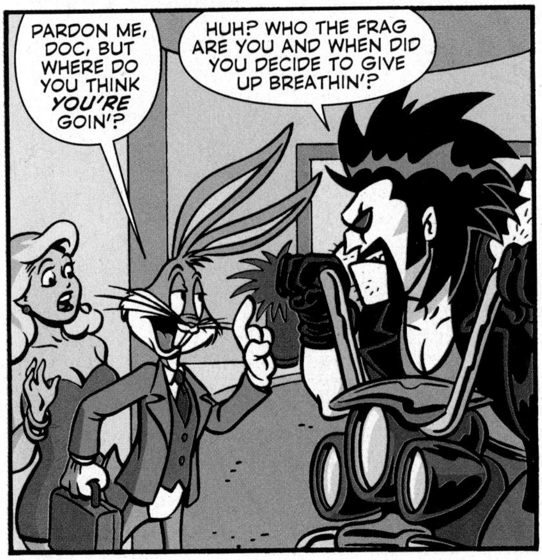
PARDON ME, DOC, BUT WHERE DO YOU THINK *YOU'RE* GOIN'?
HUH? WHO THE FRAG ARE YOU AND WHEN DID YOU DECIDE TO GIVE UP BREATHIN'?

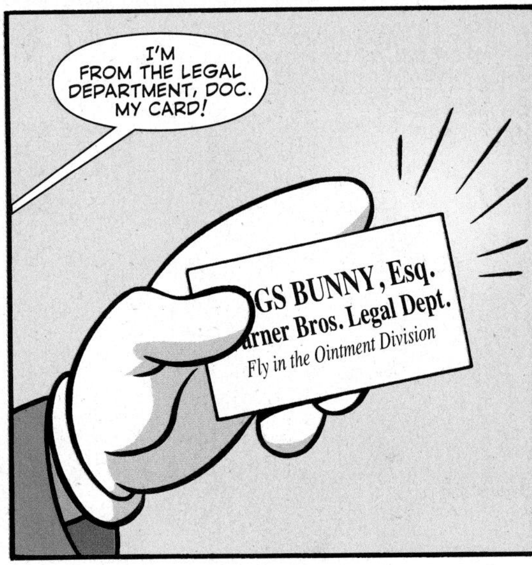
I'M FROM THE LEGAL DEPARTMENT, DOC. MY CARD!
GS BUNNY, Esq.
arner Bros. Legal Dept.
Fly in the Ointment Division

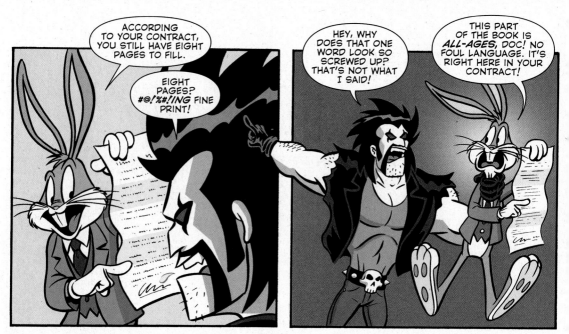

ACCORDING TO YOUR CONTRACT, YOU STILL HAVE EIGHT PAGES TO FILL.

EIGHT PAGES? #@!%#!ING FINE PRINT!

HEY, WHY DOES THAT ONE WORD LOOK SO SCREWED UP? THAT'S NOT WHAT I SAID!

THIS PART OF THE BOOK IS ALL-AGES, DOC! NO FOUL LANGUAGE. IT'S RIGHT HERE IN YOUR CONTRACT!

WHY IN THE #%@!! ARE THESE PAGES ANY DIFFERENT FROM THE REST OF THE BOOK?

BECAUSE IN THESE PAGES YOU HAVE TO TRY TO BEAT THE ROAD RUNNER IN THE LOONEY TUNES STYLE, AND WE HAVE A BRAND TO PROTECT. IT'S ALL IN THE CONTRACT.

LOONEY WHAT--?

HOLY FRAGARONI! WHAT HAPPENED TO ALL MY GRIM AND GRITTY REALISM?

YOU'RE KID-FRIENDLY NOW, DOC! IT'S ALL IN THE--

YEAH, THE CONTRACT, I KNOW, I KNOW. WELL THE 'BO ALWAYS HONORS HIS CONTRACTUAL OBLIGATIONS, SO LET'S GET THIS OVER WITH.

EXCELLENT, DOC! NOW EXCUSE ME WHILE I GO AIR OUT MY BRIEFS!

KRAK

HELLO, ACME? I WANNA PLACE A RUSH ORDER...

ACME CATALOG

CUSTOMER OF THE YEAR

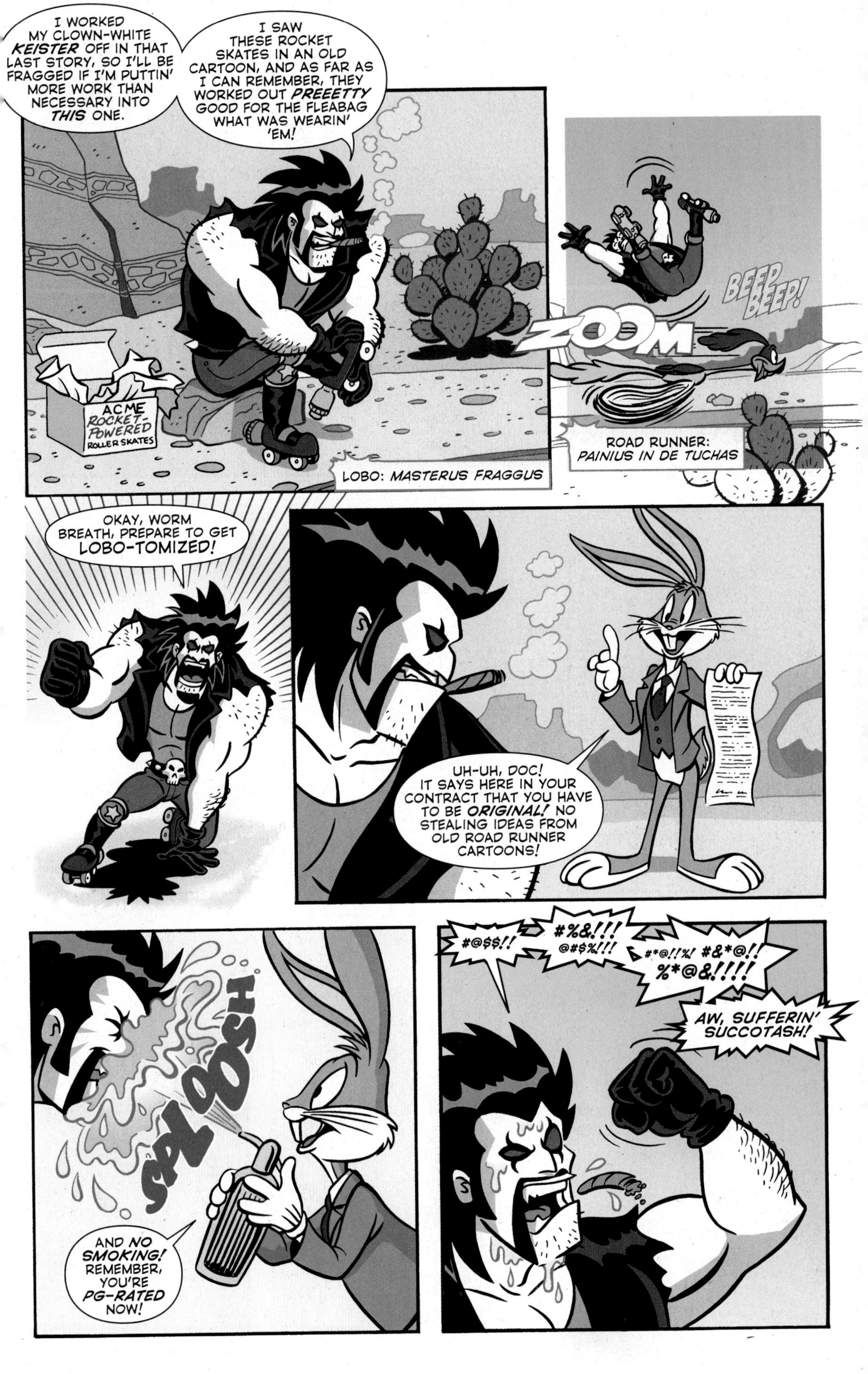
I WORKED MY CLOWN-WHITE KEISTER OFF IN THAT LAST STORY, SO I'LL BE FRAGGED IF I'M PUTTIN' MORE WORK THAN NECESSARY INTO THIS ONE.
I SAW THESE ROCKET SKATES IN AN OLD CARTOON, AND AS FAR AS I CAN REMEMBER, THEY WORKED OUT PREEETTY GOOD FOR THE FLEABAG WHAT WAS WEARIN' 'EM!
ACME ROCKET-POWERED ROLLER SKATES
LOBO: MASTERUS FRAGGUS
BEEP BEEP!
ZOOM
ROAD RUNNER: PAINIUS IN DE TUCHAS
OKAY, WORM BREATH, PREPARE TO GET LOBO-TOMIZED!
UH-UH, DOC! IT SAYS HERE IN YOUR CONTRACT THAT YOU HAVE TO BE ORIGINAL! NO STEALING IDEAS FROM OLD ROAD RUNNER CARTOONS!
SPLOOSH
AND NO SMOKING! REMEMBER, YOU'RE PG-RATED NOW!
#@$$!!
#%&!!!
@#$%!!!
#*@!!%! #&*@!!
%*@&!!!!
AW, SUFFERIN' SUCCOTASH!

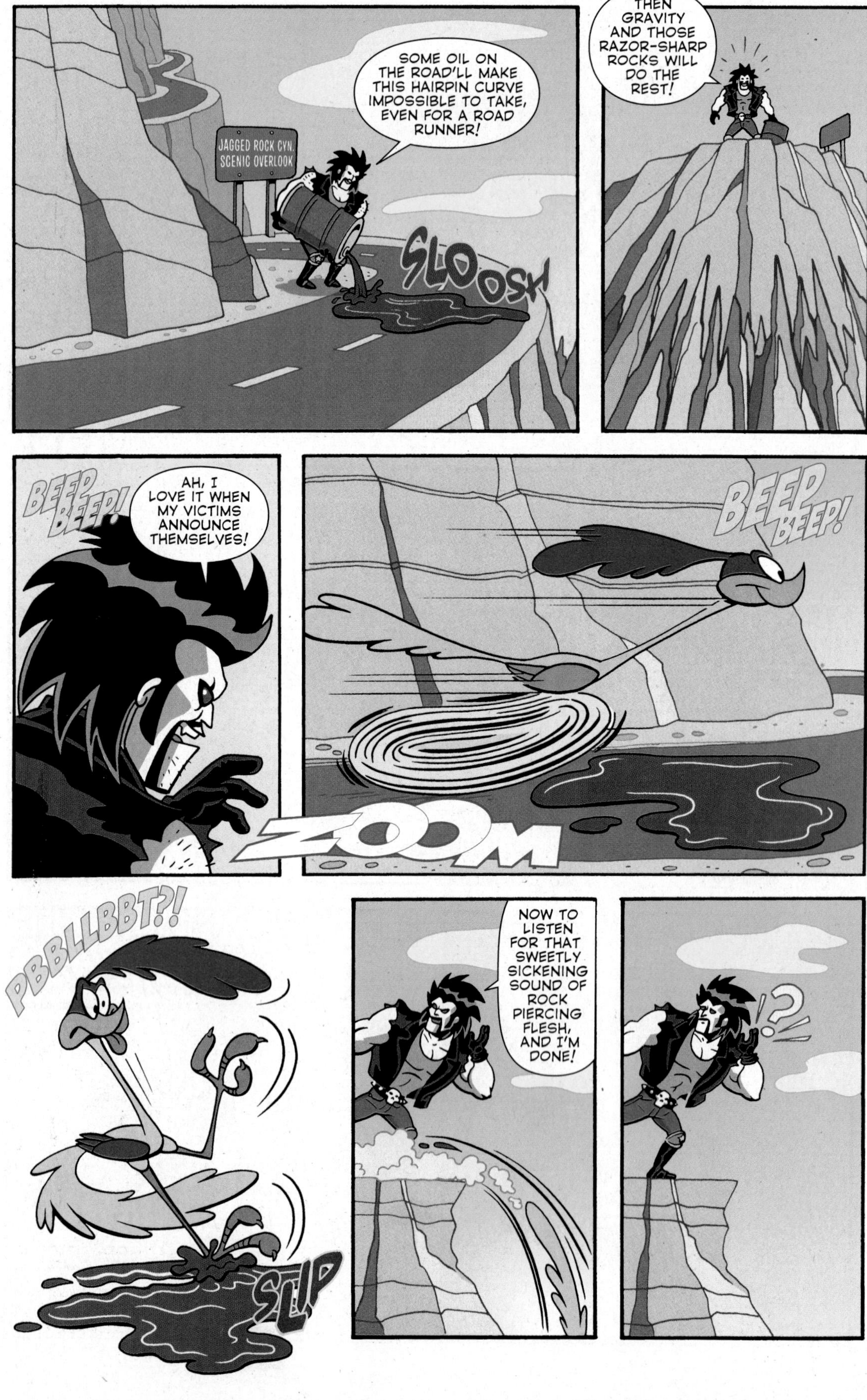
JAGGED ROCK CYN. SCENIC OVERLOOK
SOME OIL ON THE ROAD'LL MAKE THIS HAIRPIN CURVE IMPOSSIBLE TO TAKE, EVEN FOR A ROAD RUNNER!
SLOOSH
THEN GRAVITY AND THOSE RAZOR-SHARP ROCKS WILL DO THE REST!
BEEP BEEP!
AH, I LOVE IT WHEN MY VICTIMS ANNOUNCE THEMSELVES!
BEEP BEEP!
ZOOM
PBBLLBBT?!
SLIP
NOW TO LISTEN FOR THAT SWEETLY SICKENING SOUND OF ROCK PIERCING FLESH, AND I'M DONE!
!?

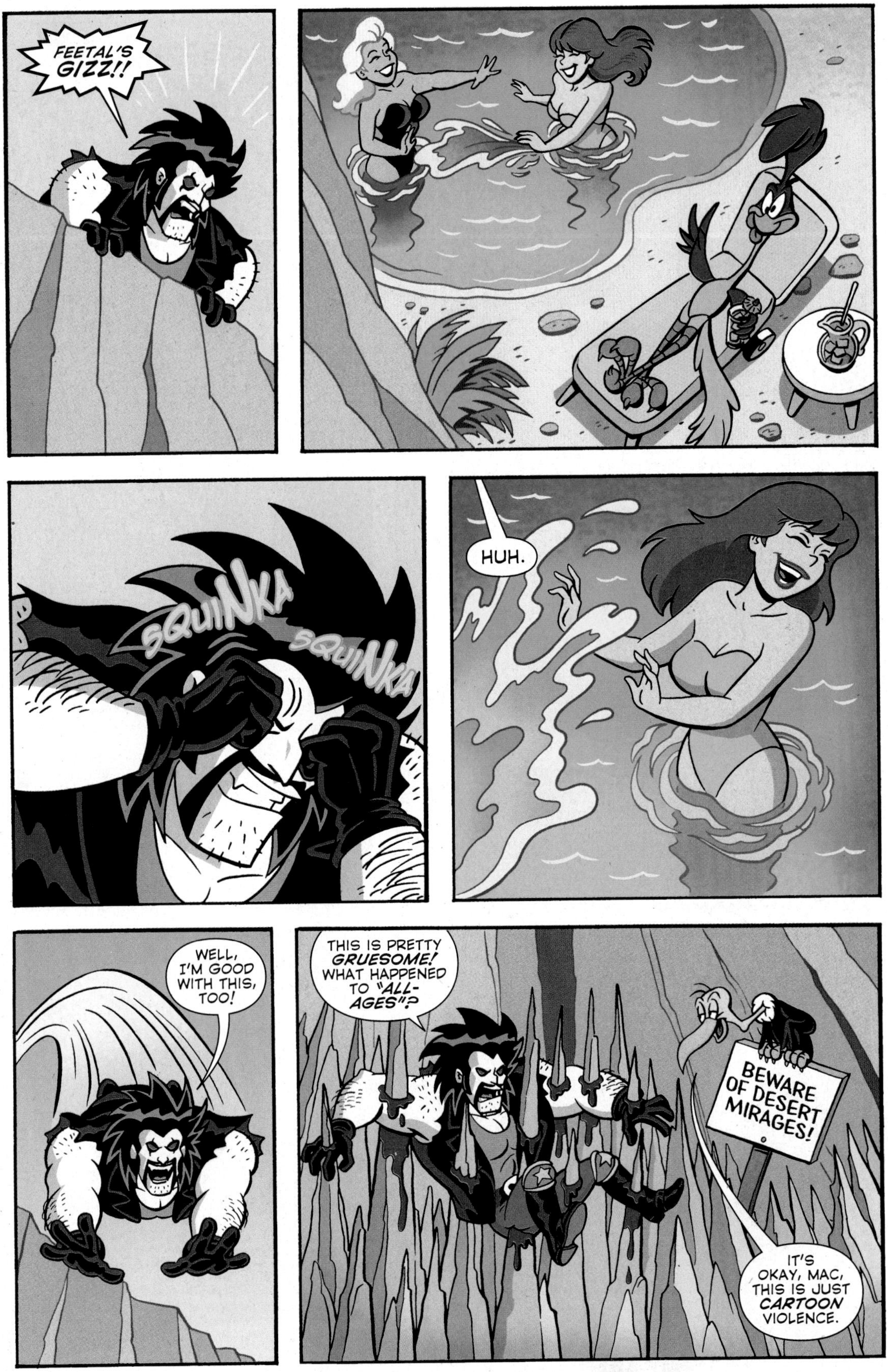

FEETAL'S GIZZ!!
SQUINKA SQUINKA
HUH.
WELL, I'M GOOD WITH THIS, TOO!
THIS IS PRETTY GRUESOME! WHAT HAPPENED TO "ALL-AGES"?
BEWARE OF DESERT MIRAGES!
IT'S OKAY, MAC, THIS IS JUST CARTOON VIOLENCE.

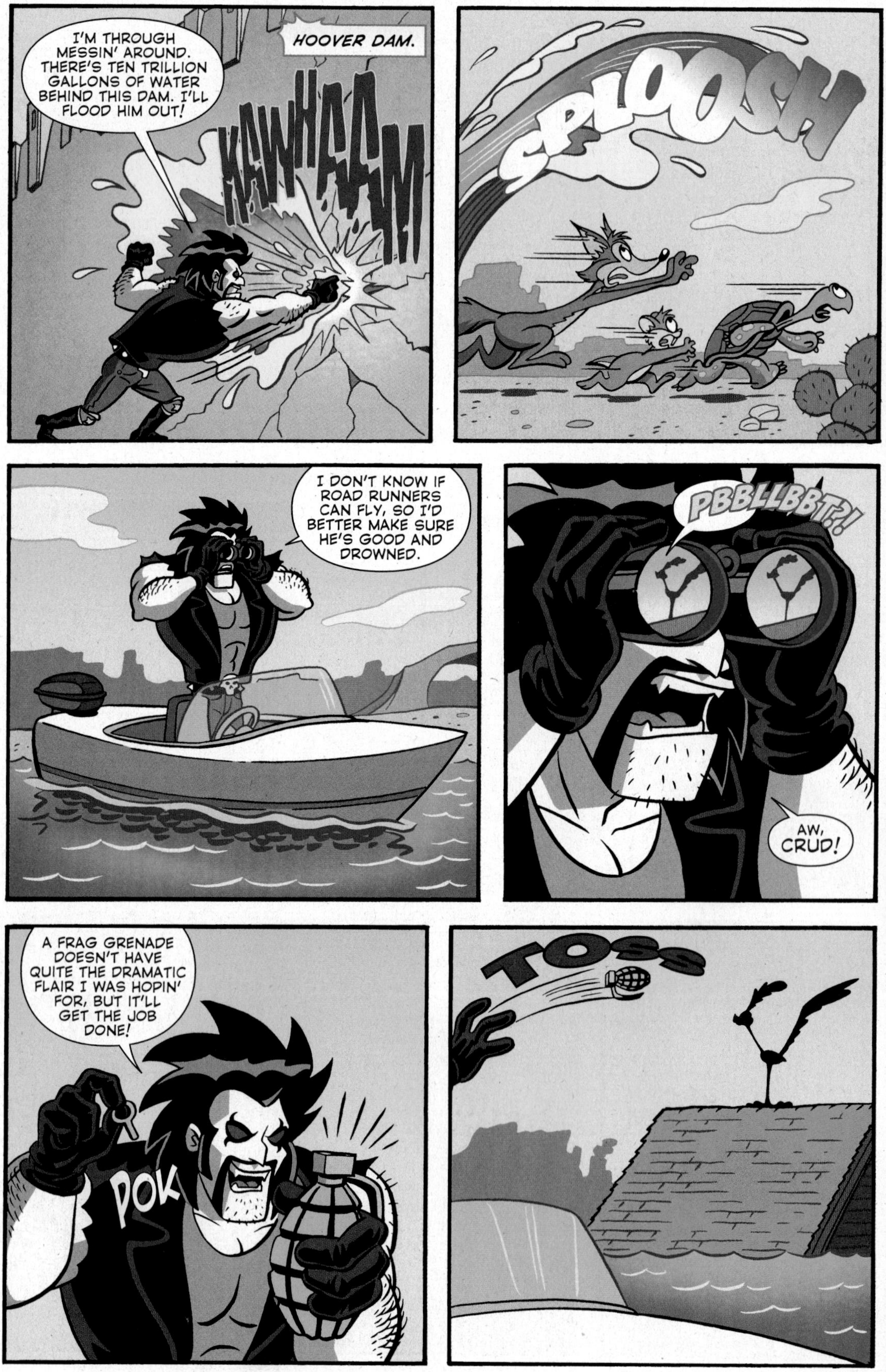
HOOVER DAM.
I'M THROUGH MESSIN' AROUND. THERE'S TEN TRILLION GALLONS OF WATER BEHIND THIS DAM. I'LL FLOOD HIM OUT!
KAWHAAM
SPLOOSH
I DON'T KNOW IF ROAD RUNNERS CAN FLY, SO I'D BETTER MAKE SURE HE'S GOOD AND DROWNED.
PBBLLBBT?!
AW, CRUD!
A FRAG GRENADE DOESN'T HAVE QUITE THE DRAMATIC FLAIR I WAS HOPIN' FOR, BUT IT'LL GET THE JOB DONE!
POK
TOSS

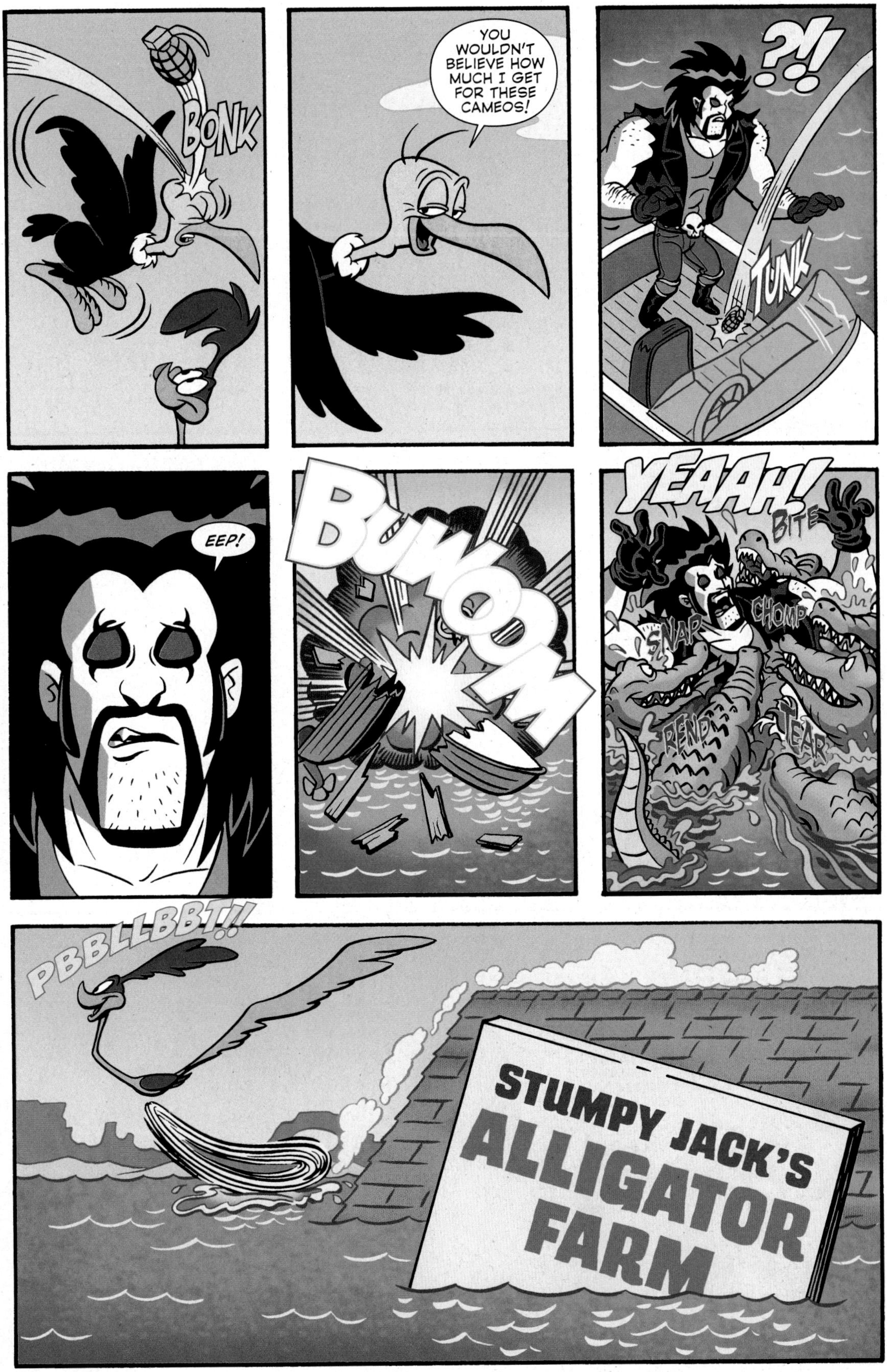
BONK
YOU WOULDN'T BELIEVE HOW MUCH I GET FOR THESE CAMEOS!
?!!
TUNK
EEP!
BUWOOM
YEAAH!
BITE
CHOMP
SNAP
REND
TEAR
PBBLLLBBT!!
STUMPY JACK'S ALLIGATOR FARM

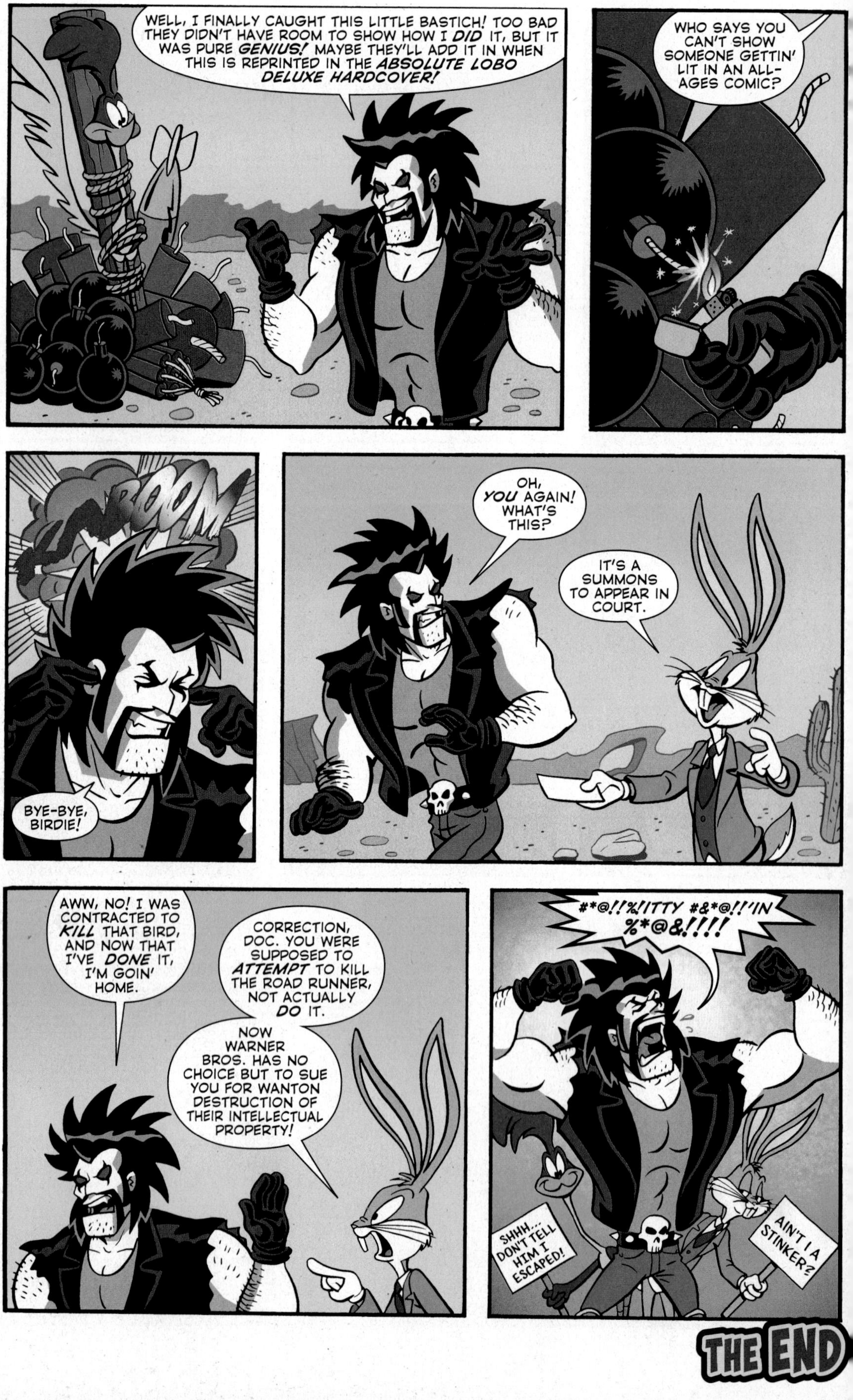
WELL, I FINALLY CAUGHT THIS LITTLE BASTICH! TOO BAD THEY DIDN'T HAVE ROOM TO SHOW HOW I DID IT, BUT IT WAS PURE GENIUS! MAYBE THEY'LL ADD IT IN WHEN THIS IS REPRINTED IN THE ABSOLUTE LOBO DELUXE HARDCOVER!
WHO SAYS YOU CAN'T SHOW SOMEONE GETTIN' LIT IN AN ALL-AGES COMIC?
BOOM
BYE-BYE, BIRDIE!
OH, YOU AGAIN! WHAT'S THIS?
IT'S A SUMMONS TO APPEAR IN COURT.
AWW, NO! I WAS CONTRACTED TO KILL THAT BIRD, AND NOW THAT I'VE DONE IT, I'M GOIN' HOME.
CORRECTION, DOC. YOU WERE SUPPOSED TO ATTEMPT TO KILL THE ROAD RUNNER, NOT ACTUALLY DO IT.
NOW WARNER BROS. HAS NO CHOICE BUT TO SUE YOU FOR WANTON DESTRUCTION OF THEIR INTELLECTUAL PROPERTY!
#*@!!%!ITTY #&*@!!'IN %*@&!!!!
SHHH... DON'T TELL HIM I ESCAPED!
AIN'T I A STINKER?
THE END

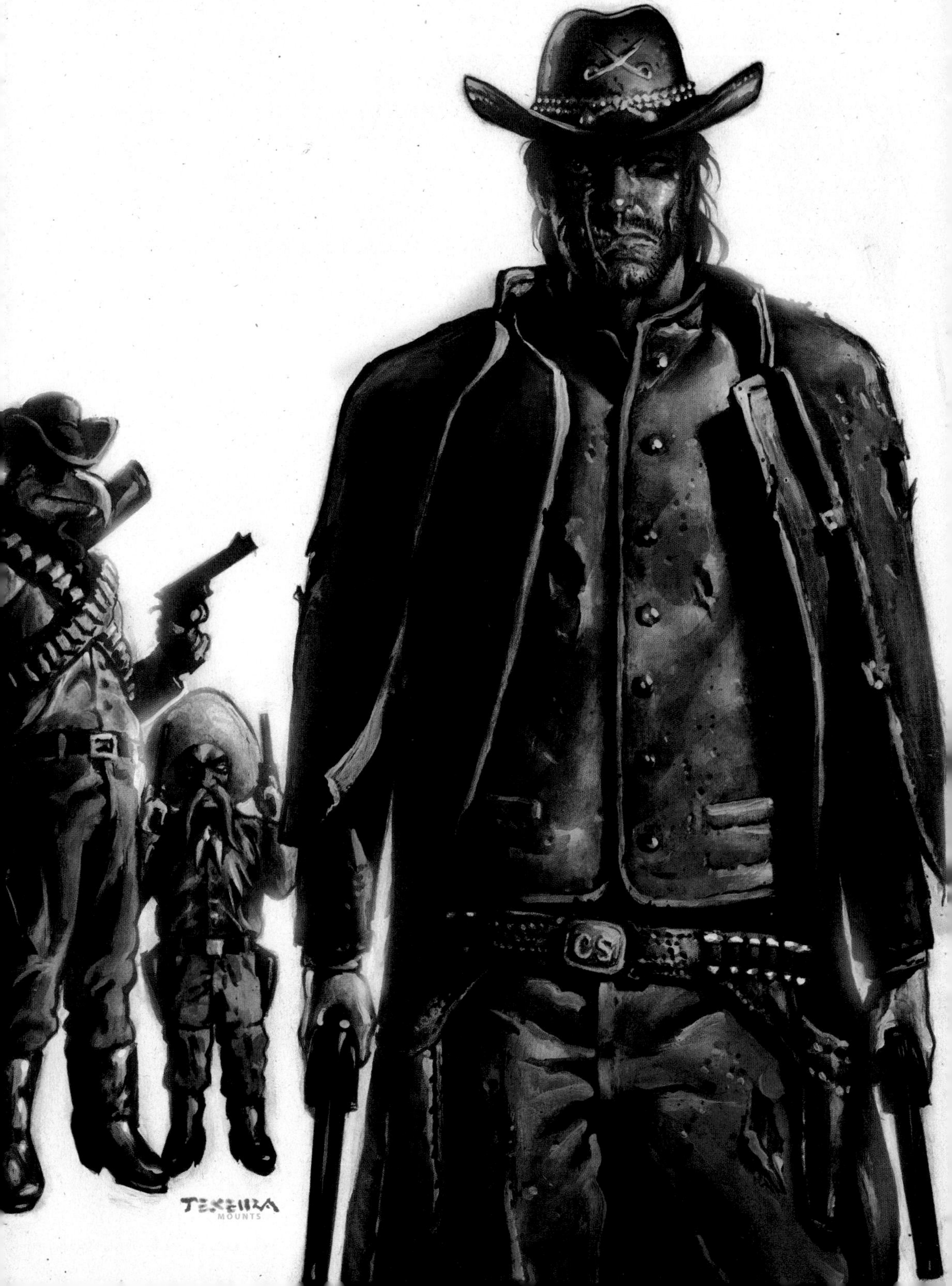

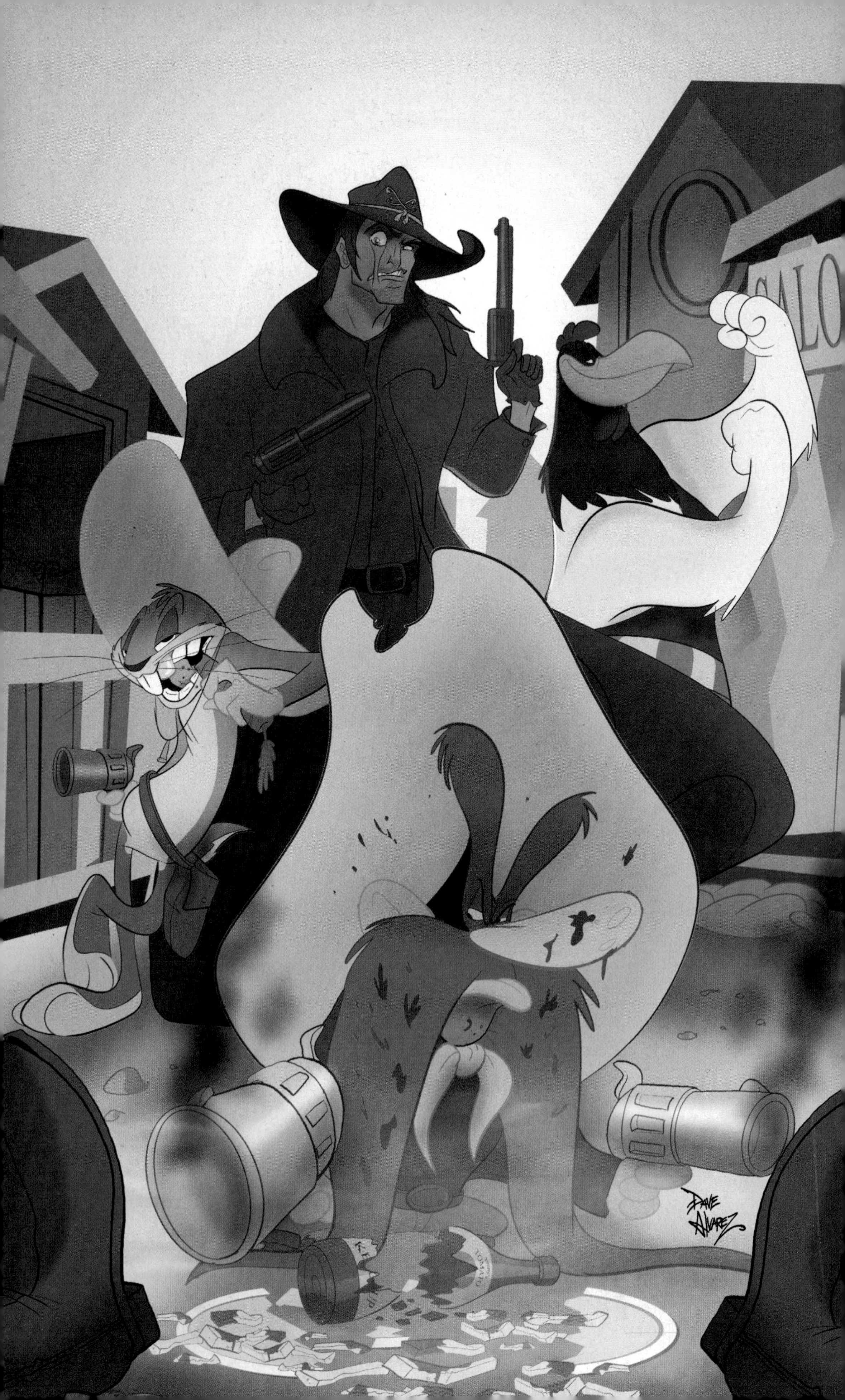
SALO
TOMATO
DAVE ALVAREZ

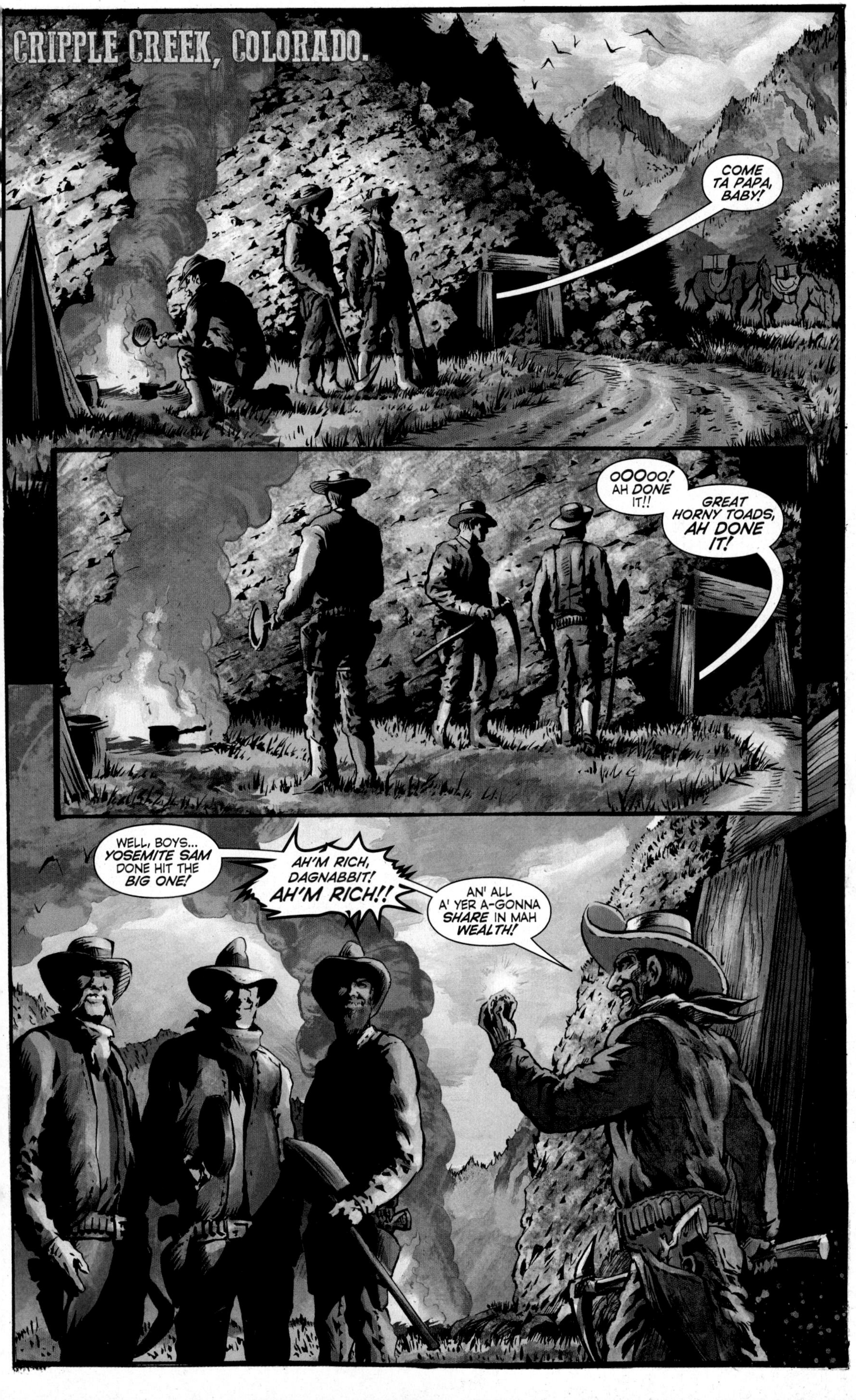
CRIPPLE CREEK, COLORADO.
COME TA PAPA, BABY!
OOOOO! AH DONE IT!!
GREAT HORNY TOADS, AH DONE IT!
WELL, BOYS... YOSEMITE SAM DONE HIT THE BIG ONE!
AH'M RICH, DAGNABBIT! AH'M RICH!!
AN' ALL A' YER A-GONNA SHARE IN MAH WEALTH!

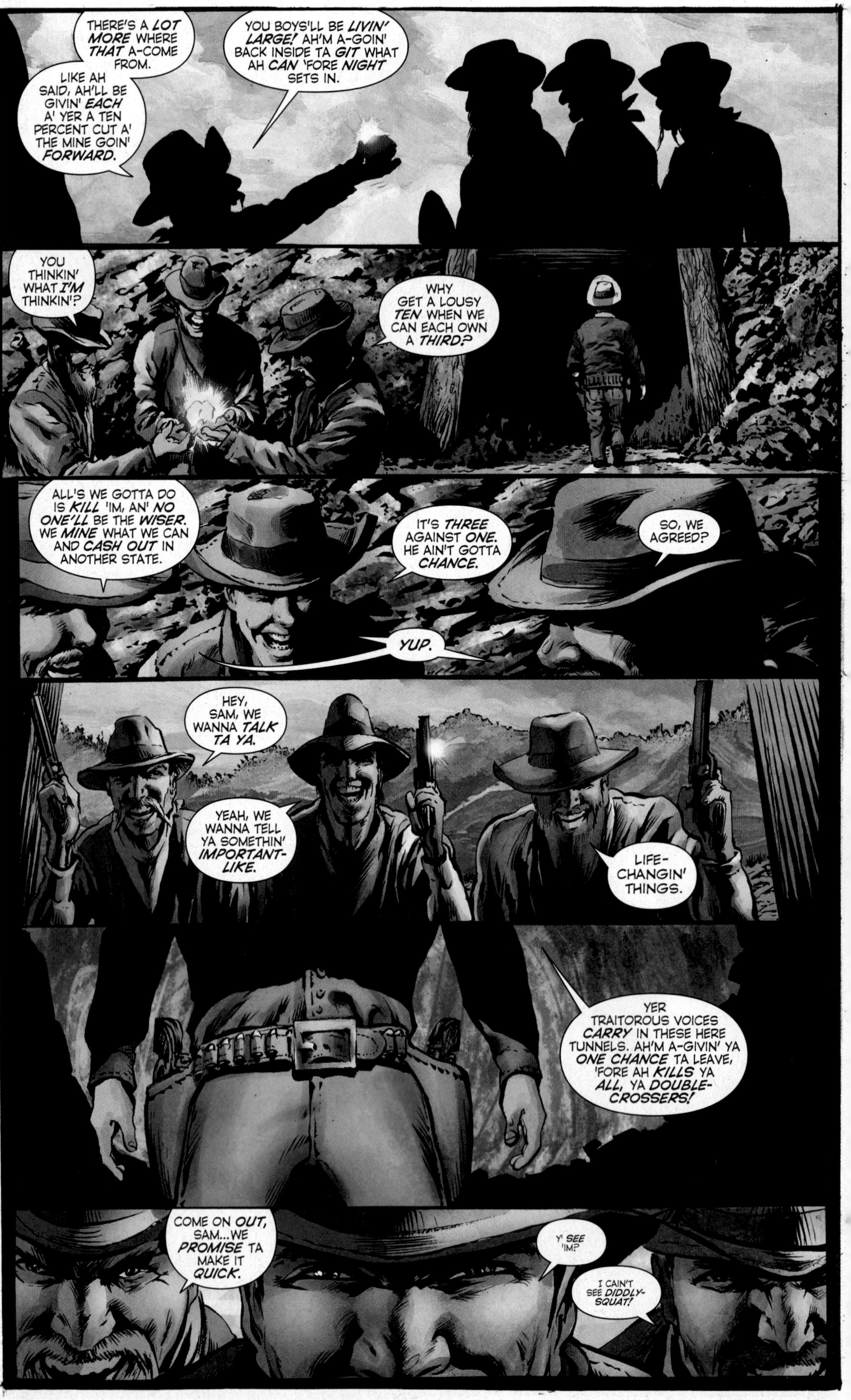
THERE'S A LOT MORE WHERE THAT A-COME FROM.
LIKE AH SAID, AH'LL BE GIVIN' EACH A' YER A TEN PERCENT CUT A' THE MINE GOIN' FORWARD.
YOU BOYS'LL BE LIVIN' LARGE! AH'M A-GOIN' BACK INSIDE TA GIT WHAT AH CAN 'FORE NIGHT SETS IN.
YOU THINKIN' WHAT I'M THINKIN'?
WHY GET A LOUSY TEN WHEN WE CAN EACH OWN A THIRD?
ALL'S WE GOTTA DO IS KILL 'IM, AN' NO ONE'LL BE THE WISER. WE MINE WHAT WE CAN AND CASH OUT IN ANOTHER STATE.
IT'S THREE AGAINST ONE. HE AIN'T GOTTA CHANCE.
SO, WE AGREED?
YUP.
HEY, SAM, WE WANNA TALK TA YA.
YEAH, WE WANNA TELL YA SOMETHIN' IMPORTANT-LIKE.
LIFE-CHANGIN' THINGS.
YER TRAITOROUS VOICES CARRY IN THESE HERE TUNNELS. AH'M A-GIVIN' YA ONE CHANCE TA LEAVE, 'FORE AH KILLS YA ALL, YA DOUBLE-CROSSERS!
COME ON OUT, SAM...WE PROMISE TA MAKE IT QUICK.
Y' SEE 'IM?
I CAIN'T SEE DIDDLY-SQUAT!

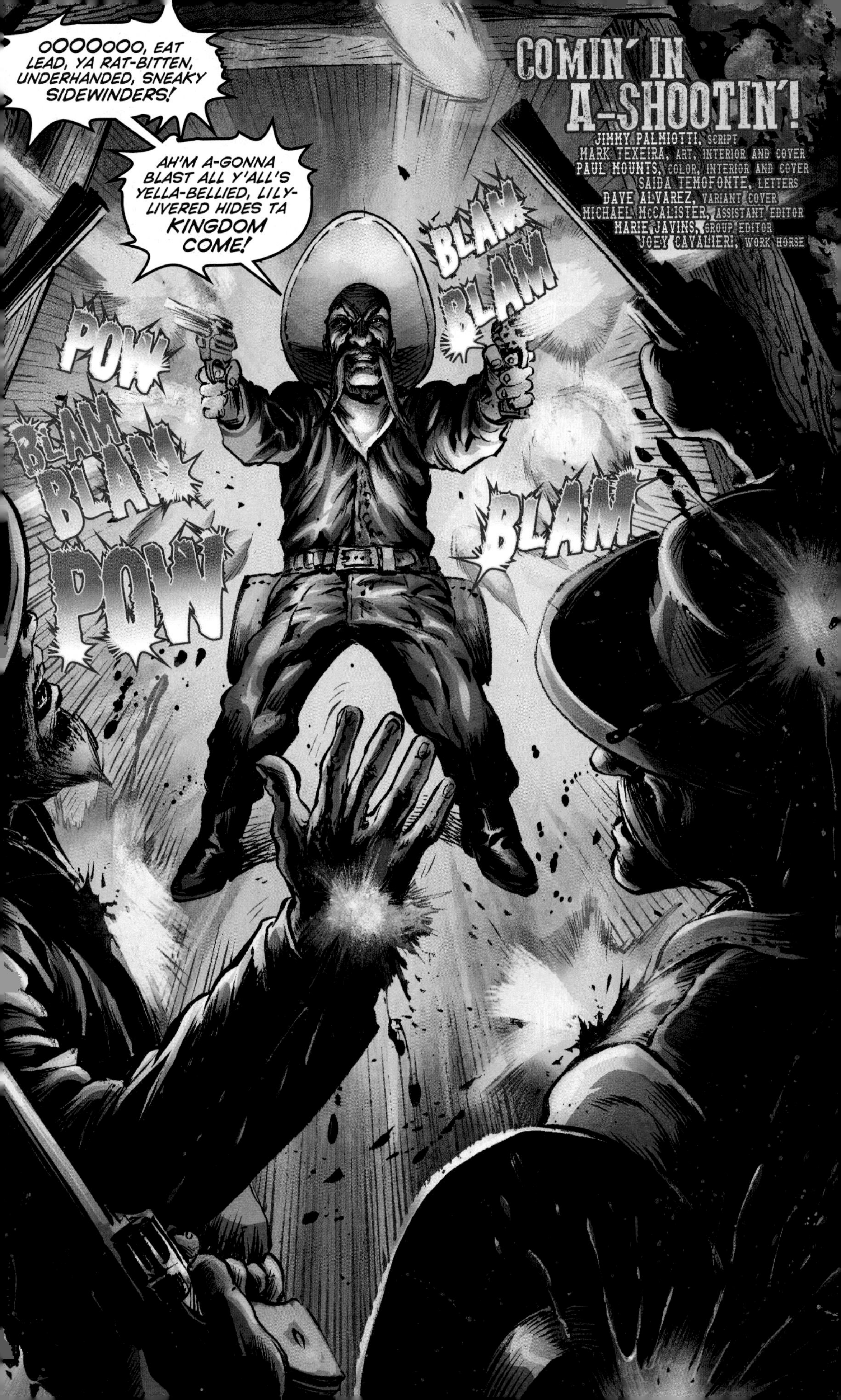
COMIN' IN A-SHOOTIN'!
JIMMY PALMIOTTI, SCRIPT
MARK TEXEIRA, ART, INTERIOR AND COVER
PAUL MOUNTS, COLOR, INTERIOR AND COVER
SAIDA TEMOFONTE, LETTERS
DAVE ALVAREZ, VARIANT COVER
MICHAEL McCALISTER, ASSISTANT EDITOR
MARIE JAVINS, GROUP EDITOR
JOEY CAVALIERI, WORK HORSE
OOOOOOO, EAT LEAD, YA RAT-BITTEN, UNDERHANDED, SNEAKY SIDEWINDERS!
AH'M A-GONNA BLAST ALL Y'ALL'S YELLA-BELLIED, LILY-LIVERED HIDES TA KINGDOM COME!
BLAM BLAM
POW
BLAM BLAM
POW
BLAM

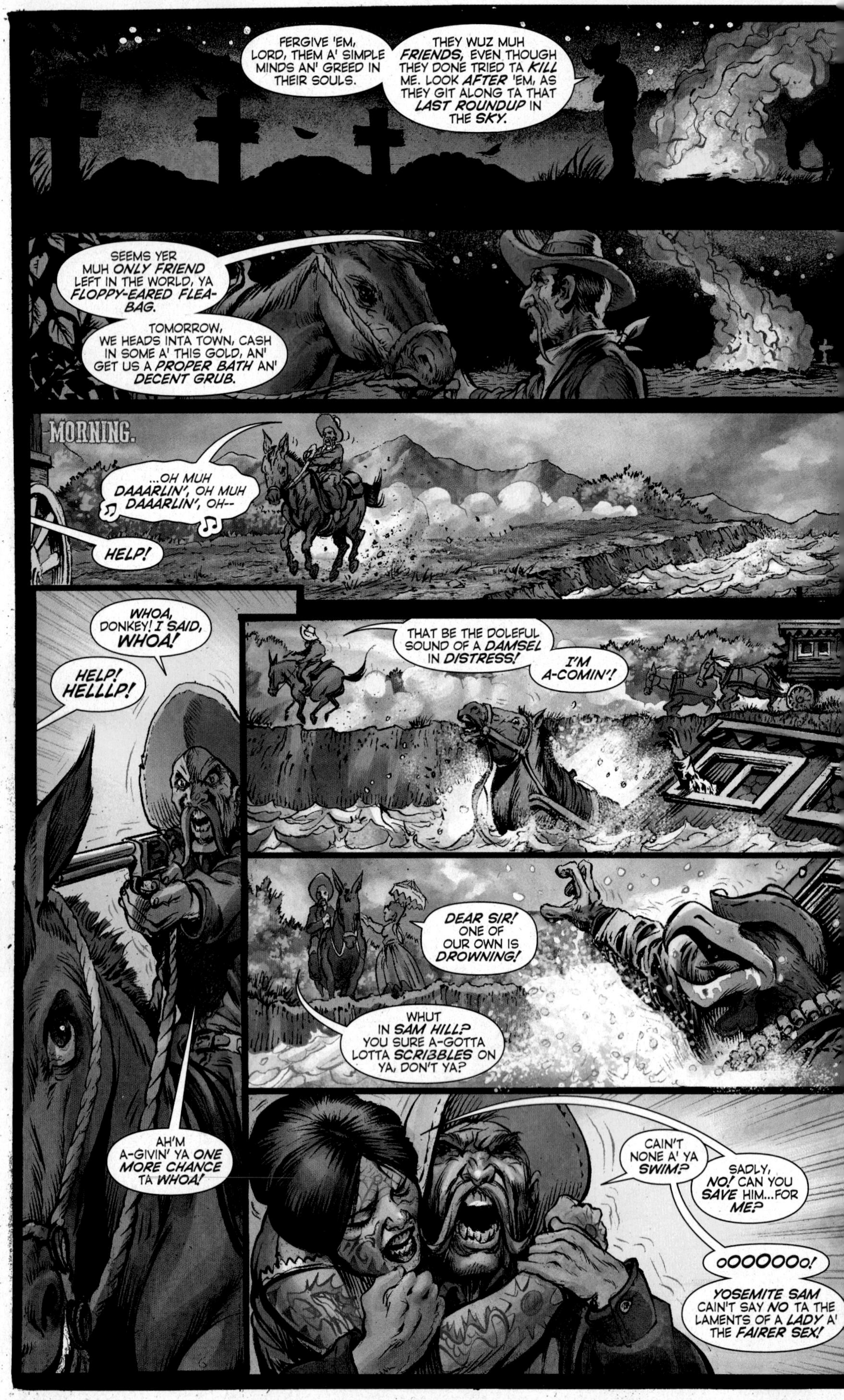

FERGIVE 'EM, LORD, THEM A' SIMPLE MINDS AN' GREED IN THEIR SOULS.
THEY WUZ MUH FRIENDS, EVEN THOUGH THEY DONE TRIED TA KILL ME. LOOK AFTER 'EM, AS THEY GIT ALONG TA THAT LAST ROUNDUP IN THE SKY.
SEEMS YER MUH ONLY FRIEND LEFT IN THE WORLD, YA FLOPPY-EARED FLEA-BAG.
TOMORROW, WE HEADS INTA TOWN, CASH IN SOME A' THIS GOLD, AN' GET US A PROPER BATH AN' DECENT GRUB.
MORNING.
...OH MUH DAAARLIN', OH MUH DAAARLIN', OH--
HELP!
WHOA, DONKEY! I SAID, WHOA!
HELP! HELLLP!
THAT BE THE DOLEFUL SOUND OF A DAMSEL IN DISTRESS!
I'M A-COMIN'!
DEAR SIR! ONE OF OUR OWN IS DROWNING!
WHUT IN SAM HILL? YOU SURE A-GOTTA LOTTA SCRIBBLES ON YA, DON'T YA?
AH'M A-GIVIN' YA ONE MORE CHANCE TA WHOA!
CAIN'T NONE A' YA SWIM?
SADLY, NO! CAN YOU SAVE HIM...FOR ME?
oOOOOOo!
YOSEMITE SAM CAIN'T SAY NO TA THE LAMENTS OF A LADY A' THE FAIRER SEX!

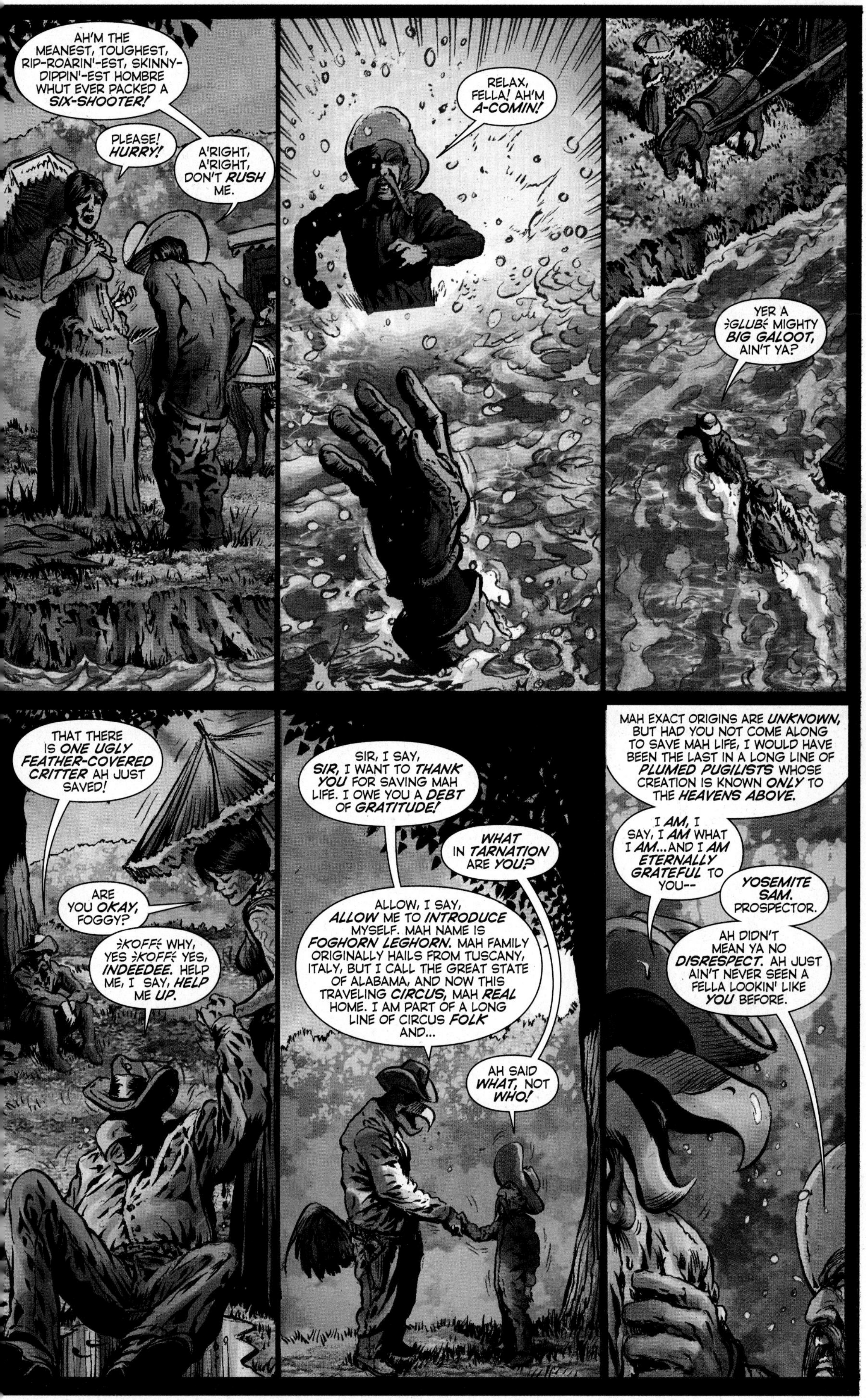
AH'M THE MEANEST, TOUGHEST, RIP-ROARIN'-EST, SKINNY-DIPPIN'-EST HOMBRE WHUT EVER PACKED A SIX-SHOOTER!
PLEASE! HURRY!
A'RIGHT, A'RIGHT, DON'T RUSH ME.
RELAX, FELLA! AH'M A-COMIN!
YER A -GLUB- MIGHTY BIG GALOOT, AIN'T YA?
THAT THERE IS ONE UGLY FEATHER-COVERED CRITTER AH JUST SAVED!
ARE YOU OKAY, FOGGY?
-KOFF- WHY, YES -KOFF- YES, INDEEDEE. HELP ME, I SAY, HELP ME UP.
SIR, I SAY, SIR, I WANT TO THANK YOU FOR SAVING MAH LIFE. I OWE YOU A DEBT OF GRATITUDE!
WHAT IN TARNATION ARE YOU?
ALLOW, I SAY, ALLOW ME TO INTRODUCE MYSELF. MAH NAME IS FOGHORN LEGHORN. MAH FAMILY ORIGINALLY HAILS FROM TUSCANY, ITALY, BUT I CALL THE GREAT STATE OF ALABAMA, AND NOW THIS TRAVELING CIRCUS, MAH REAL HOME. I AM PART OF A LONG LINE OF CIRCUS FOLK AND...
AH SAID WHAT, NOT WHO!
MAH EXACT ORIGINS ARE UNKNOWN, BUT HAD YOU NOT COME ALONG TO SAVE MAH LIFE, I WOULD HAVE BEEN THE LAST IN A LONG LINE OF PLUMED PUGILISTS WHOSE CREATION IS KNOWN ONLY TO THE HEAVENS ABOVE.
I AM, I SAY, I AM WHAT I AM...AND I AM ETERNALLY GRATEFUL TO YOU--
YOSEMITE SAM. PROSPECTOR.
AH DIDN'T MEAN YA NO DISRESPECT. AH JUST AIN'T NEVER SEEN A FELLA LOOKIN' LIKE YOU BEFORE.

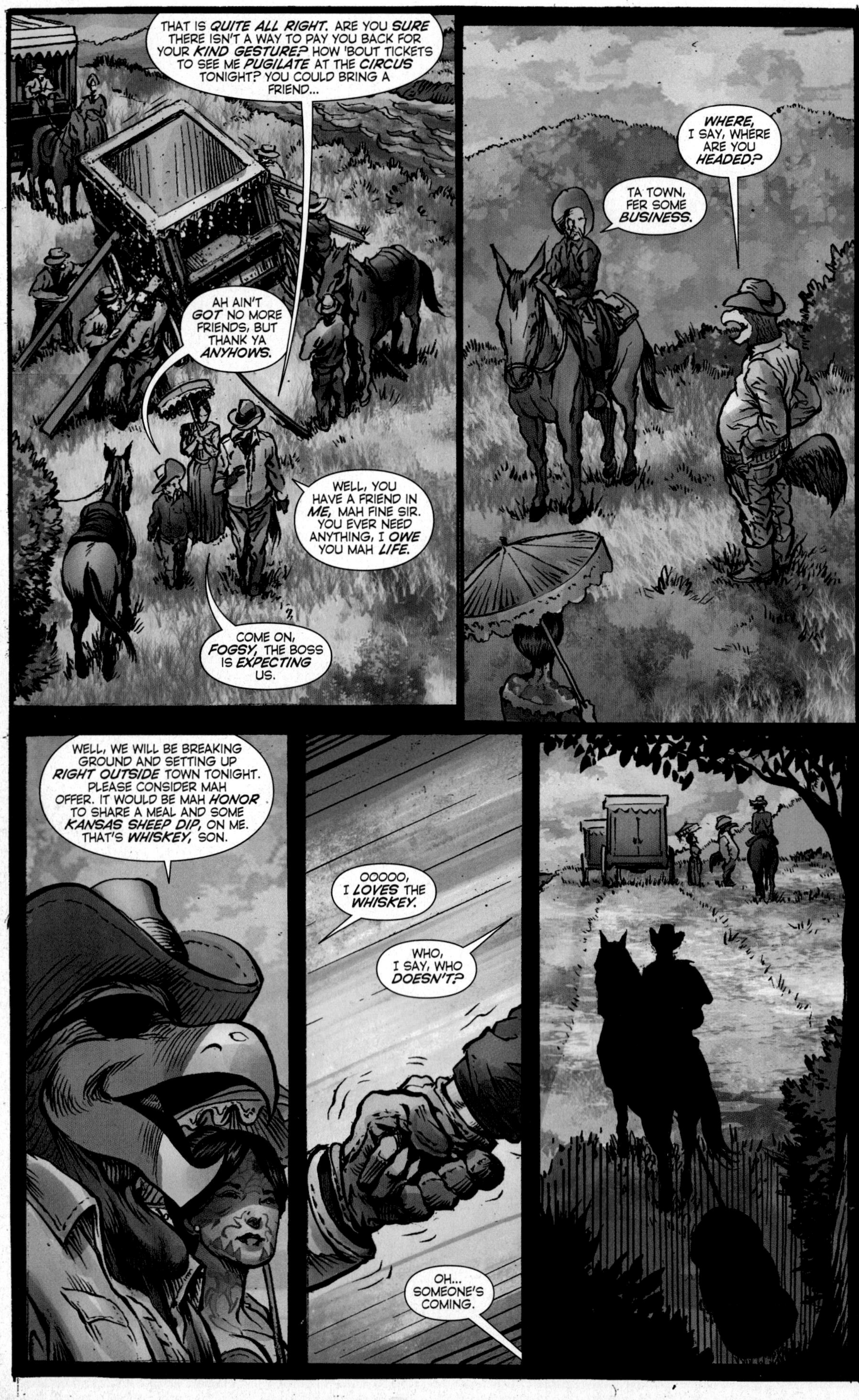
THAT IS QUITE ALL RIGHT. ARE YOU SURE THERE ISN'T A WAY TO PAY YOU BACK FOR YOUR KIND GESTURE? HOW 'BOUT TICKETS TO SEE ME PUGILATE AT THE CIRCUS TONIGHT? YOU COULD BRING A FRIEND...
AH AIN'T GOT NO MORE FRIENDS, BUT THANK YA ANYHOWS.
WELL, YOU HAVE A FRIEND IN ME, MAH FINE SIR. YOU EVER NEED ANYTHING, I OWE YOU MAH LIFE.
COME ON, FOGSY, THE BOSS IS EXPECTING US.
WHERE, I SAY, WHERE ARE YOU HEADED?
TA TOWN, FER SOME BUSINESS.
WELL, WE WILL BE BREAKING GROUND AND SETTING UP RIGHT OUTSIDE TOWN TONIGHT. PLEASE CONSIDER MAH OFFER. IT WOULD BE MAH HONOR TO SHARE A MEAL AND SOME KANSAS SHEEP DIP, ON ME. THAT'S WHISKEY, SON.
OOOOO, I LOVES THE WHISKEY.
WHO, I SAY, WHO DOESN'T?
OH... SOMEONE'S COMING.

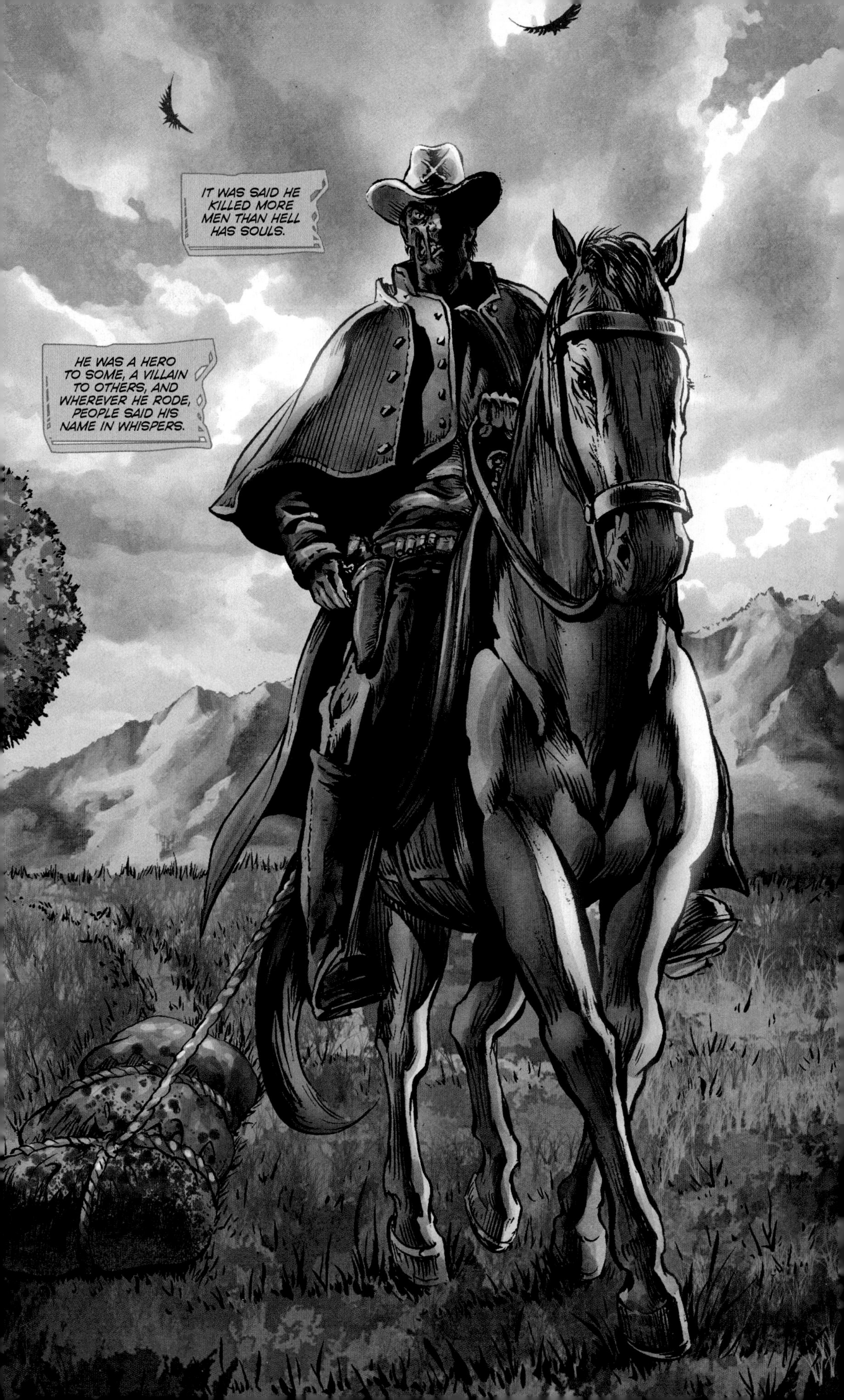
IT WAS SAID HE KILLED MORE MEN THAN HELL HAS SOULS.
HE WAS A HERO TO SOME, A VILLAIN TO OTHERS, AND WHEREVER HE RODE, PEOPLE SAID HIS NAME IN WHISPERS.

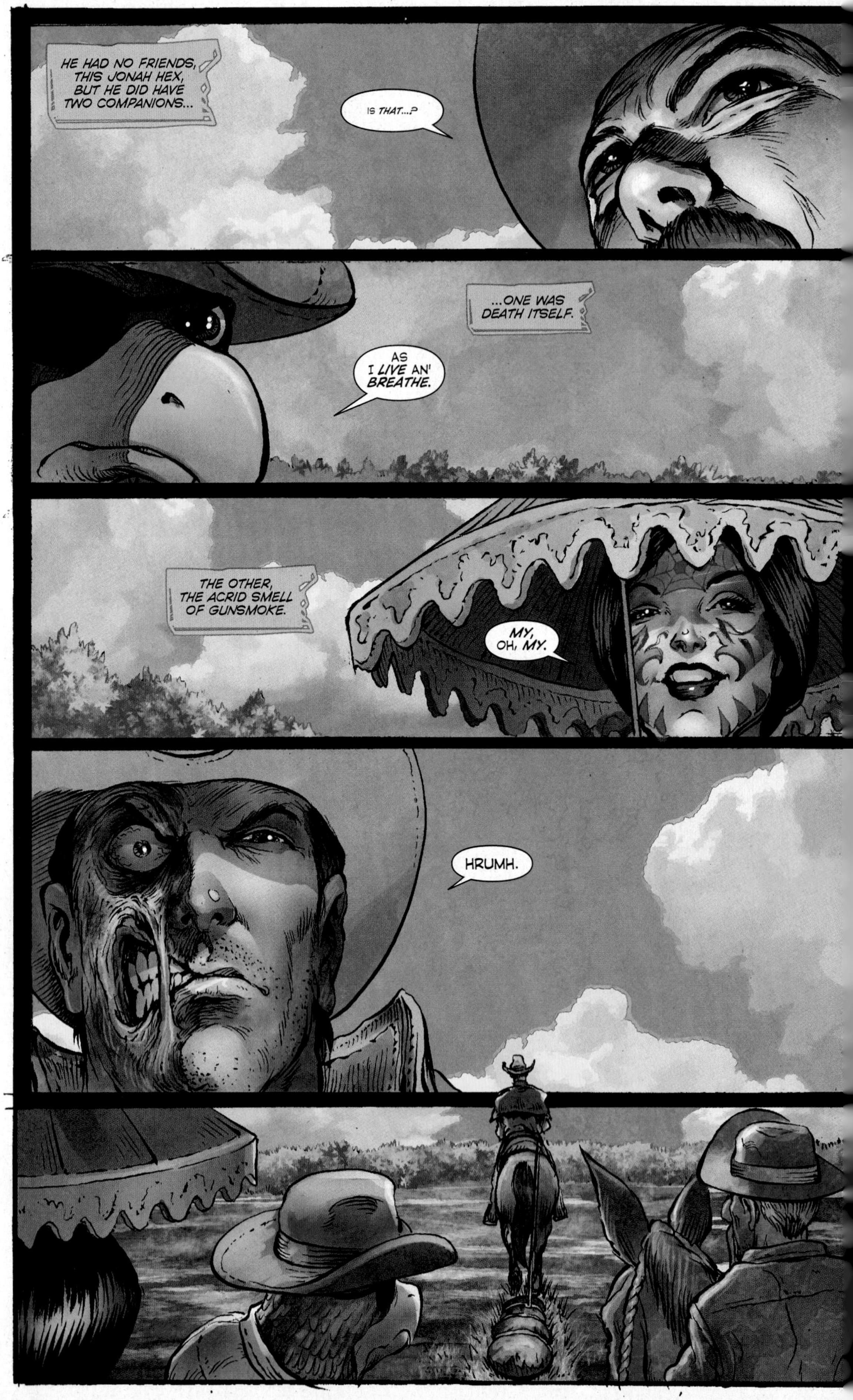
HE HAD NO FRIENDS, THIS JONAH HEX, BUT HE DID HAVE TWO COMPANIONS...
IS THAT...?
...ONE WAS DEATH ITSELF.
AS I LIVE AN' BREATHE.
THE OTHER, THE ACRID SMELL OF GUNSMOKE.
MY, OH, MY.
HRUMH.

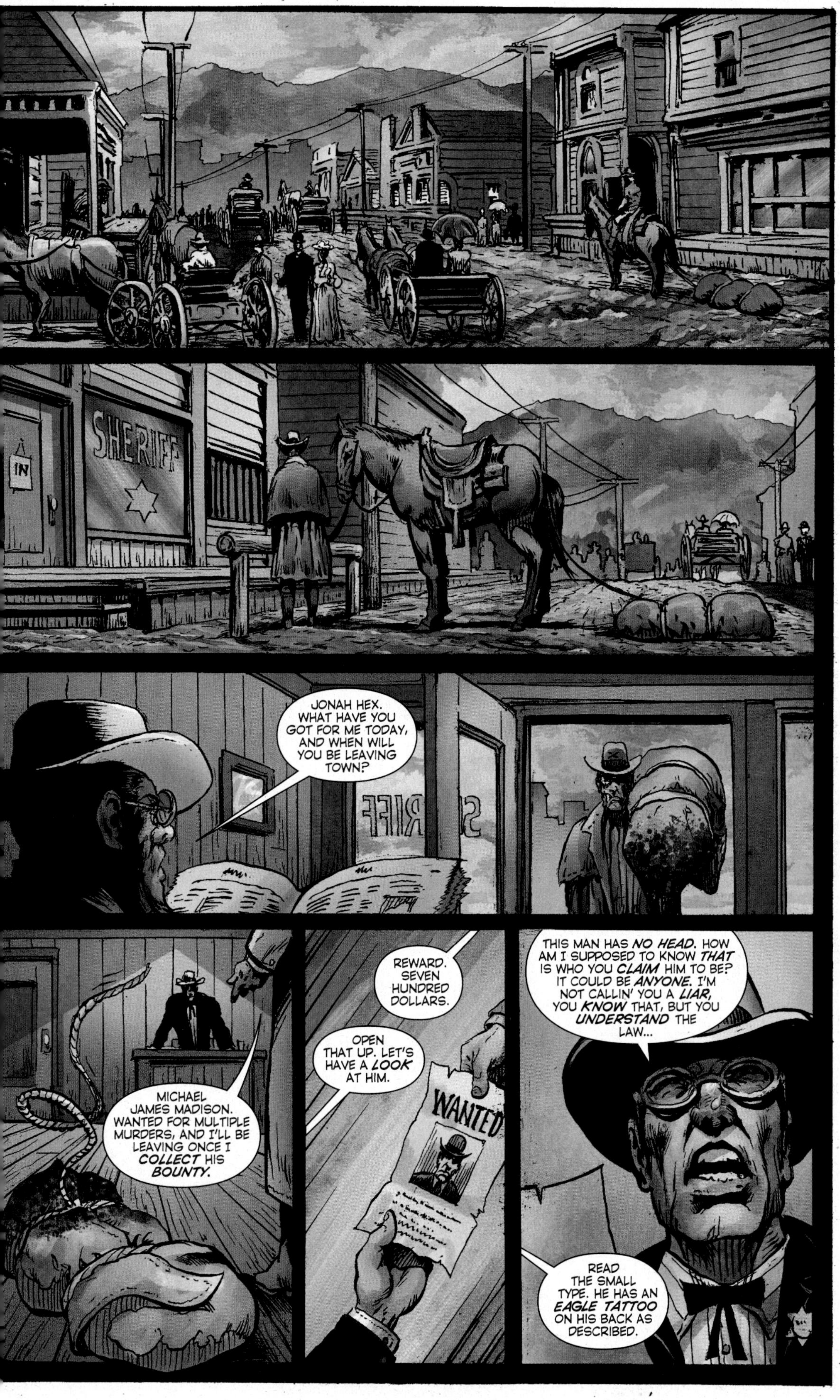

SHERIFF
IN
JONAH HEX. WHAT HAVE YOU GOT FOR ME TODAY, AND WHEN WILL YOU BE LEAVING TOWN?
MICHAEL JAMES MADISON. WANTED FOR MULTIPLE MURDERS, AND I'LL BE LEAVING ONCE I *COLLECT* HIS *BOUNTY.*
REWARD. SEVEN HUNDRED DOLLARS.
OPEN THAT UP. LET'S HAVE A *LOOK* AT HIM.
WANTED
THIS MAN HAS *NO HEAD.* HOW AM I SUPPOSED TO KNOW *THAT* IS WHO YOU *CLAIM* HIM TO BE? IT COULD BE *ANYONE.* I'M NOT CALLIN' YOU A *LIAR,* YOU *KNOW* THAT, BUT YOU *UNDERSTAND* THE LAW...
READ THE SMALL TYPE. HE HAS AN *EAGLE TATTOO* ON HIS BACK AS DESCRIBED.

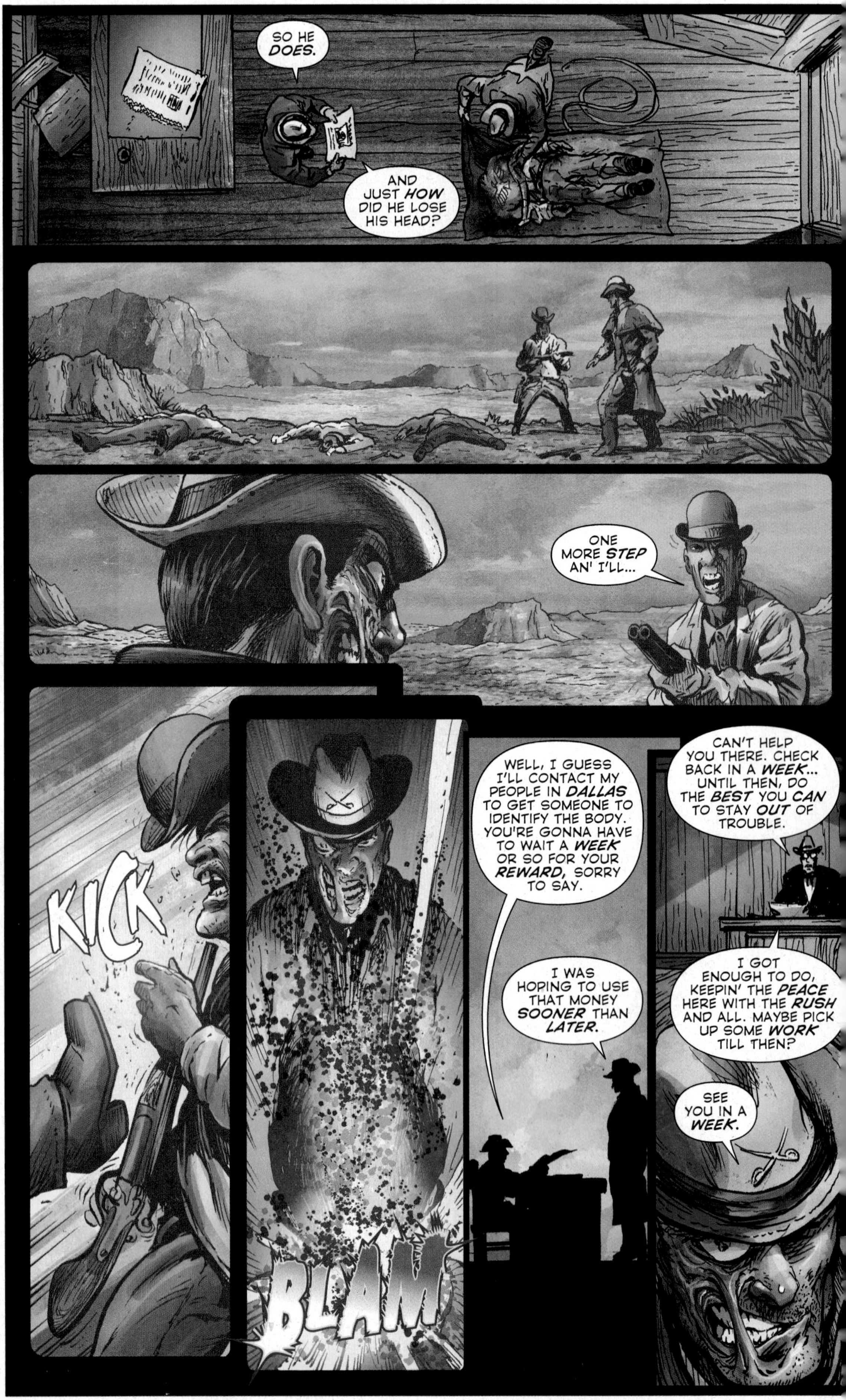

SO HE DOES.
AND JUST HOW DID HE LOSE HIS HEAD?
ONE MORE STEP AN' I'LL...
KICK
BLAM
WELL, I GUESS I'LL CONTACT MY PEOPLE IN DALLAS TO GET SOMEONE TO IDENTIFY THE BODY. YOU'RE GONNA HAVE TO WAIT A WEEK OR SO FOR YOUR REWARD, SORRY TO SAY.
I WAS HOPING TO USE THAT MONEY SOONER THAN LATER.
CAN'T HELP YOU THERE. CHECK BACK IN A WEEK... UNTIL THEN, DO THE BEST YOU CAN TO STAY OUT OF TROUBLE.
I GOT ENOUGH TO DO, KEEPIN' THE PEACE HERE WITH THE RUSH AND ALL. MAYBE PICK UP SOME WORK TILL THEN?
SEE YOU IN A WEEK.

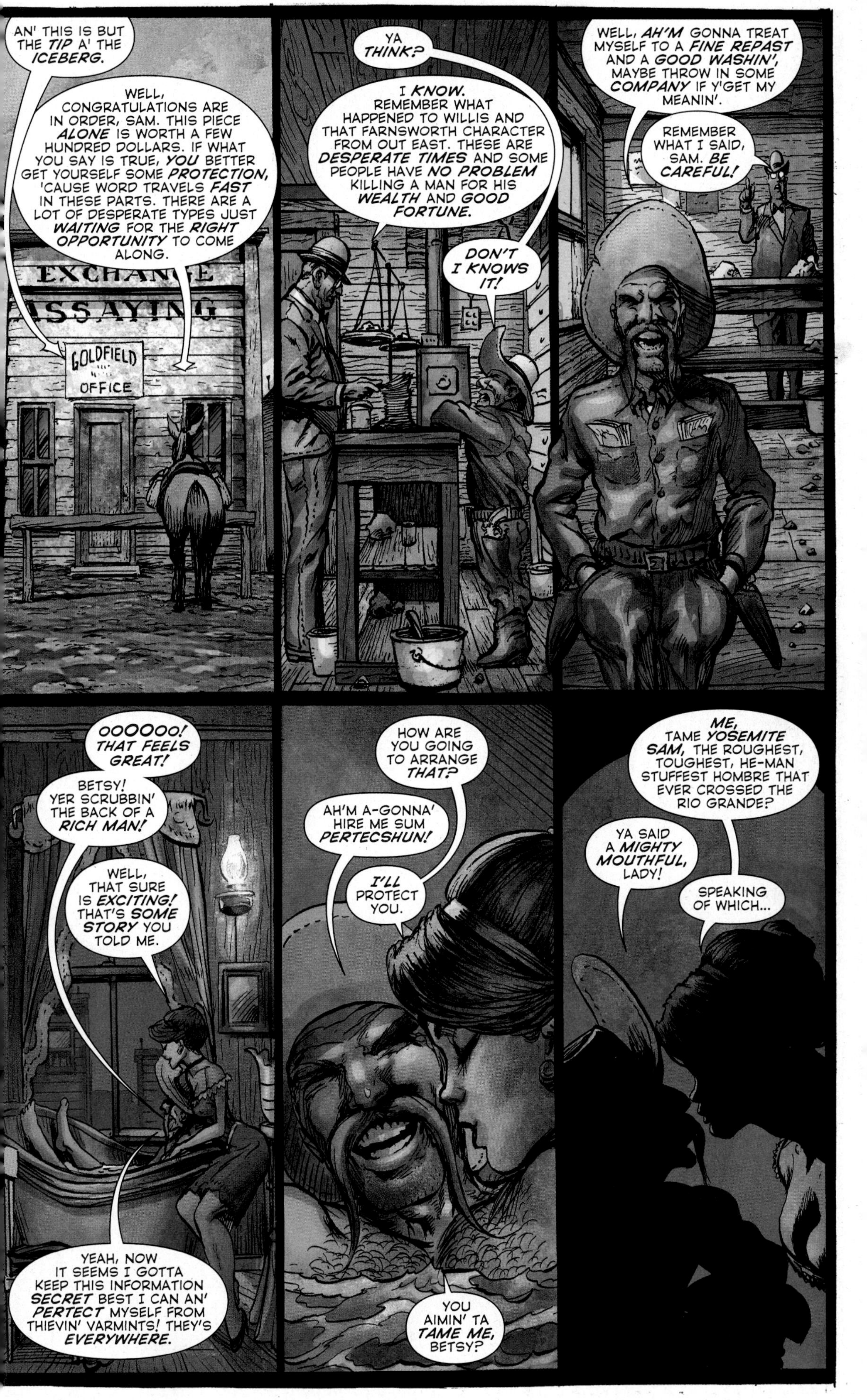

AN' THIS IS BUT THE *TIP* A' THE *ICEBERG.*
WELL, CONGRATULATIONS ARE IN ORDER, SAM. THIS PIECE *ALONE* IS WORTH A FEW HUNDRED DOLLARS. IF WHAT YOU SAY IS TRUE, *YOU* BETTER GET YOURSELF SOME *PROTECTION,* 'CAUSE WORD TRAVELS *FAST* IN THESE PARTS. THERE ARE A LOT OF DESPERATE TYPES JUST *WAITING* FOR THE *RIGHT OPPORTUNITY* TO COME ALONG.
EXCHANGE
ASSAYING
GOLDFIELD
OFFICE
YA *THINK?*
I *KNOW.* REMEMBER WHAT HAPPENED TO WILLIS AND THAT FARNSWORTH CHARACTER FROM OUT EAST. THESE ARE *DESPERATE TIMES* AND SOME PEOPLE HAVE *NO PROBLEM* KILLING A MAN FOR HIS *WEALTH* AND *GOOD FORTUNE.*
DON'T I KNOWS IT!
WELL, *AH'M* GONNA TREAT MYSELF TO A *FINE REPAST* AND A *GOOD WASHIN',* MAYBE THROW IN SOME *COMPANY* IF Y'GET MY MEANIN'.
REMEMBER WHAT I SAID, SAM. *BE CAREFUL!*
OOOOOO! THAT FEELS GREAT!
BETSY! YER SCRUBBIN' THE BACK OF A *RICH MAN!*
WELL, THAT SURE IS *EXCITING!* THAT'S *SOME STORY* YOU TOLD ME.
YEAH, NOW IT SEEMS I GOTTA KEEP THIS INFORMATION *SECRET* BEST I CAN AN' *PERTECT* MYSELF FROM THIEVIN' VARMINTS! THEY'S *EVERYWHERE.*
HOW ARE YOU GOING TO ARRANGE *THAT?*
AH'M A-GONNA' HIRE ME SUM *PERTECSHUN!*
I'LL PROTECT YOU.
YOU AIMIN' TA *TAME ME,* BETSY?
ME, TAME *YOSEMITE SAM,* THE ROUGHEST, TOUGHEST, HE-MAN STUFFEST HOMBRE THAT EVER CROSSED THE RIO GRANDE?
YA SAID A *MIGHTY MOUTHFUL,* LADY!
SPEAKING OF WHICH...

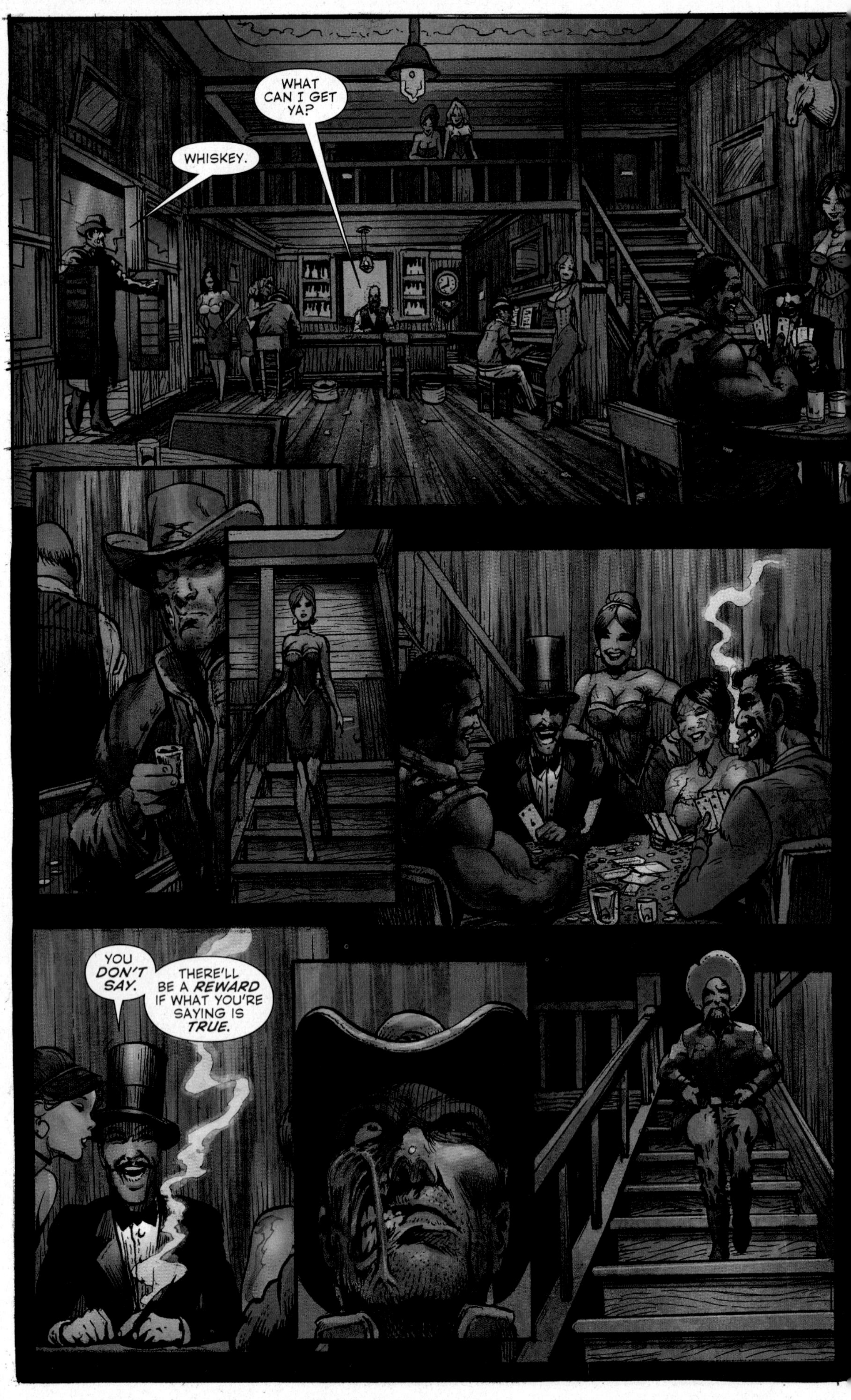
WHAT CAN I GET YA?
WHISKEY.
YOU DON'T SAY.
THERE'LL BE A REWARD IF WHAT YOU'RE SAYING IS TRUE.

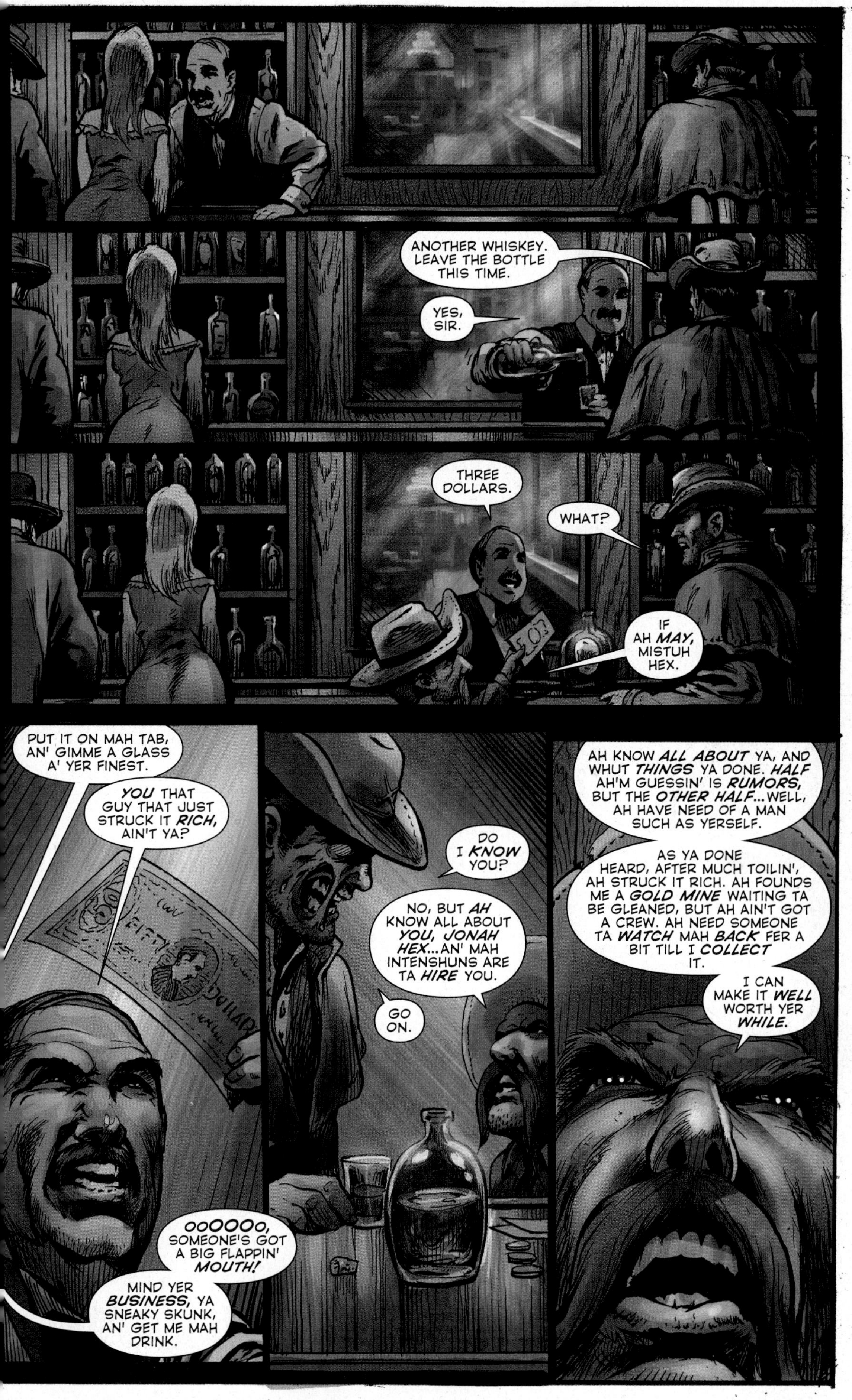

ANOTHER WHISKEY. LEAVE THE BOTTLE THIS TIME.
YES, SIR.
THREE DOLLARS.
WHAT?
IF AH MAY, MISTUH HEX.
PUT IT ON MAH TAB, AN' GIMME A GLASS A' YER FINEST.
YOU THAT GUY THAT JUST STRUCK IT RICH, AIN'T YA?
OOOOOO, SOMEONE'S GOT A BIG FLAPPIN' MOUTH!
MIND YER BUSINESS, YA SNEAKY SKUNK, AN' GET ME MAH DRINK.
DO I KNOW YOU?
NO, BUT AH KNOW ALL ABOUT YOU, JONAH HEX...AN' MAH INTENSHUNS ARE TA HIRE YOU.
GO ON.
AH KNOW ALL ABOUT YA, AND WHUT THINGS YA DONE. HALF AH'M GUESSIN' IS RUMORS, BUT THE OTHER HALF...WELL, AH HAVE NEED OF A MAN SUCH AS YERSELF.
AS YA DONE HEARD, AFTER MUCH TOILIN', AH STRUCK IT RICH. AH FOUNDS ME A GOLD MINE WAITING TA BE GLEANED, BUT AH AIN'T GOT A CREW. AH NEED SOMEONE TA WATCH MAH BACK FER A BIT TILL I COLLECT IT.
I CAN MAKE IT WELL WORTH YER WHILE.

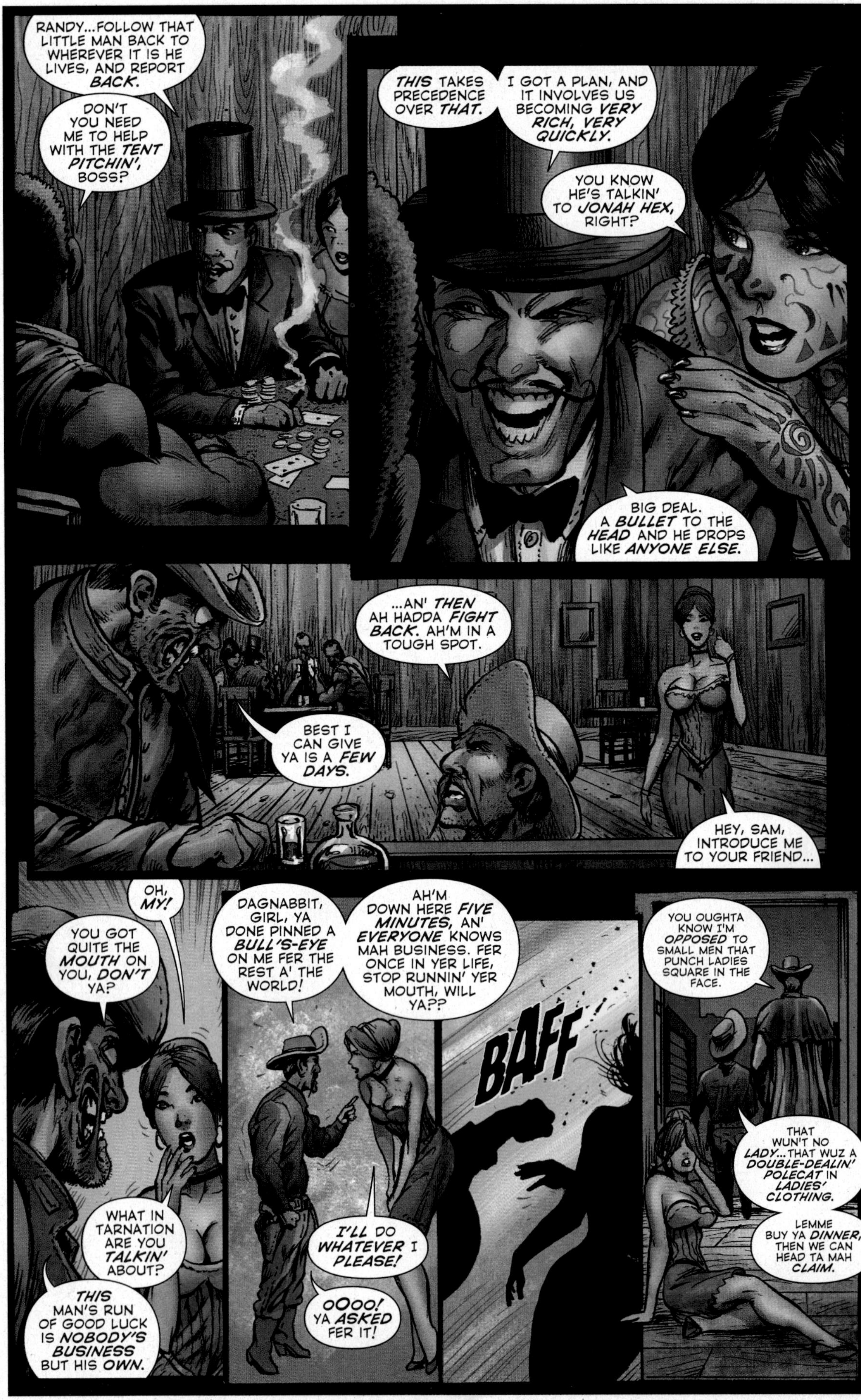

RANDY...FOLLOW THAT LITTLE MAN BACK TO WHEREVER IT IS HE LIVES, AND REPORT BACK.
DON'T YOU NEED ME TO HELP WITH THE TENT PITCHIN', BOSS?
THIS TAKES PRECEDENCE OVER THAT.
I GOT A PLAN, AND IT INVOLVES US BECOMING VERY RICH, VERY QUICKLY.
YOU KNOW HE'S TALKIN' TO JONAH HEX, RIGHT?
BIG DEAL. A BULLET TO THE HEAD AND HE DROPS LIKE ANYONE ELSE.
...AN' THEN AH HADDA FIGHT BACK. AH'M IN A TOUGH SPOT.
BEST I CAN GIVE YA IS A FEW DAYS.
HEY, SAM, INTRODUCE ME TO YOUR FRIEND...
OH, MY!
YOU GOT QUITE THE MOUTH ON YOU, DON'T YA?
WHAT IN TARNATION ARE YOU TALKIN' ABOUT?
THIS MAN'S RUN OF GOOD LUCK IS NOBODY'S BUSINESS BUT HIS OWN.
DAGNABBIT, GIRL, YA DONE PINNED A BULL'S-EYE ON ME FER THE REST A' THE WORLD!
AH'M DOWN HERE FIVE MINUTES, AN' EVERYONE KNOWS MAH BUSINESS. FER ONCE IN YER LIFE, STOP RUNNIN' YER MOUTH, WILL YA??
I'LL DO WHATEVER I PLEASE!
OOOO! YA ASKED FER IT!
BAFF
YOU OUGHTA KNOW I'M OPPOSED TO SMALL MEN THAT PUNCH LADIES SQUARE IN THE FACE.
THAT WUN'T NO LADY...THAT WUZ A DOUBLE-DEALIN' POLECAT IN LADIES' CLOTHING.
LEMME BUY YA DINNER, THEN WE CAN HEAD TA MAH CLAIM.

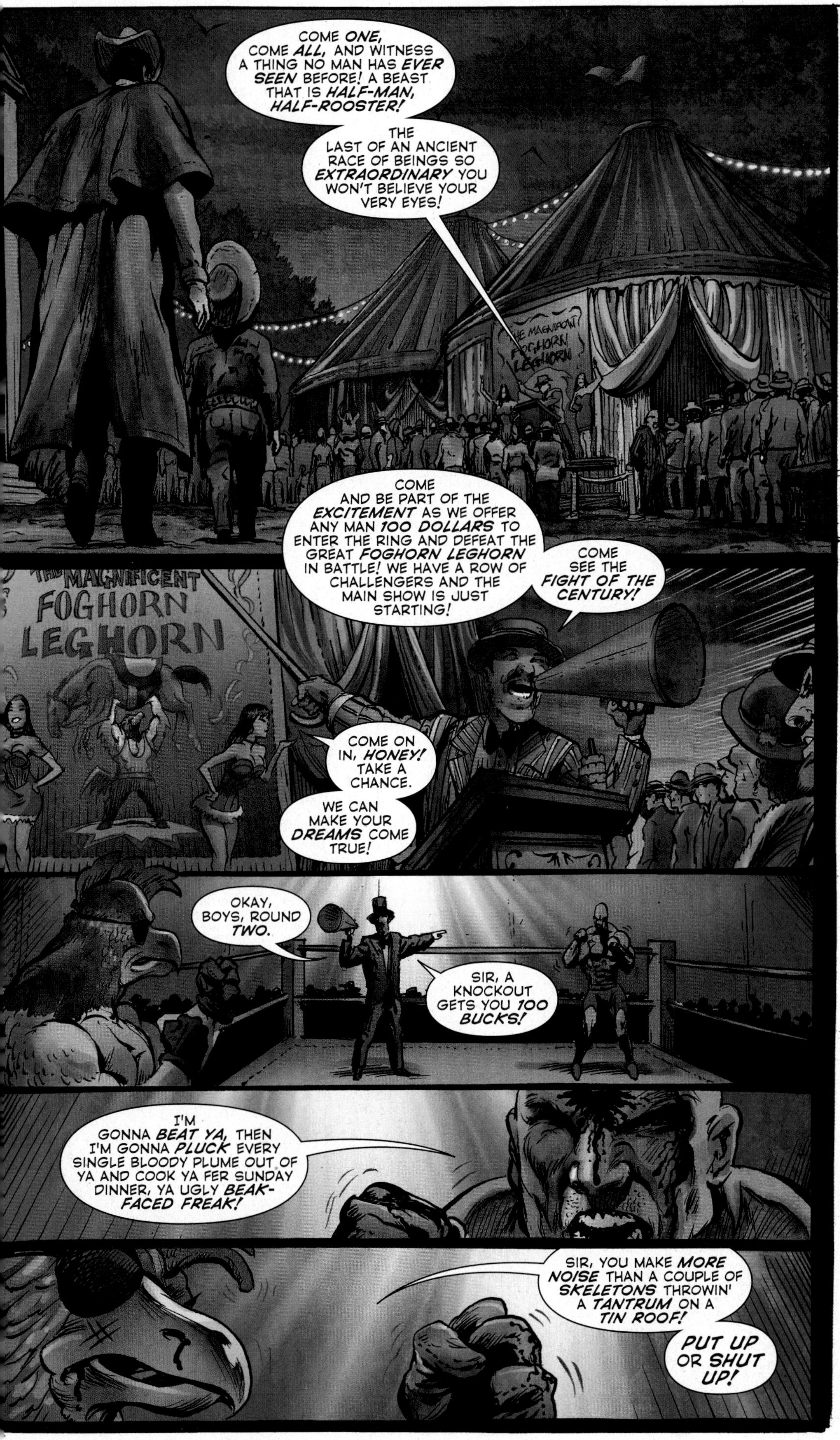
COME ONE, COME ALL, AND WITNESS A THING NO MAN HAS EVER SEEN BEFORE! A BEAST THAT IS HALF-MAN, HALF-ROOSTER!
THE LAST OF AN ANCIENT RACE OF BEINGS SO EXTRAORDINARY YOU WON'T BELIEVE YOUR VERY EYES!
THE MAGNIFICENT FOGHORN LEGHORN
COME AND BE PART OF THE EXCITEMENT AS WE OFFER ANY MAN 100 DOLLARS TO ENTER THE RING AND DEFEAT THE GREAT FOGHORN LEGHORN IN BATTLE! WE HAVE A ROW OF CHALLENGERS AND THE MAIN SHOW IS JUST STARTING!
COME SEE THE FIGHT OF THE CENTURY!
THE MAGNIFICENT FOGHORN LEGHORN
COME ON IN, HONEY! TAKE A CHANCE.
WE CAN MAKE YOUR DREAMS COME TRUE!
OKAY, BOYS, ROUND TWO.
SIR, A KNOCKOUT GETS YOU 100 BUCKS!
I'M GONNA BEAT YA, THEN I'M GONNA PLUCK EVERY SINGLE BLOODY PLUME OUT OF YA AND COOK YA FER SUNDAY DINNER, YA UGLY BEAK-FACED FREAK!
SIR, YOU MAKE MORE NOISE THAN A COUPLE OF SKELETONS THROWIN' A TANTRUM ON A TIN ROOF!
PUT UP OR SHUT UP!

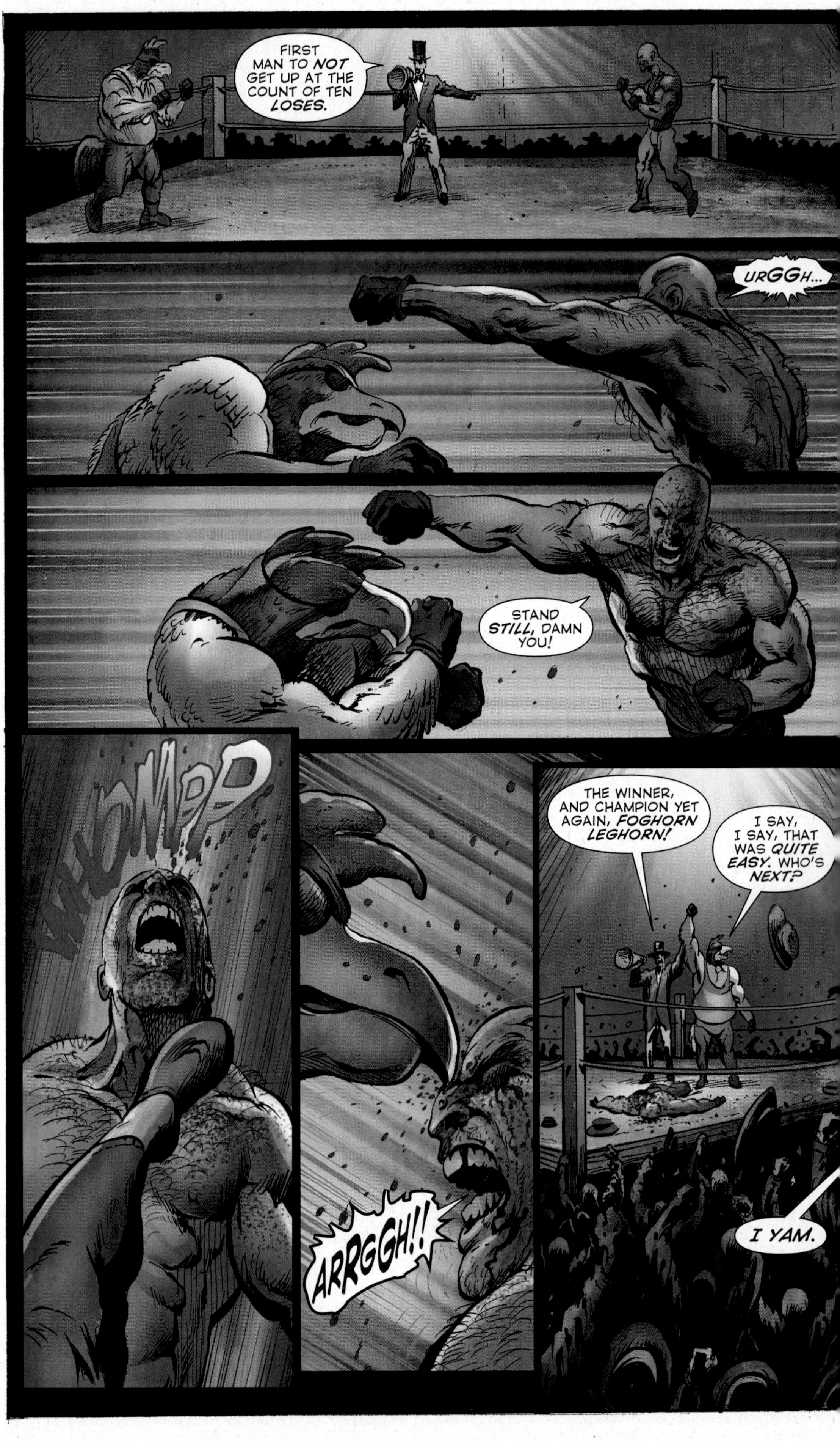
FIRST MAN TO *NOT* GET UP AT THE COUNT OF TEN *LOSES*.
URGGH...
STAND *STILL*, DAMN YOU!
WHOMPP
ARRGGH!!
THE WINNER, AND CHAMPION YET AGAIN, *FOGHORN LEGHORN!*
I SAY, I SAY, THAT WAS *QUITE EASY*. WHO'S *NEXT?*
I YAM.

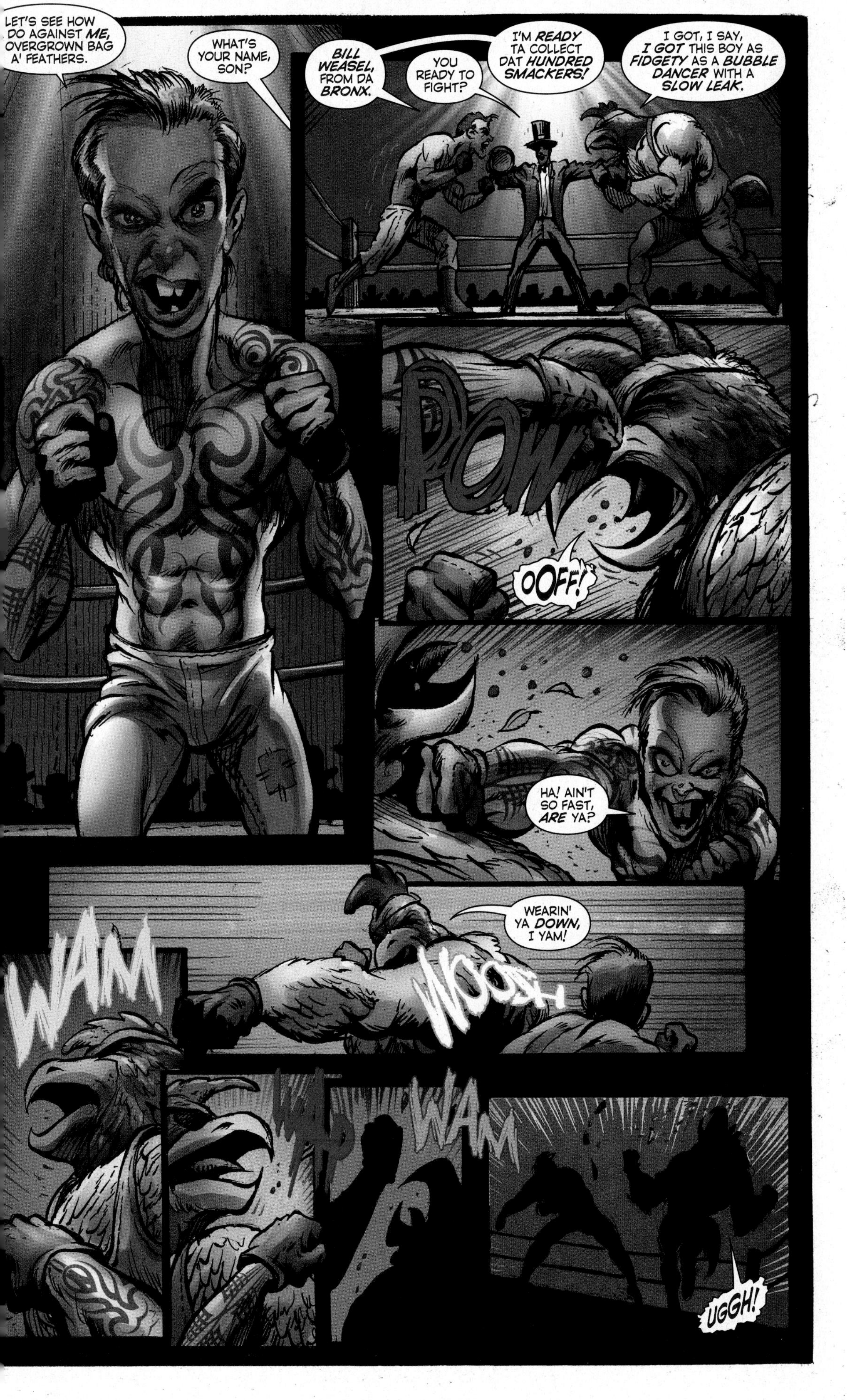
LET'S SEE HOW DO AGAINST ME, OVERGROWN BAG A' FEATHERS.
WHAT'S YOUR NAME, SON?
BILL WEASEL, FROM DA BRONX.
YOU READY TO FIGHT?
I'M READY TA COLLECT DAT HUNDRED SMACKERS!
I GOT, I SAY, I GOT THIS BOY AS FIDGETY AS A BUBBLE DANCER WITH A SLOW LEAK.
POW
OOFF!
HA! AIN'T SO FAST, ARE YA?
WEARIN' YA DOWN, I YAM!
WAM
WOOSH
WAM
UGGH!

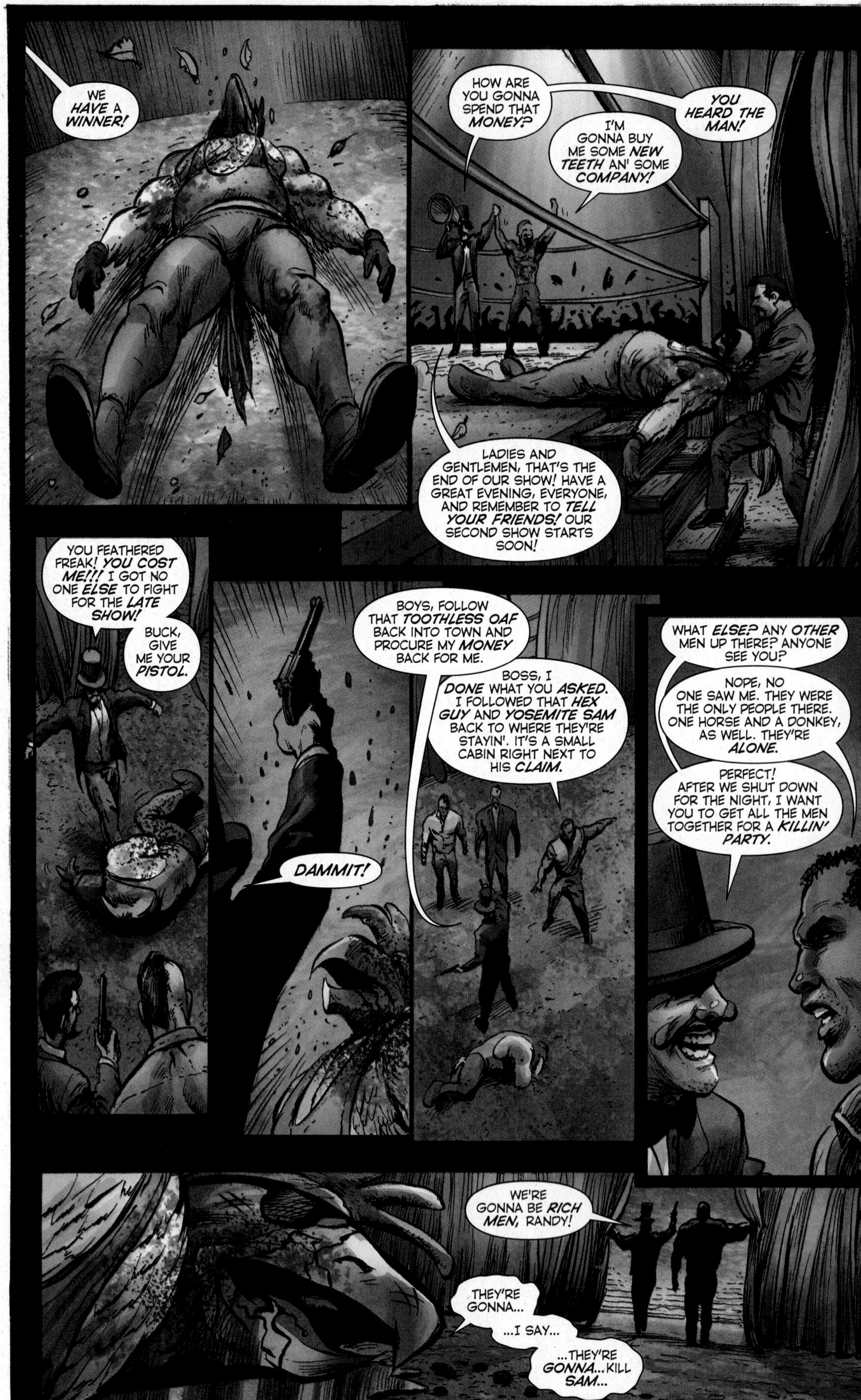
WE HAVE A WINNER!
HOW ARE YOU GONNA SPEND THAT MONEY?
YOU HEARD THE MAN!
I'M GONNA BUY ME SOME NEW TEETH AN' SOME COMPANY!
LADIES AND GENTLEMEN, THAT'S THE END OF OUR SHOW! HAVE A GREAT EVENING, EVERYONE, AND REMEMBER TO TELL YOUR FRIENDS! OUR SECOND SHOW STARTS SOON!
YOU FEATHERED FREAK! YOU COST ME!!! I GOT NO ONE ELSE TO FIGHT FOR THE LATE SHOW!
BUCK, GIVE ME YOUR PISTOL.
DAMMIT!
BOYS, FOLLOW THAT TOOTHLESS OAF BACK INTO TOWN AND PROCURE MY MONEY BACK FOR ME.
BOSS, I DONE WHAT YOU ASKED. I FOLLOWED THAT HEX GUY AND YOSEMITE SAM BACK TO WHERE THEY'RE STAYIN'. IT'S A SMALL CABIN RIGHT NEXT TO HIS CLAIM.
WHAT ELSE? ANY OTHER MEN UP THERE? ANYONE SEE YOU?
NOPE, NO ONE SAW ME. THEY WERE THE ONLY PEOPLE THERE. ONE HORSE AND A DONKEY, AS WELL. THEY'RE ALONE.
PERFECT! AFTER WE SHUT DOWN FOR THE NIGHT, I WANT YOU TO GET ALL THE MEN TOGETHER FOR A KILLIN' PARTY.
WE'RE GONNA BE RICH MEN, RANDY!
THEY'RE GONNA...
...I SAY...
...THEY'RE GONNA...KILL SAM...

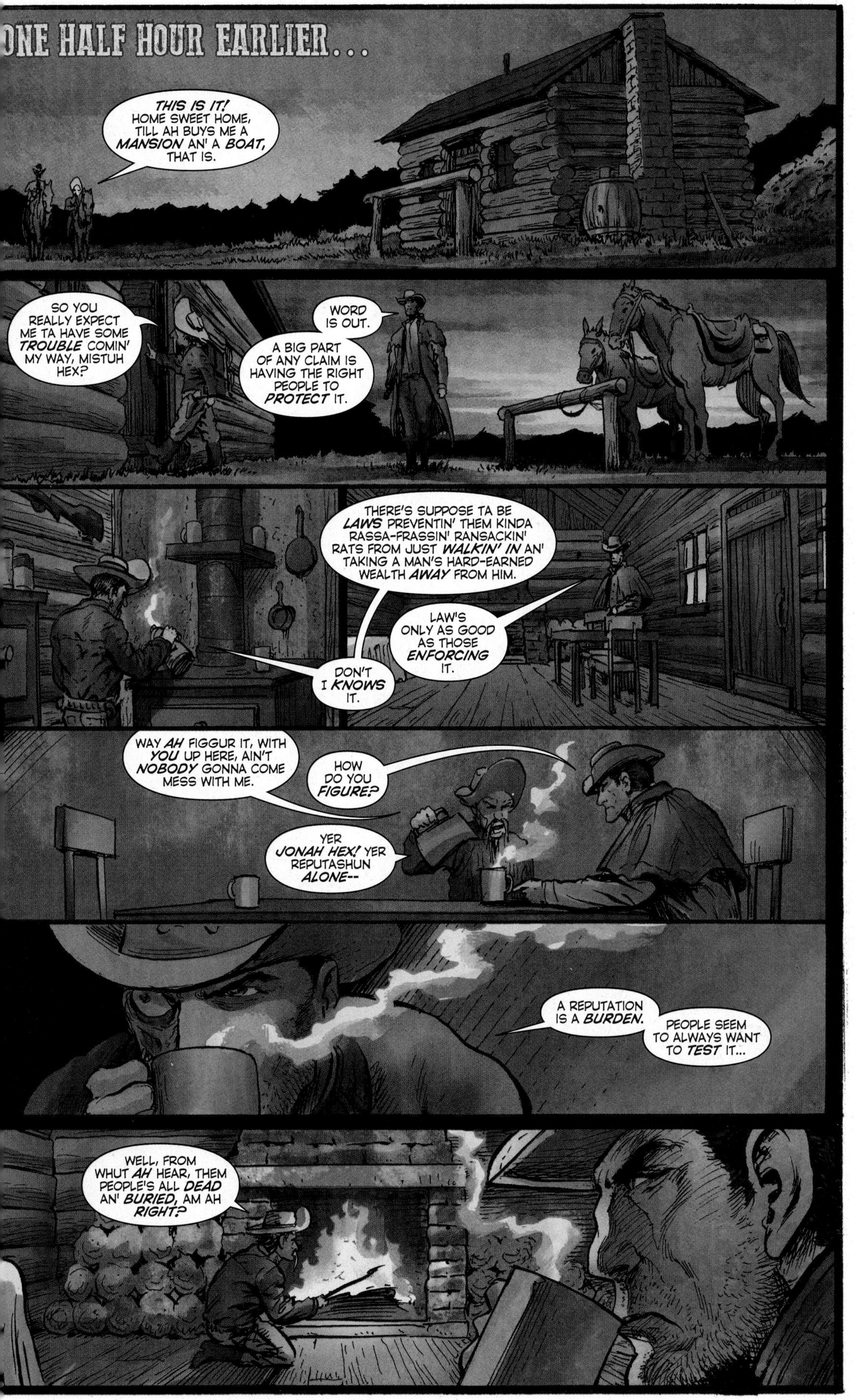
ONE HALF HOUR EARLIER...
THIS IS IT! HOME SWEET HOME, TILL AH BUYS ME A MANSION AN' A BOAT, THAT IS.
SO YOU REALLY EXPECT ME TA HAVE SOME TROUBLE COMIN' MY WAY, MISTUH HEX?
WORD IS OUT.
A BIG PART OF ANY CLAIM IS HAVING THE RIGHT PEOPLE TO PROTECT IT.
THERE'S SUPPOSE TA BE LAWS PREVENTIN' THEM KINDA RASSA-FRASSIN' RANSACKIN' RATS FROM JUST WALKIN' IN AN' TAKING A MAN'S HARD-EARNED WEALTH AWAY FROM HIM.
LAW'S ONLY AS GOOD AS THOSE ENFORCING IT.
DON'T I KNOWS IT.
WAY AH FIGGUR IT, WITH YOU UP HERE, AIN'T NOBODY GONNA COME MESS WITH ME.
HOW DO YOU FIGURE?
YER JONAH HEX! YER REPUTASHUN ALONE--
A REPUTATION IS A BURDEN.
PEOPLE SEEM TO ALWAYS WANT TO TEST IT...
WELL, FROM WHUT AH HEAR, THEM PEOPLE'S ALL DEAD AN' BURIED, AM AH RIGHT?

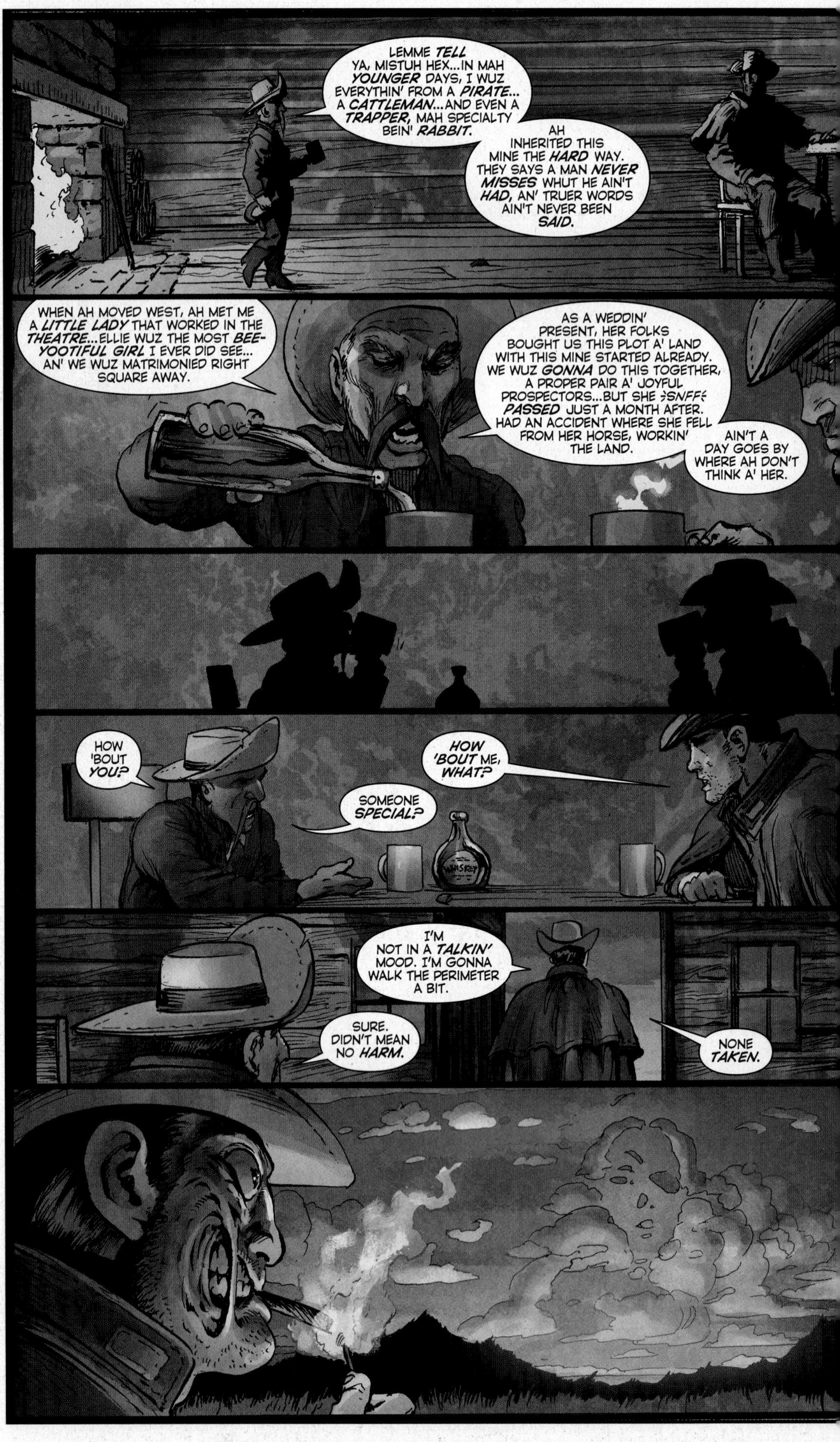

LEMME TELL YA, MISTUH HEX...IN MAH YOUNGER DAYS, I WUZ EVERYTHIN' FROM A PIRATE... A CATTLEMAN...AND EVEN A TRAPPER, MAH SPECIALTY BEIN' RABBIT.
AH INHERITED THIS MINE THE HARD WAY. THEY SAYS A MAN NEVER MISSES WHUT HE AIN'T HAD, AN' TRUER WORDS AIN'T NEVER BEEN SAID.
WHEN AH MOVED WEST, AH MET ME A LITTLE LADY THAT WORKED IN THE THEATRE...ELLIE WUZ THE MOST BEE-YOOTIFUL GIRL I EVER DID SEE... AN' WE WUZ MATRIMONIED RIGHT SQUARE AWAY.
AS A WEDDIN' PRESENT, HER FOLKS BOUGHT US THIS PLOT A' LAND WITH THIS MINE STARTED ALREADY. WE WUZ GONNA DO THIS TOGETHER, A PROPER PAIR A' JOYFUL PROSPECTORS...BUT SHE *SNFF* PASSED JUST A MONTH AFTER. HAD AN ACCIDENT WHERE SHE FELL FROM HER HORSE, WORKIN' THE LAND.
AIN'T A DAY GOES BY WHERE AH DON'T THINK A' HER.
HOW 'BOUT YOU?
HOW 'BOUT ME, WHAT?
SOMEONE SPECIAL?
WHISKEY
I'M NOT IN A TALKIN' MOOD. I'M GONNA WALK THE PERIMETER A BIT.
SURE. DIDN'T MEAN NO HARM.
NONE TAKEN.

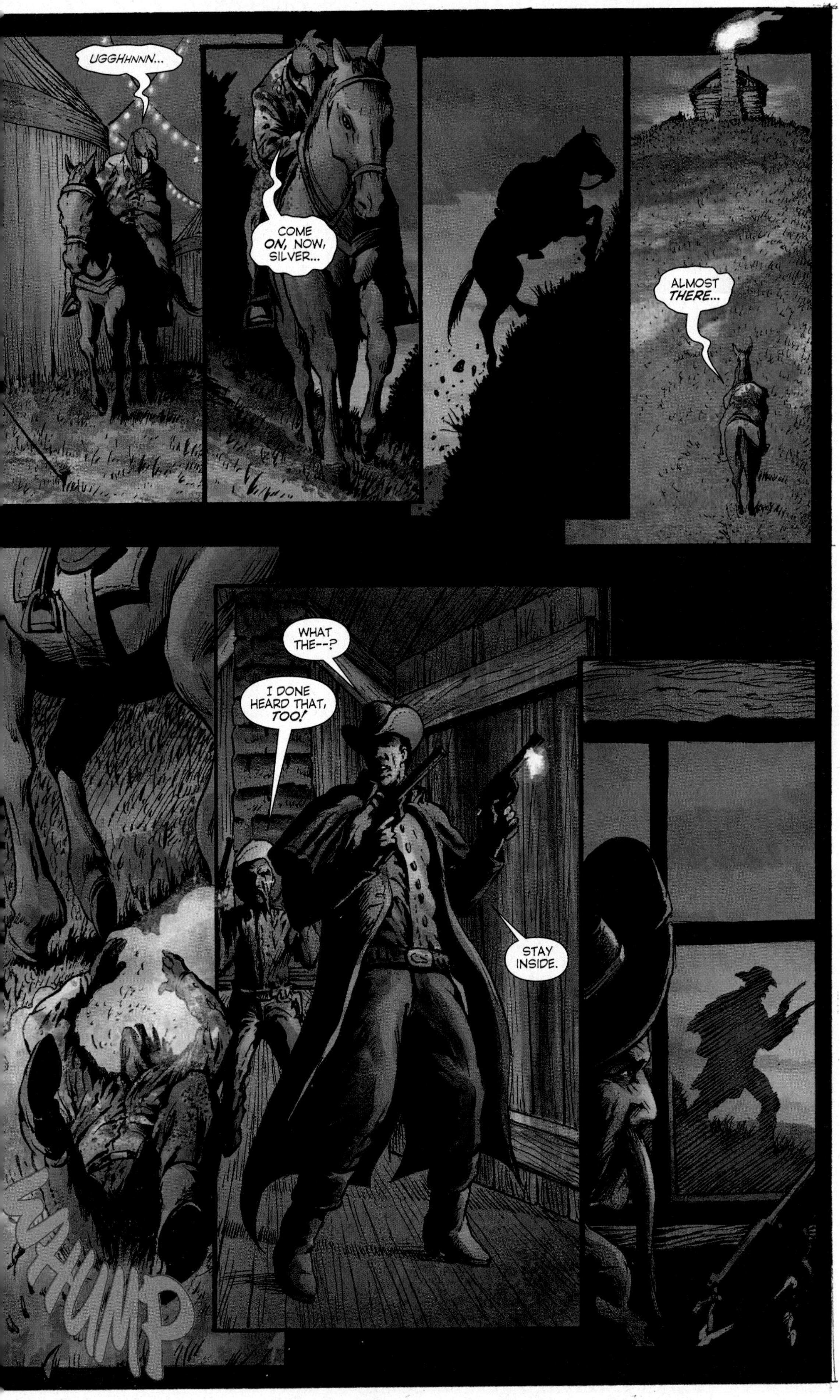
UGGHHNNN...
COME ON, NOW, SILVER...
ALMOST THERE...
WHAT THE--?
I DONE HEARD THAT, TOO!
STAY INSIDE.
WHUMP

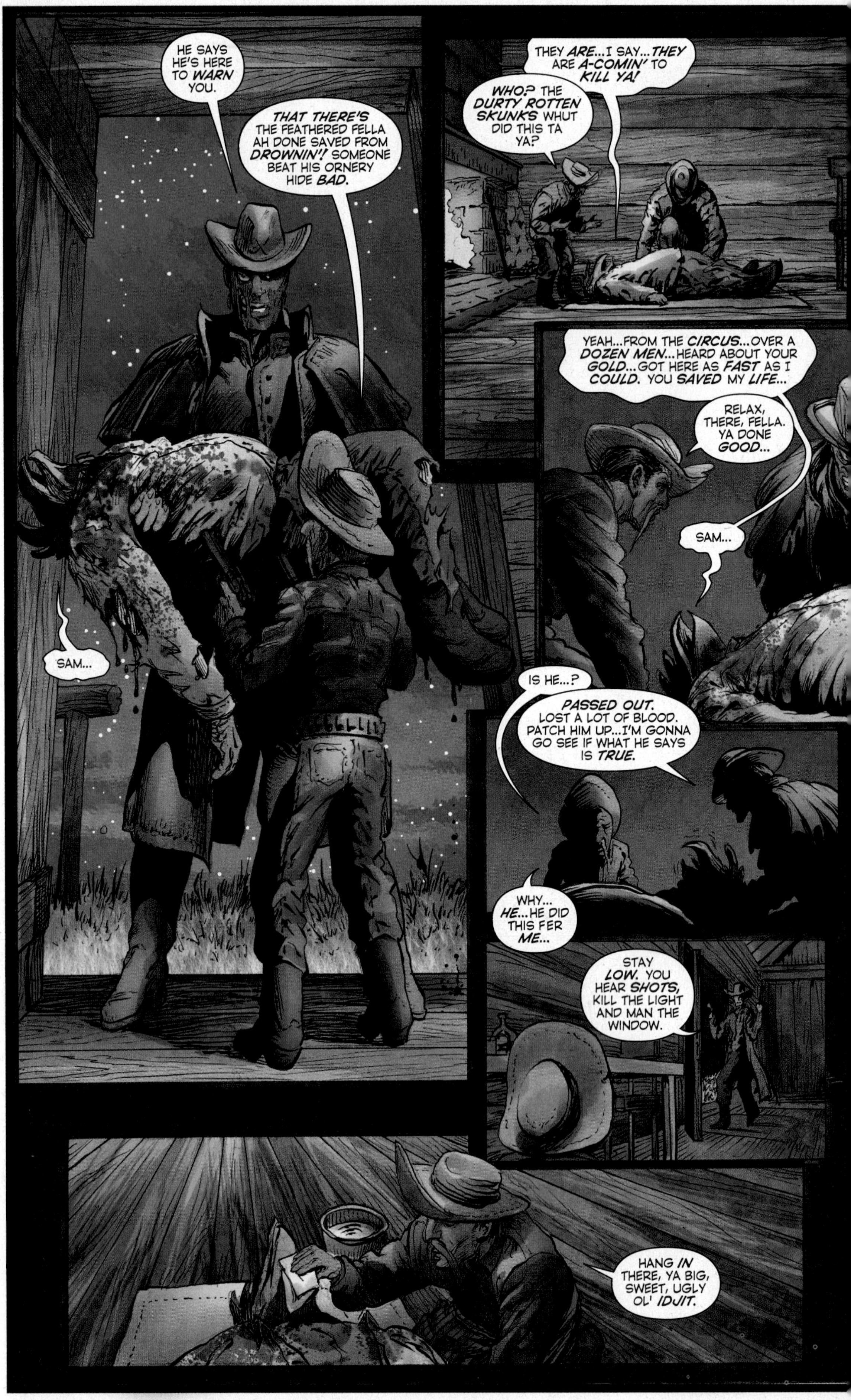
HE SAYS HE'S HERE TO WARN YOU.
THAT THERE'S THE FEATHERED FELLA AH DONE SAVED FROM DROWNIN'! SOMEONE BEAT HIS ORNERY HIDE BAD.
SAM...
THEY ARE...I SAY...THEY ARE A-COMIN' TO KILL YA!
WHO? THE DURTY ROTTEN SKUNKS WHUT DID THIS TA YA?
YEAH...FROM THE CIRCUS...OVER A DOZEN MEN...HEARD ABOUT YOUR GOLD...GOT HERE AS FAST AS I COULD. YOU SAVED MY LIFE...
RELAX, THERE, FELLA. YA DONE GOOD...
SAM...
IS HE...?
PASSED OUT. LOST A LOT OF BLOOD. PATCH HIM UP...I'M GONNA GO SEE IF WHAT HE SAYS IS TRUE.
WHY... HE...HE DID THIS FER ME...
STAY LOW. YOU HEAR SHOTS, KILL THE LIGHT AND MAN THE WINDOW.
HANG IN THERE, YA BIG, SWEET, UGLY OL' IDJIT.

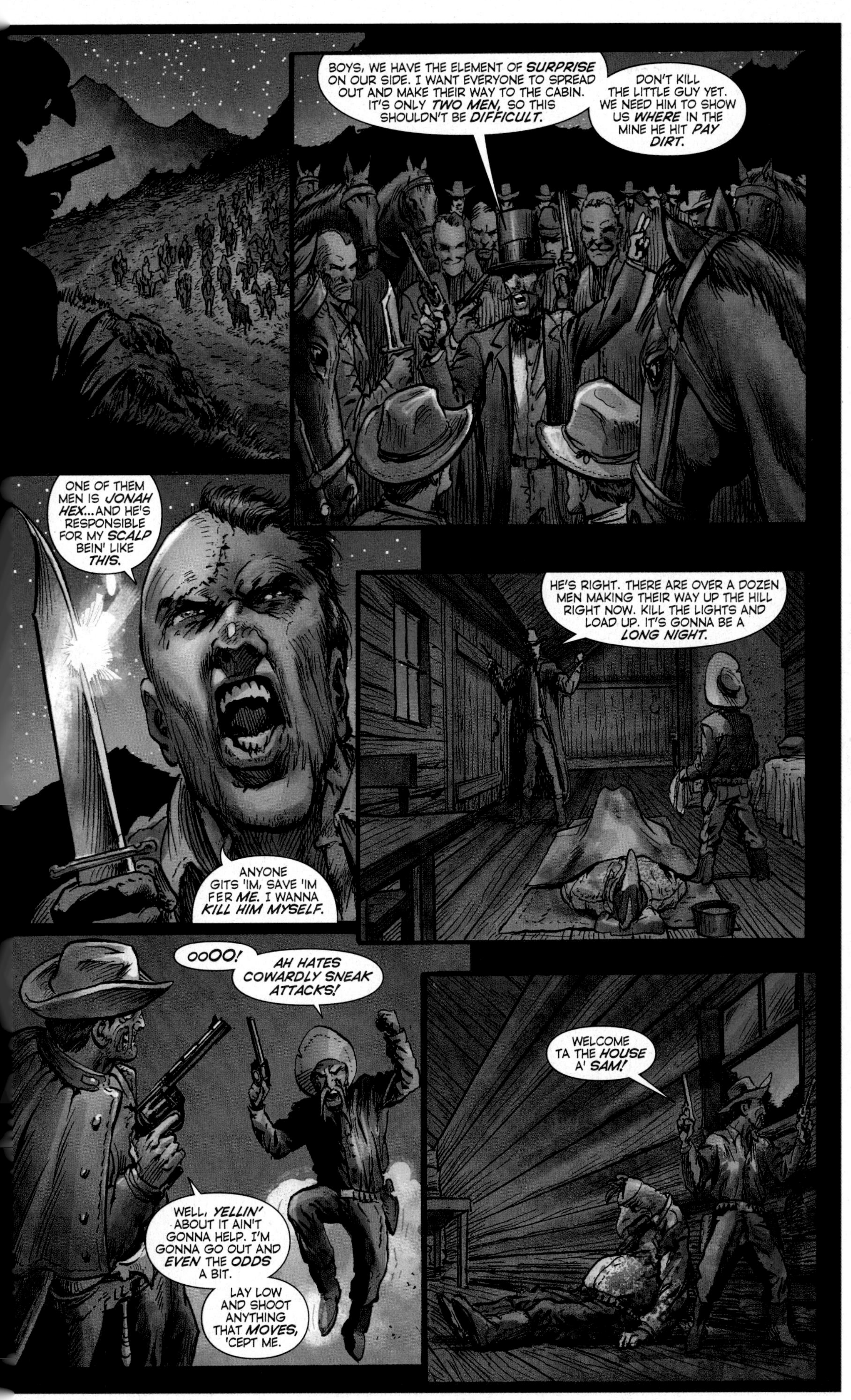
BOYS, WE HAVE THE ELEMENT OF SURPRISE ON OUR SIDE. I WANT EVERYONE TO SPREAD OUT AND MAKE THEIR WAY TO THE CABIN. IT'S ONLY TWO MEN, SO THIS SHOULDN'T BE DIFFICULT.
DON'T KILL THE LITTLE GUY YET. WE NEED HIM TO SHOW US WHERE IN THE MINE HE HIT PAY DIRT.
ONE OF THEM MEN IS JONAH HEX...AND HE'S RESPONSIBLE FOR MY SCALP BEIN' LIKE THIS.
ANYONE GITS 'IM, SAVE 'IM FER ME. I WANNA KILL HIM MYSELF.
HE'S RIGHT. THERE ARE OVER A DOZEN MEN MAKING THEIR WAY UP THE HILL RIGHT NOW. KILL THE LIGHTS AND LOAD UP. IT'S GONNA BE A LONG NIGHT.
OOOO!
AH HATES COWARDLY SNEAK ATTACKS!
WELL, YELLIN' ABOUT IT AIN'T GONNA HELP. I'M GONNA GO OUT AND EVEN THE ODDS A BIT.
LAY LOW AND SHOOT ANYTHING THAT MOVES, 'CEPT ME.
WELCOME TA THE HOUSE A' SAM!

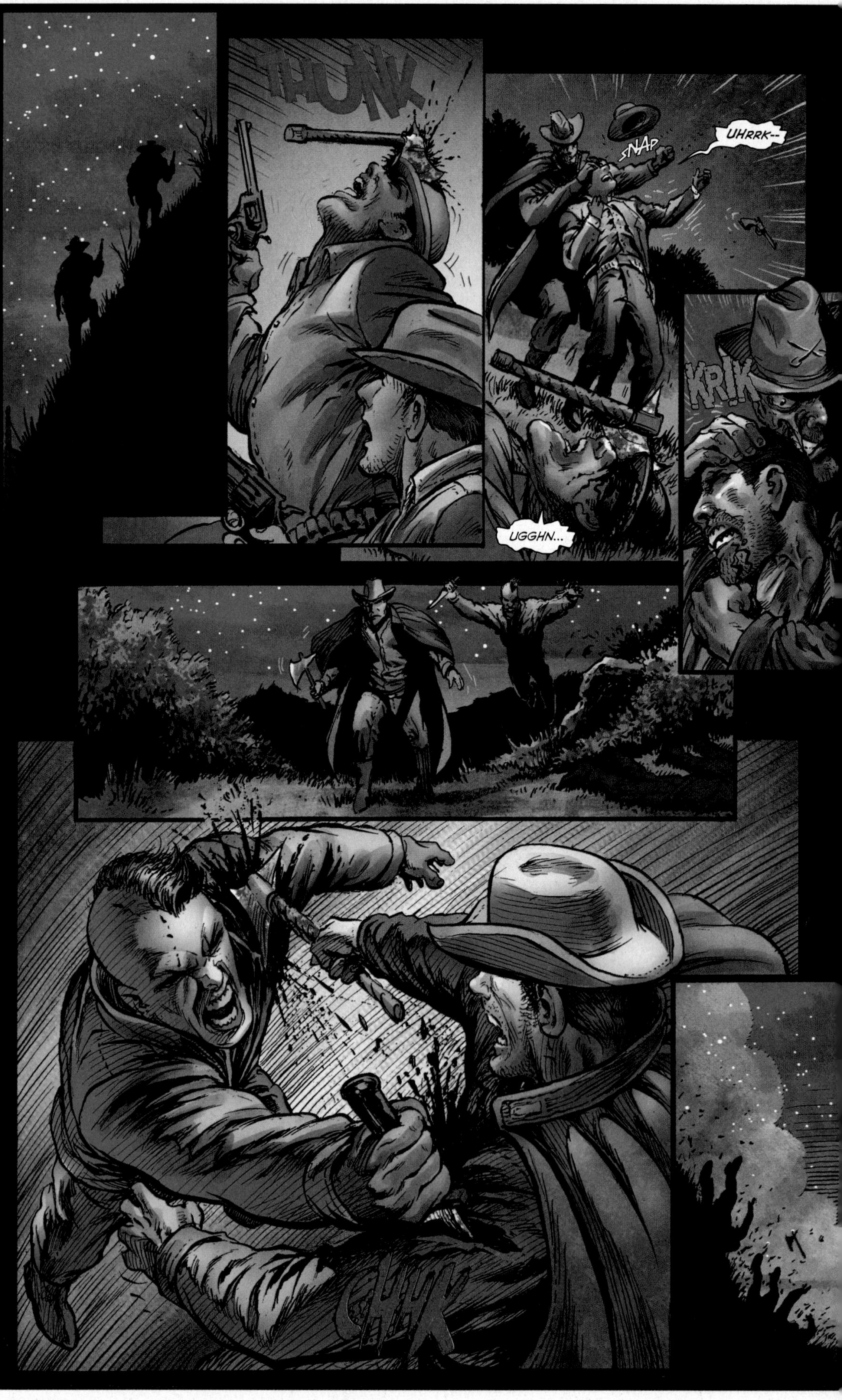
THUNK
SNAP
UHRRK--
UGGHN...
KRIK

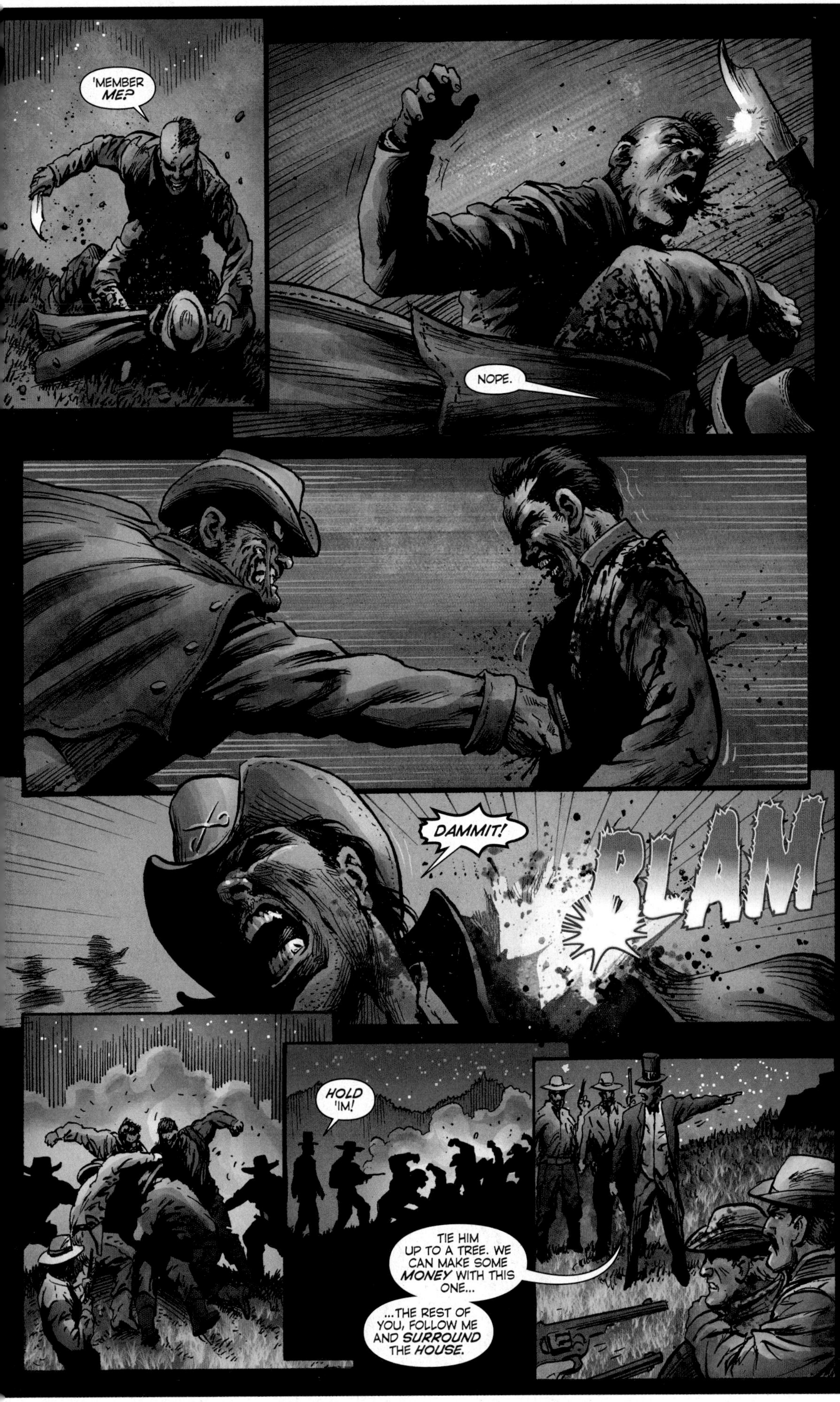
'MEMBER ME?
NOPE.
DAMMIT!
BLAM
HOLD 'IM!
TIE HIM UP TO A TREE. WE CAN MAKE SOME MONEY WITH THIS ONE...
...THE REST OF YOU, FOLLOW ME AND SURROUND THE HOUSE.

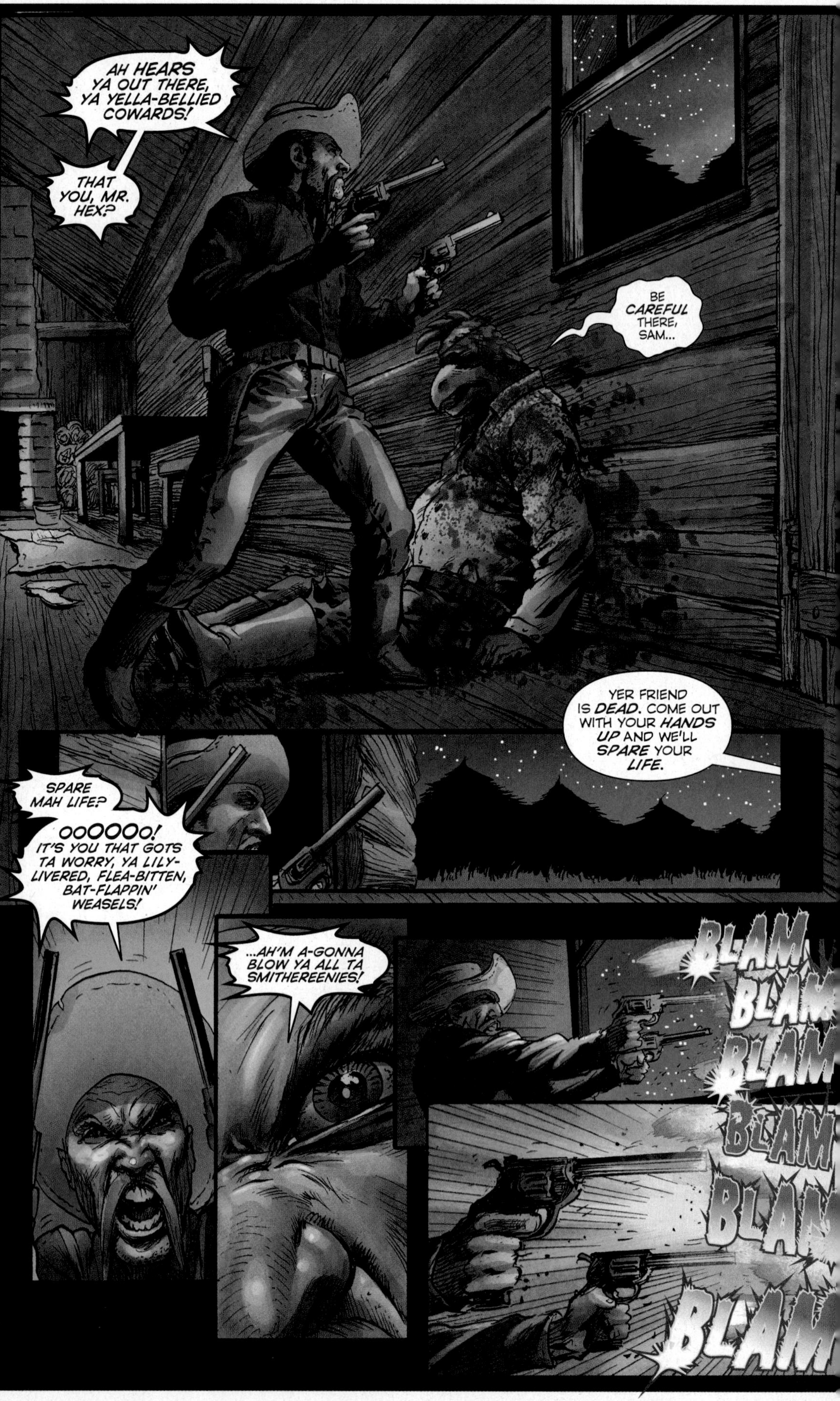
AH HEARS YA OUT THERE, YA YELLA-BELLIED COWARDS!
THAT YOU, MR. HEX?
BE CAREFUL THERE, SAM...
YER FRIEND IS DEAD. COME OUT WITH YOUR HANDS UP AND WE'LL SPARE YOUR LIFE.
SPARE MAH LIFE?
OOOOOO! IT'S YOU THAT GOTS TA WORRY, YA LILY-LIVERED, FLEA-BITTEN, BAT-FLAPPIN' WEASELS!
...AH'M A-GONNA BLOW YA ALL TA SMITHEREENIES!
BLAM
BLAM
BLAM
BLAM
BLAM
BLAM

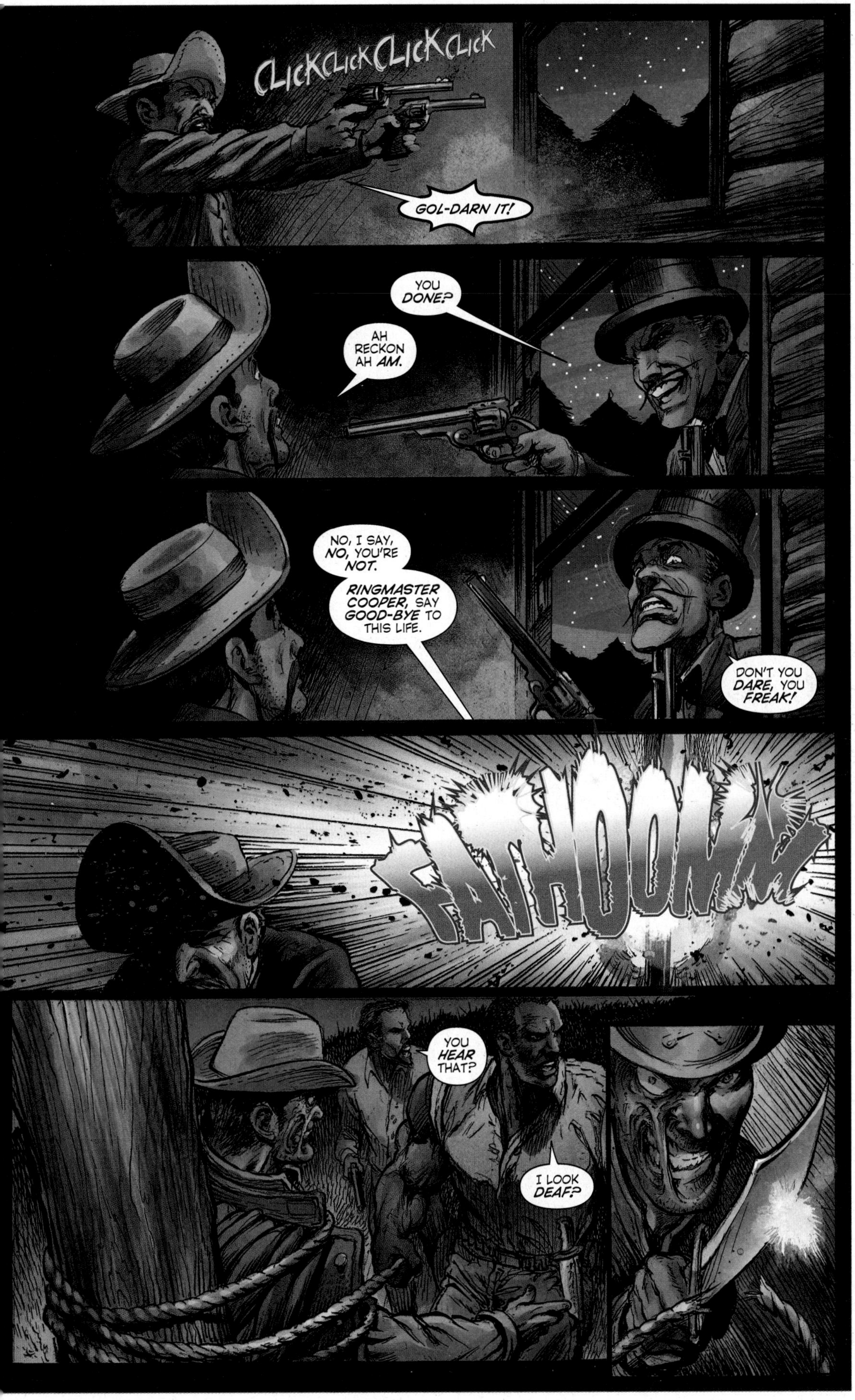
CLICK CLICK CLICK CLICK
GOL-DARN IT!
YOU DONE?
AH RECKON AH AM.
NO, I SAY, NO, YOU'RE NOT.
RINGMASTER COOPER, SAY GOOD-BYE TO THIS LIFE.
DON'T YOU DARE, YOU FREAK!
FATHOOMM
YOU HEAR THAT?
I LOOK DEAF?

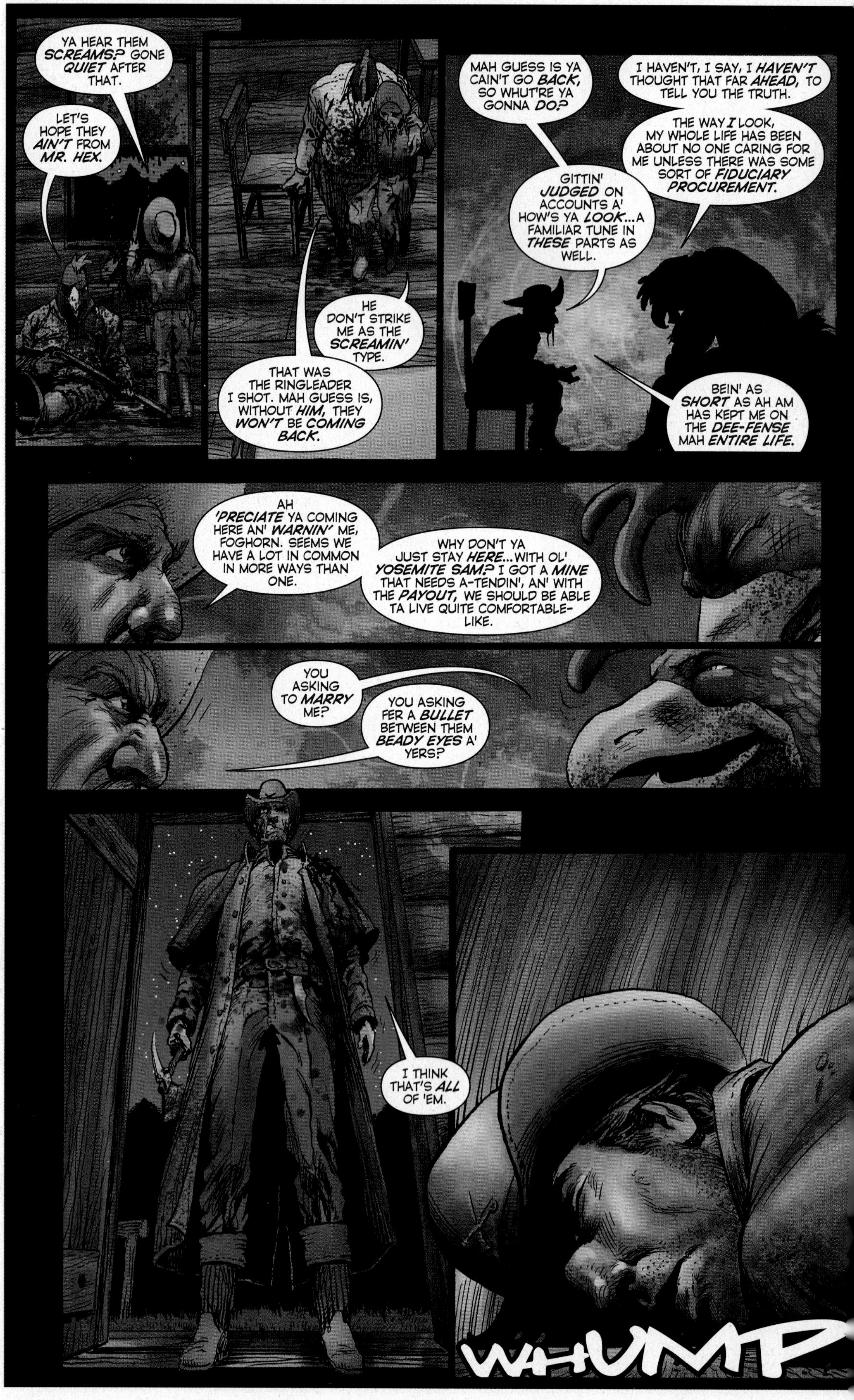
YA HEAR THEM SCREAMS? GONE QUIET AFTER THAT.
LET'S HOPE THEY AIN'T FROM MR. HEX.
HE DON'T STRIKE ME AS THE SCREAMIN' TYPE.
THAT WAS THE RINGLEADER I SHOT. MAH GUESS IS, WITHOUT HIM, THEY WON'T BE COMING BACK.
MAH GUESS IS YA CAIN'T GO BACK, SO WHUT'RE YA GONNA DO?
I HAVEN'T, I SAY, I HAVEN'T THOUGHT THAT FAR AHEAD, TO TELL YOU THE TRUTH.
THE WAY I LOOK, MY WHOLE LIFE HAS BEEN ABOUT NO ONE CARING FOR ME UNLESS THERE WAS SOME SORT OF FIDUCIARY PROCUREMENT.
GITTIN' JUDGED ON ACCOUNTS A' HOW'S YA LOOK...A FAMILIAR TUNE IN THESE PARTS AS WELL.
BEIN' AS SHORT AS AH AM HAS KEPT ME ON THE DEE-FENSE MAH ENTIRE LIFE.
AH 'PRECIATE YA COMING HERE AN' WARNIN' ME, FOGHORN. SEEMS WE HAVE A LOT IN COMMON IN MORE WAYS THAN ONE.
WHY DON'T YA JUST STAY HERE...WITH OL' YOSEMITE SAM? I GOT A MINE THAT NEEDS A-TENDIN', AN' WITH THE PAYOUT, WE SHOULD BE ABLE TA LIVE QUITE COMFORTABLE-LIKE.
YOU ASKING TO MARRY ME?
YOU ASKING FER A BULLET BETWEEN THEM BEADY EYES A' YERS?
I THINK THAT'S ALL OF 'EM.
WHUMP

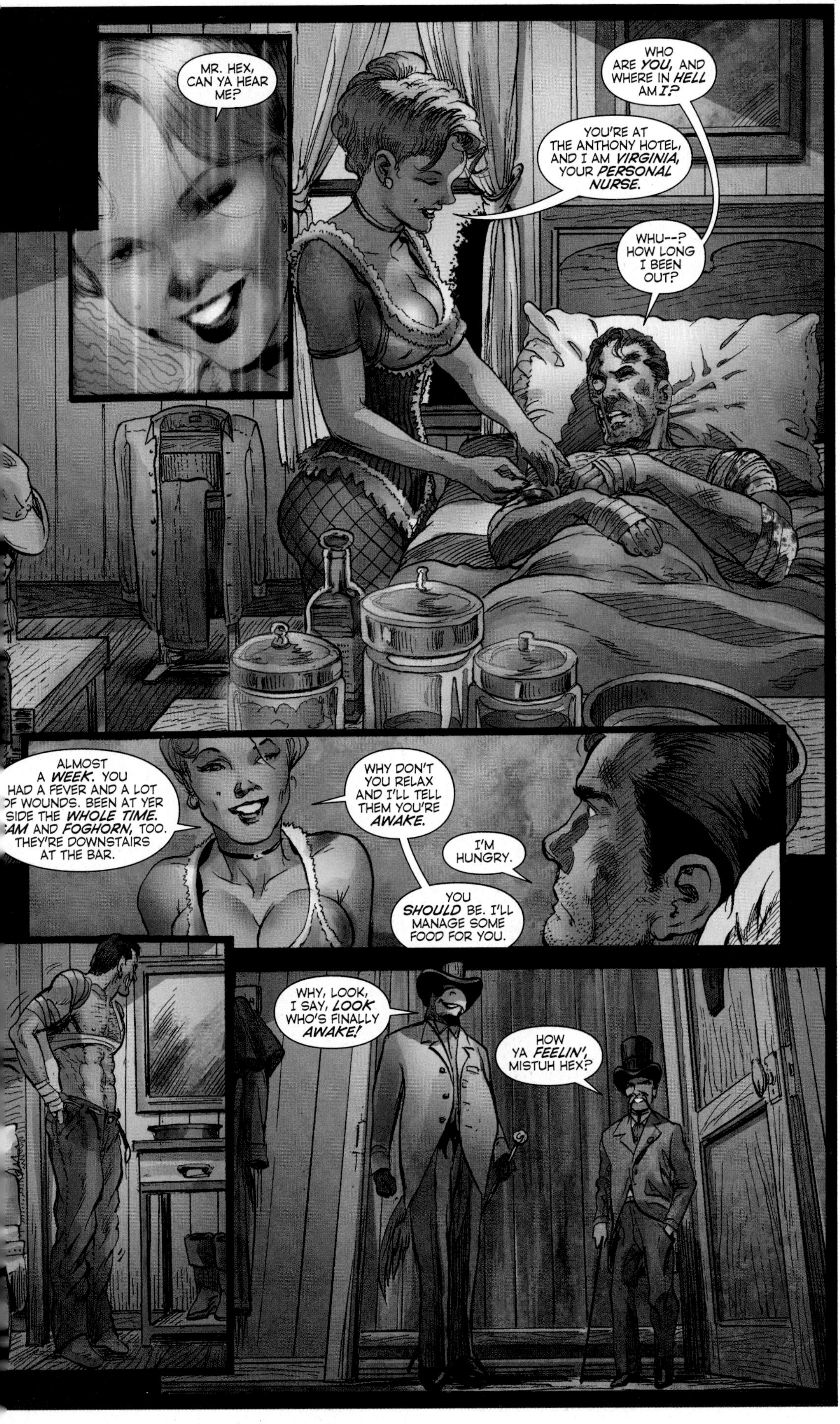
MR. HEX, CAN YA HEAR ME?
WHO ARE *YOU*, AND WHERE IN *HELL* AM *I?*
YOU'RE AT THE ANTHONY HOTEL, AND I AM *VIRGINIA*, YOUR *PERSONAL NURSE*.
WHU--? HOW LONG I BEEN OUT?
ALMOST A *WEEK*. YOU HAD A FEVER AND A LOT OF WOUNDS. BEEN AT YER SIDE THE *WHOLE TIME*. SAM AND *FOGHORN*, TOO. THEY'RE DOWNSTAIRS AT THE BAR.
WHY DON'T YOU RELAX AND I'LL TELL THEM YOU'RE *AWAKE*.
I'M HUNGRY.
YOU *SHOULD* BE. I'LL MANAGE SOME FOOD FOR YOU.
WHY, LOOK, I SAY, *LOOK* WHO'S FINALLY *AWAKE!*
HOW YA *FEELIN'*, MISTUH HEX?

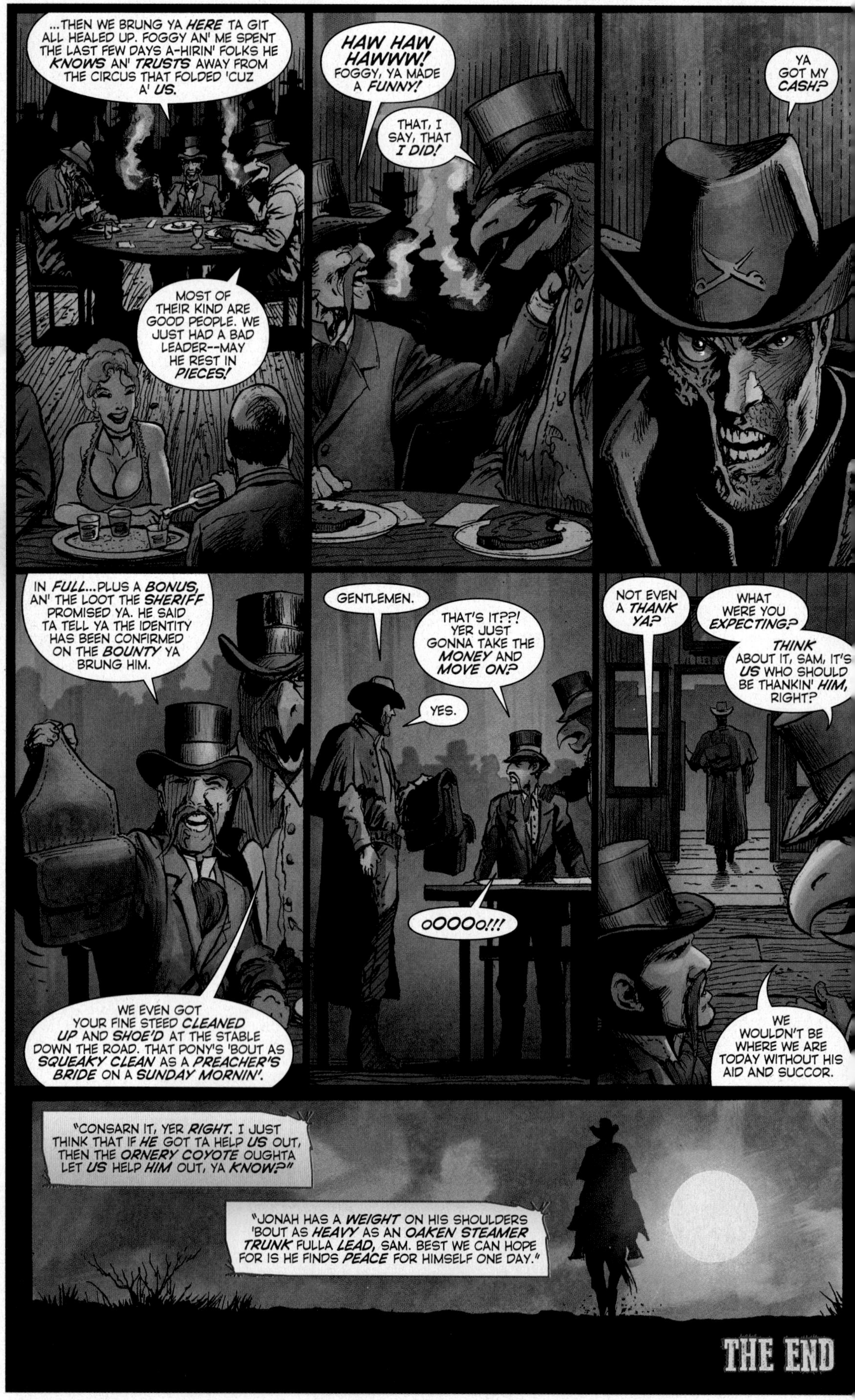
...THEN WE BRUNG YA HERE TA GIT ALL HEALED UP. FOGGY AN' ME SPENT THE LAST FEW DAYS A-HIRIN' FOLKS HE KNOWS AN' TRUSTS AWAY FROM THE CIRCUS THAT FOLDED 'CUZ A' US.
MOST OF THEIR KIND ARE GOOD PEOPLE. WE JUST HAD A BAD LEADER--MAY HE REST IN PIECES!
HAW HAW HAWWW! FOGGY, YA MADE A FUNNY!
THAT, I SAY, THAT I DID!
YA GOT MY CASH?
IN FULL...PLUS A BONUS, AN' THE LOOT THE SHERIFF PROMISED YA. HE SAID TA TELL YA THE IDENTITY HAS BEEN CONFIRMED ON THE BOUNTY YA BRUNG HIM.
WE EVEN GOT YOUR FINE STEED CLEANED UP AND SHOE'D AT THE STABLE DOWN THE ROAD. THAT PONY'S 'BOUT AS SQUEAKY CLEAN AS A PREACHER'S BRIDE ON A SUNDAY MORNIN'.
GENTLEMEN.
THAT'S IT??! YER JUST GONNA TAKE THE MONEY AND MOVE ON?
YES.
oOOOo!!!
NOT EVEN A THANK YA?
WHAT WERE YOU EXPECTING?
THINK ABOUT IT, SAM, IT'S US WHO SHOULD BE THANKIN' HIM, RIGHT?
WE WOULDN'T BE WHERE WE ARE TODAY WITHOUT HIS AID AND SUCCOR.
"CONSARN IT, YER RIGHT. I JUST THINK THAT IF HE GOT TA HELP US OUT, THEN THE ORNERY COYOTE OUGHTA LET US HELP HIM OUT, YA KNOW?"
"JONAH HAS A WEIGHT ON HIS SHOULDERS 'BOUT AS HEAVY AS AN OAKEN STEAMER TRUNK FULLA LEAD, SAM. BEST WE CAN HOPE FOR IS HE FINDS PEACE FOR HIMSELF ONE DAY."
THE END

SAY YER PRAYERS, YA BUCK-TOOTHED CARROT CRUNCHER. YOU AIN'T NO BUGS BUNNY, BUT YOU'LL BE SUPPER FOR YOSEMITE...

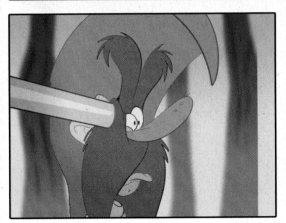

...SAM?

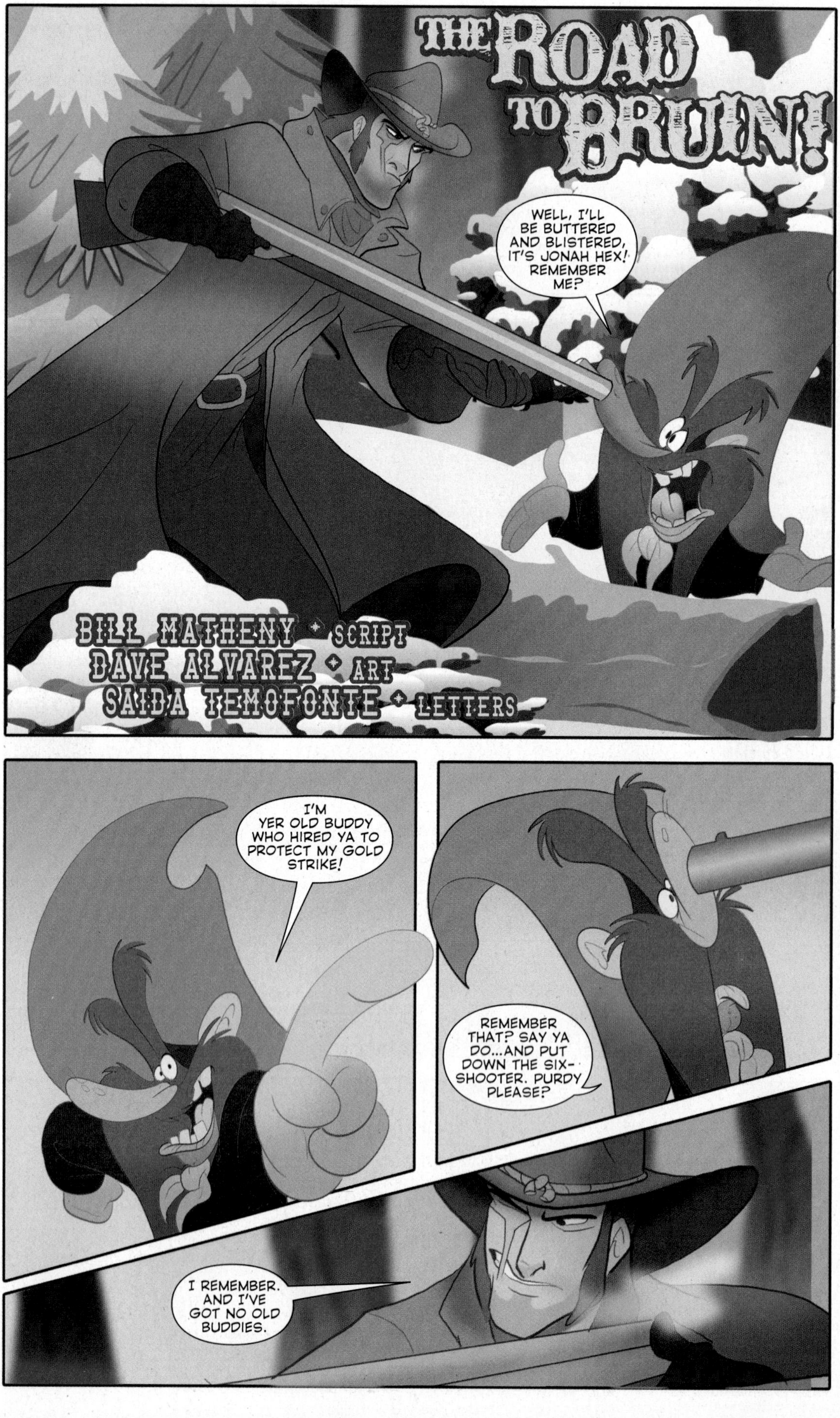
THE ROAD TO BRUIN!
WELL, I'LL BE BUTTERED AND BLISTERED, IT'S JONAH HEX! REMEMBER ME?
BILL MATHENY • SCRIPT
DAVE ALVAREZ • ART
SAIDA TEMOFONTE • LETTERS
I'M YER OLD BUDDY WHO HIRED YA TO PROTECT MY GOLD STRIKE!
REMEMBER THAT? SAY YA DO...AND PUT DOWN THE SIX-SHOOTER. PURDY PLEASE?
I REMEMBER. AND I'VE GOT NO OLD BUDDIES.

JUST OLD BOUNTIES.

A BEAR? SOMEONE PUT A BOUNTY ON A HONEY-STEALIN', FLEA-BITTEN BEAR?

DEAD OR ALIVE. AND I AIM TO COLLECT IT.

WANTED

DEAD OR ALIVE

YOSEMITE SAM AIN'T SCARED OF NO BEAR, BE HE GRIZZLY OR POLAR!

THIS ONE'S AN OUTLAW. FOLKS ARE WORRIED THAT HE MAY BECOME A MAN-EATER.

EEWWW!

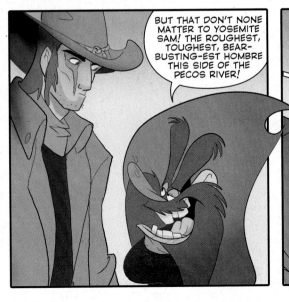

BUT THAT DON'T NONE MATTER TO YOSEMITE SAM! THE ROUGHEST, TOUGHEST, BEAR-BUSTING-EST HOMBRE THIS SIDE OF THE PECOS RIVER!

THAT SIDE, TOO, BUT I DON'T WANT TO BRAG!

HUNHH...

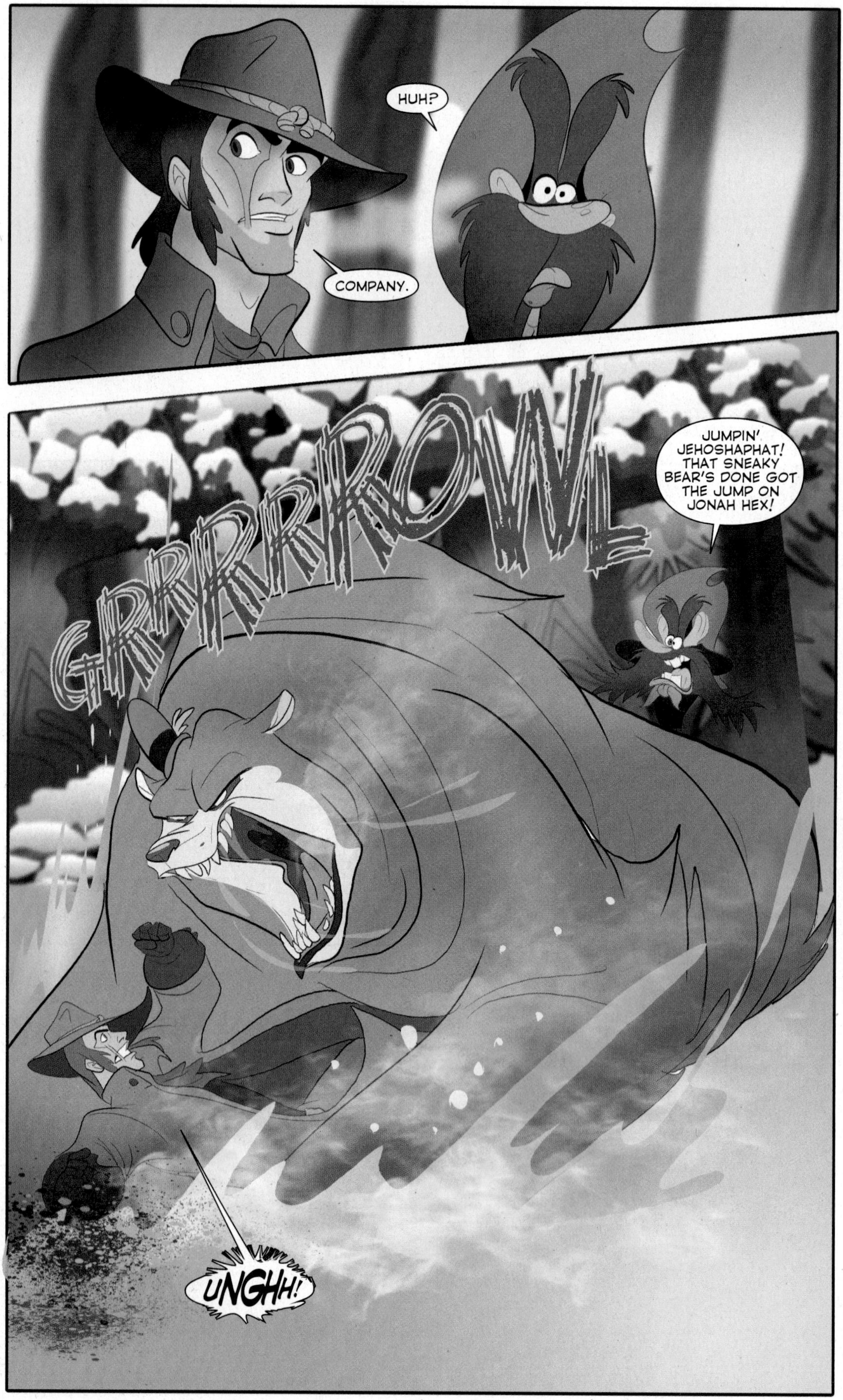
HUH?
COMPANY.
GRRRRROWL
JUMPIN' JEHOSHAPHAT! THAT SNEAKY BEAR'S DONE GOT THE JUMP ON JONAH HEX!
UNGHH!

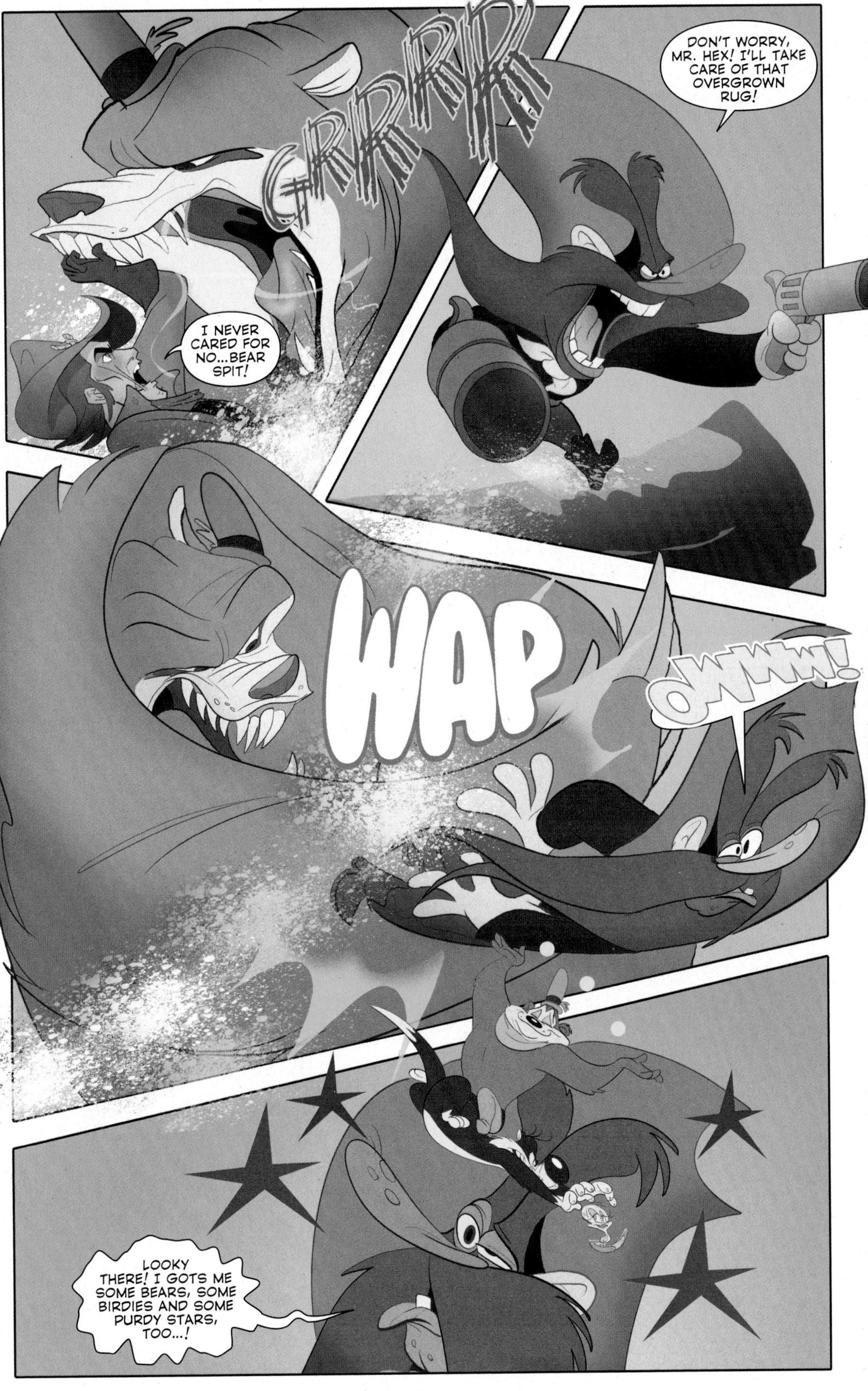
CRRRRR
DON'T WORRY, MR. HEX! I'LL TAKE CARE OF THAT OVERGROWN RUG!
I NEVER CARED FOR NO...BEAR SPIT!
WAP
OWWW!
LOOKY THERE! I GOTS ME SOME BEARS, SOME BIRDIES AND SOME PURDY STARS, TOO...!

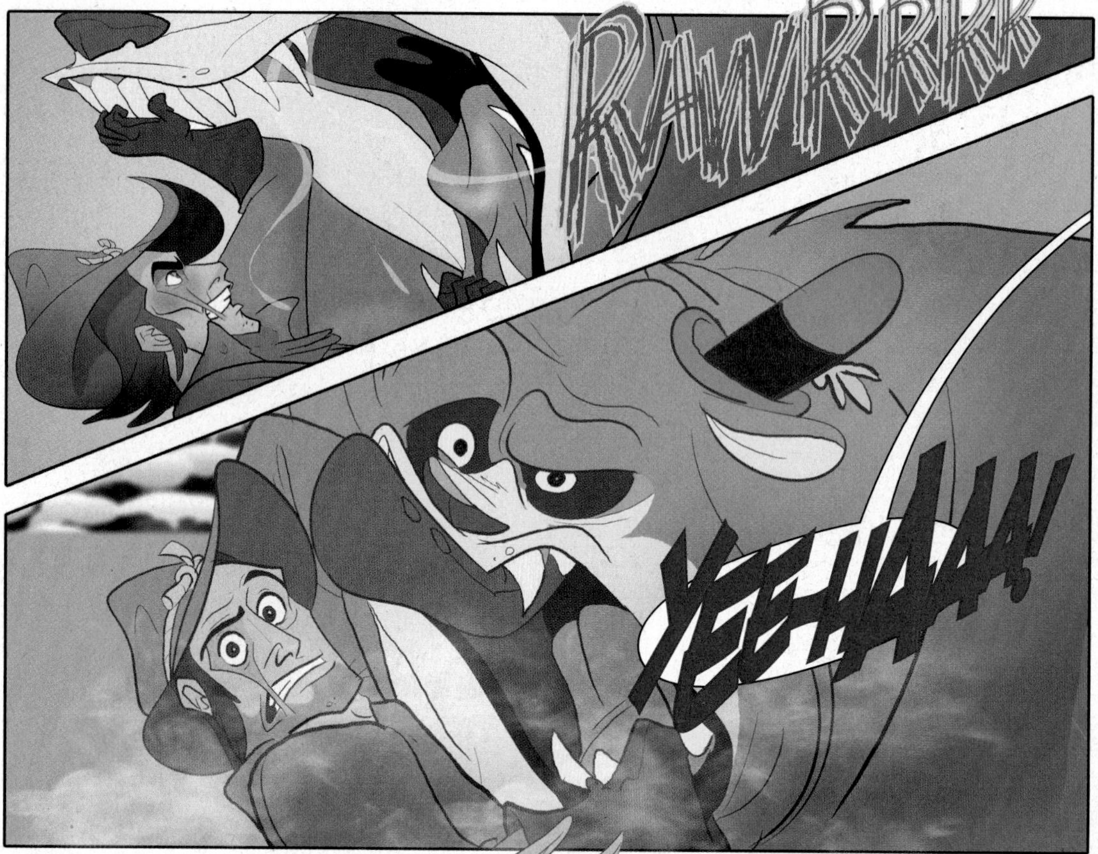
RAWRRRRR
YEEHAAA!

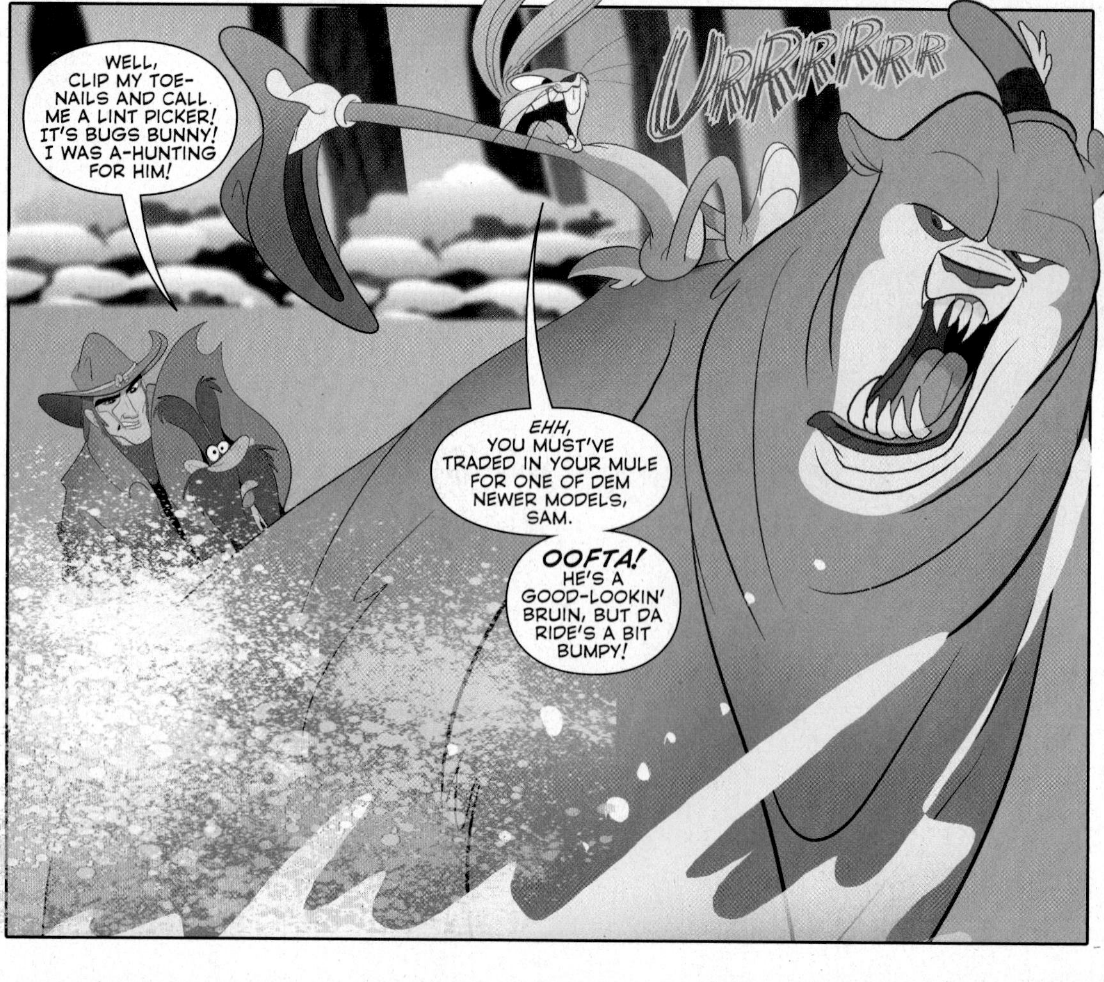
WELL, CLIP MY TOE-NAILS AND CALL ME A LINT PICKER! IT'S BUGS BUNNY! I WAS A-HUNTING FOR HIM!
URRRRRR
EHH, YOU MUST'VE TRADED IN YOUR MULE FOR ONE OF DEM NEWER MODELS, SAM.
OOFTA! HE'S A GOOD-LOOKIN' BRUIN, BUT DA RIDE'S A BIT BUMPY!

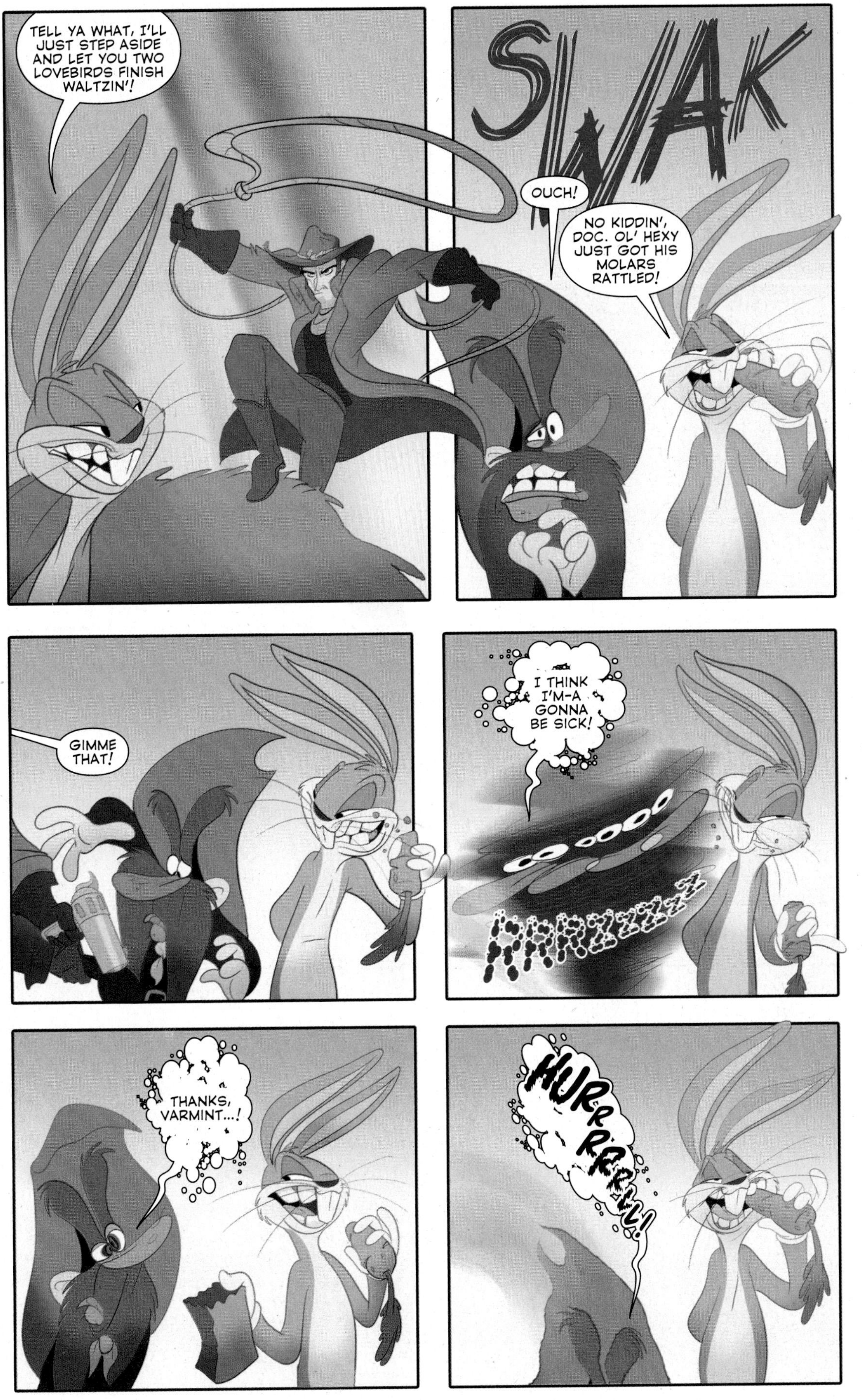
TELL YA WHAT, I'LL JUST STEP ASIDE AND LET YOU TWO LOVEBIRDS FINISH WALTZIN'!
SWAK
OUCH!
NO KIDDIN', DOC. OL' HEXY JUST GOT HIS MOLARS RATTLED!
GIMME THAT!
I THINK I'M-A GONNA BE SICK!
RRRBZZZZ
THANKS, VARMINT...!
HURRRRRL!

YOU'RE THE BEAR-WRESTLING-EST HOMBRE I EVER SEEN, MR. HEX. HOW COME YOU TOOK HIM ALIVE INSTEAD OF REAL DEAD-LIKE?

'CAUSE I'M PARTIAL TO ANIMALS. HUMANS...NOT SO MUCH.

I'M WIT'CHA DERE, DOC!

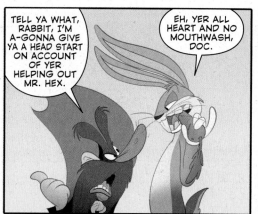

TELL YA WHAT, RABBIT, I'M A-GONNA GIVE YA A HEAD START ON ACCOUNT OF YER HELPING OUT MR. HEX.

EH, YER ALL HEART AND NO MOUTHWASH, DOC.

SO LONG, SAMMY, SEE YOU IN MIAMI!

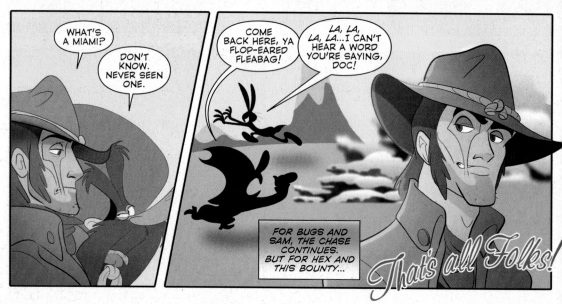

WHAT'S A MIAMI?

DON'T KNOW. NEVER SEEN ONE.

COME BACK HERE, YA FLOP-EARED FLEABAG!

LA, LA, LA, LA...I CAN'T HEAR A WORD YOU'RE SAYING, DOC!

FOR BUGS AND SAM, THE CHASE CONTINUES. BUT FOR HEX AND THIS BOUNTY...

That's all Folks!

LEE WEEKS

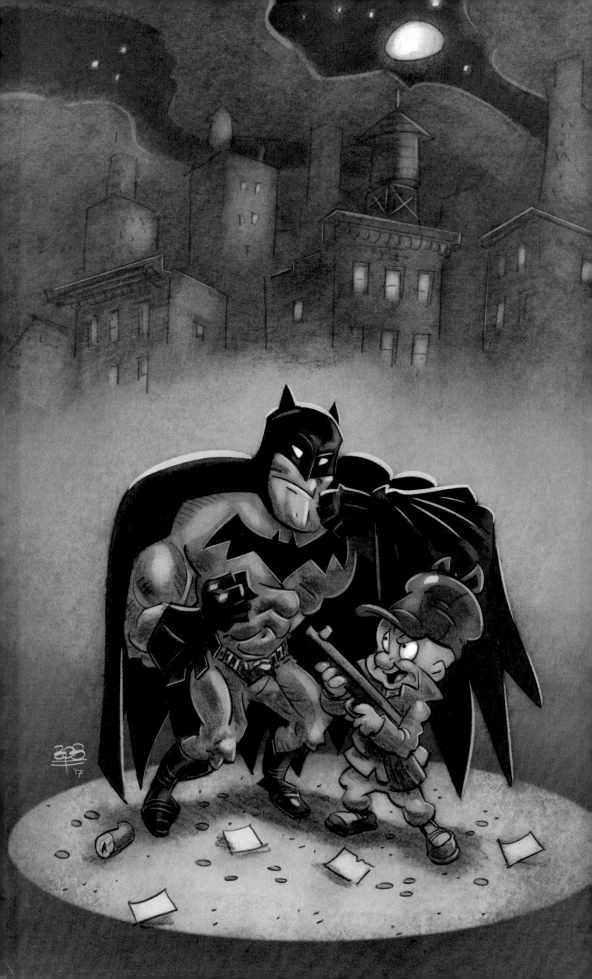

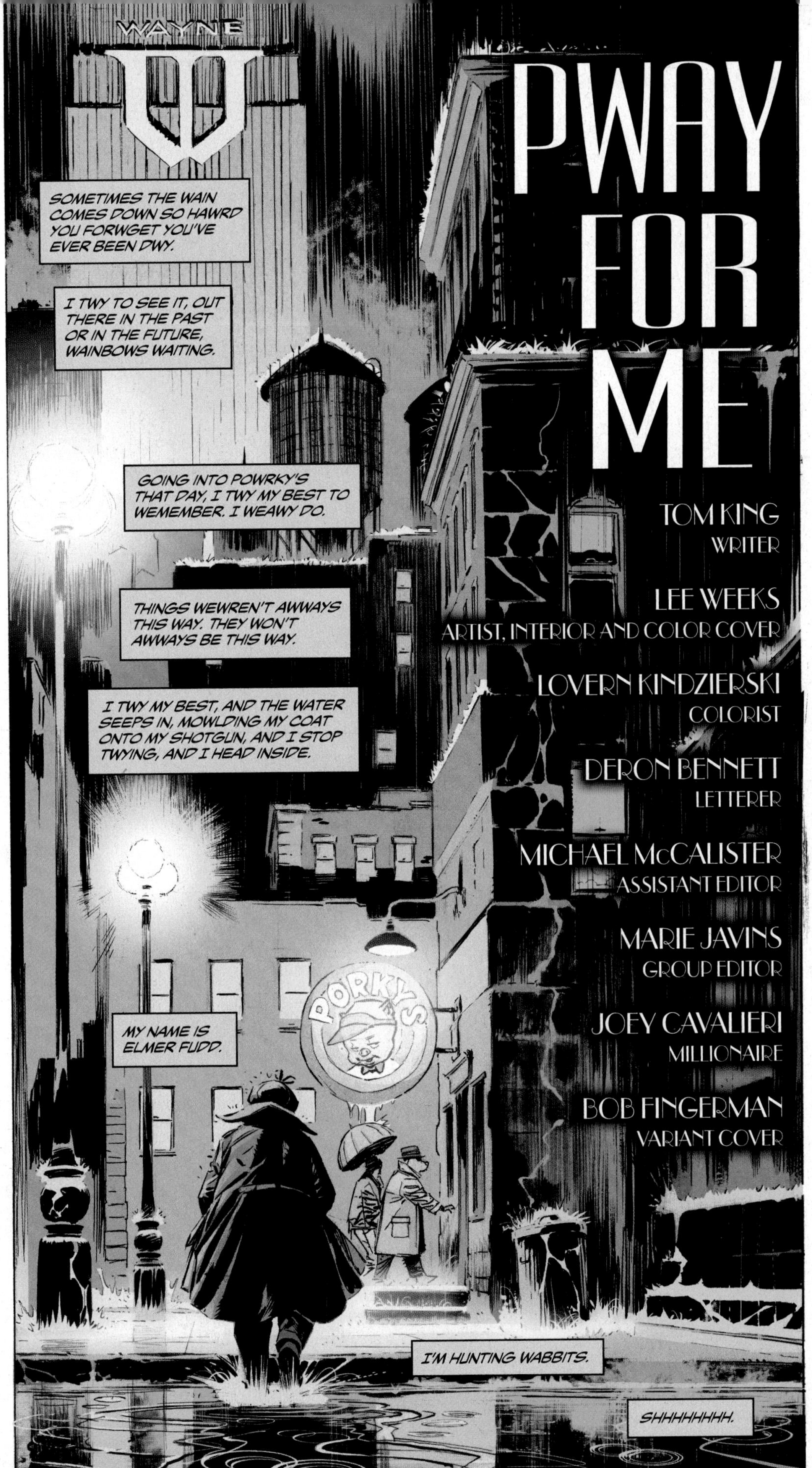
WAYNE
PWAY FOR ME
SOMETIMES THE WAIN COMES DOWN SO HAWRD YOU FORWGET YOU'VE EVER BEEN DWY.
I TWY TO SEE IT, OUT THERE IN THE PAST OR IN THE FUTURE, WAINBOWS WAITING.
GOING INTO POWRKY'S THAT DAY, I TWY MY BEST TO WEMEMBER. I WEAWY DO.
THINGS WEWREN'T AWWAYS THIS WAY. THEY WON'T AWWAYS BE THIS WAY.
I TWY MY BEST, AND THE WATER SEEPS IN, MOWLDING MY COAT ONTO MY SHOTGUN, AND I STOP TWYING, AND I HEAD INSIDE.
TOM KING
WRITER
LEE WEEKS
ARTIST, INTERIOR AND COLOR COVER
LOVERN KINDZIERSKI
COLORIST
DERON BENNETT
LETTERER
MICHAEL McCALISTER
ASSISTANT EDITOR
MARIE JAVINS
GROUP EDITOR
JOEY CAVALIERI
MILLIONAIRE
BOB FINGERMAN
VARIANT COVER
PORKY'S
MY NAME IS ELMER FUDD.
I'M HUNTING WABBITS.
SHHHHHHHH.

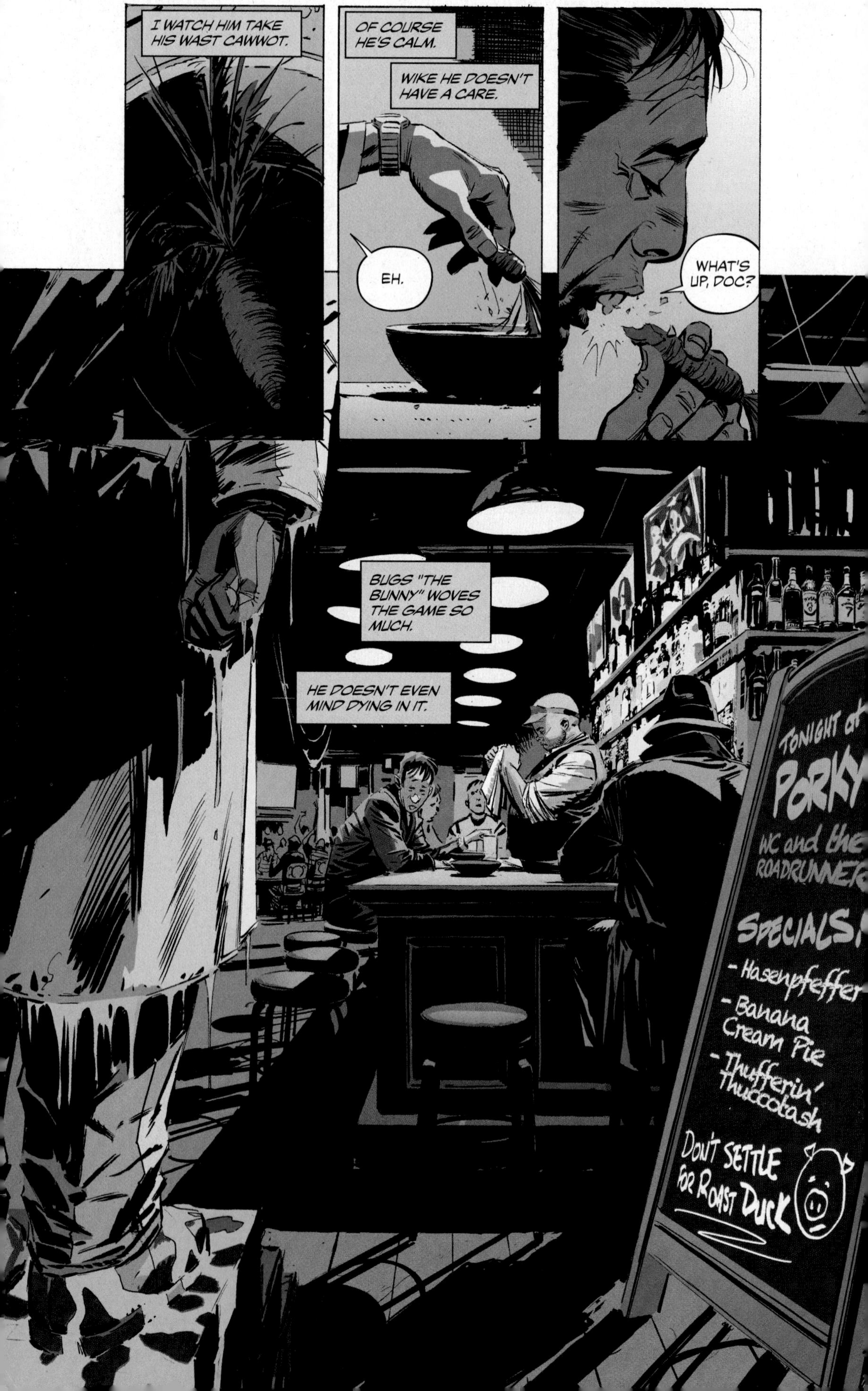
I WATCH HIM TAKE HIS WAST CAWWOT.
OF COURSE HE'S CALM.
WIKE HE DOESN'T HAVE A CARE.
EH.
WHAT'S UP, DOC?
BUGS "THE BUNNY" WOVES THE GAME SO MUCH.
HE DOESN'T EVEN MIND DYING IN IT.
TONIGHT at
PORKY
WC and the ROADRUNNERS
SPECIALS!
- Hasenpfeffer
- Banana Cream Pie
- Thufferin' Thuccotash
DON'T SETTLE FOR ROAST DUCK

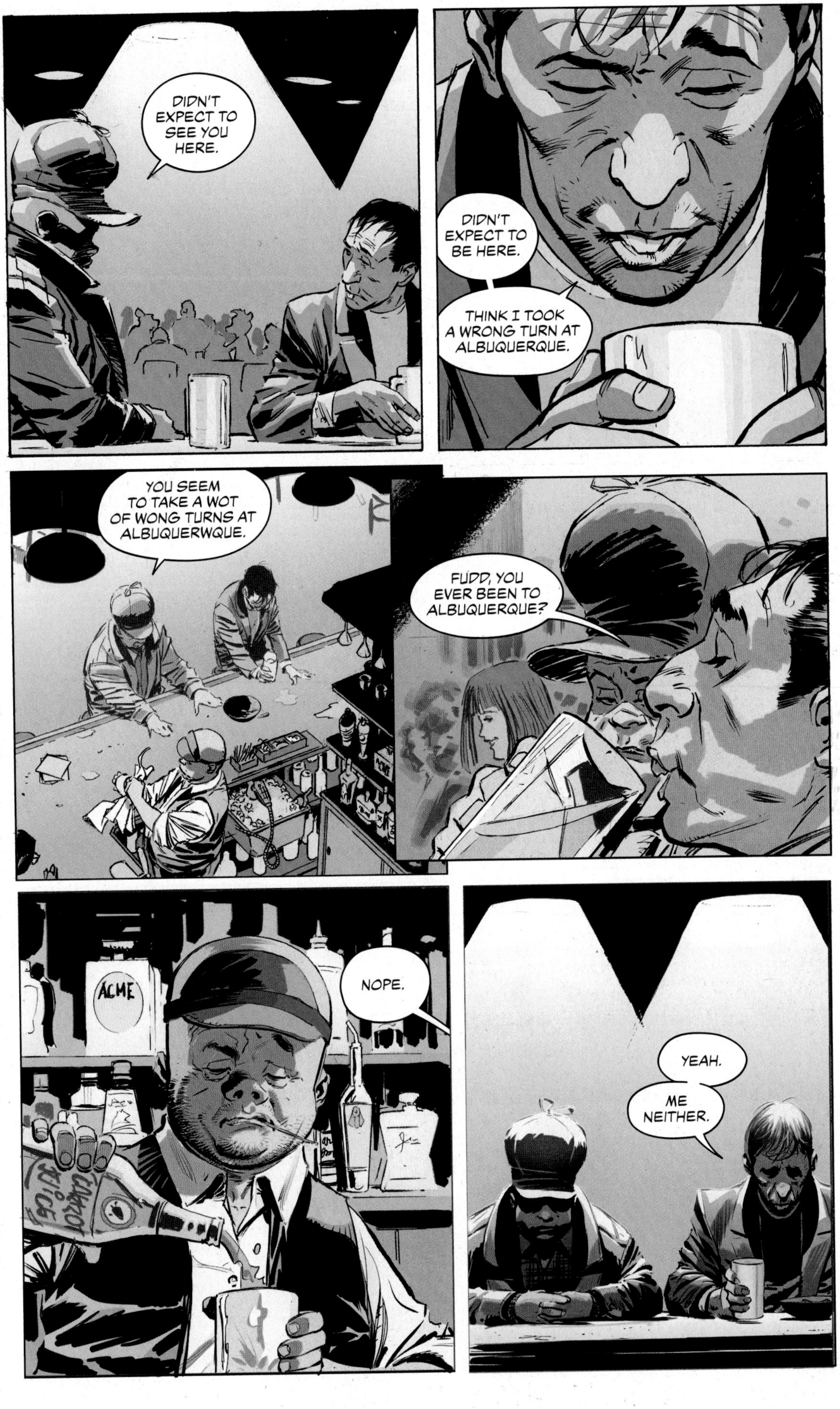
DIDN'T EXPECT TO SEE YOU HERE.
DIDN'T EXPECT TO BE HERE.
THINK I TOOK A WRONG TURN AT ALBUQUERQUE.
YOU SEEM TO TAKE A WOT OF WONG TURNS AT ALBUQUERWQUE.
FUDD, YOU EVER BEEN TO ALBUQUERQUE?
ACME
NOPE.
YEAH.
ME NEITHER.

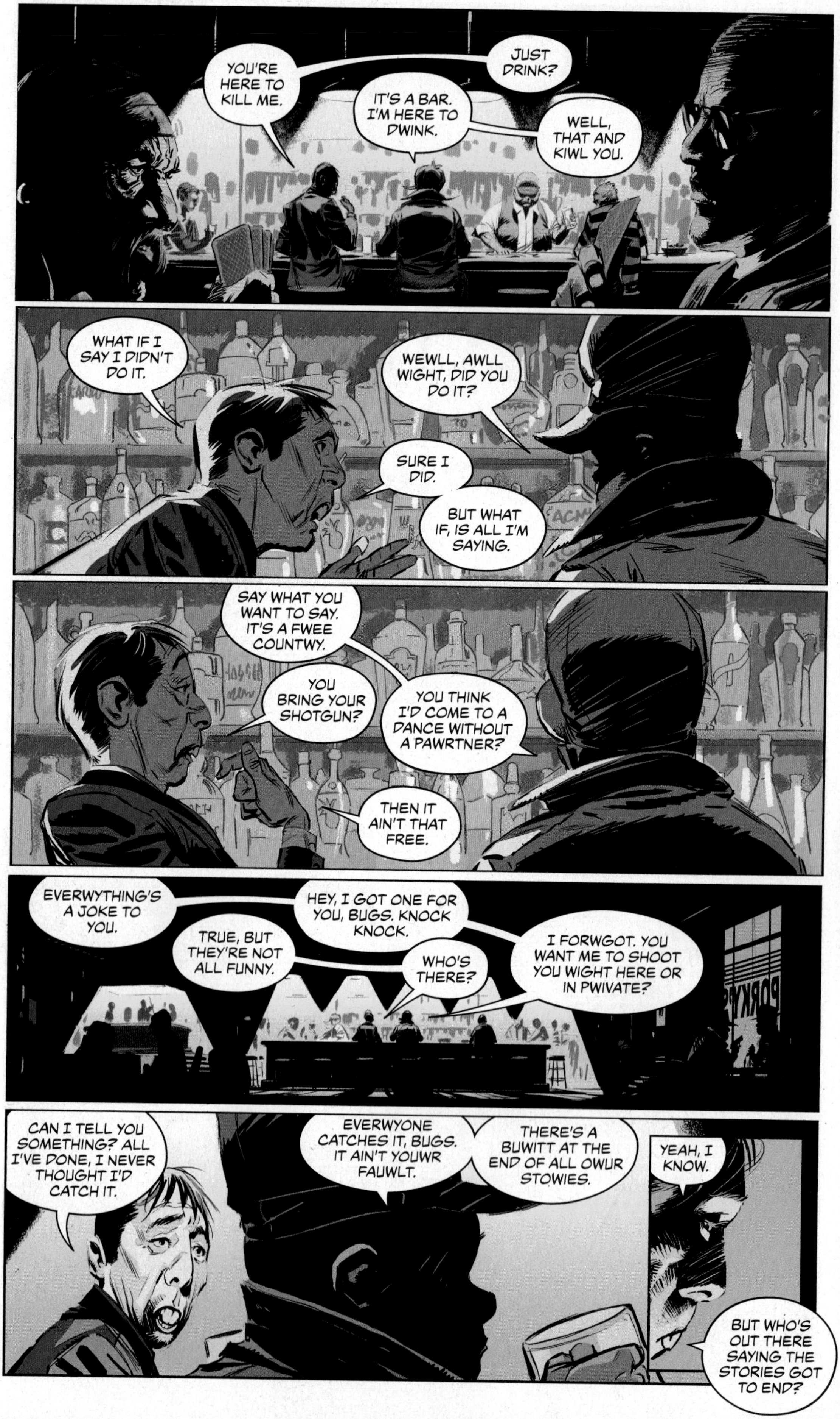
YOU'RE HERE TO KILL ME.
JUST DRINK?
IT'S A BAR. I'M HERE TO DWINK.
WELL, THAT AND KIWL YOU.
WHAT IF I SAY I DIDN'T DO IT.
WEWLL, AWLL WIGHT, DID YOU DO IT?
SURE I DID.
BUT WHAT IF, IS ALL I'M SAYING.
SAY WHAT YOU WANT TO SAY. IT'S A FWEE COUNTWY.
YOU BRING YOUR SHOTGUN?
YOU THINK I'D COME TO A DANCE WITHOUT A PAWRTNER?
THEN IT AIN'T THAT FREE.
EVERWYTHING'S A JOKE TO YOU.
TRUE, BUT THEY'RE NOT ALL FUNNY.
HEY, I GOT ONE FOR YOU, BUGS. KNOCK KNOCK.
WHO'S THERE?
I FORWGOT. YOU WANT ME TO SHOOT YOU WIGHT HERE OR IN PWIVATE?
CAN I TELL YOU SOMETHING? ALL I'VE DONE, I NEVER THOUGHT I'D CATCH IT.
EVERWYONE CATCHES IT, BUGS. IT AIN'T YOUWR FAUWLT.
THERE'S A BUWITT AT THE END OF ALL OWUR STOWIES.
YEAH, I KNOW.
BUT WHO'S OUT THERE SAYING THE STORIES GOT TO END?

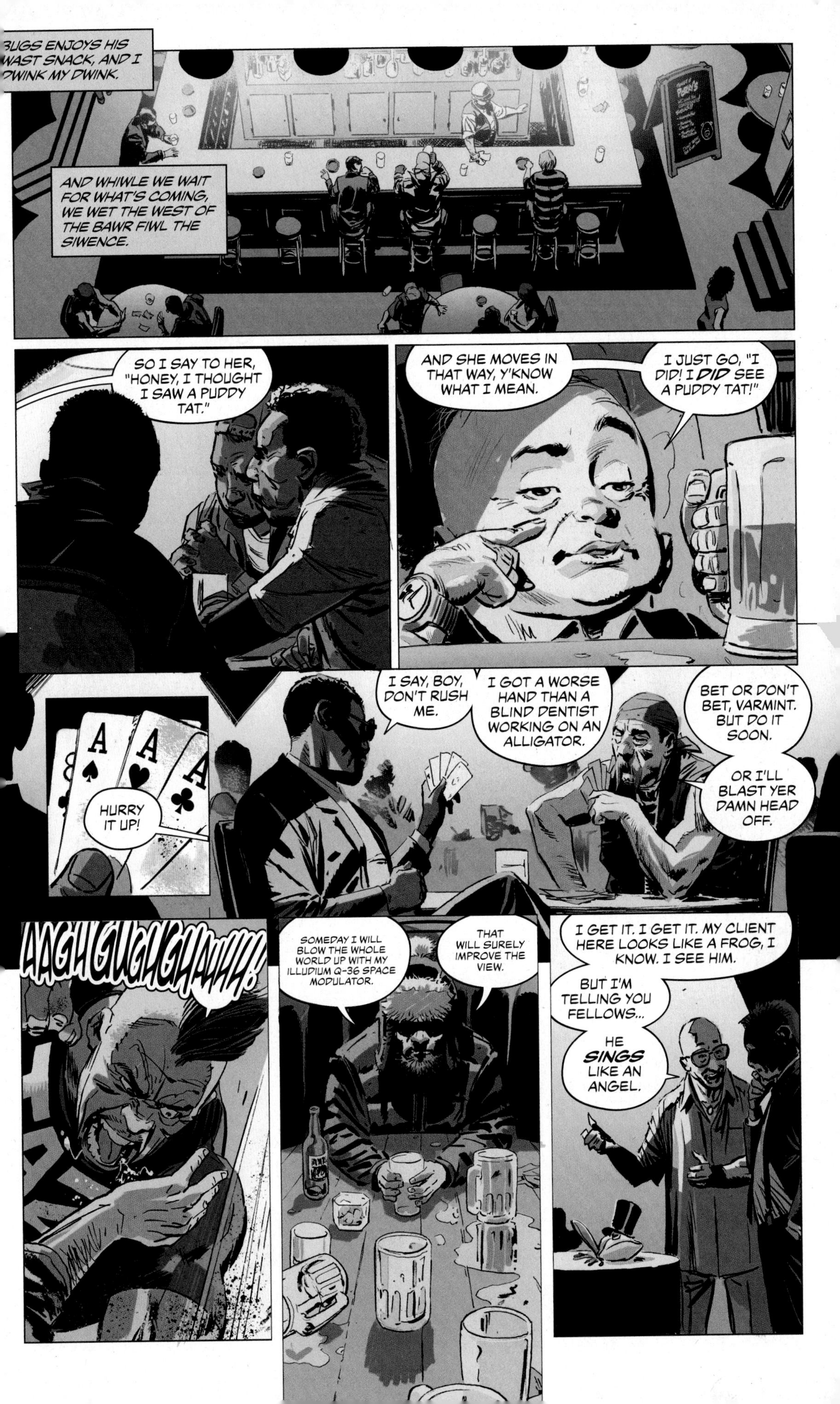
BUGS ENJOYS HIS WAST SNACK, AND I DWINK MY DWINK.
AND WHIWLE WE WAIT FOR WHAT'S COMING, WE WET THE WEST OF THE BAWR FIWL THE SIWENCE.
SO I SAY TO HER, "HONEY, I THOUGHT I SAW A PUDDY TAT."
AND SHE MOVES IN THAT WAY, Y'KNOW WHAT I MEAN.
I JUST GO, "I DID! I DID SEE A PUDDY TAT!"
HURRY IT UP!
I SAY, BOY, DON'T RUSH ME.
I GOT A WORSE HAND THAN A BLIND DENTIST WORKING ON AN ALLIGATOR.
BET OR DON'T BET, VARMINT. BUT DO IT SOON.
OR I'LL BLAST YER DAMN HEAD OFF.
AAAGHGUGHGHAHHH!
SOMEDAY I WILL BLOW THE WHOLE WORLD UP WITH MY ILLUDIUM Q-36 SPACE MODULATOR.
THAT WILL SURELY IMPROVE THE VIEW.
I GET IT. I GET IT. MY CLIENT HERE LOOKS LIKE A FROG, I KNOW. I SEE HIM.
BUT I'M TELLING YOU FELLOWS...
HE SINGS LIKE AN ANGEL.

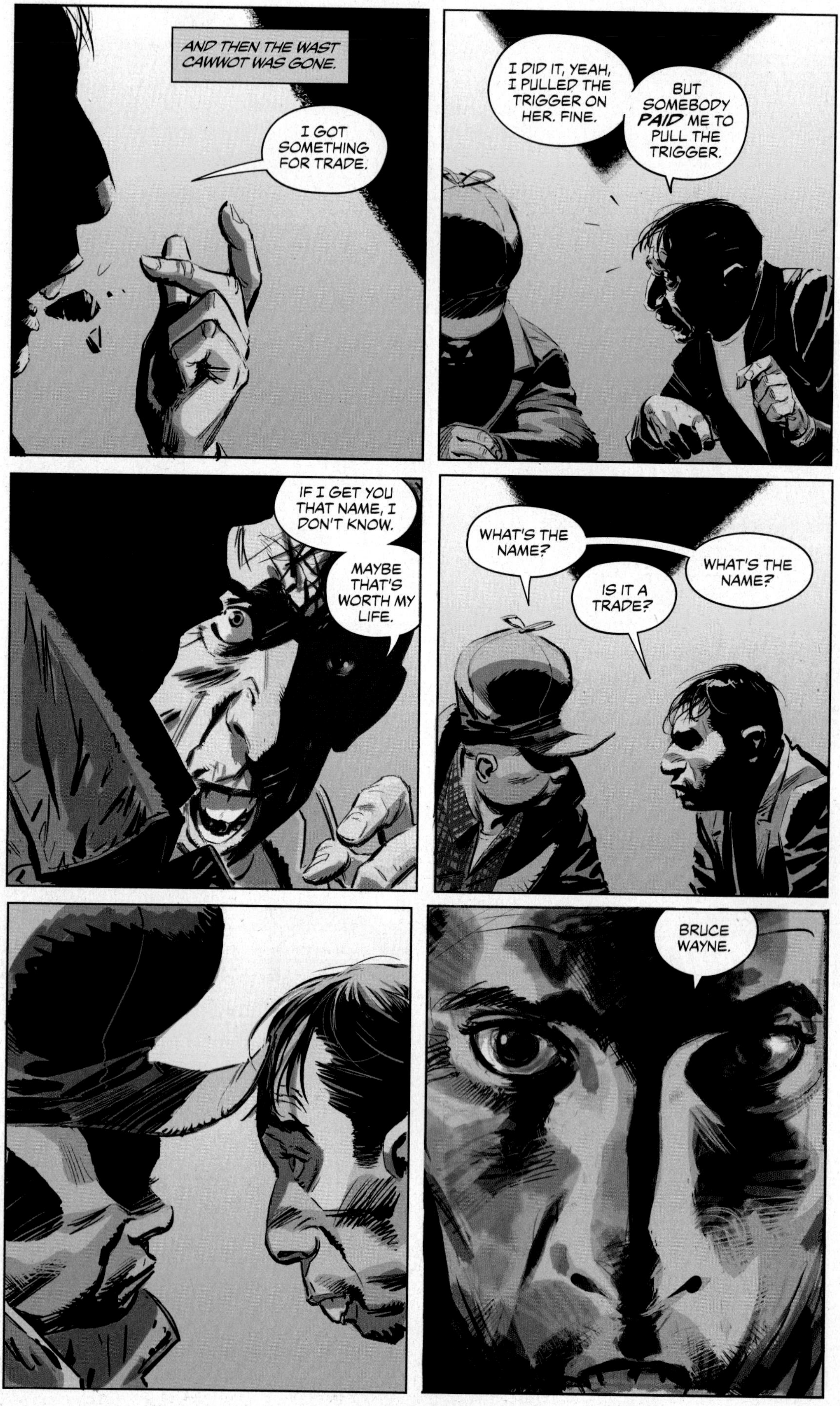
AND THEN THE WAST CAWWOT WAS GONE.
I GOT SOMETHING FOR TRADE.
I DID IT, YEAH, I PULLED THE TRIGGER ON HER. FINE.
BUT SOMEBODY PAID ME TO PULL THE TRIGGER.
IF I GET YOU THAT NAME, I DON'T KNOW.
MAYBE THAT'S WORTH MY LIFE.
WHAT'S THE NAME?
IS IT A TRADE?
WHAT'S THE NAME?
BRUCE WAYNE.

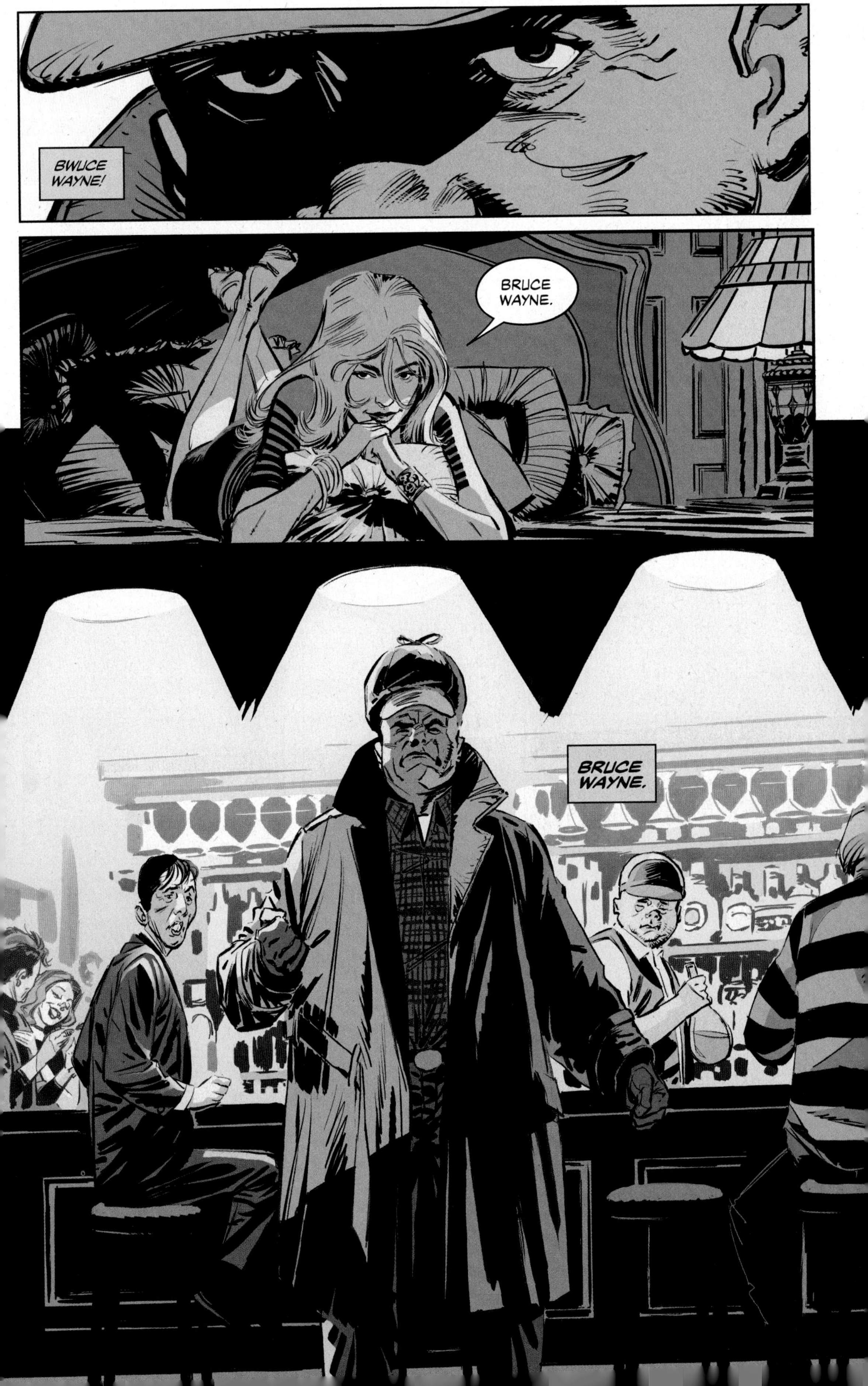
BWUCE WAYNE!
BRUCE WAYNE.
BRUCE WAYNE.

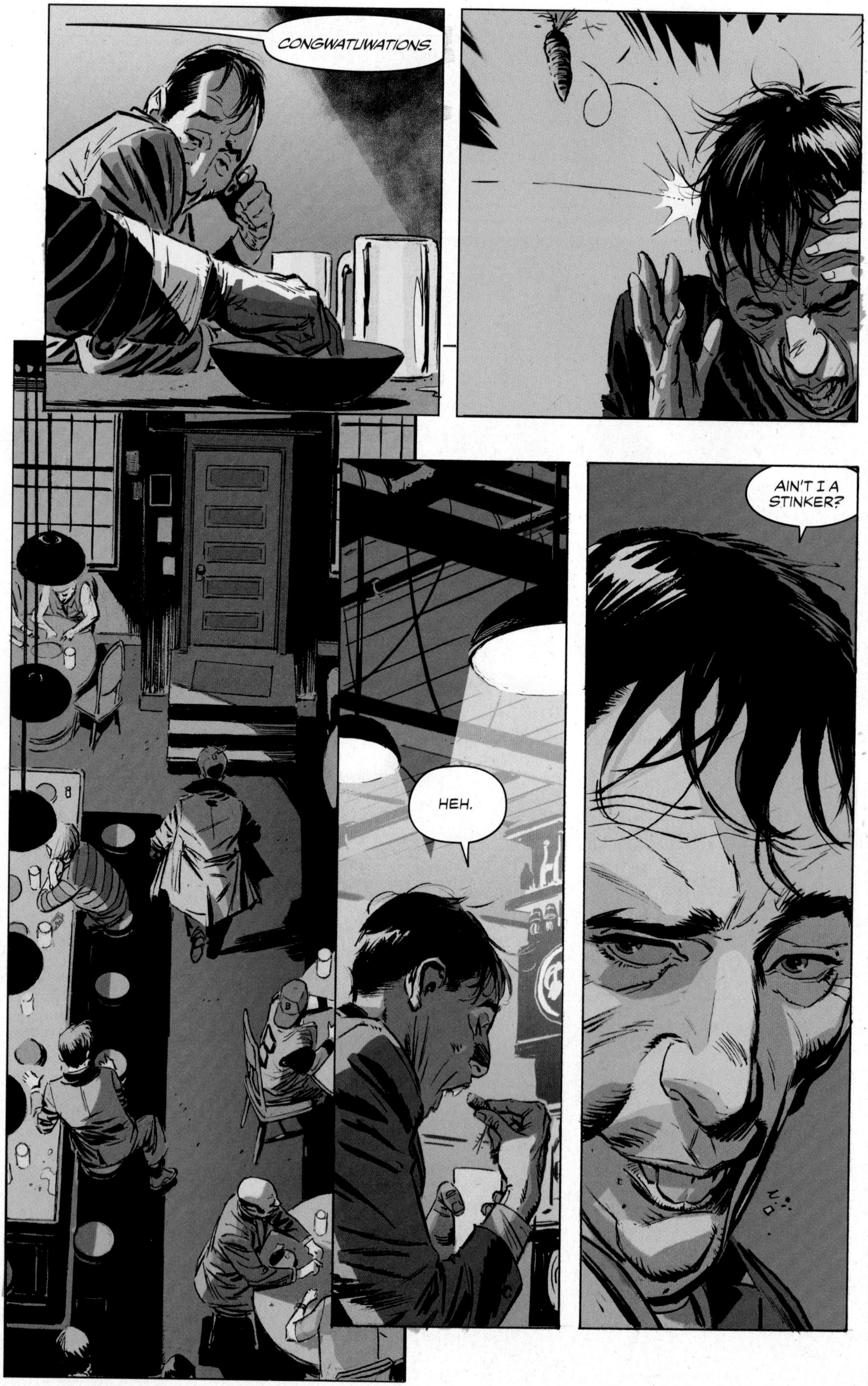
CONGWATUWATIONS.
HEH.
AIN'T I A STINKER?

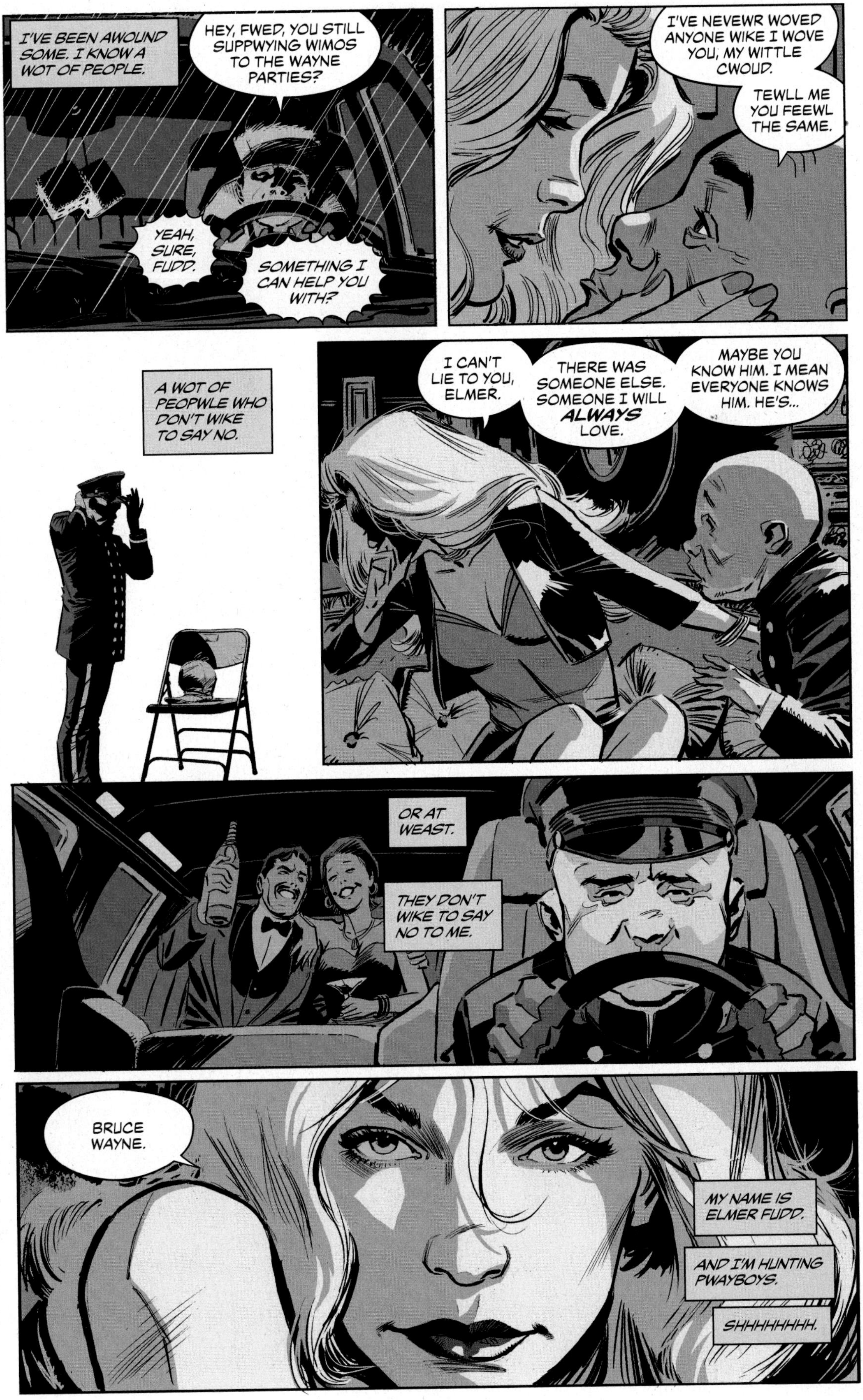
I'VE BEEN AWOUND SOME. I KNOW A WOT OF PEOPLE.
HEY, FWED, YOU STILL SUPPWYING WIMOS TO THE WAYNE PARTIES?
YEAH, SURE, FUDD.
SOMETHING I CAN HELP YOU WITH?
I'VE NEVEWR WOVED ANYONE WIKE I WOVE YOU, MY WITTLE CWOUD.
TEWLL ME YOU FEEWL THE SAME.
A WOT OF PEOPWLE WHO DON'T WIKE TO SAY NO.
I CAN'T LIE TO YOU, ELMER.
THERE WAS SOMEONE ELSE. SOMEONE I WILL ALWAYS LOVE.
MAYBE YOU KNOW HIM. I MEAN EVERYONE KNOWS HIM. HE'S...
OR AT WEAST.
THEY DON'T WIKE TO SAY NO TO ME.
BRUCE WAYNE.
MY NAME IS ELMER FUDD.
AND I'M HUNTING PWAYBOYS.
SHHHHHHH.

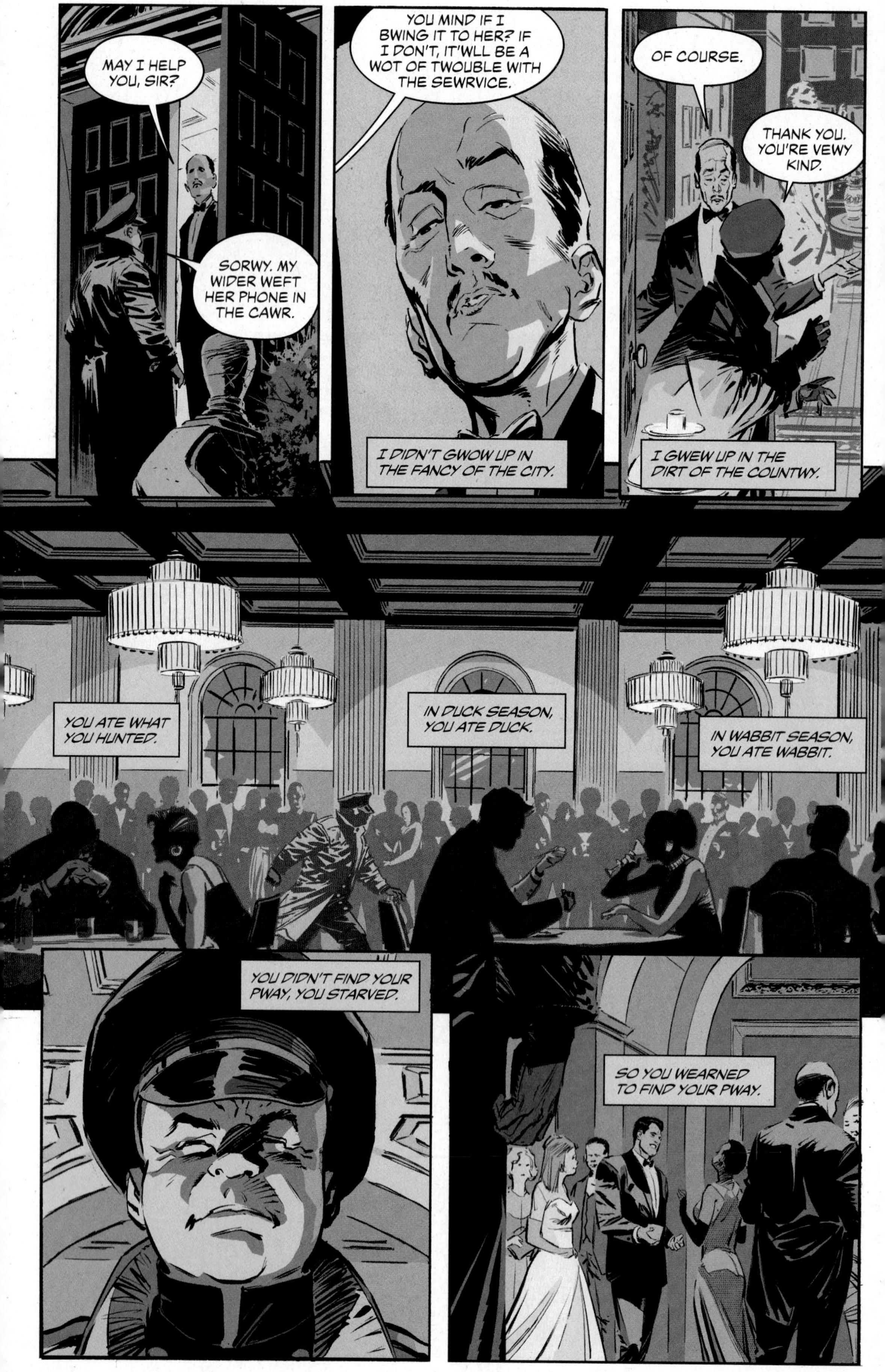
MAY I HELP YOU, SIR?
SORWY. MY WIDER WEFT HER PHONE IN THE CAWR.
YOU MIND IF I BWING IT TO HER? IF I DON'T, IT'WLL BE A WOT OF TWOUBLE WITH THE SEWRVICE.
I DIDN'T GWOW UP IN THE FANCY OF THE CITY.
OF COURSE.
THANK YOU. YOU'RE VEWY KIND.
I GWEW UP IN THE DIRT OF THE COUNTWY.
YOU ATE WHAT YOU HUNTED.
IN DUCK SEASON, YOU ATE DUCK.
IN WABBIT SEASON, YOU ATE WABBIT.
YOU DIDN'T FIND YOUR PWAY, YOU STARVED.
SO YOU WEARNED TO FIND YOUR PWAY.

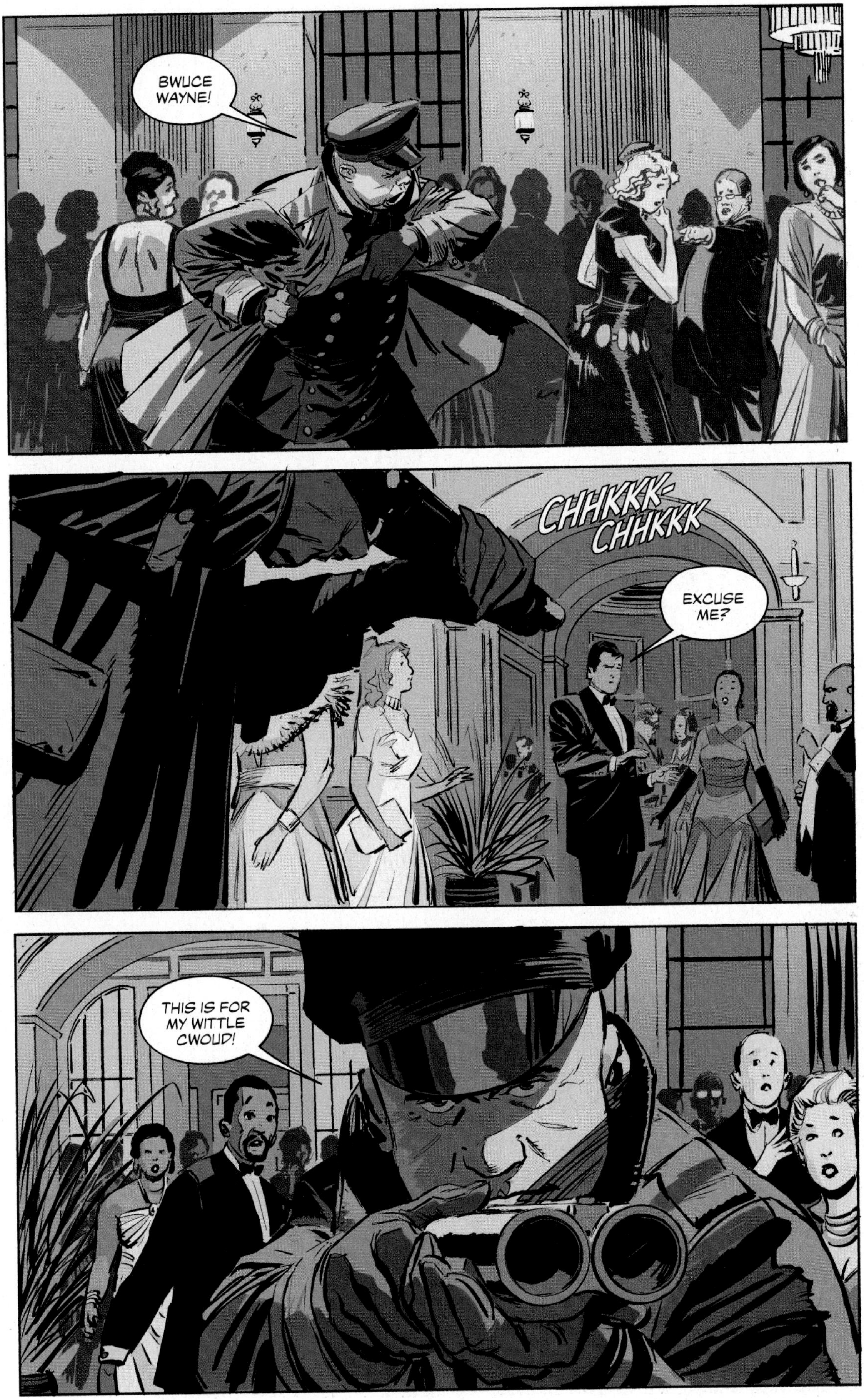
BWUCE WAYNE!
CHHKKK-CHHKKK
EXCUSE ME?
THIS IS FOR MY WITTLE CWOUD!

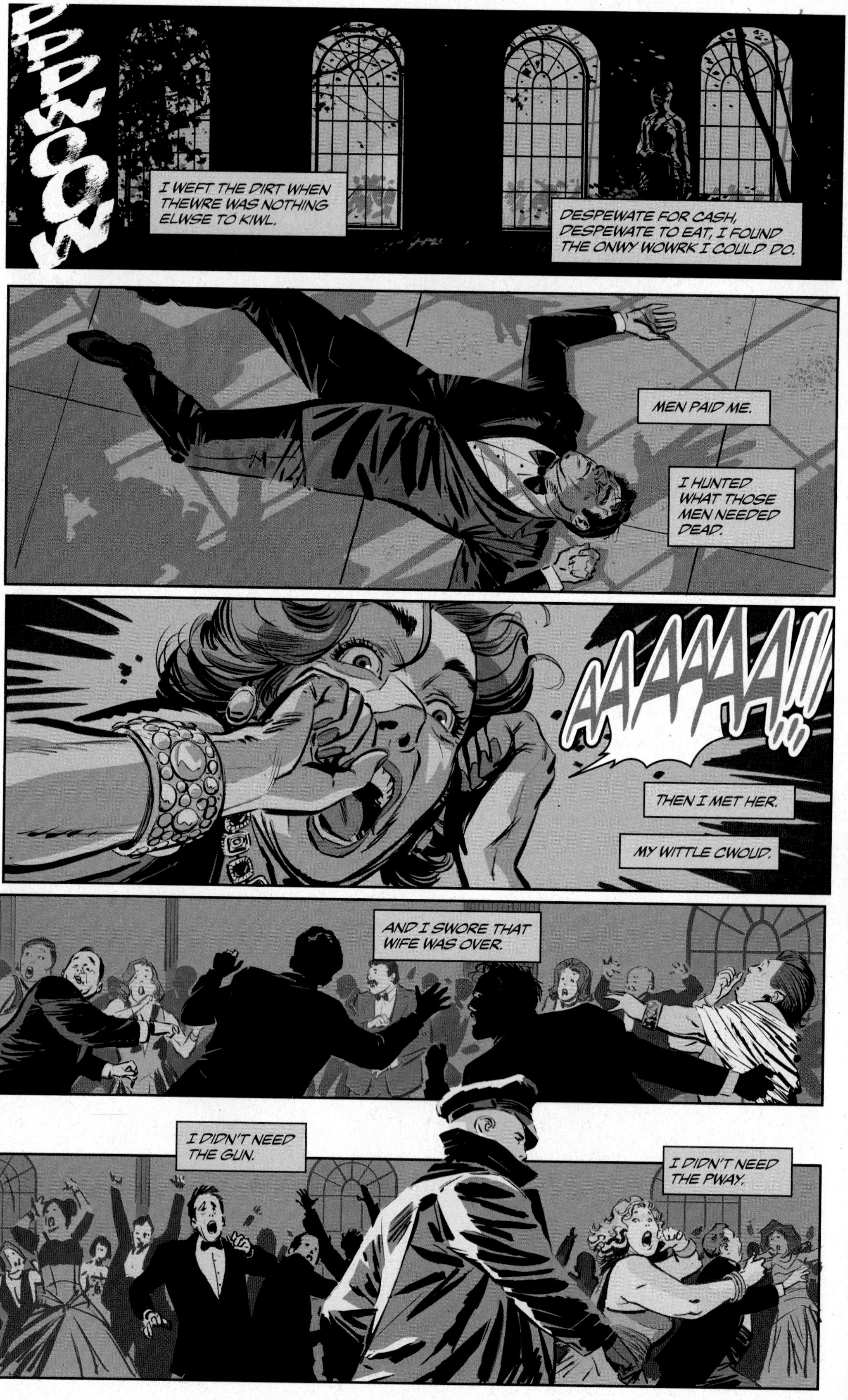
DDDWOOW
I WEFT THE DIRT WHEN THEWRE WAS NOTHING ELWSE TO KIWL.
DESPEWATE FOR CASH, DESPEWATE TO EAT, I FOUND THE ONWY WOWRK I COULD DO.
MEN PAID ME.
I HUNTED WHAT THOSE MEN NEEDED DEAD.
AAAAAA!!!
THEN I MET HER.
MY WITTLE CWOUD.
AND I SWORE THAT WIFE WAS OVER.
I DIDN'T NEED THE GUN.
I DIDN'T NEED THE PWAY.

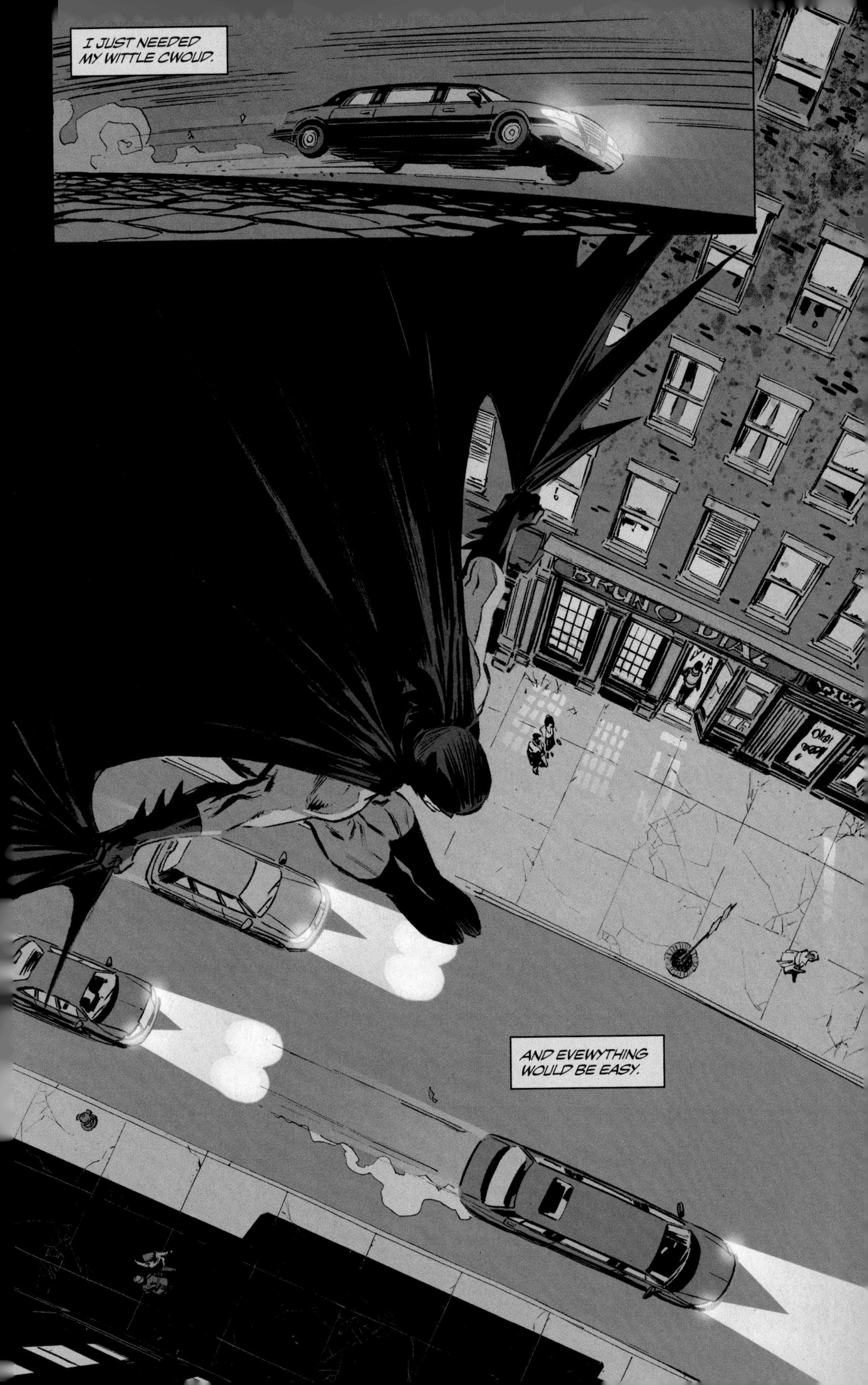
I JUST NEEDED MY WITTLE CWOUD.
AND EVEWYTHING WOULD BE EASY.

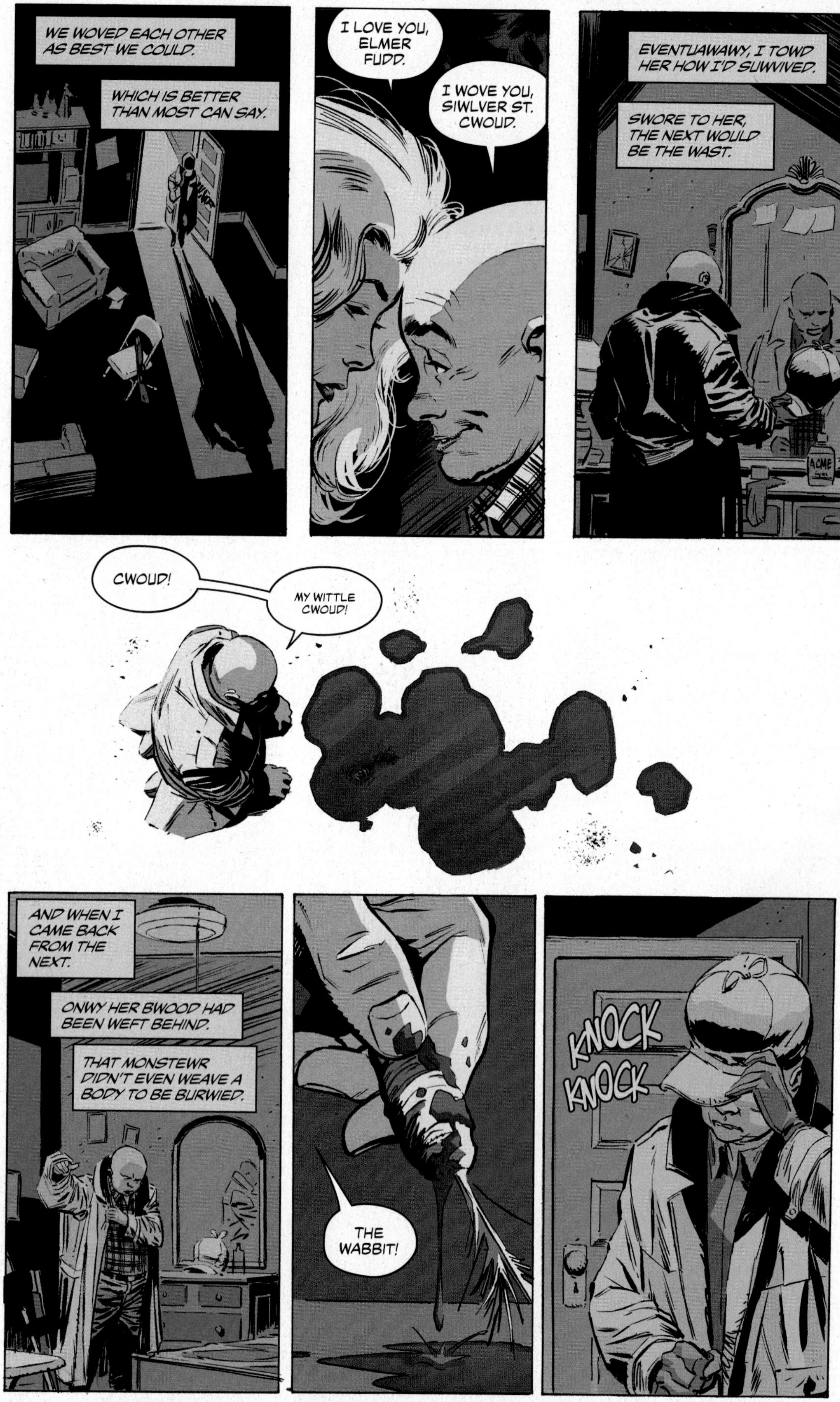

WE WOVED EACH OTHER AS BEST WE COULD.
WHICH IS BETTER THAN MOST CAN SAY.
I LOVE YOU, ELMER FUDD.
I WOVE YOU, SIWLVER ST. CWOUD.
EVENTUAWAWY, I TOWD HER HOW I'D SUWVIVED.
SWORE TO HER, THE NEXT WOULD BE THE WAST.
ACME
CWOUD!
MY WITTLE CWOUD!
AND WHEN I CAME BACK FROM THE NEXT.
ONWY HER BWOOD HAD BEEN WEFT BEHIND.
THAT MONSTEWR DIDN'T EVEN WEAVE A BODY TO BE BURWIED.
THE WABBIT!
KNOCK KNOCK

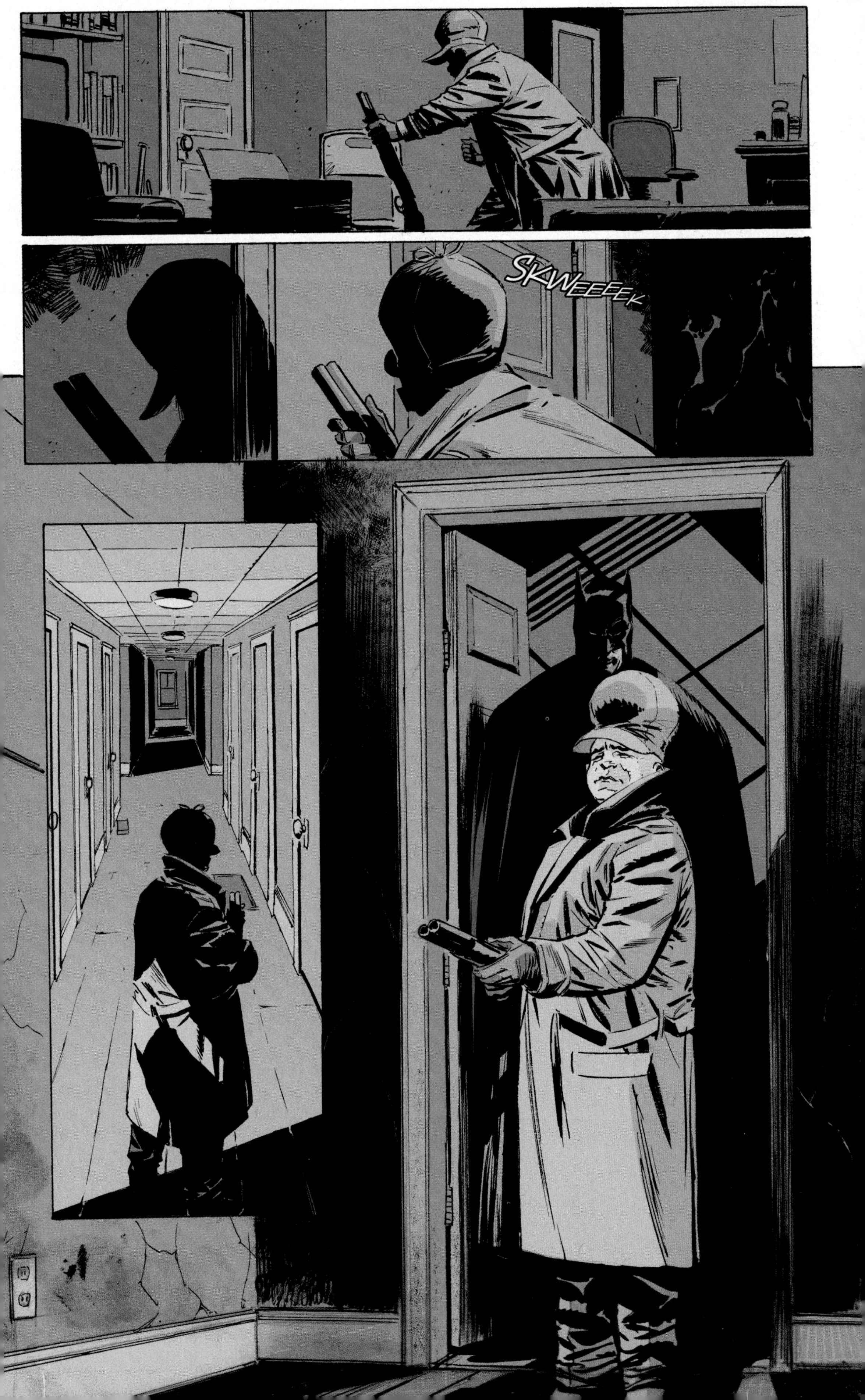
SKWEEEEEK

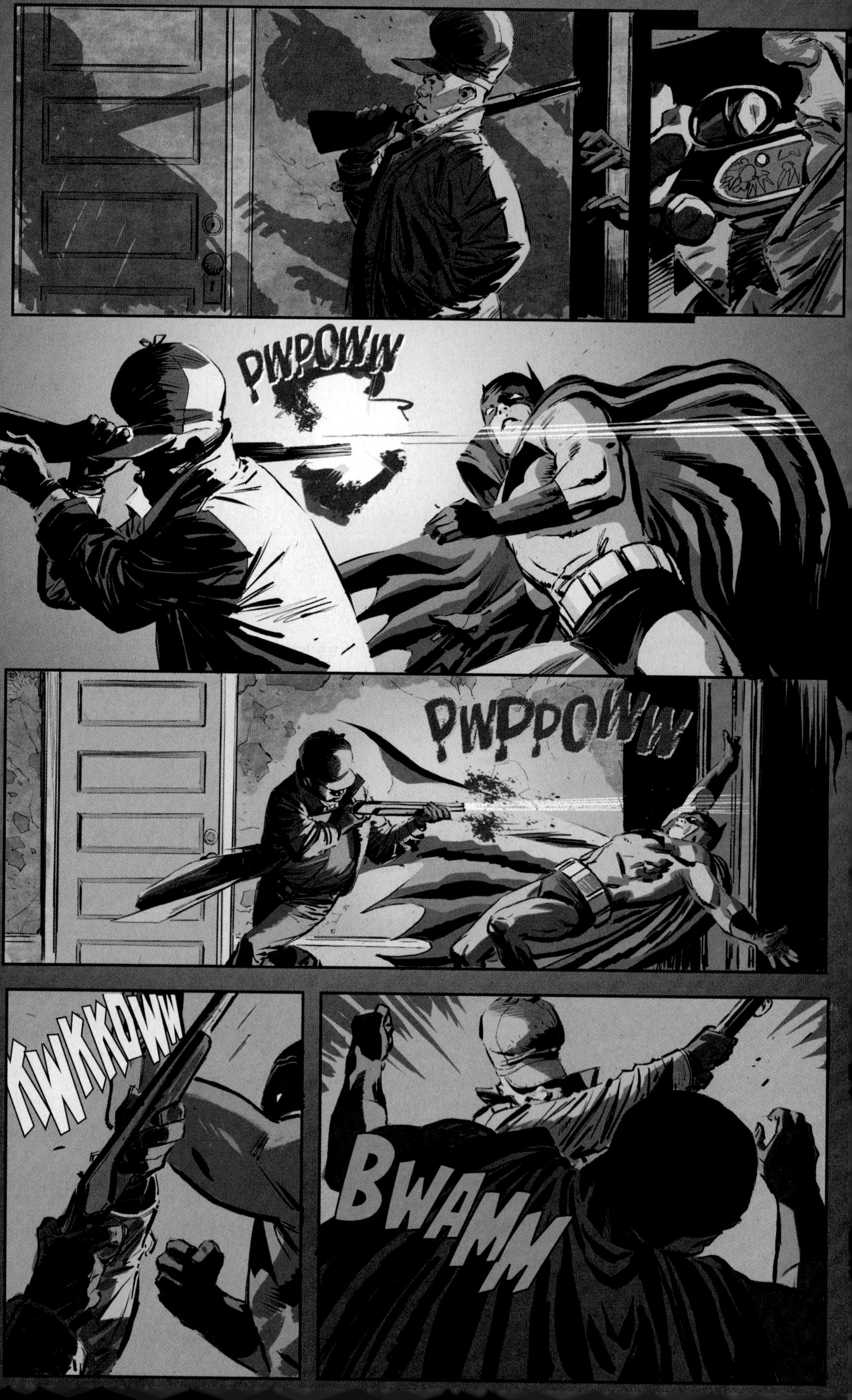
PWPOWW
PWPPOWW
KWKKOWW
BWAMM

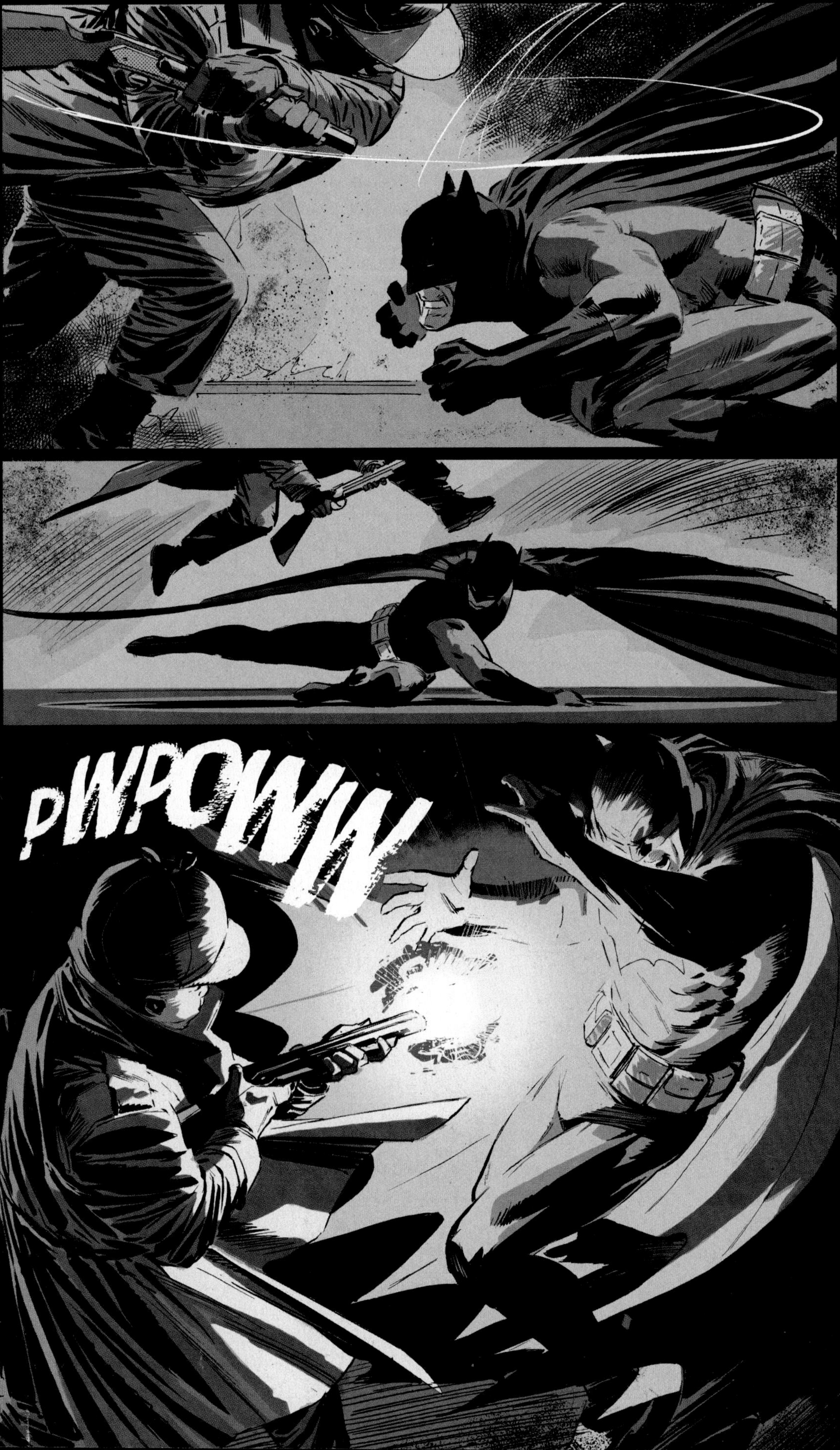
PWPOWW

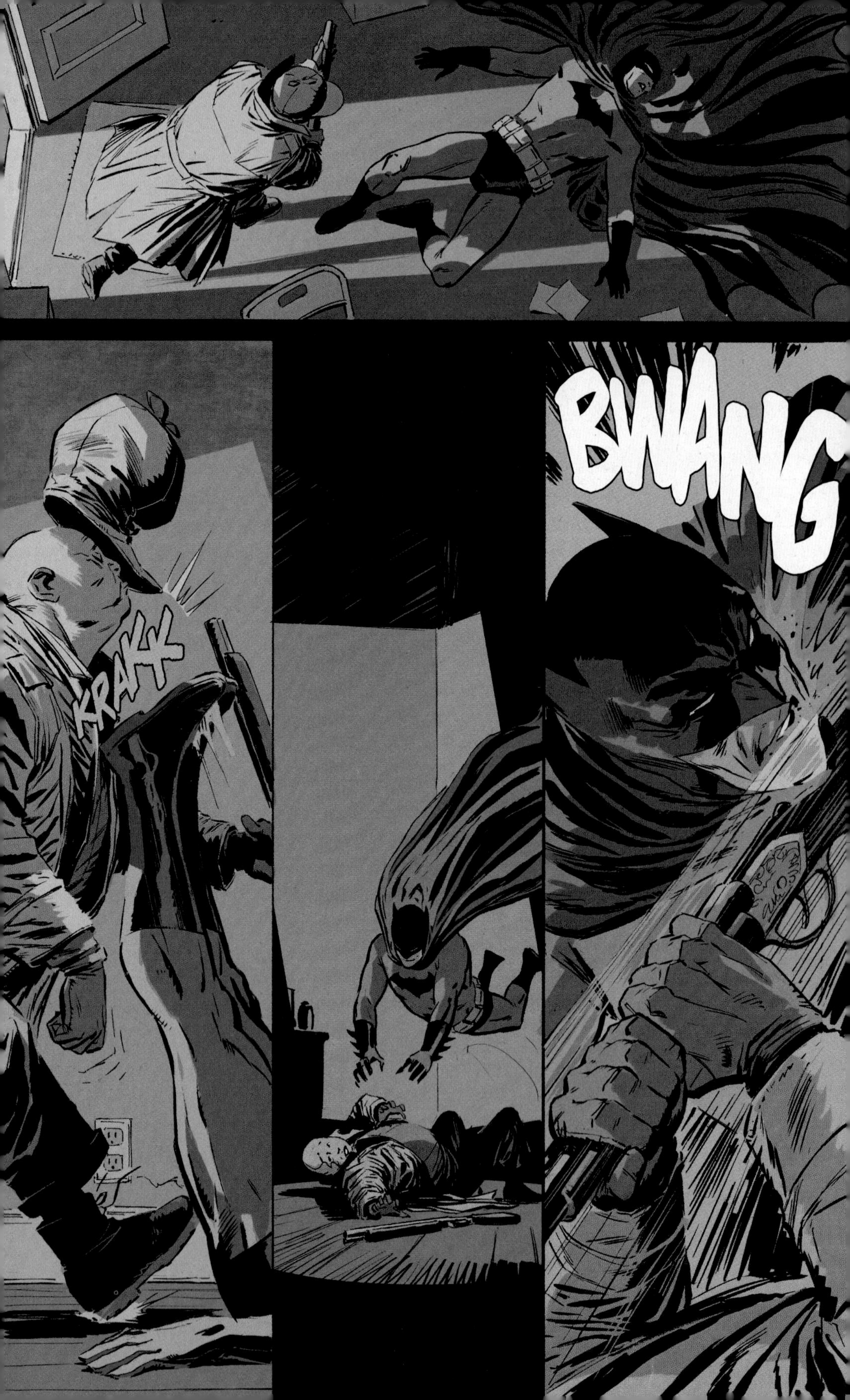
KRAKK
BWANG

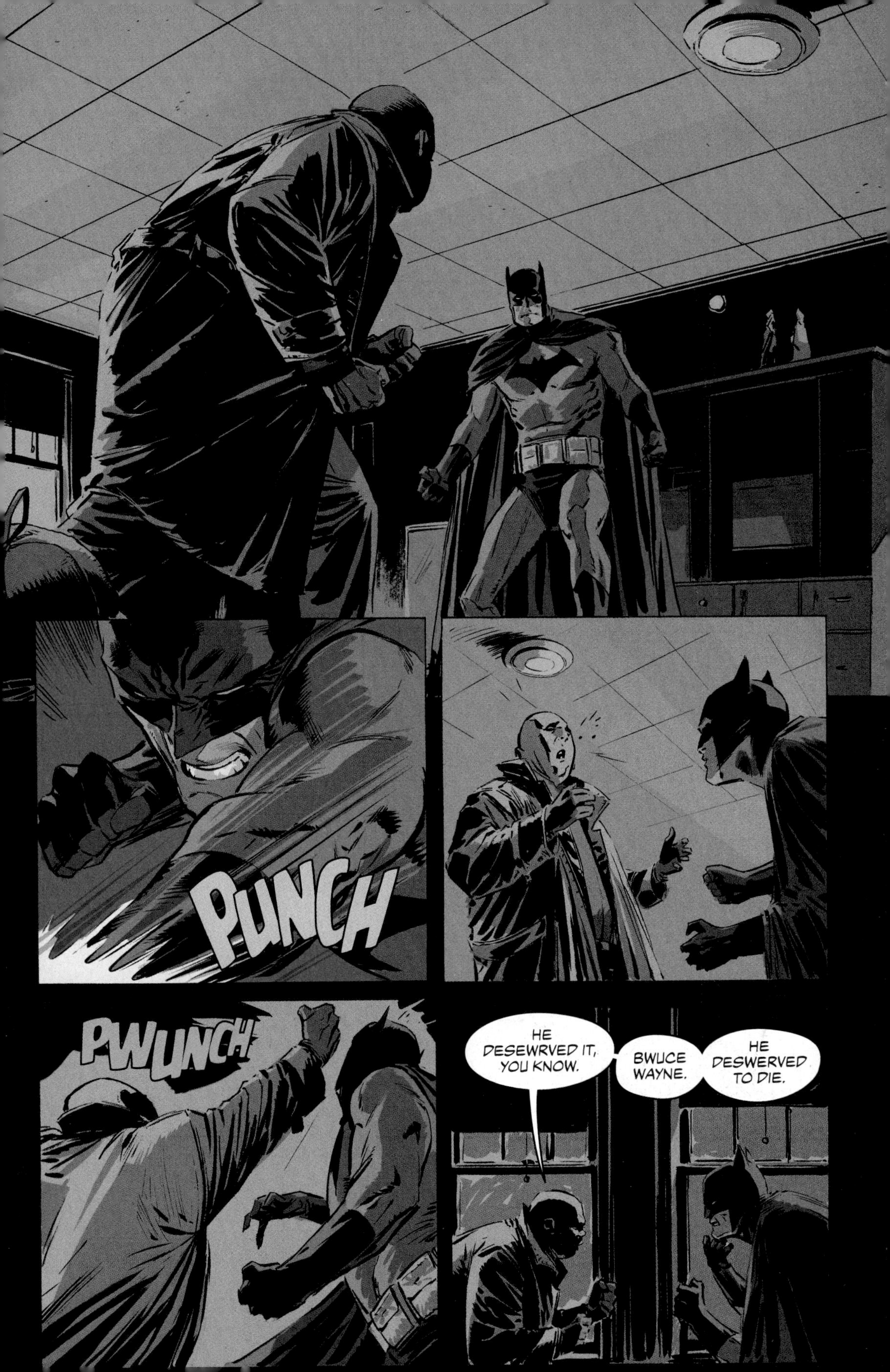
PUNCH
PWUNCH
HE DESEWRVED IT, YOU KNOW.
BWUCE WAYNE.
HE DESWERVED TO DIE.

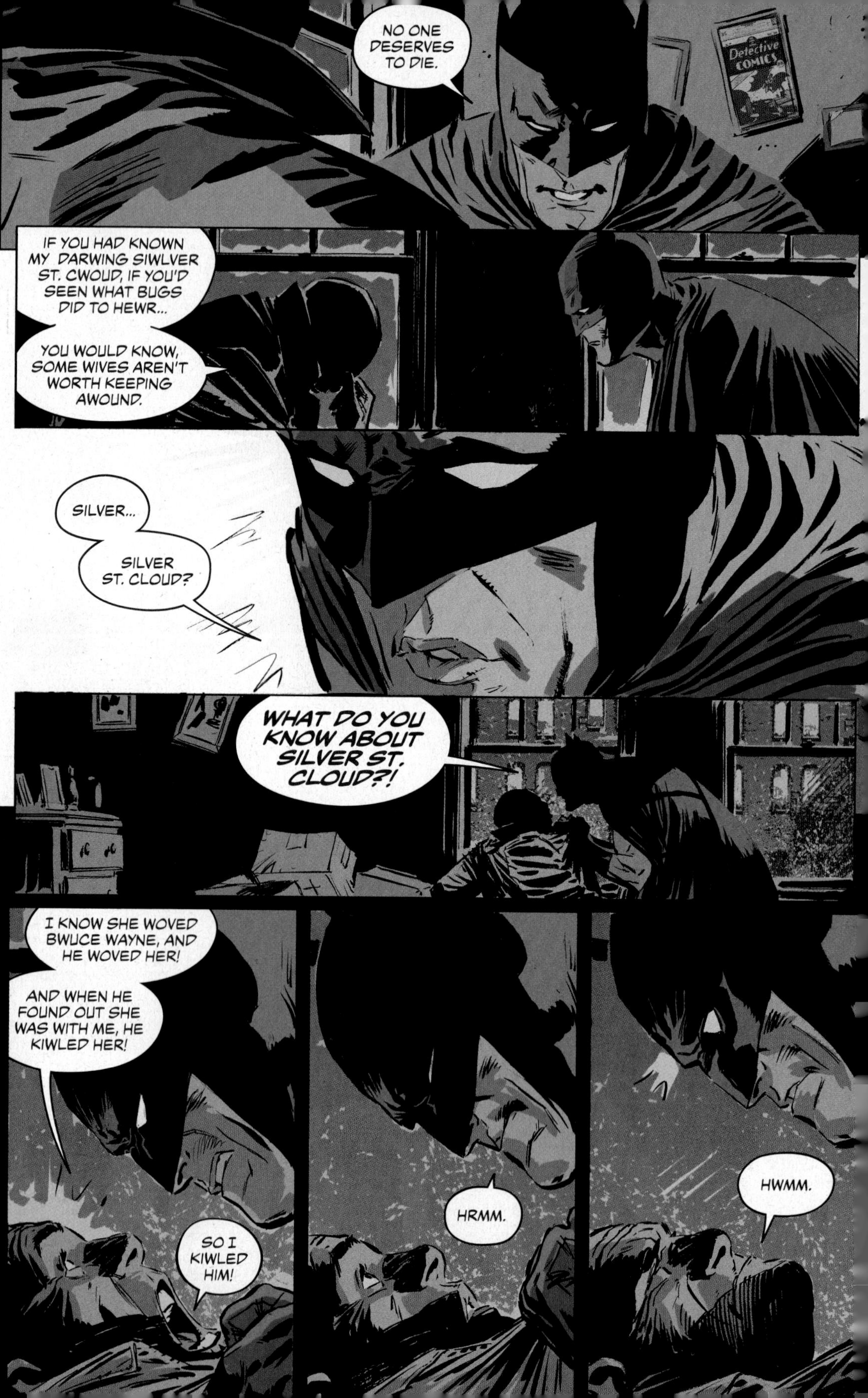
NO ONE DESERVES TO DIE.
Detective COMICS
IF YOU HAD KNOWN MY DARWING SIWLVER ST. CWOUD, IF YOU'D SEEN WHAT BUGS DID TO HEWR...
YOU WOULD KNOW, SOME WIVES AREN'T WORTH KEEPING AWOUND.
SILVER...
SILVER ST. CLOUD?
WHAT DO YOU KNOW ABOUT SILVER ST. CLOUD?!
I KNOW SHE WOVED BWUCE WAYNE, AND HE WOVED HER!
AND WHEN HE FOUND OUT SHE WAS WITH ME, HE KIWLED HER!
SO I KIWLED HIM!
HRMM.
HWMM.

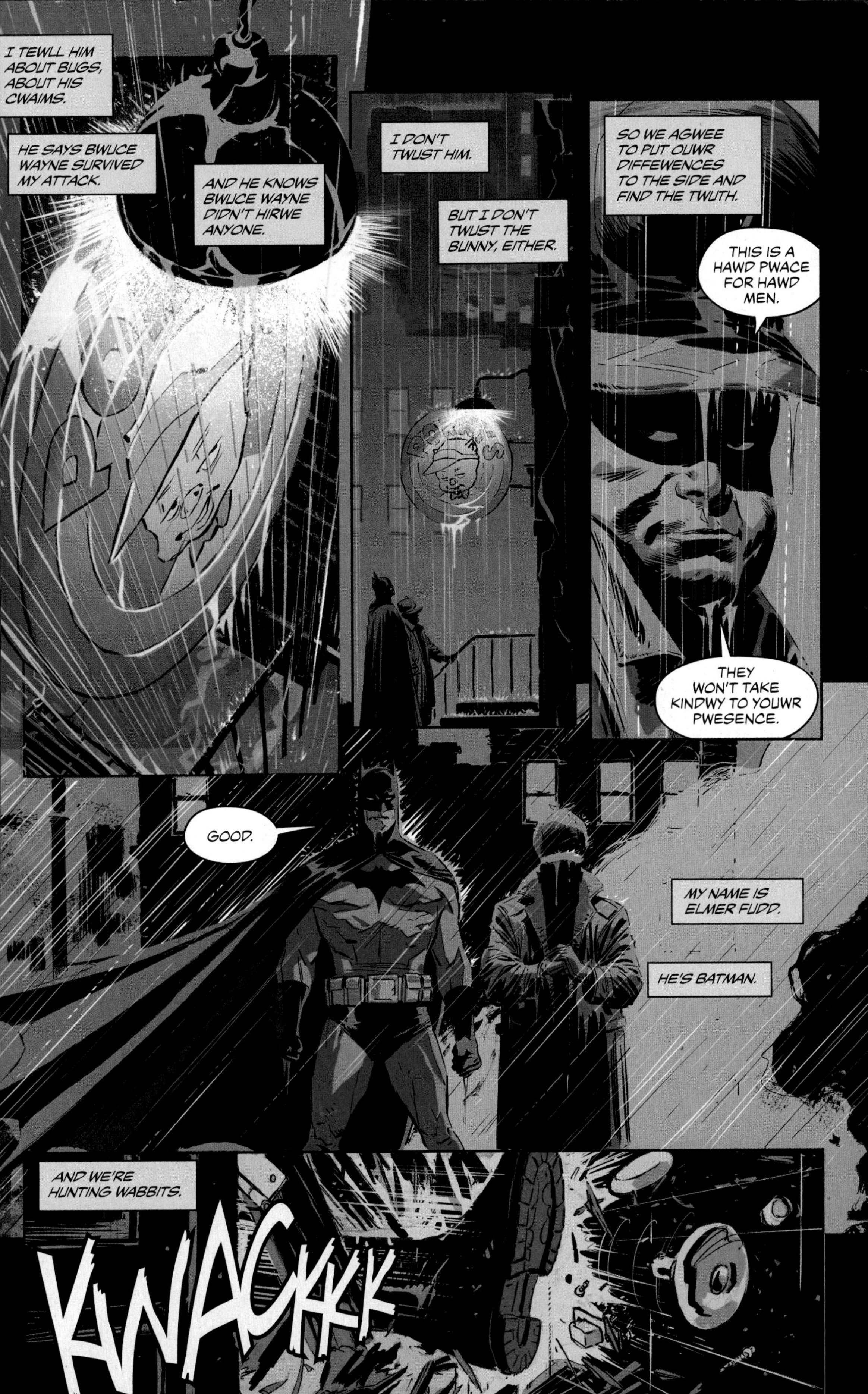

I TEWLL HIM ABOUT BUGS, ABOUT HIS CWAIMS.
HE SAYS BWUCE WAYNE SURVIVED MY ATTACK.
AND HE KNOWS BWUCE WAYNE DIDN'T HIRWE ANYONE.
I DON'T TWUST HIM.
BUT I DON'T TWUST THE BUNNY, EITHER.
SO WE AGWEE TO PUT OUWR DIFFEWENCES TO THE SIDE AND FIND THE TWUTH.
THIS IS A HAWD PWACE FOR HAWD MEN.
THEY WON'T TAKE KINDWY TO YOUWR PWESENCE.
GOOD.
MY NAME IS ELMER FUDD.
HE'S BATMAN.
AND WE'RE HUNTING WABBITS.
KWACKKK

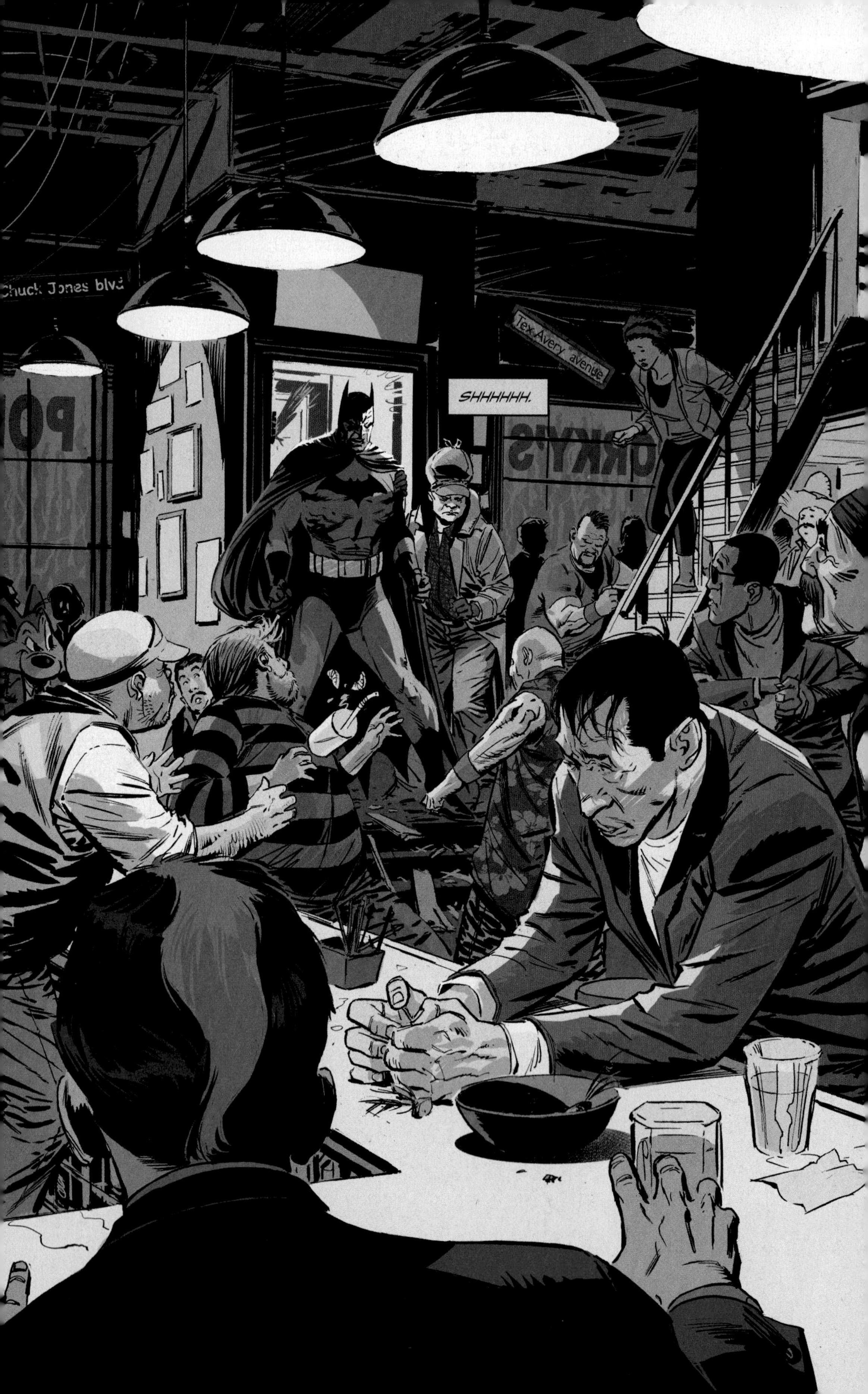
Chuck Jones blvd
Tex Avery avenue
SHHHHHH.

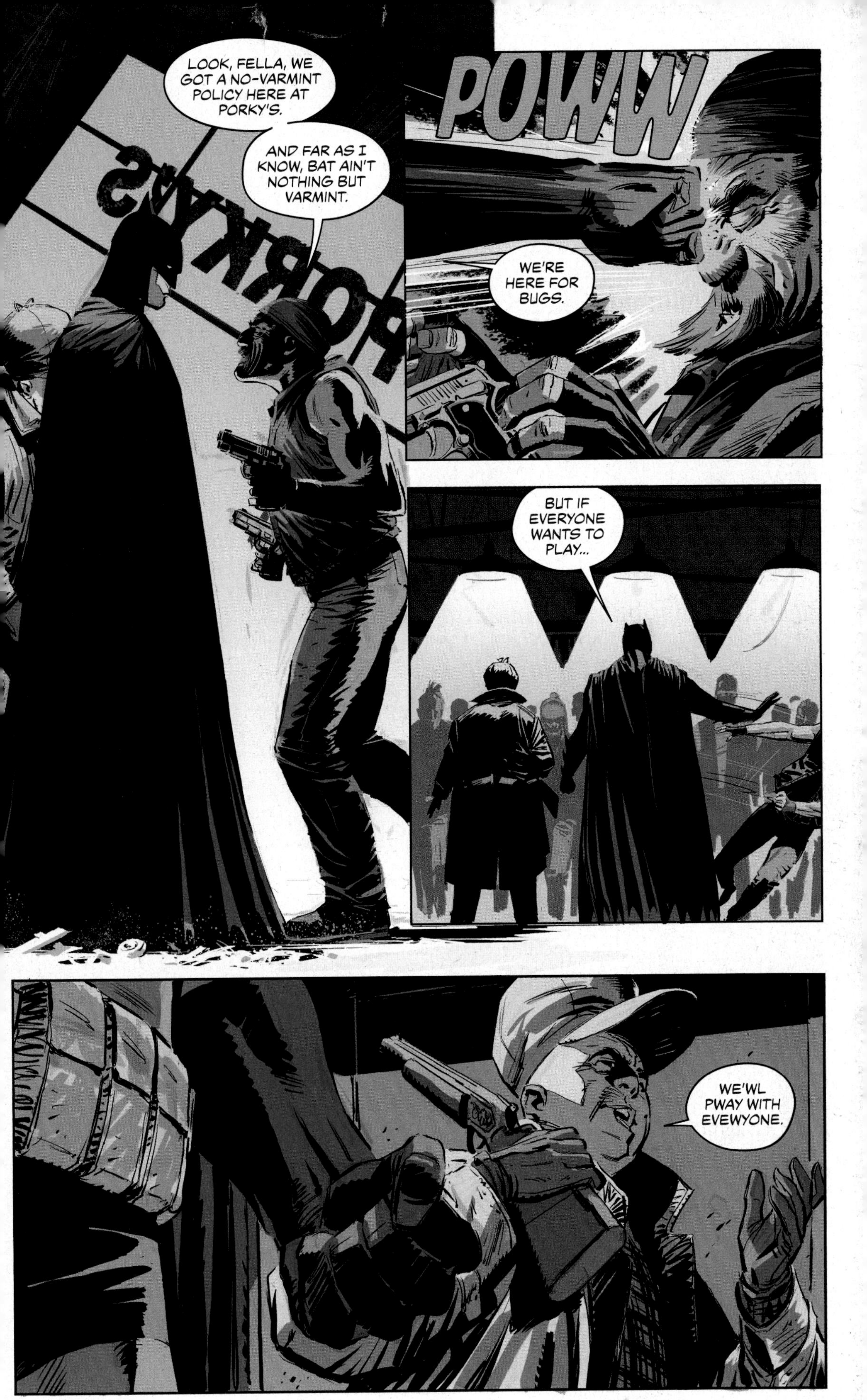
LOOK, FELLA, WE GOT A NO-VARMINT POLICY HERE AT PORKY'S.
AND FAR AS I KNOW, BAT AIN'T NOTHING BUT VARMINT.
PORKY'S
POWW
WE'RE HERE FOR BUGS.
BUT IF EVERYONE WANTS TO PLAY...
WE'WL PWAY WITH EVEWYONE.

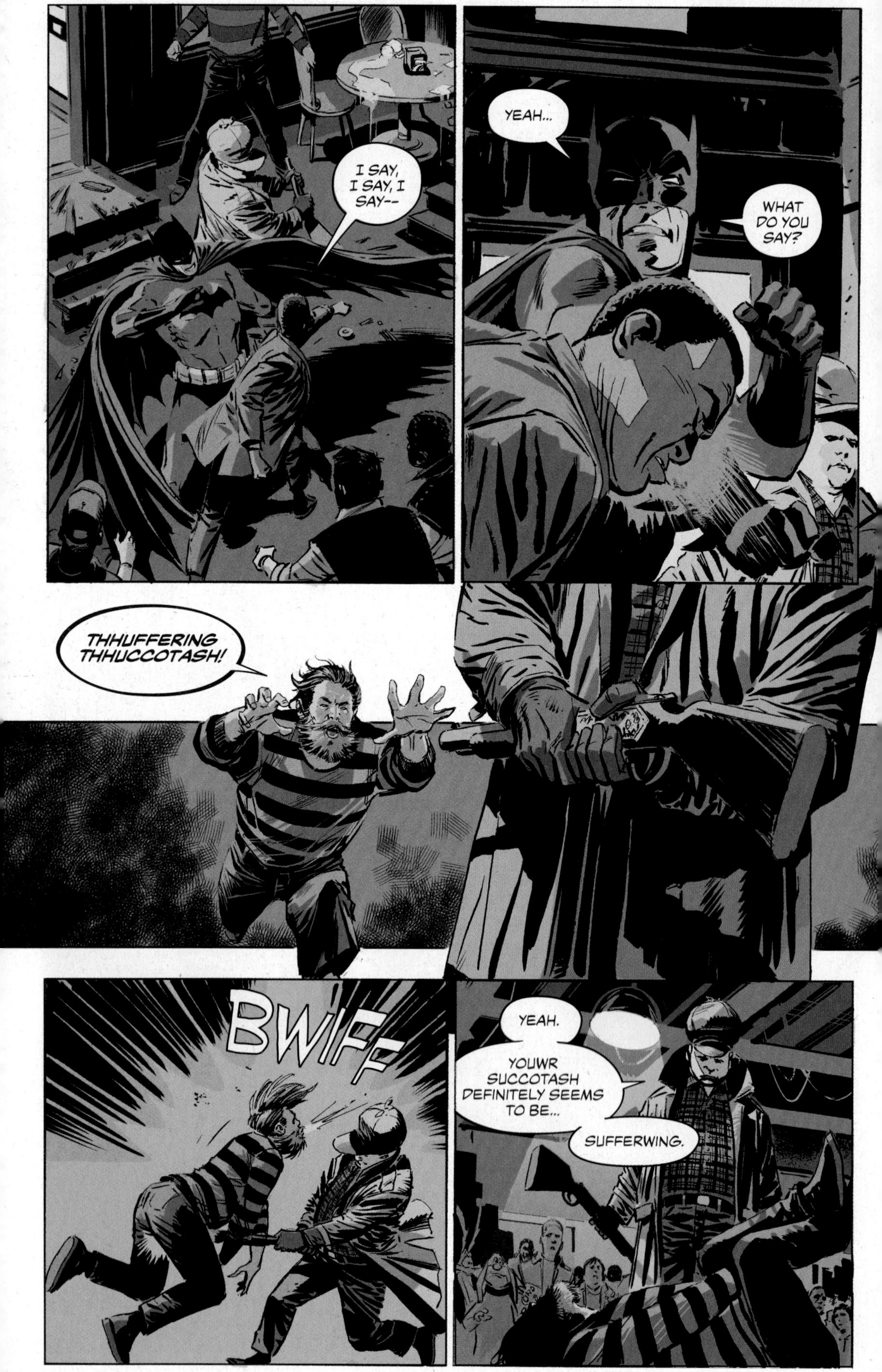
I SAY, I SAY, I SAY--
YEAH...
WHAT DO YOU SAY?
THHUFFERING THHUCCOTASH!
BWIFF
YEAH.
YOUWR SUCCOTASH DEFINITELY SEEMS TO BE...
SUFFERWING.

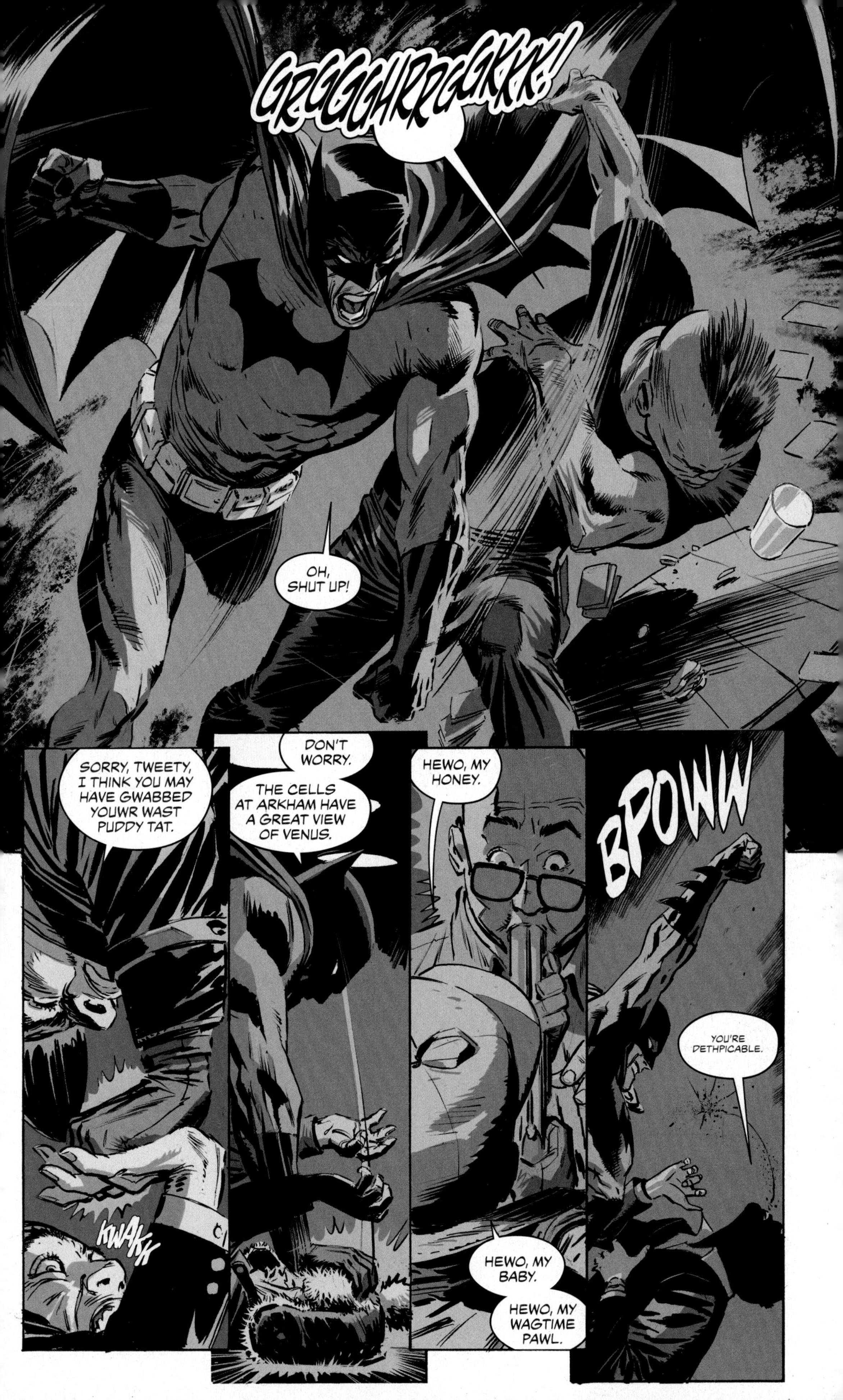
GRGGGHRRGGKKK!
OH, SHUT UP!
SORRY, TWEETY, I THINK YOU MAY HAVE GWABBED YOUWR WAST PUDDY TAT.
KWAKK
DON'T WORRY.
THE CELLS AT ARKHAM HAVE A GREAT VIEW OF VENUS.
HEWO, MY HONEY.
HEWO, MY BABY.
HEWO, MY WAGTIME PAWL.
BPOWW
YOU'RE DETHPICABLE.

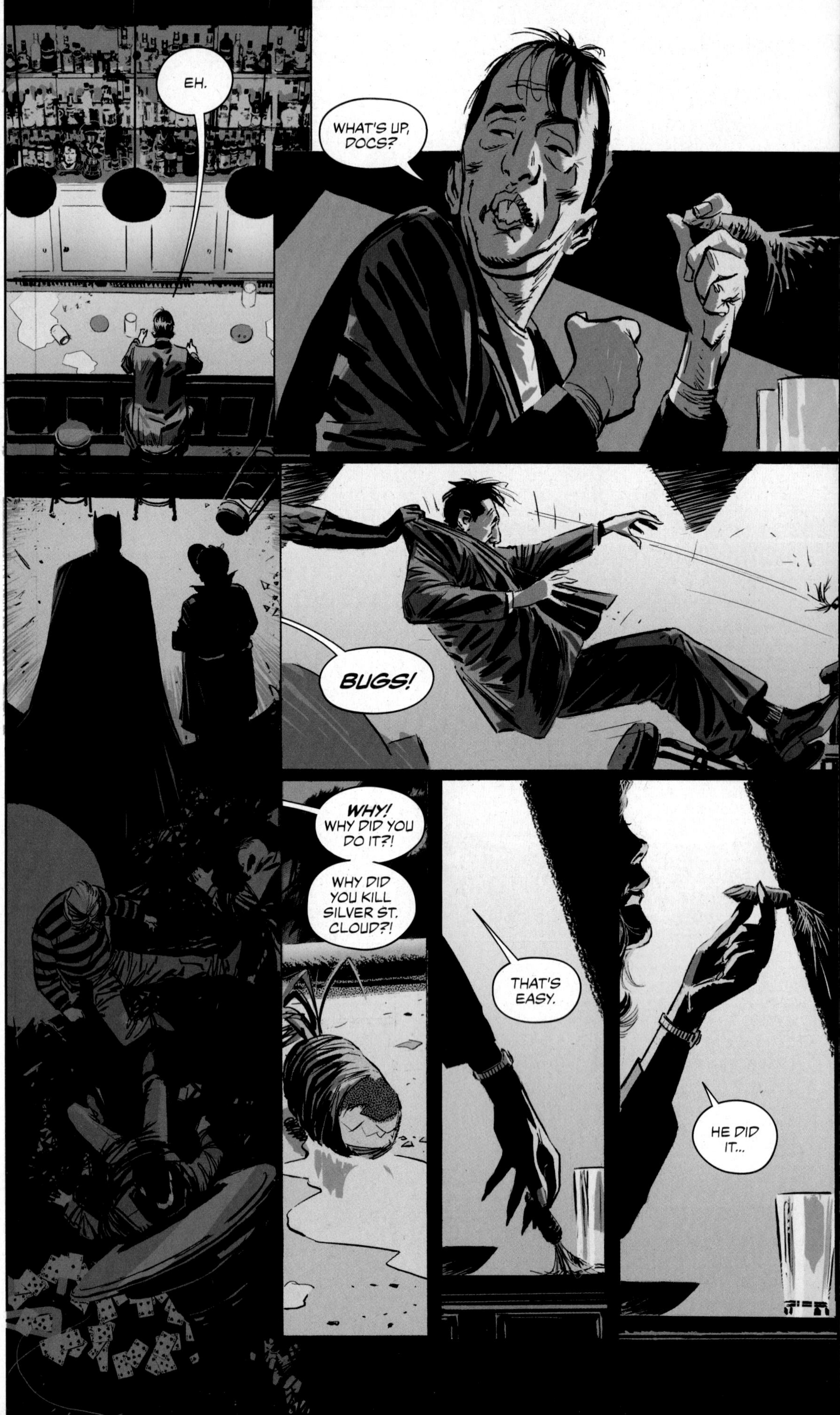
EH.
WHAT'S UP, DOCS?
BUGS!
WHY! WHY DID YOU DO IT?!
WHY DID YOU KILL SILVER ST. CLOUD?!
THAT'S EASY.
HE DID IT...

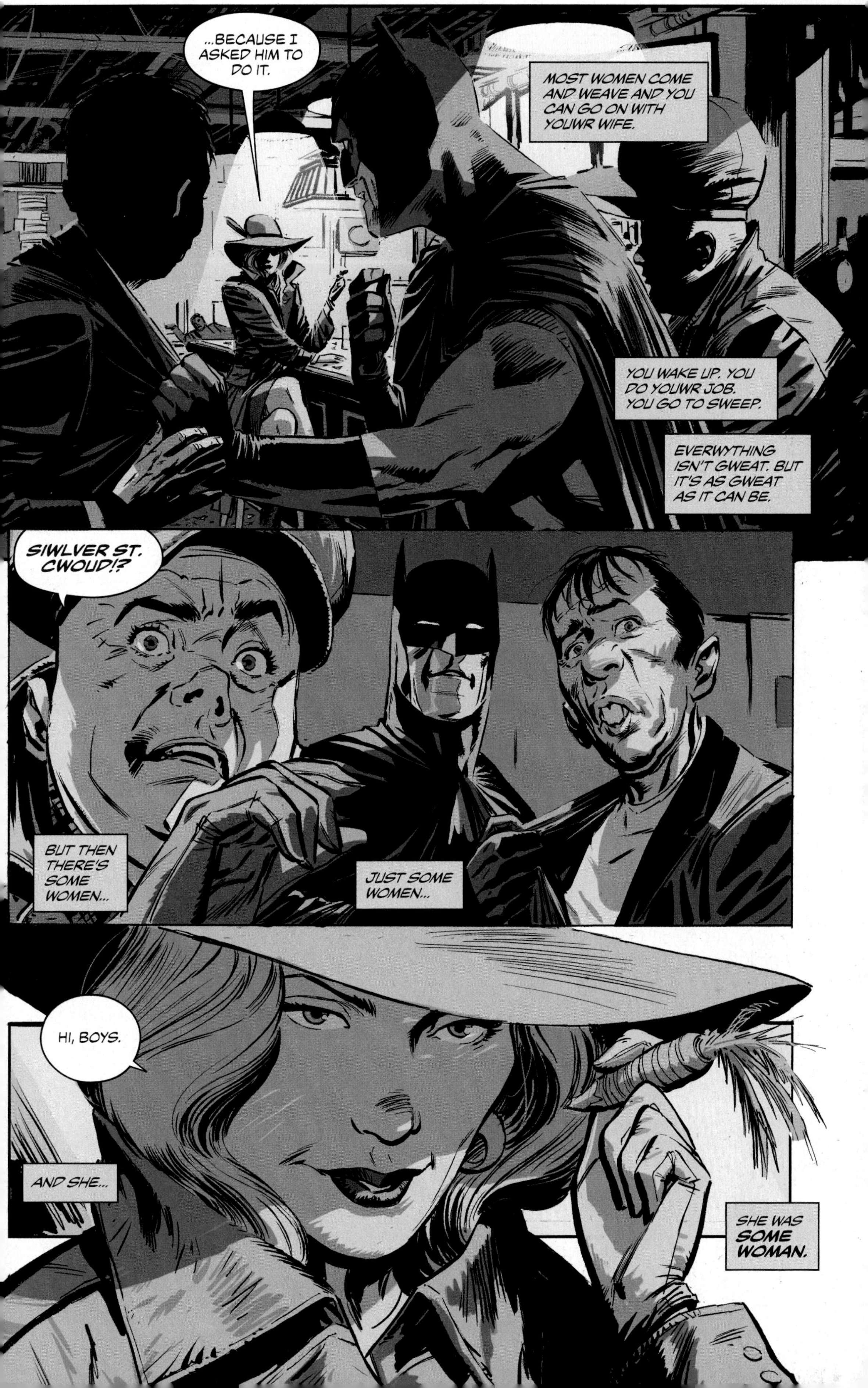
...BECAUSE I ASKED HIM TO DO IT.
MOST WOMEN COME AND WEAVE AND YOU CAN GO ON WITH YOUWR WIFE.
YOU WAKE UP. YOU DO YOUWR JOB. YOU GO TO SWEEP.
EVERWYTHING ISN'T GWEAT. BUT IT'S AS GWEAT AS IT CAN BE.
SIWLVER ST. CWOUD!?
BUT THEN THERE'S SOME WOMEN...
JUST SOME WOMEN...
HI, BOYS.
AND SHE...
SHE WAS SOME WOMAN.

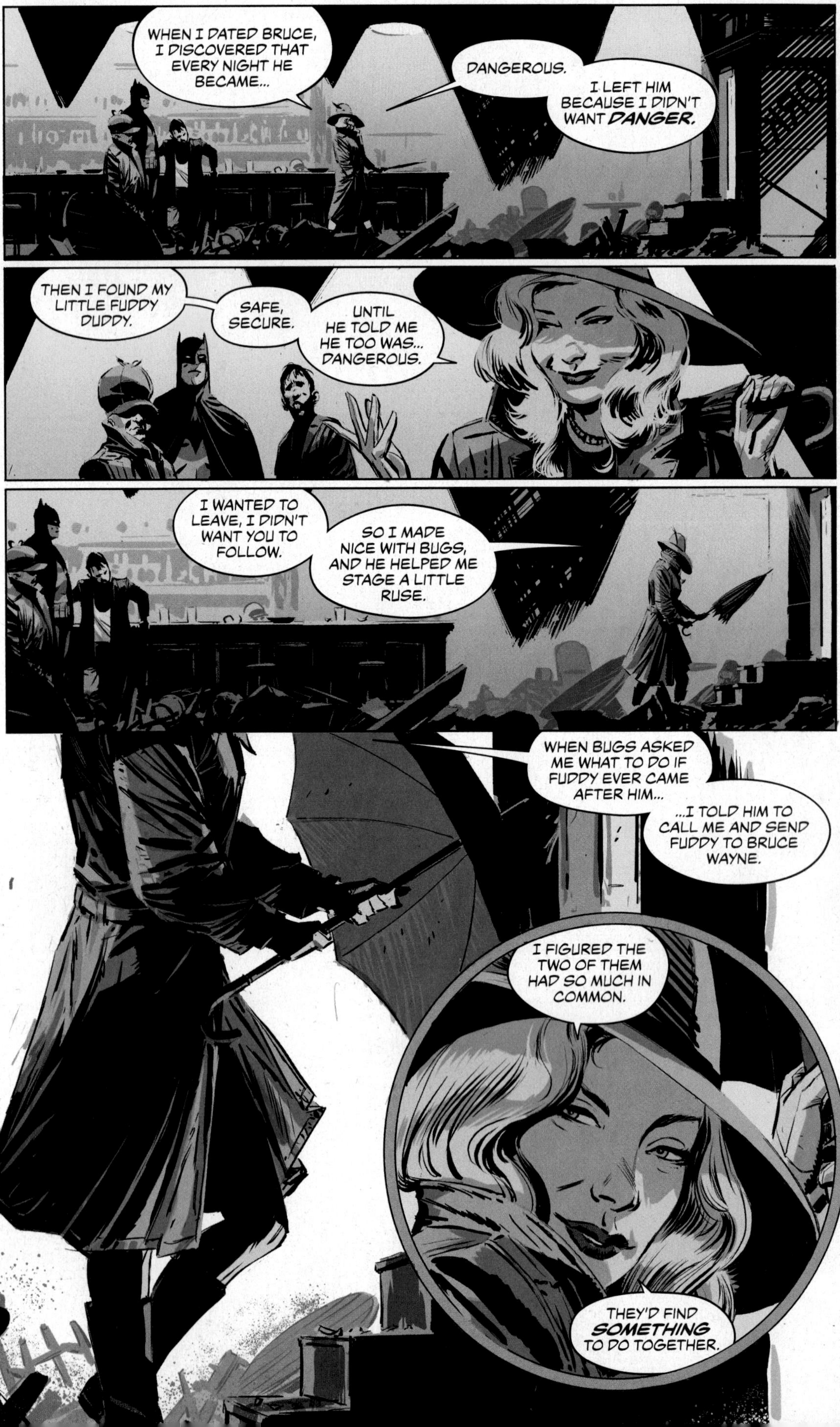
WHEN I DATED BRUCE, I DISCOVERED THAT EVERY NIGHT HE BECAME...
DANGEROUS.
I LEFT HIM BECAUSE I DIDN'T WANT DANGER.
THEN I FOUND MY LITTLE FUDDY DUDDY.
SAFE, SECURE.
UNTIL HE TOLD ME HE TOO WAS... DANGEROUS.
I WANTED TO LEAVE, I DIDN'T WANT YOU TO FOLLOW.
SO I MADE NICE WITH BUGS, AND HE HELPED ME STAGE A LITTLE RUSE.
WHEN BUGS ASKED ME WHAT TO DO IF FUDDY EVER CAME AFTER HIM...
...I TOLD HIM TO CALL ME AND SEND FUDDY TO BRUCE WAYNE.
I FIGURED THE TWO OF THEM HAD SO MUCH IN COMMON.
THEY'D FIND SOMETHING TO DO TOGETHER.

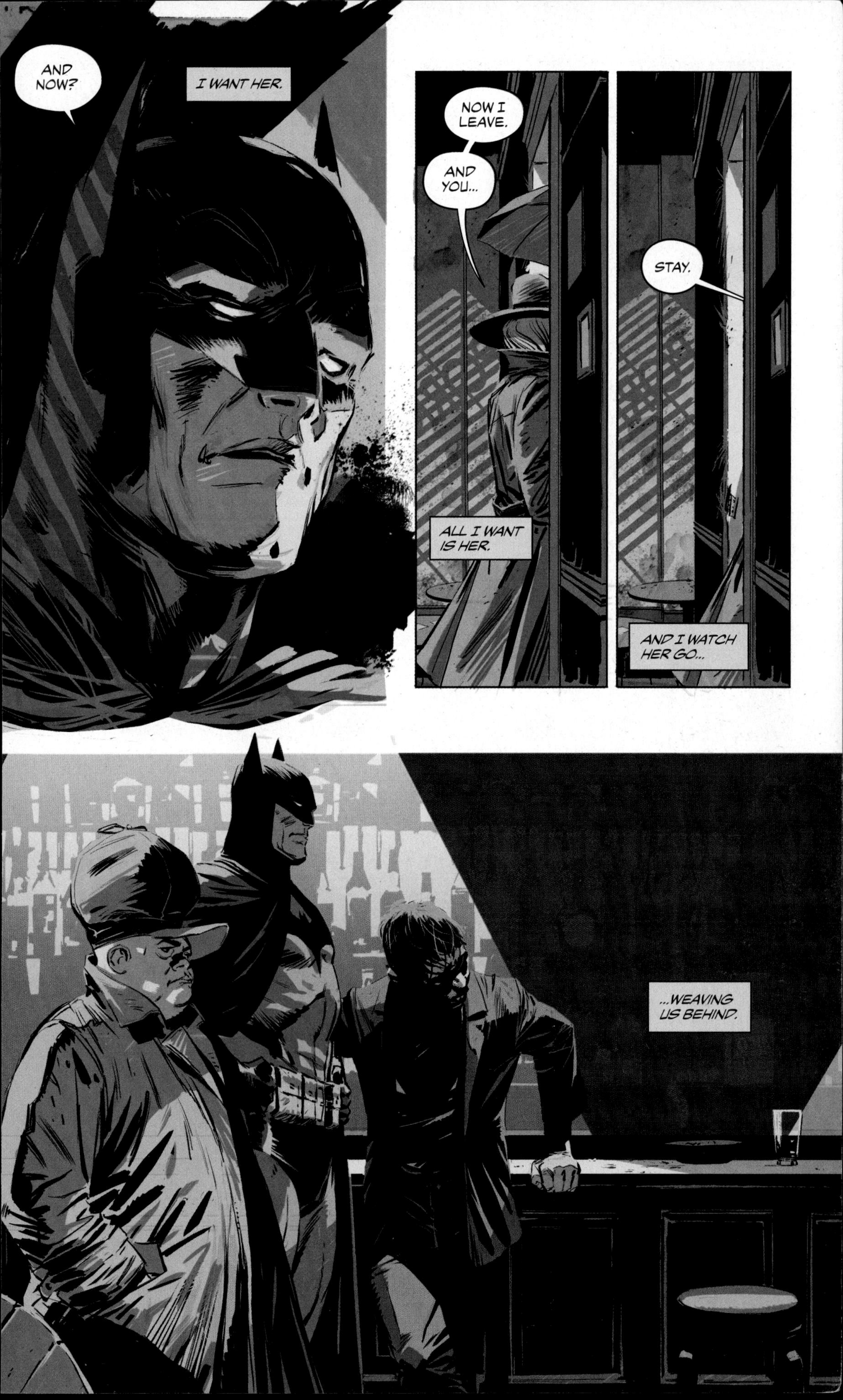
AND NOW?
I WANT HER.
NOW I LEAVE.
AND YOU...
STAY.
ALL I WANT IS HER.
AND I WATCH HER GO...
...WEAVING US BEHIND.

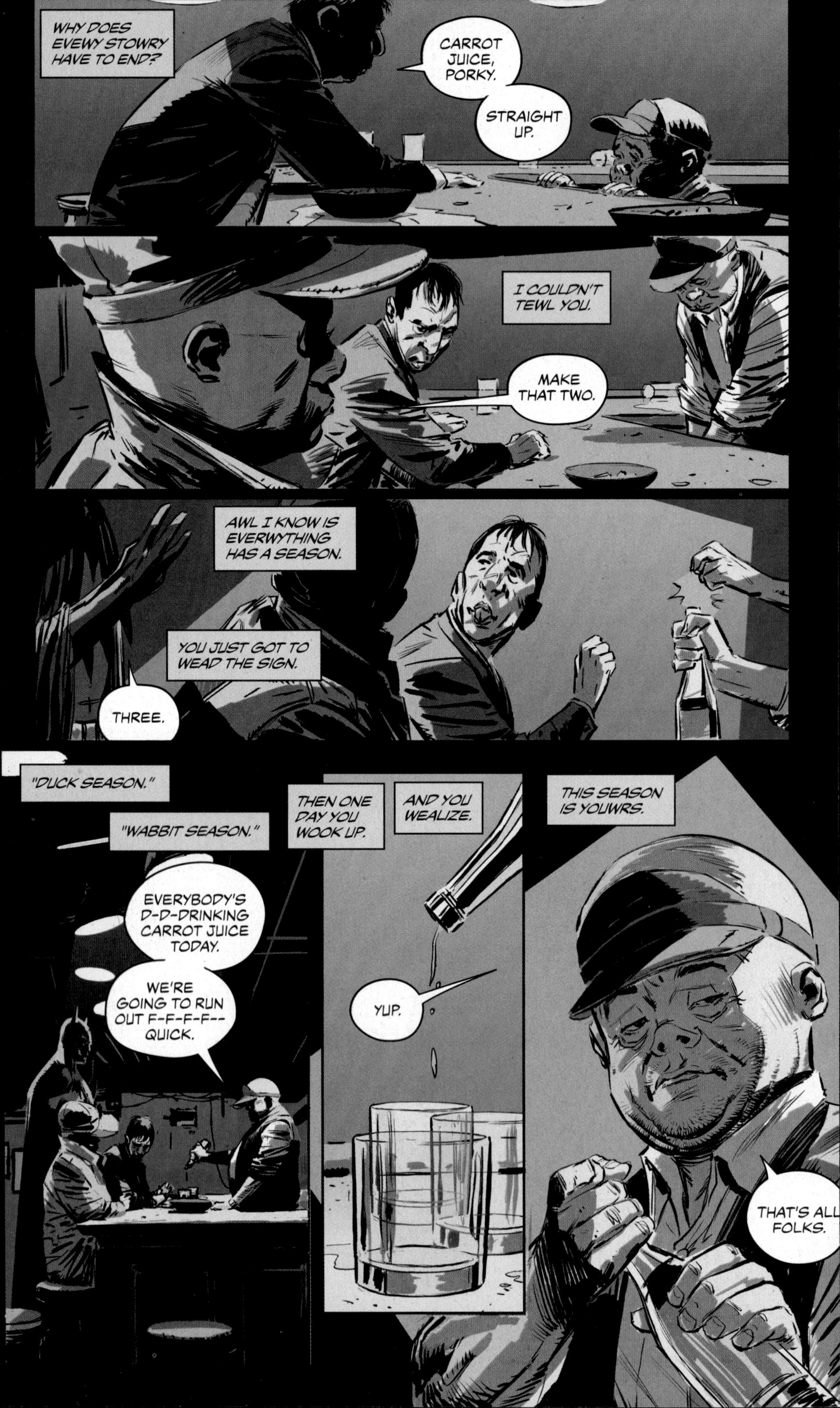

WHY DOES EVEWY STOWRY HAVE TO END?
CARROT JUICE, PORKY.
STRAIGHT UP.
I COULDN'T TEWL YOU.
MAKE THAT TWO.
AWL I KNOW IS EVERWYTHING HAS A SEASON.
YOU JUST GOT TO WEAD THE SIGN.
THREE.
"DUCK SEASON."
"WABBIT SEASON."
EVERYBODY'S D-D-DRINKING CARROT JUICE TODAY.
WE'RE GOING TO RUN OUT F-F-F-F-- QUICK.
THEN ONE DAY YOU WOOK UP.
AND YOU WEALIZE.
YUP.
THIS SEASON IS YOUWRS.
THAT'S ALL FOLKS.

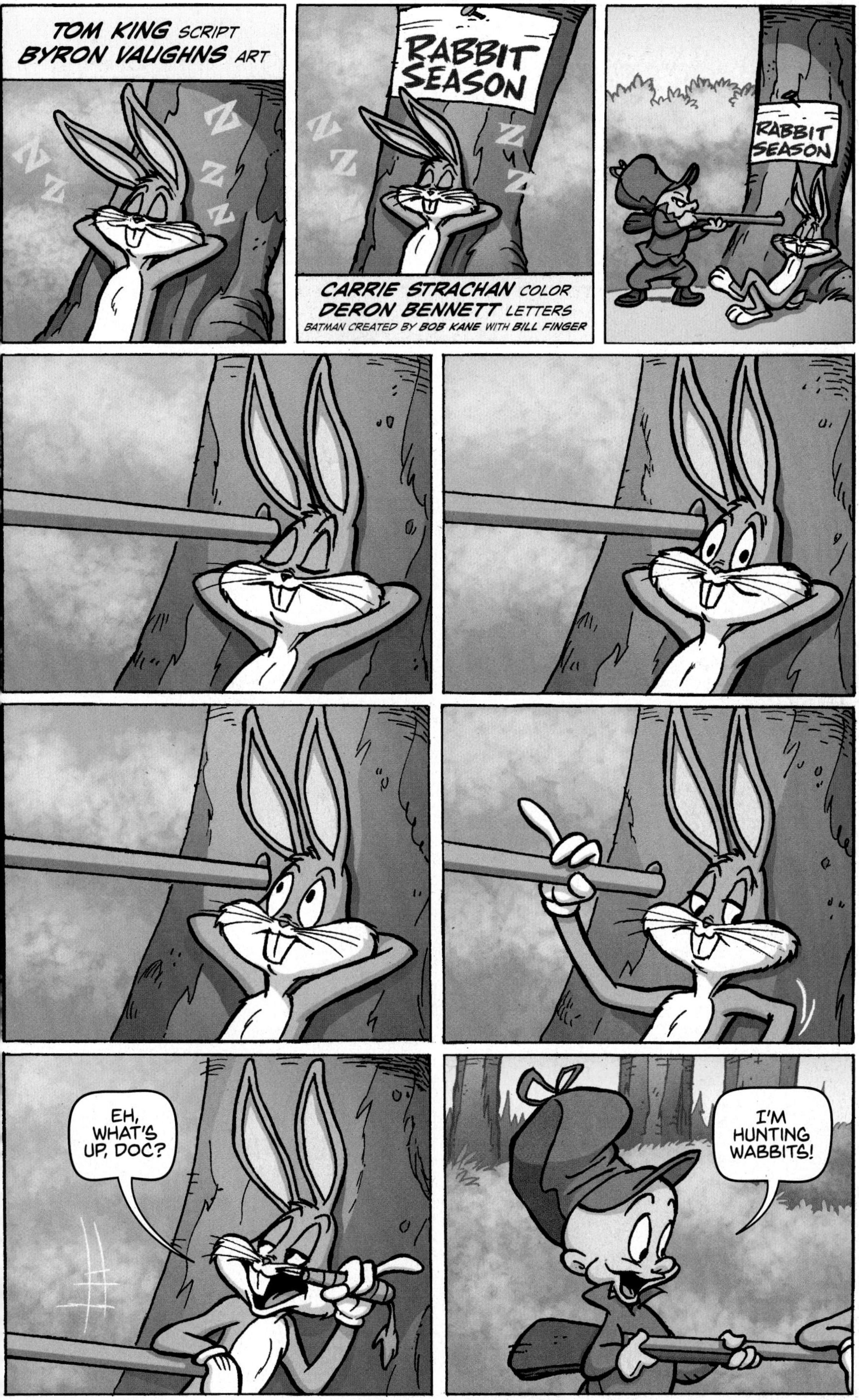
TOM KING SCRIPT
BYRON VAUGHNS ART
RABBIT SEASON
CARRIE STRACHAN COLOR
DERON BENNETT LETTERS
BATMAN CREATED BY BOB KANE WITH BILL FINGER
RABBIT SEASON
EH, WHAT'S UP, DOC?
I'M HUNTING WABBITS!

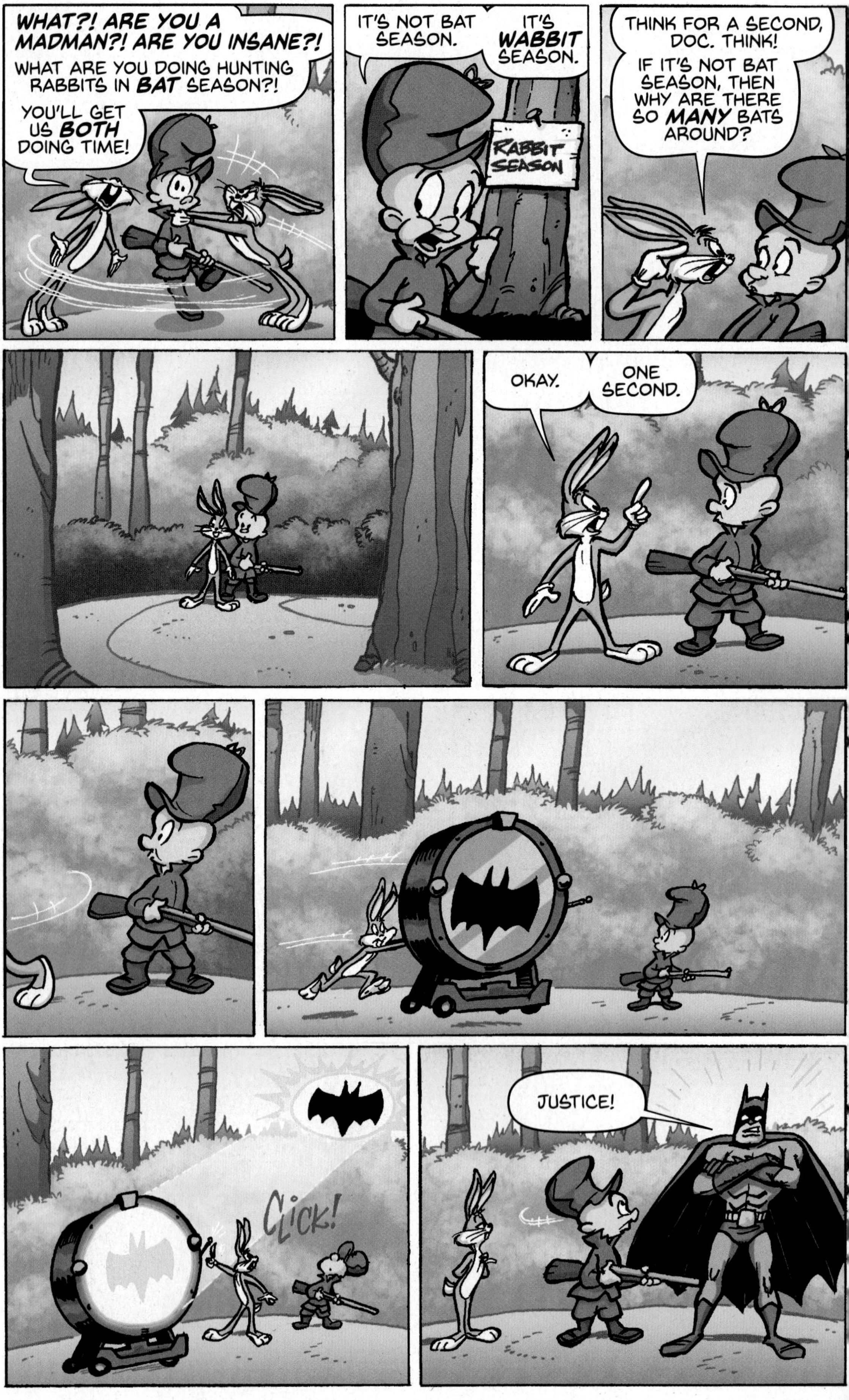

WHAT?! ARE YOU A MADMAN?! ARE YOU INSANE?!
WHAT ARE YOU DOING HUNTING RABBITS IN BAT SEASON?!
YOU'LL GET US BOTH DOING TIME!
IT'S NOT BAT SEASON.
IT'S WABBIT SEASON.
RABBIT SEASON
THINK FOR A SECOND, DOC. THINK!
IF IT'S NOT BAT SEASON, THEN WHY ARE THERE SO MANY BATS AROUND?
OKAY.
ONE SECOND.
CLICK!
JUSTICE!

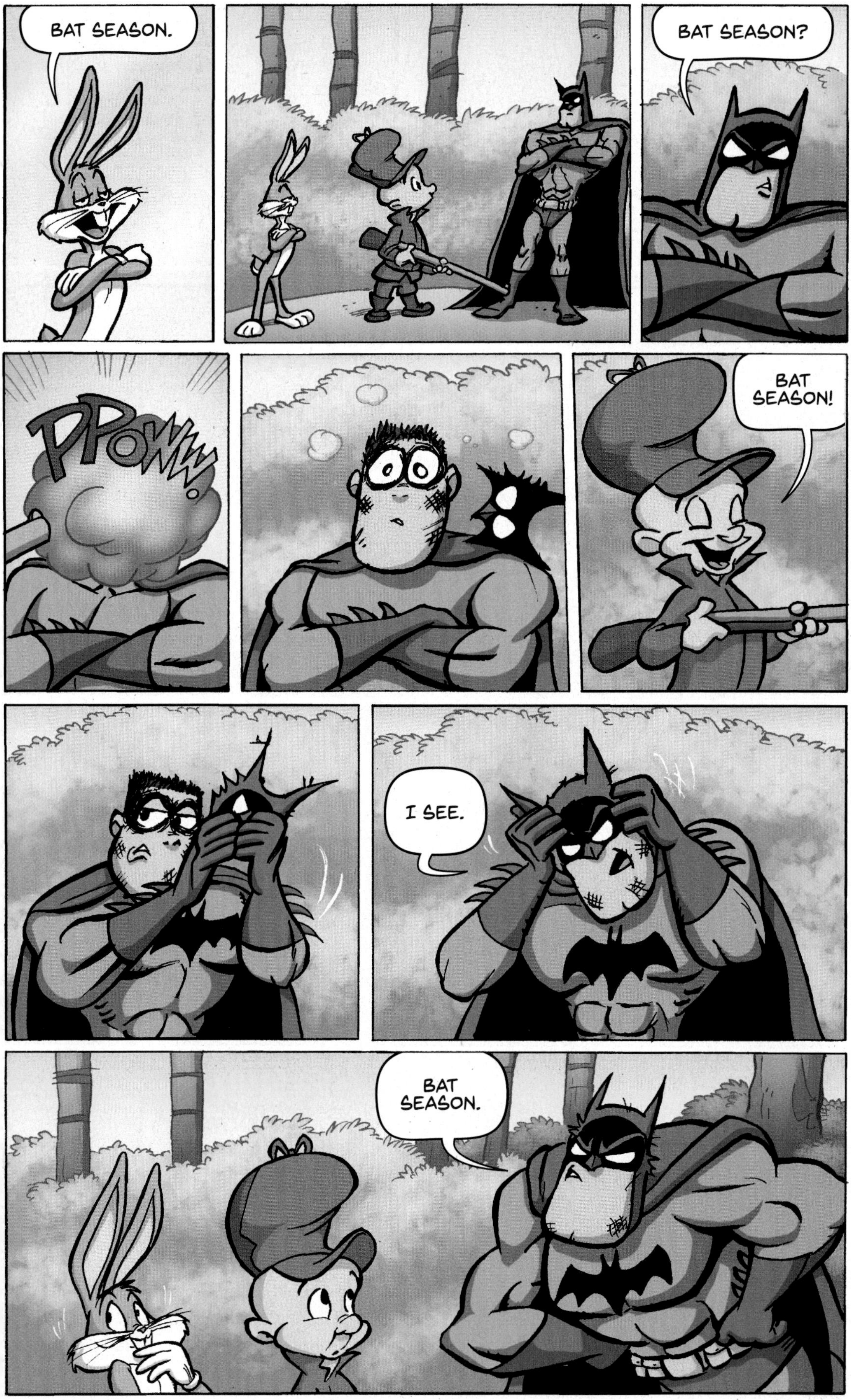
BAT SEASON.
BAT SEASON?
PPOWW
BAT SEASON!
I SEE.
BAT SEASON.

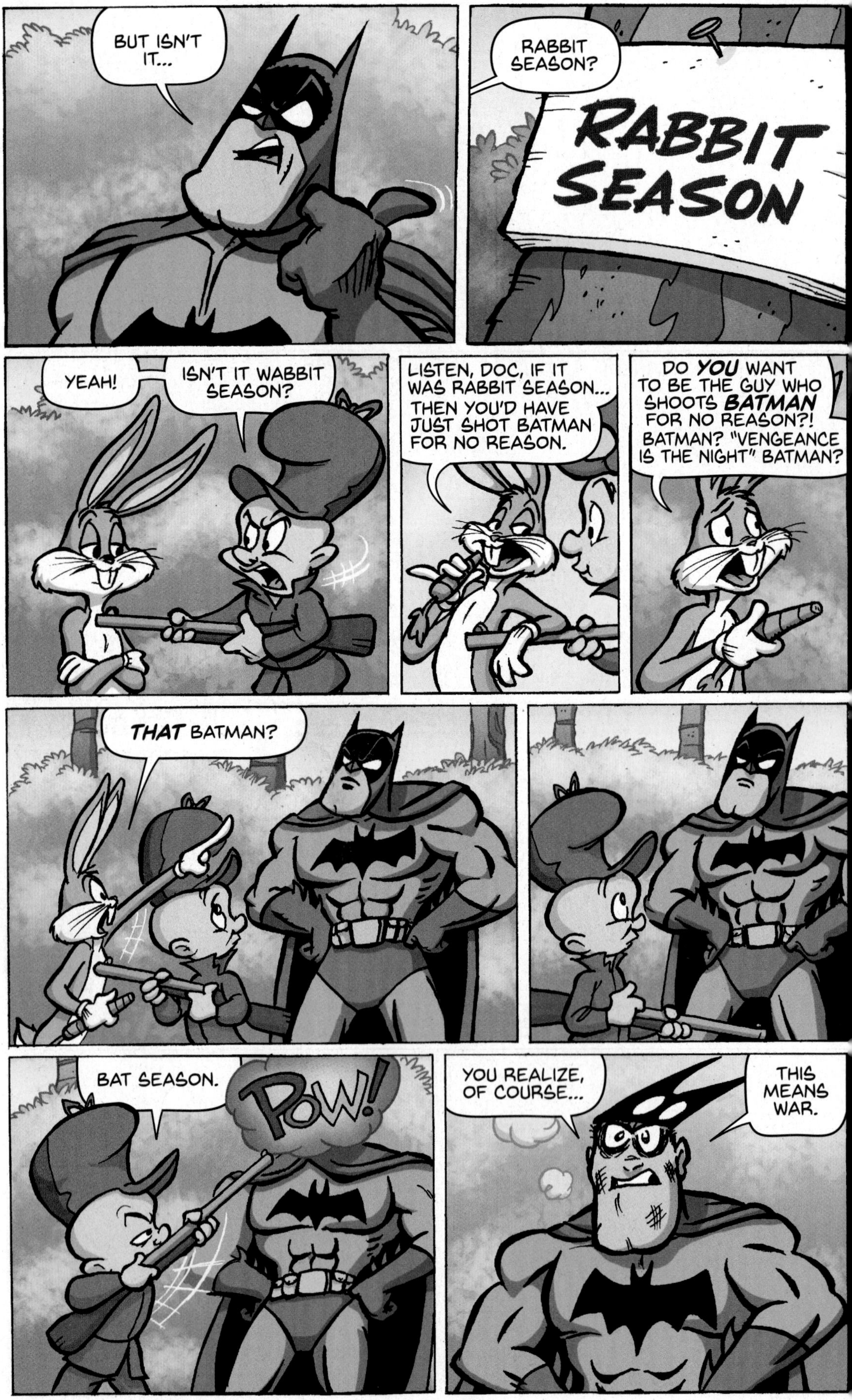
BUT ISN'T IT...
RABBIT SEASON?
RABBIT SEASON
YEAH!
ISN'T IT WABBIT SEASON?
LISTEN, DOC, IF IT WAS RABBIT SEASON... THEN YOU'D HAVE JUST SHOT BATMAN FOR NO REASON.
DO YOU WANT TO BE THE GUY WHO SHOOTS BATMAN FOR NO REASON?! BATMAN? "VENGEANCE IS THE NIGHT" BATMAN?
THAT BATMAN?
BAT SEASON.
POW!
YOU REALIZE, OF COURSE...
THIS MEANS WAR.

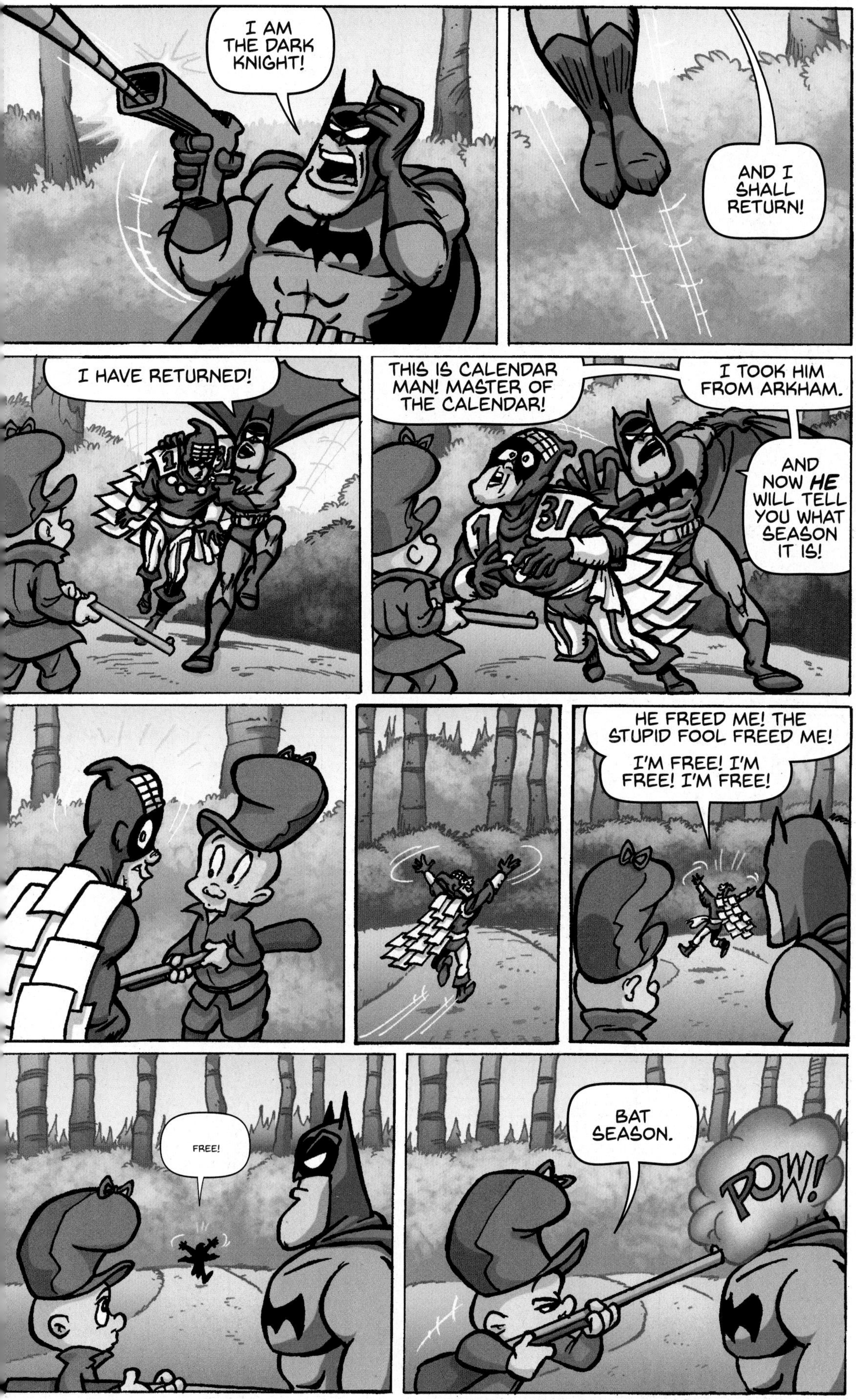
I AM THE DARK KNIGHT!
AND I SHALL RETURN!
I HAVE RETURNED!
THIS IS CALENDAR MAN! MASTER OF THE CALENDAR!
I TOOK HIM FROM ARKHAM.
AND NOW **HE** WILL TELL YOU WHAT SEASON IT IS!
HE FREED ME! THE STUPID FOOL FREED ME!
I'M FREE! I'M FREE! I'M FREE!
FREE!
BAT SEASON.
POW!

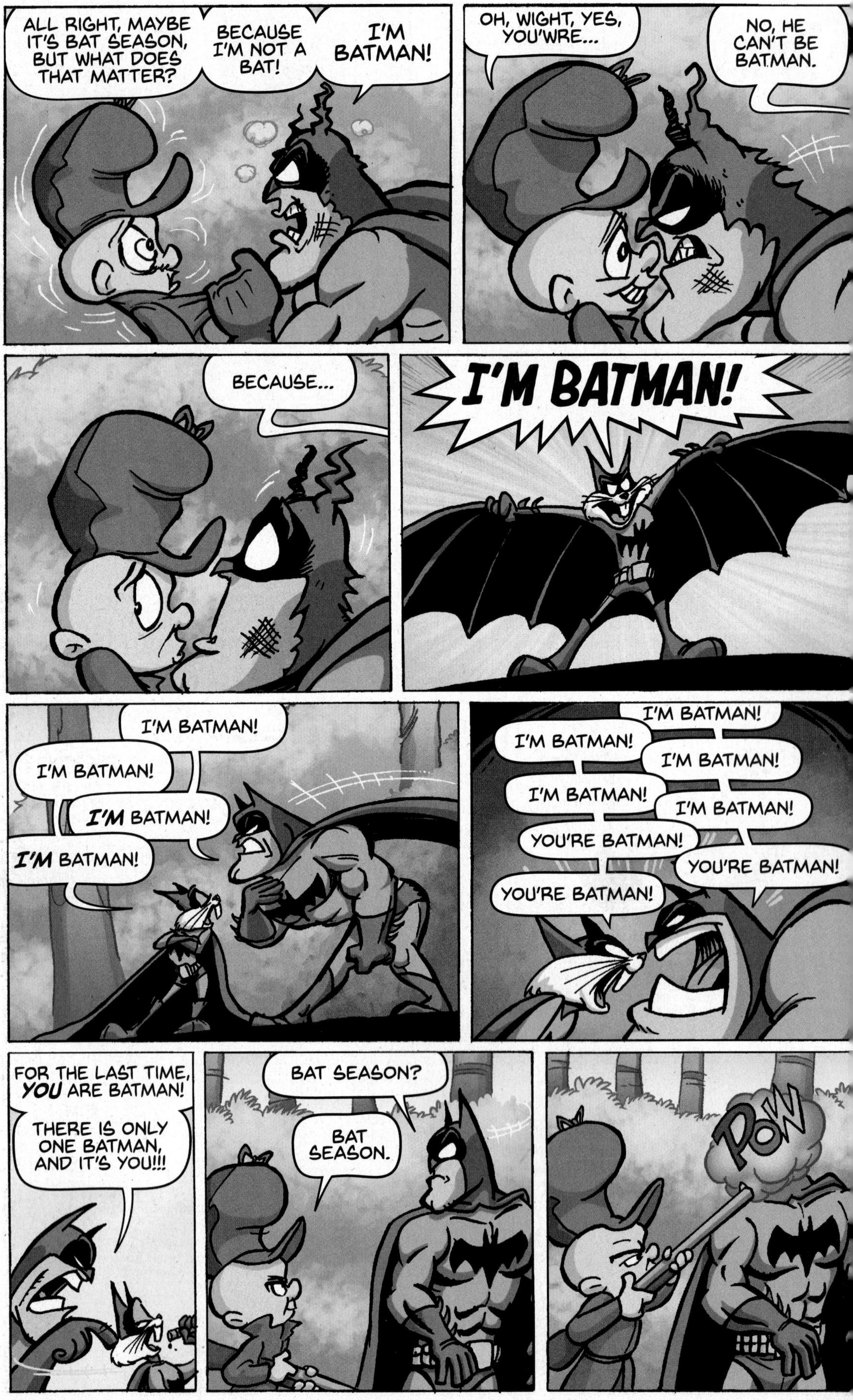
ALL RIGHT, MAYBE IT'S BAT SEASON, BUT WHAT DOES THAT MATTER?
BECAUSE I'M NOT A BAT!
I'M BATMAN!
OH, WIGHT, YES, YOU'WRE...
NO, HE CAN'T BE BATMAN.
BECAUSE...
I'M BATMAN!
I'M BATMAN!
I'M BATMAN!
I'M BATMAN!
I'M BATMAN!
I'M BATMAN!
I'M BATMAN!
I'M BATMAN!
I'M BATMAN!
I'M BATMAN!
YOU'RE BATMAN!
YOU'RE BATMAN!
YOU'RE BATMAN!
FOR THE LAST TIME, *YOU* ARE BATMAN!
THERE IS ONLY ONE BATMAN, AND IT'S YOU!!!
BAT SEASON?
BAT SEASON.
POW

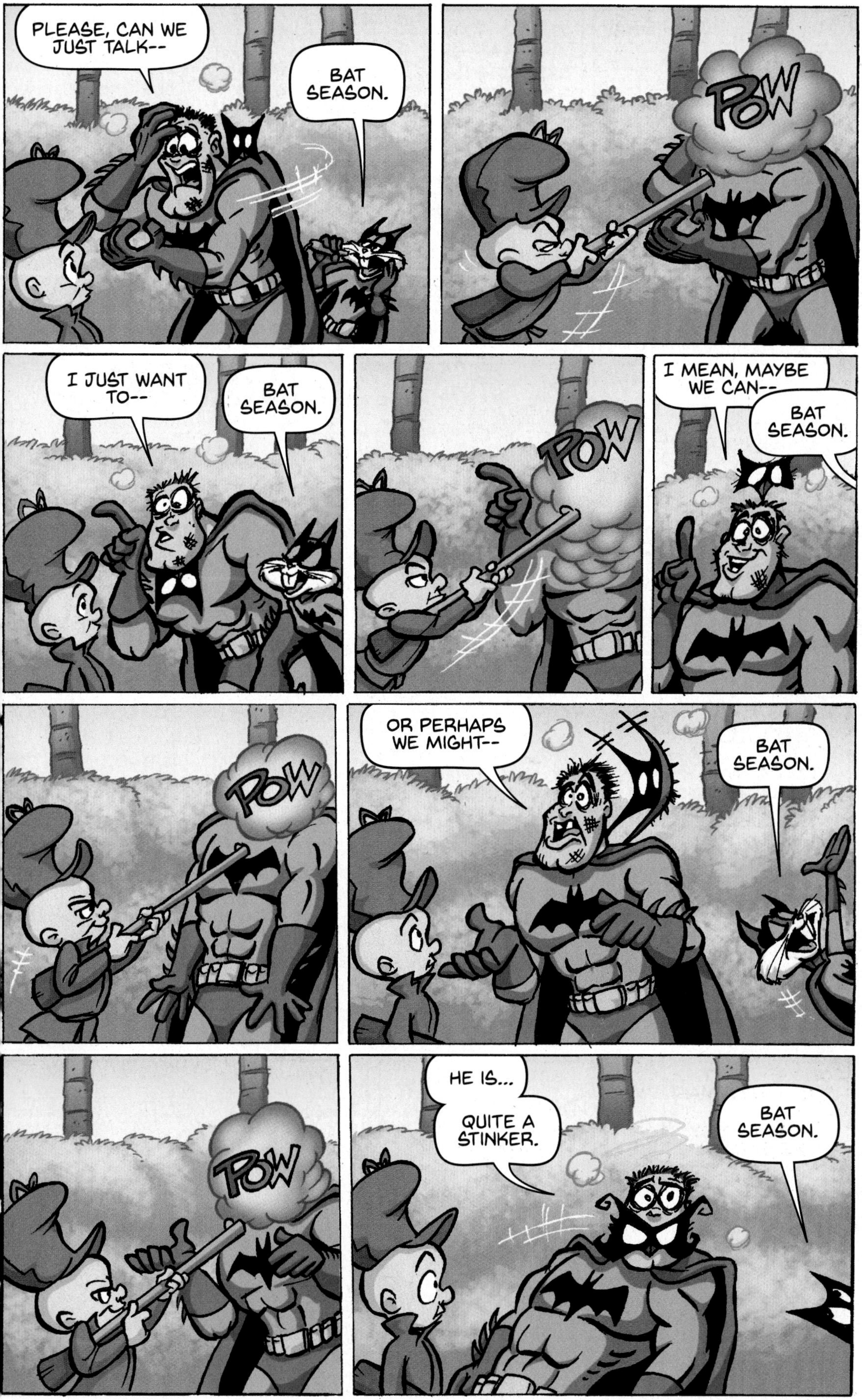
PLEASE, CAN WE JUST TALK--
BAT SEASON.
POW
I JUST WANT TO--
BAT SEASON.
POW
I MEAN, MAYBE WE CAN--
BAT SEASON.
POW
OR PERHAPS WE MIGHT--
BAT SEASON.
POW
HE IS...
QUITE A STINKER.
BAT SEASON.

ALL RIGHT! **ALL RIGHT!**

IS THERE **ANY WAY** TO STOP THIS?!

OKAY. UH-HUH.

YEAH, YEAH, THAT SEEMS FAIR.

BOYS.

BATMAN!

RABBIT SEASON

ROBIN ~~RABBIT~~ SEASON

WOBIN SEASON?

ROBIN SEASON.

WOBIN SEASON!

THANK YOU. TO RETURN THE FAVOR, I'D LOVE TO INTRODUCE YOU TO A FRIEND OF MINE.

OH?

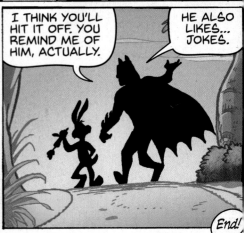

I THINK YOU'LL HIT IT OFF. YOU REMIND ME OF HIM, ACTUALLY.

HE ALSO LIKES... JOKES.

End!

TASMANIAN DEVIL design by JIM LEE

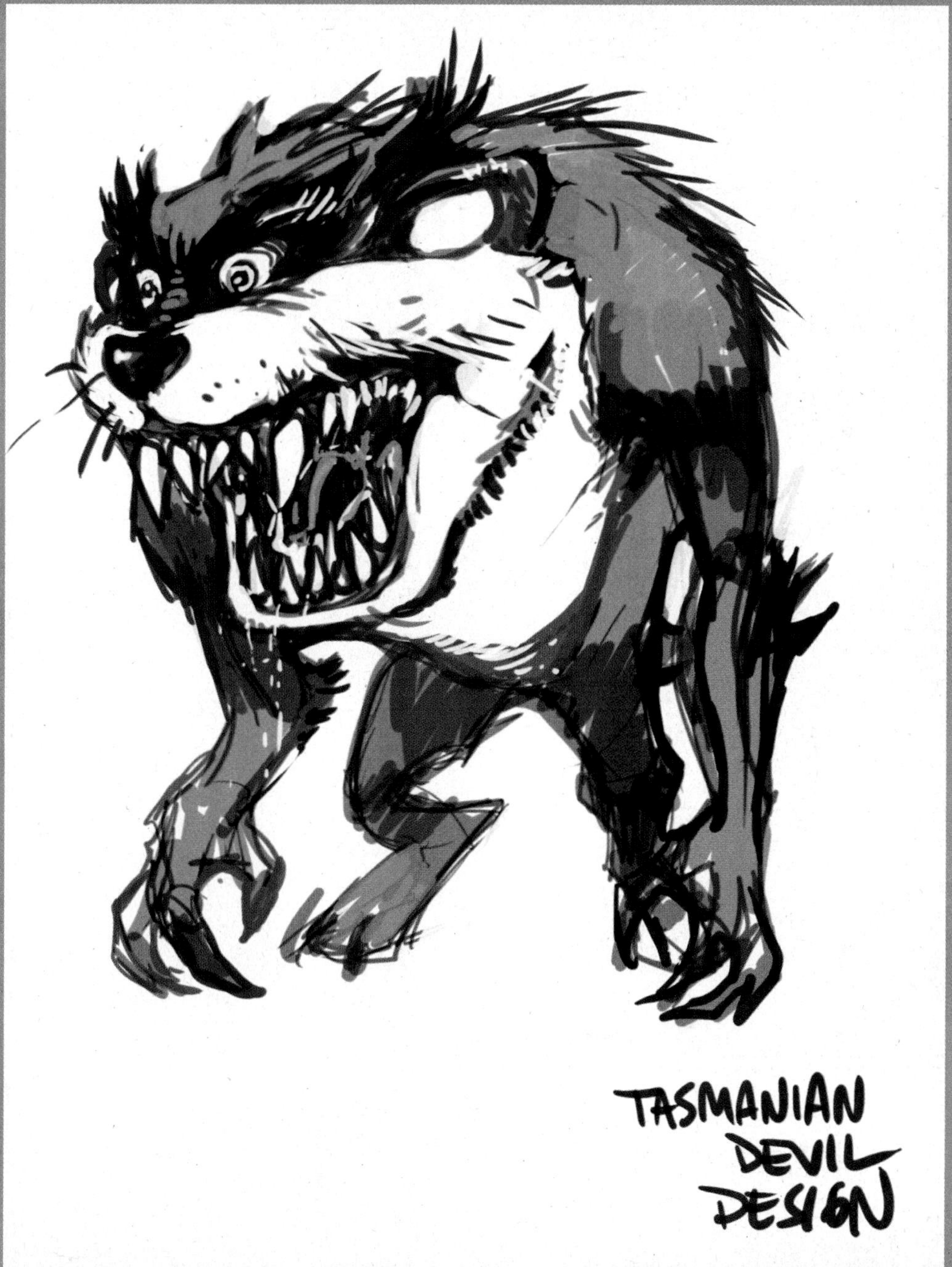
TASMANIAN
DEVIL
DESIGN

JONAH HEX/YOSEMITE SAM SPECIAL #1 cover sketches by MARK TEXEIRA

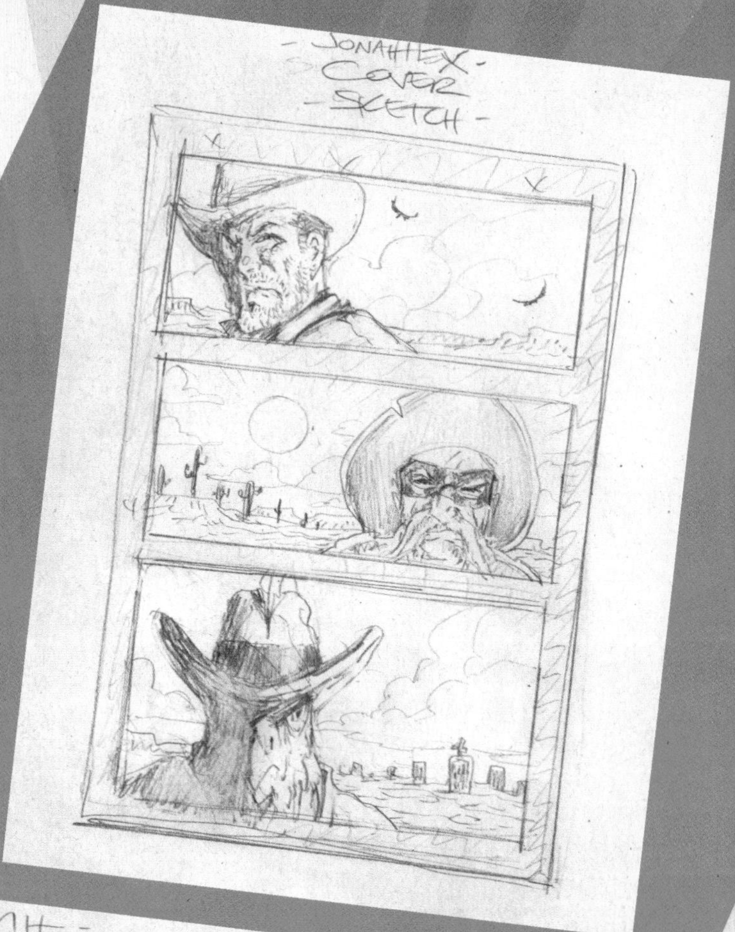
-JONAH HEX-
COVER
-SKETCH-

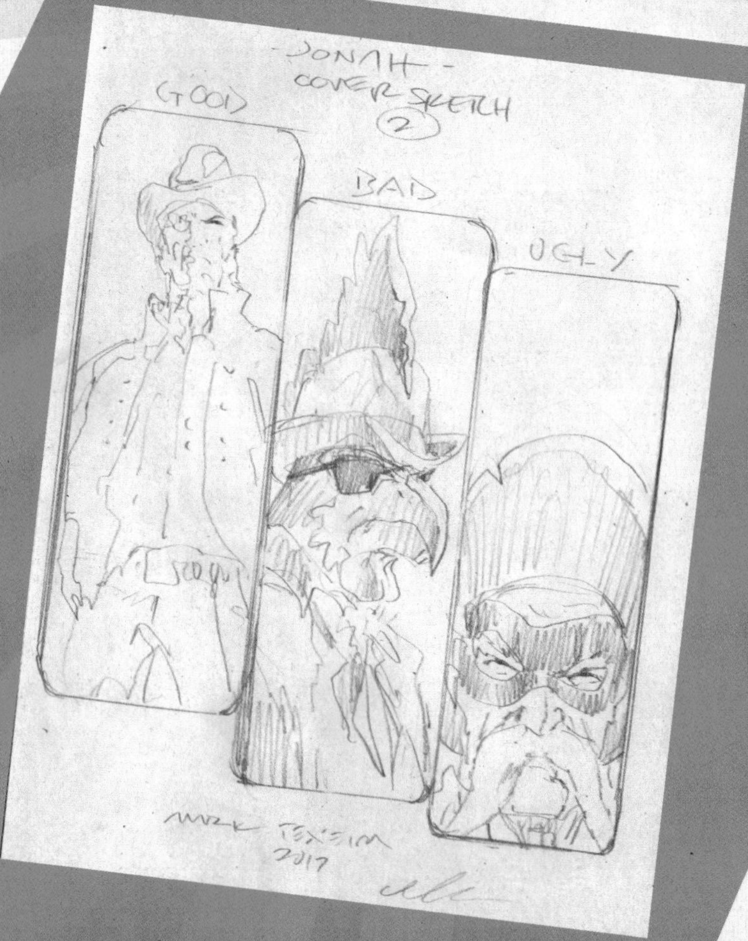
-JONAH-
COVER SKETCH
2
(GOOD)
BAD
UGLY
MARK TEXEIRA
2017

FOGHORN LEGHORN sketches by MARK TEXEIRA

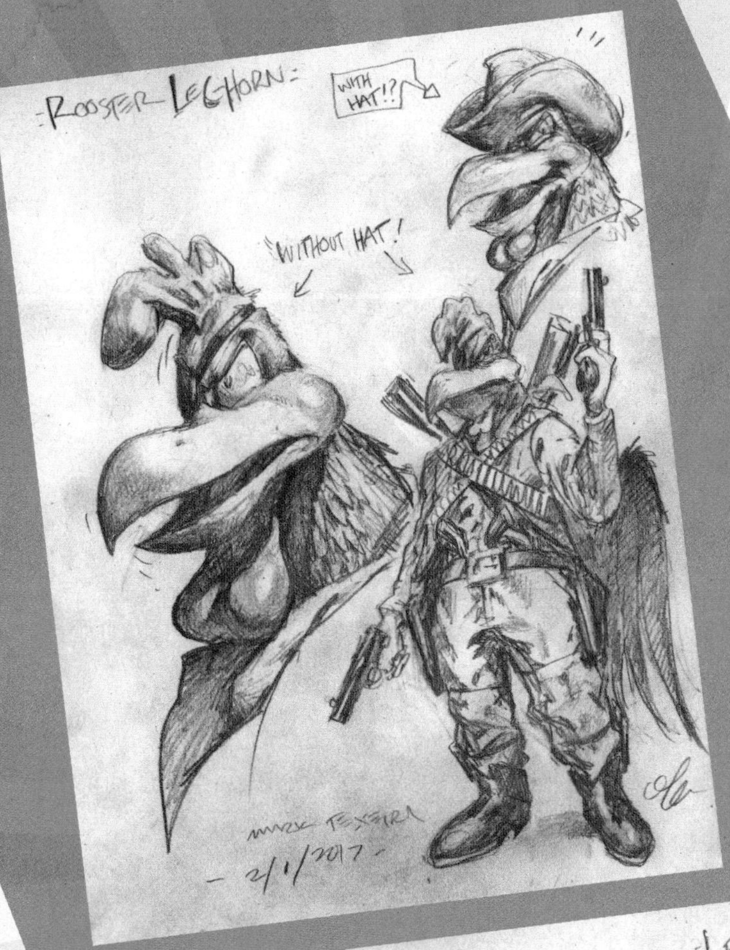
ROOSTER LEGHORN
WITH HAT!?
WITHOUT HAT!
MARK TEXEIRA
2/1/2017

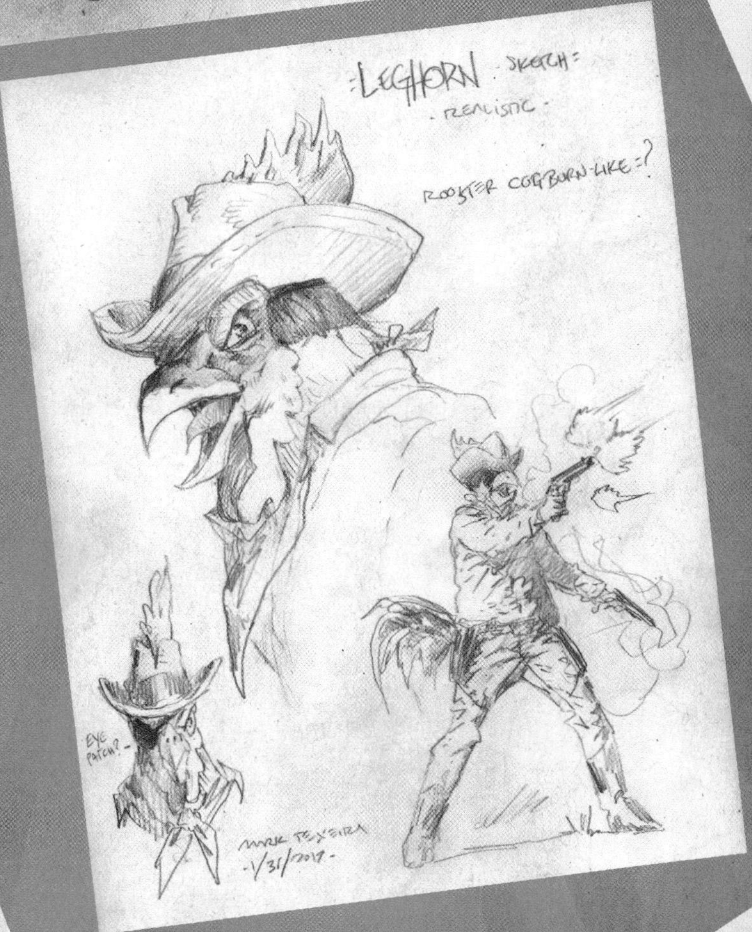
LEGHORN SKETCH
REALISTIC
ROOSTER COGBURN-LIKE?
EYE PATCH?
MARK TEXEIRA
1/31/2017

WONDER WOMAN/TASMANIAN DEVIL SPECIAL #1
variant cover layout by BYRON VAUGHNS

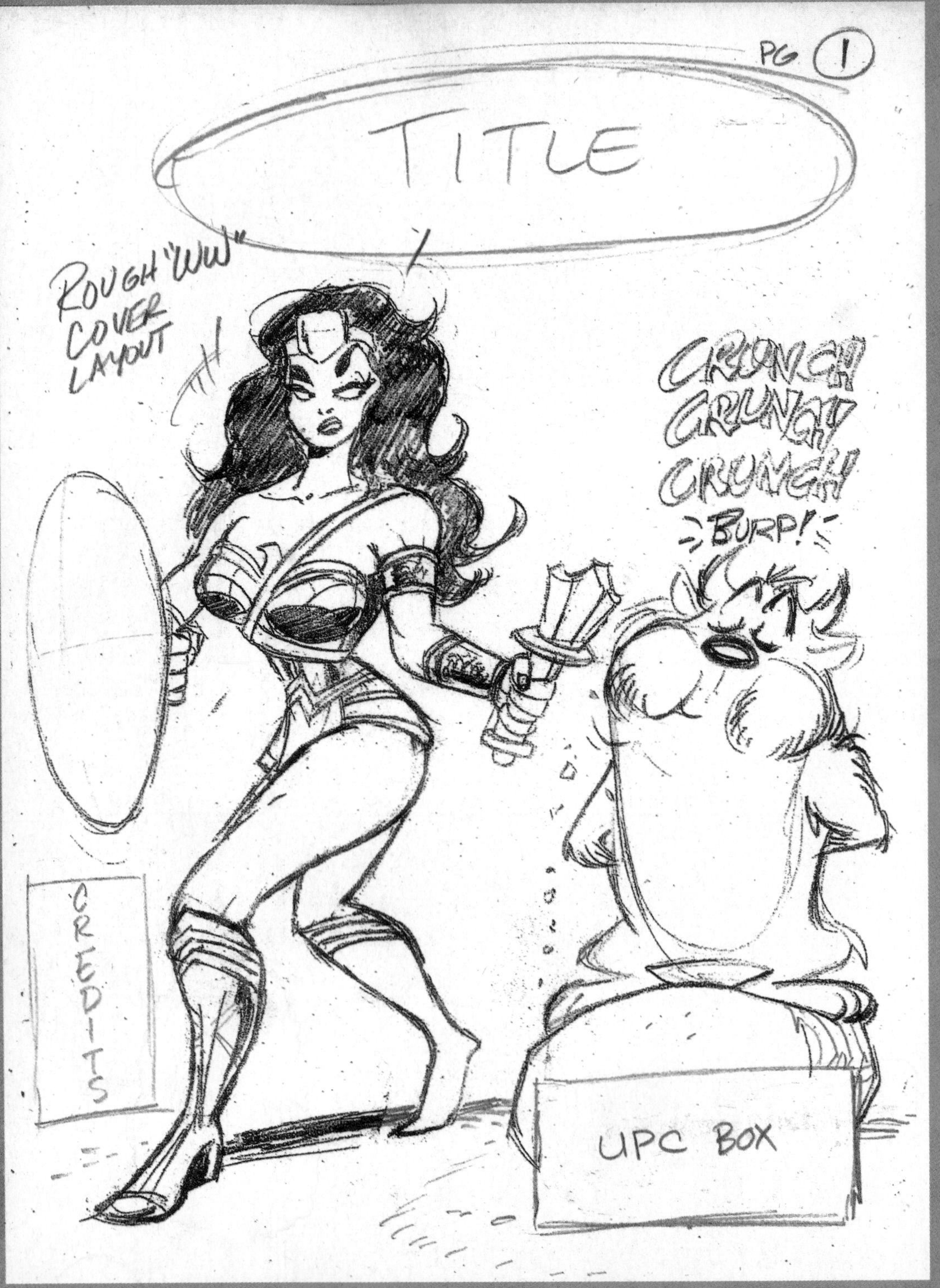
PG 1
TITLE
ROUGH "WW" COVER LAYOUT
CRUNCH
CRUNCH
CRUNCH
BURP!
CREDITS
UPC BOX